Georg Simmel and the Disciplinary Imaginary

Georg Simmel
and the Disciplinary Imaginary

Elizabeth S. Goodstein

Stanford University Press
Stanford, California

Stanford University Press
Stanford, California

©2017 by the Board of Trustees of the Leland Stanford Junior University.
All rights reserved.

This book has been published with the assistance of Emory University.

No part of this book may be reproduced or transmitted in any form or by any means, electronic or mechanical, including photocopying and recording, or in any information storage or retrieval system without the prior written permission of Stanford University Press.

Printed in the United States of America on acid-free, archival-quality paper

Library of Congress Cataloging-in-Publication Data Names: Goodstein, Elizabeth S., author. Title: Georg Simmel and the disciplinary imaginary / Elizabeth S. Goodstein. Description: Stanford, California : Stanford University Press, 2017. | Includes bibliographical references and index. Identifiers: LCCN 2016037992 (print) | LCCN 2016038968 (ebook) | ISBN 9780804798365 (cloth : alk. paper) | ISBN 9781503600737 (pbk. : alk. paper) | ISBN 9781503600744 (ebook) Subjects: LCSH: Simmel, Georg, 1858-1918—Influence. | Philosophy, Modern—20th century. | Philosophy and social sciences. | Social sciences—Philosophy. | Money—Philosophy. Classification: LCC B3329.S64 G66 2017 (print) | LCC B3329.S64 (ebook) | DDC 193—dc23 LC record available at https://lccn.loc.gov/2016037992

Typeset by Bruce Lundquist in 10/13 Minion

Contents

Acknowledgments   vii

List of Abbreviations   ix

Prologue: Modernist Philosophy and the History of Theory   1

PART I: COLD CASH AND THE MODERN CLASSIC

1. Introduction: Simmel's Modernity   15
   Marginality at the Center: Georg Simmel in Berlin, 15   Modern Culture and the Problem of Disciplinarity, 25   Disciplining Simmel, 35   Simmel's Philosophical Modernism and the History of Theory, 48

2. Simmel as Classic: Representation and the Rhetoric of Disciplinarity   52
   A Modern Classic?, 53   Simmel's Self-(Re)Presentation, 61   Simmel's "Formalism," 66   Form in Context: Theorizing Culture, 78   Modernist Identity and the Self-Overcoming of Relativism, 83

3. Memory/Legacy: Georg Simmel as (Mostly) Forgotten Founding Father   96
   Simmel in America: The Disciplinary (Pre-)History, 96   Discipline/History: Theorizing Misrecognition, 104   Rereading Misreading: "Simmel" in America, 113   Styles of Thought and the Rhetoric of Disciplinarity, 121   Disciplining Culture, 125

PART II: *PHILOSOPHY OF MONEY* AS MODERNIST PHILOSOPHY

4. Style as Substance: Simmel's Modernism and the Disciplinary Imaginary   137
   Reading Simmel's *Philosophy of Money*, 140   Simmel's Philosophical Modernism, 146   Rethinking Thinking: Culture, Relativism, and *das Geistesleben*, 156

5. Performing Relativity: Money and Modernist Philosophy   168
   From a Psychology to a Philosophy of Money, 172   Money in Action: Value, Life, Form, 179   Money, Representation, and "the Cultural Process," 186   Money and Metaphysics: Relativism as Modernist Method, 199

6. Disciplining the *Philosophy of Money*   211
   A Disciplinary Rorschach: Early Responses to the *Philosophy of Money*, 212
   The *Philosophy of Money* as "Social Theory," 221   Interdisciplinarity before Disciplines: Simmel's Phenomenology of Culture, 226   Metaphysical Relativism and Modernist Praxis, 234

   PART III: THE CASE OF SIMMEL

7. Thinking Liminality, Rethinking Disciplinarity   249
   Method and Change: Thinking Liminality, 249   Beyond the (Philosophy of the) Subject: Thinking Relatively and the "Problem of Sociology," 259   Laws, Norms, and the Relativity of Being, 272   Form, Figuration, and the Disciplinary Imaginary, 278
   Canonization Reprised, 284

8. The Stranger and the Sociological Imagination   296
   Reading Simmel: Appropriation by Fragments, 300   Rereading Rereading: Estranging the Stranger, 306   Becoming Social, Figuring Strangeness, 310   Disciplinarity and the Cultural Process, 321

Epilogue: Georg Simmel as Modernist Philosopher   331
   Simmel in Strasbourg, 337

Select Bibliography   347

Index   359

Acknowledgments

Every book bears the traces of a life. I thank my friends, family, neighbors, and colleagues who have supported, sustained, and challenged me in and through the many permutations of a project that has occupied me intermittently for a great many years.

This book would not exist had I not had the excellent fortune to find my way to Emory's Graduate Institute of the Liberal Arts, where I enjoyed unparalleled intellectual freedom to pursue interdisciplinary research and teaching. I am especially grateful for the support of Robert Paul and the late Ivan Karp, admirers of Simmel who brought me to Emory in 1999, and for the wisdom, kindness, and unwavering solidarity of Kevin Corrigan and Sander Gilman, who demonstrate that the life of the mind is truly worth living. I thank all of the students who read and reread Simmel and thought with me as I found my way through to what really mattered. Special thanks go to Zak Manfredi and to Jean-Paul Cauvin, who survived reading the *Philosophy of Money* in just two weeks and went on to teach me so many things. Now that the Graduate Institute of the Liberal Arts is no more, I am grateful to have found a congenial new home in Emory's English Department, and my warm thanks go to Walter Kalaidjian for his thoughtful support during the recent transition, when Walt Reed's generosity and kindness have also been more welcome than ever.

In a world where sustained projects of the sort represented by this book have become most untimely, it is a pleasure to thank those who supported and advanced my work both intellectually and materially along the way. An Alexander von Humboldt Foundation Research Fellowship provided an invaluable opportunity to work in Berlin and Leipzig with the late Klaus Köhnke, whose formidable scholarship and compelling vision of Simmel's significance have left an indelible legacy. The Humboldt provided a front-row view of the monumental undertaking that was the *Georg Simmel Gesamtausgabe*, without which this book would not be thinkable. Years later, a residency at the American Academy in Berlin provided a new impetus to reimagine my project under extremely congenial conditions, and my special thanks go to the Academy and its wonderful staff for all they did to make my stay on the Wannsee so special and so productive. More recently, a residency at Emory's Fox Center for Humanistic Inquiry at Emory afforded me time and space to rethink this work yet again under changed conditions both local and global. I am very grateful, too, to the wonderful librarians at Emory who have so often gone the extra mile for me.

I thank the colleagues here and abroad who have provided opportunities to share and test my evolving vision of Simmel. Kieran Keohane invited me to give a keynote address at a remarkable Social Theory Consortium Conference at University College, Cork. Dan Purdy introduced me to the lively interdisciplinary community at the Max Kade Institute at Penn State. Don Levine invited me to join the party for Simmel's *Lebensanschauung* at the Franke Institute for the Humanities at the University of Chicago. Michael Gardiner and Tilottama Rajan welcomed me at the Center for the Study of Theory and Criticism at the University of Western Ontario. Brigid Doherty brought me into the interdisciplinary conversation about European Cultural Studies at Princeton. Special gratitude goes to Martin Kagel, who inspired new directions by seeing the path I needed to follow before I knew it myself and finally getting me to Athens. Thanks, too, to the readers for Stanford University Press, whose invaluable feedback came at a crucial juncture, and to my editor, Emily-Jane Cohen, for her discerning support.

There is not room to thank everyone whose friendship and support has accompanied and sustained me over the past years, but I can't imagine how it would have been without Delia Angiolini, Jay Bernstein, David Carr, Petra Coronato, Kari Dianich, Gabrielle Goodstein, Klio Goodstein, May Goodstein, Sam Goodstein, Peter Hoeyng, Li Jiang, Susan Katrin, Richard Kopffleisch, Kim Loudermilk, Carla Mays, Diane McWhorter, Judith Miller, Helen Nash, Christina Oberstebrink, Rachel Saltz, Dirk Schumann, Birgit Tautz, Pedro Vasquez, Katrin Volger-Schumann, and Cindy Willett. Thank you all very much.

The completion of this book is ringed with sadness for those who are no longer here to receive it, including three very different Simmel partisans, Ivan Karp, Klaus Köhnke, and Don Levine. My uncle Eldon and aunt Marian are deeply missed, as is my dear friend Leslie Graham. Most of all, I mourn the loss of my father, Bernard J. Goodstein, whose faith in me never wavered, and who would have rejoiced to hold this volume in his hands. I am so grateful that my mother, May, and brother, Sam, are here to celebrate and to remember.

The final years of this evolving project have brought the great joy of joining my life to Klaus van den Berg's. I thank him for solidarity, kindness, and patience, for good humor and transcendent music, and for all varieties of insight and support. Klaus has thought with me and challenged me, and his help, not least with translating many an opaque passage, has been invaluable in bringing my latest vision of Simmel to the present conclusion. In love, I dedicate this book to the memory of my father, and also to the hope of the future that is dawning even now for the two of us—together, at long last, in one place.

Abbreviations

AJS	*American Journal of Sociology*
AuS	*Äesthetik und Soziologie um die Jahrhundertwende: Georg Simmel*, ed. Hannes Böhringer and Karlfried Gründer (1976)
BdD	*Buch des Dankes an Georg Simmel: Briefe, Erinnerungen, Bibliographie. Zu seinem 100. Geburtstag am 1. März 1958*, ed. Kurt Gassen and Michael Landmann (1958)
DGS	Deutsche Gesellschaft für Soziologie; German Sociological Society
GSG	*Georg Simmel Gesamtausgabe*, ed. Otthein Rammstedt (1989–2015)
IIS	Institut internationale de sociologie
TCS	*Theory, Culture & Society* (journal)
WS	Winter Semester (at the Berlin [Friedrich-Wilhelms] University)

Georg Simmel and the Disciplinary Imaginary

Prologue: Modernist Philosophy and the History of Theory

> I know that I shall die without spiritual heirs (and it is a good thing). My legacy is like one in cold cash divided among many heirs, and each converts his portion into an enterprise of some sort that corresponds to *his* nature: whose provenance in that inheritance is not visible.
>
> Georg Simmel[1]

Certain figures in the history of thought seem to derive their significance from their marginality. Never quite forgotten, often the objects of devoted scholarly followings yet largely unread by nonspecialists, they enjoy wider fame mainly in the form of cliché—thus Herodotus is said to be the father of lies, Montaigne the inventor of the essay, Musil the chronicler of a Vienna that perished in the Great War. So, too, Georg Simmel (1858–1918) is known, if at all, as one of the founding fathers of modern social science and the author of a single work, the *Philosophy of Money*, which remains by and large unread. This truncated form of memory contains *in nuce* the dynamic of marginalization: a complex intellectual legacy reduced to a work that is itself misunderstood when Simmel is celebrated as the first sociologist of modernity.

By the mid-nineteenth century, the human costs of progress were inescapably apparent. What we have come to think of as the founding texts of modern social science were part of a broader discourse on modern society and culture suffused with ambiguity and contradiction; they belong to the world that gave rise to Spengler and Nordau, Nietzsche and Weininger. The same ambivalence concerning the meaning and value of what has come to be called modernization also shaped efforts by Marx and Weber, Durkheim and Freud, to forge conceptual means for coming to terms

---

1. This is the epigraph to a collection of aphorisms that the poet and art historian Gertrud Kantorowicz, Georg Simmel's lover, presented as selections from his "diary" (my trans.; unless otherwise noted, translations throughout this book are my own). At Simmel's request, Kantorowicz traveled to Strasbourg in August 1918, and in the final weeks of his life, she worked with him there on editing papers that were to be published posthumously. Selections first appeared in *Logos* in December 1919 and were reprinted with other material from Simmel's papers in *Fragmente und Aufsätze: Aus dem Nachlaß und Veröffentlichungen der letzten Jahre*, ed. Gertrud Kantorowicz (Munich: Drei-Masken, 1923). The "diary" is included in the *Georg Simmel Gesamtausgabe* (henceforth *GSG*), ed. Otthein Rammstedt (Frankfurt am Main: Suhrkamp, 1989–2015), 20: 261–96; quotation here from p. 261. The original manuscript has been lost, and as the editors of the critical edition of the "diary" remark, "Since [Kantorowicz] does not provide an account of her interventions in the text, no conclusions can be drawn concerning its original form (*GSG* 20: 546). Simmel's (incomplete) correspondence is collected in *GSG* vols. 22 and 23, but a number of additional letters are included with other documents in vol. 24.

with what was happening around them. The resulting tensions between analysis and interpretation, objectivity and critique, empiricism and moralism mark their work and inflect their methodological strategies and theoretical perspectives.

The complexity and nuance of what came to be canonical texts tend to be obscured when the story of the emergence of the social sciences is being told. In the case of Simmel, simplifying his highly multivalent undertakings into cliché allows a thinker who fits only with difficulty into the dominant disciplinary paradigm to be assimilated to the contemporary social sciences. At the same time, it obscures how the origins of sociology are related to a new kind of philosophical investigation both defined by and centered on specifically modern cultural circumstances.

Such clichés and misprisions are, then, not without interest for the history of thought in general and for reflection on the emergence of modern social and cultural theory in particular. Intellectual history lives from the reduction of ideas to sound bites—but also from the recovery of ambiguities flattened out by narratives that have lost their force. In the case of the history of modern social thought, questions about the philosophical status of reflection on social structures and mechanisms are, furthermore, imbricated with problems of historiography tout court. What constitutes the history of (cultural) theory? How can it be distinguished from the disciplinary histories of the social sciences? Where do silences, gaps, and obfuscations fit into the story? What, in the final account, is the meaning of marginality in theory?

The case of Georg Simmel underlines how epistemological questions concerning the status of social scientific concepts and methods are linked to historiographical concerns of both a general and a specific, institutional or disciplinary, nature. Simmel's significance as a cultural and social theorist comprises both his philosophical achievements and a considerable, yet largely unrecognized, impact on his students and readers. His innovative approach to cultural interpretation brought the legacy of the German philosophical tradition into conversation with the phenomena of everyday modern life, and the influence of his ideas and modernist style of philosophizing extends through figures as diverse as Walter Benjamin, Martin Buber, György Lukács, Robert Musil, and Robert Park.

But this very diversity—or put in another way, the absence of a "school" or doctrine of any sort—has helped to render Simmel's intellectual influence virtually invisible. To write his conceptual and methodological innovations into the history of twentieth-century thought therefore requires not just an encounter with his writings but also an interrogation of the nature of his influence and of the reasons it has gone unrecognized. And it entails taking seriously Simmel's insistence, expressed as early as 1899, that despite his reputation abroad, he was not, in fact, a sociologist: "I am a philosopher, see my life's vocation in philosophy, and only pursue sociology as a sideline."[2] In a word, the case of Simmel foregrounds how fundamental questions

---

2. Simmel to Célestin Bouglé, December 13, 1899 (*GSG* 22: 342–44). Simmel would use stronger words on other occasions, as when he wrote Georg Jellinek that it was an "idiocy" to regard him as a sociologist (March 20, 1908; *GSG* 22: 617).

about what used to be called the history of ideas are for understanding our own disciplinary context and intellectual world.

In the pages that follow, I hope to avoid both the Scylla of overspecialization—taking Simmel's importance for granted and treating his texts as canonical ends in themselves—and the Charybdis of appropriation—making the case for Simmel's significance by situating his oeuvre in relation to a metanarrative defined by contemporary interests tangential or even foreign to his self-professed understanding of his work. In the first instance, it is a matter of taking seriously the question of how to read him. Simmel was a lavishly published author, not only of sociological treatises but also of popular works on philosophy, meditations on canonical and contemporary artists and writers, scores of essays on cultural phenomena from fashion to cities to femininity—and criticism, poetry, and fiction to boot. The sheer complexity of his texts makes demands on the reader that call for more thorough conceptualization, while the diversity and range of his oeuvre (or to put it less generously, his lack of clearly defined disciplinary identity) pose challenges of another order.

This book does not attempt to give a comprehensive account of this formidable body of work, let alone an exhaustive one. Rather, by approaching Simmel as a modernist philosopher—by foregrounding his innovative style of thought and drawing attention to the affinity between his methods of interpretation and broader modernist cultural developments—I hope to persuade my own readers to (re)turn to the texts themselves in a new way. To approach Simmel as a modernist in this writerly sense decenters not only received accounts of his significance as a thinker but also of the fin de siècle origins of modern social thought and cultural theory in general and of the discipline of sociology in particular. Embracing rather than erasing his marginality, I reframe the question of how to read this multiform oeuvre in relation to the disciplinary traditions that have shaped Simmel's reception. Attending to the legacy of his style of thought casts new light on the history of social and cultural theory, enabling us to ask anew what constitutes rigorous inquiry into the constitutive structures of collective existence in the modern world.

My project depends on a body of specialized scholarship—most notably on the work of those who labored over more than two decades on the historical-critical edition of his works—of which it cannot, properly speaking, form a part. To be sure, it is grounded in textual and contextual evidence amassed, often for the first time, in the *Georg Simmel Gesamtausgabe* (*GSG*) realized under the general editorship of Otthein Rammstedt between 1989 and 2015. However, my project parts ways, of necessity, with the philological objectives and hermeneutic principles that define a historical-critical edition as such and that make faithful reconstruction and historical contextualization ends in themselves. Insisting on the importance of critical and theoretical self-reflection on the categories and perspectives in and through which such (canonizing) reconstruction and narrative contextualization take place, this book aims to liberate resources in Simmel's oeuvre for our own time and for the future.

In the final instance, the plausibility of my interpretation depends on a vision of the tasks of thought in modernity that cannot, *sensu strictu*, be derived from empirical evidence. Historical-critical contextualization is important. But giving a plausible account of Simmel's intellectual contributions entails imaginatively reconstructing a vision of philosophy and an approach to philosophizing in many ways quite foreign to contemporary sensibilities. Representation and understanding are intertwined, for the thinker cannot be entirely separated from the thought.

We cannot simply return to the texts themselves to disclose what Simmel might have called "the individual law" of his oeuvre. Another history, that of generations of interpretation, stands between the reader and this thinking. To determine what his texts mean for us, we must first free them—and Simmel himself—from the effects of a reception history that has obscured much of what is most interesting and important about his work. The historical and sociological task of contextualization and the hermeneutic and philosophical challenges of interpretation intermingle.

Georg Simmel and the Disciplinary Imaginary thus sets out onto the territory disclosed by the historical and critical work of the *Georg Simmel Gesamtausgabe*, but it explores that terrain to very different and often diametrically—or dialectically—opposed ends. The critical edition has established Simmel's place in what one of the most distinguished members of the editorial group, the late Klaus Christian Köhnke, called "the classical period *[Klassik]* of the human and social sciences."[3] *Georg Simmel and the Disciplinary Imaginary* returns him to his historical and cultural context with the aspiration of helping to disclose the unrealized and as it were unclassical potential of his texts and practices. In calling attention to the ways in which unrecognized investments of the "cold cash" of Simmel's legacy have shaped our contemporary intellectual landscape, my object is to draw attention to what institutionalized modes of commemorating the "founding father" exclude or forget: the Simmel who did not and perhaps could not become a "classic" in the canonical sense, whose oeuvre arguably calls into question the institutional framework of canonicity itself.

From the beginning, Simmel's thought transgressed disciplinary and institutional strictures. In the course of the twentieth century, as the contours of the contemporary disciplines emerged, what is known in German as the *Wirkungsgeschichte*—literally, the history of effects—of his work in sociology took on contours that obscured the breadth and complexity of his philosophical and theoretical achievement, particularly in the Anglophone world. To appreciate the significance of the new vistas on Simmel's oeuvre opened up by the critical edition, it will be necessary to clarify how his reception has been shaped by a disciplinary ordering of knowledge practices that we take for granted today—in particular, by the very different modes of reading and understanding both texts and historical evidence proper to social scientific as opposed to humanistic inquiry. Simmel's identification as a (mostly forgotten) founding father of sociology has given him a role in modern intellectual history at the cost of obscuring his substantial philosophical contributions. But this is getting ahead of the story.

Simmel is often classified as a neo-Kantian. His concern to link epistemological and ethical frames of reference and his distinctive approach to the problem of form

---

3. Klaus Christian Köhnke, *Der junge Simmel in Theoriebeziehungen und sozialen Bewegungen* [The Young Simmel in Theoretical Relations and Social Movements] (Frankfurt am Main: Suhrkamp, 1996), 23.

speak for such a contextualization of his thought, as do his many books and essays dealing directly with Kant's philosophy, which he taught throughout his entire career, and, indeed, his long friendship with Heinrich Rickert.[4] Even if Simmel cannot properly be regarded as belonging to a neo-Kantian "school,"[5] his work is in many ways recognizably and undeniably Kantian in inspiration. The signs of Simmel's allegiance to a Kantian idiom and sensibility are pervasive: his emphasis on the epistemological foundations of inquiry and on the ethical self-determination of the individual; his recurrent invocation of the tenet of the ultimate inaccessibility of the thing in itself; even the division of the *Philosophy of Money* into "analytic" and "synthetic" parts.

And yet, as the existence of a radically different competing characterization of Simmel as a *Lebensphilosoph*, a "philosopher of life,"[6] underlines, this is hardly the whole story. In a 1908 letter to Hermann Graf Keyserling, Simmel confessed that he had again become embroiled in the sort of "epistemological-metaphysical questions" that had occupied him earlier in his career,

> once again with the feeling that we are just going round like squirrels on a wheel in this whole epistemology that rests on Kantian presuppositions. What a thing this man did to the world by declaring it to be a representation! When will the genius come along who frees us from the spell of the subject as Kant freed us from that of the object? And what will "the third" be?[7]

To pigeon-hole Simmel as a neo-Kantian is to discount the depth and significance of this epistemological crisis. It entails ignoring his flirtation with irrationalism; his recurrent attention to materiality, embodiment, and the emotions; his fascination with historical specificity and cultural difference, with the challenges of thinking a world gripped in flux.

In a word, Simmel is as much a reader of Nietzsche as of Kant. Indeed, as I shall show, he is one of the greatest and most subtly influential readers of Nietzsche alto-

---

4. However, Rickert complained to Emil Lask (unpublished letter of July 13, 1902, cited in editorial notes to Simmel's letter to Rickert of June 23, 1902, *GSG* 22: 422) about Simmel's "arrogance," saying: "As much as I recognize Simmel's superiority . . . I also think that I objectively deserve a bit more respect than Simmel is inclined to dispense to me from his infinite height."

5. See Klaus Christian Köhnke, *Entstehung und Aufstieg des Neukantianismus* (Frankfurt: Suhrkamp, 1986), 305.

6. In the first (and still most recent) book in English on Simmel as philosopher, Rudolph Weingartner writes, "Simmel's philosophy is but one of life—human life—and its products: culture." Weingartner, *Experience and Culture: The Philosophy of Georg Simmel* (Middletown, CT: Wesleyan University Press, 1962), 12.

7. Simmel to Keyserling, October 13, 1908 (*GSG* 22: 666). Simmel has sometimes been portrayed as a Bergsonian, so it is worth noting that immediately before the passage just cited, he remarks that since Keyserling and others had suggested that Bergson's *tournure d'esprit* ["mind-set"; in French in the original], was "related to my own," he would "try to incorporate" his work "despite having 'quite enough of myself through the daily 24-hour-long being-myself." Gregor Fitzi dates the beginning of closer contact between Bergson and Simmel to this period (1908–9), when Simmel had long since reached his mature views, but notes that "they had opportunities to become aware of one another earlier through the mediation of Léon's journal [i.e., the *Revue de métaphysique et de morale*—EG] and through international philosophical congresses" (Fitzi, *Soziale Erfahrung und Lebensphilosophie: Georg Simmels Beziehung zu Henri Bergson* [Konstanz: UVK Verlagsgesellschaft, 2002], 50).

gether, for in his modernist approach to culture the inherited resources of the philosophical tradition are transformed before our eyes. As in the case of Kant, Simmel creatively and constructively appropriates his predecessor's insights and strategies of thought. The significance for his work of what Nietzsche called the death of God can hardly be overestimated; Simmel's metaphysical relativism and emphasis on the perspective nature of truth and his distinctive approach to ethics are clearly Nietzschean in inspiration; and his sociology involves, among other things, a rethinking of genealogy itself.

Like Nietzsche, Simmel was profoundly concerned with the question of the future of European culture in general in light of the rise of modern science—and with the problem of the future of *Bildung*, of the cultural task of education, in the post-1871 German university in particular. Like Nietzsche, he was profoundly influenced by Goethe as a thinker and artist and as the exemplar of a specifically human vitality and integrity. In a 1913 monograph, Simmel described his life as a "flowing unity": "Goethe's unceasing experimenting and reformulating of possible standpoints, the development that flowed through all the contradictions of his long life" permits endless possible "interpretations of that unity and totality"; it also provides a model for integrating multiple, changing perspectives and development through contradiction without sublation.[8] Not least, Simmel, too, found inspiration in the (Goethean, but also romantic) fascination with synecdoche and developed philosophical strategies that elevated fragments into windows onto sociocultural and historical wholes.

Yet Simmel's writing, like Nietzsche's, is self-consciously situated at a moment when the rationalist pieties of nineteenth-century *Wissenschaft* were coming into crisis: when the realities of industrialization were undermining faith in technological progress, and Goethean holism and organicism were beginning to give way to more sinister forms of longing for totality. It is in this broader intellectual-historical context that the question of whether and in what sense Simmel ought to be characterized as a philosopher of life must be posed. This question is imbricated with the more general issue of his place in intellectual history altogether—and especially with the implications of Simmel's thinking for the return to the topos of life in contemporary theoretical work. Here, too, his modernist style of thought, with its self-reflexive relation to problems of life and form, lends Simmel's writing a new actuality.

In her incisive monograph *Die geistige gestalt Georg Simmels* (Georg Simmel [as] Spiritual Gestalt), the philosopher and poet Margarete Susman (Margarete von Bendemann) (1872–1966), a former student who belonged to Simmel's close circle of friends, highlights his striving to find a new way of philosophizing beyond dualities: "With his disinclination for the system, which was grounded for him in the essence

---

8. In his *Goethe*, Simmel set out to "project the Goethean life, this restlessness of self-development and productivity, onto the plane of the timelessly significant thought" by exploring what he identified as "a third" distinct from both the life and the work in which it found expression: "the pure meaning, the rhythm and significance of the essence," analogous to "a concept, which is realized both in the soul that thinks it and in the thing whose content it defines." Riffing on Goethe's characterization of his own oeuvre, Simmel admits that such a writing of "this third, this 'idea Goethe'" must become "the exegete's own confession" (*GSG* 15: 7–270; all citations here from pp. 9–10).

of thinking itself, Simmel never represented the three and the third in systematic form. Nonetheless it permeates his philosophy. Always it is something unreachable, for which he seeks names and concepts."[9]

Susman goes on to cite the first aphorism in Simmel's posthumously published journal, where he takes issue with the received view that we must belong either to "the natural" or "the transcendent" world. Rather, Simmel writes, "we belong to a third, unutterable [world], of which the natural and the transcendent alike are mirrorings, discharges, falsifications, interpretations" (*GSG* 20: 261). According to Susman, "All of Simmel's efforts as a thinker are to be understood as such mirrorings and interpretations of a third. Subject and object, life and death, being and duty [*Sein und Sollen*], reality and idea are to be reconciled in a third, still undiscovered, yet to be discovered spirit- and life-form [*noch zu entdeckenden Geistes- und Lebensform*]."

In recent years, Simmel has become increasingly recognized as a key avatar of a thinking of the "third," and in this there is still much to be learned from him.[10] Yet his vision of spiritual and cultural renewal belong to a world utterly lost to us. As Susman underlined, "Simmel's death at the end of the First World War marks the boundary at which a new form of thinking commences." Looking back, she reflected on its origins: "in the two great wars the human being had lost its countenance," and thus "Western philosophy as a whole had really arrived at its end. A new thinking and a new language were needed to express the thinking of a new time."[11]

It is misleading to think of Simmel either as a sociologist who also philosophized or as a philosopher who happened to participate in the emergent discipline of sociology. Both views project into the past a professionalized disciplinary order that was still being constituted during his lifetime. Simmel's vision of the tasks of thought in the modern world led him to make significant practical as well as theoretical contributions to the founding of the modern social sciences. But these contributions were by no means as extrinsic to his philosophical agenda as they appear from contemporary, disciplinary perspectives. Rather, Simmel's preoccupation with the status and nature of sociology is a constitutive feature of the modernist approach to philosophizing that evolved out of his early proto-positivist conviction that philosophy was becoming obsolete in a world where "the science of man has become the science of human society."[12] Placing that intellectual evolution in the context of the global shifts in modes of inquiry and in rhetorics of reflection under way in this period will throw seemingly self-evident distinctions between social science and philosophy, and more generally between empirical and theoretical inquiry, into relief.

---

9. Margarete Susman, *Die geistige Gestalt Georg Simmels* (Tübingen: Mohr-Siebeck, 1959), quoted here from pp. 4–5. See also www.margaretesusman.com/index.html.

10. See Thomas Bedorf, Joachim Fischer, and Gesa Lindemann, eds., *Theorien des Dritten. Innovation in Soziologie und Sozialphilosophie* (Munich: Fink, 2010), and my "Simmel's Stranger and the Third as Imaginative Form," *Colloquia Germanica* 45, nos. 3–4 (2012): 239–63.

11. Susman, *Die geistige Gestalt Georg Simmels*, 35–36.

12. "Die Wissenschaft vom Menschen ist Wissenschaft von der menschlichen Gesellschaft geworden" ("Das Problem der Soziologie [1894], *GSG* 5: 52–61; here p. 52). I generally translate *Mensch* as "human being" but defer to the (sexist) tradition in this case to avoid obscuring the historiographical and theoretical resonance of the phrase.

With the canonizers, then, I urge a return to Simmel's oeuvre as the crucial repository of largely forgotten resources for social and cultural theory. One of the principal objects of this book is to uncover something of the history of effects through which, in the course of the twentieth century, Simmel's ideas and strategies of thought were absorbed and transformed in ways that not only rendered their origins illegible but also squandered their full theoretical and practical potential for reflection on modern life. If we are to recover that potential, we need to understand the larger philosophical project from which even the most sophisticated readings of Simmel as sociologist abstract his ideas and methods. We cannot brush away ambiguity by returning to "the texts themselves," because an adequate account of Simmel's thought must also explain the peculiarities of his reception, including the fact that the same texts are regularly understood to substantiate diametrically opposed positions and methodological commitments.

To be sure, Simmel has been read selectively; misleading and even distorting appropriations have decisively shaped his reception. Yet doing justice to his internally complex oeuvre entails more than correcting errors. The question—as with Freud, Durkheim, or Weber, for that matter—is how to come to terms with the ambiguity and opacity that mark the path of thought that has not yet solidified into certainty regarding the meaning or even the nature of its objects. In Simmel's case, this difficulty is exacerbated by the fact that his modernist approach to philosophizing entails a radical openness to interpretation. The multivocity of Simmel's texts reflects a sophisticated awareness of the relativity of thought and of the challenges of capturing symbolically and intersubjectively constructed realities in concepts.

Simmel was acutely aware of the limits and contingency of his own insights and approach, yet he was explicitly committed to a vision of thought as exceeding its own time. As a self-consciously historical thinker of the social, he strove to develop methods of analysis and strategies of interpretation that could be extracted from their contexts of origin and put to use for quite different purposes. However important and necessary it is to identify some of the unmarked bills of Simmel's legacy, this is not the same thing as coming to terms with his oeuvre itself.

The mature Simmel embraced a perspectival relativism that feels very contemporary today—yet, by its very nature, we cannot simply adopt it. For he wrote in ways that invite, indeed, demand, reflection on the relativity and contingency of his own claims. His texts are modernist in drawing attention to their own writtenness so as to catalyze awareness of the constitutive role of perspective in human understanding—and hence of the relativity of every knowledge claim, including Simmel's own. To address texts that formally evoke reflection on the relativity of perspectives in this way, methodological and theoretical discussions must be enriched by critical and historical modes of thinking about form. *Georg Simmel and the Disciplinary Imaginary* attempts, then, both to clarify how and why Simmel arrived at his relativist understanding of culture, society, and the human and to grasp the strategies of thought and writing through which he inscribed openness to multiple interpretations in his philosophizing.

To read Simmel not only as a modern thinker, or even a thinker of modernity, but as a modern*ist* entails reconceiving the relationship between his oeuvre and its historical, cultural, and theoretical context. To do justice to the historicity as well as the philosophical seriousness of his modernist conception of form also requires a broader reconsideration of received narratives about the emergence of modern social science. My examination of Simmel's reception reveals how the genealogy that bifurcates those disciplines from their origins in philosophy and history also severs the methodological questions that animate today's social sciences from the concerns of "theory" as understood in the contemporary humanistic disciplines. To draw attention to the synthetic features of Simmel's thought is to underline the continuity of his approach to theorizing the social with the practices of interpretation and representation that defined modernist culture more broadly—and thereby to illuminate the prehistory of the contemporary disciplinary imaginary.

Simmel's oeuvre is situated at what were during his lifetime relatively permeable boundaries between philosophy and social science, academic and popular writing. His thinking was shaped by a perspectival relativism that, even as it draws attention to its own conditions of possibility in the phenomenon of subjective experience, exposes the supplementary relations between the knowledge practices of distinct disciplines, particularly between philosophical modes of reflection and social scientific ways of knowing. Read with sensitivity to their historical, cultural, and intellectual context—that is, to the past of our own theoretical practices—Simmel's writings cast a fresh light on the contemporary disciplinary landscape, providing new perspective on the categories and conceptual divisions that came to structure Western intellectual culture and shape quotidian understandings of modern life in the course of the twentieth century.

The network of assumptions and practices that frame readings of Simmel in disciplinary terms blockades recognition of this wider, transdisciplinary theoretical and historical significance of his work. Not only do we miss a great deal that is of interest when we slice up his oeuvre into disciplinary "parts"; we reinforce a fragmentation of scholarly life that presents very real institutional and conceptual barriers to meeting the intellectual and cultural challenges of the twenty-first century.

My objective, then, is not simply to show that what have been categorized as Simmel's "sociological" works have implications for philosophy and humanistically oriented social and cultural inquiry more generally. Thinking his liminal position can open a new and urgently needed perspective on the contemporary intellectual world, where disciplinary divisions of dubious ontological purchase have become deeply naturalized features of our mental and institutional landscapes. Consider, to take two current trends as examples, that efforts to bring together psychological and philosophical perspectives on the self or to integrate biological perspectives into social science are commonly taken for cutting-edge scholarly innovations. Without historical awareness, such efforts to bring together ideas from different disciplinary spheres all too often culminate in what amounts, as in these cases, to the rediscovery of the wheel—that is, to work that uncovers the shared problematics lurking behind different idioms and methods of intellectual traditions that in fact have common origins.

Failure to reflect on the contingency and perspectival specificity of (naturalized) disciplinary perspectives thus compounds the sort of epistemic errors that

Marx and Nietzsche both criticized as the consequence of forgetting (or willfully ignoring) that the conceptual structures and standards that organize our world are themselves produced by human beings. That is, the apparent stability (and institutional reality) of disciplinary categories depends on the same ahistorical confusion of concepts with realities, subjectivity with the world, that issues in the embarrassing spectacles skewered by Nietzsche as analogous to the practice of seeking out "truths" behind the very shrubbery where one has hidden them. To forget the significance of the subject in the creation of objects in this way is both epistemologically and ethically suspect. As Nietzsche puts it, "at bottom the searcher after such truths seeks the metamorphosis of the world into the human being" and, in failing to recognize the difference that separates us from the nonhuman, "wins at best a feeling of assimilation."[13]

Like both Nietzsche and Marx, Simmel believed that the necessary first step in moving philosophy beyond such anthropomorphic circling and toward a more adequate, historically and culturally articulated conception of truth was to expose the historicity and contingency of our ways of seeing. While his dialectical strategies of interpretation were deeply inflected by Hegel's phenomenological approach to philosophizing, Simmel did not aspire to overcome contingency by creating a system, but rather maintained a Kantian modesty about the limits of human understanding and self-understanding. Like Nietzsche but unlike Marx, rather than attempting, even imaginatively, to overcome contingency and individuality in an integrative totality, he espoused a perspectival view of truth that affirmed the radical difference and multiplicity of situated points of view. As we shall see, Simmel's efforts to reconcile this historicist commitment to a perspectival understanding of reality with an old-fashioned aspiration to higher truths animates his evolving conception of his work—and the shifting disciplinary identifications that accompanied it. Along the way, he developed strategies of thought that remain of considerable interest in an intellectual context where fundamental questions about knowledge and identity, culture and perspective, have lost none of their urgency in the intervening generations.

Even though frankly old-fashioned historical questions about Simmel's intellectual accomplishments and the vicissitudes of his influence over time play a central role in my arguments, the present project is thus far from being what Nietzsche called "antiquarian" in intent. Indeed, quite in the spirit of a man whose work often flouted scholarly conventions, including, not coincidentally, the footnote,[14] it advocates an appropriation of his thought for present needs. Such appropriation should not be conflated with a collapse of scholarly horizons. It is essential to attend to the

---

13. Friedrich Nietzsche, *Sämtliche Werke: Kritische Studienausgabe,* ed. Giorgio Colli and Mazzino Montinari (Munich: Deutscher Taschenbuch, 1999), 1: 883.

14. In Simmel's defense, as Anthony Grafton writes, "the intellectuals of the nineteenth century did not view [footnotes] with the unmixed admiration and affection one might expect. Hegel, for example, clearly rebelled against the idea that a philosopher's text should use footnotes to exemplify and carry on a dialectical argument" (Grafton, *The Footnote: A Curious History* [Cambridge, MA: Harvard University Press, 1997], 97).

differences between his intellectual and cultural starting points and our own. In returning to his texts, it is just as crucial to ask what cannot or should not be appropriated as to discover what can. The pages that follow call for a return to Simmel, but by no means for an uncritical one. Indeed, aspects of his work that are of the greatest interest from a historical perspective—his conception of culture, his reflections on gender—underline the distance between his philosophical perspectives and contemporary points of departure.

As appealing and timely as many of Simmel's writings remain, and as important as it is to attend not only to his many substantive contributions but also to his methodological achievements, we may in fact have the most to learn from him where the distance is greatest. Simmel's writing is remarkable in its reflective openness to the sociocultural transformations under way in his lifetime and its author's wholehearted efforts to discover genuinely new strategies of reflection adequate to the shifting realities of modern life. But the similarities and indeed continuities between the circumstances of our own dawning century and the previous one notwithstanding, there can be no question of identifying our modernity with Simmel's. Even if the encounter with his ideas can do much to clarify what is at stake today, neither his questions nor his answers can finally be ours.

Georg Simmel and the Disciplinary Imaginary attempts to return to his oeuvre with an awareness of this historical and conceptual distance. It sets out, to be sure, to examine seriously and thoroughly what remains an underappreciated theoretical and philosophical legacy, to identify Simmel's recognized and unrecognized contributions to the theoretical and cultural debates of the twentieth century, and to demonstrate the continuing relevance of his methods of cultural analysis. But my guiding purpose is neither to defend his philosophy nor to make the case for the timeliness of his ideas. Instead, I want to ask what we might learn from Simmel about what we most need to know: how to find ways to think differently.

Today, as at the nineteenth-century fin de siècle, inherited strategies of thought have come to seem increasingly inadequate—culturally, politically, theoretically. Simmel, whose fame rested in no small part on his emphatic embrace of modern life, found ways of moving forward without rejecting the achievements of the past. The wager of this book is that his significance as a thinker cannot be captured by a straightforwardly historicist or antiquarian approach—that we must ask, instead, whether Simmel's oeuvre can provide a model of innovation, a touchstone in our efforts to come to terms with the very different challenges of our own rapidly changing world.

Scholarly enterprise began to take on its contemporary disciplinary contours in the world where he was an internationally famous philosopher and pioneering theorist of the social. To return—in medias res—to Simmel's texts in search of what has not yet been read into the canonical interpretations entails reflecting on the origins and limitations of our own intuitions and self-understandings in an era when the Western world was being transformed at least as rapidly as it is today—when the organization of knowledge and practices of inquiry, the meaning of art, science, culture, indeed of life itself, already seemed quite radically unsettled.

Part I addresses the relation between history and disciplinarity, exploring how Simmel became who he was—how he came to be represented and understood as a figure at once canonical and marginal in and through a reception that indeed resembles a diffusion of "cold cash." As I demonstrate, the very process that established his canonical position as a founding figure of modern social science also obscured the way his work addresses (rather than simply describing) the philosophical dilemmas of that complex, liminal moment when the modern disciplinary imaginary was coming into being. Focusing on the tensions in Simmel's reception history between attempts to draw attention to his status as a major thinker and innovator and a persistent pattern of selective reading and textual distortion, Part I analyzes how problematic strategies of reading have been made productive for a tradition of thought with which Simmel himself ultimately declined to identify.

In delineating what it means to read him as a (modernist) philosopher rather than a sociologist (of modernity), Part I lays the groundwork for a return in Part II to his 1900 masterpiece, the *Philosophy of Money*, situating this pivotal work—"one of the few after Nietzsche that does or will belong to the canon" of philosophy, according to Hans Blumenberg[15]—in the larger arc of Simmel's intellectual and professional development. In the first extended philosophical treatment of the work to appear in English, I demonstrate that Simmel's phenomenologically articulated, self-consciously relativist approach to the study of social and cultural life remains a valuable theoretical resource for the twenty-first century. Finally, Part III reconsiders the larger meaning of Simmel's place in the Western scholarly imaginary, reading the reception of his sociology against the grain to illuminate the historical ordering of inquiry today and reveal undisclosed possibilities in the liminal moment before the distinctions between diverse knowledge practices had ossified into the lived boundaries we call "disciplines."

---

15. Hans Blumenberg, "Geld oder Leben. Eine metaphorologische Studie zur Konsistenz der Philosophie Georg Simmels," in *Ästhetik und Soziologie um die Jahrhundertwende: Georg Simmel* (henceforth *AuS*), ed. Hannes Böhringer and Karlfried Gründer (Frankfurt am Main: Klostermann, 1976), 130.

PART I

Cold Cash and the Modern Classic

Simmel did not become a "classic" . . . [he was] more a philosophizing diagnostician of his era with a social-scientific touch than a philosopher and sociologist solidly rooted in the scientific enterprise.

Jürgen Habermas (1983)

CHAPTER 1

Introduction: Simmel's Modernity

Marginality at the Center: Georg Simmel in Berlin

Georg Simmel's marginality began during his lifetime, with an academic career that combined international fame with a long series of rejections and professional slights at the hands of the German professoriate. The author of more than two dozen books and hundreds of articles—an oeuvre comprising everything from thick tomes on moral philosophy and sociology to feuilletonistic fluff—Simmel published best-selling works of metaphysical speculation as well as a remarkably diverse range of essays on art historical, literary, sociological, and cultural topics. The critical edition of his works runs to twenty-four volumes, including two of letters, which by no means capture the original breadth of his correspondence, much of which has been lost forever. With his capacious and flexible mind and wide-ranging interdisciplinary interests came notable rhetorical talent, and Simmel enjoyed considerable fame in his own lifetime as a writer and speaker both in Germany and abroad. Significantly, though, he remained at the margins of the academic establishment.

Simmel was a philosopher and sociologist of recognized scholarly stature; he was also what we would today call a public intellectual. Recent research has underlined his impact beyond academic circles, including on key figures in the new social movements of the day, such as the feminist Helen Stöcker and the expressionist writer and pathbreaking homosexual rights activist Kurt Hiller.[1] He was also a fabled conversationalist, whose circles extended from Marianne and Max

---

Part I epigraph: Jürgen Habermas, "Georg Simmel über Philosophie und Kultur" (1983), in Habermas, *Texte und Kontexte* (Frankfurt am Main: Suhrkamp, 1991, 157–69); here p. 158.

1. As Klaus Christian Köhnke has shown in *Der junge Simmel in Theoriebeziehungen und sozialen Bewegungen* [The Young Simmel in Theoretical Relations and Social Movements] (Frankfurt am Main: Suhrkamp, 1996), the young Simmel was associated with social democratic activities as well as a wide range of contemporary life-reform movements. He published essays (often pseudonymously or anonymously) intervening in contemporary controversies concerning everything from prostitution and girls' schools to debates about national as well as academic political matters. Regarding his impact on Stöcker and Hiller, see Ralph M. Leck, *Georg Simmel and Avant-garde Sociology: The Birth of Modernity, 1880–1920* (Amherst, NY: Humanity Books, 2000). Klaus Lichtblau, *Kulturkrise und Soziologie um die Jahrhundertwende. Zur Genealogie der Kultursoziologie in Deutschland* (Frankfurt am Main: Suhrkamp, 1996) also discusses Simmel's political activities.

Weber to Rainer Maria Rilke,[2] from Edmund Husserl and Heinrich Rickert to Auguste Rodin and Stefan George. George Santayana called him "the brightest man in Europe."[3]

For many years one of Berlin's Friedrich-Wilhelms-Universität's most prominent intellectual figures, Simmel was a popular and influential teacher in the philosophy department (where he had also studied) from 1885 to 1914. His lecture courses, ranging over all five branches of philosophy—metaphysics, epistemology, ethics, aesthetics, and logic—in addition to sociology, became a "Berlin tradition." Hearers came from far and wide to experience a thinker who, in the words of one of the many eulogies published at his death, fostered the "rehabilitation of philosophy" and "exercised a more powerful influence on the spiritual development of the younger generation than the majority of his colleagues in the philosophical chairs of Germany."[4]

With his vibrantly embodied delivery, Simmel appeared to be thinking aloud, and he was able to convey the most abstract ideas in such an animated fashion that, as the literary critic Paul Fechter recalled, "the listener's thinking along also came to life and understanding arose of its own accord."[5] According to his admirers, Simmel's popularity was not due merely to his rhetorical brilliance. In the presence of this "genuinely cosmopolitan intellect," the philosopher Karl Joël wrote, one felt that "the zeitgeist itself had come to life."[6] For Fechter, he had a *Zeitinstinkt*, an instinctive feel for the times, that allowed him to give form to the intellectual and social transformations under way and provide what his hearers most needed, "an interpretation of the era [*Zeitdeutung*] starting from the modern."[7]

Many others remembered him in similar terms. Simmel's unusually public success as a philosopher was grounded in a cosmopolitan sensibility that resonated powerfully with his Berlin audiences. Skeptical, analytical, and highly sensitive, he experienced the modern world with visceral intensity—and strove to capture that

---

2. Rilke studied with Simmel in Berlin on and off beginning in 1897 (*GSG* 22: 1060) and they were in occasional contact. Two of the letters that have been preserved, from Simmel to Rilke, August 9, 1908, and from Rilke to Simmel, August 26, 1908, provide moving evidence of their mutual esteem (*GSG* 22: 642–43 and 646–47).

3. Quoted in Donald N. Levine and Dan Silver, Introduction to Georg Simmel, *The View of Life: Four Metaphysical Essays with Journal Aphorisms*, trans. John A. Y. Andrews and Donald Levine (Chicago: University of Chicago Press, 2010), x.

4. Quotations in this paragraph: Kurt Gassen and Michael Landmann, *Buch des Dankes an Georg Simmel: Briefe, Erinnerungen, Bibliographie. Zu seinem 100. Geburtstag am 1. März 1958* [henceforth *BdD*] (Berlin: Dunker & Humboldt, 1958), 154, 157. Hans Simmel recalled that although generally tolerant of unregistered auditors, including intellectually qualified outsiders, his father "placed great value on the 'niveau' [level] of his students" and did not like an uncomprehending audience, however large. When too many members of the public seemed to be motivated by the wish to make an appearance at a fashionable lecture, Simmel had student ID's checked at the door for a few sessions. Hans Simmel, "[Lebenserinnerungen] 1941/43," *Simmel Studies* 18, no. 1 (2008): 70.

5. Fechter quoted in *BdD*, 160. According to an anecdote related by Michael Landmann, in a moment of despondency about his legacy, Simmel asked Martin Buber "what he really had given his students in Berlin," to which Buber responded: "You taught them to think" (*BdD*, 223). For Emil Ludwig [Cohn], Simmel was "the artists' teacher" (*BdD*, 156).

6. *BdD*, 166.

7. *BdD*, 159.

experience and make it intelligible in speech and writing.[8] Simmel regarded a wide range of hitherto unexamined phenomena as worthy of philosophical attention, and he was often accused of uncritically embracing all things new. In fact, his analytic attitude was considerably more ambivalent. If his contemporaries saw him as a personification of the zeitgeist, it was not simply because he epitomized the hypersensitive modern urban subject, but also on account of his deep awareness of the cultural costs of freedom and of the intimate losses suffered in pursuit of subjective autonomy.

Simmel's cosmopolitan sensibility, a distinctive combination of immersion in and distanced reflection upon the complex and contradictory achievements of modern society, provided the lived foundation for what I call his modernist style of philosophizing. His texts do not, as has so often been asserted, simply affirm or uncritically register modern experience, with all its fragmentation and contradictoriness, but embody a mode of reflection deliberately shaped by the striving to make the modern world intelligible on its own terms. From his genuinely cosmopolitan, that is to say, reflective and self-reflective, perspective, the fascination of the moment, the allure of the particular, provided an occasion, not an end, for thought. But the philosophical sophistication of Simmel's approach to the contradictory plenitude of modern experience has gone largely unrecognized, with even his advocates tending to overemphasize moments of apparent immediacy, of immersion in particularity, while downplaying and neglecting the countervailing movements of negation and distancing that also mark his style of thought.

Writing in the *Hannoverscher Kurier* on the tenth anniversary of his teacher's death, the philosopher, critic, and literary scholar Ludwig Marcuse attempted to capture what made him stand out as a philosopher, "and not only among those of this century." Recalling Simmel's objection to "imprison[ing] the fullness of life in a symmetrical systematic," he powerfully evokes an intellectual style that combined "a maximum of receptivity, of experiential breadth and depth with a maximum of intellectuality, scholasticism, Talmudism, addiction to rationalization," adding that Simmel's "sensual-soulful sensitivity created an uncommonly rich substance for his possession by thought" (*BdD*, 189).

Marcuse goes on to describe Simmel's distinctive form of dialectical thought, his "relativism," as lived experience: "We loved in Simmel the fascinating event that a human being of enormous experiential capacity repeatedly penetrated through all conceptual boundaries into unconceived spaces of the soul," then captured them in concepts only to find these in turn "left behind by new experiencing" (*BdD*, 189–90). Writing for an audience that shared this living memory of the teacher and philosopher, Marcuse invoked and affirmed Simmel's posthumously published prediction:

---

8. *BdD*, 204. For the art historian Werner Weisbach, Simmel was "a typical representative of the epoch Karl Lamprecht called the age of nervous sensitivity [*Reizbarkeit*]." Leopold von Wiese echoed the same perspective, calling Simmel's work "the sociology of an aesthete, a sociology for the literary salon. Simmel is a cultural psychologist with a cosmopolitan cast of mind" (*Archiv für Sozialwissenschaft und Sozialpolitik* 31 [1910]: 882–907, quoted in Lewis A. Coser, *Georg Simmel* (Englewood Cliffs, NJ: Prentice-Hall, 1965), 56, trans. modified.

"Why did he die without spiritual heirs? Because he was (as Rickert once called him) the systematizer of the unsystematic." However, Marcuse writes, "Only the dogmatic concept can become tradition" (*BdD*, 190).

Simmel's cosmopolitan fascination with emerging forms of individual and collective experience gave rise to a new "relativist" approach to philosophizing, to new kinds of cultural inquiry and modes of reflection on the phenomena of everyday life. Such investigations always had high theoretical stakes: Simmel was striving to modernize philosophy, to achieve reflective traction on the historical and philosophical situation of modern western Europe and on the lived experience of those inhabiting and constituting that world.

Yet it is a mistake to think of this modernist philosopher as a philosopher of *modern* experience. For Simmel the entire relation between philosophy and experience was at stake, as it was for Kant and Hegel, Schopenhauer and Nietzsche before and Husserl and Heidegger after him.[9] While emphasizing philosophical problems that had gained particular urgency under modern historical and sociocultural circumstances, he did not develop a philosophy, much less a sociology, of modernity. Beginning with the phenomena of everyday life, Simmel led his listeners to timeless questions using a distinctive synecdochic logic that anchored the most abstract ideas in historical particularity. As the testimony of contemporaries shows, it was most of all this gift for making philosophical questions relevant to human existence that accounted for his appeal.

Like Hegel, that other great master of synecdoche, Simmel found philosophical entrée in the most insignificant features of everyday life. The novelist Frank Thiess recalled his "incredible ability to concretize an abstract process" and knack for discovering "the most inspired examples":[10] "in two years of study in Berlin, I never heard an hour that was more interesting, riveting, animated, and exciting, than Simmel's 'logic' lectures" (*BdD*, 177).

Simmel's modernist pedagogy opened up new vistas for thought. For the novelist Georg Hermann, he was an "anatomist of the ultimate stirrings of the soul that in others took place deep in the darkness of the subconscious," the "idol of youth" who became "the greatest experience of our years at the university" (*BdD*, 163). Simmel "proclaimed a 'turning away from mere thought' and believed that the immediacy

---

9. As a series of letters that have been preserved attest, Simmel enjoyed a lively philosophical friendship with his contemporary and colleague Edmund Husserl (1859–1938) during the period when the latter was rethinking his conception of phenomenology. Many of the works for which Husserl is best known today were written after the war, including the crucial second and third volumes of his *Ideen* (*Ideas*), both of which appeared posthumously. Regarding the relations between Simmel's philosophy of history and phenomenology, see Gary Backhaus, "Husserlian Affinities in Simmel's Later Philosophy of History: The 1918 Essay," and, with Richard Owsley, "Simmel's Four Components of Historical Science," *Human Studies* 26 (2003): 223–58 and 209–22. Exploring the personal relations and intellectual connections between Simmel and Husserl would be a worthy topic for a dissertation.

10. That is to say, Simmel had what Aristotle identifies in the *Poetics* (1459a) as a singular and unteachable natural and implicitly philosophical as well as poetic gift: the ability to create metaphors, which is a kind of thoughtful seeing (*theōrein*): "For to employ a metaphor well is to see (have insight into) the similar" (τὸ γὰρ εὖ μεταφέρειν τὸ τὸ ὅμοιον θεωρεῖν ἐστιν). Thanks to Kevin Corrigan for help with this translation and with Simmel's tricky Latin phrases.

of existence could be experienced 'only in its own profundity,'" Ludwig Marcuse recalled. This thinker who "abhorred the robustness of manipulable formulations" thus lived on in the memory of his students as "the original image of a philosopher" (*BdD*, 190–91).

Simmel's rhetorical brilliance and his gift for connecting philosophizing to lived experience were, then, placed at the service of the most intimate, yet most traditional, of pedagogical ends. In the words of the twentieth-century Dutch American geostrategist Nicholas Spykman,[11] Simmel "aided his students in finding themselves" rather than propagating a doctrine of his own (*BdD*, 187).[12] His private seminars were formative philosophical experiences for thinkers as diverse as Ernst Bloch, Martin Buber, Bernhard Groethuysen, György Lukács, Karl Mannheim, Gustav Radbruch, Max Scheler, Margarete Susman, and Leopold von Wiese.

Simmel's cosmopolitan approach attracted a cosmopolitan audience. From early in his career, his lectures and private seminars drew admirers from afar—from North and South America as well as eastern and western Europe and Japan.[13] Before the turn of the century, his lecture courses had already taken on the character of public events and were held in the largest auditoria of the Berlin University. But Simmel's popularity and the diversity of his audience were a source of suspicion. In a fateful denunciatory letter, the historian Dieter Schäfer, a student of the nationalist Heinrich von Treitschke's, called attention, not only to the large numbers of women attending Simmel's lectures,[14] but to many listeners from "the Oriental world . . . streaming toward [Berlin] out of eastern lands" among his audience.[15]

If Simmel's public success reflected the rhetorical talent that made him an unusually gifted teacher and lecturer, it nonetheless rested on solid academic credentials.

---

11. Spykman (1893–1943), whose 1923 University of California dissertation became the first monograph on Georg Simmel in English, was a political theorist and the founding director of the Yale Institute of International Studies. Spykman was an early geostrategical realist whose ideas were influential in the development of the field of international politics during the Cold War.

12. The testimonials to Simmel's pedagogical impact may be contrasted with the panegyrics to Martin Heidegger's charismatic effect on a younger generation of students after World War I, who, like Simmel's listeners before them, were seeking something more from philosophy than its academic adepts had to offer. Heidegger's esotericism and hostility to modernity are, however, the antipode of Simmel's eclectic approach and pluralistic embrace of contemporary culture.

13. In a letter to Célestin Bouglé on November 10, 1995, Simmel noted that "the interest in my conception of sociology is growing greatly among the students, especially among the foreigners; my listenership in this semester extends from Italy to Russia and Japan to America" (*GSG* 22: 157).

14. Women could not study formally in Berlin until 1908/9 but could attend lecture courses with the instructor's permission, which Simmel had been "among the first" to grant. Hans Simmel, "[*Lebenserinnerungen*]," 69.

15. Schäfer's poison-pen response (letter, February 26, 1908, *GSG* 24: 286–88) to an inquiry from Franz Böhm in Baden's Ministry of Education is generally recognized as accounting for the derailing of Simmel's seemingly assured call to Heidelberg in 1908. But Schäfer's letter, which also questioned sociology's status as science and attacked the idea that "society" could replace the role of "state and Church in human collective life" (English in Coser, *Georg Simmel*, 37–39), did not come to light until 1950. The unsavory terms of the opposition to Simmel filtered through, but the speculations of Simmel and his supporters were not directed toward Böhm or Schäfer himself. Since the publication of that letter in *BdD*, Schäfer's anti-Semitic rhetoric has frequently served to illustrate the sort of opposition Simmel faced over many years from the establishment.

In no small part due to his attempts to lay the theoretical groundwork of sociology, Simmel gained international scholarly recognition well before the publication of his masterwork, *Philosophie des Geldes* (translated as *The Philosophy of Money*), in 1900. The earliest commentaries on his work appeared not in Germany but in France, the first in 1894—a full twenty years before he finally received a regular professorship. The first book-length monograph on his work (likewise in French) was published the same year he left Berlin for Strasbourg,[16] but well before 1914, Simmel's intellectual impact had been reflected in literature in Czech, Russian, and Italian as well, and his work had been translated into an even wider range of languages, including Danish and Polish. The earliest English translation was an excerpt from his *Einleitung in die Moralwissenschaft* (Introduction to Moral Science) that appeared in the *International Journal of Ethics* in 1893, shortly after the German original was published.

The efforts of Simmel and his supporters to secure him a position commensurate with his talents and achievements were nevertheless repeatedly rebuffed. In the charged atmosphere of fin de siècle Berlin, his public success only exacerbated his status as academic outsider. By 1910, he had acquired a certain ironic resignation, writing a colleague: "German officialdom takes me for a kind of 'corrupter of the young,' and I shall thus surely never receive a professorship—even when, as happened two years ago, the Heidelberg department, indeed, the whole university (as the rector at the time put it), supported me in a way that had not happened for any appointment in years."

Simmel added that he enjoyed great pedagogical success—"numerically speaking" among the best in the country—and that "the area of my philosophical activity is about the most extensive of any German professor. It encompasses the *entire history* of philosophy, logic and psychology, ethics and aesthetics, the philosophy of religion, sociology, and the philosophy of right."[17] But neither his success as a teacher nor the breadth of his course offerings necessarily accrued to his advantage. There was considerable hostility to Simmel, as well as to what he represented—not only the entry of Jews into the university, but also unconventional scholarship that questioned established assumptions and even institutions.[18]

Correspondence with the aforementioned rector of Heidelberg University, the legal philosopher Georg Jellinek, in early 1908 illustrates Simmel's considerable insight into the difficulty of his position. His appointment to the Heidelberg chair formerly held by Kuno Fischer initially seemed virtually assured—he was in the second position on the list sent to the ministry in February, and Heinrich Rickert, whose name was first,

---

16. Albert Mamelet, *Le relativisme philosophique chez Georg Simmel* (Paris: Alcan, 1914).

17. Simmel to Samuel Singer, who had attempted to arrange an appointment for him in Bern, March 3, 1910 (*GSG* 22: 797). Here, as throughout, unless otherwise noted, all emphases in citations are also in the originals. Regarding Bern, see also *GSG* 24: 327–33, where Wilhelm Worringer's engagement on his former teacher's behalf is also documented.

18. Most "Jews" in the professoriate tended—like Husserl, Georg Jellinek, and Simmel himself—to be converts to Christianity. Regarding the racialized perception of Simmel as a "typical" Jew, as distinguished from his (in religious terms, apparently nonexistent) Judaism, and his theoretical and practical engagement first with socialism and then with the "new social movements" of his day striving for ethical and cultural reform, see Köhnke, *Der junge Simmel*, 122–49, 459–73.

wanted to remain in Freiburg.[19] Upon learning that the minister of culture "was reconsidering the matter for various reasons," Simmel responded with considerable equanimity, treating the delay as a routine bureaucratic development and proceeding to put forward tentative plans for taking up the post in Heidelberg in the coming semester.[20]

But a conversation with an unnamed official of his acquaintance awakened familiar concerns and prompted him to write to Jellinek again the following day. Simmel was widely regarded, he had been told, as "a purely critical spirit, who teaches students only the critique of everything and thus has a destructive effect, tending toward mere negation"—an "opinion," the man had assured him, that was "consistently joined with the greatest recognition of your professional achievement." Palpably alarmed, Simmel continued,

> As I heard these words, it suddenly went through my head—with the conviction that we sometimes have for entirely unproven things—that the minister's reservations of which you hinted to me can be traced to this, probably only to this "opinion." He will have heard from someone or other that I am a hypercritical, merely analytical thinker who corrupts the young in a properly Socratic way.[21]

His letter attempts both to explain and to combat the putative charge.

The source of the problem lay, Simmel thought, in a work he had published sixteen years earlier, *Einleitung in die Moralwissenschaft*, "admittedly a critical book. Since then I have been cursed for only offering negativities, and everything positive that I have done since then has been unable to eliminate this *aliquid haerens* [thing sticking to me]." But he had long since left behind his youthful stance: "I don't believe that there can be a book more averse to mere critique and more positively oriented toward the understanding of history and life than the *Philosophy of Money*." As for his teaching, one could dispute the worth of his lectures, but to call them merely critical would be nothing less than a "*falsification of the facts*," for he shared "Nietzsche's view: 'where you don't love, you should pass over.'"[22]

Simmel had correctly discerned that his seemingly certain appointment in Heidelberg was endangered. He wrote Max Weber the same day, beginning by rehearsing the accusation that he was "an exclusively critical, even destructive spirit and that [his] lectures lead only to negation" and continuing:

> Probably I don't need to tell you that this is a terrible falsehood. Like all of my work, my lecture courses have for many years been directed exclusively toward the positive, toward

---

19. *GSG* 22: 606. The list proposal (February 17, 1908, signed by the historian Karl Hampe, then chair, but actually composed by the historian of philosophy Wilhelm Windelband) praised Simmel as "the most singular" philosopher of his generation. His "main impact lay in the sociological works," with their "philosophical penetration" and "mastery of the research material pertaining to the most diverse disciplines"; Simmel was capable of "elevating sociology out of the state of empirical collecting and general reflections to the level of a truly philosophical investigation." With him on the faculty, Heidelberg would represent "the social sciences in their totality and in all relations" (*GSG* 24: 277–83; here pp. 279–80).

20. Simmel to Georg Jellinek, March 17, 1908 (*GSG* 22: 611). Jellinek (1851–1911), one of the founding members of the German Sociological Society (DGS), was professor of *Staatsrecht, Völkerrecht und Politik* in Heidelberg from 1891 on. During 1907–8, he held the post of prorector (*GSG* 22: 1050).

21. Simmel to Georg Jellinek, March 18, 1908 (*GSG* 22: 613–15).

22. As the *GSG* editor notes (22: 614), Simmel alludes to *Also sprach Zarathustra*, pt. 3, *Vom Vorübergehen*.

the establishment of a deeper understanding of world and spirit, with a complete abstention from polemic and critique with respect to other positions and theories. Anyone who understands my lectures and books at all *can* only understand them thus."[23]

Beneath his exasperation at the idea that the professional judgment of the Heidelberg philosophical faculty might be set aside on the basis of deliberate distortions of the record, Simmel was clearly beginning to come to terms with the possibility that this prestigious and seemingly assured professorial appointment would come to nought. He closed on a high note, remarking that however things turned out, what the whole process had revealed was "a thousand times more valuable to me than any sort of external success can be, the respect and love of so many and of *such* people."[24]

In fact, the defamation of Simmel as a "purely critical spirit" was only part of the story. Like other humanistic traditions in the rapidly evolving intellectual landscape of the previous fin de siècle, the discipline of philosophy was being professionalized and institutionalized, and its academic representatives were engaged in very practical struggles to defend the integrity of their enterprise in the face of the meteoric rise of new kinds of scientific enterprises. Social and natural scientific approaches were making both theoretical and practical inroads into formerly philosophical territory. With upstarts like sociology and experimental psychology competing for intellectual adherents and institutional resources, it was becoming necessary to differentiate and define the discipline in new ways.

In this context, Simmel's frankly modernist mode of philosophizing—from his avowed "relativism" and unusual topics and style of thought to unconventional behavior that included publicly engaging in contemporary political controversies and associating himself with movements striving for social and cultural change—was hardly conducive to academic success. Moreover, despite his philosophical qualifications, including publications that from the beginning of his career ranged over ethics, aesthetics, the philosophy of history, and the history of philosophy, Simmel had become indelibly associated with an emergent field widely identified, not without reason, with socialist tendencies. Even his institutional supporters regarded sociology as a hotbed of superficial scholarship.[25]

---

23. Simmel to Max Weber, March 18, 1908 (*GSG* 22: 61). As he put it to Jellinek, a listener who had followed for a semester and failed to grasp his positive orientation must be "either malevolent or entirely without comprehension" (*GSG* 22: 614).

24. Weber's own estimation of Simmel and engagement on his behalf are amply demonstrated in his correspondence—as is his consideration for his friend's feelings. In writing Simmel, Weber attributed the problems to "Berlin influences," but he in fact faulted Windelband, then chair, mentioning "disloyal behavior on W[indelband]'s part" to his wife Marianne and writing Rickert that those influences "would have had no significance if W[indelband]'s *report* [on behalf of the faculty-EG] had been different" (*GSG* 22: 616, 624). Windelband had cleverly conveyed his own view that "S. was actually not a philosopher" but a sociologist and thus might not support the appointment of a "'real' philosopher" in the future (*GSG* 24: 291–92). The concerted action of Weber and Rickert was decisive in securing Simmel his appointment in Strasbourg (*GSG* 24: 362–65, 376–78), although Weber was somewhat ambivalent—see his letter to his brother Alfred of November 9, 1912, cited in *GSG* 24: 294–95), and his uncompleted review of the *Philosophy of Money*, "Georg Simmel as Sociologist," trans. Donald N. Levine, *Social Research* 39 (1972): 155–63.

25. See the Berlin faculty's letter of February 2, 1900, requesting a position for Simmel, where sociology is described as "a playground for semi-science" (*BdD*, 24).

By 1908, Simmel's professional difficulties were already long-standing. Thanks to his experimental spirit and unconventional behavior, he had already encountered considerable institutional difficulties with the philosophical faculty at the Berlin University. His proposed dissertation, "Psychological-ethnological Studies on the Origins of Music," seems to have been regarded as wildly inappropriate, and he was encouraged to submit in its place his prize-winning paper about Kant's views on matter. A few years later, the efforts of Wilhelm Dilthey and Eduard Zeller in overcoming their colleagues' objections to Simmel's *Habilitation* submission (once again on Kant) had been rewarded by the candidate's publicly insulting Zeller during the colloquium after his qualifying lecture.[26] Simmel had failed and been obliged to wait six months before repeating the process that would allow him to be officially accepted as a member of the faculty in 1885.[27]

Predictably, in light of this rocky beginning, there was some hesitation among the members of Berlin's philosophical faculty about promoting him. Simmel spent fifteen years as *Privatdozent* before at last receiving the title of *Professor Extraordinarius* in 1900, the year *Philosophie des Geldes*, his fourth book, appeared. And that recognition took a marginalizing and even insulting form that perfectly reflected official ambivalence toward this unconventional figure: Simmel's appointment was unsalaried.[28] As *Professor Extraordinarius* he was excluded from most university business and could not supervise dissertations. While his fame continued to grow, several efforts to secure Simmel regular professorships in philosophy at other institutions were defeated at the highest levels.[29] By the time he finally received his chair in Strasbourg in 1914, he was already fifty-six and had only a few years left to live.

Despite the gratification of finally achieving the institutional recognition he had long craved, Simmel left Berlin, the city where he had lived his whole life, with a heavy heart. It was not simply that after nearly receiving an appointment in Heidelberg and apparently declining an offer to join the faculty of an unidentified Amer-

---

26. According to family lore, Simmel had behaved dismissively "when [Eduard] Zeller claimed that the seat of the soul was in a certain lobe of the brain" and been sent off "to think about how one is supposed to behave in relation to distinguished older scholars" (*BdD*, 21; see also *GSG* 24: 202).

27. Then as now, German universities filled out their offerings with courses by scholars who had qualified for university teaching with a second thesis beyond the Ph.D., the *Habilitation*, but who had not yet received appointments elsewhere. In Simmel's day, these *Privatdozenten*, private lecturers, received fees from the students who attended their courses. The next level in the hierarchy, still at a very great distance below regular, *Ordinarius* professors, were professors *Extraordinarius*, those without chairs.

28. The Berlin philosophical faculty had unsuccessfully nominated Simmel for an *Extraordinariat* in 1898. In renewing its request two years later, the faculty petitioned for an appointment "with suitable salary," but the minister took the unusual measure of obliging Simmel to renounce claims to monetary compensation for the professorship. For a discussion that places Simmel's professional woes in institutional context and clarifies the situation concerning this appointment, including the question of Dilthey's role in the whole, see Köhnke, *Der junge Simmel*, 361–78. The primary documents are reproduced in *GSG* 24.

29. Simmel is often wrongly alleged to have been uninterested in a regular professorship by reason of his personal wealth. He actively pursued a number of possibilities outside Berlin. After his near-miss in Heidelberg, Simmel was once again in first place on a list for a philosophical *Ordinarius* in 1910–11, this time in Greifswald; his appointment was once again denied at the ministerial level. Another effort to appoint Simmel at Heidelberg, in 1915, also came to naught, as did an effort in Göttingen in 1918; all available documentation is in *GSG* 24.

ican university in earlier years,³⁰ his destination was a small and relatively obscure university on the outskirts of Germany. As a "metropolitan philosopher" and a Berliner par excellence who often "emphasized, as proof of his modernity, that he had been born at the intersection of Leipziger- und Friedrichstrasse,"³¹ Simmel regarded his philosophical achievements as deeply connected with his Berlin milieu and was, as a thinker and public figure, very strongly identified with the booming capital of the young empire. In the end he took on the challenge of helping build up an innovative philosophical faculty in the provinces, but the decision was not an easy one. Such was Simmel's devotion to his Berlin public—such was his understanding of his professional identity—that, according to his son Hans, he had worried: "Would it not almost be a betrayal to give up the possibility of influencing the spiritual development of youth for the sake of an official position and salary?" Even as he prepared to depart, he was wondering whether his choice had been an act of "cowardice."³²

Simmel's reaction reflects his unacademic thinking about the role of philosophy in modern life. His sense of pedagogical mission attests to his affinity with the broader cultural tendencies associated with contemporary life-reform and youth movements. But Simmel's concern for the "spiritual development" of his students and his contempt for pecuniary motivation also resonate with the most traditional, the originary image of Western philosophy: Socrates wandering through the agora, engaging the youth of the city in conversation.

Simmel's departure did not spell the end of his intellectual influence; some of his most significant work was published in the four years that remained to him, and he by no means retreated into the provinces but continued to travel and lecture widely. Moreover, as it turned out, moving to Strasbourg placed him squarely in the middle of the most important cultural and political event of his lifetime. Yet his departure from Berlin unquestionably marked a caesura. By the time Simmel finally received his appointment in Strasbourg, he had addressed overflowing crowds from Hegel's former haunts at the Berlin University on Unter den Linden for nearly thirty tumultuous years. According to his son, Simmel's urgent sense of philosophical mission was tied up with a belief that "his own fate was strongly connected to that of the city" as an emergent modern capital, and he often observed that "[t]he development of Berlin from a big city to a metropolis in the years around and after the turn of the century coincides with the period of my own most intensive and extensive development."³³

Simmel's feelings about leaving Berlin were by no means unrequited. In the

---

30. According to Hans Simmel, "At some point my father received a job offer at an American university, so far as I know Northwestern in Chicago or Western Reserve in Cleveland"; Simmel's refusal crossed paths in the mail with the withdrawal of the American offer on the grounds of economic crisis. Hans Simmel, "[Lebenserinnerungen]," 35. Despite considerable efforts undertaken in the context of work on the *Gesamtausgabe*, no particulars about this alleged job offer have been confirmed.

31. The story has an apocryphal air (and Simmel told it playfully, *BdD*, 276), but Hans Simmel confirms that he really was "born March 1, 1858, in the house that formed the northwest side of the intersection of Leipziger and Friedrichstrasse." Hans Simmel, "[Lebenserinnerungen]," 16.

32. Ibid., 106, 107.

33. Ibid., 105.

spring of 1914, he took his leave from "a lectern overflowing with roses."[34] Kurt Gassen reports that as Simmel spoke during the final hour, his hearers "became devastatingly aware that for us something was coming to an end for which there was no substitute and that we would now have to see whether we were able to think further and to continue to act in his spirit without his presence" (*BdD*, 302). A newspaper headline lamented the prospect of "Berlin without Simmel."[35]

This broad resonance makes the timing of Simmel's departure all the more striking. His final lectures at the Berlin University took place in the Winter Semester of 1913–14; the very next semester, the Great War would begin, bringing a definitive end to Simmel's cultural and intellectual world and utterly transforming the prospects, spiritual and otherwise, of his youthful hearers.

Modern Culture and the Problem of Disciplinarity

Seen from the far side of the cataclysms of the twentieth century, the previous fin de siècle appears far more stolid than it was. If great empires (Habsburg, Romanov, British) were still in place, so too were the fault lines that would sweep all of them away in the course of the next generation.

The truly global market fostered by colonialism and borne by modern forms of transportation and new technologies of communication had already shrunk the world perceptibly. Rapid urbanization in the wake of the so-called second industrial revolution, with which Germany had entered the modern fray in earnest, was fracturing the traditional social order; new sources of energy were promising (or threatening) to replace human and animal labor with machines. These transformations laid the foundations of the twentieth-century world order: the hegemony of the money economy, the political and economic predominance of the Western powers, what today seems the self-evident domination of everyday life by technology and consumption. Developments in the natural sciences and the rapid social transformation brought on by industrialization and urbanization were simultaneously intensifying the already ongoing destabilization of inherited religious and cultural norms that was the legacy of the Enlightenment. New, democratized and democratizing forms of mass entertainment based on emergent technologies of mechanical reproduction were altering the arts and cultural life.[36]

As in the case of the technological, political, and cultural revolutions of our own era, all this happened rapidly enough to produce a palpable divide from the past in the space of far less than a single lifetime. Georg Simmel, who turned twelve in 1871, came of age, as it were, with the newly unified German state, and his life and career unfolded against a backdrop of epochal sociocultural and political change

---

34. *BdD*, 191 (Marcuse); Kurt Gassen also mentions the roses, *BdD*, 302.
35. Hans Simmel, "[*Lebenserinnerungen*]," 107. This headline is frequently invoked, as here, without attribution; my efforts to locate the original in Berlin archives have been unsuccessful. In a postcard to Susman, Simmel notes "highly lively and highly repulsive" attention from the press: "I was a 'sensation' for five minutes" (January 28, 1914; *GSG* 23, 287); a gossipy January 20th feuilleton is reproduced in *GSG* 23: 282.
36. Simmel's inheritance was derived from sheet music publication (Peters Verlag).

and scientific, technological, and aesthetic innovation. By the end of the nineteenth century, a recognizably "modern" world had taken shape: an enlightened, critical stance vis-à-vis traditions and inherited truths of all sorts penetrated deeply into elite European cultural life—though to be sure, change and the emergent culture of novelty were by no means universally celebrated, especially within conservative institutions such as the university.

The *Communist Manifesto*, written on the eve of the 1848 revolutions, vividly captures this ascendant cultural modernism: in the hands of the bourgeoisie, with their pragmatic and materialist attitude toward all established values and practices, "all that is solid melts into air." For Marx and Engels, the disappearance and destruction of the old, and the rapidity with which what succeeded it became antiquated in turn, had "finally forced human beings to gaze with sober eyes upon their life situation, their mutual relations." The material transformations that accompanied the bourgeois industrial and political revolutions had made possible a new, scientific mode of human self-understanding, one that could without ceasing to be materialist also be dialectical.

A generation later, the overall direction and prognosis for the future of European society and culture remained unclear. For all the optimism and confidence associated with the booming *Gründerzeit* (era of economic takeoff), the densely populated, soot-blackened cities and recurrent economic crises made the ambiguity of progress evident even before the Great War, challenging the web of rationalist assumptions that had sustained the identification of history and progress within "enlightened" thought. Especially before 1917, the Marxian metanarrative according to which these tensions would ultimately be resolved in a new kind of society was one among many competing socialist visions, one by no means as universally compelling as adherents of its logic believed—and, later on, attempted to compel others to believe.

Against this backdrop of emergent mass society, amidst the cultural upheaval and uncertainty regarding the political and practical implications of the changes brought by industrialization, urbanization, and (however incomplete) democratization, the problems took shape that would occupy Simmel throughout his career. He began to contemplate the nature of the society and the "problem of culture": of the origins, nature, and fates of the accumulated knowledge, values, and practices that constitute the lived and intersubjectively transmitted foundations of human collective life. "Culture [*Kultur*]: this word was a central, practically religious concept not just in Simmel's thought but also in his life," Margarete Susman writes. "The being [*Sein*] Simmel called culture was for him not only that which allows everything truly to become real, it was before all else the 'path of the undeveloped soul to its unfolding.'"[37]

Simmel's reflections on the nature and future of culture concerned both its role in the formation of individual subjects—that is, in the process of education, or *Bildung*—and its function in collective life in a more general sense—that is, as the condition of possibility of what we would call subjectivation. Like both Marx and Nietzsche, Simmel framed these questions in relation to the future of philosophy, the discipline

---

37. Susman, Die *geistige Gestalt Georg Simmels*, 28; subsequent citations are in the text.

that, par excellence, embodied and perpetuated the Humboldtian ideal of cultural education as harmonizing individual and collective life.

Simmel sometimes sounds like a conventional adherent of that tradition, but he was by no means uncritical, rejecting its idealist underpinnings in favor of the Herderian conception of objective spirit that had resonated in the *Völkerpsychologie* of his teachers Moritz Lazarus and Heymann Steinthal.[38] Yet even as he helped pave the way institutionally and conceptually for the overcoming of the idealism embedded in inherited ways of thinking about philosophy and culture alike, Simmel still found it possible (or necessary) to believe (in Susman's words) that "the grand convergence of culture itself: the speaking of spirits from summit to summit" defined "the meaning of life" (28).

Simmel lived on the cusp of a new world. As modernity took on the configuration of unending revolution, the cultural legacy was losing its aura of self-evident value, and both the place of philosophy and the conception of culture inherited from German idealism were being set aside or relegated to the ivory tower for good. The sheer rapidity of socioeconomic and technological change was palpably destabilizing traditions and inheritances of all sorts, even as exposure to other worlds accentuated the constructedness and contingency of the European worldview. In a nutshell, "culture" was changing its meaning. By 1918, a mode of philosophizing centered on that category and assuming the normative value of the Western inheritance appeared antiquated—or not originary enough. Simmel's career as a thinker registers the impacts of these tectonic changes; they can be traced in the evolution of his disciplinary self-understanding and animate his mature efforts to renew what he called "philosophical culture" both inside and beyond the university.

Like Simmel himself, this thinking is liminal. His efforts to conceive of culture, society and human existence from a perspective that sees human being as historically and culturally constituted, but also as constituting the world that shapes it, and to do so in a way that rethinks the very notion of foundations, brought Simmel to the brink of a new world, which he was barred from entering.

Thus Susman, looking back from 1959, underlined that "the new generation," those who came of age in and through World War I and its aftermath, no longer shared Simmel's quasi-organic vision of culture as means and catalyst for the de-

---

38. *Moritz Lazarus und Heymann Steinthal: Die Begründer der Völkerpsychologie in ihren Briefen*, ed. Ingrid Belke (Tübingen: Mohr, 1971) remains an invaluable introduction. The memory of these distinguished representatives of the first generation of German Jews to enter the professorate (albeit as marginalized *Extraordinarien*) has been burdened by unfortunate associations with the concept of "*Volk* [folk]" and its grim twentieth-century history. Strongly influenced by Humboldt's thinking about language, Lazarus and Steinthal promulgated a broadly humanistic, non-idealist Herderian conception of culture that should not be anachronistically conflated with the pernicious forms of nationalism that gained force after 1871. Simmel's earliest publications appeared in their journal, *Die Zeitschrift für Völkerpsychologie und Sprachwissenschaft*. Regarding the wider impact of *Völkerpsychologie* on cultural anthropology, see George W. Stocking, "Franz Boaz and the Culture Concept in Historical Perspective," *American Anthropologist* 68, no. 4 (1966): 867–82, and id., ed., *Volksgeist as Method and Ethic: Essays on Boasian Ethnography and the German Anthropological Tradition* (Madison: University of Wisconsin Press, 1996), as well as H. Glenn Penny and Matti Bunzl, eds., *Worldly Provincialism: German Anthropology in the Age of Empire* (Ann Arbor: University of Michigan Press, 2003).

velopment of the individual soul. Not only did they find the ideals that had defined bourgeois German philosophy untenable. They thought that

> culture was what had led the world that was destroying itself into ruin. They thus saw this alone in Simmel's concept of culture, they did not see that the great philosopher of history and sociologist Simmel, who had penetrated such wide swaths of events, also clearly recognized the crisis of the culture that had formed him and that he had himself formed further, who sought the way to a central depth below everything cultural and wanted to reach life and death and the human self. (28)

Today, when it seems self-evident that the engine of change is socioeconomic and technological, that erstwhile younger generation's perspective on culture, too, seems a historical relic of idealism.

Looking back across the abyss of twentieth-century history, it is striking how rapidly the classicizing philosophical ideal of the formation of cultured human beings, or *Bildung*, was decentered as the unquestioned end of higher education. A new, pragmatically oriented vision of practical training for the tasks of a changing world was gaining force and prestige; new kinds of educational institutions were founded in which such liberal educational ideals played little role. As the pragmatic requirements of modern technoscience gave rise to laboratories and research institutes that required capital investments of a new order, what have become self-evident ties between natural science and industry were forged, and fundamental changes in knowledge practices in the rest of the academy accompanied these new modes of scientific and institutional organization.

All of this formed the context for the emergence of the modern disciplinary order: the division of inquiry into areas of specialized expertise that in the course of the twentieth century came to structure both intellectual culture and the ways in which knowledge itself is understood. During Simmel's lifetime, previously unprofessionalized practices, including the critical study of literature and the arts, were taking on the trappings of disciplines—departments, professorships, journals, professional organizations, canons, methodological debates—and becoming colonized by academically sanctioned experts.[39] The rise of the modern sciences of culture and the social reflected this overall tendency to professionalize and systematize scholarly and reflective practices in emulation of the natural sciences—and the ascendance of a bureaucratic culture of expertise in modern society more generally. These new disciplines were thus also symptoms of the very changes that they reflected upon.

The modern disciplines of the social owed their very existence to intellectual and cultural developments that were shaking the foundations of Western culture, and a reflexive relation obtains between the emergent knowledge practices and their objects of study. Catalyzed by colonialism and archaeological and geographical explo-

---

39. In 1874, Nietzsche published "On the Usefulness and Disadvantages of History for Life," his first great diatribe against the transformation of culture under the sign of modern science. In 1883, the year Simmel initiated his first, unsuccessful, attempt to obtain his *Habilitation* in Berlin, Nietzsche began to publish *Thus Spoke Zarathustra*, even today the lodestar of non-academic philosophizing, and Wilhelm Dilthey's *Einleitung in die Geisteswissenschaften* (*Introduction to the Human Sciences*), the first great systematic defense of humanistic (historically, socially, psychologically articulated) inquiry, appeared.

rations, by ideas from biological thinking about evolution and population genetics, by innovative methods of historical study, new knowledge formations took shape that made society and culture objects of empirical study. These incipient disciplines were infused with the global skepticism concerning traditions and foundations of all sorts, most of all religious, that was gaining an ever-greater foothold in nineteenth-century European society. As the term "culture" began to acquire the nominally nonevaluative connotation that defines its location in the modern scientific study of human society, the groundwork was being laid for the famous battle in the next generation over the relation between "civilization" and "culture."

Today, as cultural turns and (re)turns to biology continue to proliferate through the disciplines, the Simmel who "clearly recognized the crisis of the culture that had formed him," even as he strove to maintain and perpetuate it, is worth serious consideration. He grasped the depth of the conceptual and ethical crisis that followed on the development of the modern natural sciences—from physics no less than from biology. He struggled with the implications of what Nietzsche called "the death of God": the new way of thinking about human origins and purposes in which culture was coming to be understood as an evolutionary sociohistorical process in which human beings created and perpetuated values and meanings. And, like Nietzsche, Simmel was both a catalyst for and an analyst of the epochal shifts under way in the understanding of human life in the period.

Simmel did not understand the crisis he identified in his culture as a problem of modernity per se. But he shared with many of his contemporaries—not least Nietzsche—a conviction that the transformations of the nineteenth century had brought new (intellectual, political, social) urgency to problems of meaning and value at a collective as well as individual level. Without entirely parting ways with the philosophical tradition, he redeployed its resources in ways that helped prepare its creative destruction in the coming generation. Thus Simmel questioned the foundations and status of that tradition (as by concluding *Philosophische kultur* with an essay "Weibliche Kultur" (Feminine Culture), that thematizes the gendering of the cultural project of the West), and he extended the resources of philosophical reflection and inquiry to seemingly superficial or frivolous areas and topics.

Simmel's modernist philosophizing is situated, then, between (emergent) social science and a kind of philosophy that was passing away. His formally innovative writings both reflect and reflect upon an intellectual landscape undergoing a sea change, and his sensitive, yet critical strategies for disclosing the significance even of ephemeral cultural phenomena stand in an explicitly self-reflexive relation to contemporary scientific, technological, and material developments. There is reverence, but not only reverence, for canonical cultural objects in literature and the visual arts (in the intriguing monographs Simmel devoted to Rembrandt and Goethe, for example). But Simmel also philosophizes about unconventional and innovative topics and cultural phenomena (gambling, fashion, flirtation) with the same light-handed seriousness. And in doing so, he draws on the entire philosophical tradition, but also on contemporary research in archaeology, history, psychology, political economy, and law, to name only the most prominent fields.

Simmel can sound old-fashioned; he continued to deploy concepts that would come to seem antiquated in his own lifetime. Yet his imaginative strategies of thought strikingly anticipate the emergent philosophical idiom, the vocabulary centered on life and death, being and becoming, that would displace the Hegelian and Kantian language of truth and transcendence. His liminal philosophical and theoretical idiom helped shape the language in and through which the philosophy of spirit and the subject would yield to philosophies of life and existence and ultimately to theories of the embodied self in the decades to come.

His use of the term *Kultur* is a case in point. With his typical equanimity in the face of ambiguity and contradiction, Simmel embraces the complexity of the concept: in his hands, the lexical range of "culture" encompasses the high and the low, the objective and the subjective, the unabashedly evolutionist and the unreservedly elitist. Intertwined theoretically with his thinking of the social, Simmel's conception of culture exemplifies the ways his disciplinary liminality becomes palpable in and through his lifelong striving to develop theoretical practices adequate to a world devoid even of the illusion of transcendental foundations—to do justice to the Nietzschean insight that in the aftermath of the death of God, thought must begin from human life in its full, embodied complexity. And even as his work and example helped to shape the very way of thinking that was heralding the end of philosophy and culture in their inherited senses, he strove to foster new forms of "philosophical culture" both inside and outside the academy.

Simmel was a modernist in the writerly sense who made significant formal innovations in an effort to represent and understand modern experience. Such cultural modernism should not be conflated with an embrace of the new for its own sake. Even if, in the formulation of its locus classicus, Charles Baudelaire's "Painter of Modern Life," every age has known its own modernity, the affirmative sense of the modern that emerged in the nineteenth century registers an epochal change in the experience and understanding of history and temporality as such.[40] To be a modernist was not to reject the cultural legacy, but rather, in the face of the vast changes under way, to participate in the ongoing redefinition of (aesthetic and ethical) value away from the maintenance of tradition as such: to be oriented toward the still-emergent and the unknown present and future of culture and of the palpably new forms of subjective identity and experience coming into being.

In registering and reflecting upon the effects of cultural modernization, Simmel's oeuvre inherited and transformed the German philosophical tradition's concern with the historical vicissitudes of the dialectic between subjectivity and

---

40. I draw here on my reflections on the relations between cultural modernization and the remaking of temporal experience in the nineteenth century in *Experience without Qualities*. Regarding the primacy for artistic modernity of Baudelaire's claim about the perennial significance of the new for human existence, see Hans Ulrich Gumbrecht's "Modern, Modernität, Moderne," vol. 4 of *Geschichtliche Grundbegriffe. Historisches Lexikon zur politisch-sozialen Sprache in Deutschland* (Stuttgart: Klett-Cotta, 1972–1997), 110. According to Gumbrecht, Baudelaire's essay marks a historic turning point: the modern is no longer opposed to the classical. Grasped as the quality of the historical present as such, modernity is, rather, placed in tension with the eternal itself. As Baudelaire put it, "la modernité, c'est le transitoire, le fugitif, le contingent."

objectivity. It also anticipated and prefigured developments in phenomenological and existential philosophy and critical theory in the decades to come. On one hand, Simmel drew attention to the ways the hypertrophy of "objective" culture in the modern world was undermining and threatening individual subjectivity, creating blasé, morally indifferent agents. On the other, he emphasized how an intensification of individuality and awareness of subjective freedom were emerging, not despite, but in and through the regimentation and depersonalization of collective life.

With his wide-ranging topics and sources and innovative ways of thinking about and representing the sociocultural transformations under way during his lifetime, Simmel's modernist approach to philosophizing remains of considerable theoretical value (as distinct from merely historical interest) for any effort to understand the origins of our own modernity. Yet as the very anomalousness of the category of modernist philosophy underlines, Simmel and his interpretive practices cannot be straightforwardly situated in terms of our own disciplinary categories. To attempt to do so gives rise to vexing scholarly problems, not least concerning how to define, assess, and understand his influence on what, in the course of the twentieth century, came to be thought of as distinct traditions of thought. To come to terms with the historical and theoretical challenges of writing Simmel's innovations into the story of modern intellectual history, it is necessary to examine the genealogy of the contemporary disciplinary imaginary.

It is an obvious but easily forgotten truth that disciplinary formations come into being and pass away, that our ways of thinking and knowing, our practices and theoretical strategies, are anything but necessary. The contemporary disciplines are cultural as well as intellectual formations that exist and persist as assemblages of practices with more or less implicit embedded assumptions about everything from which questions really matter to what counts as a good argument or a reliable piece of evidence. Thanks to the internal logic of sociocultural differentiation and development that Simmel parsed so persuasively, disciplines tend to become, or at least to operate as, relatively self-sufficient worlds. A field and its practitioners come to be fitted out, not just with journals, conferences, and book series, professorships, offices, and laboratories, but also with unreflective habits and unquestioned taboos, unexamined truths and ideological commitments, shared aesthetic expectations and ethical as well as intellectual standards. Disciplinary identity is produced and perpetuated via a process of acculturation into the inherited knowledge practices that define a living tradition. Through this interactive, sociocultural process, practitioners—whether budding physicists or anthropologists or literary scholars—develop the sort of proclivities and intuitions that give them a feel for what does and does not belong to their disciplinary culture—and thereby acquire their professional identities. That is, they learn, not just how to act, but also how to think.[41]

---

41. An early, still compelling account of the cultural and intellectual operations of what Kuhn would label scientific paradigms is Ludwik Fleck's 1935 *Genesis and Development of a Scientific Fact*.

Disciplinarity is an assemblage of cultural practices through which both practitioners and institutions are produced and reproduced. Qua sociohistorical process, disciplinarity is itself situated in a complex historical and cultural context, surrounded both inside and outside the university by different and often competing styles of thought and inquiry. This circumstance both directly and indirectly shapes the practices and performances that constitute the lived foundation of the (institutional and imaginary) modern disciplinary ordering of knowledge practices as a whole. Only in the lived form of a specific institutionally and intellectually articulated culture can a given disciplinary formation effectively distinguish itself from the alternative knowledge practices of other fields in order to establish or assert its institutional prerogatives—first and foremost, what has become the highly mediated and systemically regulated right to produce new generations of professional practitioners. The resulting perennial scuffles at the margins of established disciplines are not resolved but perpetuated by the combination of poaching and cooperation among fields that today goes by the name of interdisciplinarity.

Whatever the truth claims enfolded in the ways of knowing, the theoretical precepts and methodological commitments of a given disciplinary (sub)culture, every such formation is itself subject, like all forms of human existence, to the vagaries of history. Knowledge may or may not transcend its own time, but it comes into being historically and, even in the case of mathematics, must be expressed in language that mires it in the contingency of representational expression. Within contemporary academic culture—and this is as true, if not as obvious, in the sciences as in the humanities—neither what counts as a fact nor how truth is understood can be entirely disentangled from this historicity.

Whether or not there are or can be truths independent of their historical context and rhetorical framing, in the absence of any assured, stable, and ultimate foundations, every actual human way of knowing is subject to reflection on the contingency of the point(s) of view embedded in it.[42] One of the consequences of this contingency (not determination) of knowledge practices in relation to their historical, cultural, human situatedness, is that in order for new disciplines to come into being, it is not sufficient that new ways of disclosing truth emerge. Incipient disciplinary cultures must, as it were, assert themselves effectively: new strategies and practices must be deployed by individual and collective actors who can differentiate them from other existing and emergent knowledge formations and successfully represent their ideas and methods as new and distinct, as well as effective and valuable, modes of inquiry.

Like so much of what happens to exist and persist in human cultural life, disciplinary cultures thus comprise narratives and practices that are perpetuated less by virtue of their truth than on account of historical accidents. Not that the tales we tell are a matter of indifference. Stories about origins play a decisive role in stabilizing and perpetuating any sociocultural formation, and disciplinary histories—with their

---

42. Regarding the implications of such historical self-reflexivity for the history and theory of the modern natural sciences, see Jean-Paul Cauvin, "A New Machine for Thinking: Historical Epistemology in Twentieth Century France" (PhD diss., Emory University, 2014).

already noted tendency to turn into convenient, if somewhat parodic sound-bites—are no exception. As in other forms of received wisdom, how much is at stake in the "official memory" of a discipline may not always be immediately apparent, and what has been left out of account is often of as much significance as what is foregrounded.

This is also true of much of the rest of contemporary disciplinary culture. Consider the metadivision of scholarship that fragments the universe of inquiry into "natural" and "social scientific" and "humanistic" arenas. Life and work within this sociocultural framework depends in all sorts of ways on the highly questionable and largely tacit assumption (or, better, unconscious image) of a world itself divisible into human, social, and natural parts or aspects or phenomena. And that large-scale ordering of inquiry, anchored in institutions and practices in manifold ways, does not change or evolve in the same way or at the same rate that knowledge does or can. Thus the disciplinary organization of the university is hardly called into question simply because inquiry into the natural, the social, and the human alike constantly demonstrates the contingency and constructedness of the imaginative division in and through which we represent and understand disciplinary knowledge practices.

In exploring the history of Simmel's representation as (proto)sociologist, I render more visible the highly tendentious background narratives on which the plausibility of that metadisciplinary (imagined, lived) order as a whole depends—and call into question the (largely tacit) equation of the differentiation and specialization of knowledge practices with intellectual progress.[43] In the case of modern social and cultural theory, a great deal of ink has already been spilled attacking the positivistic assumptions that underlie such narratives and attempting to develop more accurate historical accounts of the emergence of the modern disciplines of the social. Retracing Simmel's reception illuminates these debates from a tangent that helps account for why such critiques have by and large failed to affect the way mainstream social science operates.

In examining that history, I am less concerned with the status of claims to scientificity than with finding ways to open up thinking to novelty and invention by fostering reflection on the limiting and enabling conditions of dominant knowledge practices and on the global disciplinary imaginary as such. I strive to approach disciplinarity in ways that point (as I contend Simmel himself was attempting to point) beyond the philosophically (epistemologically, but also ethically) unsatisfactory knowledge practices that inevitably result when we fail to reflect on the ways our own socially and culturally situated ways of knowing inflect what we believe we know.

To leave behind the sorts of approaches Nietzsche criticized as anthropomorphically remaking the world in the (or rather, *a* very specific) human image, we must meet the relativist or perspectivist challenge of grasping the actual present organization of inquiry not as an objective scientific or theoretical achievement but rather as a contingent historical state of affairs in an ongoing process of change and

---

43. My purpose is not to argue against the value of disciplines or to discount the modes of knowing they embody and perpetuate but to emphasize that meta-, inter-, pre-, trans-, and even anti-disciplinary approaches are not just supplements or correctives to disciplinary knowledge practices but are themselves valuable constitutive features of a vibrant intellectual culture.

evolution. To fail to do so is to hypostasize our disciplines and modes of knowing as they happen to exist and to elevate the partial, always flawed visions of truth and facticity embodied in our contingent present into eternal truths. In clinging to a platitudinous vision of the past and treating our accustomed ways of thinking and ordering knowledge as unquestionable, we foreshorten our vision and elide the ambiguous zones between and commonalities among the disciplines that could be a source of renovation and renewal.

In retrospect, the long period of European peace between the proclamation of the German Empire in 1871 and the beginning of World War I appears as a prelude to the cataclysms of the twentieth century. But this is not how the vast upheavals of the *Gründerzeit* were experienced at the time. We must beware of reading back from 1945 or 1933, of underestimating the importance not just of 1914 but of 1917 for our own (tacit) historical self-understanding, for the narrative and hermeneutic perspectives we bring to bear on the intellectual and cultural tumult of the nineteenth-century fin de siècle.

Such attention to the openness of history is all the more important for human beings living in a period of epochal change. The year 1989 has come to stand for the beginning of a new and still emergent political restructuring of the world order and the end of the short twentieth century. Like the geopolitical transformations that began in Simmel's own lifetime, the economic and political upheavals of the twentieth-century fin de siècle, including, notably, the rise of new forms of concentrated financial power, went hand in hand with technological developments that have altered the lived foundation, the social structuration and perceptual ordering, of human experience. The ubiquity of "personal" computers beginning at about the same time marks the inauguration of a second communication revolution: transnational and global connectivity and the permutations of economic, social, and cultural life and experience in our own networked world give new meaning to Simmel's term "technologies of life."

What I am calling the problem of disciplinarity must be situated in the context of the vast and ongoing sociocultural, political, and economic, but also intimately embodied, transformation of the lived world in modernity. That, in contrast to the German *Wissenschaft*, the English word "science" has a relatively narrow semantic compass has helped naturalize conceptual divisions, with disciplines oriented to the empirical study of society embracing and those concerned with reflection on culture and the arts mostly eschewing the claim to be "science." But as the case of the discipline of history, which belongs at once to the humanities and the social sciences, reminds us, the division of inquiry into humanistic and social and natural scientific spheres is itself a contingent and relatively recent cultural development.

Over the past century, that global ordering of ways of knowing has come to seem so self-evident that it is difficult for those who operate within it to grasp how tenuous the categorizations and subdivisions of knowledge have become. Paradoxically this naturalized, institutionalized, and internalized disciplinary imaginary, with its division of knowledge into "kinds," remains robust, even as the traditional, absolutist understanding of truth has been displaced thanks to the dissemination of a (modernist) awareness of the contingency and constitutedness of knowledge itself and of the role of historically, culturally, socially specific perspectives on truth in all forms of rigorous inquiry, up to and including physics.

A great many factors have contributed to the general paradigm crisis in the organization of knowledge production that has emerged since 1989. Within and across the disciplines—and by no means only in the fields devoted to the study of culture in all senses—there have been a series of "turns": theoretical, historical, cultural, technological, biological. Yet today, as in Simmel's own time, relatively crude forms of materialist reductionism are enjoying increasing hegemony, with phenomena such as the current enthusiasm for "images" of "brain activity" or aspirations to "genetic engineering" uncomfortably reminiscent of historical precedents whose trajectories should give us pause.

Such reductivist approaches cannot possibly do justice to the complexity of their own existence as complexes of human action and reflection. That they are nonetheless gaining sway even in humanistically oriented inquiry calls for critical interrogation. The practical and theoretical urgency of thinking differently, of modeling more complex approaches to our very complex world, can hardly be overemphasized. Notwithstanding the differences between our moment in time and his, when the modern organization of professionalized inquiry was just beginning to be consolidated, Simmel's liminality provides a valuable perspective, but one that must be recovered. For as he himself foresaw with uncanny perspicacity, the significance of his spiritual-intellectual legacy would be rendered invisible in the world that emerged in the aftermath of the Great War, which he had already judged in 1915 to be nothing short of Europe's "suicide."[44]

Disciplining Simmel

That Georg Simmel is remembered today almost exclusively as a "founding father" of modern sociology is of considerable significance both within and beyond the social sciences. This categorization belies the diversity and range of his writings and anchors a largely implicit narrative about the organization of knowledge practices that authorizes appropriating Simmelian ideas and methods while disavowing the magnitude of his theoretical and methodological contributions to modern social and cultural thought as a whole. Reducing him to this particular sound-bite is more a mode of forgetting than of recognizing Simmel's actual accomplishments

---

44. By early 1915, Simmel had already revised an initial enthusiasm for the Great War, for which he is still censured. "Europe is about to commit suicide, and America sees its chance to place itself at the helm of world history," he wrote. "It stands by like the heir lying in wait at the deathbed of the rich testator" ("Europa und Amerika. Eine weltgeschichtliche Betrachtung" (Europe and America. A World-Historical Observation), *Berliner Tageblatt*, July 4, 1915; *GSG* 13: 139). By 1918, Simmel saw "Europe's self-destruction" as a fait accompli, writing Hermann Graf Keyserling that even the "*idea* of Europe has disappeared, for it is finally not a timeless idea like humanity or beauty but a historical one." His erstwhile hope "that the horrifying epoch of the industrial age and exclusively capitalist valuations was coming to an end" in a "new spirituality" had been laid to rest. Still, one might try to "be supernational" and "think and feel beyond one's own cultural egoism," to find comfort in the notion that "one day an American world-culture may come into being whose forms we can as little imagine as the Egyptians of the Old Kingdom those of a modern state" (May 18, 1918; *GSG* 23: 952–55).

as a thinker. But it is not subject to a simple reversal, for this canonizing mode of reception has in fact been a very productive, indeed a generative approach that embeds assumptions and practices that are constitutive of both social science and modern philosophy.

Simmel saw himself as primarily a philosopher, and he was regarded as such by his contemporaries. Several of his philosophical works were instant best sellers. Indeed, although his *Hauptprobleme der Philosophie* (Main Problems of Philosophy) sold 8,500 copies within two weeks of its publication in 1910, his most important sociological books, *Über sociale Differenzierung* (1890; On Social Differentiation) and the "large" *Soziologie* of 1908, waited twelve and fourteen years respectively for their second printings. But to emphasize his self-understanding as philosopher is by no means to deny the enduring value of his contributions to the emergent knowledge practices that, regarded retrospectively, formed the canonical foundations for sociology.

Decisively, it was through that sociological work that Simmel came to understand himself first and foremost as a philosopher, albeit one for whom "official Germany simply does not have a place."[45] Many of his most significant contemporaries in philosophy thought highly of him, and during his long struggle for a position consonant with his achievements, he enjoyed considerable institutional and personal support from better-established colleagues, notwithstanding that he has since become marginal at best in disciplinary memory.[46] Ironically, his subsequent canonization in sociology has obscured the import of these struggles—and not just for understanding Simmel himself.

These very different images of the thinker point to the crucial importance of such identifications in and for the cultural and intellectual prehistory of our own theoretical and disciplinary self-representations. What has been forgotten or occluded in the institutional and cultural memory of Georg Simmel casts light on the global evolution of the contemporary disciplines and in particular the differentiation of "humanistic" from "social scientific" inquiry during the twentieth century.

Like Marx's commodity, the image of Simmel as a sociologist serves as a kind of fetish whose "metaphysical niceties" conceal very material connections among the activities of those who exchange it. Like any fetish, its appeal depends on an enacted forgetting of those lived foundations, on a mise-en-scène that mimics and obscures the practices through which the image is produced. As we shall see, "Simmel," who is barely read and then often badly, serves a crucial function for sociology—but also for philosophy. For what is obscured in and through his habituated reception

---

45. This remark appears in Simmel's letter of July 20, 1908, assuring Jellinek that he regarded the matter of the Heidelberg post as settled and was entirely at peace about it. "I can't even call it resignation, for I was always instinctively convinced about the negative outcome even when a positive one seemed outwardly to have the greatest probability. Official Germany does not have a place for me. The way that philosophy professorships are now filled makes this entirely plausible" (*GSG* 22: 640–41).

46. The correspondence concerning possible appointments attests to warm support from colleagues and implacable opposition from above. Regarding Heidelberg, for evidence of Max Weber's concern about the humiliating treatment of his "intellectually eminent" colleague by the authorities, see Köhnke's editorial notes to Simmel's letter to Weber, July 17, 1908, formerly misidentified as dated June 17, 1908 (*GSG* 22: 635–40).

is precisely that these disciplines, now situated on either side of a hypostasized divide between "social sciences" and "humanities," have only recently been distinguished—and that for all their differences they remain inseparably part of a single enterprise of thinking the human world.

As recent developments on both sides of this institutional chasm have brought into relief, the distinction between the study of "society" and reflection on "culture" is a slippery one. Today's disciplines of sociology and philosophy embody a history that exemplifies a truth of which every modern scholar is uneasily aware: the divisions in our knowledge practices by no means map onto the natural organization of reality. What we think we know depends on assumptions (methodological, theoretical, epistemological, metaphysical) whose contingency only becomes truly evident when things break down.

Not just what is known but also what is forgotten in and through our knowing is complex and multiform. Contemporaries recognized Simmel as a figure who self-consciously embodied the intellectual and cultural ferment of Berlin at the dawn of the twentieth century. Looking back over his years there on the eve of his departure in 1914, he declared himself fortunate to have "participated in the great reversal in philosophy" away from "scholasticism" and toward life: "whether it is the river that brings forth the waves or the waves that constitute the river, I have been a wave in the river of this time."[47] What is forgotten in remembering Simmel as a sociologist is this man, the philosopher par excellence of his times who, just a few short years later, was clear-sighted enough both about the nature of his fame and about the institutional operations and historical effects of the emerging disciplinary order to embrace the fact that he would "die without spiritual successors" and predict that his legacy would be like an inheritance "in cold cash."

As Simmel's university career illustrates, that self-reflexive equanimity was far from being the blithe expression of an outsider's intellectual freedom. His relativism and objectivity reflected a deeply lived encounter with the transformation of academic life, and particularly of philosophy, as the social sciences began to become institutionally established as independent academic disciplines.[48] The first depart-

---

47. The newspaper report of Simmel's final lecture on March 1 is reproduced in *GSG* 22: 210. Ludwig Marcuse recalled the final image in a variant phrasing I have quoted, adding that Simmel "was the wave who had the whole river in himself. He reflected the heaven of this time, with its passion for thinking, like no one else" (*BdD*, 191).

48. All of Simmel's classes appeared in the official catalog under "Philosophical Sciences" until 1900, when some but by no means all of his sociological offerings began to be listed under the subheading "State-, Cameral-, and Industrial Sciences," and virtually all of his courses on aesthetics under "Theory of Art and Art History" (*GSG* 24: 607–21). In Berlin as elsewhere, the process by which the incipient modern social sciences found institutional foothold within the larger *Philosophische Fakultät* gave rise to acrimonious disputes, not least because such chairs (most notably in psychology) were coming at the cost of traditional appointments in philosophy. These origins have been subject to drastic historical revisionism. Consider, for example, the creation of the "Georg Simmel Guest Professorship" in 1993 on what Köhnke called the "fully fictional" occasion of the alleged centenary of "The Institute for Sociology at the Humboldt-University" in Berlin. In fact, that winter, Simmel (already the author of a small shelf of books) had "out of embitterment over his hopeless academic situation . . . remained away in Switzerland and Italy until spring." The institute in question had actually been founded in 1979 "as [an East German] research institute with the goal of training [GDR] cadres" (Köhnke, *Der Junge Simmel*, 360-361 n.).

ments of sociology and anthropology were established in France and the United States in the 1890s and in England in the following decade, but in Germany there were no professorships in sociology until after World War I.[49] Simmel's early sociological theorizing was thus explicitly directed toward establishing disciplinary foundations. In pursuing sociology, he was in the first instance attempting to establish a specialization that would gain him institutional recognition within philosophy, the field in which he had been trained and accredited.[50]

The Berlin faculty's second, partially successful effort to have Simmel appointed *Professor Extraordinarius* of philosophy "with a suitable salary" illustrates the effectiveness, but also the perils, of this professional strategy. The official letter of nomination praised his pedagogical and scholarly achievements. While "difficult in their abstract delivery," Simmel's challenging lectures had attracted a "large and stable audience" among the best students, even as he had "accomplished something genuinely fruitful and enduringly useful for *the special area created by him* [emphasis added—EG], investigations of the forms of social connection, their social-historical modifications and developments as well as their effects."[51] That is, what are today understood as contributions to sociology constituted an innovative *philosophical* accomplishment. "In representing sociology in this entirely justified sense," Simmel had become indispensable to the faculty "for the curriculum of philosophy and the political sciences," and he had distinguished himself as a scholar by bringing "scientific precision" to a field where rigor was wanting.

In 1900, then, the Berlin philosophical *Ordinarien* (senior faculty) regarded sociology as an emergent subfield of their own discipline—or at least recognized the project of defining its methodological and epistemological foundations as a properly philosophical task. Unfortunately, while the faculty's gambit was (relatively) successful in improving Simmel's professional situation at the time, it would have adverse and lasting consequences for his reputation.

---

49. It testifies to the intellectual ferment from which the modern social sciences emerged—and to the contested status of purportedly univocal categories—that the seemingly empirical question of who held Germany's first professorship in sociology appears a matter of scholarly controversy a century later. Many authorities name Max Weber, whose new position in Munich began in 1919. For Horst Helle, it was Simmel's follower Leopold von Wiese, in Cologne, also in 1919 (Helle, *The Social Thought of Georg Simmel* [London: Sage, 2015], 15). But as Dirk Kaeseler notes in the authoritative *Neue Deutsche Biographie*, Franz Oppenheimer (whose 1909 *Habilitation* in political economy had been supervised by Simmel's mentors Gustav Schmoller and Adolph Wagner, who viewed sociology as a "universal discipline oriented by the philosophy of history," and who was an early seeker after a "third way" between capitalism and socialism), also assumed his professorship in theoretical national economics and sociology at Frankfurt am Main that year. According to Volker Kruse, the first position "advertised in sociology alone" was at Leipzig in 1925; it went to Hans Freyer (Kruse, *Geschichte der Soziologie in Deutschland* [Konstanz: UVK Verlagsgessellshaft, 2012], 212).

50. The prudence of Simmel's strategies could be questionable. Consider his March 3, 1895, letter to the head of the secondary education division in the Prussian Ministry of Culture, Friedrich Althoff, in which he declared that sociology was "winning more and more of a place in the universities and it is probably only a matter of time until it is officially recognized all round." Enclosing copies of two of his essays, Simmel commended the scientific value of his effort to replace the hitherto confused concept of sociology with "a new and clearly delineated complex of specific tasks" to Althoff's attention (*GSG* 22: 146).

51. All quotations in this paragraph are from the letter of February 2, 1900 (*GSG* 24: 252–55).

Nearly a decade later, convinced that precisely these accomplishments were being used against him at the highest levels to block his appointment at Heidelberg, Simmel complained in exasperation to Jellinek that the Prussian minister of culture's "idiotic" (or "nonsensical": *blödsinnige*) notion that he was a "mere sociologist" must be based on the official description of his "special teaching area" that had accompanied his appointment as *Extraordinarius*.[52] The Berlin faculty had situated him "at the borderline between political science and philosophy" in a strategic effort to underline for the minister how his distinctive profile would supplement their offerings: "There was never any question that it would form the mainstay of my activity; that was and remained the purely philosophical lecture courses." Simmel was probably naïve to think that drawing attention to these facts could put the misapprehension about his disciplinary allegiances to rest. To be sure, his offerings did always range widely over philosophy and the history of philosophy (and from 1911 on, he read on sociology only once every three years).[53] But that he did not receive the appointment at Heidelberg illustrates all too clearly that what was at issue was a matter of image and representation.

Simmel indisputably merits a place in the social scientific canon. In addition to publishing ground-breaking and still-canonical sociological works, he played a decisive role in helping to establish the discipline institutionally. Early in his career, he quite systematically promoted his distinctive vision of sociology in Germany and beyond, with his efforts to disseminate his 1894 essay "Das Problem der Sociologie" ("The Problem of Sociology") internationally being particularly noteworthy. Simmel enjoyed an enthusiastic reception in the United States, where his sociological essays were regularly translated and published, as well as among his European colleagues, especially in France. His work appeared in the inaugural issue of Émile Durkheim's *L'année sociologique*, and he was invited to join the Institut internationale de sociologie convened by René Worms in 1893.[54] The impact of his lectures on sociology—among the first offered in Europe—can hardly be overestimated.

The international fame that preceded official recognition of Simmel's accomplishments at home is strikingly illustrated by Célestin Bouglé's pseudonymously published *Notes d'un étudiant français en Allemagne* (Notes of a French Student in Germany), which appeared in installments in the cosmopolitan *Revue de Paris* in 1894 and were revised and published in an elegantly bound volume the following year.[55] During Bouglé's sojourn in Berlin, Simmel was still a *Privatdozent*, with even

---

52. All quotations in this paragraph are from Simmel's letter of April 29, 1908 (*GSG* 22: 625–26).

53. For Simmel's courses at Berlin and Strasbourg, see *GSG* 24: 607–24.

54. Regarding Simmel's relation to René Worms and the Institut internationale de sociologie (IIS) and its "organ" the *Revue internationale de sociologie* (*GSG* 22: 115), see Köhnke's editorial notes on the first known correspondence between Simmel and Célestin Bouglé, a letter of November 15, 1894 (*GSG* 22: 111–12), and the newly discovered letters in *GSG* 24. Simmel remained a member of the IIS from 1895 to 1899, when an unauthorized translation of his essay on social differentiation in the *Revue* led to conflict with Worms. See Gregor Fitzi, *Soziale Erfahrung und Lebensphilosophie: Georg Simmels Beziehung zu Henri Bergson* (Konstanz: UVK Verlagsgesellschaft, 2002), 19; and on the controversy over this translation, see also Köhnke, *Der junge Simmel*, 114.

55. Bouglé published *Notes d'un étudiant français en Allemagne: Heidelberg-Berlin-Leipzig-Munich* under the pseudonym Jean Breton. Bouglé's *Notes* were revised and expanded for book publication; Fitzi, *Soziale Erfahrung und Lebensphilosophie*, 22–24, reproduces the most significant passages on Simmel.

his first, unsuccessful nomination as an *Extraordinarius* several years off. Yet at the very outset, after declaring that he had come to Germany "to study a science that (I have been told) is coming to an end: philosophy, and a science just beginning: sociology," Bouglé singled Simmel out as one of Germany's prime intellectual attractions.[56] His lectures on sociology attracted "more than 150 auditors" and illustrated that the (Spencerian and Schäfflerian) "biological method" was falling out of favor in Germany.[57] Bouglé lauded Simmel's effort to define sociology as a science that could foster "the progress of the spirit" by replacing "the excessively vast syntheses of the philosopher by the partial syntheses of the specialist."

Simmel's much-cited 1894 declaration that "I am devoting myself entirely to sociological studies" came in response to an inquiry from Bouglé, who was also composing an essay entitled "Les sciences sociales en Allemagne: Mr. Simmel" for a scholarly audience.[58] But Simmel's commitments and self-understanding as a thinker changed considerably in the ensuing years. By the late 1890s—that is, when he was writing *Philosophie des Geldes*—he had become remarkably ambivalent about the international fame he had sought, and found, in sociology. Simmel was coming to regard his unfinished sociological opus as an onerous burden, and to question the professional wisdom of pursuing such studies altogether, even as his senior colleagues prepared to renew their efforts on his behalf by praising the "special area created by him" as grounds for promotion to *Extraordinarius*.[59]

In 1899, Célestin Bouglé had just completed his doctoral studies in philosophy. He would go on as founding director of the Centre de documentation sociale of the École normale supérieure in Paris to play a decisive role in the institutionalization of sociology.[60] Simmel wrote to thank Bouglé for sending him his French

---

56. "Notes d'un étudiant français en Allemagne," *Revue de Paris*, June 1, 1894, 49–80; here p. 49; http://gallica.bnf.fr/ark:/12148/bpt6k207971w.image.r=Revue+de+Paris.f500.pagination.langEN (accessed May 16, 2016). Perhaps it was Élie Halévy, to whom the *Notes* are dedicated, or Durkheim himself, who sent the gifted young student to Germany with this mandate and recommended "Kuno Fischer, Paulsen, Wagner, Simmel..."

57. The passage just cited as well as that in the following sentence appear only in the expanded edition of *Notes d'un étudiant français*, on pp. 127 and 128 respectively.

58. Simmel to Bouglé, February 15, 1894 (*GSG* 22: 111–12). Bouglé published "Les sciences sociales en Allemagne: Mr. Simmel" in the neo-Kantian *Revue de métaphysique et de morale* 2, no. 3 (May 1894): 329–55, edited by Léon Brunschvicg, Xavier Léon, and Élie Halévy, indicating the complex international landscape in which the modern disciplinary formation of sociology emerged. (Bouglé also translated "Das Problem der Sociologie" for the *Revue* during this period.) In France, Bouglé's mentor Émile Durkheim, also a philosopher by training, had managed to put sociology on the map, though not, as is often claimed, by establishing the first sociology department. "Durkheim was appointed in 1887 as 'Chargé d'un cours de science sociale et de pédagogie' at Bordeaux. *Science sociale* was a concession to Durkheim, and it was under this guise that sociology now officially entered the French university system" (Robert Alun Jones, *Émile Durkheim: An Introduction to Four Major Works* [Beverly Hills, CA: Sage, 1986], 15).

59. At its February 1, 1900, meeting, the faculty agreed (with one abstention) to renew the request on Simmel's behalf (*GSG* 24: 252).

60. Bouglé's academic trajectory parallels sociology's evolution. From 1902 to 1908, he held a professorship in social philosophy at Toulouse. In 1909, he accepted a professorship in the history of social economy at the Sorbonne. He was appointed assistant director of France's premiere institution of philosophical higher education, the École normale supérieure, in 1927, and concluded his career as its director from 1935 to 1940 (*GSG* 23: 1154; W. P. Vogt. "Un durkheimien ambivalent: Célestin Bouglé, 1870–1940," *Revue française de sociologie* 20 [1979]: 123–39).

thesis, *Les idées egalitaires: Étude sociologique*, which drew on both his own and Durkheim's conceptions of sociology. Simmel reveled in the recognition ("that such books are being written is ultimately the whole meaning of my efforts") and encouraged Bouglé to send the thesis to other colleagues abroad. But he coolly rejected the invitation to participate in the sociological congress being organized to coincide with the Paris Exposition of 1900.[61]

Simmel was, he declared, "in no position whatsoever" to provide a report on the state of the social sciences in Germany: "You must not forget that the *sciences sociales* are not my discipline [*Fach*]," he explained. Leaving aside his own "quite distinctive" sociology, Simmel insisted, his relation to the social sciences was that of a "layperson." "It is altogether rather painful for me that abroad I am only known as a sociologist—whereas I am a philosopher, see my life's vocation [*Lebensaufgabe*] in philosophy, and only pursue sociology as a sideline."

A fundamental transformation had taken place in Simmel's conception of his work in the five years since he had proclaimed to Bouglé that he was abandoning the field of moral philosophy in order to devote himself "entirely to sociological studies." Now he was nearing the completion of *Philosophie des Geldes*, which he hoped would appear in the course of the next year—a book, he added, that "aspires to be a philosophy of historical and social life as a whole." Simmel was by no means burning his bridges—in the next breath he asked Bouglé whether he ought to try to publish his book simultaneously in French and German—but he was quite deliberately resituating himself and his work outside sociology.

To be sure, Simmel's insistence that he was not a professional social scientist reflected the fact that he was operating in an institutional context considerably less receptive to sociological innovation than Bouglé's own. Troubled relations with the educational bureaucracy—the rejected dissertation, failed *Habilitations-Colloquium*, and the Berlin faculty's unsuccessful 1898 attempt to secure him even a nominal professorship—had already checkered his academic career. Still, Simmel's ambivalence regarding his fame as a sociologist cannot be reduced to professional calculations.

However flattering he found Bouglé's attention, he also knew that the issues that most concerned him were growing increasingly illegible from the point of view of the sociological mainstream. In its ambivalence, that is, his letter to Bouglé reflects not only Simmel's growing sense of the professional costs of his identification with sociology but also his awareness that it was evolving in directions that rendered his interest in it marginal or seemingly eccentric. In placing himself on the other side of a disciplinary divide, Simmel was pointing to an emerging disjunction between

---

61. The quotations are from Simmel's letter to Bouglé of December 13, 1899 (GSG 22: 342–43). Bouglé's letter has been lost, but the invitation presumably concerned the Institute international de sociologie congress to be held at the Sorbonne the following September. The IIS congress was not officially part of the Paris Exposition of 1900, but its meeting "in Paris during the progress of the Exposition rendered it practically such, and it was generally so regarded by the world at large," according to Lester Ward, "Sociology at the Paris Exposition of 1900," chap. 28 in U.S. Bureau of Education, *Report of the Commissioner of Education, 1899–1900* (Washington, DC: GPO, 1901), 1571.

philosophy and sociology, a disjunction that established the latter as a separate field of inquiry with an autonomy very different from that envisioned by Auguste Comte or Herbert Spencer.

Still, despite declaring that "the *sciences sociales* are not my discipline," Simmel did not cease to advance his vision of sociology, with results that are still recognized as canonical contributions to the field. When his "large" *Soziologie* was finally published in 1908, he had, by his own accounting, labored on the project, circumscribed by its subtitle, *Untersuchungen über die Formen der Vergesellschaftung* (Investigations into the Forms of Association), off and on for fifteen years.[62] Nor, even then, was his institutional engagement at an end. In 1909, he helped found the professional organization of German sociologists, the Deutsche Gesellschaft für Soziologie (DGS). Simmel gave the opening address, on "The Sociology of Sociability," at the society's inaugural meeting in Frankfurt the following year, and he served as one of its first presiding officers.[63] In 1911, his activities "as founder of the science of sociology" were recognized with an honorary "doctorate of political sciences" from Freiburg University. Finally, at the end of his life, after largely eschewing sociology for many years, Simmel published his "small" *Grundfragen der Soziologie* (Fundamental Questions of Sociology) in 1917.

The tensions and ambiguities in Simmel's professional activities and identity only become legible when they are placed in a larger, intellectual-historical and cultural context. On his view, and not only on his view, what was at stake in the emergence of the social sciences was of philosophical significance. A historic transformation of scholarly endeavor as a whole was under way—a consequence, as Simmel put it in 1894 in "Das Problem der Sociologie," of the contemporary shift in the way human being itself was understood, an "overcoming of the individualistic way of seeing" (*GSG* 5: 52).

Simmel's institutional involvement and intellectual engagement with sociology continued even as he reframed his sense of what it meant to reflect philosophically on the historic changes under way. His central concerns remained: the fate of the subject in a world where inherited values and frameworks of meaning have dissolved, and the meaning and direction of culture and knowledge under such circumstances. Simmel's enthusiastic efforts to disseminate his vision of the discipline as the study of "forms of association" as such had met with little success. By 1899, advocacy for his methodological breakthrough had given way to a recognition that his vision of sociology was marginal at best—and had, as he put it to Bouglé, "no representatives except me in Germany." Although this pessimistic self-assessment was not entirely unwarranted, his innovative approach nonetheless became a source

---

62. Simmel to Bouglé, March 22, 1908 (*GSG* 22: 619).

63. In 1913, after a dispute at the Second German Sociological Congress over the role of value in social scientific inquiry, Simmel and his fellow officers Max Weber and Alfred Vierkandt resigned from the leadership. Simmel does not, however, mention this dispute as the cause of his decision in his letter of resignation but explains it as a consequence of a turn to "pure philosophy" so radical as to make his continuing in the leadership role tantamount to "inner dishonesty" (Simmel to DGS board, October 11, 1913; *GSG* 23: 208–10).

of (often unacknowledged) inspiration for many better-known figures.[64] Simmel posed questions about the nature and scope of sociology that remain significant, and his analyses of social phenomena constitute still untapped theoretical resources. These only really become available when his specifically philosophical objectives and achievements in theorizing social and cultural life are recognized.

This book seeks to render visible the broader impact of Simmel's style of thinking, by exploring both his evolving conception of his intellectual tasks and his influence on sociology. The figure of Simmel plays an important role in sociology's evolving self-representation as a discipline, embodying the legacy of a philosophical past it had purportedly subsumed and transcended. His career sheds light on the prehistory of what we have come to call "theory" and its relation to fin de siècle European intellectual culture.

Simmel's irascible refusal of Bouglé's invitation to Paris in the name of his disciplinary identity as a philosopher should be seen in the larger context of his evolving historical, philosophical, and professional-institutional self-reflexivity. It echoes nearly a decade later in a letter to his supporter Jellinek during the crucial days in March 1908 when the chair in Heidelberg was plainly slipping away. His opponents, Simmel explained, had successfully disseminated the "idiocy" that he was really a sociologist although "in reality I pursue sociology only 'as a sideline' [*im Nebenamt*]." He added ruefully that when this misrepresentation had originally come up in official deliberations, there had been no one present to testify to his indisputable philosophical bona fides by way of "a glance at the title of my lectures and my books (or even better, a look *into* the latter)."[65]

Simmel's acerbic assessment of his reception was hardly an exaggeration—even his proponents often ignored the words on the page in their reception of his writings. When he wrote this letter to Jellinek, however, he was putting the finishing touches to his nearly 800-page opus *Soziologie. Untersuchungen über die Formen der Vergesellschaftung*, encouraged by the prospect of the post in Heidelberg.[66]

---

64. According to Heinz-Jürgen Dahme, Simmel's reception followed a pattern: "the phase of an enthusiastic assimilation of his works was followed by a phase of rejection and eventually . . . neglect." Not just "Durkheim, Weber, Lukács, Park, and Parsons" but also Alfred Vierkandt and Leopold von Wiese, who both built on his formal sociology, ceased to invoke Simmel's role as "the founder of German sociology as an independent empirical science" and focused on "promoting their own image as sociologists" after his death. Von Wiese in particular (who was active in the leadership of the DGS before 1933, spearheaded the refounding of the organization in 1946, served as its first postwar president, and founded one of German sociology's most important journals) "went so far [as] to disclaim the cognitive significance that Simmel had had for his theorizing, although an inspection of his writings indicates that the contrary was the case." Dahme, "On the Current Rediscovery of Simmel's Sociology—A European Point of View," in *Georg Simmel and Contemporary Sociology*, ed. Michael Kaern, Bernard S. Phillips, and Robert Sonné Cohen (Dordrecht: Kluwer Academic, 1990), 16.

65. Simmel to Georg Jellinek, March 20, 1908 (*GSG* 22: 617). See my "Sociology as a Sideline: Does it Matter That Georg Simmel (Thought He) Was a Philosopher?" in *Anthem Companion to Georg Simmel*, ed. Thomas Kemple and Olli Pyyhtinen (New York: Anthem Press, 2016).

66. The manuscript was corrected in late March, and *Soziologie: Untersuchungen über die Formen der Vergesellschaftung* [Sociology: Investigations into the Forms of Association] appeared in June (see Rammstedt's editorial report to *GSG* 11). A collection of essays and excerpts, including some selections from the latter work, long circulated under the title *The Sociology of Georg Simmel* (New York: Free Press,

In his 1971 study *Masters of Sociological Thought: Ideas in Historical and Social Context*, Lewis A. Coser calls *Philosophie des Geldes* (which would not be fully translated into English as *The Philosophy of Money* until 1978) "a much neglected classic." Coser speculates that sociologists might have avoided the book on account of "the title, which could have led many to infer that this is one of Simmel's metaphysical works."[67] On his reading, this was an error: "Although this large book does contain certain important philosophical ideas, it is mainly a contribution to cultural sociology and to the analysis of the wider social implications of economic affairs," and is thus "indispensable for an understanding of his cultural analysis and his cultural criticism."

Treating his *Philosophy of Money* as a contribution to (interdisciplinary) social science has helped Simmel's advocates advance his cause. Its author continues to be fêted as the "first sociologist of modernity" today, at the cost of underestimating the unsettling implications of the work's actual title. Nor is this by any means the only example that appears to warrant Simmel's plaint that he had been misread or not read at all. The same rhetorical strategy has also served to help assimilate other of his explicitly philosophical books and essays into the ambit of social science. But the approach is built on shaky scholarly foundations, and its plausibility depends on seemingly willful blind spots.

It is remarkable that even Lewis Coser—who not only translated and edited Simmel's texts but also, as a writer and teacher, effectively brought some of his most challenging ideas into the sociological mainstream—read him so poorly. *Philosophy of Money* does not simply "contain important philosophical ideas." The metaphor, which is hardly without its own metaphysical implications, is extraordinarily misleading. It would be more accurate to invert Coser's claim and characterize Simmel's "contribution to cultural sociology" as a philosophical interpretation of the social, cultural, and historical "implications of economic affairs."

The *Philosophy of Money* is the work of a culturally engaged thinker aspiring to transcend his own historical moment. Simmel only rarely referred to "modernity" as a historical period,[68] and what he has to say about modernity and modern experience is grounded in philosophical views concerning time and history, subjectivity and the social, knowledge and reality, that are not in fact about a particular era at all. To subordinate Simmel's philosophical ends to his argumentative and analytic means is to miss what makes his *Philosophy of Money*—and his work more generally—such a significant contribution to social and cultural theory.

As Coser's example shows, a great deal is at stake theoretically in the ways Simmel has been represented. He has in effect been consigned to the margins of modern intellectual history in being (re)defined as a sociologist. Rectifying the problem is

1950), but a full English translation of it did not in fact become available until 2009 (*Sociology: Inquiries into the Construction of Social Forms*, trans. and ed. Anthony J. Blasi, Anton K. Jacobs, and Mathew Kanjirathinkal, Boston: Brill, 2009). Regarding the issues with that translation, see Lawrence Scaff, "Simmel Redux," *Contemporary Sociology* 40, no. 1 (2011).

67. *Masters of Sociological Thought* was first published in 1971 and issued in a revised and expanded second edition in 1977, from 193–94 of which the quotations here are drawn.

68. To designate the contemporary era, he generally employs *die moderne Welt* (the modern world) or *die moderne Zeit* (modern times) rather than the German terms *die Moderne* or *die Neuzeit*.

thus not simply a matter of establishing—or restoring—his status as philosopher, but also entails examining the relationship between philosophy and the social sciences. To do justice to Simmel's accomplishments requires reexamining assumptions about disciplinarity, about modernism, and about culture itself—assumptions that became intellectual commonplaces during the twentieth century in the course of the very developments that both canonized and marginalized him as a thinker of the social.

The reversals in Simmel's stance have often been interpreted as an index of his loss of faith that he could make a career in sociology, an oversimplification that helps obscure the importance of his liminal institutional and intellectual position. What has been construed in biographical terms has broader historical and theoretical significance and calls for both philosophical and sociological interpretation. In considering the evidence, it is crucial to bear in mind that in the late nineteenth century, "sociology" did not refer to an institutionally established discipline—nor, more generally, had systematic, empirically oriented inquiry into society and culture become clearly differentiated from its philosophical origins.[69]

The whiggish tendency of disciplinary histories to assume the inevitability of subsequent institutional developments retrospectively[70] has fostered a highly selective approach to Simmel's oeuvre. Like other narrated traditions, disciplinary histories are imagined into being through iterative practice: "a look *into*" the complexity and range of his German oeuvre reveals that Simmel's venerable location within sociology's master narrative depends on selective practices of editing and reading that have helped obscure and even distort his theoretical accomplishments. His canonization thereby continues a trend he had criticized even before its practical impact on his career had really become clear.

---

69. The status and potentialities of inquiry into culture was an object of considerable philosophical discussion during this period. To name what are probably the two most significant examples of attempts to delineate a philosophical as opposed to empirical approach: Wilhelm Dilthey published the first version of his *Einleitung in die Geisteswissenschaften* in 1883 and Heinrich Rickert his *Kulturwissenschaft und Naturwissenschaft* in 1899. Regarding Simmel's strained relations with Dilthey, who assumed his chair in Berlin in 1892, see Köhnke, *Der junge Simmel*.

70. The brief official history by E. L. Pattullo posted on the web site of Harvard University's Department of Psychology, the home institution of William James, one of those rare figures recognized today in both philosophy and psychology, illustrates the significance for social scientists of a presentist perspective on the intellectual and institutional history of their disciplines, particularly in relation to their philosophical origins. Pattullo's narrative and rhetoric are especially noteworthy, since Harvard's institutional permutations exemplify the complex and historically shifting interrelations between diverse "humanistic" and "(social) scientific" knowledge practices as philosophy, psychology, sociology, and anthropology became distinct disciplinary formations. James initiated the scientific study of psychology in the 1870s, but psychology did not become a separate department until 1936. Ten years later, all subfields except the experimental (which remained independent as the Department of Psychology) were merged with other social science disciplines in the Department of Social Relations. However, Pattullo writes, "The demise of Social Relations as a separate entity was heralded by the decision of the sociologists to withdraw into their own Department of Sociology in 1970. Shortly thereafter (1972) the branches of psychology recombined as the Department of Psychology and Social Relations, soon after which the social anthropologists retreated to their (never abandoned) association with the Anthropology Department. The circle was completed in the spring of 1986 when, just fifty years after an independent department under that name first appeared at Harvard, the name was shortened and the present Department of Psychology emerged" (http://psychology.fas.harvard.edu/history [accessed July 19, 2016]).

Isolating Simmel's "sociological" from his "philosophical" work is misleading both theoretically and historically: what made him a "founding father" of sociology can only be understood in relation to his pursuit of properly philosophical objectives. The not insignificant matter of his shifting self-definition bears careful consideration. But in the end, his own assessment can be affirmed: it was as a philosopher that Simmel made his contributions to sociology, and it is necessary to grasp what this means both institutionally and theoretically in order to appreciate his importance.

My aim, however, is not to reclaim Simmel for philosophy but to reframe the questions surrounding the significance of his work in a way that illuminates the contemporary disciplinary imaginary and the challenges of cultural theory in our own time. For Simmel's ambivalence about his relation to sociology was related to very real difficulties in situating his work in the contemporary university that were by no means simply a function of his rather precarious professional status.

As a writer and teacher, Simmel worked to sustain and strengthen the resources of reflection, demonstrating the value and importance of examining a wide range of phenomena that had previously been ignored or deemed beneath serious philosophical attention. His pathbreaking achievements are imbricated with the question of disciplinarity in both the institutional-historical and theoretical-philosophical senses. When these dimensions are thought together, the question of how and why Simmel's self-understanding as a thinker and scholar evolved as it did leads to the heart of the issue of what constitutes (cultural, social) theory in modernity—and indeed to the question of the status of the disciplinary order itself as we know it today, when the wholesale turn to interdisciplinarity in cultural inquiry invites us to reenvision both the methodological and institutional divisions among the "social" and "natural" "sciences" and the "humanities."

Nor does Simmel's career simply illustrate this complex of problems. All of these dimensions—philosophical, sociological, historical, disciplinary, and cultural—come quite explicitly and self-consciously into play in the course of his intellectual evolution. Simmel developed his modernist approach to philosophizing as he grappled simultaneously with where he belonged institutionally and how to reflect theoretically on the rapidly changing world around him. And that style of thought played a significant, largely unacknowledged role in twentieth-century intellectual history well beyond the boundaries of "sociology."

Simmel's theoretical innovations, circulating forgotten or as alienated gestures in the work of thinkers including Husserl and Heidegger, Benjamin and Adorno, helped pave the way for the transformation of philosophy that took place after 1914.[71] Once we recognize his stylistic impact on writing across a wide range of fields both within and beyond the academy, his significance as a thinker becomes palpable.

---

71. The (largely unacknowledged) impact of Simmel's late reflections on life, death, and the question of immanent transcendence on the twentieth-century phenomenological tradition, and on the early Heidegger in particular, is especially noteworthy. Regarding Simmel's influence on Heidegger, see Michael Grossheim, *Von Georg Simmel zu Martin Heidegger: Philosophie zwischen Leben und Existenz* (Bonn: Bouvier, 1991), and John E. Jalbert "Time, Death, and History in Simmel and Heidegger," *Human Studies* 26, no. 2 (2003): 259–83.

The innovative approach to philosophical reflection often referred to as Simmel's "essayism" has had a history of effects that extends beyond the critical and reflective traditions, social scientific and humanistic alike, that inherited the concerns of the German philosophical tradition he espoused. But this wider legacy of his work and strategies of thought in European prewar thought and culture continues to be obscured through the anachronistic perspectives and assumptions borne by the disciplinary divisions and historical classifications that subsequently came to shape the recollection of modernist thought and culture more generally.

Situating Simmel's efforts to discern the larger (theoretical, historical, philosophical) significance of the changes under way as European society modernized and industrialized within the broader context of cultural modernism draws attention to the resonance of his writing, in terms both of style and theoretical and cultural concerns, with modernist problematics and strategies of thought in general. The cross- and transdisciplinary influence of his style of thought in the genealogy of what we now call (cultural) "theory" underlines the significance of Simmel's pathbreaking methodological contributions to rhetorical strategies and knowledge practices that combine elements of literary and aesthetic as well as empirical traditions in reframing the philosophical legacy.

As both writer and teacher, Simmel helped shape the metaphoric foundations of the modern theoretical imaginary. He drew attention to the sociological and philosophical significance of distance and speed; to the constitutive role of conflict and gender for culture; to the aporetic relations between concept and experience, life and form; to the pervasive and alienating effects attendant on the increasing objectification, rationalization, and instrumental and materialist orientation of contemporary culture; to the distinctive role of awareness of mortality for human existence in a period when religious horizons were disappearing or collapsing into immanence; but also to the importance of aesthetics and style in every sphere human life and to the possibilities of a new kind of awareness of subjectivity and of noninstitutional forms of religiosity under modern conditions. An index of the eminence of Simmel's largely unrecognized conceptual and methodological contributions to the wider reframing of the philosophical inheritance evident in all these themes is the fact that a number of terms that have had important histories in twentieth-century cultural theory—constellation [*Konstellation*], condensation [*Verdichtung*], configuration [*Gebilde* and occasionally *Konfiguration*], form of life [*Lebensform*], and life-world [*Lebenswelt*], to name a few decisive examples—can be traced to his work.

To give an accounting of the unmarked bills of Simmel's intellectual legacy, it will be necessary to clear away some methodological as well as historical obstacles embedded in his reception. It is, then, for both historical and theoretical reasons that chapter 2 examines Simmel's intellectual and professional development before the publication of the *Philosophy of Money*—according to Klaus Christian Köhnke, "in the eminent sense his first original 'work.'"[72] Simmel's evolving self-definition as

---

72. Klaus Christian Köhnke, *Der junge Simmel in Theoriebeziehungen und sozialen Bewegungen* (Frankfurt am Main: Suhrkamp, 1996), 29. In this context, it is worth noting that Simmel's title *Philosophie*

a thinker both reflects and illuminates an intellectual context that remains of considerable interest for contemporary cultural theory. A new disciplinary imaginary was emerging as diverse knowledge practices were reorganized and professionalized into the emerging modern research university, and the revisions of Simmel's self-definition cast light on the theoretical as well as institutional evolution of disciplinarity as we know it. This discussion will prepare the way for a reconsideration of Simmel's reception history that illuminates the prehistory of contemporary work on culture in theoretical and empirical, social scientific and humanistic contexts alike—and lay the groundwork for the constructive task of presenting new readings of Simmel's mature texts that demonstrate their theoretical vitality.

Part I explores Simmel's modernity, placing our view of his thinking (to invoke his concept) in "reciprocal interaction" with its sociocultural and historical contexts. After considering the theoretical and historiographical issues involved in (mis)remembering Simmel, we then turn to the question of his status as a "classic." Focusing on the relation between Simmel's evolving self-understanding as a thinker and the paradigm shift by which the modern social sciences came into being, chapter 2 lays out the lineaments of the relativism (in particular, the relativistic rethinking of concepts) that formed the basis of his mature work. Chapter 3 then considers how Simmel has been represented and read into the disciplinary canon and history of sociology. Centered on a close examination of the American reception that was so decisive in establishing his reputation as a founding father of modern social science, it explores how Simmel's ideas and strategies of thought were appropriated—or not.

Part I thereby lays the groundwork for reflection on how Simmel is read, especially in relation to our own modernity, an issue that will be pursued in the remainder of the book. Through (re)readings of key Simmelian texts that reconnect these historical and disciplinary reflections to still-urgent theoretical and methodological concerns, I then place the evolution of Simmel's scholarly self-understanding in historical and institutional context, reopening the question of disciplinarity by reframing Simmel's relation to modernism and his intellectual legacy in order to ask anew what constitutes cultural theory in modernity. In closing these introductory remarks, I would like to comment briefly on the larger stakes of this effort to foster a return to Georg Simmel's texts as resources for our own time.

Simmel's Philosophical Modernism and the History of Theory

In returning to paradigmatic predecessors, we must always be prepared to recognize systematic distortions in the inheritance, and it should be emphasized that Simmel can by no means be pronounced free of the biases of his era. If we take seriously the notion that human existence is radically historical, there can in principle be no

---

des Geldes lacks an initial article. This absence, awkward in German as well, is significant. In contrast to the published English translation, *The Philosophy of Money*, I have followed Simmel's own practice. En passant: we do not add an article in translating Adorno's titles "Aesthetische Theorie" (Aesthetic Theory) or "Negative Dialektik" (Negative Dialectics).

simple recovery of past models; we should not aspire to find in the past answers to our present dilemmas. But exploring the practices of innovation that animate his writings and taking seriously Simmel's efforts to invent new strategies of thought at once rigorous and playful in their approach to modern life can provide important orientation for the tasks of contemporary cultural theory. Such constructive, future-oriented appropriation entails reflection on the historicity of the disciplinary imaginary that has evolved since what Simmel identified as a fundamental reorientation of attention from the individual to the collective, the subject to the social, changed the very meaning of inquiry into human existence and brought new questions, methods, and assumptions into being in the second half of the nineteenth century.

Simmel's own intellectual praxis is marked by indistinction among what we have come to think of as disciplinarily and even ontologically distinct objects and practices. The resulting blurring between society and culture; analysis and interpretation; and philosophical and social scientific perspectives and methods makes it challenging to assess his contributions, even as this multiplicity and ambiguity draws us in. Yet Simmel's facility at moving among social, intellectual, and broadly cultural objects and themes in ways that integrate strategies of thought that have subsequently come to be distributed among and identified with very diverse disciplines makes his texts still inspiring more than a hundred years later.

My point, to anticipate an important objection, is by no means that Simmel is the only relevant figure for studying the theoretical and methodological sea change under way at the nineteenth-century fin de siècle or identifying resources in that past that may help us understand our own period of cultural and theoretical transformation. Widespread interest in once-forgotten thinkers (including Walter Benjamin and Siegfried Kracauer, both influenced by Simmel) attests to the importance of the view from the margins. What becomes visible at the disciplinary and institutional interstices is crucial for grasping the historical significance and contemporary theoretical resonance of the paradigm shift in humanistic inquiry at the end of the nineteenth century, when the meaning of culture itself was changing and a new disciplinary and institutional order was beginning to emerge. Other thinkers, only some of whose names are still obscure to American readers—Weber, Dilthey, Rickert, Tönnies, Cohen, Cassirer—also need to be reread in the double context of the two fins de siècle.

Yet Simmel, not least as a consequence of the vicissitudes of his professional life, is exemplary. With his continually evolving self-understanding, he belies the clichéd image of Wilhelmine stability and mandarin detachment from the commotion of modern life, anticipating the intellectual style of more famous students and readers who came of age after World War I. Simmel's intellectual openness, the flexibility of his attitude toward the transformations under way, reflects a moment before many promises hardened into disappointing realities or faded away entirely. Although he lived long enough to witness the cataclysm of 1914–18 remake the face of European culture, Simmel did not experience the drastic sociopolitical upheavals that came in the aftermath of the war. In a very real way, he was writing before the thoroughgoing politicization of culture that came to characterize European intellectual life after

1917—at a moment when, for better and for worse, it was possible to believe in culture both as the vehicle of subjective self-realization and as "the being" that "allows everything truly to become real."

Moreover, the course of his intellectual evolution registers, and Simmel explicitly reflects upon, the process by which innovative knowledge practices and new forms of disciplinarity emerged from the scientific, industrial, and political upheavals of the nineteenth century. His story thereby illuminates the conjunction of institutional and theoretical transformation that defines the site where philosophy began to give way to the science of the social as inherited understandings of culture and of human being itself were taking on recognizably contemporary contours.

That Simmel's work does not situate these changes in an explicitly political fashion need not be regarded as a weakness. Rather, recognizing the theoretical complexity and fecundity of his struggle to discover strategies of thinking and writing appropriate to that historic moment underlines the need to clarify our own relation to this theoretical, historical, and disciplinary prehistory. At a moment when the political-historical metanarratives that framed Western intellectual history during the short twentieth century have lost their purchase and the question of the relation between politics and the being of culture is being posed anew, telling this story also provides an opportunity to explore how our own thinking has been configured by a historically, culturally contingent account of the social conditions of modern knowledge formation.

Unlike many of Simmel's current proponents, I do not advocate a renewed encounter with his work in an attempt to recover and perpetuate his "philosophy of culture" or to defend the accomplishments of his philosophy of life. Such approaches do not go far enough beyond the old model of reception that has given us, in turn, Simmel as "formal sociologist," as "sociologist of conflict," and as "sociologist of modernity." To do justice to the methodological significance of his style of thought, it is essential to grasp the formal, the philosophical, and the historical significance of Simmel's heightened self-reflexivity. At the same time, it is crucial to incorporate a perspective that of necessity exceeds his own self-understanding: to read his work as symptomatic or typical (or, as Simmel might have put it, at once bearer and symbol) of what we can recognize as the larger historical transformations during his lifetime.

What was finding expression in the new discourse on culture, in the emergent sciences of the social, in the new, materialist conception of human existence, amounted to nothing less than a historic transformation in the collective self-understanding of the West. As philosopher and sociologist, but also as a writer and public figure attempting to come to terms with the literary, artistic, and more broadly cultural, legacy, Simmel tracks this transformation. Through methodologically and stylistically innovative conceptual strategies grounded in a philosophical interpretation of the meaning of the historical situation, his writing attempts to come to terms with a world changing in most fundamental ways, to construct means of thinking about culture that built on the inheritance of the past without abandoning the responsibility of thought to the present. The self-reflexive relation between his approach and the historical and cultural circumstances in which Simmel was writing assures the enduring theoretical interest of his philosophical modernism—and, perhaps, provides a model of innovation for us today.

Located in the vertiginous space opened up by the ambiguous liberation known as the death of God, Simmel's writing strives to come to terms with the way epistemological and ethical questions had come unmoored from their inherited metaphysical foundations. From *Einleitung in die Moralwissenschaft* to the *Philosophie des Geldes*, through his writings on society and culture, art and aesthetics, all the way to his final meditations on life and death in the *Lebensanschauung* (*View of Life*), Simmel was engaged in a modernist effort to invent strategies of thought and interpretation adequate to a world in which experience seemed to have lost its contours, in which the very possibility of relying on inherited truths appeared to have been foreclosed forever.

Operating at the junctures where new knowledge practices were taking shape in response to this epochal shift, his texts trace the fault lines of emergent forms of experience—modern existence coming into being. In Simmel's writing, but also in the course of his intellectual evolution, questions of historiographical method as such therefore gain practical force. Exploring what is most interesting and innovative in his oeuvre simultaneously entails uncovering the importance of the wider prehistory of the contemporary disciplinary imaginary for work on culture today. Only such methodological illumination can surmount the obstacles of Simmel's puzzling and ambivalent reception and render visible the significance of his largely anonymized influence on modern thought.

CHAPTER 2

Simmel as Classic: Representation and the Rhetoric of Disciplinarity

In 1908, the publisher Wilhelm Crayen proposed that Simmel write a book on a subject of his choice to appear as the "Jubilee" 500th volume of the popular Sammlung Göschen series. Crayen was delighted with the result, which he clearly felt confirmed the wisdom of his giving Simmel the place of honor in the collection. "I regard you as a genuine philosophical classic whose works one will read later on just like Hegel, Schopenhauer, and so on."[1] Upon its publication in 1910, the slender volume Simmel produced, *Hauptprobleme der Philosophie* (Main Problems of Philosophy), became an immediate best seller.[2]

Simmel wrote *Hauptprobleme* in the months after the latest debacle in his university career—which in July 1909 he called the "tragicomedy of my Heidelberg professorship, of blessed memory."[3] The volume's popularity attests to the pivotal tension between Simmel's public success and his professional difficulties—to the accuracy of his self-assessment that he had "a not entirely small circle of loyal devotees" despite his being "rather isolated and a sort of outsider [in English in the original] with respect to 'official' academic philosophy in north Germany."[4]

Today, with the twenty-four-volume historical-critical Georg Simmel *Gesamtausgabe* on library shelves throughout the world, one might argue that Crayen's judgment has been vindicated. Simmel is a recognized classic of modern sociology, remembered as a forerunner of cultural studies and credited with theoretical innovations associated variously with modernity and postmodernity, with critical theory and deconstruction. Yet he has never really been integrated into the philosophical canon, and there is no shortage of historians, not only of philosophy, who would dismiss Simmel as being, in words of his erstwhile acolyte György Lukács, an *Übergangserscheinung*, a "transitional phenomenon."[5] This ambivalent reception is the-

---

1. Wilhelm Crayen to Simmel, December 10, 1909 (*GSG* 22: 746–48). Crayen announced the publication itself in a letter of November 11, 1910 (*GSG* 22: 868).

2. On February 19, 1911, Simmel reported to Edmund Husserl that it had sold 13,000 copies in ten weeks (*GSG* 22: 940–41).

3. Simmel to Jellinek, July 20, 1909 (*GSG* 22: 716).

4. Simmel to Crayen, March 7, 1910 (*GSG* 22: 801–2).

5. *BdD*, 171. Lukács's obituary, reproduced in *BdD*, 171–76; English translation by Margaret Cerullo in *Theory, Culture & Society* [*TCS*] 8 (1991): 145–50. Reproduced in David Frisby, ed., *Georg Simmel: Critical Assessments* (New York: Routledge, 1994), 1: 98–101.

oretically as well as historically significant. Precisely because so much is excluded in representing him as canonical sociologist, grasping what is truly innovative in Simmel's thinking requires a critical genealogy that both interrogates the way he has been assimilated into the social scientific canon and uncovers the distorting effects of his own self-representations.

As a young man, Simmel quite emphatically and openly embraced the notion that philosophy in the traditional sense was reaching an end, but he would come to regret the hypercritical, reductivist stance of his early works. Although the relativism of the mature thinker was if anything more radical philosophically than the sociologism out of which it evolved, Simmel adopted more conciliatory modes of argument and more pragmatic strategies of self-representation, which effectively downplayed the novelty of his ideas and the discontinuities of his approach with the tradition in which he was operating. His own rhetoric has thereby helped obscure the (often disavowed) impact of what were in fact quite innovative ideas and methods on students and readers who took a more provocative stance toward the tradition and more directly attacked the network of assumptions and ideals of academic philosophy.

To discover how Simmel became who he was, let us commence, then, with an earlier period, before his public successes and professional debacles alike. In a world unapologetically oriented both intellectually and culturally toward the new, where the imperative to cast off the burdens of the past in the name of the future sets the dominant tenor, such an exploration may appear superfluous. But Simmel's innovations must be understood in self-reflexive relation to the very different historicity of the Wilhelminian world, where change was by no means universally identified with progress. In that era it was innovation, rather than continuity with tradition, that bore the burden of self-justification. Tracing the development of Simmel's thinking and of his distorting image as a sociologist illuminates the historical, cultural, and intellectual evolution of the disciplinary imaginary that has come to enframe scholarly work in the intervening century.

A Modern Classic?

The point of departure for any discussion of Simmel's early work remains Klaus Christian Köhnke's magisterial effort to establish Simmel as a "classic" of modern cultural philosophy. His 1996 book *Der junge Simmel in Theoriebeziehungen und sozialen Bewegungen* (The Young Simmel in Theoretical Relations and Social Movements), the first and most important of a number of *Habilitation* projects to grow out of work on the Simmel *Gesamtausgabe*, set out "to disclose or expose the backgrounds of [Simmel's] theoretical development step by step beginning with the early work."[6] For Köhnke, exploring the foundations and genesis of Simmel's thought was,

---

6. Köhnke, *Der junge Simmel*, 18; subsequent citations given parenthetically in the text. Köhnke was professor of cultural theory and cultural philosophy at the Cultural Sciences Institute in Leipzig from 1997 until his untimely death in 2013 and edited or co-edited a number of volumes in the critical *Gesamtausgabe*.

like the *Gesamtausgabe* itself, part of a wider ongoing process of consolidating a new theoretical canon at the turn of the twenty-first century.

"The reevaluation of the science of the fin de siècle is in full swing," Köhnke observed of the mid-1990s. Other previously largely forgotten figures were also being showered with meticulous scholarly attention and "honored with collected works and yearbooks, seminars and conferences"; "we are presently living in—and taking part in—the constitution . . . of the classical period [*Klassik*] of the human and social sciences, just as the end of the nineteenth century defined for itself and for us the classical era of German literature." Köhnke saw this historical and philological enterprise as a "medium of self-reflection for contemporary inquiry," the "so-called 'Simmel Renaissance'" being "just one of many symptoms" of the "revitalization" of contemporary thought via encounters with the newly discovered classics of the nineteenth-century fin de siècle—that is, with what is now seen as a period of "transition to so-called modernity . . . as the beginning of an epoch in which we too still stand."[7]

Der junge Simmel embraces its status as symptom of this turn to historical-critical self-reflection at the end of the twentieth century. By probing the vicissitudes of his early professional life and exploring the larger sociocultural context in which Simmel's thinking developed, Köhnke aimed to elucidate the "prehistory" of his *Philosophy of Money* and the "large" *Soziologie* of 1908, seen as "classic works of the theory of so-called modernity" (22). To this end, he carefully reconstructs the ups and downs of the young thinker's intellectual and professional evolution in the 1880s and 1890s, drawing on published and unpublished early writings, as well as on unpublished letters and other documents, to redefine Simmel's image in fundamental ways.

Precisely because Simmel's epoch-defining "attempt to modernize philosophy and science" took place from a point of view "outside or at least at the periphery of 'normal science' at the fin de siècle," Köhnke contends, what might seem to be biographical contingencies, "merely individual conditions," can also be understood "as more general conditions of possibility of philosophical-scientific [*philosophisch-wissenschaftlicher*] innovation" (22). Simmel's oeuvre thereby becomes "a case study for scholarly [*wissenschaftliche*] innovation" in the face of the "limitations and restrictions" that characterized "the discipline of philosophy and normal science" at the turn of the twentieth century, a case "not so much for biographical as for institutional- and disciplinary-historical [*wissenschafts-geschichtliche*] treatment"(22).

Der junge Simmel thereby challenges established disciplinary narratives, even if its author's claims for Simmel as a classic are less surprising in the European context, where he has always been regarded as a cultural philosopher as well as a sociologist—and where the lines between philosophy and sociology are more permeable in any case. In this chapter, I build on Köhnke's account of the contextual conditions of possibility for Simmel's theoretical breakthroughs, emphasizing the

---

7. Köhnke, *Der junge Simmel*, 23. Köhnke dated the beginnings of this process to the 1980s. Whereas Dilthey, Husserl, and Weber "had enjoyed nearly continuous attention," he noted, others who, like Simmel, had been neglected and more or less forgotten ("Ernst Cassirer, Werner Sombart, Ernst Troeltsch, Ferdinand Tönnies, and Hermann Cohen, to name only a few examples") were also being recovered and republished (22–23).

links between liminal disciplinary status and the capacity for radical intellectual innovation, even as my own interpretation of Simmel as modernist philosopher parts ways with Köhnke's vision of him as representative of a "classical modernity."

Der junge Simmel tracks its subject's intellectual and professional path up to the point of intellectual maturity, the publication of *Philosophie des Geldes* (*The Philosophy of Money*): "the first [work]," Simmel declared, "that is really *my* book."[8] Köhnke concentrates in particular on the 1890s—"the phase of transition into an original conception of sociology and philosophy" whereby Simmel's "attempts to know the social" yielded "an entirely new consciousness of his own position and thought as well" (28).

Köhnke argues that it was Simmel's self-reflexive relation to the challenges of reflection in a rapidly changing world that turned him into a modern classic. His early work illustrates "a successful development toward a philosophical thinking that unified science, philosophy, and life: in the form of . . . universal self-reflection." Simmel started out with a positivist "belief in science" that led him to advocate the sociological demystification of the human, then turned back to a quasi-transcendental attention to "the achievements of the cognizing subject" in the early 1890s, and finally attained his mature conception of the "creative individual" subject of life and art. His path as a thinker is thus "roughly parallel to that of German philosophy as a whole at the fin de siècle" (28–29). This exemplary philosophical development not only accounts for Simmel's popularity. Because each phase involved a new understanding of his own subjectivity, "from the perspective of the history of philosophy, it poses—and purports to answer—the question of the relation of the individual to the whole in a unique way" (29) as well. For Köhnke, Simmel is a paradigmatically modern philosophical classic—a hermeneutically unified subject who both embodies and reflects upon a new form of identity grounded in a self-reflexive relation to that subject's own sociohistorical conditions of possibility.

Whether or not one accepts Köhnke's interpretation, *Der junge Simmel* demonstrates that the process by which Simmel became who he was is of considerable historical and philosophical interest—in itself a significant scholarly accomplishment, since it entailed reconstructing the biographical and historical context in the absence of the *Nachlaß*[9] and in the face of an almost total lack of contemporary sources. The

---

8. Simmel to Rickert, February 27, 1904 (*GSG* 22: 471–72): "I have lost interest in everything that I wrote before the *Philosophy of Money*. That is the first that is really *my* book, the others appear entirely colorless to me and as if they could have been written by any one else at all."

9. Simmel had most of his drafts and lecture notes burned, and manuscripts designated for posthumous publication, as well as some intended only for private consumption, notably, "On the Essence of Truth, " were lost or destroyed under the NS regime. In 1921, a suitcase with writings on art and aesthetics meant for posthumous publication was stolen from Gertrud Kantorowicz's train compartment while she was in the dining car (*GSG* 20: 501–3; the editors speculate about papers on poetics, painting, and aesthetic theory). In May 1933, Simmel's books were burned in the infamous Nazi demonstration against "un-German" authors. After Gertrud Simmel's apparent suicide in July 1938 (according to her grandson Arnold, she did not want to stand in the way of her son's emigration; *GSG* 20: 522n75) and Hans Simmel's release from Dachau in December, the Simmels fled in early 1939. During the war, trunks of household goods placed in storage remained in Hamburg. All such property was "Aryanized," that is to say, stolen, by the Gestapo in 1941, and efforts to ascertain the fate of an inheritance that also included

textual basis has improved, but Köhnke's caution is still worth noting: Simmel did not simply see to it that most of his unpublished work was consigned to flames; he also actively produced and propagated a "stylized" self-image that elided significant aspects of his early life and thought—a (re)writing that inflects the primary evidence available. Thus, Köhnke warns, the extant reminiscences of Simmel's students and friends cannot be taken at face value. Precisely because they evoke a "relatively consistent image," they must be treated "with circumspection" (18). Most such portraits are retrospective, dating "almost exclusively from the period *after* 1900"—that is to say, after Simmel had abandoned the hypercritical stance of his youth. Since, as Köhnke puts it, they betray "the hand of the master," a "simple citation cannot escape the danger of uncritically perpetuating Simmel's self-stylization" (18–19).

Köhnke's title thus refers not to a "biographical treatment" but to a "hermeneutic problem and the attempt to resolve it" (18). To understand how Simmel became the self-reflexive, self-consciously public philosopher of his maturity, it was necessary to explain both how and why he had rewritten and obscured the history of his own thought. The first step was to uncover the facts about his intellectual and professional evolution to develop a "critique of the tradition," of the received view reflected in Simmel's own "self-presentations as well as in the reminiscences" of others (18). Here Köhnke alludes to a key source in a fashion that at once underlines the multiplicity and ambiguity of these representations and blurs the line between (canonical) text and (classical) author, exposing how indebted his conception of hermeneutics—and of critique—remained to his nineteenth-century predecessors.

The terms "self-presentations [*Selbstdarstellungen*]" and "reminiscences [*Erinnerungen*]" both refer to the *Buch des Dankes an Georg Simmel* (Book of Thanks to Georg Simmel) produced by Kurt Gassen and Michael Landmann to commemorate the hundredth anniversary of Simmel's birth on March 1, 1958. The earliest fruit of the Simmel Archive established ten years earlier, it defined the beginning of Simmel Studies in multiple ways. Introduced by Gassen and Landmann as at once a *Gedenkbuch* (memorial book) and a *Zeitbild* (image of its times) (*BdD* 5), the *Buch des Dankes* contained the first scholarly bibliography (compiled by Gassen and including an invaluable chronological listing of Simmel's university courses) and made key primary documents and letters available to a wider public for the first time, albeit largely without critical commentary. As the editors conceded, while the effort to render "Simmel's personality" had made the volume into an "image of its times," many of the relations and connections it revealed would appear only to those "for whom the intellectual history of the fin de siècle is alive" (*BdD* 5). In fact, most of the volume consists of "reminiscences" by students and friends. Culled from widely scattered books, newspapers, journals, and letters or solicited for the volume itself, these texts remain an invaluable resource for Simmel Studies, even if, as Köhnke emphasizes, their testimony must be approached with a critical eye.

---

a valuable library, antiques, and letters from Bergson, Rilke, and Rodin were fruitless (*GSG* 20: 529–30). See also Rüdiger Kramme, "Wo ist der Nachlaß von Georg Simmel? Spurensuche zwischen Klein- und Großkriminalität," *Simmel Newsletter* [*Simmel Studies*] 2 (1992): 71–76.

This caveat holds all the more for the other source to which Köhnke alludes in calling for a critique of the received view of his subject. Less than a page long and of uncertain provenance, this text came to be known as the "Self-Presentation" because it was published for the first time under the rubric *Anfang einer unvollendeten Selbstdarstellung* (Beginning of an Unfinished Self-Presentation) at the very beginning of the *Buch des Dankes*. While situating it in the place of honor in their memorial volume, Gassen and Landmann made no editorial remarks on its origin or purpose, nor did they in any way elaborate on their implicit claim in the title that the text was a fragment of a larger, uncompleted work. It was thereby enshrined as a founding document for Simmel Studies, although its purportedly autobiographical narrative can by no means be uncritically accepted. This decontextualized "Beginning" thus epitomizes the ambiguous scholarly contribution of the volume itself—at once a memorial act and propaedeutic to a critical edition, the *Buch des Dankes* played a key role in perpetuating what Köhnke later characterized as Simmel's self-stylization.

That being said, Gassen and Landmann were not wrong to place the "Self-Presentation"—or, as *Selbstdarstellung* might better be translated, "Self-Representation"—so prominently. As Simmel's only comprehensive characterization of his own intellectual development, the text provides an essential touchstone for scholarly interpretation, despite the fact that its documentary value is hardly unambiguous. For, as Köhnke demonstrates, the text reflects Simmel's habit of dismissing the works of "his entire early period as stupidity and 'sins of youth'" (31). It represents the author "as he wanted to be seen" (165), setting aside the biographical facts in favor of "an idealized youthful development from the standpoint of the essential philosophical results" as Simmel saw them circa 1905–7 (160). Its customary title notwithstanding, in this sense at least, the text is thus, as Köhnke puts it, in fact "quite finished" (164).

Simmel is an unreliable narrator, eliding all evidence of the rocky path by which he came into his own as a thinker and appropriating an autobiographical form to put forward a stylized image of himself as philosopher that stands, in Köhnke's words, "directly in opposition to his own early works" (164). And yet, he insists, this very "Self-Representation" can be read against the grain to reveal the "historical Simmel" (164) obscured by that idealizing narrative—a thinker whose works, with their inconsistencies, complexities, and reversals, register a "genuine inner development" (165). Köhnke seems rather too sanguine that he can read his way into the man himself, but Simmel's rather hermetic gloss on his philosophical evolution indeed merits very careful attention. For the "Self-Representation" reveals a good deal about the challenges of attaining the paradoxical subject position, at once canonized and marginalized, known as "Georg Simmel." Grasped as an act of self-stylization, the text casts an entirely new light on Simmel's self-understanding as a thinker and thereby helps to clarify key problems with his reception.

Let us begin by reviewing Köhnke's reconstruction of Simmel's path to intellectual maturity in order to illuminate why he would eventually elide and obscure so much of his story. The young Simmel, it turns out, was more radical philosophically, politically, and personally, than has generally been acknowledged—and far more of a materialist than the admirer of Stefan George he became cared to admit. Moreover, the man whom the politically engaged thinkers of the next generation would dismiss as a rentier aesthete by no means held himself aloof from the new social movements of his day. In the first half of the 1890s, Simmel participated in a range of broadly speaking political activities, published anonymously in social democratic journals, and generally functioned as a "connecting link between sociology, social scientific student organizations, and socialism" (455).

Simmel's practical orientation was anchored in the vision of philosophy that gave rise to his preoccupation with the social, and while his modes of engagement changed in the years to come, he never abandoned his aspiration to make a concrete impact on contemporary society. His efforts to nurture what he called "philosophical culture" after the turn of the century attest to the continuing importance of praxis, broadly conceived, for his self-understanding as a thinker.

To anticipate the larger course of my argument, while Simmel sometimes sounds like an idealist, his philosophical position is in fact a good deal more complex. What makes it so difficult to grasp that complexity—and contributed to a history of neglecting and misreading his work—lies less in what Simmel did or did not say than in a complex of assumptions about the nature of knowledge and disciplinarity that endured well into the twentieth century. These assumptions have eroded considerably over the past twenty years. The evolution of theory as genre has brought a new sort of attention not only to the linguistic but also to the historical and cultural construction of meaning, and we have come to conceive of the relation between thought and reality, to recognize and reflect on the contingency of our knowledge of the world, in new ways. It is from this perspective that I shall, in due course, come back to the questions Köhnke raised about the (historical, cultural) significance of the current return to Simmel. But this is getting ahead of the story.

As Köhnke demonstrates, the young Simmel stood under the twin influences of evolutionary thought and an incipient cultural (as opposed to philosophical) anthropology.[10] The interplay between naturalist and culturalist tendencies was decisive for Simmel's intellectual development—and, along with his turn to Kant, helps clarify the origins of the innovative conception of sociology he first formulated in 1894.

Like so many of his generation, Simmel was profoundly influenced by Herbert Spencer and his vision of rational social progress. But whereas his first book, *Über sociale Differenzierung. Sociologische und psychologische Untersuchungen* (On Social Differentiation: Social-Psychological Studies), published in 1890, evinced a none too cryptic Spencerianism, just two years later, Köhnke says, his "separation from evolutionism [was] already complete" (424), and Simmel was advancing a culturalist philosophical critique of its foundational assumptions. In the first, 1892, edition of *Die Probleme der Geschichtsphilosophie* (*The Problems of the Philosophy of History*),

---

10. More precisely, under the influence of Moritz Lazarus and Heymann Steinthal's *Völkerpsychologie*. For the impact of Simmel's teachers on the foundations of cultural anthropology, see George W. Stocking, *Volksgeist as Method and Ethic: Essays on Boasian Ethnography and the German Anthropological Tradition* (Madison: University of Wisconsin Press, 1996).

he had already abandoned the perspective that characterized his earliest works and, as Wilhelm Windelband put it at the time, had become an opponent of "positivistic and sociological theories" altogether.[11]

Köhnke contends that the author of *Die Probleme der Geschichtsphilosophie* had begun to come into his own as a thinker in advancing his "decided countertheses" (417) to the most basic historical and historiographical assumptions of evolutionism in 1892. Yet the fact that Simmel's conception of the fundamental, framing problems of social science had undergone a conceptual transformation went unrecognized by many of his colleagues in philosophy, most significantly, as Köhnke notes, by Wilhelm Dilthey, who as late as 1898 continued to refer to Simmel as a Spencerian.

Simmel's post-Spencerian conception of sociology quickly took on definite contours. The first version of his essay "Das Problem der Sociologie" ("The Problem of Sociology"), published in 1894, already incorporated a historicist perspective conscious of the limitations of materialism and of a positivist conception of science. His attitude toward the discipline and his place in it, as well as his interpretation of sociology's place in modern intellectual life, would, however, change dramatically in the years to come.

Köhnke integrates cultural and institutional history into his genealogy of the mature thinker, delving into the previously largely unexplored archives of the former Friedrich-Wilhelms-Universität in Berlin to reconstruct what he calls Simmel's "academic path of sorrows [*Leidensweg*]" (20). The young scholar's difficulties at the university were overdetermined: hostility on account of Simmel's purported Judaism or apparent areligiosity, objections to what was alleged to be an excessively critical turn of mind, and antipathies of a personal nature, as well as generalized opposition to sociology on the part of some of his senior colleagues in philosophy, all came into play (20).

But over and above all of these factors, Köhnke shows that it was Simmel's originality as a thinker, his failure to fit the established disciplinary mold, that led to his professional woes:

> Georg Simmel's intellectual profile, his works, and his personality, simply did not suit the required profile for promotion of the successor generation in German academic philosophy at the turn of the century: his extreme individualism, his themes, extremely critical and transdisciplinary methods, preferred means of demonstration, professional foci and forms of teaching, modes of argument, and style of thought did not recommend him for a philosophical professorship. (20–21)

---

11. Wilhelm Windelband in his 1894 review in the *Jahresbericht der Geschichtswissenschaft* (quoted in Köhnke, *Der junge Simmel*, 425). Simmel's attempt to place morality on a naturalist foundation in his *Einleitung in die Moralwissenschaft. Eine Kritik der ethischen Grundbegriffe* (Introduction to Moral Science: A Critique of the Foundational Concepts of Ethics) belongs to substantially the same conceptual universe as 1890's *Über sociale Differenzierung* (On Social Differentiation). Köhnke demonstrates that the second volume of the *Einleitung*, although published more than a year after the 1892 *Probleme der Geschichtsphilosophie*, must therefore predate it. As he points out, *Probleme* would be revised and reworked repeatedly, whereas Simmel's other early works were simply reprinted—or rather, in the case of the two-volume "youthful indiscretion" (*BdD* 314) that was the *Einleitung*, not reprinted at all after a certain point—a strategy that did not prevent its continuing to fuel Simmel's professional difficulties.

In a period of disciplinary consolidation and professionalization, what was called for was duly representing normal science by teaching established "subdisciplines of philosophy and the history of philosophy." From the point of view of the Wilhelminian academic establishment, Simmel's methodological and intellectual individualism, his penchant for "philosophical and indeed sociological innovation," and his associated popularity with students rendered him anything but promotable (21).

As Köhnke shows, Simmel's "distinctive position" emerged over time, "simultaneously the consequence and cause of his entirely individual profile," that is, of the original turn of mind that enabled him "in contrast to many other successful, tenured [ordinierten] colleagues—to become a classic" (21). Simmel's innovativeness as a thinker was, in turn, fostered by his failure to achieve conventional forms of scholarly recognition.[12] In examining why and how his academic career failed to proceed in a normative fashion, Köhnke thus elucidates the institutional conditions through which Simmel became a teacher and "philosophical author" (21) of enduring interest—and exposes the extent to which what is regarded as the "classical" theory of modernity entailed a break with established patterns of thought.

Simmel's departure from the Wilhelminian academic norm had begun with his youthful embrace of evolutionary ideas and a more generally "scientific" approach to philosophy, as well as engagement with the new social movements of his day. But just a few years later, he was already disseminating an image that elided his nonconformity. In the highly compact and stylized "Self-Representation," Simmel refers neither to his early materialism nor to his preoccupation with ethics and practical philosophy in the widest sense; indeed, he occludes the cultural and political stakes of his early, more overtly socially engaged conception of philosophy entirely. Not coincidentally, Simmel's idealizing account of his intellectual development—what Köhnke dubs his retrospective self-stylization "from the point of view of the essential philosophical results"—thereby set aside the most painful episodes of his early career: the rejected dissertation and failed *Habilitations-Colloquium* that turned out to be only the beginning of his academic "path of sorrows."

Simmel's narrative also implicitly registers his status as an outsider in an environment where anti-Semitic discrimination was the norm. Köhnke offers a sensitive and nuanced reading of the subjective as well as objective consequences of the institutional and social pressures on "Simmel as 'Jew,'" that is, as someone who was perceived as such and treated accordingly, religious affiliation and personal inclination aside (122–48).[13] By centering the story of his intellectual development on "the area of theoretical philosophy," he argues, Simmel was at once capitulating to "the other's image [*Fremdbild*]" (156) and writing the associated institutional humiliations out of the story.

---

12. Coser's influential related argument is that lack of recognition from scholarly peers and superiors and significant—hence highly reinforcing—appreciation from students led Simmel to cultivate those traits that appealed to the latter. See Lewis A. Coser, *Georg Simmel* (Englewood Cliffs, NJ: Prentice-Hall, 1965).

13. The son of Jews who had converted to Christianity, and married to a Christian himself, Simmel nonetheless, like many bourgeois Germans with similar backgrounds, self-identified as a Jew.

To emphasize his self-stylization is thus by no means to assert that what is at stake in his narrative is merely rhetorical or in a narrow sense subjective. On the contrary: as Köhnke suggests, Simmel's trajectory as a whole—"perhaps even the change from social engagement to the 'formal' sociological, from naturalism and social democracy to aestheticism and the [Stefan] George circle, from sociology to the metaphysics of life, etc."—may reflect a need to fit in or assimilate, that is, in this sense, too, Simmel's outsider status not only conditioned his abandonment of the direct forms of critique that characterized his youthful life and work but also shaped the (stylized) "classical" subject position he came to occupy (144).

What is at issue is not simply Simmel's personal story but, to put it in contemporary terms, his subjectivation and its relation to a broader disciplinary and institutional metanarrative about the emergence of modern social and cultural theory in the early twentieth century. Historical and methodological issues are deeply imbricated in academic narratives of origin. Examining the rather cryptic "self-presentation" in light of Köhnke's critical reconstruction not only reveals the repressed traces of Simmel's "genuine inner development"; it opens up broader questions about how to interpret the origins and development of the modern social sciences. This discussion will pave the way for an exploration of Simmel's reception in twentieth-century thought that reveals how the history of failed attempts to integrate his ideas into the disciplinary mainstream betrays the broader methodological significance of Simmel's marginalization for the institution and institutionalization of sociology.

Simmel's Self-(Re)Presentation

The text presented in the *Buch des Dankes* as the "Beginning of an Unfinished Self-Presentation" now appears in the *Gesamtausgabe* under the title "Fragment einer Einleitung [Fragment of an Introduction]" (*GSG* 20: 304–5). The new editors derive this title from a single clause in the penultimate paragraph, where Simmel alludes to his "special concept of metaphysics, which I set out in the following pages" (*GSG* 20: 305). Those pages were either lost or never written, and there is no external evidence that Simmel's autobiographical reflections were intended as part of a larger whole, yet the editors confidently announce:

> It is a fragment of an introduction to a text on metaphysics about which we know nothing else. At the earliest, this introduction can have been written in 1910, when Simmel's first publications on metaphysical themes had appeared in print; it may also be that it is a first draft of an introduction to the *Mélanges de philosophie relativiste: Contribution à la culture philosophique*. (*GSG* 20: 549)

Both of these possibilities can account for Simmel's promise to explicate his metaphysical conception of relativism "in the following pages," but neither explains the text's autobiographical framing. In fact, the actual *Préface* to Simmel's contribution to French "philosophical culture"—a collection of essays and excerpts from longer works published at Bergson's instigation in 1912 by Félix Alcan under a title that might be somewhat irreverently translated as "A Relativist Philosophical Mash-Up"—evinces no overlap with the purported "fragment." The second option is thus hardly less speculative than the notion that it might be "an introduction to a text on metaphysics about which we know nothing else."[14]

Given the level of philological uncertainty, the editorial confidence evinced is noteworthy. Since Köhnke had demonstrated nearly a decade earlier that, upon a close reading, the text is hardly "unfinished," hermeneutically speaking, it is the interpolated reference to a larger whole that requires explanation. What is actually at stake literally falls between the two possibilities entertained by the editors: their unsubstantiated assertion that the text cannot be dated earlier than 1910, when Simmel allegedly first began to publish on metaphysical themes.

As a matter of fact, by the time *Philosophie des Geldes* appeared in 1900, Simmel's metaphysical relativism was already well established. The Preface to that work describes his approach by contrasting it to "philosophical system-building," and the text is suffused with metaphysical themes and concerns. If the *Philosophy of Money* is seen as a pioneering work of philosophical modernism, as I contend it must be, it becomes clear that the distance between Simmel's objectives there and the project of fostering "philosophical culture" that provided the rhetorical framing for the French volume and oriented the even later essays to which the editors refer should not be overstated. The narrative that has its author "still" a "sociologist" in 1900, rather than the "philosopher of life" he became later on, leaves a great deal out of account to undergird an extraordinarily persistent, whiggish framing of Simmel's work as moving "from" sociology "to" a "philosophy of life" in his later years.

Simmel's autobiographical "Self-Representation" calls for most careful and critical reading. But the very different disciplinary narrative in which it situates his metaphysical relativism rewards serious consideration. First, though, a brief reflection on the question of its provenance, which Gassen and Landmann passed over in silence upon its initial publication, will prove illuminating.

Köhnke reports that while collecting materials for the memorial volume, Landmann had written Simmel's friend Margarete Susman to inquire about papers he had been told were in her possession, "including an autobiographical sketch that was intended for the Ueberweg." While "it is no longer possible to determine in detail how Landmann actually came by the sketch," Köhnke judged it highly probable that Simmel had in fact composed the text in question for the register of contemporary philosophers included in the reference work *Friedrich Ueberwegs Grundriss der Geschichte der Philosophie vom Beginn des neunzehnten Jahrhunderts bis auf die Gegenwart* (11th ed., 1916), also known, with a nod to its editors Friedrich Ueberweg and Max Heinze, as the "Ueberweg-Heinze." If so, far from being the aborted beginning of a larger whole, as both teams of editors implied, the purported fragment is instead a rather well-rounded apologia aimed at an audience of professional philosophers.[15]

---

14. The editors of the critical edition of the *Mélanges* make no reference whatsoever to the purported "fragment" in discussing the origins of the collection (*GSG* 19: 407–19). Simmel included long passages from the introduction to his 1911 essay collection *Philosophische Kultur* in its preface.

15. Köhnke credits Angelika Rammstedt with discovering the documentation that "clarifies the origin of the self-presentation," in the Susman (von Bendemann) papers deposited in the Deutsche Literatur-

Approached from this point of view, the text provides an invaluable lens for examining Simmel's disciplinary self-understanding. This point is underlined by another piece of evidence that Köhnke brings in support of his identification, one of the striking "sayings" Ernst Bloch included in his own contribution to the "Reminiscences" section of the *Buch des Dankes*. "Today," Bloch recalled Simmel telling him,

> I am having the saddest day of my life. I was supposed to summarize the content of my philosophy in a half-page for the latest volume of Ueberweg-Heinze. Epigones can still write books about their thoughts, but the abstract of a half-page brings to light how little unity there is [*bringt die Sache an den Tag, die so wenig eine ist*]. Schopenhauer could express his entire teaching in just six words, in the title of his main work [i.e., *Die Welt als Wille und Vorstellung* (*The World as Will and Representation*)].[16]

For Köhnke, Simmel's melancholy words register the pain of submitting to (disciplinary) unification. Writing from a "fallback position after countless failed hopes and projects" for genuine integration into "the Wilhelminian and academic lifeworld" (165) and the disciplinary mainstream, he had composed an account intended for philosophical posterity that disowned most of his early work—a text that at once illuminated and obscured his achievements by representing his thinking, so Köhnke, "without genuine inner development, unhistorically."

That what actually appeared in the Ueberweg was clearly not Simmel's own writing speaks volumes about his situation vis-à-vis the institutions of academic philosophy. Despite a strenuous effort to assimilate, epitomized by a "Self-Representation" that rewrote and disguised his differences from the disciplinary mainstream, he did not really fit in. Today, it is Simmel's distance from the dominant paradigms regnant in the normal science of his day that is of the greatest interest—but also, thanks to his reception history, most difficult to grasp. Severing Simmel's "sociological" from his "philosophical" accomplishments underpins a narrative that belies the significance of his thinking for the theory and practice of interpretation well beyond the social sciences.

We shall return in due course to the remarks recalled by Bloch, as well as to the question of when "metaphysical themes" entered into Simmel's work. First, though, we need to understand how and why Simmel constructed the unified image of his intellectual evolution that appears in the "Self-Representation." Uncovering and recovering what he wrote out of the story is the first, essential, step if, as Köhnke puts it, we are to stop seeing Simmel through the distorting mirror of "the eyes of others" (165–66). As he shows, the "Self-Representation" must be read against the grain if we are to gauge the full significance of Simmel's distance and difference from the disciplinary mainstream, for it was quite literally composed for the scrutinizing gaze of those who "caused him to disavow . . . his own youth and these stations of his development" (165).

---

archiv in Marbach. (For the remarks quoted here, along with an extended citation from Landmann's letter of November 10, 1956, see Köhnke, *Der junge Simmel*, 161n236.)

16. *BdD*, 251. Like Kantorowicz and Susman, Bloch presents his memories via a sort of ventriloquism. For an alternative version of this story, see Michael Landmann, "Ernst Bloch über Simmel," in *AuS*, 269–71.

Simmel's "Self-Representation" begins with a remarkable elision: he declares that his point of departure had been "epistemological [*erkenntnistheoretischen*] and Kantian [*kantwissenschaftlichen*] studies that went hand in hand with historical and social scientific ones" (*GSG* 20, 304). As Köhnke observes, in circumscribing his "point of departure" in Kantian terms, Simmel tailors his intellectual biography to suit his mature philosophical convictions and disciplinary image.

Not only does this retrospective rewriting effectively exclude Simmel's "two most comprehensive early publications in [Lazarus and Steinthal's—EG] *Zeitschrift für Völkerpsychologie*—the first, rejected dissertation and the study on Dante's psychology," Köhnke notes in *Der junge Simmel* (149).[17] The text also passes in silence over his first two books, mentioning neither the "social and psychological studies" of his 1890 *Über sociale Differenzierung* (On Social Differentiation) nor the "ethical- and moral-philosophical studies" undertaken in the nearly 900-page *Einleitung in die Moralwissenschaft. Eine Kritik der ethischen Grundbegriffe* (Introduction to Moral Science: A Critique of the Foundational Concepts of Ethics), published in two volumes in 1892–93. Glossing over the devastating materialist critique of ethics that remained a major source of hostility toward his person long after he had abandoned its premises, Simmel begins by tacitly foregrounding the prize-winning essays on Kant, written during the same period, that had eventually served as his dissertation and *Habilitation*.[18] He then jumps directly to his third book, *Die Probleme der Geschichtsphilosophie* (*The Problems of the Philosophy of History*), passing over his Spencerian phase in silence and entirely eliding his even more decisive involvement with Moritz Lazarus and Hermann Steinthal's *Völkerpsychologie*—that is to say, his participation in the field of (broadly speaking) psychological and proto-anthropological studies.

The latter omission is significant biographically as well as theoretically. Unlike a Comte or Spencer, whose aspirations to create comprehensive philosophical systems place them firmly in the nineteenth century, the efforts of Lazarus and Steinthal on behalf of what they called *Völkerpsychologie*, "the psychology of peoples," pointed firmly to the future. Their work was part of a field of emergent social scientific practices that extended materialist and evolutionist paradigms, setting aside totalizing philosophical ambitions in favor of a new ideal of empirically grounded scientific knowledge. The young thinker's engagement with those practices, as Köhnke puts it, thus attests to the considerable "difference between Simmel's own cognitive interests and the existing realities and requirements of normal science" as understood by the philosophical establishment (150). In redacting himself into a more mainstream disciplinary narrative, the text occludes not just his liminal institutional status during

---

17. As Köhnke notes, the article on "Psychological and Ethnological Studies of Music" published in the *Zeitschrift für Völkerpsychologie* 13 in 1882 (now in *GSG* 1: 45–87) is not "strictly speaking" identical with the (rejected) dissertation on "Psychological-Ethnographic Studies on the Beginnings of Music" submitted in December 1880 (Köhnke, *Der junge Simmel*, 51). "Dante's Psychology" is in *GSG* 1: 91–177.

18. See Köhnke's discussion in *Der junge Simmel*, 104 passim, of the second (lost) paper and its relation to the (likewise lost) *Habilitation*.

the first phase of his career but also theoretical differences that remained decisive for the thinker he became.

Simmel's retrospective rewriting of his intellectual and professional trajectory not only drastically redescribes his intellectual starting points. The "Self-Representation" as a whole adopts what Köhnke refers to as an "idealist" perspective on his intellectual development that conceals how methodologically significant Simmel's interest in, broadly speaking, materialist explanation and the related interdisciplinary pursuits remained for his mature philosophical work. As Köhnke shows, the subtle presence of *völkerpsychologischen* ideas and methods in Simmel's self-description is striking. Indeed, the subterranean influence of Lazarus, whom he credited with awakening his interest in "the problem of the super-individual and its depths," is evident in the very second sentence.[19]

There Simmel asserts that the "first result" of his early work had been

> the fundamental motif [*Grundmotiv*][20] (developed in *Probleme der Geschichtsphilosophie*) that "history" signifies the formation [*Formung*] of immediate, merely experienceable events according to the apriorities of the spirit that forms science [*die Apriolitäten des wissenschaftsbildenden Geistes*], just as "nature" signifies the formation of sensually given material via the categories of the understanding. (*GSG* 20: 304)

Simmel's "fundamental motif" expands the conventional understanding of apriority considerably. Kant had focused on how subjective experience must be constituted so that reliable empirical and scientific knowledge is possible. Simmel, as Köhnke puts it, uses the term "a priori" to refer to "an answer to the universalized question of the 'conditions of possibility'" (426). This usage, which extends the notion of epistemological prerequisites to include their cultural-psychological and sociological formation, had its intellectual roots in *Völkerpsychologie*. It was by setting aside the reductive and determinist materialism of his early, Spencerian work and adopting an anthropologically inflected, generalized understanding of a priori "formation," then, that Simmel came to understand "'history' [*Geschichte*] as created by science" (425). To translate Köhnke's point into rather different terms, Simmel abandoned his naturalism because he came to recognize the constructive role of culture and narrative framework in constituting and maintaining knowledge practices.

But Simmel's idealizing account of his intellectual development elides the role of empirical—"historical and social scientific"—studies in fostering this extension of Kantian ideas. As he represents it, recognizing the logic of the historical a priori was what led him to conceive of the investigation of the social in a new way. Epistemology became theory, as it were, as Simmel's insight into "the spirit that forms

---

19. Simmel sent the first version of "Das Problem der Sociologie" to Lazarus as a belated seventieth birthday gift. In an accompanying letter (November 5, 1894), he characterized the essay as "the most recent result of lines of thought that you first awakened in me. For however divergent and independent my subsequent development became, I shall nonetheless never forget that before all others, you directed me to the problem of the superindividual and its depths [*des Überindividuellen u. seine Tiefen*], whose investigation will probably fill out the productive time that remains to me" (*GSG* 22: 132).

20. Simmel employs the musical concept *Grundmotiv* (which I have sometimes also translated "fundamental motive") at a number of crucial points.

science" gave rise to the practical task of establishing the (methodological) foundations of a new discipline. The text continues:

> This division between the form and content of the historical image [*Bild*], which came to me purely epistemologically, I then extended into a methodological principle within a single discipline:[21] I attained a new concept of sociology by dividing the forms of association from the contents, that is, from the drives, purposes, content matter which only become social when taken up by the reciprocal interactions [*Wechselwirkungen*] between individuals; in my book, I therefore undertook the treatment of these types of reciprocal interaction as the object of a pure sociology. (*GSG* 20: 304)

On Simmel's retrospective account, a philosophical insight thus enabled the emergence of a new knowledge practice: a new strategy for attaining knowledge of the social and a new definition of sociology.

Simmel rightly emphasized the magnitude of this conceptual breakthrough to a new concept of form(ation). In focusing on what he called the "forms of association" (the forms of *Vergesellschaftung*, literally, "becoming-society" or "becoming-social," variously translated as "association" or "sociation"), Simmel set aside his early reductive naturalism, while maintaining a significant orientation toward phenomenal reality. Far from denying or abstracting from the complexity of the world, his conception of form disclosed a new dimension of meaningfulness.

What has been construed as Simmel's "formalism" has fostered a good deal of misunderstanding, so before continuing our examination of the "Self-Representation," it will be helpful to look more closely at his "new concept of sociology," to consider the theoretical implications of his emphasis on social form as such, and to examine how Simmel's theoretical approach came to be understood—and misunderstood—by his contemporaries. Since the thinking of form remained so significant within his oeuvre well beyond his "sociological" writings, contextualizing the theoretical move involved in Simmel's adoption of this venerable category helps make clear what was at stake in his subsequent turn back from discipline-building in sociology to a renewed identification with philosophy. For that return would be a consequence of Simmel's insight into the historical and philosophical significance of the conception of human cultural existence that he had begun to develop under the rubric of a "sociology of form."

Simmel's "Formalism"

In setting out his vision of sociology, beginning with "Das Problem der Sociologie," his crucial and explicitly programmatic essay of 1894, Simmel was intervening in the larger fin de siècle discourse on the stakes and future of the human and cultural sciences as such in modernity.[22] Keeping this broader intellectual context in view helps counterbalance the (often unconscious) presentism that reads his the-

---

21. Simmel's syntax foregrounds the relation between (philosophical/epistemological) theory and (sociological) practice. The division between form and content, he writes, "setzte sich mir dann in ein methodisches Prinzip innerhalb einer Einzelwissenschaft fort" (literally, "extended itself for me into a methodological principle within a single science").

22. *Probleme der Geschichtsphilosophie* (1892), which Simmel identified as his first significant book,

oretical and methodological innovations from the perspective of the social sciences as they subsequently took form and became institutionalized in the course of the twentieth century. Simmel's writings, self-consciously situated in a context of institutional and disciplinary transformation where questions of representation, interpretation, causality, and evidence were all being confronted in new ways, cannot be understood in terms of a straightforward opposition between (what is retrospectively construed as) the "hermeneutic" orientation of the (traditional) humanities (*Geisteswissenschaften*) and (incipient) "empirical" social science. And since what animated Simmel's sociological labors amounts to an alternative vision of inquiry into human cultural or social life as a whole, historical self-reflexivity is crucial in assessing the nature and importance of his achievements as a thinker.

Simmel defined his "pure sociology" in terms of a focus on types of interactive patterns rather than on static structures, social or otherwise. As Friedrich Tenbruck showed in a 1959 essay devoted to his "Formal Sociology," for him, social forms have, by definition, a kind of transcendent, transcultural meaning: Forms are "reciprocal orientations which go with typical situations," and "no culture is entirely free to 'define' typical situations." Yet Simmel was no structuralist *avant la lettre* for whom the individual subject was "a mere functionary in society."[23] As Tenbruck stressed, his vision of sociology could not have been further from an approach in which "the structural pattern is conceived as a social system, and society, as such a system, is the object of investigation and the ultimate unit of reference" (86).

In "Das Problem der Soziologie," Simmel distanced himself from such a totalizing vision of the social even as he set out his strategy for defining sociology as "a specific, independent science" without hypostasizing "society" as independently existing reality. He thereby quite explicitly situated the question of sociology's disciplinarity at the center of the generally recognized historical turn within the cultural and human sciences as a whole during this period.

He begins with an intriguing observation about the intrication of historical narrative, discursive construction, and representational regimes in the emergence of the modern category of the social:

> The most significant and consequential progress that the historical sciences and the understanding of the human altogether have made in our time is usually understood as the overcoming of the individualistic way of seeing [*die Uberwindung der individualistischen Anschauungsart*]. In place of the individual fates that formerly stood in the foreground of the historical image [*des historischen Bildes*], what has come to seem genuinely effective and decisive to us are social forces, collective movements out of which it is rarely possible to discern the part of the individual with full certainty: the science of the human has become the science of human society.[24]

---

also contributed to these debates, which form the background of his professional development and shaped his relations with Dilthey, Tönnies, Rickert, Weber, Cassirer et al.

23. Friedrich Tenbruck, "Formal Sociology," first published in K. H. Wolff, ed., *Georg Simmel: 1858–1918* (Columbus: Ohio University Press, 1959), 61–99, and partially reprinted in Coser, *Georg Simmel* (1965). Both of these quotations are from Wolff, 86; subsequent citations, also to the Wolff volume, are in the text.

24. "Das Problem der Soziologie," *GSG* 5: 52–61; here p. 52. Parenthetical citations in the following paragraphs also refer to this edition.

The historical or social turn through which the modern human and social sciences had "overcome the individualistic mode of seeing" reflected a fundamental transformation of human self-understanding itself in modernity. "No object of the human sciences can escape this turn," he insisted. Simmel's faith in the power of sociology would wane, but he never abandoned this conviction that all modern forms of thought have to incorporate a fundamental shift of perspective, that historical and social reflective self-awareness had altered the foundations of systematic inquiry as such.

The opening of "Das Problem der Sociologie" makes palpable Simmel's intellectual evolution away from his early reductive materialism and evolutionism. It reflects the methodological and historical self-awareness that ensued once he had grasped "history" by analogy with the Kantian transcendental synthesis of nature as the product of the mediation of human ways of knowing. This essay thereby proclaims the new, anti-naturalistic "fundamental motif" of his work in this period: the notion "that 'history' signifies the formation" of the matter of immediate experience "according to the apriorities of the spirit that forms science." Beginning in the mid-1890s, for all the variations of subject matter, formal structure, disciplinary location, and stylistic approach in his subsequent writings, this idea indeed became an underlying theme. Simmel never turned back to a "pre-critical" stance.

However, he had by no means simply become a (neo-)Kantian. The new motif was more complicated and (from the perspective of mainstream academic philosophy) unconventional. A new dimension of theoretical reflection had entered into his thinking along with an understanding of objective *Geist* as a formative force that, as Köhnke shows, owed much to Moritz Lazarus and *Völkerpsychologie*. Recognizing and participating in the "overcoming of the individualistic way of seeing" entailed more than adding a new dimension of methodological self-reflection, for it required thinking about subjectivity and subject-formation in new ways. This conceptually articulated awareness of "the super-individual," and what we might call the anthropological a priori—that is, the ways in which human sensibility itself is always already culturally and historically shaped—constitutes the point of departure for Simmel's mature work.

In this double sense, the recognition of historicity—not just that "history" is a human construct but also that human beings themselves are historically (culturally) constituted—becomes the "fundamental theme" of his mature work. This shift marks a sea change in Simmel's approach to cultural analysis. He abandoned the certitudes of his early, more derivative works and began to rethink the philosophical implications of the evolutionary paradigm. From this point forward, he was always trying to theorize how perception and cognition varied over time and place and to think crucial categories—individuality, objectivity, particularity, truth, value—as both relative and absolute.

Simmel's anthropological or cultural understanding of the historical a priori cast a fresh light on very old philosophical problems. Connecting his reflections on modern experience to issues that had occupied (among others) the Stoics and Skeptics gave Simmel a new sensitivity for the complexity and ambiguity of human cultural life and a subtlety both in questions and answers. Even if his understanding of form(ation) is not unproblematic, the notion that human sensibility is culturally and historically formed and formative helped him articulate connections between what were increasingly being approached as disparate domains and to link the dilemmas of modern subjectivity to that very historical-methodological self-awareness.

While the theme would undergo considerable development, Simmel's understanding of history as a spiritual-intellectual formative process indeed set the tone for his subsequent theoretical innovations. Thus, as he put it in the "Self-Representation," the distinction between (cultural) form and (material) content of the "historical image" was expanded into "a methodological principle within a single science" to define a new concept of sociology that stood in a self-reflexive relation to the writer's own historical situation. The ascendance of the sociological way of seeing was symptomatic of a global transformation under way in the human and social or cultural sciences: the discipline of sociology was both a response to and a catalyst for the process of historical transformation associated with the "overcoming of the individualistic way of seeing."

For Simmel, "The Problem of Sociology" had both scholarly and pragmatic urgency precisely because the impulse and sensibility that define sociology were widely diffused in modern culture. "The tendency to trace every individual occurrence to the historical circumstance, the needs and achievements of the whole, extends equally into religion as into economic life, into morality as into technical culture, into politics as into the health and sickness of soul and body" (52). On account of its general applicability, this cognitive tendency may well provide a "regulative principle for all the human sciences" (52). But for that very reason, it is ill-suited to defining a specific science (*Wissenschaft*). To identify what distinguishes sociology's intellectual practices as those of a well-defined discipline or "scientific" mode of inquiry, it is necessary to clarify its relation to this larger sociocultural and intellectual transformation of sensibility.

If "sociology" is taken "in the sense of an explanation of everything that happens via social forces and configurations," the term ceases to refer to a systematic intellectual practice or discipline at all. Rather, like "induction," it designates "a method of cognition, a heuristic principle" of potentially infinite extension (53). So defined, "sociology" is simply a synonym for the contemporary historical turn in reflection on human life as a whole. Understood in this overly expansive sense, as "comprising the totality of processes in society and every reduction of individual events to the social," Simmel declares, "sociology" becomes "nothing but a unifying *name* for the totality of the human sciences approached in a modern fashion" (52).

To accept such a generalizing definition of the discipline, he warns, would lead sociology away from science and back toward the sort of "empty universals and abstractions that had spelled the fate [*Verhängnis*] of philosophy." Attempts to force the most diverse aspects of reality into a "conceptual or merely external unity to create a scientific empire" are doomed to fail (52–53). These epistemological issues are not limited to the methodology and logic of social scientific inquiry but go to the heart of the discipline as such: if "sociology" is to signify more than "a mere research tendency falsely hypostasized into a science of society" and become a specific and productive *Wissenschaft*, its object must be more narrowly specified.

Simmel advances his methodological solution via a critique of sociological reasoning, supplementing his case for a narrower definition of the discipline by drawing an analogy with psychology: "Just as everything that happens is a happening in the soul, so too, seen in another way, it is a happening in society." However, just as the fact that consciousness is a necessary condition of an event does not make that event, per se, into a psychological object, it does not follow that "everything that happens only *in* society and under the condition that society exists belongs in sociology" (54). Rather, what is "specifically social" are simply "the form and forms of association [*Vergesellschaftung*] as such, in abstraction from the individual interests and contents that are realized in and through association" (54).

Simmel objected on both philosophical and pragmatic, methodological, grounds to hypostatizing processes of social interaction into a totality, "society," that could then be construed as the unified object of sociological inquiry. The discipline's object must be conceived in a way that reduced without denying the complexity of reality. Sociology should be the "investigation of the forces, forms, and developments of association, the being-with, -for, and -beside one another of individuals," including the material and other "determinations which the form of association receives from the specific content through which it finds expression." Delimiting sociology as the study not of *society* but of the trans- and intersubjective *forms of association* among individuals would place the discipline on a firm epistemological and methodological foundation: sociology "extracts the social moment out of the totality of human history, that is, out of what happens *in* society, for specialized observation or, to express it with somewhat paradoxical brevity, it investigates that which in society is society" (57).

Grounded in a new understanding of the epistemic stakes of the process of historical and sociocultural formation, Simmel's phenomenological approach takes self-reflexive awareness of the historical and cultural constitution of human sensibility as the point of departure, balancing the encounter with cultural-historical particularity and variability with an aspiration to universalizing claims about human collective life as such. Far from turning analysis of social form into a protostructuralist end in itself, treating the "forms of association" as the unique object of the discipline also entails that the same empirical phenomena may, in other contexts of inquiry, be legitimately considered in terms of their psychological, historical, political, or other content(s).

Simmel's approach opens up strategies for interpretation—for understanding the distinctiveness of the social as an object—that have implications for the humanities and cultural and social sciences more generally. His own thinking about the social changed considerably as he integrated the theoretical and practical consequences of his new way of understanding both the subjects and the objects of these modes of inquiry. After exploring Simmel's intellectual evolution, we shall turn to his mature (re)delimitation of this "problem" in the drastically revised and expanded version of "The Problem of Sociology" that introduces his 1908 book *Soziologie. Untersuchungen über die Formen der Vergesellschaftung* (Sociology: Investigations into the Forms of Association [or, more literally, "of Becoming-Social"]) to ask about the larger implications of his theoretical and methodological insights for contemporary cultural theory. For now, though, what is at issue is the nature of his claims regarding form.

In Simmel's view, putting sociology on a firm foundation required, not defining human being or culture or society, but establishing a method for examining the flux that constitutes the actuality of individual and collective existence. Just as the objects of natural science are not "things in themselves" but "things for us"—objects as constituted by and for the subject who knows them—the objects of the human sciences are not abstract particulars but temporally extended multiplicities: events, interactions, processes. Simmel's purported formalism thereby opens onto dimensions that he is not, at least initially, able to master conceptually. For what corresponds to the synthesis of the manifold of sensation in the Kantian account of the a priori structures of objectivity is not a transcendental act of the subject as such but the historical (we would probably say "cultural") a priori as enacted in the complexity of collective life. The temporally extended multiplicities it generates—the phenomena of interpersonal, historical, cultural life—cannot in principle be exhaustively known from any single perspective.

To put it anachronistically, for Simmel, the social and human sciences must be radically interdisciplinary since the condition of possibility for systematic inquiry into human individual and collective existence is a constitutive multiplicity of interpretive perspectives. Far from being vitiated by an excessive formalism, his conception of sociology's disciplinarity gives rise to a philosophical vision of inquiry into social, cultural, and human life that is an implicit challenge to formalism and structuralism of all stripes. That vision would lead Simmel back to an identification with the discipline of philosophy and give rise to his efforts to produce a coherent account of epistemological relativism (or perspectivism) that could ground his pluralistic approach to reflection on cultural life. Before returning to our examination of his autobiographical account, it will be helpful to explore his colleagues' objections to Simmel's conception of sociology.

The key figure in the opposition to Simmel's purported formalism was Émile Durkheim himself. In an essay published in 1900, Durkheim vehemently objected to Simmel's effort to delimit sociology as the study of social forms. He attacked as a "gratuitous assertion" Simmel's distinction between form and content, and, in a move that prefigured Talcott Parsons's subsequent dismissal of Simmel, glossed content as "the content of conduct."[25] For Durkheim, it was

> easy to see at a first glance that the traditions and common practices of religion, law, morality, and of the political economy are no less social phenomena than the external forms of sociability. . . . They are society itself, living and acting. What a queer notion it would be to imagine the group as a sort of empty form, any sort of mold whatsoever which could receive, indifferently, any sort of content! (84)

In a word, Simmel's "use of abstraction [was] methodologically unsound" (85).

---

25. Émile Durkheim, "The Realm of Sociology as a Science," trans. Everett K. Wilson, reproduced in *Georg Simmel: Critical Assessments*, ed. David Frisby (New York: Routledge, 1994), 1: 84. My citations (henceforth in the text) refer to this volume.

Durkheim's critique misunderstands, even distorts, Simmel's views. Leaving aside for the moment the difficulties with his own assumption that society can be construed as a "living and acting" totality, it is worth emphasizing that Durkheim's argument turns on a significant mistranslation—one that his translator Everett Wilson did readers the service of both exposing and correcting. In criticizing Simmel's allegedly "radical separation between form and content of society" (84), Durkheim juxtaposes not, as one might assume, *forme* and *contenu* but rather *le contenant du contenu* (84; "the container of the contents"). *Contenant* is not simply an oddly unidiomatic translation of Simmel's *Form*. As the reader may see for herself by substituting "container" for "form" in the passages I have just cited, this translation misses—and distorts—Simmel's way of approaching the question entirely. Nevertheless, and this is the crucial point, the metaphorics Durkheim thereby introduced help anchor his argument that Simmel had not provided an adequate foundation for a science of sociology.

According to Durkheim, "form" was too vague an object of inquiry; in focusing on it, Simmel failed to establish essential distinctions between orders of analysis that would enable sociology's progression toward rigorous science. For all the "shrewdness and ingenuity" of his work (86), Durkheim held, Simmel's vision of the discipline was fundamentally flawed. His method "lends itself to individual whim. There is no rule, no guideline which allows one to determine in an objective fashion where the circle of sociological phenomena begins and ends" (85). Simmel had, furthermore, betrayed the weakness of his conceptual apparatus by using "form" to refer, not only to the "external and morphological characteristics" of association, but also to "the most broadly conceived forms of relationship of all sorts which are bound into the life of society" (85). On these grounds, Durkheim rejected as only "seemingly fundamental" the method of abstraction of which Simmel was so proud. The "appearance deriving from the opposing of form to content [*le contenant au contenu*] disappears as soon as one specifies more precisely the meaning of these terms and sees that they are only loosely used metaphors" (85).

The question of the role of metaphor is crucial. Durkheim's own language is by no means beyond reproach with respect to the covert importation of figures. However, since the problem of metaphoricity cannot be limited in this way but goes to the heart of what constitutes a discipline, it cannot in fact be resolved as neatly as Durkheim implies. What is at stake is how to read the social itself: how overcoming "the individualistic way of seeing" becomes the condition of possibility for social science as such. As the following passage illustrates, Simmel's approach—and, ipso facto, its philosophical motivation—was in fundamental ways illegible to Durkheim. The sentence in which he praises the "shrewdness and ingenuity" of Simmel's writings continues:

> but we do not believe it possible to outline the chief divisions of our discipline as he understands them. We see no connections among the issues he suggests as objects of sociological inquiry. They are matters for reflection which do not tie together into a *scientific system which forms a whole* [my emphasis—EG]. Furthermore, the proofs he relies on are usually a number of examples. Facts are cited which are drawn from the most disparate

sources and with no assessment of them, and consequently with no conception of their worth. If sociology is to merit the name of a science, it must consist in something other than a number of philosophical variations on the theme of social life, chosen more or less randomly, according to the inclinations of particular individuals. The problem must be posed so as to enable a logical solution. (86)

Durkheim's critique of Simmel in the name of a properly scientific sociology exemplifies the objections that would become the commonplaces of the reception. His work, while brilliant, is too subjective; it fails to achieve systematicity; examples are arrayed in an insufficiently argumentative manner.

It is an interpretation that misreads and underestimates Simmel's intellectual achievement on every point. At the same time, Durkheim's assessment makes strikingly clear how fundamental the issues are. What underlies accusations about loose language and shoddy argumentation, about the "gratuitous assertion" of "methodologically unsound" abstractions, is a basic disagreement about the nature of concepts and the logic of social scientific inquiry itself.

Two very different visions of objectivity were at stake. Durkheim thought that the scientific enterprise of sociology should be oriented toward the collective phenomena of "social facts" as such. He objected to Simmel's methodological individualism, failing to grasp his Kantian perspective and therefore construing as psychological what for Simmel were epistemological claims. For his part, by the mid-1890s, Simmel had come to the conclusion that objectivity could only be anchored via a quasi-transcendental operation. For him, defining sociology as a science depended on delineating the conditions of possibility of higher-order collective phenomena classed as "society" as such. The study of social forms was a strategy for linking the phenomenal back to the transcendental in this sense—an approach that from Durkheim's point of view constituted an unwarranted abstraction from the palpable reality of social facts and could therefore only lead sociology back toward metaphysics.

It is, then, a fundamental philosophical disagreement that animates the accusations that Simmel wanted to build a science on mere metaphors. If we understand a constitutive multiplicity of interpretive perspectives to be the condition of possibility for systematic investigation in the social and human sciences, what appeared to Durkheim as an overly subjective and unsystematic accumulation of "philosophical variations on the theme of social life" looks quite different. Like other modernist texts, Simmel's writings do not cohere in a conventional fashion. His mode of narration—metaphors and all—is highly significant, and it is necessary to reflect on his formal strategies to grasp what he is saying. The considerable philosophical stakes of Simmel's approach, and hence the theoretical and methodological achievement of his sociological analysis, do not really become legible until we reflect on his modernist strategies of argumentation directly and as such.

Durkheim's objections thus amount to far more than a simple misunderstanding of Simmel's conception of sociology. His critique is symptomatic of fundamental philosophical disagreements about language, science, and rationality that, as our consideration of the reception history in the next chapter will show, have rendered Simmel's approach opaque to all who conceive of society as a substantive totality accessible to scientific investigation. From that point of view, in Durkheim's concise formulation, Simmel's approach "serves only to keep sociology in a metaphysical state from which, on the contrary, it should above all else be emancipated" (84) so that knowledge of the social can be put to pragmatic use.[26]

In the course of the twentieth century, a Durkheimian notion of social totality provided both philosophical inspiration and methodological orientation for a diverse array of efforts to integrate analytic and disciplinary perspectives to unify, consolidate, and expand the range of social scientific inquiry. For all their differences, Lévi-Straussian anthropology, Lacanian psychoanalysis, Althusserian political theory, and Braudelian historiography all enshrine Durkheim's precept that the particular, the individual form, is analytically secondary to the universal, the social whole. Totalizing (inter)disciplinary master discourses focused on the operations of features of human life that transcend historical and cultural particularity were its legacy.

A Simmelian emphasis on flux over order and on form as opposed to structure yields a very different vision of the social scientific enterprise, one that anticipates many of the insights associated with poststructuralism. For Simmel, there can be no ultimate units of analysis and no "social facts" as such in isolation from their interpretive framing. To do justice to social formation in this sense means to attend to the complexity of sociocultural phenomena that arise from reciprocal interactions among human beings, whether at the macro- or micro-sociological level. It is a vision of social theory that is decentered rather than integrative, for attention to form in Simmel's sense reveals the necessity of developing multiple, only sometimes interrelated disciplinary perspectives in order to grasp the complexity of historical (social, cultural) life.

In setting out his account of his intellectual development more than a decade later, Simmel thus rightly emphasized the distinctiveness and methodological importance of his conception of form(ation). Its epistemological (as opposed to metaphysical or ontological) grounding in "history" as a human construct—rooted in praxis yet transcending the (apparent) immediacy of subjective experience—allowed Simmel to turn his self-reflective approach to form (in the words of his "Self-Representation") into "a methodological principle" for his new vision of a "pure sociology." The purity or abstraction in question is by no means formalistic.

Crucially, Simmel understood the forms of association themselves to be constituted through intersubjective *Wechselwirkung*, or reciprocal interaction—a view considerably closer to Hegel than Kant. To put it somewhat paradoxically, while the objects of other social sciences are sociocultural "contents" of various sorts (e.g., political or economic facts and relations), in Simmelian sociology, "form" is content. In one sense, then, the discipline exists at a higher degree of abstraction than the other cultural or social sciences—its object being "what in society is society." Yet thanks to his robust conception of interactive causation, sociology had (no less than those

---

26. For Simmel, the primary task of sociology was not practical or political but analytic, and, as we shall see in due course, he was (on good philosophical grounds) less sanguine than Durkheim about instrumental applications of sociological ideas and methods.

other disciplines) a means of analytically delineating an orderliness that had already found expression in human activity.

Simmel's theoretical self-understanding stands at a considerable distance from the conceptual strategies that came to define the disciplinary mainstream, and the sort of objections Durkheim raised suffuse his subsequent reception. As the modern social sciences became established, the philosophical rhetoric of reflection in which he had couched his insights grew increasingly foreign and illegible. Even if Simmel's groundbreaking strategies for abstracting patterns of social interaction had been foundational for sociology, from the empiricist point of view that came to dominate the social sciences, the very idea of form was suspiciously metaphysical. Less than a decade after his death, the Harvard sociologist and advocate of statistical methods Pitirim Sorokin was declaring that a formal approach to sociology could only lead to "a purely scholastic and dead science."[27]

In fact, the liveliness and inventiveness of Simmel's sociological imagination have been repeatedly remarked by his successors, and his by no means formalistic analyses of social forms have continued to inspire very diverse thinkers. Yet what was and is truly challenging about Simmel's analyses cannot be probed too deeply without calling into question very fundamental theoretical and methodological assumptions of modern social science in general—and of mainstream sociology in particular. The symptom of this disjuncture has been misprision and defensive rejection. Thus it is that the very critics who object to his definition of sociology as the study of forms invoke Simmel's failure to restrict his analyses to the purely formal as a performative self-refutation of his purported theory.

This objection has persisted even though, as Tenbruck wryly pointed out nearly fifty years ago in the first paragraph of an essay that should have put a decisive end to such misreadings (or at least motivated a few of his critics to take a much more thorough "look into" Simmel's books!), "the very crudeness and continuance of the alleged transgressions should have cautioned against the formalistic interpretation" of his work.[28] As Tenbruck elegantly demonstrated, what were styled as principled objections to Simmel's "formal sociology" were based on a misunderstanding. His approach by no means, as Sorokin, Abel, Aron, and others had misconstrued it, attempted to establish a scholastic system of abstract categories that captured the most general features of society and social relations.

Ironically, Simmel's emphasis on the category of form had obscured his conceptual innovations. In fact, as Tenbruck put it, his sociology "provides little basis for the criticisms which are usually leveled against him": Simmel was neither excessively formalistic nor unsystematic (61). If his texts sometimes lacked conceptual clarity, it was because he was initiating a new way of thinking, or perhaps, recalling

---

27. Pitirim Sorokin, *Contemporary Sociological Theories* (New York: Harper, 1928), 495, cited by Tenbruck, "Formal Sociology," 74. That Coser's 1965 *Georg Simmel* includes an excerpt from Sorokin's 1928 critique of Simmel attests to the importance of Sorokin (and his *Contemporary Sociological Theories*) for sociology—and legitimates his attack on Simmel's alleged formalism.

28. Tenbruck, "Formal Sociology," 62. The passages cited here and in the following paragraphs are from the first pages of the essay, which were omitted when it was reprinted in Coser's 1965 *Georg Simmel*.

Simmel's own formulation at the outset of "Problem," a new way of seeing. "Simmel was the first, or among the first, to uncover for sociology a specific 'layer' of reality, its 'social dimension,'" and if his writings seemed disparate and fragmentary, his purpose was clear and well-defined: Simmel was attempting to explore "this novel perspective and the world of new phenomena it opened up" (65). This (phenomenological) agenda thus echoes the "fundamental motif" he had identified in his "Self-Representation" as the first result of his early work: recognition of the role of human consciousness in synthesizing historical and social unities out of the fragmentary particulars of experienced events—of the quasi-a-priori synthesis that gives knowable form to the flux and multiplicity of historical and cultural existence.

In Tenbruck's formulation, Simmel's basic, groundbreaking insight was that "objects and phenomena reveal their full significance only when questioned in respect to their social dimension, a dimension which possesses an order of its own." This questioning—the attention to formation in Simmel's sense—may be understood as the immediate consequence of "the overcoming of the individualistic way of seeing" in modern, historically self-conscious scholarship. However, as Tenbruck continues:

> The originality and novelty of this idea have been obscured for us by subsequent advances in sociology, psychology, and social psychology. Today, we take Simmel's basic perspective for granted, no matter how much his particular insights may still impress us. We are used to exploring the social presuppositions and implications of phenomena. (66)

Tenbruck rightly emphasizes both the "originality and novelty" of Simmel's perspective and the fact that the flowering of the social sciences in the first half of the twentieth century had rendered it ubiquitous. Then as now, the question remains of how to understand the relation between Simmel's epistemological and methodological insights and the larger historico-cultural, theoretical, and institutional evolution under way at the nineteenth-century fin de siècle.

For Tenbruck, the advance of (social) science had (by 1953) made possible a level of conceptual clarity regarding the "social dimension" that had been inaccessible to Simmel. His breakthrough was still of great methodological significance. But in disclosing his novel perspective, Simmel himself had simply been "unable to articulate his fundamental idea programmatically and thus, in order to illuminate it, he had had to rely on its illustrative applications in concrete analyses" (65).

This brings us back once again to the question of structuralism—and points up the need in a poststructuralist (or perhaps post-poststructuralist) period to take up aspects of Simmel's thought that remained illegible to Tenbruck. Setting aside the latter's evident certainty that the emergence of the modern social sciences represented rational progress, we may put the methodological point even more forcefully: Simmel's basic insight about social form required a performative demonstration. However (to impose more anachronistic language on Tenbruck's account), once the paradigm shift had taken place and focusing on "social presuppositions and implications" came naturally, it was easy to forget that, as he put it, "in Simmel's time, things in general were conceived from the standpoint of their objective qualities; actions in particular, from that of the individual ends pursued in them" (66).

In defending Simmel's conception of formal sociology as a way of getting at a newly identified aspect of reality, Tenbruck's essay helps clarify what was at stake in the paradigm shift that gave rise to modern social science. But Simmel did not, in fact, remain satisfied to work on elaborating the disciplinary consequences disclosed by his new way of seeing. Indeed, the implications of his concept of *Wechselwirkung*, reciprocal interaction, for understanding objectivity and subjectivity—that is to say, the philosophical implications of regarding the interpretation of phenomena, both external and internal, as requiring attention to a third perspective or "dimension" of formation—would soon lead Simmel, by his own account, beyond the sociological point of view.

In reading Simmel as modernist, I am challenging Tenbruck's view that Simmel's mode of argumentation reflected an inability "to articulate his fundamental idea programmatically." But Tenbruck correctly and eloquently drew attention to Simmel's distinctive strategy of thought as a point of departure for social science, and he rightly emphasized the hermeneutic significance of Simmel's conception of form, once again pointing to what we would call its performative dimension. When he wrote of "abstracting the forms of sociation from reality," Tenbruck explained, Simmel was emphasizing not their "abstract character" qua forms but rather "the process of abstracting" forms that "inhere in the totality of reality" and "have no separate existence" (74).

> Abstraction for Simmel is not—it could not be—abstraction from content-*phenomena*, in which the forms inhere and through which alone they can be set forth, but abstraction from a content-*perspective*.... Forms are not general concepts arrived at by generalization and abstraction, and formal sociology is not the analysis of such general concepts. "Abstracting" must be understood in the radical sense of extracting or extricating from reality something which is not a directly observable and common element in it. (75)

Simmel (to translate Tenbruck's point into a philosophical idiom) was neither a Platonist nor a positivist. He emphasized attention to form as a means of achieving a new perspective for cultural analysis—what I characterize as a phenomenological perspective. Thus, as Tenbruck put it, social forms do not explain interaction as such. Rather, as "reciprocal orientations which go with typical situations" (86), "they account for its patterns" (85), for the shape of human interactions as they actually take place. Simmel's emphasis on the "social dimension" reveals modes of regularity inscribed within social reality itself.

There are, then, good reasons for emphasizing the impact of Kantian thought on Simmel. In his programmatic essay on "The Problem of Sociology," even as he rejected the generalizing view that threatened to lead to the same "empty universals and abstractions that had spelled the fate of philosophy," he advocated a vision of sociology that implied its quasi-philosophical role in and for the social sciences as a whole as a general or "pure" science of the social. The frequent complaint of later sociologists that his approach neglects empirical data is not entirely unjustified, but Simmel was no idealist. He was quite interested in the wealth of information about human cultural life being amassed and circulated in the late nineteenth century and regularly invoked anthropological and historical findings to ground his claims, whether of the sociological or psychological or more properly philosophical variety.

For Simmel, distinguishing form from content and classifying diverse forms of association were means of defining and exemplifying and thereby demonstrating the viability of a new strategy of thinking—means of theoretically articulating a way of seeing that takes into account the formation of human existence through an anthropological or cultural a priori. The fundamental idea, in Tenbruck's terms, that "objects and phenomena reveal their full significance only when questioned in respect to their social dimension, a dimension which possesses an order of its own" (66) is the start of his sociology—but also of his philosophy. To come back to our point of departure in 1894's "Problem," for Simmel, reflective awareness of this "new" dimension was part and parcel of a historic shift in scholarly life: moving beyond the "individualistic way of seeing" involved, in my terms, a fundamental paradigm shift in the rhetoric of reflection on human experience in modernity.

A great deal is at stake, theoretically but also practically, in Simmel's aspiration, as Tenbruck put it, to convey "this novel perspective and the world of new phenomena it opened up" (65) to his students and readers. What constitutes a modern, post-individualistic way of seeing the world? Through a phenomenological approach, Simmel conveyed a new style of thought, a self-reflexive way of thinking about society and culture, history and objects and subjects alike—one in and through which, as Otthein Rammstedt put it in the editorial report on the critical edition of Simmel's *Soziologie,* the conditions of possibility for forms "emerge through reciprocal interaction with knowing" itself (*GSG* 11: 898).

Form in Context: Theorizing Culture

Simmel's vision of the creative role played by human formative (historical, cultural) activity needs to be situated in the context of reflection on the evolving logic of scientific inquiry as a whole. In the decades before World War I, the neo-Kantians, with their preoccupation with the delineation of disciplines and distinctions among the spheres of cultural, psychological, and natural science, played a key role in laying the foundations of the modern philosophy of science. As his invocation of the rhetoric of the synthetic a priori attests, Simmel participated in this wider discourse, but he cannot properly be regarded as belonging to any "school," and the "Self-Representation," written "for the eyes of others," must be situated in a wider hermeneutic context. A new intellectual landscape was taking shape, and it was by no means only those we have come to call neo-Kantians who were working to delineate differential logics of inquiry and establish distinctions among disciplines. The place of knowledge in society was changing, and philosophical attention to the logic of inquiry took place in a context that rendered it urgent.

Even as the foundations of twentieth-century industrial Germany were being laid in the so-called *Gründerzeit,* the dark side of modernization was becoming ever more evident. Since 1871, an extremely rapid urbanization process had transformed the newly unified country, disturbing the established social order and upending traditional mores. While there were those whose faith in progress was unshaken by this upheaval—many even saw in it grounds for the renewal of revolutionary hopes—the perception that the modern world had taken a wrong turn was also widespread. Among the mandarins, there was much talk of threats to the cultural inheritance as a consequence of developments emanating from technology and the natural sciences. Fueled by the organicist metaphorics according to which *Kultur* is a product of the *Bildung*—signifying both knowledge or education and the resulting cultural formation—of *Geist*, spirit or mind, the discourse on *Kultur* would in the ensuing years rapidly take on rather sinister nationalist connotations. But especially before World War I, that discourse was in fact far less univocal; it cannot simply be dismissed as ideological or identified with a particular political direction.

The notion that the fragmentation and instrumentalization of knowledge in modernity was imperiling culture and indeed humanity itself has a long history in German thought; what became a mainstay of romantic anti-capitalism can be traced back at least to Schiller's meditations on aesthetic education at the end of the previous century. It was by no means exclusively within conservative or reactionary circles that this discourse proliferated. The multivalent, often contradictory tendencies classed together as the *Jugendbewegung* (youth movement) and the even more amorphous so-called *Lebensreform* (life-reform) movement are a case in point. An acute awareness of the cultural threat posed by technological and industrial progress (increasingly also labeled "Americanization") was characteristically intertwined with an urgently felt need to escape or overcome the strictures of the past. In recalling this period—the era of Simmel's greatest fame and most profound pedagogical impact—it is crucial to keep this pervasive ambivalence about modernity and modernization in mind. For the Janus-faced "new social movements" of the fin de siècle melded socially revolutionary aspirations (for women's rights and for sexual liberty; for a renewed connection to the body and to nature; for new forms of community and new pedagogical visions) with politically regressive tendencies. As such, they were the precursors both of the second wave of new social movements in the twentieth century and of National Socialism.

These "movements" flourished in Berlin, where the intrication between technological-industrial progress and social suffering and impoverishment was particularly palpable. A mélange of hope and malaise, of discontent with the present and inchoate longing for new forms of community and more holistic forms of knowledge charged the atmosphere of the fin de siècle German university. The discourse on culture, at once popular and academic, reflected very real upheavals in contemporary society—transformations that were, in turn, intertwined with natural scientific developments. Well before the end of the nineteenth century, the life sciences had thrown the privileged status of human being into question, and physics had begun to propagate an unsettlingly dark vision of a random, entropic universe in some ways even more challenging to religious precepts than Darwin's natural selection. Natural philosophy had yielded the field to modern, experimentally oriented natural science. The perilous balance Kant had advocated between freedom of inquiry and conformity of action seemed threatened by the latest scientific and cultural developments. Unsurprising, then, if the notion was gaining traction that progress was undermining the established social and moral order, indeed, culture itself.

The rather dubious political and scientific reputation of sociology (not least its association with socialism) attests to the imbrication of the young discipline with this cultural upheaval. Its emergence was in many ways a symptomatic response to a changing intellectual landscape in which traditional assumptions about objective truth and rationality had been called into question. Many of sociology's proponents were philosophers attempting to address the intellectual and moral upheaval of the times. Through their efforts to gain theoretical and practical purchase on the changing landscape of modern intellectual and cultural life, they came to play key roles in remaking the disciplinary structure of the modern research university—and became the founding figures of modern social science.

In 1894, Simmel identified the methodological dilemma he was addressing in "The Problem of Sociology" as a consequence of the ways in which old pieties were being undermined and destabilized by scientific and technological progress. The sociological turn in the generic sense—the eclipse of the "individualistic way of seeing" in which "the science of the human" had become "the science of human society"—could be seen as "a unifying name for the totality of the human sciences approached in a modern fashion." What was at stake for Simmel intellectually as well as biographically in the problem of sociology's disciplinarity attests to the intertwining of these ideas with developments in what we have come to think of as the natural sciences—and to the considerable and ongoing influence of the (broadly speaking) materialist concerns of his youth on his mature thinking.

As a writer and teacher, Simmel reframed very old philosophical questions in innovative ways. His search for viable resources in the cultural inheritance, exemplified by his reinterpretation of the notion of *Geist* in terms of an anthropological or cultural a priori, subsequently led him to redeploy this historically and philosophically decisive category to articulate the epistemological, historico-cultural, and ultimately metaphysical stakes of inquiry in modernity. In setting aside his sociologism and taking up the conceptual resources of the philosophical tradition, including the key terms of the inherited discourse on culture, in his mature work, Simmel was not (re)turning to an idealist position but resignifying terms laden with idealist connotations to make them serviceable for a new kind of reflective project. In so doing, he helped lay the foundations of modern humanistic inquiry and social and cultural theory more broadly. How much is ultimately in play in Simmel's assertion that "history" is the product of a synthesis analogous to that by which "nature" becomes an object of knowledge will become clearer in the next chapter through my examination of his classic essay on urban life, "Die Großstädte und das Geistesleben" ("The Metropolis and Mental Life").

First, though, it will be helpful to translate his neo-Kantian rhetoric into a different idiom in order to foreground how the practice of resignifying the philosophical legacy shaped Simmel's mature thinking. In setting aside the naturalism and positivism of his earliest work, he had begun to develop a new, more sophisticated approach to the problem of meaning in culture, charting out new theoretical territory under the aegis of a sociology of forms of association. His mature theoretical approach—his philosophical relativism—elaborated and extended this rich vision of *Formung* (formation) as a collective, historical-cultural process. Drawing on the dialectical philosophical tradition, Simmel anchored his phenomenological understanding of form in material reality in the widest sense. Thus, as Rammstedt argues, the "Self-Representation" attests to the evolution in Simmel's understanding of sociology toward his mature view of "the human not as the *product* of society but as its *producer*."[29] The new, "future-directed program" that resulted from reconceiving the social in this way, Köhnke observes, "cannot be understood as a pure theoretical development—and by no means as a merely individual achievement of Simmel's—but proceeded from a specific spiritual [*geistige*] milieu" (432) defined by the new social as well as artistic movements of the fin de siècle.

In a period of unceasing scientific and cultural change, Berlin rapidly urbanized and industrialized, and the social was thrown into relief in an entirely new way. As in Paris a few decades earlier, sociocultural and material upheaval produced not only poverty and alienation but also an exhilarating atmosphere of intellectual ferment that fostered novelty in life, art, and thought.[30] The "Kaiser's Era" is often downplayed as the site of Weimar's conservative prehistory, but many of the cultural and artistic innovations associated with the Weimar Republic in fact had their beginnings in Wilhelmine Germany. Simmel's phenomenological approach must be seen in this wider modernist context; his efforts to represent his ideas as a unified and as it were "timeless" philosophical achievement effectively obscure his importance for cultural modernism.

In the broadest sense, Berlin's metropolitan context provided the concrete conditions of possibility for the new mode of writing Simmel did so much to inaugurate, the modernist "essayism" that would be of such great significance for twentieth-century thought. The development Simmel framed in the "Self-Representation" as a purely philosophical insight took place in a historical and intellectual context in which new, empirically oriented strategies of reflection on human existence had already gained considerable traction both inside and outside the academy. Simmel's work is part of a broader discursive paradigm shift in this period in which the question of what constitutes rigorous reflection on collective life was being posed in entirely new ways. The problem of disciplinarity was not merely a logical or theoretical matter.

To describe the same phenomena from a somewhat different angle: against the background of new social movements animated by strivings to revitalize and reform modern life and rejuvenate art and culture, "theory" in the social scientific sense

---

29. As paraphrased by Köhnke, *Der junge Simmel*, 431.

30. The accelerating effects of industrialization and urbanization also marked Simmel's existence materially. His son Hans recalls the family moving house at least seven times in Berlin (moves detailed in *GSG* 24: 657–61). Simmel bicycled to the university and made extensive use of modern forms of transportation and communication, engaging in frequent and wide-ranging international travel that also fostered his networks of contacts. Many sources also emphasize his being in virtually incessant movement while lecturing.

was becoming differentiated from traditional philosophical reflection. By occluding Simmel's connections to the wider field of discourses and practices surrounding the emergence of the category and experience of the social—and in particular by effacing the philosophical impact of a range of broadly speaking materialist strategies of thought on his writing, the mature thinker's idealizing rhetoric deliberately obscured the persisting difference between his thought and writing, on the one hand, and the increasingly professionalized world of mainstream academic philosophy, on the other.

Precisely through its reframings and lacunae, the "Self-Representation" Simmel constructed for the "eyes of others" thus powerfully attests to the centrality for him of the problem of disciplinarity. If it betrays the high personal costs of the choices he had to make, it also suggests the emblematic significance of Simmel's story. The line between social scientific and philosophical reflection was by no means unwavering, but the stakes were becoming clear, and by the early 1900s, Simmel saw himself constrained to adopt a mode of self-representation that in effect endorsed the very marginalization of "sociological" theorizing that had plagued his efforts to establish himself in the discipline of philosophy.

Simmel's "Self-Representation" assimilates his sociology to the idealizing rhetoric of mainstream philosophical discourse in a way that occludes the influence of multiple traditions of materialist philosophical thought, among them those represented by Spencer, Marx, and the experimental psychologist Gustav Fechner (1801–87). Most decisively, it omits all mention of *Völkerpsychologie* and of the man to whom Simmel had sworn eternal loyalty for drawing his attention to "the problem of the super-individual," Moritz Lazarus.[31] For it was Lazarus's Herderian conception of *objektiver Geist* (a term probably best rendered by the English word "culture"), which expanded the notion of epistemological conditions of possibility to include their cultural-psychological and sociological formation and thereby pointed the way toward Simmel's rethinking of apriority and hence to his breakthrough concept of social form.

In his retrospective account, Simmel passed over not only his teacher but also many of his own earliest publications in silence, thereby, as it were, editing himself out of the multivalent (pre)history of the modern social sciences and asserting his place in the discipline of philosophy. The idealist vocabulary and dehistoricizing rhetorical strategies Simmel deployed in the service of what Köhnke called his "self-stylization" became the mature thinker's habitual strategy for representing himself and his work. Especially as these strategies and the image thereby cultivated had considerable unintended consequences for the fate of his oeuvre, many larger issues concerning Simmel's reception become visible through a close examination of the "Self-Representation."

31. A protean figure who also influenced Dilthey, Lazarus not only helped bring cultural anthropology and modern linguistics and religious studies into being; he also played a decisive role both intellectually and institutionally in the evolution and flowering of Jewish life, thought, and culture in Berlin during this period. Lazarus's key theoretical texts are reproduced in *Grundzüge der Völkerpsychologie und Kulturwissenschaft*, ed. Klaus Christian Köhnke (Hamburg: Meiner, 2003).

The story Simmel tells there virtually invites the "formalist" (mis)reading that has so bedeviled his reception. In effacing his "materialist" interests and deploying the category of form in a way that assimilates his thinking to the idealist rhetoric of the Wilhelminian philosophical mainstream, this text epitomizes the mature mode of self-representation through which, ironically, in distancing himself from social science for philosophical reasons, Simmel succeeded in laying the groundwork for the wider misrecognition of his theoretical achievements. In short order, the very ideas and methods that made him a founding father of modern social science came to be misunderstood along lines that he himself had begun to trace. Intriguingly, though, Simmel was deploying a conception of form more sophisticated and considerably more interesting (and innovative) than the (idealizing) story he was telling could accommodate. To grasp what is at stake theoretically in this interpenetration of image, representation, and disciplinarity, we need to turn back to the autobiographical text itself.

Modernist Identity and the Self-Overcoming of Relativism

Within the idealizing narrative framework of Simmel's "Self-Representation," all that matters is the logical progression of his thinking toward his mature philosophical convictions. To recap, he claimed that the first step in his intellectual evolution was the (neo-Kantian) recognition of the epistemological significance of formation in and for history. Reflection on "the apriorities of the spirit that forms science" had led him to a (neo-Hegelian) attention to the vicissitudes of form as the framework of lived experience and to the sociohistorical process by which such forms are generated and perpetuated. This dual attention to structure and process, as captured by the (phenomenological) concept of *Wechselwirkung*, had then given rise, quasi-organically, to a further, self-reflexive turn. As Simmel (re)presented it, by the logic of the concept of reciprocal interaction itself, the notion of a "pure sociology" taking such "forms of association" as its object had led him back once again to philosophy, but in a new key. Keeping this Hegelianizing logical framework in mind, let us return to the text, taking up Simmel's account just after his description of his sociological method in the lines that prompted our excursus on form.

As he continues his account of the evolution of his thinking, Simmel's narrative fluctuates briefly into the present tense:

> Starting with its sociological significance, the concept of reciprocal causation gradually grew into an entirely comprehensive metaphysical principle. The contemporary dissolution of everything substantial, absolute, eternal into the flux of things, into historical mutability, into merely psychological reality is, it appears to me, only secure against an unstable subjectivism and skepticism, if one sets in the place of the substantial fixed values the living reciprocity [*lebendige Wechselwirksamkeit*] of elements, which themselves are subject to the same dissolution ad infinitum. The central concepts of truth, of value, of objectivity, etc. appeared to me as reciprocalities, as contents of a relativism that now no longer signified the skeptical dissipation of all that is solid but precisely protection against this via a new concept of solidity ("Philosophy of Money"). (*GSG* 20: 304–5)

Simmel's claim for his concept of reciprocal interaction resonates with Kant's account of experience as structured via transcendental "pure concepts of the understanding" proper to human sensory-intellectual existence as such.[32] As noted, his ideas about the synthesis of the a priori were unorthodox. A (neo)Kantian conception of experience provided the logical foundation, but he expanded the notion of reciprocal causation beyond its originally "sociological significance" in ways considerably indebted to post-Kantian thought. Drawing on a tradition identified with Goethe, whom he construed as Kant's great antipode, Simmel emphasized the distinctiveness of the categories through which historical and cultural life becomes intelligible.[33]

Wechselwirkung—the relations or interactions that constitute form in his sense—thereby becomes the (onto)logical foundation of what in Simmel's later work is referred to as the philosophy of life. His concept of a "living reciprocity of elements" epitomizes his phenomenological strategy for coming to terms with the ethical and epistemological challenges of a world marked by incessant transformation: by the "dissolution of everything substantial, absolute, eternal into the flux of things, into historical mutability, into merely psychological reality." The historical transformation Simmel describes has philosophical implications well beyond an "overcoming of the individualistic way of seeing" in the initial sociological sense.

For all its Heracleitan resonance, his relativism is deeply imbued with a Hegelian and post-Hegelian conception of dialectics. Although he rejected the Marxian account of meaning in history, Simmel, too, found it necessary to embrace as inevitable the process by which, in the fancifully translated words of the *Communist Manifesto*, "all that is solid melts into air" ("Alles Ständische und Stehende verdampft"; more literally, All estates, everything standing, evaporates). We shall return to this matter and to Simmel's very important account of his relativism in our discussion of the *Philosophy of Money* in Part II. As his "Self-Representation" suggests, that text indeed turns the process of dissolution—what we have come to think of as the historical and cultural effects of modernity on inherited institutions, values, and so on—into an occasion for rethinking the nature of concepts and even rationality itself.

Simmel's strategy for saving the phenomena that threatened to dissolve in the face of an "unstable subjectivism and skepticism" thereby gave rise to new ways of apprehending and analyzing the relations between subjective experience and sociocultural reality, between reflection and history. For, having abandoned his early materialism along with his faith in historico-evolutionary progress, Simmel could not stop the dialectical movement at the Marxian reduction of sociocultural and political phenomena to their material "bases." Rather, in his mature work, "living reciprocity" (or "interactivity"), understood as the logico-experiential ground of the

---

32. Since Simmel taught both logic (that is, epistemology) and the history of philosophy regularly and published extensively on Kant, it is worth noting that the term *Wechselwirkung* appears in Kant's table of categories in *The Critique of Pure Reason* as an explication of the meaning of *Gemeinschaft*, the third type of Relation: "Community (Reciprocity between Agent and Patient)" (*Kritik der reinen Vernunft*, A 80/B 106).

33. See Donald N. Levine, "*Soziologie* and Lebensanschauung: Two Approaches to Synthesizing 'Kant' and 'Goethe' in Simmel's Work," *TCS* 29 (2012): 26–52.

intersubjective, historical constitution of the "central concepts of truth, of value, of objectivity, etc.," becomes the basis of a "new concept of solidity" (*Festigkeitsbegriff*)—of a new kind of foundation.

The late Simmel has often been accused of retreating into philosophical idealism. However, this line of criticism, often bearing telltale marks of self-interest and not infrequently resulting in rather obtuse readings of Simmelian texts, underestimates the methodological sophistication of his theoretical style and misrecognizes strategies of thought that are at once sociological and philosophical. In 1951, Michael Landmann wrote: "what is today falling apart into the philosophy of existence and the philosophy of mind [*Existenz- und Geistesphilosophie*] was for Georg Simmel still meaningfully integrated." Simmel's distinctive approach to dialectics—what Landmann called the "philosophical expression of a specifically modern feeling for life"[34]—anticipates both Heidegger's turn to the existential analytic of *Dasein* and Adorno's negative dialectics.

All of this being said, as Köhnke warned, if we are to grasp the significance of his intellectual evolution, Simmel's "Self-Representation" must be treated with circumspection. Its narrative as a whole is unreliable, and the text retroactively translates the messiness and contingency of living thought into an idealist rhetoric that systematically obscures not only Simmel's sources but also his process of intellectual innovation. Nevertheless, in the third paragraph, that strategy of abstraction enables Simmel to characterize his mature style of thought, with its convergence of form and substance and interpenetration of materialist and idealist dimensions, quite precisely.

Both in its internal structure and its rhetorical framing, the "Self-Representation" may thus be read as Simmel's defense of his method—a defense that turns on (performatively) conveying his distinctive conception of form. What has so often been misunderstood as fragmentary and unsystematic in his writings in fact reflects a commitment to a "comprehensive metaphysical principle" of an innovative sort. Embracing living reciprocity as the anti-foundational essence of concepts and values, Simmel synthesizes a neo-Hegelian reinterpretation of the logic of dissolution with a Nietzschean affirmation of perspectivism. His innovative interpretations performatively demonstrate the philosophical conviction articulated in the passage just cited: that embracing flux—affirming the "living reciprocity" of values, concepts, and ideals—would make it possible to attain a subjective and collective stability in the face of the radical and irreversible shift into an innerworldly perspective that defines modernity itself. In the years to come, his ideas about form and the logic of history would be further elaborated, but the relativist strategy of thought that Simmel first put forward in 1900 as a sort of homeopathic conceptual means of overcoming "skeptical dissipation" would characterize his writing and thinking from then on.

This point is worth emphasizing. *The idealizing "Self-Representation" is quite illuminating theoretically, despite the fact that it is not a historically accurate account*

---

34. Michael Landmann "Konflikt und Tragödie. Zur Philosophie Georg Simmels," *Zeitschrift für philosophische Forschung* 6, no. 1 (1951): 116, 125.

of Simmel's intellectual evolution. Taking seriously what this text reveals about the interpenetration of "sociological" and "philosophical" ideas and methods in his mature self-understanding entails reconsidering the oft-refuted, still robust received account of his evolution as a thinker. Simmel's "Self-Representation" reveals that he understood himself to have been engaged in a performative proof of the value of epistemic relativism as "an entirely comprehensive metaphysical principle" eight years before the publication of the text regarded as the high point of his "formal" sociology. What is at stake in Simmel's late work by no means emerges after his encounter with Bergson, but rather (like his invocation of the language of "life") predates it by at least a decade, and it reflects an ongoing engagement with theoretical difficulties that he understood as proper to his own historical (philosophical, cultural) situation.

In the next, penultimate paragraph of the "Self-Representation," Simmel continues to elaborate a defense of his method in which his idealist rhetoric obscures considerable historico-cultural self-reflexivity: "My special concept of metaphysics is tied up with this relativism as cosmic and epistemic principle that replaces the substantial and abstract unity of the world-image [*Weltbild*] with the organic unity of *Wechselwirkung* (reciprocal interaction)" (*GSG* 20: 305).

After we have considered Simmel's vision of an alternative to such philosophical system constructions, we shall return again to this passage, since the link, jarring to contemporary ears, between relativism and metaphysics bears further reflection. For now let me simply underline the difficulty of situating his theoretical position. Simmel's conception of form as "comprehensive metaphysical principle"—methodologically speaking, the very antipode of a structuralist approach—has profound implications for the social (cultural) sciences. Conversely, it is philosophically significant that social life provides the model for the "living reciprocity of elements" that Simmel regards as the logical alternative to foundationalisms of all stripes. The strategy of thought described here may be found in his "sociological" and "philosophical" writings alike—as well as in the texts, more difficult to categorize, that have often been dismissed as popularizations and that more recently have been assimilated to the "sociology of culture."

Simmel deployed epistemic relativism in very different intellectual and disciplinary contexts as a means of overcoming what appear to be aporetic dualisms—between materialism and idealism, determination and freedom, life and form; but also inside and outside, change and constancy; masculinity and femininity.[35] Deconstructing binaries never became an end in itself, however. On the contrary, Simmel was engaged in a Promethean effort to embrace and affirm the Heracleitan flux in which "everything substantial, absolute, and eternal" had dissolved—and thereby to establish a new, relativist conception of meaning upon the ashes of the philo-

---

35. The last opposition is on Simmel's understanding deeply connected with metaphysical problems; he was, generously speaking, a "difference feminist" avant la lettre. See Inke Mülder-Bach, "'Weibliche Kultur' und 'stahlhartes Gehäuse': Zur Thematisierung des Geschlechterverhältnisses in den Soziologien Georg Simmels und Max Webers," in *Triumph und Scheitern in der Metropole: zur Rolle der Weiblichkeit in der Geschichte Berlins*, ed. Sigrun Anselm and Barbara Beck (Berlin: Dietrich Riemer, 1987), 115–40.

sophical inheritance itself. In his own terms, in redefining the "central concepts" of truth, value, and objectivity as effects of the "living reciprocity of elements," Simmel aspired to avoid "an unstable subjectivism and skepticism," not by establishing a new sort of foundation, but by rethinking solidity—foundations—as such.

Attending to the consistency of his performative philosophical (depending on one's perspective, pragmatic or metaphysical) strategy brings both the methodological coherency of Simmel's texts and the significance of his oeuvre into relief. For all their diversity, his mature writings are marked by an effort to show that it is possible to accept, even embrace, the seemingly devastating epistemic consequences of the actual cultural and historical situation in modernity—the "contemporary dissolution of everything substantial, absolute, eternal into the flux of things"—without abandoning the philosophical aspiration (or obligation) to attempt to give a coherent account of the conditions of possibility of knowledge and of what it means to live a meaningful life.

In Simmel's view, relativism properly understood entails that it is not necessary to sacrifice the ideals of freedom, self-determination, of ethical subjectivity. Rather than conceding in despair that the examined life is probably not worth living, he suggests reframing the philosophical inheritance such that it becomes possible to live a meaningful *modern* life with a *stable* "subjectivism and skepticism" that recognizes and incorporates the contingency of human existence. Then, in the fifth and final paragraph of the "self-representation," Simmel links his metaphysical views to his philosophy of religion. What he has to say vividly illustrates the cultural stakes of his modernist strategies of thought:

> For I believe that critique leaves not a single content of historical religion standing, yet does not trouble religion itself. For as this is a *being* [*Sein*] of the religious soul, an a priori forming function [*formende Funktion*] that makes its life as such a religious one, it can no more be disproved than a being altogether can be disproved. This being or this function, but not the *content* of belief that is then representatively formed out of it, is the bearer of religious-metaphysical value.

Simmel's closing remarks attest to the actuality of his thought today, in an era marked by the persistent power of religious identifications and practices in the face of pervasive skepticism and relativism.[36] They also underscore the complex modernist cultural origins of social science, reminding us that the constitutive elements of problems of value and objectivity have roots in the cultural cataclysm Nietzsche called the death of God.[37]

---

36. Simmel, who wrote a brief but important monograph on the sociology of religion for Martin Buber's *Gesellschaft* series, was not religious in any conventional way. But as he wrote to Jellinek on June 22, 1908, religious matters remained unusually "close to his heart." Most of his philosophical contemporaries were "entirely without understanding and without any interest in religious questions. However, I suspect that my positive relation to these matters is more dubious to the preachers than the absolute indifference of the others" (*GSG* 22: 630).

37. As noted, Simmel's modernist relativism and his cosmopolitan attitude to culture have a subterranean connection to the origins of modern religious studies in *Völkerpsychologie*. The same Moritz Lazarus who had drawn his attention to the profundity of "the problem of the superindividual" was the founding force behind the Lehranstalt [later Hochschule] für die Wissenschaft des Judentums in Berlin.

Köhnke thought it was the pain of submitting to (disciplinary) unification in writing the *Selbstdarstellung* that had evoked Simmel's plaint to Ernst Bloch, cited earlier, that "the abstract of a half-page brings to light how little unity there is." However, Simmel's ironic, cosmopolitan tone must, as it were, be taken seriously. He was neither wistful nor nostalgic about lost or absent totalities. His remark—less lament than bon mot—is a wry commentary on the problem of philosophical coherence in the twentieth century. The "Self-Representation" is, in fact, a reasonably unified account of Simmel's philosophical evolution, albeit at the cost of a number of inconvenient facts. The lack of unity—or, to translate more literally, "the thing . . . that is so little one [*die Sache . . . die so wenig eine ist*]"—brought to light via his attempt to construct an intellectual biography was less individual than symptomatic. It was the fate of epigones so vividly described by Nietzsche in his *Unzeitgemäße Betrachtungen* ("Untimely Observations") on history.

In light of his broader analysis of the situation of philosophy in modernity, Simmel's remark about Schopenhauer's ability to capture his teaching in a single phrase is sharply double-edged. The unity of *The World as Will and Representation* was hardly comparable to the unity of the Kantian system of which Schopenhauer was an epigone. In any case, Simmel regarded his effort to circumvent Kantian critique and reintegrate experience and stabilize its meaning (or lack thereof) by regrounding philosophy in the Will as a failure.[38]

Simmel's attitude toward Schopenhauer resonates with Nietzsche's own profound ambivalence about his "most important teacher." For Simmel, Schopenhauer was "without a doubt the greater philosopher," for he "possessed the mysterious relation to the absolute in things which the great philosopher shares only with the great artist," while Nietzsche, moved not by "the metaphysical but the moralistic drive," lacked this "extending of subjective life into the ground of existence [*Dasein*] itself." Yet it was Nietzsche, with his secular vision of immanent transcendence, who provided "the much more adequate expression of the contemporary feeling for life." In Simmel's view, "that he used his superior forces to defend the inferior cause is part of Schopenhauer's tragedy."[39] The unity of the world as Will and Representation

---

Lazarus served as the longtime rector, with a faculty that included Steinthal and other path-breaking scholars, such as Abraham Geiger and Ismar Ellbogen, and helped develop a new model of rabbinical training integrating the academic study of religion with Talmudic study.

38. As Simmel put it once in conversation, "Schopenhauer may be right [that] the world is Will, but this table is not Will." Arthur Stein recalled this remark in a conversation with Michael Landmann as Simmel's illustration of the difficulty that "individual experience does not confirm the general metaphysical view without falsifying it" (*AuS*, 274).

39. *Schopenhauer und Nietzsche: Ein Vortragszyklus* (Leipzig: Duncker & Humblot, 1907), trans. Helmut Loiskandl, Deena Weinstein, and Michael Weinstein as *Schopenhauer and Nietzsche* (Amherst: University of Massachusetts Press, 1986); *GSG* 10: 167–408; here p. 188). Simmel's point is thus not in the least that "an aspect of the tragedy in Schopenhauer is that he defends the weaker cause with more impact," as Loiskandl et al. have it (13). Thanks to his embrace of evolution and change over stasis, Nietzsche was in Simmel's view more sympathetic to the "modern human being" than Schopenhauer. In particular, he writes (invoking the musical term that plays a key role in his "self-representation"), despite the "anti-social elaboration" Nietzsche gave to this "fundamental motif," his affirmation of life as striving toward self-overcoming in the creation of new forms—that is, his understanding of life as "more than life" (here Simmel already invokes a key concept purportedly from his "late" metaphysics) "appears the

could not be maintained in the face of Nietzsche's radicalization of his attack on the metaphysics of subjectivity. Philosophical reflection would have to synthesize a new sort of unity—or rather write into being a means of coming to terms with the absence in modernity of the sort of cohesion once provided by metaphysical foundations.

By the time of the putative composition of the "Self-Representation," shortly before the publication of his *Soziologie* in 1908, Simmel had already arrived at what the eventual entry on him in the Ueberweg termed his "relativistic reinterpretation of critical philosophy."[40] As a mature thinker, he abandoned the naturalism of his earliest writings, deploying the resources of the Kantian and post-Kantian tradition from within a cosmopolitan Nietzschean perspectivism[41] that eschewed appeals to absolute visions of self and world. Simmel aspired instead to develop strategies of thought adequate to the existential and epistemic circumstance of modern epigones, for whom the experience of unity, of the convergence of the True, the Good, and the Beautiful evoked in the Platonic dialogues, could be no more than a beautiful philosophical dream.

Simmel's "Self-Representation" does not simply compose a pleasing image for the eyes of others. The narrative he puts forward represents a considerable challenge to the disciplinary mainstream of the day, and he sets out a cogent account of a philosophical strategy inspired by Nietzschean perspectivism for addressing the problem of thought in the absence of the sort of foundations that once allowed concepts and values to cohere into meaningful unity—for the modernist approach to philosophizing that characterized his work from the *Philosophy of Money* on.

To be sure, Simmel's refusal or inability to produce a more definitive philosophical position than the one articulated here—one less tied up with a "sociological" or historicist analysis of the situation of philosophy in modernity—in fact caused him no end of professional difficulties. It does not follow, though, that Simmel was at a loss conceptually or methodologically. On my reading, his remark to Bloch is thus not the index of a perceived philosophical failure but the recognition of a historic fate. What Köhnke calls "the courageousness of Simmel's thinking" (163) in identifying himself with (pejoratively tinted) "relativism" is indeed noteworthy. And so perhaps it is not too much to see in his remark to Bloch—that summing up his work "brings to light how little unity there is"—Simmel's ironic recognition that in developing this modernist approach to philosophy, he had chosen a path that opened his work up to the very charges of incoherence and fragmentariness that still dog his

---

much more adequate expression of the contemporary feeling for life" (*GSG* 10; 188). In a letter of July 17, 1906, Simmel wrote Rickert "*Schopenhauer & Nietzsche* is intended as a counterpart to my Kant. I would wish to live long enough to write a Hegel as the third in this series . . . but it is probably not to be" (*GSG* 22: 545–46).

40. Cited (and characterized as "entirely to the point") in Köhnke, *Der junge Simmel*, 164.

41. Nietzsche too had gone through a quasi-positivist phase before arriving at his mature epistemological views. For both, the later attitude was tied to a "European" vision of the tasks of thought. In light of this—and apropos of Simmel's oft-repeated association with "neo-Kantianism" in general—it is worth noting the next item in the list of Simmel's sayings recalled by Ernst Bloch, a jab at Marburg's Paul Natorp: "There are not only minor [*kleine*] but also provincial [*kleinstädtische*] philosophers" (*BdD*, 251).

reputation. In putting forward what he saw as the only way out of the epistemological dilemmas of contemporary thought, Simmel, like Nietzsche, could not avoid the risk of being mistaken for what he was not.

The question of relativism—and of the importance of Nietzsche's vision of philosophy for Simmel's thinking about the tasks of philosophy in modernity—brings us back to our point of departure in his correspondence and to the question of what was at stake in his shifting disciplinary self-understanding. How, in particular, are we to understand the convergence between Simmel's renewed allegiance to philosophy and his conviction that (as he put it in the letter from July 1908, written after the effort to secure him an appointment at Heidelberg had definitively come to nought) "official Germany simply has no place for me"? To be sure, the verdict proved premature; six years later, a place was found, after all—albeit, quite literally, at the very margins of official Germany. But Simmel's attitude (in his own words "not even resignation") was decisive. Like Nietzsche before him, he had come to regard the Wilhelminian University as inimical to genuine intellectual innovation.[42] Still, his professional travails fostered spiritual and intellectual independence and effectively freed Simmel to write and teach in ways less compromised by institutional demands. To put the point in extreme form, his marginality enabled him to become an original thinker—one whose writing helped bring about a paradigm shift that has inflected both humanistic inquiry and social science.

As Köhnke demonstrated, Simmel's first, crucial step toward real intellectual autonomy and innovation was the auto-critique of his earlier way of thinking—and indeed of the entire paradigm that had given rise to his mammoth attempt to place ethics on a naturalistic foundation in his *Einleitung in die Moralwissenschaft*. This self-reflexive turn, complexly indebted to *Völkerpsychologie*, led to his breakthrough conception of a sociology of forms. Convinced he had made a major, career-changing innovation with the first, 1894, version of "Das Problem der Sociologie," Simmel initially saw himself as putting philosophy behind him in an approach to form that established a new way of understanding and studying the social and provided not just a new method of interpretation but a reliable foundation for sociology as a science.

However, as the ambivalent reception of Simmel's conception of form in the social sciences attests, the questions he posed in defining that discipline turned out to involve a good deal more: a new conception of science, *Wissenschaft*, and of interpretation altogether. He was grappling with the philosophical significance of the "overcoming of the individualistic point of view" in a fashion that truly parted ways with the idealist legacy. Simmel had come to see it as necessary to reframe the most fundamental epistemological questions in terms of collective practices. It was no longer sufficient to focus on the logical criteria for truth: the question had become how meaning is made in history, in sociocultural reality.

---

42. In the same letter, Simmel cites the appointment of one Paul Menzer in Halle as an example of "the tendency . . . to bring *colorless* personalities into the most important philosophical positions," adding: "He has not even written a *bad* book, but absolutely nothing. . . . The charming bon mot has been circulating here that if Menzer manages . . . to prove that he never wrote his dissertation, he will become professor in Berlin" (*GSG* 22: 640–41).

It was at this point in his life, when Simmel identified most strongly with the sociological discipline he was actively engaged in helping bring into being, that he responded to Célestin Bouglé's query about the future direction of his work, declaring: "I am devoting myself entirely to sociological studies and for the foreseeable future will indeed not reenter any other area, particularly not that of moral philosophy."[43] And yet, by the following summer there were already signs of a fresh evolution in his self-understanding. In June 1895, Simmel wrote to update Bouglé, who was preparing his 1894 articles on German social science for book publication, about his activities. The passage is worth quoting at length, for it includes the first mention of the work that would become the *Philosophie des Geldes*:

> Please don't mention my plans to work on an epistemology of the social sciences; it lies too far off. At the moment, I am working on a "Psychology of Money" that hopefully will be finished in the next year. But please do take my little essay on the problem of sociology into account. I myself attach the greatest value to it and it contains the agenda for my work (& the essential part of my curriculum). By the way, it will soon appear with a postscript from me in the Annals of the American Academy.[44]

Even as he succeeded in publishing his programmatic essay on sociology in multiple languages, Simmel's interpretive framework was shifting. This invocation of the language of psychology represents a transitional phase in which he assimilated the conceptual strategies of Lazarus and Steinthal into his own, increasingly original, mode of thought. Just three years later, Simmel's concept of form would have evolved beyond sociology, and his "psychology" become a "philosophy of money."

By 1899, as Simmel was completing the first edition of the work that marked his emergence as a mature and independent scholar—a work in which, among other things, he would build on his "sociological" conception of form to develop an original interpretation of the problem of value—he had made a complete about-face and come to regard his sociological work as a burdensome duty. In December he declined the invitation from Bouglé to participate in the 1900 World Congress of Sociology in Paris. After declaring flatly that "the *sciences sociales* are not my discipline [*Fach*],"[45] Simmel confided:

> it is altogether rather painful for me that abroad I am only known as a sociologist—while I am a philosopher, see my life's vocation in philosophy, and only pursue sociology as a sideline [*Nebenfach*]. Once I have fulfilled my obligation to it by publishing a comprehen-

---

43. Simmel to Bouglé, February 15, 1894 (*GSG* 22: 112).
44. This letter of June 22, 1895, attests to Simmel's friendly relations with his French colleagues in the circle of the *Revue de métaphysique et de morale* during this period. After informing Bouglé that the just-published *Notes d'un etudiante française* had been "generally recognized as agreeable and witty" by the acquaintances in Berlin to whom he had lent it, he offers several criticisms (*GSG* 22: 149–50).
45. In July, Simmel had already accepted Xavier León's invitation to join the Comité de patronage for the Philosophical Congress being organized for the same time as the World Exposition. Although Simmel was for unknown reasons unable to come to Paris himself, he sent an essay on the philosophy of religion ("de la religion au point de vue de la théorie de la connaissance" (*GSG* 19: 117–28), which León read, and which was published in the proceedings. For the connections between this essay and the conflict with Durkheim unfolding in this period, see *GSG* 19: 404–5. See also letters to León, July 26, 1899, and June 9, 1901 (*GSG* 22: 332–33 and 387).

sive sociology—which will probably happen in the course of the coming years—I shall probably never again return to it.[46]

By the time he wrote these lines, of course, Simmel was already indelibly identified with his sociological work, and as a matter of fact, neither his sociological publications nor his activities on behalf of the emergent discipline were at an end.

Among the consequences of this continued engagement with sociology is the circumstance that today, particularly in the Anglophone world, it seems surprising to speak of Georg Simmel as a philosopher at all. That he and his contemporaries saw things so differently underlines the profound impact of the institutional framework in which inquiry takes place on the ways intellectual practices are and can be understood. Thus while it is essential to recognize the philosophical as well as philosophical-historical significance of his oeuvre, my objective in pursuing an encounter with Simmel as philosopher is not, per se, to expand the philosophical canon. In exploring this much neglected precursor of modern cultural theory, I hope to foster new and more flexible ways of thinking about our practices of reflection on modern life and to disclose strategies of inquiry that are freer from the strictures of the disciplinary order in which contemporary theoretical work continues to be located.

It is worth emphasizing that, although frustrated by what he regarded as a basic misunderstanding of himself as a thinker and scholar, Simmel did not wish to disavow his sociological achievements. On the contrary, even as he entered the final phase of work on his *Philosophie des Geldes*, Simmel remained convinced of the distinctiveness and value of the project whose foundations he had set forth beginning with 1894's programmatic "Das Problem der Sociologie." In a letter of July 1898 to Georg Jellinek, Simmel affirmed his considerable faith in the synthetic power of "the theory [*Lehre*] of the forms of association as such": "The problem that I posed for sociology opens a new and important field of knowledge [*Erkenntnisfeld*]."[47] Being himself more an explorer than a settler, he would, however, have preferred that the task of demonstrating "the practicability and fertility of the idea" fall to others. Following his "own scholarly inclinations and proclivities" into other, as yet uncharted areas would have allowed him to "achieve far more fruitful and . . . valuable things" than writing "an exhaustive sociology, whose subsequent parts can furthermore in principle result in nothing new."

Despite his disinclination, however, Simmel regarded himself as responsible for producing such a work, that is, for proving that a fruitful sociological praxis could be centered on *Vergesellschaftung*, on the forms of association or becoming-social. Unfortunately, other established scholars had not stepped forward to carry out the task, and as he explained to Jellinek: "I cannot in good conscience chain young people who wish to attach themselves to me to a field that is not officially recognized, in which it is not possible to take exams, and for which one in the foreseeable fu-

---

46. *GSG* 22: 342. These phrases recur nearly verbatim in a 1913 letter to Robert Michels: sociology was "always only a 'sideline'"; "[my] heart always belonged to philosophy" (*GSG* 22: 201).

47. All citations refer to a letter of July 15, 1898, to Georg Jellinek (*GSG* 22: 297–99). My discussion draws on Otthein Rammstedt's editorial report in *GSG* 11, which places Simmel's relation to sociology in biographical and scholarly context. See particularly 891–82, where the letters cited here are discussed.

ture will not even be able to habilitate; that would seem to me to be an abuse of my personal power." Having set out his theoretical claims, he would, out of scholarly obligation (*wissenschaftlicher Moral*), eventually have "to write a large sociology" himself in order to vindicate them.

In a word, Simmel accepted his responsibilities as a founding father of the discipline, but his sense that his obligation to sociology amounted to "an almost tragic fate," that his intellectual honor was at stake, seems to have embittered the fruits of these labors, which stretched over many years. Ironically, in the end, Simmel hurriedly concluded his sociological opus in the hope of improving his chances for the second chair in philosophy at Heidelberg. As he confided to Jellinek at the end of 1907:

> I publish this book with a very heavy heart. . . . For since it is a very first beginning that builds on no tradition and existing technique—a great deal in it will be imperfect, groping, mistaken. . . . No one knows the weaknesses and gaps of this book better than I and it is a slight comfort that a book whose principle has no predecessor cannot be as complete as one that is integrated into an already-existing science and works according to an already-proven method.[48]

The loneliness of Simmel's intellectual path is palpable here. The following sentence renders the sacrifice he was making for the sake of his scholarly honor even more vividly. Once he finished the book, he declared, "the sociological existence of my life will be concluded along with it, and I shall dedicate the remainder entirely to philosophy, in which I think I still have a few things to say and to which my heart belongs quite differently than to sociology."[49]

In the course of 1907, it had become ever more evident to Simmel that the widely disseminated "idiocy that I am actually not a philosopher but a sociologist" had hurt him professionally. While by no means always the most astute judge of his own professional travails, he was probably correct in this case. It had in fact initially seemed the chair would be his, but Franz Böhm in the Baden Ministry of Education solicited what turned out to be a notorious anti-Semitic denunciation by the right-wing historian Dieter Schäfer, who, among other things, drew associations between sociology and socialism, fuming, "I cannot believe that it would elevate Heidelberg to provide an even greater space than they already have in the faculty for the life- and worldviews that Simmel advocates, views that are clearly distinct from our German Christian-classical culture."[50] Schäfer's intervention seems to have been decisive in blocking Simmel's appointment despite the countervailing efforts of Jellinek, Max Weber, and others.[51] As in the case of the earlier struggle over his appointment as

48. Simmel to Jellinek, December 23, 1907 (*GSG* 22: 597–99).

49. The gap between these letters to Jellinek covers a period in which many of the most prominent among Simmel's peers and younger associates received their first regular professorships—including Weber (1894), Rickert (1896), and Husserl (1901).

50. Schäfer to Böhm, February 26, 1908 (*GSG* 24: 286–88).

51. Schäfer's defamation was being anonymously disseminated. As Jellinek wrote Weber on March 23, 1908, "the resistance is exclusively from Berlin. The hatefulness with which things are being stirred up against S. is visible from the fact that his listeners are represented as consisting primarily of inferior Russian elements" (*GSG* 22: 624).

Extraordinarius, personal, sometimes anti-Semitic hostility to Simmel mingled with skepticism about his unconventional views and scholarship; his identification with a new and marginal field, and one not merely lexically but also practically associated with socialism, was polarizing.

For Heinrich Rickert, Max Weber, and other supporters, Simmel's effort to provide a systematic alternative to the "semi-science" reigning in sociology belonged to his philosophical accomplishments. But the disciplinary ground was shifting, and as subsequent developments confirmed, more conservative philosophers were not wrong to feel threatened. The ascendance of social science endangered the moral and institutional primacy their discipline had enjoyed since Humboldt's (re)founding of the German university after the Napoleonic wars. The discipline of sociology was gaining autonomy internationally, notably among Germany's industrial rivals: the United States, France, and England. In all of those contexts, sociology was taking on an ever more empirical and quantitative cast, which increasingly differentiated it from its philosophical origins. On this basis, the discipline would rapidly gain societal power in the following generation and eventually become deeply integrated into the apparatus of modern bureaucratic state administration.

Unsurprisingly, then, sociology's reputation for fostering perniciously critical attitudes toward established institutions—and the association of its practitioners with progressive politics of various sorts—fed hostility to the discipline on the part of the traditional philosophical establishment in imperial Germany. As Köhnke, Klaus Lichtblau, and others have demonstrated, his more conservative colleagues were right to identify Simmel and his theoretical innovations with the new social movements of the day. To recognize his sociology as a distinctive, original, theoretical achievement must have seemed tantamount to many to endorsing a threat to philosophy's institutional role in the imperial state.

This disciplinary flux underlines the difficulty in determining how personal, substantive, political, and institutional factors should be weighted in assessing the course of Simmel's professional career. What appeared to some contemporaries as "negativity" marked a theoretical praxis attempting to take historical, cultural reality into account, to come to terms with a rapidly changing world. But as sociology became established institutionally, Simmel's work became assimilated to disciplinary narratives that helped obscure the specifically philosophical virtues of his innovative strategies for intellectual pathfinding of all sorts. Indeed, categorizing him as a sociologist aligned his thought with institutional transformations that rendered it difficult to discern what had been at stake for Simmel in setting out on the path of defining sociology.

His innovative strategies of thought soon become appropriated into practices aimed at institutionally anchoring and professionalizing the new discipline, including by creating a historical narrative that profoundly altered the landscape his explorations had aimed to disclose—not simply, as its "makers" implied, widening routes Simmel had laid out, but, as it were, bulldozing the winding paths he preferred and replacing them with paved highways with well-defined entrances and exits. Yet even if the institutional as opposed to intellectual development of the discipline during his lifetime doubtless affected Simmel's shifting attitude toward sociology over time, the sea change evident in his self-understanding as a scholar even before the publication of his *Philosophy of Money* reflects a significant development in Simmel's thinking that must be understood on its own terms, and whose meaning has been rendered virtually illegible by the actual historical and institutional trajectory of the social sciences.

CHAPTER 3

Memory/Legacy: Georg Simmel as (Mostly) Forgotten Founding Father

Especially in the Anglophone context, Simmel's champions and translators have almost all been sociologists. But even within the narrow terms of his reception in sociology, he plays a marginal role in the dominant disciplinary narratives, particularly in the United States.[1] To be sure, this reflects a more general neglect of classic European social theorists as a consequence of the empirical orientation of American sociology, but it also registers peculiarities in his scholarly reception in particular.[2]

Paradoxically, Simmel's work is represented as at once foundational for and marginal to the modern social sciences. Tracing the process by which Simmel (in contrast to his contemporaries Weber and Durkheim) came to occupy this distinctive liminal position casts considerable light on the historical constitution as well as the rhetorical organization of modern social scientific thought. At the same time, the history of Simmel's reception in American sociology illuminates the occlusions and misapprehensions his thought has suffered in the Anglophone world more generally. In the course of that history, a range of textual practices—ways of reading but also of editing his oeuvre—became established that have rendered it both theoretically and practically difficult for Anglophone readers to get beyond the clichéd understanding of Simmel as a social scientist manqué.

Simmel in America: The Disciplinary (Pre-)History

Unlike Max Weber and Sigmund Freud, Georg Simmel never visited the United States, but his ideas nonetheless had a considerable impact there during the years when academic social science was becoming established.[3] As Donald Levine and his

---

1. Two telling examples: the American Sociological Association's centennial volume, *Sociology in America: A History* (Chicago: University of Chicago Press, 2007), ed. Craig J. Calhoun, has just seven indexed references to Simmel—not one of which engages his work or examines the influence of his ideas. *The Cambridge History of Science*, vol. 7: *The Modern Social Sciences*, ed. Theodore M. Porter and Dorothy Ross (Cambridge: Cambridge University Press, 2003), indexes just five—none of which refers to a substantive discussion of Simmel's work.

2. On the neglect of history in sociology, see *Reclaiming the Sociological Classics: The State of the Scholarship*, ed. Charles Camic (Malden, MA: Blackwell, 1997), particularly the essays by Camic and Sica, and *Social Theory and Sociology: The Classics and Beyond*, ed. Stephen P. Turner (Cambridge: Blackwell, 1996). On the evolution of the American discipline toward a hegemonic "methodological positivism," see Steinmetz 2005.

3. Weber's work was, in contrast, not even available in English until after 1927, aside from his contri-

co-authors note in "Simmel's Influence on American Sociology" published in the *American Journal of Sociology* (*AJS*) in 1976, Simmel "stands in the unusual position of being the only European scholar who has had a palpable influence on sociology in the United States, throughout the course of the 20th century."[4] This fact is "particularly noteworthy," since "when sociology was becoming established within the American academic system during the first few decades of this century, it was truly a homegrown product."[5] Simmel's influence took an unusual form, however: "although literate American sociologists today could be expected to produce a coherent statement of the theoretical frameworks and principal themes of Marx, Durkheim, and Weber, few would be able to do the same for Simmel" (Levine et al., I, 814). "Simmel's Influence on American Sociology" casts considerable light on why this was (and arguably still is) the case.

According to Levine et al., "the fragmentary picture of Simmel's sociology held by American sociologists" in 1976 reflected not only "the bewildering variety of topics he treated and the disorganized manner in which he presented his general principles" but also "the disjointed manner in which his ideas entered the mainstream of American sociology" and "the transmutations they underwent in the process" (I, 814). In two long synthetic essays, they presented a nuanced account of Simmel's "recurrent, variegated, and erratic" impact on American sociology up to that point (II, 1127). After examining the processes of transmission that established Simmel as a "classic" thinker by the mid-1950s, Levine et al. reviewed his contribution to sociological research on "the social psychology of the stranger and social distance . . . urbanism, small groups, interpersonal knowledge, conflict, and exchange" (II, 1112). While their selection of topics was by no means exhaustive, it was more than wide-ranging enough to demonstrate the breadth of Simmel's impact.

And yet the story Levine et al. tell makes clear that it was no accident that Simmel's larger intellectual objectives remained obscure to American sociologists. In a discipline defined by an empirical and pragmatic orientation, questions about theoretical foundations were—and are—a distinctly minority concern. The history

---

bution to the proceedings of the St. Louis Congress of Arts and Sciences in 1904. See Lawrence A. Scaff, *Max Weber in America* (Princeton, NJ: Princeton University Press, 2011), 207.

4. Donald Levine, Ellwood B. Carter, and Eleanor Miller Gorman, "Simmel's Influence on American Sociology, I," *AJS* 81, no. 4 (1976): 813–45; here, p. 813. Part II of the article appeared in the next issue, *AJS* 81, no. 5 (1976): 1112–32. These articles remain (in the words of the author of the only book-length exploration of the same topic) "a key reference for all students of Simmel's American reception" (Gary Jaworski, *Georg Simmel and the American Prospect* [Albany: State University of New York Press, 1997], x). Unless otherwise noted, references in this chapter refer to these texts (as I and II).

5. In a 1927 survey of 258 American sociologists, "only 20% . . . mentioned any European author as having exerted a significant influence on their intellectual outlook" (Levine et al., I, 813). To be sure, in that survey, Simmel came in a not very close second to Herbert Spencer, with Gabriel Tarde bringing up the rear. (Durkheim, Comte, and Hobhouse lagged further behind; neither Marx nor Weber appeared at all.) According to Levine et al., "general treatises on sociology and social psychology of that period" follow the same patterns of citing American rather than European sociologists and of referring to Spencer and Simmel far more often than to others (I, 813). But even as most of the thinkers who dominated the earlier period were forgotten in favor of Vilfredo Pareto, Karl Marx, "and, slowly but more durably, Émile Durkheim and Max Weber," Simmel continued to be influential. Although interest in his thought was "subdued" in the 1930s and 1940s, it "thereafter revived to become more extensive then ever" (I, 814).

of Simmel's impact on American sociology is in very significant ways a history of misreading—or to put the point less prejudicially, of selective appropriation. With most of his oeuvre still unavailable in English (as was, until 1978, almost the entire *Philosophy of Money*), even today his reputation in the United States is largely based on a few essays taken out of their larger context and often read badly to boot.[6] Throughout that reception, questionable interpretations have been exacerbated by patent errors of fact—thus Simmel was neither (as has often been claimed) politically disengaged nor so wealthy that the lack of a salaried academic position was a matter of indifference to him.

But efforts to rescue Simmel from the clichés and distortions that have shaped his Anglophone reception have repeatedly failed. The sheer resilience of such misunderstandings suggests that his image as brilliant outsider constitutes and sustains the marginality it purports to describe. My aim is less to correct the received readings than to contextualize and interpret them to make visible how they have obscured Simmel's significance as a thinker. This complex reception history reveals a great deal about the discipline of sociology in America and brings the theoretical, methodological, and institutional issues at stake in reading Simmel as a sociologist rather than a philosopher into relief; it needs to be understood if its effects are to be overcome.

During the late nineteenth and early twentieth centuries, German scholarship set a recognized and distinguished standard, and a pilgrimage, often extended, to one or more German universities was an important mark of distinction for aspiring American academics. Levine et al. underline that Simmel's fame was a powerful draw. "No fewer than six men who became sociologists as the discipline was starting to gain footing in American universities" attended his lectures, including three future presidents of the American Sociological Association, all of whom would also produce influential textbooks—Charles A. Ellwood, Edward C. Hayes, and Robert E. Park.[7]

The most decisive relationship for the future course of Simmel's influence had even earlier roots, however. Albion W. Small, who left the presidency of Colby Col-

---

6. Problems arising from the scope and quality of translations plague the wider Anglophone reception of European sociology. The responses to critical scrutiny of Talcott Parsons's English translations of Max Weber's works illustrate how significant these canonical versions remain. Thus Keith Tribe defended Parsons against the charge that his translation and recontextualization of the first chapters of Weber's *Economy and Society* "systematically distorts the original sense," as other scholars had argued, with a virtual apologia for the disciplinary status quo, contending that Parsons's "introduction directs the reader to think of the text as a methodological statement linked to Parsons' own conceptions of the social sciences, while his presentation and translation of the text itself obscures the structure that Weber gave it, making it easier for the text to be thought about in the way Parsons, not Weber, intended" (Tribe, "Talcott Parsons as Translator of Max Weber's Basic Sociological Categories," *History of European Ideas* 33, no. 2 [2007]: 233). Similarly, Uta Gerhardt defends Parsons's controversial translation of the *Protestant Ethic and the Spirit of Capitalism* as "a stepping stone in the emergence of scientific sociology in the twentieth century," criticizing Stephen Kalberg's 2002 retranslation for failing to provide "an uncontroversial text for the average undergraduate" (Gerhardt, *Idealtypus: Zur methodologischen Begründung der modernen Soziologie* [Frankfurt am Main: Suhrkamp, 2001], 59).

7. Levine et al., I, 815. Until the mid-1950s, "nearly every translation of Simmel into English and nearly every major presentation through university instruction had been the work of Americans who had been in Germany, immigrants from central Europe, or students of either or both of these two small groups" (ibid., 820).

lege in 1892 to assume the first professorship in sociology in the United States at the newly founded University of Chicago, had met Simmel when they were both studying in Berlin and remained in collegial contact with him in the years to come. Small is remembered mainly for his "crucial administrative role as gatekeeper in the early stages of the development of sociology in America."[8] He was the founder, not only of the first sociology department in the country, but also, in 1895, of the *AJS*, of which he was the editor-in-chief for over thirty years; Small also co-authored the first sociology textbook.[9] He held the presidencies of both the American Sociological Association and the Institute international de sociologie in Paris.[10] Simmel and Small corresponded regularly, and Small ensured Simmel's early reception in the United States, sending his students to Berlin and translating and publishing Simmel's sociological essays.[11]

Under Small's leadership the University of Chicago became a "center of diffusion" for Simmel's thought, Levine et al. observe.[12] Long after his death, Simmel's writings continued to enjoy canonical status in the Chicago sociology curriculum. Small's protégé and successor, and the guiding spirit of the "Chicago School,"[13] Robert Park, who received from Simmel "the only formal instruction in sociology he ever had" (I, 816), continued this tradition.[14] Although neither Park nor Small can really be regarded as Simmelians, as discipline builders they valued and drew upon his efforts. As Small put it, "The desideratum is to start with the spirit of Simmel's desire for a

---

8. James J. Chris, "Albion Small," in *Fifty Key Sociologists: The Formative Theorists*, ed. John Scott (New York: Routledge, 2007), 156.

9. Small's *An Introduction to the Study of Society* (1894), which consisted "mostly of extracts from German social thinkers and philosophers," was technically his second sociology textbook: he had privately published a volume with the same title in 1890 for the course in sociology at Colby that had "replaced the traditional course in moral philosophy taught by the president" with "one of the first three sociology courses in the nation" (Cheryl Laz, "Albion Small," *American National Biography*).

10. See Thomas W. Godspeed's charming commemoration, "Albion Woodbury Small," *American Journal of Sociology* 31, no. 6 (1926): 1–14.

11. Levine et al., I, 816, note that "15 such entries appeared [in the *AJS*] between volumes 2 and 16 [that is, between September 1896 and November 1910—EG], most translated by Small himself." Small sought "to stimulate social scientists in the English-speaking world to begin with beginnings by devoting themselves to fundamental problems of methodology" (Albion Small, "Review of *The Social Theory of Georg Simmel* by Nicholas J. Spykman," *AJS* 31, no. 1 [July 1925]: 84). On Small's appropriation of Simmel's ideas, see also Gary D. Jaworski, *Georg Simmel and the American Prospect* (Albany: State University of New York Press, 1997), chap. 1.

12. In the 1927 survey, among the eleven American sociologists cited as most influential, "six were directly and one indirectly associated with the University of Chicago" (Levine et al., I, 816).

13. The literature on this (semi-mythical) formation is extensive. For an especially instructive synthesis, see Andrew Abbott, *Department & Discipline: Chicago Sociology at One Hundred* (Chicago: University of Chicago Press, 1999).

14. Until well into the twentieth century, sociologists were of necessity trained in other fields. Park, who started out in journalism and always maintained an activist orientation, studied philosophy and psychology under William James at Harvard before receiving his doctorate for a pioneering study of mass communication written under Wilhelm Windelband at Heidelberg. Max Weber was a legal historian whose first position was as a professor of political economy; Durkheim took his Ph.D. in philosophy. Small first trained as a theologian and eventually received his Ph.D. in history at Johns Hopkins in 1888 while on sabbatical from teaching history and political science at Colby; Talcott Parsons held a D.Phil. from the London School of Economics; Pitirim Sorokin did advanced work in psycho-neurology and earned two law degrees before turning to sociology.

methodology, not necessarily with his specific conclusions."¹⁵ The popular textbook Park edited with his Chicago colleague Ernest Burgess, *Introduction to the Science of Sociology*, which appeared in many successive editions between 1921 and 1979, included ten selections from Simmel's work. It "became the most influential introduction to sociology in the United States in the 1920s and 1930s, playing a major role in the exposure of generations of sociology students to Simmel's writings" (I, 817).

From the perspective of Simmel's thought as a whole, however, this exposure took a highly problematic form. Park and Burgess helped canonize Simmel's contributions to sociology by decontextualizing and reframing his ideas, extracting from his texts thematically organized "contributions to" various subfields of a sociological discipline conceived very differently than Simmel had envisioned it.

Thus even as Simmel's importance became established in the United States, the contradictions and lacunae that would lead to his ambiguous status as a founding father about whom little was known were already taking shape. Fueled by the limited corpus of texts available in English, Simmel's reception took place by bits and pieces, with his work often being misconstrued even by his declared advocates. In 1925, the University of Chicago Press published the first English monograph devoted to him, Nicholas J. Spykman's *The Sociological Theory of Georg Simmel*, which summarized sociological works unavailable in English "in a systematic, albeit uninspired, fashion" (Levine et al., I, 817).¹⁶ In surveys of sociological theory published in 1928 and 1929 respectively, Pitirim Sorokin (who in 1930 became the founding chair of the Harvard Sociology Department)¹⁷ and Theodore Abel (of Columbia) criticized Simmel's approach as insufficiently scientific.¹⁸ Unfortunately, as Levine et al.

---

15. Small, "Review of *The Social Theory of Georg Simmel* by Nicholas J. Spykman," 87. Writing the year before he died, Small lamented: "Up to the present time the Americans who have given indubitable evidence of having considered Simmel thoroughly might be counted on the fingers of one hand." Nor was this neglect limited to the United States—a point he makes vividly by describing "the translator's" dismaying discovery that at the library at the London School of Economics in the volumes of the *AJS* containing his renderings of Simmel, "the leaves were uncut!" For Small, widespread ignorance of Simmel's work was symptomatic of more general methodological problems in the nascent social science disciplines: "It was not conscious hypocrisy—it was the expediency of semiconscious desperation for the sociologists of the passing generation to claim for their specialty as a science more than it has performed." He urged his colleagues to turn their attention to establishing the scientific foundations of their endeavors now that they had survived their "gallant fight for existence" (ibid., 84 and 86).

16. To Albion Small, whose enthusiastic review included the dire assessment of the social sciences just cited, Spkyman's effort to shore up scientific foundations appeared considerably more impressive: "We hope that Dr. Spykman will prove to have done for Simmel and for social science what this *Journal* was unable to do thirty years ago" (84). Spykman's book had its origins in a 1923 Berkeley dissertation written under the historian Frederick Teggart. See Frederick J. Teggart, "In Memoriam: Nicholas John Spykman, 1893–1943," *AJS* 49, no. 1 (1943): 60. Spykman's book was reissued in 2004 with an introduction by David Frisby.

17. The son of a peasant icon maker, Sorokin had also founded the sociology department at the University of St. Petersburg in 1919 before being forced into exile in 1922 for his political views (Barry V. Johnston, "Sorokin Lives! Centennial Observations," *Footnotes* 17, no. 1 (January 1989): 1, 5 (www.asanet.org/about/presidents/Pitirim_Sorokin.cfm [accessed July 19, 2016]).

18. As Levine et al. note, Abel would later reverse his assessment of Simmel in his *Systematic Sociology in Germany* (New York: Columbia University Press, 1929). In a paper with its origins in the 1958 Durkheim-Simmel centenary session of the American Sociological Association, Abel declared that Simmel "belongs to the small company of men who have opened up an entirely new path of inquiry" and

write, all three "grossly misrepresented the scope of Simmel's achievement." While Spykman gave "no hint of the luminosity of Simmel's mind or the trenchancy of his sociological perceptions," Sorokin and Abel "misunderstood Simmel's distinction between form and content" and "failed to represent any of his substantive materials adequately" (I, 818).

This tension between recognition and misrecognition by admirers and foes alike has remained characteristic of Simmel's reception more generally. In his influential courses on social theory at Harvard in the 1930s, Talcott Parsons treated Simmel at some length, and he included selections from Simmel in an influential anthology he coedited in 1961. But a discussion of Simmel was edited out of Parsons's book *The Structure of Social Action* (1937),[19] a work that set the theoretical agenda for much of twentieth-century social science, and the question of the significance of Parsons's omission remains a matter of controversy.[20] Robert K. Merton, a graduate student of Sorokin's who took Parsons's course on social theory, conceived an enduring interest in Simmel that he passed on to generations of his own students at Columbia and disseminated more widely through his influential and oft-revised *Social Theory and Social Structure* beginning with the 1957 edition. A number of Merton's students

---

"can justifiably be regarded as the founder of modern sociology" (Theodore Abel, "The Contribution of Georg Simmel: A Reappraisal," *American Sociological Review* 24, no. 4 [1959]: 473–74).

19. Talcott Parsons had drafted a chapter on Simmel and Tönnies for *The Structure of Social Action: A Study in Social Theory with Special Reference to a Group of Recent European Writers* (New York: McGraw Hill, 1937) but included only his treatment of Tönnies. There is a considerable literature on this redaction and on the significance for the discipline of Simmel's absence from *Structure*, which helped set "the base line vocabulary for modern sociology" (Jeffrey C. Alexander, "Against Historicism/For Theory: A Reply to Levine," *Sociological Theory* 7, no. 1 [1989]: 97). For Donald Levine, the "peculiar selectivity" of Parsons's historiography led to the "exclusion of Simmel from the pantheon of sociological classics" despite his long-standing recognition "as a preeminent originative thinker" before *Structure*'s 1937 publication (Levine, "Parsons' *Structure* (and Simmel) Revisited," *Sociological Theory* 7, no. 1 [1989]: 114). The excised discussion of Simmel was finally published in 1993 with an introduction by Giuseppe Sciortino and commentaries by some of the major interlocutors in that literature—Levine, Alexander, and Parsons's literary executor, Victor Lidz—in the first volume of the short-lived journal *Teoria sociologica*. Then, in 1996, Kiyomitsu Yui discovered another manuscript in the Harvard archives in which Parsons repeatedly referred to Simmel's alleged "dilettantism" and twice denoted his methodological doctrine as "pernicious" for sociology (Yui, "Parsons' 'Lost Fragment' on Simmel: Pivoting around an Unpublished Manuscript," *Annual Reports of Humanities and Social Sciences, Kobe University* 17 [March 1998]). Both the previously identified "missing fragment" of Parsons's original Simmel–Tönnies chapter and this newly identified "lost manuscript" were published in the Summer 1998 issue of *American Sociologist*, where the editor, William J. Buxton, revealed that the latter MS had turned up in 1990 when a trove of new materials from Parsons made their way to the Harvard archive. Although clearly "a previously undiscovered manuscript of great importance for understanding the development of Talcott Parsons's thought," its provenance and significance were still being evaluated when Yui came upon it in the archives. Giuseppe Sciortino, "The *Structure of Social Action*'s 'Missing' Chapter on Simmel: An Introduction. Appendix: Talcott Parsons, Letter to J. C. Alexander, January 19th, 1979," in *Parsons' "The Structure of Social Action" and Contemporary Debates*, ed. Gabrielle Pollini and Sciortino, 45–69 (Milan: Franco Angeli, 2001), surveys these debates and reproduces the salient primary texts, including the 1979 letter to Jeffrey Alexander with Parsons's own much-discussed assessment of his reasons for omitting his discussion of Simmel from *Structure*.

20. Jaworski's view that "theoretical incompatibility" but also Parsons's "resistance to incorporate Simmel's . . . tragic vie[w] of life" were at stake would seem to be supported by Scaff's observation (in a chapter titled "The Creation of the Sacred Text") that Parsons's *Protestant Ethic* translates away a whole family of terminology with a "Simmelian cast" involving compounds with "*Leben* [life]" (Jaworski, *Georg Simmel*, 63, and Scaff, *Max Weber in America*, 226).

would play important roles in the revival of interest in Simmel that ensued in the 1950s. But like their teacher, most tended to treat his work as "an indispensable point of departure" in developing "a style of theorizing [Simmel] could never bring himself to do."[21] The somewhat distorted impact of Simmel's ideas on the various sociological subfields Levine et al. survey enfolds a failure to appreciate the theoretical importance of his distinctive style of thought.

American sociology has never abandoned its pragmatic orientation to focus on the sorts of philosophical questions about society and culture that preoccupied Simmel. But after World War II, in good part due to the influence of émigré European scholars, as Levine et al. describe it, a discipline largely defined by "what has been called the dominant American ethic of instrumental activism" (I, 818) started "to become more self-conscious," to examine its history and "reconsider its theoretical orientations" (I, 820).

Simmel's work featured prominently in that reorientation, with Kurt H. Wolff's volume of new translations, published in 1950 under the misleading title *The Sociology of Georg Simmel*, "more than any other single factor responsible for the revival of American students' interest in Simmel in the postwar years" (I, 819). More translations, mostly from the corpus of sociological texts, followed. Simmel's work was included in a series of influential anthologies of sociological classics, and the centenary of his birth in 1958 saw a further upswing of interest in his work.

By 1976, there was a significant body of secondary literature on Simmel and his impact on the discipline. Nonetheless, Levine et al. tempered their upbeat assessment that his "work has been diffused to the point where its status as a significant component of American sociology now seems assured" with a reminder of how much remained to be done. With so much of his oeuvre untranslated and no "thorough, critical study of Simmel's sociology" in existence, "the task of integrating Simmel into American sociology remains a challenge" (I, 822). And despite their optimism that "the luxuriantly rich personal knowledge and subtle imagination which inform his investigations" (II, 1129) would keep future sociologists returning to Simmel's writings, the authors stressed the contradictions of his reception up to that point.

"Simmel's Influence on American Sociology," Levine et al. concluded, had established that Simmel served as a source of "scientific identity, theoretical ingenuity, and substantive generalizations" (II, 1129)—that his work played a key role in defining the "subject matter" of the discipline, in helping to orient "analytic perspectives," and in providing a rich variety of "novel topics and propositions" for sociological investigation (II, 1127). However, Simmel's ideas had been used in a "highly selective and often arbitrary way" (II, 1128). While attributing these weaknesses in the sociological literature partly to the lack of "readily accessible" translations of many texts and partly to the author's own unsystematic approach, Levine

---

21. So Merton's own self-characterization in a personal communication to Levine et al., cited in I, 820. One of the most influential of Merton's students for Simmel's future reception in the United States was Lewis A. Coser, whose work on the sociology of conflict came out of his dissertation on Simmel, and who edited a series called "The Makers of Modern Social Science" that included the 1965 volume on Simmel already cited.

et al. also identified the "relatively weak institutionalization of rigorous scholarly standards within American sociology" as a factor. "In many instances scholars have erroneously faulted Simmel for neglecting crucial considerations" or neglected to cite confirming passages "because of ignorance of the relevant texts, including those in translation" (II, 1128). Critical literature was treated with the same cavalier attitude: "the research tradition on social distance is to some extent cumulative, but it is also marked by considerable discontinuity and disjointedness" (I, 835).

These problematic reading practices have proved extremely resilient. Simmel's stature as a thinker continues to be obscured by a reception that, recurrent proclamations of a "Simmel renaissance" notwithstanding, has not completed "the task of integrating Simmel into American sociology." Nearly forty years after Levine et al.'s thorough demonstration of his historical and theoretical significance, Simmel remains a marginal figure. A few of his essays are invoked with almost ritualistic regularity, but his theoretical and methodological achievements are generally poorly understood, and his work barely appears in the dominant narrative about the development of the discipline. It remains true that, as Stanley Aronowitz put it in 1994, although "there is much talk of a Simmel 'revival' in the secondary literature," the efforts of scholars from Coser to Frisby to draw attention to Simmel's contributions have not yet had "much impact on the theoretical orientation of most of the discipline."[22]

Simmel's persistent marginality is at least partly due to larger historical factors. Twenty years later, Donald Levine revised his optimistic assessment of 1976: "efforts to recover Simmel were eclipsed in the 1960s by the surge of interest in Marxian writings, which led to Marx's joining Durkheim and Weber to form a canonized trinity of sociological founders."[23] Significantly, the most influential Anglophone advocate of a return to Simmel to emerge in the intervening years, the British sociologist David Frisby, initially framed his arguments in the idiom of Marxian cultural theory. He, too, located Simmel's achievement at the margins of the discipline—but as that of a *flâneur* whose aesthetic approach to cultural analysis amounted to an alternative form of sociological thought.[24]

While Frisby's approach remains influential, the displacement of Marxist paradigms has also contributed to an increased interest in Simmel since 1989. If a renaissance is indeed under way, its epicenter is in Germany, where work on the *Gesamtausgabe* spawned multiple research initiatives, but renewed interest in Simmel

---

22. Stanley Aronowitz, "The Simmel Revival: A Challenge to American Social Science," Sociological Quarterly 35, no. 3 (1994): 401. The over 900-page essay collection *Sociology in America* (2007) includes not a single sustained discussion of Simmel, and there are no references to his works (in contrast to Marx, Durkheim, and Weber's) in the extensive resource bibliography.

23. Donald Levine "Simmel Reappraised: Old Images, New Scholarship," in *Reclaiming the Sociological Classics: The State of the Scholarship*, ed. Charles Camic (Malden, MA: Blackwell, 1997), 174. For a critique of the role of this sociological "holy trinity" from the point of view of standpoint theory that does not, however, mention Simmel at all, see Joey Sprague, "Holy Men and Big Guns: The Can[n]on in Social Theory," *Gender and Society* 11, no. 1 (February 1997): 88–107.

24. For an objection to this approach from the point of view of one of Simmel's most effective advocates in the previous generation, see Lewis Coser, "The Many Faces of Georg Simmel." *Contemporary Sociology* 22, no. 3 (May, 1993): 452–53.

is palpable in the European scholarly community more generally. How much such international developments in social theory affect the practices of sociologists in the United States is another matter. At a 2003 Paris symposium on the prospects of general sociological theory in a globalized world, an American participant emphasized the persistent force of "indigenous pathways" in the United States. According to Stephen Kalberg, "The discipline's longstanding orientations remained for the most part intact and, in the 1980s and 1990s, erected obstacles against modes of analysis and schools emanating from Europe."[25]

Indeed, as the story Levine et al. told made quite clear, such obstacles are anchored in the dominant sociological paradigm as such, and raising the discipline's historical consciousness, as it were, is no simple matter. It is worth considering Simmel's reception in U.S. sociology quite closely, since the process by which his thought was at once assimilated and excluded was both conceptually and institutionally constitutive for the discipline. From a genealogical perspective, the difficulty of "integrating Simmel into American sociology" is not simply a function of the prevailing, fundamentally ahistorical, understanding of theory. It is a symptom of what must be forgotten if the discipline is to remain secure in the concomitant understanding of sociology as a scientific endeavor: its origins in a conceptual world defined by a very different kind of disciplinary and scientific ideal, the deeply historical models of fin de siècle German philosophy and the *Geisteswissenschaften*.

Discipline/History: Theorizing Misrecognition

Simmel's ambiguous status as a (mostly) forgotten founding father—his marginalization despite his demonstrable impact on modern social thought—is theoretically significant. As the fact that his contributions to sociology are so consistently misconstrued (when they are not being written out of the story entirely) attests, the history of theory is anything but an objective account of a rational progression. And a great deal is at stake both institutionally and conceptually in misreading Simmel. His vision of sociology differs fundamentally from the paradigm of quantitatively oriented social science that gained wide adherence in the United States early on— the paradigm that, despite assaults from poststructuralism on the one hand and cultural studies on the other, continues to govern the disciplinary mainstream today. Both the questions Simmel asked and the ways he went about seeking answers to them continue to be dismissed as "philosophical," if not "metaphysical." But that is to say that the very things that make his work foundational for sociology must be forgotten in order to assimilate him to the dominant disciplinary paradigm.

---

25. Stephen Kalberg "A Cross-National Consensus on a Unified Sociological Theory? Some Inter-Cultural Obstacles," *La revue du M.A.U.S.S.* [Mouvement anti-utilitariste dans les sciences sociales], no. 24 (2004): 210, in French; reproduced in English in the *European Journal of Social Theory* 10, no. 2 (2007): 179–83. The passage continues: "Highly influential European approaches grounded in the works of Elias, Baumann, Giddens, Habermas, Luhmann, Foucault, Bourdieu, Simmel, Marx, and Weber became visible on the American landscape only on the margins." Regarding the symposium, see Roger Caillé's Introduction to the collection of papers in the *European Journal of Social Theory* 10, no. 2, that includes the English version of Kalberg's essay.

This ambivalent process of assimilation is well illustrated by the reception of what is today probably Simmel's best-known essay, "Die Großstädte und das Geistesleben" ("The Metropolis and Mental Life" [1903]). Originally a talk at the first conference on the metropolis ever held in Germany, it examines the "intellectual/spiritual" [*geistige*] significance of the metropolis as an historical and cultural formation—the meaning of this "product of specifically modern life" in and for the evolution of human subjectivity.[26] Simmel uses the resonant notion of the *Geistesleben*, literally, the "life of the spirit," to bridge between a perspective rooted in the philosophical tradition and contemporary psychological and sociological approaches to understanding human life.

This essay, which presents central theses from his *Philosophy of Money* in compact form, is justly famous for its combination of acute phenomenological observation and suggestive theoretical formulations. However, in line with the misleading translation of the title—Simmel's use of *Geist* is neither idealist nor psychological— the essay's sociological readers have tended to conflate Simmel's philosophical objectives with, and thereby reduce them to, the psychological analysis he provides along the way. His notion that "the intensification of nervous life" provides the "psychological foundation" for a new form of subjective existence under conditions where shock has been normalized (116) has thereby taken on a life of its own, and passages about the impact of nervous overstimulation are cited and recited out of context—by no means only within sociology.

Thanks in large part to Walter Benjamin, the metropolis essay is often invoked as the locus classicus of the idea that traditional modes of subjective experience have been destroyed in modernity. In fact, Simmel drew on a well-established scientific and popular discourse about how the permanent vigilant awareness demanded by the urban environment leads to nervous exhaustion, apathy, atony, and indifference. As in the *Philosophy of Money*, he integrates such materialist tropes into an innovative philosophical interpretation of the sociohistorical development of rationality. Ironically, Simmel's contribution to theorizing the rationalization process remains widely unrecognized even as his account of how people adapt via "intensification of consciousness" (117) to permanent nervous stimulation by the incessant stream of ever-changing impressions under urban conditions has become a commonplace of contemporary cultural theory. In particular, Simmel's remark that the hyperattentive metropolitan subject thereby "creates a protective organ against the deracination threatened by the flux and contradictions of his external environment" (117), which Benjamin influentially assimilated to Freud's similar claims regarding the structuration of the ego as a defense against the external world, has attained canonical status as a phenomenological description of the subjective consequences of the shock structure of modern experience. This psychologizing interpretation has turned "Die Großstädte und das Geistesleben" into a classic at the cost of occluding what Simmel

---

26. "Die Großstädte und das Geistesleben," in *Die Großstadt. Vorträge und Aufsätze zur Städteausstellung. Jahrbuch der Gehe-Stiftung Dresden*, ed. Th. Petermann, 9 (1903): 185–206; quotation from *GSG* 7: 116 (subsequent parenthetical citations in this section also refer to this text). Simmel's articulation of his purpose is in the first paragraph of the essay.

presented as its philosophical stakes: the way the "most profound problems of modern life" (116) become visible in the metropolis as sociohistorical, cultural life form.[27]

The essay's reception illustrates how Simmel's oeuvre came to be understood as simultaneously foundational for and marginal to the modern social sciences—a liminal position that epitomizes the troubled relation between those disciplines and the philosophical traditions out of which they developed. Here, as elsewhere, mining Simmel's texts for lapidary insights turns him into a source of theoretical inspiration at the cost of obscuring questions about the broader significance of his philosophical and methodological achievements.

Simmel's remarks about physiology concern only one dimension of what for him makes the metropolis "one of the great historic configurations [*Gebilde*] in which the antithetical currents that comprise life . . . conjoin and unfold" (131). By extracting this (narrowly "psychological") moment from Simmel's larger account of the dialectic between subjectivity and cultural development, both empiricist and historical materialist appropriations of this essay have rendered illegible his claims for the world-historical significance of modern cities: their place in the evolution of human *Geistesleben* in both the subjective and collective senses. In so doing, they render illegible what Simmel understood by "psychology," which was inseparably sociocultural, historical, and philosophical. Read, not as an exercise in sociological or socio-psychological analysis, but as a philosophical intervention, his exploration of the historic transformation of individual and collective experience, of the reflective existence of the embodied human being, as such, under modern metropolitan conditions epitomizes the way Simmel reframed philosophical problems in terms we would today call "cultural."

As in the *Philosophie des Geldes*, he places sociological and psychological analyses quite explicitly at the service of a philosophical interpretation of the crisis of the modern subject: of the individual striving for autonomy and freedom in the face of the overwhelming collective "superpowers" [*Übermächte*] of society, tradition, culture, and technology (116). Again, Simmel's conception of the historical life of spirit is by no means idealist but drew on a tradition of reflection on the development of "objective culture" that may be traced back at least to Herder.[28] His conception of *Geistesleben*—and thus his way of thinking the place of the metropolis in the "world history of spirit" (130)—refigures the meaning of *Geist* and of "life" alike. Incorporating materialist analytic perspectives, his interpretation situates the dilemmas of the modern subject in what the *Philosophy of Money* calls "the cultural process" (*Kulturprozeß*), in which "forms of life" evolve over time. To be sure, this approach contributed to the emergent discipline of sociology by illuminating the

---

27. I discuss "Die Großstädte und das Geistesleben" at greater length in the context of Simmel's invocation of blaséness as a "lived philosophical problem" in my book *Experience without Qualities: Boredom and Modernity* (Stanford: Stanford University Press, 2005).

28. In his discussion of objectifications of spirit in the final chapter of the *Philosophy of Money*, Simmel notes the philosophical-historical significance of the opposition to the "strict individualism" of Enlightenment "rationalism," that "went from Herder through romanticism, and that with its recognition of life's superintellectual powers of feeling also recognized the superindividual collectivities as unities and historical realities" (*GSG* 6: 606).

nature, status, and meaning of the shifting relations between subjective experience and social formations. But for Simmel, these are not per se sociological problems: the spiritual-historical-cultural life of the metropolis both exacerbates and democratizes the philosophical problems of the modern subject through what he calls "the atrophy of individual via the hypertrophy of objective culture" (130).

When Simmel's phenomenology of metropolitan subjectivity is treated as an empirical psychology, the dialectical stakes of his argument are obscured. Without wishing to recuperate the notion of *Geist*, I want to underline that Simmel is using the term to anchor an inquiry into the historical and cultural significance of urban life that is both theoretically and methodologically far richer than the materialist accounts of the modern psyche that snippets from this text are so often brought forward to support.

A superb reader of Nietzsche, Simmel took his questions about the history of reason as well as his elevation of the category of life most seriously. In arguing that nervous overstimulation creates the "psychological conditions" and "the sensual foundations" for "the intellectualistic character of metropolitan psychic life" (117), he weaves questions about the body and the emotions into an account of the rationalization process. Thus even as he asserts that the onslaught of rapidly changing impressions in the modern city fosters an "intensification of consciousness" and of rationality, Simmel denies that it is possible to live entirely on the surface; consciousness has its limits as a "protective organ." Physical proximity to other people calls forth a continual "activity of our souls that answers nearly every impression of another human being with a sensation that is in some way distinct, whose unconsciousness, fleetingness, and fluctuation only appears to neutralize it into indifference" (123). But Simmel's theoretical achievement—a multivalent and nonreductive approach to interpreting the effects of cultural-historical transformations on human subjects understood as embodied, reflective beings—has been obscured by the modes in which this text has been appropriated.

When *Geist* is translated as "mind" or "intellect," questions that are constitutive for the discipline of sociology are literally written out of consideration. In the metropolis essay, as elsewhere in his oeuvre, Simmel's interpretations of social phenomena serve to articulate a wider "spiritual"—historico-philosophical, psychological, cultural—significance with material reality, to identify dimensions of meaning incorporated and enacted in trans-subjective forms of life. What matters to him are not the effects of nervous overstimulation as such or even giving a causal account of the pervasive rationalism of life in large and intricately interdependent social formations, but rather the larger significance of such sociocultural phenomena. What do individual and collective "adaptations" to urban life reveal about the status and future of subjectivity? How does the historical evolution of autonomy and individuality under the complex social, cultural, and material conditions of modern, metropolitan existence illuminate philosophical questions about the meaning of subjective freedom?

At stake in these inquiries is neither the status and limits of reflection on society in the abstract nor the philosophical aporiai of subjectivity as such. Simmel is exploring the question of how a historicizing, relativizing (that is to say, a modern) understanding of culture and human being refigure the core concerns of the classical German philosophical tradition. The sociological moment is, as it were, interior to his philosophy. Ironically, even as "Großstädte" became the founding text of the sociology of urban life, the questions Simmel was raising about the human significance of the transformations associated with rationalization and urbanization were marginalized as metaphysical. Selective strategies of reading helped (re)define sociology as a positive enterprise that could eschew the self-reflexive tangles of the dialectical tradition.

The fate of this essay typifies Simmel's impact on the discipline with which he is primarily identified: his psychological and sociological insights are celebrated while his theoretical and methodological contributions go unrecognized or misunderstood. For when the questions Simmel defined as central are set aside, the ways his analyses link sociological and philosophical dimensions become unrecognizable. In this formal respect, too, the history of Simmel's ambivalent reception in mainstream empirical sociology is theoretically significant. The selective citation and misleading translation of key concepts that have shaped the reception of the metropolis essay both reflect and perpetuate a way of reading Simmel that helps obscure the questions his work raises about the status of sociological analysis and indeed of sociology itself.

For Simmel, the social is a process, and in a very significant sense, his sociological work is not "about" anything outside that process itself. In his approach, style is substance. The "luxuriantly rich personal knowledge and subtle imagination" Levine et al. praised find expression in a distinctive mode of writing characterized by series of phenomenological descriptions formulated and arranged to foster philosophical self-reflection by the reader—an approach celebrated by enthusiastic contemporary witnesses as modernist *Zeitdeutung*. When Simmel is read from within the discipline of sociology, however, it is in search of something categorically different from such a self-reflexive encounter with sociocultural reality: non-contingent, generalizable, objective—"scientific"—truth. Thus on one hand, his descriptions of the psychological effects of metropolitan existence are given independent existence as empirical claims, while, on the other, his analyses of social "forms" are abstracted from their larger argumentative context and assimilated to a quasi-structuralist "formal sociology." Simmel's strategies of thought have thereby been appropriated for an understanding of social theory in which the pragmatic ethical and epistemological questions that concerned him fall out of the picture.

As in the case of any dialectical thinker, readings that assume that form can be distinguished from content are guaranteed to miss the point. What might be called Simmel's "unscientific method," his modernist challenge to the reader to think with him about the world he describes, is rendered unrecognizable when his texts become quarries for gleaning acutely observed examples and abstracting out reified "theories of" various sociological phenomena.

The proliferation of seemingly incompatible readings and images of Simmel—excessively formalist; immersed in particulars; metaphysical; psychologizing—is symptomatic of something more than quotidian misunderstanding. It suggests that in some very basic way, what is going on in his texts is illegible from within the discipline of sociology. Precisely because his work challenges foundational (and thus often largely tacit) conceptual and methodological assumptions, the distortions and misunderstandings that characterize Simmel's reception in sociology are not easily corrected. The consequences of the psychologizing translation of *Geistesleben* illustrate the larger difficulty: such hermeneutic practices both produce and reinforce an understanding of concepts and of legitimate modes of argumentation that is fundamentally at odds with his philosophical approach.

Simmel's dialectical strategies of interpretation are incompatible with the rhetoric of reflection that has come to define the parameters of acceptable social scientific discourse. His marginalization within the dominant narrative thus exposes how disciplinary history serves present needs even as the ways his texts are (mis)read reveal a great deal about what, in both the genetic and explanatory senses, constitutes sociology as a discipline. For if Simmel's marginalization within sociology registers the illegibility of his work from within the dominant disciplinary paradigm, his status as (mostly) forgotten founding father marks a blind spot within the rhetoric of inquiry that constitutes social science itself. The tension between acknowledgment and disavowal that runs through his reception history is theoretically as well as historically significant. Not only has neglecting or misconstruing Simmel's methodological achievements helped establish a focus on structure over process in the modern social sciences, a strategy for (seemingly) transcending the contingency and historicity of thought. Marginalizing Simmel as (too) "philosophical" has also helped occlude the metaphysical striving that shapes those disciplines as sciences—the drive to establish a perspective for reflection securely outside the historical fray and thereby to render the irrational dimensions of human existence manageable and even predictable.

What remains a mostly unrecognized methodological contribution to social and cultural theory both in and beyond sociology turns on Simmel's nuanced understanding of the status of rationality in human life and on his sophisticated vision of inquiry into culture and society as a self-reflexive process. Drawing on the German philosophical tradition, with its emphasis on the complexities of interpreting reality that is (partially) constituted by one's own participation in it, Simmel develops strategies for pursuing objectivity while remaining aware of the effects of subjectivity. Keeping the perspectival aims of interpretation in the foreground, he integrates philosophical reflection into the practice of cultural analysis. His later work, with its emphasis on the category of life and the dilemmas of modern existence, brings into relief what is problematic in the notion of a science of the social: the question of whether it is possible, even in principle, to attain definitive and univocal transhistorical truths concerning the multifarious, historically changing reality of human interaction and cultural endeavor. As his account of the ways historically and socially developed forms of life shape and define subjective experience grew more subtle, Simmel increasingly emphasized the radically individualizing experience of problems of meaning that constitute humans as ethical-political beings.

Simmel's texts are often praised for their originality and insight and, as Levine et al. showed, his work provided topical and analytical orientation for sociology, as well as founding multiple lines of inquiry that have since become established subfields. And yet, because that discipline has remained largely blind to the meaning of Simmel's style of thought, in an important sense, his oeuvre has still not been read. Disavowing the significance of style in the broader sense means his texts can at once be recognized as original (and acknowledged as historically significant points of origin) and dismissed as theoretically incoherent (and thus methodologically irrelevant today). What makes Simmel a forgotten founding father—the disavowed significance of his dialectical style of thought—is also the blind spot of contemporary social scientific modes of inquiry. The genealogical significance of his oeuvre and of his modernist approach to philosophy for the disciplines that both subsume and exclude him is revealed by the imbrication of theoretical and historical dimensions in the story of Simmel's ambivalent reception.

This larger genealogical significance illuminates the pattern of failed renaissances in his reception history. Even demonstrating that Simmel was (as Levine et al. put it) "the only European scholar who ha[d] had a palpable influence on sociology in the United States throughout . . . the 20th century" does not necessarily change anything. Recognizing him as "founding father" is perfectly compatible with continuing to read his texts in the same ways; it need not lead to reexamination, let alone revision, of the scientific self-understanding dominant in the discipline.

The history of sociology in general and of sociological theory in particular remains, on the whole, a strikingly unhistorical enterprise. Robert Alun Jones's characterization from 1983 still holds: "most people who write the history of sociology . . . call themselves "theorists". . . . [and] view themselves as providing the *normative* framework within which the more *empirical* study of society *ought* to take place." To put it polemically, as social scientists, they have a fundamentally instrumental attitude toward theory. While such work may be enframed in historical narratives, these serve to consolidate and perpetuate the discipline rather than to examine or criticize its foundational epistemological or ontological assumptions. "Theory" in this sense is oriented, to invoke Robert K. Merton's classical distinction, toward systematic as opposed to historical questions about the development of sociology. From a systematic perspective, what Merton called "reading the masters" helps consolidate disciplinary achievements by redressing "the imperfect retrieval of past sociological theory that has not yet been fully absorbed in subsequent thought."[29] Such a broadly normative systematic orientation still survives even if suspicion of origins

---

29. Robert Alun Jones, "On Merton's 'History' and 'Systematics' of Sociological Theory," in Functions and Uses of Disciplinary Histories, ed. Loren Graham, Wolf Lepenies, and Peter Weingart (Dordrecht: D. Reidel, 1983), 123. In what quickly became a canonical essay, "On the 'History' and 'Systematics' of Sociological Theory," in his *On Theoretical Sociology: Five Essays, Old and New* (New York: Free Press, 1967), Robert K. Merton argued that the properly historical interest in the development of a scientific discipline must be distinguished from the way contemporary practitioners approach the works of their intellectual predecessors. For the latter, what is at stake is not the history of ideas per se but the "systematic substance" (1) of theories currently in use, for their goal is to be "effective rather than merely pious . . . to *use* earlier formulations of theory rather than simply commemorate them" (37). This essay forms the

in general and canons in particular has made it less true that, as Alun Jones put it, sociological theorists "ultimately... regard themselves as the guardians of a sacred canon of 'classic texts' whose pages yield timeless truths of continuing relevance to their contemporaries."[30]

From the point of view of historians of the social sciences, this systematic approach appears methodologically problematic: the normative orientation covers a range of historiographical sins. Thus in his introduction to a 1997 volume of essays, *Reclaiming the Sociological Classics*, directed against the predominant, "presentist," approach to social theory, Charles Camic echoed the complaints about scholarly standards made by Levine et al. more than twenty years earlier. Even leaving aside those who in principle opposed invoking canonical "dead theorists" to advance contemporary work, the discipline appeared to Camic to be on shaky ground. The systematic understanding of sociological theory provided carte blanche for a perpetual return to an imagined ground zero. Thus, Camic wrote, "the massive disregard, even by those sociologists who remain interested in classical sociological theory, of the findings and interpretations contained in the existing scholarly literature" had produced "an academic area largely bereft of cumulative development: an area where one sees, in paper after paper, article after article, book after book, a repetition of the same misleading stereotypes and distorting clichés about the classical theorists that serious scholarship on the subject dissolved long ago, though to very little avail."[31]

In this respect, the peculiarities of Simmel's reception reflect more general features of the ahistorical understanding of theory dominant in sociology. In "systematic" approaches, the epistemological assumptions that anchor the discipline's self-understanding vis-à-vis philosophy have been institutionalized in reading practices that reinforce that very ahistorical self-understanding. Sociology is thereby assimilated to the dominant social scientific rhetoric of inquiry, which eschews historicizing self-reflection while laying claim to theoretical transparency and objectivity—the rhetoric that, in a word, denies the claims of history in the name of (scientific) truth.

But it is far easier to criticize the claims to transhistorical validity made on behalf of the social sciences than to define what constitutes an adequately historical perspective on theory. Despite what often appears to be a radical disjunction between Simmel's texts and the ways they have been understood and appropriated, as the history of his reception attests, clichés and misreadings cannot simply be set aside. As appealing as the notion of a "return to the texts themselves" might be, every attempt to enact such a return is beset by genuine difficulties, some of which are rooted in the historicity of texts and the ways ideas are embedded in culture. It is not

---

first chapter of Part I of Merton's much-revised *Social Theory and Social Structure* (New York: Free Press, 1968), from which it is quoted here and in subsequent parenthetical citations in the text.

30. Jones, "On Merton's 'History,'" 123. Jones illustrates what he calls "disgraceful practices in the history of sociology" with an example of "the theorist, committed to present 'truths'" who "quickly reduces the task of *reading* the *Elementary Forms* to one of 'finding' within it Durkheim's 'contribution' to those ideas, themes, or problems currently regarded as constitutive of the discipline" (124).

31. Camic, ed., *Reclaiming the Sociological Classics*, 6–7.

just that problematic interpretations may have had a significant impact on how texts are understood within disciplinary traditions. In the case of classic texts, it is probably the rule rather than the exception that their canonical status has been (partly) constituted by readings that are, philologically speaking, demonstrably inaccurate. Moreover, since reading is itself embedded in history and context, it is no simple matter to return to forgotten or misread predecessors. We must first become aware of the distortions and difficulties that arise out of habitual practices of interpretation, examine the web of assumptions and expectations with which we have always already begun to read "classic" thinkers.

If Simmel's stature as a thinker is to be recognized, it is necessary to rediscover what the discipline of sociology has systematically forgotten in remembering him as a founding father. For while his person and selected elements of his work continued to be invoked throughout the twentieth century, the history of reception—of appropriation—traced by Levine et al. illustrates the dashing of Albion Small's hope that sociology might build secure scientific foundations starting from "Simmel's desire for a methodology." Instead, Simmel's conception of sociology was marginalized in the very process through which the modern discipline became institutionally established and sociologists came to understand themselves as "social scientists" in possession of reliable methods. The pattern of selective appropriation that characterizes Simmel's reception reflects this disciplinary evolution: philosophical questions about the status of inquiry into the social were largely set aside as not just dialectical but qualitative approaches and styles of thought of all stripes increasingly took a back seat to quantitative methods, utilitarian considerations, and instrumentalist modes of reasoning. Read against the grain, the history and historiography of sociology make visible the process that constituted the methodological blind spot that marginalizes Simmel and his vision of (social, cultural) theory.

For Simmel did not just emphasize the importance of understanding sociology as a historical formation constituted by the turn to historical and cultural self-reflexivity that marked all modern disciplines in (what subsequently came to be called) the humanities and social sciences. He rejected what effectively became naturalized as an ontological postulate of modern social science: that society as such exists and thus can serve as an independent object of empirical investigation. As that way of thinking gained sway, what Simmel viewed as central philosophical problems—from the threat to subjective freedom and autonomy in a bureaucratized world to the ascendance of the intellectual and calculative over the emotional and creative dimensions of human life, from the dominance of instrumental rationality in everyday interactions to the wholesale eclipse of ends by means—also became naturalized as objective features of the modern world.

The decoupling of the "sociological" from the "philosophical" takes place through practices of reading that are ways of both remembering and forgetting Simmel's achievements. The example of the metropolis essay illustrates how decontextualizing and abstracting his "sociological" insights served to extend his analyses in new directions at the expense of rendering his method illegible and thereby foreclosing what was at stake for Simmel philosophically in reflecting on social and cultural phenomena—stakes that are no means merely historical.

The mode of reading I call appropriation by fragments is articulated through specific sorts of editorial practices that function institutionally to reinforce the categorization of Simmel as sociologist—and obscure his philosophical achievements. As bits and pieces of his texts are cited and recited, his complex, yet coherent modernist approach to thinking social and cultural life, encompassing innovative theoretical strategies for interpreting subjective and objective developments alike as forms of life change over time and in different settings, is obscured. To render visible what made Simmel's work so influential for all sorts of reflection on culture in the twentieth century will therefore entail both exposing the ways philosophical questions motivated and shaped his conception of sociology and considering the theoretical significance of his methods and style of thought.

It will be helpful to examine Simmel's reception history more closely before turning to the constructive task of reading him as (modernist) philosopher. The significance of his approach only becomes apparent when the history of contemporary cultural and critical theory is understood to include the (institutional and theoretical) process by which he was at once canonized and marginalized, for his approach to theorizing social and cultural life was rendered invisible as part of the very process of establishing the reigning understanding of sociology in the United States. Recovering his reception history is theoretically and methodologically crucial, for Simmel's strengths are the discipline's blind spots, and what is foreclosed when he becomes a forgotten founding father constitutes sociology institutionally and as such.

Rereading Misreading: "Simmel" in America

In his 1997 book *Georg Simmel and the American Prospect*, Gary D. Jaworski developed a new reading of the history of Simmel's impact on American sociology that emphasized the importance of interpretive traditions over fidelity to original sources. Jaworski charged that in privileging the category of influence, with its "astrological origins," Levine et al.'s "approach neglects to consider the interpretive dialectic between Simmel's writings and their readers."[32] From a perspective that emphasizes reception, what they had regarded as misreadings appear in a different light: as "strategic social action" (2). Jaworski proposed to produce an alternative account that emphasized "the interpretive creativity of Simmel's readers as opposed to the sheer force of his ideas" (x) by focusing on "the practical meaning or significance of his ideas for a range of American social thinkers" (xi). Bracketing concerns about philological accuracy and intellectual genealogy, he approached "translations as strategic resources in contests over moral or political issues" in which the texts themselves and the ideas and interpretations put forward became "forms of social action" (26) for Simmel's American readers.

Jaworski reframes the story of Simmel's reception in relation to broader themes in American cultural history. Inspired by Dorothy Ross's exploration of the political

---

32. Jaworski, *Georg Simmel*, x. Subsequent citations in the text refer to this source.

and cultural stakes of social science in the United States,[33] his narrative centers on the role of "national ideals" such as "democracy, individuality, [and] racial tolerance" in the constructive use of Simmel's work by thinkers who aspired "to transform American society, to shape its future, to influence the American prospect" (xii). Jaworski's history draws on archival and biographical sources to illuminate both the social sciences' "dialogue with American ideals and ideologies" (xi) and the ways in which Simmel's ideas were deployed in American sociology. In the story he tells, what for Levine et al. are misreadings become productive appropriations.

There is considerable merit in Jaworski's approach. Not only is the line between original and interpretation necessarily blurred in the case of texts that function as canonical sources for disciplinary formations. An openness to appropriation is inscribed in Simmel's own writing, and his modernist style of theorizing stands in a complex relation to his canonical status. However, Jaworski's support of readers' prerogatives extends too far, obscuring the significance of the tension between recognition and misrecognition that marks his reception history. In affirming the strategic appropriation of Simmel's ideas through the prism of American sociology's ideological and pragmatic orientation, he comes dangerously close to taking the self-understanding of the disciplinary mainstream at face value.

For example, even though he acknowledges that Simmel himself upheld an ethic of individual autonomy, rather than that of "reciprocity and mutual dependence" favored by Park and Small (127, n. 12), he endorses the way Park's anthologization of a selection from Simmel's *Soziologie* of 1908 supports the latter's own position. "When read along with the two essays that precede it," Jaworski asserts, "the ethical import of Simmel's ideas become [*sic*] manifest" (19).[34] Surely this is taking the emphasis on the reader's "interpretive creativity" too far: however legitimate it may be to deploy texts for purposes foreign to their authors' stated positions and intentions, that such appropriation is possible hardly proves that one is thereby accessing a deeper truth about the original.[35]

This point bears special emphasis because Simmel's reception in the Anglophone world has in fact largely come in the form of excerpts in anthologies. Even today, only seven of Simmel's many books have been rendered into English in their entirety,[36] and a fraction of his hundreds of essays have been translated. Conversely, much of what has been anthologized and continues to be treated in the secondary

33. Dorothy Ross, *The Origins of American Social Science* (Cambridge: Cambridge University Press, 1991).

34. Similarly, in his discussion of Simmel's impact on functionalist sociology, Jaworski takes the demonstration that Parsons, Merton, Naegele, and Coser "found in Simmel not only intellectual inspiration, but moral wisdom" as a proof that "rather than being peripheral to functional sociology . . . Simmel was a key architect of its intellectual and moral vision" (44).

35. On the contrary: since Simmel wrote extensively about ethical matters throughout his career, if American readers placed his sociological texts in the service of positions incompatible with his articulated philosophical positions, it would seem to be prima facie evidence that such a selective reception has distorted the ethical import of his work.

36. *The Problems of the Philosophy of History, Philosophy of Money, Schopenhauer and Nietzsche, Rembrandt, Sociology, View of Life*, three of which appeared in the last decade. *Kant and Goethe*, originally a monograph, also appeared in *TCS* in 2007. See Thomas Kemple, "Simmel in English," in Thomas M.

literature as "essays" are actually excerpts from longer works. Those who do not read German receive Simmel's texts in and through frames created by editors with objectives by definition distinct from the author's.

Even when such editing does not, as in the case of Park and Burgess, entail reframing his ideas in terms Simmel would have rejected, it inevitably obscures even as it reveals. By grouping essays and fragments of larger texts together under overarching thematic categories, anthologization fosters a mode of reception centered on Simmel's contributions to fields and areas of inquiry (conflict theory, organizational theory, the study of small groups, etc.) alien to his own conceptual horizon. This systematizing approach also tends to elide the changes in his thought over time. Even anthologies produced by scholars like Levine or Frisby who regard intellectual history as substantively relevant for social theory have adopted these disciplinary editing conventions and thereby contributed to the resulting abstraction of Simmel's sociological thought from his philosophy as a whole. That abstraction, in turn, has encouraged reading practices that are especially problematic in light of Simmel's modernist style and perspectivist philosophical commitments: a presentist approach to theorizing that appropriates Simmel by fragments, deploying isolated "ideas" or "concepts" without regard for textual or argumentative context.

Jaworski's contextualist reception history opens a new perspective on Simmel's impact on American social thought. Shifting the emphasis from fidelity to interpretation, from origin to appropriation, reveals a history of thought distinct from the traditional history of ideas, a history that bears consideration even—perhaps especially—when the readings in question are poorly anchored in Simmel's texts. The ways readers' purposes and horizons of expectation have shaped his image in America constitutes, for better or worse, the point from which new thinking must proceed. Situating the multivalence of canonical texts in historical context demonstrates that the history of theory must take account of the sociology of knowledge and shows that an adequate account of disciplinary history must encompass cultural perspectives.

In his book and in subsequent work on the history of sociology in New York City, Jaworski demonstrated that a great deal was at stake institutionally as well as intellectually in the selective ways Simmel was read after World War II. Beginning in the 1940s, Albert Salomon, who had studied with both Simmel and Max Weber, offered "penetrating insights into Simmel's links to the phenomenological tradition" at the New School.[37] However, neither Salomon's interpretation nor his style of reading achieved real traction. The sociological tradition represented by the New School, which even today retains its orientation toward Europe and (continental) philosophy, became increasingly marginal to the disciplinary mainstream in postwar America. Uptown, at Columbia, beginning in the mid-1950s, "Merton and his colleagues abandoned continental intellectual styles" (7) to develop their anti-historicist and

---

Kemple and Olli Pyyhtinen, *The Anthem Companion to Georg Simmel* (London and New York: Anthem Press, 2016), 191–98, for an updated bibliography.

37. Gary D. Jaworski. "Contested Canon: Simmel Scholarship at Columbia and the New School," *American Sociologist* 29, no. 2 (1998): 1.

overtly anti-philosophical mode of theorizing—and an approach to disciplinary history likewise rooted in Parsonian structural functionalism.

The rise of this new paradigm defined sociology as a modern, scientific discipline by transforming its relation to the past. As Jaworski shows, Merton's vision of sociology "as a 'special science' focused on the structural factors of social life" helped Columbia invent a tradition with institutional as well as conceptual cohesion. Merton and Paul Lazarsfeld "joined formal theory with research methodology" to integrate faculty and student research into a coherent and fundable collective research program and "helped form a school of thought that ensured Columbia's place as one of the country's leading departments" (7). As the increasingly complex governmental and bureaucratic apparatus of postwar U.S. society established new standards and practices for institutional success, the hegemonic function acquired by social scientific strategies of thought within the disciplinary regime of the modern research university was taking on contours. The emerging institutional and intellectual landscape was built upon a new kind of narrative imagining of the discipline's past. Merton's "rereading of the sociological tradition, not as a history of great thinkers or a tale of theoretical convergence, but as a repository of structuralist insights" (7) was of great consequence for the social sciences as a whole. While earlier social theorists, including his predecessors at Columbia, had emphasized the links between sociology and philosophy, "Mertonian structural-functionalism . . . severed the connection" between them (7), passing over the philosophical (pre) history of modern social science and social theory largely in silence.[38]

Severing Simmel's sociological work from its larger philosophical context in this way helped Merton to turn structuralism into the dominant research program in the United States after World War II. Merton's work also led to a Simmel renaissance of sorts by placing his ideas at the service of a new "style of theorizing." Yet Merton not only explicitly excluded Simmel's philosophical and cultural texts from the sociological canon. As Jaworski shows, he also established a practice of reading that eschewed the standards of conventional humanistic scholarship by making no effort "to better understand Simmel on his own terms" (8). "In place of a historical and systematic examination of Simmel's writings, Merton developed a strategy of extracting and extending Simmel's structuralist insights" that began with a distinctive method of teaching (7). In his seminars, there was "neither an exegesis nor a contextual examination of the text" (8). "The basic approach of each seminar session" was to take up the "raw material" of selected passages and "rephrase" its intellectual content "in terms of contemporary issues or concepts in order to extend, revise,

---

38. Merton more or less excluded philosophy from his theoretical canon altogether, Jaworski points out: "In more than 600 pages, Hegel and Nietzsche are cited once each, and there are no citations of Plato or Aristotle, Kant or Kierkegaard, Schopenhauer or Bergson." Drawing on interviews with participants and on documentation supplied by Merton himself, he also notes the narrow focus on Simmel's early sociological writings to the exclusion of other texts: "Simmel's cultural or philosophical works, indeed even his other sociological writings, would have been read by Merton's students only either outside class or later in their careers" (ibid., 7).

or update the ideas"(7). This practice established sociology's autonomy at the cost of abandoning the connection not only to philosophy but to the wider history of reflection on culture, performatively anchoring a new, distinctively social scientific relation to the traditions out of which the discipline had emerged.

The result was less an alternative history of sociology than a way of writing history out of social science. Although himself a distinguished exponent of "literate" sociology who both advocated and practiced engagement with classical social thinkers, Merton saw the future of the discipline in a systematic, progressive, and "scientific" approach to social theory. For him, paradoxically, undertaking the "historical analysis of the development of theory" as a whole therefore meant abandoning the "humanistic" approach to disciplinary history and eliminating what would come to be seen as an irrelevant emphasis on origins and originality.[39] This valorization of work on the putatively cumulative body of "systematic" social theory over "the scholastic practice of commentary and exegesis" (37) profoundly impacted sociological praxis. Merton can hardly be regarded as a Nietzschean, yet his methodological innovations form an important thread in the resistance of contemporary social theory to questions of origin once fetishized in the sort of historicism Nietzsche skewered.

"Reading the masters" was a means of retrieving past insights and consolidating the intellectual legacy of sociology into a constructive and forward-looking enterprise that replaced (humanistic) self-reflexivity with social scientific objectivity. Distinguishing a systematic from an historicist approach to social theory made it possible to uphold the normative model of scientific progress supposedly embodied in the physical and life sciences even though, as Merton conceded, the "process of obliteration by incorporation [of past knowledge] is still rare in sociology" (35). But this ahistorical approach to history established sociology as a science at the cost of occluding reflection on its historicity—that is to say, on its cultural existence. Indeed, as Alun Jones pointed out, Merton's now-classic meditation on history and theory in sociology suffers from a "glaring omission ... of any discussion whatever of the putative value of the authentic "history" of theory for its "systematic" counterpart."[40] This omission is all the more striking in that Merton explicitly recognizes the achievements of contemporary historians such as Thomas Kuhn, who had appropriated sociological methods to write new kinds of "analytic histories" of science (3).

Sociology's intellectual origins in the rise of historical consciousness are indisputable, and exclusion of historical self-reflection as "humanist" marked a discursive paradigm shift of profound consequence. By redefining the history of social thought as a "repository of structuralist insights" accessible via a decontextualizing method of analysis, Merton decisively shaped what would become the dominant rhetoric of reflection in twentieth-century sociology. For a discipline that understood itself as "scientific" and "objective" both in contrast to and in relation to its predecessors, the history of ideas was not per se of interest. Contemporary

---

39. Merton, "On the History and Systematics of Sociological Theory" (1967), in id., *Social Theory and Social Structure*, 23. All parenthetical citations of Merton in this and the following paragraph refer to this source.

40. Jones, "On Merton's 'History,'" 135.

standards defined what constituted well-formed sociological questions and acceptable modes of argumentation, and the development of social thought came to be identified with a logical evolution whose culturally contingent vicissitudes were not theoretically relevant. This ahistorical approach to history effectively limited reflection on the significance of ideas to examining the formal, functional, and logical relations among them, creating an account that reflexively reinforced its own epistemological and ontological assumptions. History was not simply excluded: the complex web of contextual connections between ideas was emptied out and converted into scientifically accessible propositions. The success of structural functionalism in postwar America established this practice of selective reading—which treated other kinds of questions about the history of social and cultural thought as anachronistic throwbacks to a prescientific era—as the dominant approach within the social sciences as a whole.

There have, of course, always been alternative streams that emphasize the vital links between sociological thought and older cultural traditions, but these are situated outside the disciplinary mainstream and tend to be identified with European scholarship. The ascendance of "systematic" social theory redefined the disciplinary past in a way that marginalized historical self-reflection itself. From the point of view of the broader (intellectual and cultural) history of thought, what is at stake here is not the historiography of theory as such but the way this discursive organization and the assumptions about method it embodies established disciplinary claims to scientific status. "Explication du texte is a dying art, while methods that ape the natural sciences are de rigueur in graduate schools across the United States. European-style scholarship, with its ties to philosophy and literature, has been rejected as old-fashioned and replaced by an American brand of academic work tied to scientific advance and social improvement," Jaworski observed of the disciplinary status quo "in the American academy" in 1998 ("Contested Canon," 6). If in the early years what Small dubbed "the expediency of semiconscious desperation" (Small, "Review of *The Social Theory of Georg Simmel*," 86) led sociologists to make inflationary claims about the discipline's scientific accomplishments that pushed aside questions about philosophical foundations, the legacy of structural functionalism is a disciplinary rhetoric proudly blind to its intellectual origins.

Among theorists, sociology's ahistorical and scientistic self-understanding would increasingly come under fire as the foundational assumptions of structuralism began to be called into question. But the developments that followed hardly entailed a return to history or a wholesale rethinking of the discipline's relationship to philosophy. On the contrary, in the face of critics who, for all sorts of reasons, tended to regard the canon with suspicion, the normative and pragmatic understanding of sociological theory (which had always been compatible with a vision of the discipline as socially engaged) proved adaptable. Disciplinary traditions and habits die hard, and, as the frustrated remarks of their historically trained colleagues signal, properly historical concerns about sociology's past remain largely illegible for many of those who understand themselves as sociological theorists. In the end, though, these may be internecine battles, for despite the purported "cultural(ist) turn" around the advent of the twenty-first century, mainstream American sociological praxis is still characterized by a fairly unsophisticated empiricism and the inherited "ethic of instrumental activism."

Simmel's thought, with its intertwining of "sociological" and "philosophical" perspectives, fits most uneasily into that larger American tradition. How much is at stake is obscured by a reception still implicitly shaped by structural functionalism and especially by translations produced in dialogue with the scientistic sociological tradition. Only a small portion of Simmel's properly philosophical writings have even been rendered into English, and by shaping readers' perceptions of his significance in terms of topics and themes external or tangential to the original context of his writing, practices of selective anthologization have helped widely to establish the notion that Simmel was primarily a sociologist—if an unusual and interesting one. In methodological terms, it can hardly be regarded as surprising that Anglophone readers tend to emphasize the fragmentary quality of Simmel's writing, his essayistic tendencies, and the prismatic and incomplete character of his works, when the textual basis consists almost exclusively of short essays and fragments of longer works! In this formal sense, too, Simmel's reception history has obscured the philosophical significance of his style of thought.

This brings us back to the problem of misreading. "Full appreciation of Simmel has been hampered by widespread clichés about his life and work that are misleading when not distorting. Many of those misleading notions have been purveyed by scholars who, for a time or in certain respects, sought to champion Simmel," Donald N. Levine observes in his contribution to *Reclaiming the Sociological Classics* ("Simmel Reappraised," 175). Levine advanced example after example of distortions that scholarship on Simmel had long since redressed. Unfortunately, his eloquent attempt to let the facts speak for themselves and thereby to undo the clichés "pertaining to Simmel's place in intellectual history," as well as "to the substance of his theories" (176), seems to have fallen on deaf ears. Even today, Simmel's reputation as an unsystematic dilettante, a rich aesthete dabbling in a philosophy that amounts to thinly disguised bourgeois ideology persists, as does the potted intellectual history according to which he "started as a positivistic Darwinist, became a neo-Kantian in mid-life, and was converted to a Bergsonian *Lebensphilosophie* during his last decade" (179). And it remains true that Simmel's reputation as an unsystematic thinker "persists tenaciously, in spite of the fact that numerous scholarly investigations have revealed a striking degree of coherence in Simmel's thought" (196). All too often, these clichés continue to be "purveyed" by those who really ought to know better, masquerading under a positive sign, as in the assimilation of Simmel to a nebulously defined "postmodernism" or in affirmations of his "essayism" that fail to interrogate the dialectical significance of his fragmentary style of thought.

However much leeway one is willing to grant to Jaworski's emphasis on readerly creativity and on the relativity of modes of knowing, there is certainly an argument to be made that Simmel's reception in the United States registers the effects of a "weak institutionalization of rigorous scholarly standards" in the discipline of sociology. Yet this is also a matter of perspective and theoretical framework. What counts as a good argument—what constitutes a well-formed claim, solid evidence, and a sufficiently persuasive account of the significance of the relations among those elements—is highly contextual. As the misunderstandings and misprisions within the Simmel literature show, historians and theorists do not always agree on these matters even among themselves. That his texts seem to embrace a profusion of incommensurable differences only complicates matters. As Levine put it, "the experience of coherence in Simmel's thought" is not immediately accessible to the reader struggling with "the undeniable experience of disjointedness . . . and with his apparent espousal of contradictory positions in different places" (202).

The question of how to read his texts thus opens onto a much larger matter: the theoretical and philosophical significance of Simmel's intellectual style, which could not be further from the contemporary social scientific ideal of empirically grounded exposition. The "experience of coherence in Simmel's thought" only becomes available to a reader willing and able to work through a textual surface wrought of tensions and contradictions: his philosophical and methodological achievements are tied up with a complex convergence of form (which can paradoxically appear as a lack of form) and method. Simmel's reputation as an unsystematic thinker reinforces the widespread incomprehension of his style of thought that is both a product and a symptom of the vicissitudes of his reception history in American sociology—that is to say, of the very process that established the selective textual foundation in and through which his reputation as the essayistic master of the fleeting insight is anchored in the Anglophone context.

The difficulty of reading Simmel's texts, then, is a complex function of (largely unarticulated), historically and culturally situated, disciplinarily specific assumptions about the nature of social and cultural theorizing. But what makes such assumptions so practically as well as theoretically intractable? When Levine et al. drew attention in their study "Simmel's Influence on American Sociology" to the effects of Simmel's style of thought on American readers in 1976, they ventured a sociological explanation for the history of incomprehension they had traced. A cultural intolerance for complexity and indeterminacy was at work: "the ambiguities, dualistic conceptions, and dialectical aspects of Simmel's thinking have often been screened out by those trained in American modes of thought, which stress univocality and one-dimensional metrics" (II, 1128). The result was a practice of reading characterized by systematic distortion: "even when American sociologists have drawn on Simmel's ideas in their own research, they have often patently misrepresented what Simmel was saying" (I, 822). Such errors and clichés were grounded, then, in what might be called stylistic features of American intellectual culture: an intolerance for ambiguity, itself codified into an ahistorical rhetoric of reflection that characterizes so much theorizing both in and beyond the social sciences.

Simmel's style of thought, deeply embedded in continental philosophical traditions, appears incompatible with that culturally dominant rhetoric of reflection. His strategies for getting his ideas across were ill-suited to an audience with a highly pragmatic, even instrumentalist, approach to theoretical foundations and an allergic attitude toward philosophical reflection. What Levine et al. characterize as an indigenous intolerance for the complexity and indeterminacy of Simmel's thought, the "ambiguities, dualistic conceptions, and dialectical aspects" of his writings, literally led American readers to "screen out" much of what is most interesting and most important in his work—those ideas and methods most challenging to what, given the international hegemony of American social science in the postwar period, would become very much the dominant conception of sociology internationally. Since this screening process literally shaped the corpus of texts available, at every level, the occlusions that characterize Simmel's reception in the United States are as much about style as substance.

Styles of Thought and the Rhetoric of Disciplinarity

Argumentative style is a function of disciplinary culture: Sociological discourse is defined by a rhetoric of reflection that embodies a quite specific (though not unchanging) vision of what makes for a good argument. If this rhetoric is viewed historically, Simmel's status as forgotten founding father appears as a symptom of the way the discipline's cultural and historical origins were systematically obscured in the course of sociology's becoming a "science"—that is to say, casting aside the remnants of its origins in German *Wissenschaft*, with its associations with the European philosophical tradition, and establishing the modes of inquiry and conventions of presentation and argument that characterize the contemporary discipline.

But rhetorical effects extend beyond exclusion and forgetting. If the intolerance for ambiguity and dialectics that has characterized Simmel's reception is a positive feature of a characteristically American social scientific disciplinary culture, the peculiarities of his reception cannot be treated as errors in a straightforward sense—or explained as the consequence of a "relatively weak institutionalization of rigorous scholarly standards within American sociology." However understandable it is that historians of the discipline, confronted with a problematic and inaccurate image of Simmel that seems quite resistant to correction, have echoed that assessment, such an interpretation betrays a quite un-Simmelian (and undialectical) attachment to a particular interpretive framework.

Doubtless a broadly ambivalent attitude among practicing sociologists toward the discipline's history and in particular toward the history of social theory becomes visible in the selective attention to the theoretical corpus and frequent neglect of predecessors Levine et al. described. But the ahistorical rhetoric of reflection that dominates social scientific discourse more generally, and the hermeneutic practices that correspond to it, are not simply a consequence of the dominant empiricist orientation of those disciplines. That rhetoric and those practices also register the theoretical legacy of structuralism and of the full range of late twentieth-century rebellions against canons and canonical thinkers within American social science.

On George W. Stocking Jr.'s Kuhnian reading, the ordinary operation of these disciplines more or less precludes historical (self)-reflection: "the more a social scientific practitioner is committed to the 'scientism' of his discipline, the less likely he is to see it as an historical growth conditioned in a variety of subtle ways by an intricate complexity of contextual influences."[41] The striving after an a- or transhistorical perspective is a constitutive feature of the social scientific rhetoric of reflection.

Precisely because Simmel's ambiguous status as a (mostly forgotten, disavowed) founding father is theoretically significant for American sociology, it is no simple matter to overcome the clichés and distortions that continue to characterize his reception. Placing his reception history in historical and theoretical context opens up a new perspective on the significance of such persistent misreadings—and on his importance for twentieth-century intellectual history. Beginning in the 1890s, Simmel eloquently and consistently raised philosophical questions about the nature and status of sociology. If these questions have more or less been written out of the story of the discipline in the United States despite the efforts of generations of scholars to bring them to the fore, it is not only because they have been misunderstood and ignored but also, at least in part, because their importance has been denied and rejected. As they "patently misrepresented what Simmel was saying" to translate his ideas into an American idiom, Simmel's sociological readers were creating, as it were, the disciplinary unconscious.

In their ambiguity or, better, multivocity, Simmel's texts point beyond their ostensible objects of analysis to a realm of epistemological self-reflection foreclosed by the systematic approach to social theory. Forced into the procrustean bed of positivist sociology, they literally become illegible. The incomprehension and misreadings rampant within the Anglophone literature are both effect and cause of a reception that disregards Simmel's philosophical oeuvre almost entirely.

The paradoxical combination of recognition and misrecognition, acknowledgement and disavowal, of Simmel's contributions to twentieth-century social thought reflects the ambivalent relationship to the philosophical tradition that continues to characterize the discipline of sociology in the United States more generally. If Simmel's approach is illegible from within the dominant rhetoric of sociological reflection, it is not simply because a historical relationship is being disavowed. His peculiar position as forgotten founding father marks a constitutive blind spot in the disciplinary rhetoric of reflection. For Simmel, the "problem of sociology" is itself the issue of the situatedness of modes of reflection. But in pursuit of a scientific sociology that could transcend its own contingency and situatedness, the discipline's "scientific" status was performatively constituted by obscuring its philosophical origins. That Simmel has been so persistently and seemingly systematically misunderstood thus reveals the theoretical significance of his liminal disciplinary location—and suggests the urgency of returning to his work in a less blinkered fashion.

What is at stake in the (mis)readings of Simmel is not so much the status of sociology as a discipline as the question of the historicity of thinking, at least insofar as it is (reflection on) culture. If the history of theory is to evade the perils of idealism, it is crucial to grasp the historicity of the conceptual categories and strategies

---

41. Stocking, "The History of Anthropology: Where, Whence, Whither?" *Journal of the History of the Behavioral Sciences* 2, no. 4 (1966): 286, cited in Robert Alun Jones, "The New History of Sociology," *Annual Review of Sociology* 9 (1983): 451.

of thought that constitute the contemporary theoretical repertoire. In urging a return to Simmel's oeuvre as a site that can illuminate the contemporary disciplinary imaginary, my point is not simply that he has been underestimated as a philosopher. What from a contemporary point of view are his inter- or trans-disciplinary strategies of reflection preceded and helped constitute our distinctions between philosophy and sociology and more generally between social scientific and humanist modes of interpretation. If Simmel's work is to help us gain perspective on the disciplinary imaginary that shapes our own ways of understanding society and culture, we must beware anachronistically interpreting his work in the terms of the present configuration of inquiry. Grasping the subtlety and complexity of his modernist approach to philosophizing opens up a new way of getting at the importance of the cultural and discursive origins of the contemporary disciplinary order as a whole.

As my brief survey will have made clear, the readings and misreadings of Simmel that were constitutive for American sociology are emblematic of broader historical developments. The eclipse of historicist modes of thinking that helped bring the modern social sciences into being is part of a global shift in the dominant rhetoric of reflection in modernity through which instrumental styles of reasoning and modes of argument that take a reified conception of the (natural) scientific method as their ideal displaced dialectical strategies of thought. The practices of decontextualization so marked in Simmel's sociological reception may be regarded as paradigmatic for a new, self-consciously post-philosophical culture of inquiry marked simultaneously by a refusal of self-reflexivity and allegiance to this new a- or transhistorical "scientific" rhetoric of reflection.

Even those who would regard the fact that "explication du texte is a dying art" in sociology as a fatal methodological flaw often share the ahistorical understanding of theory that is part of the wider legacy of structuralism. It is by no means only within sociology that theory is treated as a "systematic" enterprise in which the interpretation of ideas is separable from historical and cultural contextualization. And it is by no means only in the social sciences that ideas are approached ahistorically and passages excised from larger works and treated as freestanding "theoretical contributions" to areas of inquiry defined in ways not just extrinsic to the original context but even hostile to an author's self-understanding. The same practices of decontextualization that became part of the basic methodological repertoire of the modern social sciences also shaped analytic philosophy and—however paradoxical this fact appears—helped define the wider set of practices that have come to be called "theory." To paraphrase Simmel, the fate of his thought is at once "symbol and mirror" of the development of (social, cultural) theory as a whole in the twentieth century.

Much of this book consists of precisely the sort of old-fashioned engagement with texts that is no longer "de rigueur" in the social sciences—not for antiquarian ends but rather in the service of what is at stake in the social sciences and the humanities alike: discovering resources for reflection on our collective situation. The history of Simmel's reception in American sociology is not simply "background" but reveals what cannot be seen when his thought is approached as the foundation of a science. And it suggests how much is rendered invisible when theorizing about culture and society is approached ahistorically and the modes of writing that constitute the modernist enterprise of creating a theoretical account of social and cultural life as such are treated as methodologically neutral. Simmel's way of approaching the sociohistorical situatedness of thought and his understanding of sociology amount to an implicit critique of what have since become established paradigms of interpretation and explanation.

Unsurprisingly, Simmel's work has remained most influential among those (whether inside or outside the discipline) who are most suspicious of the institutional success attained by sociology—that is to say, of the integration of a sociological vision of the social as an object of knowledge into the disciplinary and regulatory practices of modern bureaucratic institutions. On the whole, though, since sociologists both as readers and translators have largely established the terms for Simmel's reception in the wider Anglophone world, the lacunae that result from the illegibility of his approach from within the dominant social science paradigm have shaped the way he is read and perceived more generally. Unlike in the continental European literature, there is almost no reception of Simmel as a philosopher, and he is known more widely, if at all, as a founding father of sociology.[42]

To be sure, that image has been updated somewhat in recent years, but representations of Simmel as the "first sociologist of modernity" still bear the traces of his ambivalent embrace by the social sciences. In truncating his memory into a marginalizing sound bite that at once recognizes and obscures his theoretical achievements, contemporary (cultural) sociology continues to occlude its debt to philosophy. From a genealogical perspective, however, the marginal is anything but inessential. The blind spot in the rhetoric of inquiry made visible by Simmel's reception history is constitutive for modern social science itself, with its preference for quantitative over qualitative evidence and instrumental over dialectical modes of argumentation. For sociology, forgetfulness of its own origins—or, more precisely, of the significance of the history of the discipline—simultaneously defines it as a social science and blinds those who practice it to the limitations of their perspective.

Simmel's status as forgotten founding father of sociology epitomizes the discipline's troubled relationship to its philosophical origins. For him, truth could not be reduced to objectivity nor reason to rationality. In his work, this broader vision of logic—the legacy of the dialectical tradition—merges with a new kind of awareness of the historicity and perspectival nature of knowledge rooted in the ways Schopenhauer and Nietzsche linked meaning to value. Simmel's insistence that relativizing self-reflexivity characterizes all "the human sciences approached in a modern fashion" (*GSG* 5: 52) is a key element of his often unacknowledged legacy in continental

---

42. Remarkably, not a single American or British philosopher seems to have devoted a book to Simmel since Rudolph H. Weingartner's *Experience and Culture: The Philosophy of Georg Simmel* appeared (Middletown, CT: Wesleyan University Press, 1962). Nor, since Weingartner's 1959 Columbia dissertation of the same title, has his work been the focus of a North American dissertation in philosophy—though a 46-page MA thesis on "The Problem of Transcendence in Georg Simmel's Philosophy of Culture" was accepted at Clark University in 1979. As of February 2016, of the only twelve dissertations in the Proquest Dissertations and Theses database with "Simmel" in their titles, not one is in philosophy.

social and cultural theory. Reflection on the historical contingency and theoretical significance of the desubstantializing and contextualizing tendencies that constitute social science itself is strikingly lacking from the social scientific mainstream. In uncovering Simmel's achievement, we explore the significance of dimensions of the (historical, philosophical, cultural) imaginary that are constitutive for social scientific praxis but that do not form part of methodological self-consciousness.

Disciplining Culture

To conclude this examination of Georg Simmel as (mostly) forgotten founding father, let us revisit the methodological and historiographical issues raised by Klaus Christian Köhnke's effort to elevate him into a pantheon of human- and social scientific "classics" and anchor contemporary cultural philosophy through Simmel's "self-reflexive theory of the modern."[43] Delving a bit more deeply into this matter will help to clarify my own purpose in returning to Simmel and to differentiate this return from Köhnke's two decades ago.

The prehistory of contemporary cultural and critical theory takes on special interest and importance today. The institutional and intellectual transformations under way on the shifting disciplinary landscape of the contemporary academy reflect a social and cultural world gripped in change arguably as profound as that which marked the emergence of the "classical modern" in Simmel's lifetime. It is now amply clear that the political revolutions of the final decades of the twentieth century exacerbated an already virulent crisis of metanarrative frameworks. Within theoretical as well as practical life, the venerable modern optimism that change over time is tantamount to progress has come to appear increasingly dubious.

The conceptual scaffolding of cultural theory—the regime of oppositions, as it were, that stabilized the rhetoric of reflection through the Cold War period—having collapsed, the central terms of inherited theoretical discourse—"materialism," "science," "culture," and "criticism," to name a few—have been problematized in new ways. At the same time, the digital revolution is posing new challenges for scholarship. Critical, rigorous cultural inquiry must be redefined in a world where divisions between ideal and material, theoretical and empirical have been transformed by technology and reformed by virtual dimensions of representation, communication, and identity formation. With the terms of reflection and the disciplinary order itself in flux, the point when the modern social sciences emerged is particularly instructive.

Taking a broader view of the theoretical antecedents and intellectual as well as sociopolitical context of systematic reflection on society and culture at the previous fin de siècle significantly expands our perspective on the importance of Simmel's work. That as philosopher he provided intellectual inspiration for the new social movements, for literary theorists, and for the social sciences also throws into relief

43. Klaus Christian Köhnke, *Der junge Simmel in Theoriebeziehungen und sozialen Bewegungen* (Frankfurt am Main: Suhrkamp, 1996), 508. Regarding modernity and postmodenity, see my "Georg Simmels Phänomenologie der Kultur und der Paradigmenwechsel in den Geisteswissenschaften," in Willfried Geßner and Rüdiger Kramme, eds., *Aspekte der Geldkultur. Neue Studien zu Georg Simmels Philosophie des Geldes* (Berlin: Edition Humboldt, 2002), 29–62.

how much has been neglected within a theoretical discourse shaped (both positively and reactively) by Marxist conceptual categories.[44] Once it is no longer measured against its success or failure in advancing historical materialism, Simmel's oeuvre can be seen to make available a range of interpretive resources, and Köhnke did contemporary cultural theory and the historiography of the social sciences an important service by contextualizing those strategies of reflection, and in particular Simmel's breakthrough conception of social form, in a long and complex genealogy of systematic reflection on culture very much alive in Moritz Lazarus and Heymann Steinthal's *Völkerpsychologie,* with its non-idealist vision of *Geist.*[45] Foregrounding Simmel's place in an often-neglected philosophical tradition stretching back beyond Humboldt to the cosmopolitan Kant and his renegade student Herder, resituates our understanding of the emergence of the modern social sciences in relation to a more public sense of philosophizing in tension with the professionalization of humanistic inquiry in the same period.

Yet Köhnke was committed to a disciplinary project—developing a historically articulated philosophy of culture to provide a theoretical foundation for the human and cultural sciences—that does not really coincide with Simmel's own conception of the task of philosophy in modernity. What now appear as Simmel's inter- or transdisciplinary theoretical contributions reflect a synthetic, nonprofessionalized vision of philosophy that consistently interrogated disciplinary and other boundaries that seem self-evident today.

From the beginning of his studies, Simmel's thinking was shaped by multiple perspectives on human cultural life: by art history and Schmoller's political economy; by Darwin, Spencer, and Adolf Bastian;[46] by literature, music, and the Italian Renaissance. His position on the margins of the university allowed for considerable freedom in his intellectual pursuits, and his prominence made him influential, both

---

44. The image of Simmel as a disengaged aesthete has in recent years yielded in the German literature to a more complex recognition of his engagement with a variety of modernist cultural movements, at least in the early years. Ralph Leck attempted to square the circle by drawing attention to what he calls "Geist-Politik" and "highlighting the political ambiguity of Simmel's Nietzschean legacy: a combination of anti-capitalist egalitarianism and cultural elitism" (Leck, *Simmel and Avant-Garde Sociology: The Birth of Modernity, 1880–1920* [Amherst, NY: Humanity Books, 2000], 17). Focusing on Simmel's impact on a modernist avant-garde that included politically radical figures such as Kurt Hiller and first-wave feminists such as Marianne Weber and Helene Stöcker, Leck rightly points out that the received view of Wilhelminian Berlin ignores considerable cultural ferment. Unfortunately, his lack of critical attention to the question of disciplinarity issues in an account that fails to address Simmel's importance as a philosopher independently of the question of his historical significance.

45. Lazarus had the greater personal impact on Simmel. But as Köhnke notes (*Der junge Simmel*, 58), his rejected dissertation on the origins of music drew on Steinthal's "epoch-making" work on the origins of language (*Der Ursprung der Sprache im Zusammenhange mit den letzten Fragen alles Wissens* [4th rev. ed., Berlin, 1988]). A distinguished and influential linguist and philologist who held an extraordinary professorship at the Berlin University, Steinthal was also a founding member of the Berlin Society for Anthropology, Ethnology, and Primitive History and among other things edited Wilhelm von Humboldt's linguistic works and established the methodological foundations of linguistic anthropology.

46. Another of Simmel's teachers who, like Lazarus, also influenced Franz Boas, Bastian was the founder both of the German Anthropological Society and Berlin's Ethnographic Museum; his conception of a "world archive" was the guiding principle for the practice of collecting that defined this new sort of museum.

directly, through his teaching and writing, and indirectly, through his dialogues with friends and colleagues. An active participant in the literary and artistic culture of his time, not least through the famous *jours* that made his and Gertrud Simmel's home a latter-day salon, he taught and mentored younger figures who shaped social and cultural movements now recognized as the (often extra-institutional) precursors of various interdisciplinary formations, including not just critical theory but also film and media studies, gender studies, and religious studies.

Theoretical, aesthetic, and practical dimensions must all be taken into account to understand Simmel's significance as a modernist thinker and writer. His attention to the "details on the surface" of everyday modern life returned philosophy to the oldest questions of all—the problem of the meaning and value of life itself and the challenge of giving an account of oneself—and had a significant impact on diverse theoretical developments in the early twentieth century. Significantly, the same strategies that belong to the prehistory of the modern social sciences also paved the way for philosophical phenomenology and existentialism.[47] To assess Simmel's contributions, it is necessary to reexamine his role in the wider confluence of hermeneutic, phenomenological, linguistic, literary, and cultural theory—but also to question the tacit assumption that the evolution of social theory can be understood in isolation from the diverse cultural, intellectual, and political developments that accompanied the emergence of the modern social science disciplines.

Such attention to disciplinary history and the history of disciplinarity must be distinguished from traditional *Geistesgeschichte* in the sense of the history of ideas. Disciplines are not simply intellectual but also cultural and institutional formations.[48] As Köhnke pointed out, heroizing narratives centered on founding fathers belie the widespread "public and academic interest" in social scientific knowledge and strategies of thought that provided "the decisive preconditions" for the successful establishment of the modern disciplines. The larger modernist cultural context, including the political reality that, in Germany as elsewhere, efforts to develop systematic knowledge in the service of social improvement facilitated establishment of the academic social science disciplines, is significant.[49]

The legitimacy, value, and importance of Köhnke's effort to situate Simmel in an emerging canon of cultural philosophy—and, more broadly, in a narrative about

---

47. In "Geld oder Leben. Eine metaphorologische Studie zur Konsistenz der Philosophie Georg Simmels" (*AuS*, 121), Hans Blumenberg calls Simmel the discoverer of life-philosophy. See also Gary Backhaus, "Georg Simmel as an Eidetic Social Scientist," *Sociological Theory* 16, no. 3 (1998): 260–81. And consider that in 1913, Simmel sent Husserl an essay titled "The Problem of Fate," with the inscription: "Is this, too, phenomenology?" (*GSG* 23: 211).

48. Recent work on the cultural history of the modern social sciences has enriched our understanding of how liberal and progressive political strivings to bring science to bear in improving modern society shaped the wider intellectual and social context in which these new disciplines took form. Consider, to name only a few decisive examples, the work of Dorothy Ross on the politics of American social science, of Anson Rabinbach on the history of the science of work, of Mary Poovey on British economics, and of Ian Hacking on the evolution of the science of probability.

49. Köhnke, *Der junge Simmel*, 432. Köhnke documents how the activities of the *Studentenvereine* (before whom Simmel gave a series of important early papers) paved the way for the founding of the Deutsche Gesellschaft für Soziologie.

the emergence of the *Kulturwissenschaften*, the sciences of culture, beginning in the nineteenth century—in order to help foster a self-reflexive historical and institutional revitalization of the texts and thinkers whose work forms the theoretical and historical horizon of modern cultural theory are, I think, unquestionable. Simmel's struggles with materialism as well as the sophisticated relativism of his mature thinking belonged to the same milieu that shaped the thinking of the late Dilthey and Cassirer, of Rickert, Weber, Husserl, and the young Heidegger, and it is in this larger context that both his shifting relations to sociology and his place in intellectual history more generally must be understood.

Yet Simmel's interest as a thinker does not lie simply or even principally in his contributions, recognized or unrecognized, to the establishment of modern intellectual formations. There is as much to be learned from the ways his oeuvre confounds subsequently established disciplinary boundaries and expectations—and thereby invites us to rethink our own historical and theoretical sensibilities. Thus while I hope that the present book will do its part to draw attention to the stature of a thinker who thoroughly merits being treated as "a genuine philosophical classic," I believe we must question whether such an approach honors the distinctiveness of Simmel's accomplishments and ask instead whether he provides a model of innovation that might inspire new directions today.

We are in many ways at the end of a development that was just getting under way in Simmel's lifetime, in and through which the very idea of "a genuine philosophical classic" has, along with so much else, been radically called into question. What is most interesting, impressive, and modern in Simmel is far more complex than a backward-looking, canonizing mode of reception can capture.

To emphasize Simmel's place within a longer tradition stretching back, via Humboldt, to antiquity is to risk underplaying his striving to transform philosophy and culture. It was Simmel's critical embrace of the dissolution or relativization of inherited values and the resulting cultural transformations that gave him such affinity for Nietzsche—who began his own career by deconstructing the concept of *Kultur* and the ideal of *Bildung*, and, through his radical reinterpretation of the cultural reality and meaning of tragedy, the very foundation of those ideals in the Winkelmannian vision of Greek art as "noble simplicity and quiet grandeur."

As he came to terms with the ethical and epistemological impact of the radical decentering of received values and truths that became acute in the years before World War I and set aside his too-simplistic youthful materialism in favor of a more nuanced, phenomenological understanding of reality, Simmel anticipated many significant developments in twentieth-century philosophy—not least the embrace of that philosophical outsider Nietzsche. The mature thinker's philosophical achievements—his understanding of individuality as giving itself its own law, his conception of philosophical culture, his emphasis on the immanence of death and the relativity of truths, to name only a few examples—anticipate and prefigure developments identified with postwar thinkers whose debt to him has been obscured, in many cases rather deliberately. There is a great deal of work to be done to uncover Simmel's history of effects. Illuminating his specifically philosophical contribution to the study of art and culture and clarifying his historical and theoretical contribution to a reorientation of philosophy away from intellect and toward life are of singular importance.

Approaching Simmel as a modernist philosopher foregrounds underappreciated aspects of his work and suggests strategies for (re)reading him that have different, trans- or meta- as well as cross- and interdisciplinary implications. It casts new light on the ways Simmel's strategies of thought have been appropriated into a range of disciplines and applied to very diversely grounded projects, and it gives rise to different and more future-oriented questions regarding the interplay between theory and history. And probing the relations between Simmel's evolving epistemological convictions and disciplinary identifications and his ambiguous status in the modern social scientific canon reveals his representation in modern intellectual history to be tied up with deep and perhaps insoluble questions about disciplinarity and modern intellectual life that remain of the greatest urgency.

Part II thus considers Simmel's self-reflexivity from a perspective diametrically opposed to Köhnke's historicist effort to situate his modernist innovations in "theoretical movements." Taking him seriously as a modernist writer both illuminates his concept of form and counters the persistent, misleading view of Simmel as a mandarin aesthete. His cosmopolitan approach to philosophizing, epitomized by the "essayism" of his later work, is a strategy for revitalizing the (cultural, philosophical) tradition. Simmel's evolving self-representation is part of a praxis of self-fashioning that is in itself philosophically and theoretically significant, and the shifting categories that track the philosophical development of his thinking should be interpreted within this framework.

In emphasizing the dynamic of innovation over consolidation, the story I tell also calls into question the clear division between systematic inquiry (*Wissenschaft*) and "culture" that Köhnke's approach presupposes. What is at issue in remembering and returning to Simmel in the twenty-first century is not the reconstruction of historical truth concerning "the" origins of modern social science. It is grasping the philosophical significance of a problematic narrative framework that underpins the institutional and cultural ordering of reflection on and inquiry into human social and cultural life and that thereby helps undergird the modern disciplinary order as a whole. I aim, then, to make legible how Simmel's efforts to understand and theorize human collective life illuminate the (cultural, historical, philosophical) constitution of the discourse on culture and of knowledge of the social as a distinct object of scientific inquiry.

For reasons of both practice and principle—reasons that I believe are exemplified by Simmel's work—I am dubious not just about the desirability but also about the possibility of rigorously distinguishing "scientific" or "theoretical" reflection on society and culture from other sorts of cultural practices. To put it quite prosaically, thought is social thought; thinking about culture—about values, practices, ideas, but also about their conditions of possibility or the modes by which they ought to be evaluated—is part of culture. As the preoccupation with narrative in contemporary history and anthropology and the recent turn to culture in sociology attest, mainstream social science has, at least to a certain extent, embraced the self-reflexive task of grasping its own activity as part of the human context within which it takes place; today the distinction between theory and praxis appears, not just methodologically but also historically and conceptually, rather shaky.

My point is by no means that all stories have equal value, let alone that the striving for objectivity or empirical knowledge is unimportant. But in an era conspicuous for its dizzying proliferation of perspectives—a consequence of globalization, but also of the entry of previously unheard and silenced voices into the public sphere—to aspire to establish a uniquely privileged position of reflection outside the messy flux of cultural life seems, at the very minimum, unrealistically idealistic.

Not least because there are very good theoretical reasons for taking Simmel's relativism seriously, we need to leave open the question of how the continuity or discontinuity between the modernist streams of thought he embodied and represented and the older discourse on culture stretching back to the turn of the nineteenth century should be understood. Securing Simmel his rightful place in the genealogy of a style of thinking that cannot be confined to a single discipline raises a new set of questions about the history of theory, and emphasizing his modernism makes it possible to ask how to reflect upon a style of cultural interpretation and on the theoretical and methodological gestures and practices common to very diverse disciplines in a coherent way without integrating the diverse threads and practices into a single philosophical master-narrative.

The struggles with questions of historicity and relativism that continue to define our own theoretical landscape and to shape the study of culture, whether under the aegis of the human, the social, or the cultural sciences, belong to the legacy of modernism. Exposing the imbrication between modernism and social science cannot be an end in itself; the project of historicizing social science is a cultural as well as theoretical one. Both theoretically and practically, we need a more nuanced understanding of the discursive specificity of our practices of theoretical reflection on culture.

The distinctions between "high" and "low," and "mass" versus "popular" forms, so recently a matter of virulent debate, have by and large lost their force within the academy. Like the broadly speaking Marxist rhetoric of reflection with which they were associated, these distinctions have lost their progressive edge as the terms of political reflection and the parameters of subjective identity as such are reconfigured by new technological and socioeconomic conditions. And yet cultural theorists today confront many of the same issues faced by Simmel and his contemporaries. Then as now, there is considerable hostility to the specialization of knowledge in the contemporary humanistic disciplines and no shortage of appeals to return to an idealist understanding of humanistic inquiry oriented toward the normative and substantive value of culture in the Humboldtian sense. The same hostility Simmel faced from those who believed that sociological modes of thought had undermined and defiled that ideal of culture, which reached a fevered pitch during the notorious debates opposing *Kultur* to *Zivilisation*, echoes through the "culture wars" of the late twentieth century and beyond.

Strikingly, the ideological force of appeals to "culture" appears to have survived the wholesale transformation of literature, philosophy, and the arts by the depredations of the market. The political rhetoric of reflection that until very recently still shaped debates about such matters seems largely to have lost its hold on critical theory even as the wholesale commodification of everyday life proceeds apace and once sacrosanct liberal ideals such as individual privacy dissolve. Since 1989, economic and political phenomena predicted by Marxist theory—the increasing concentration of capital, globalization of markets, and concomitant systemic crises, as well as the intensification both nationally and internationally of differences between rich and poor—have proliferated. And yet, among those who do not reach for their pistols when they hear the word, attention to culture has grown ever more disconnected from the analysis of society.

What might be called the problem of culture has contributed to the increasingly precarious situation of the humanities in general and of theory in particular within the academy itself. The contemporary turn to interdisciplinarity remains situated in a discursive space shaped and reinforced by disciplinary divisions that continue to oppose (humanistic) "scholarship" to (scientific) "research" and thus to disempower the (implicitly evaluative and normative) humanistic approaches to culture vis-à-vis (putatively objective and descriptive) anthropological, psychological, and sociological analysis. If we are to develop genuinely new and rigorous strategies of inquiry and interpretation that will allow us to analyze and understand the very real contradictions of late-modern life, it is crucial for us to overcome the strictures of a disciplinary imaginary shaped a hundred years ago under very different intellectual and cultural-institutional conditions.

As we attempt to come to terms with the contemporary remaking of the university, it can serve as a source of practical and theoretical inspiration that the modern social sciences have roots in the very tradition that brought us the modern humanities—that the same Humboldt whose conception of education did so much to bring the modern research university into being was also the great-grandfather of contemporary anthropology. Recognizing Simmel as both philosopher and sociologist provides a crucial opening to rethinking the links between "social scientific" and "humanistic" understanding of culture.

We must beware overemphasizing continuities stretching back into the era before industrialization and urbanization transformed collective life—and before the political and cultural upheavals of the twentieth century had given way to a new political order centered on the nation-state. As Foucault so forcefully demonstrated, the modern social sciences emerged as politics in the old sense was giving way to the management of populations and as the strengths and perils of capitalism and of the politics of national identity were becoming apparent. The new knowledge practices were shaped both practically and theoretically by strivings to come to terms with the global transformations we think of as defining modernity. Thus there were efforts to understand the operations and implications of social differentiation and the division of labor (the first association remains Marx, but Spencer, Durkheim, and Simmel all wrote books on the topic as well); to conceptualize the emergent structures of mass society (Durkheim, Tönnies, Veblen, Tarde); to theorize the convergence of political, technological, and sociocultural transformations in the rise of the modern nation-state (Marx, Sombart, Simmel, Weber).

Emergent sciences such as epidemiology and demographics were not simply a response to the challenge of managing the intertwining social effects of technological progress: urbanization, industrialization, and the emergence of mass society. They were significantly shaped by the profound moral shocks emanating from the natural sciences, which had been busily undermining hallowed beliefs about human beings and their place in a divinely ordered world for some time before Darwin published *On the Origin of Species* in 1859. It is also crucial to bear in mind that many of the most significant scientific advances in the period went hand in hand with the needs of industry and colonialism.[50]

In institutional terms, the emergent sciences of society were both a product of these developments—political, social, scientific—and a symptom of the growing division between philosophical reflection and natural scientific inquiry. They reflected the increasing hegemony of disenchanted, materialist strategies of thought that had reshaped Europe's intellectual landscape since the Enlightenment. The new concept of culture emerging in the far more globalized and interconnected, rapidly electrifying world of the late nineteenth century reflected the recognition that progress was a two-edged sword, bringing social, cultural, and religious destruction in its wake. From Comte to Spencer to Dilthey, there was no shortage of efforts to synthesize totalizing visions that could contain these difficulties theoretically and help orient social, political, and cultural practices.

How, then, are these efforts themselves to be understood today? The urgency, pervasiveness, and scale of the problems as well as the continuing widespread consensus that a modern, scientific approach to human collective life is called for complicate the historiographical situation. As the case of Simmel shows, the history of social and cultural theory has been, by and large, a partisan affair, with methodological convictions masquerading as objectivity and theoretical assumptions guiding the description of facts. There is, too, a fundamental difficulty in writing the history of these ideas: any description of or thesis about the social has self-reflexive implications for the narrative itself. Just as, quite generally, there can be no history of philosophy without philosophical implications, the history of the social has social implications.

Rather than attempting to lay claim to a transhistorical objectivity, I want to emphasize the distinctive historiographical possibilities of the present moment, with its peculiar mélange of sociocultural self-reflexivity and drastically curtailed temporal horizons. Until very recently, the dominant narratives about the emergence and evolution of modern social thought centered on the political ideology of theories—the measure, often quite explicitly, being Marx and Engels and whether a given thinker could be regarded as historically progressive or not. Now that the under-

---

50. New geological theories inspired by evidence unearthed in the process of mining for mineral resources undermined the authority of the Bible; paleontology and archaeology grew in tandem with colonial power; Darwin's discoveries while voyaging on the HMS *Beagle* were made possible by the British government's investment in hydrographic charting of the coasts of South America.

lying metanarratives have lost their allure, and in the context of what I believe it is no exaggeration to call a crisis in and of the contemporary disciplinary imaginary, the emergence of this body of theoretical and cultural practice can be integrated into a wider account of the vicissitudes of social and cultural modernism in the late nineteenth and early twentieth centuries that does better justice to the rhetorical and cultural contingency of the modern Western conception of the political itself.

As I have argued elsewhere, the emergence of the modern disciplines of society and culture is coeval with a profound internal crisis within the dominant Western rhetoric of reflection on human existence. Sociopolitical and cultural transformation within European societies, exacerbated by the stimulating as well as disturbing effects of incipient globalization and colonial expansion, reinforced the sense that words were losing their meaning, that the very foundations of sense and value needed to be reestablished on a new basis.

This crisis of language and reflection registered within the institutions of German philosophy in various ways. There were the debates over the status of language itself and its relation to the human; efforts at rethinking subjectivity in light of developments in psychology; the displacement of the category of *Geist* by that of life; the question of the status of history in philosophical explanation; the emergence of a philosophy of (natural) science as distinct from logic and epistemology. The modern social sciences took form in an intellectual and cultural context characterized by competing conceptions of science and drastically different understandings of the logic and proper justification of inquiry into the human and social worlds; a new, objectifying attitude toward culture and society gained sway as idealist and religious rhetoric yielded to the predominantly materialist modes of explanation and interpretation that came to dominate European intellectual life by the early twentieth century. The aporetic relations between the still-dominant and emergent paradigms profoundly inflected not only Simmel's intellectual formation but also the course of his philosophical career.

Beginning, then, from this broader sense of Georg Simmel as an important theoretical innovator and critical progenitor of a modernist style of thought in situ, let us explore the genealogy of a mode of thinking and writing that has since become deeply rooted in theoretical practices across a number of disciplines. As we examine some of Simmel's most theoretically significant and historically consequential texts, we shall simultaneously attend to how and why the problem of reflection on society and culture as such took on such urgency at the previous fin de siècle. Appropriately contextualized, historical and theoretical reflection on his oeuvre can, I hope, contribute to a more differentiated response to our own intellectual and cultural situation in which rigorous inquiry, most vividly but by no means exclusively in the the humanities and social sciences, is confronting methodological as well as practical crises that are deeply rooted in the institutional and more broadly cultural circumstances of the modern disciplinary imaginary.

PART II

Philosophy of Money as Modernist Philosophy

[A]ctually, the *Philosophy of Money* is objectively the most significant [of my books] as a *first* attempt to represent the development of the psychic culture of humanity as a whole through a single symbol. Of course, the attempt is quite imperfect and incomplete, but [it is] as such entirely novel. Unfortunately, thus far, this significance of the book has neither been recognized nor rendered fertile.

Georg Simmel (1918)

CHAPTER 4

Style as Substance: Simmel's Modernism and the Disciplinary Imaginary

Georg Simmel's *Philosophy of Money* may well be the twentieth century's most significant mostly unread theoretical text. Weighing in at over seven hundred pages, it is remarkable for its breadth of culture, philosophical discernment, and unrelenting celebration of the complexity of human existence. Simmel's virtual absence from the grand narratives of twentieth-century intellectual history is overdetermined, and nowhere is his paradoxical role as (mostly) forgotten founding father more evident than in the case of the *Philosophy of Money*. Indeed, the book's reception may be regarded as symptomatic, at once registering and obscuring the significance of Simmel's place between philosophy and social science.

Although the *Philosophy of Money* was well received upon its publication in 1900, it was already difficult to assimilate into the emerging disciplinary division of intellectual labor. During the twentieth century, the book was mostly ignored by philosophers, being regarded as a work of sociology, notwithstanding its title. Lewis Coser's warning against misconstruing it as "one of Simmel's metaphysical works" has already been noted.

A great deal, up to and including its author's declared intention, must be quite literally set aside to avoid this "misunderstanding" and establish the book's sociological bona fides. Within the social scientific mainstream, it has been read selectively and, as it were, retrospectively, through disciplinary lenses that obscure its historical significance and theoretical ambition. By approaching the text with an eye to how contemporary (sub-)disciplinary enterprises could be enriched by his investigations, Simmel's social scientific advocates have appropriated his insights into the sociological and cultural implications and psychological effects of the modern money economy for purposes quite alien to the author's own, philosophical understanding of his enterprise.

Part II epigraph: These remarks are from "1918—Unzweideutiges Bild meiner geistigen Individualität" (1918—An Unambiguous Image of My Spiritual Individuality), the later of two newly published excerpts from Simmel's lost "family chronicle" (*GSG* 24: 71–72). Gertrud Simmel provided the selections for research purposes, describing them in a letter dated December 31, 1926, as comprising "an objective report and not Simmel's subjective opinion of himself and his life's work" (*GSG* 24: 691). My epigraph presents the text in its entirety, save for the fragmentary beginning, which I have elided. With my interpellations, the opening sentence runs: "What matters is [the essay collection] Philosophical Culture, the [books about] Goethe and Rembrandt, actually..."

By the time he was writing it in the late 1890s, Simmel had already begun to distance himself from sociology, notably in the 1899 letter to Célestin Bouglé in which he declared his "life's work" to be that of a philosopher and called his sociological labors a "sideline."[1] The work's reception has obscured the decisive question of why he so radically redefined his disciplinary allegiances at that point in his life, something that is by no means only of biographical interest.

To be sure, Simmel's pathbreaking approach to theorizing the social is rightly recognized as foundational for the social sciences. But his intellectual legacy was also appropriated and rewritten to help build the theoretical frameworks and hermeneutic practices of the contemporary humanistic disciplines. Through students and readers who adopted and adapted his methods of inquiry and style of interpretation, the strategies of thought that made possible a *Philosophy of Money* thus achieved a profound, yet largely subterranean influence on the study of "society" and "culture" alike.[2] Though barely remembered today, Simmel's philosophical oeuvre thereby helped lay the conceptual, methodological, and rhetorical groundwork for the remaking of the disciplinary order over the past hundred-odd years.

In emphasizing the significance of Simmel's position between (nineteenth-century) philosophy and (twentieth-century) social science, I hope to provide a way of stepping back from the resulting network of assumptions and presuppositions. My point is not that Simmel was a critical theorist *avant la lettre*—though he can sometimes sound like one. In reading him, it is crucial to attend to the distance between our own intellectual-historical and disciplinary horizon and that of the nineteenth-century fin de siècle, since without adequate historical self-reflection, his theoretical accomplishment is rendered invisible.

Through a reception history in which decontextualization has gone hand in hand with a very selective canonization, Simmel's advocates in sociology have reframed his contributions in ways that conceal the challenge his writing poses to prevailing assumptions and intuitions concerning methods of analysis and interpretation, and even the nature of evidence, in the social sciences. His work has thereby been deployed to help naturalize understandings of the foundations and ultimate ends of inquiry into social and cultural life that he did not actually share.

Crucially, following Coser's lead, the metaphysical and epistemological concerns that motivated Simmel to philosophize about money have mostly been set aside. His *Philosophy of Money* has, after a fashion, entered the theoretical canon through readings that anachronistically take the basic assumptions and orientations of twentieth-century social science as a point of departure, focus almost exclusively on its final chapter, "The Style of Life," and culminate in the now conventional celebration of Simmel's contributions to the "sociology of modernity." But his masterwork remains unknown to most professional philosophers today,

---

1. Simmel to Célestin Bouglé, December 13, 1899 (*GSG* 22: 342–43).
2. In English, see Frisby's prefaces and "Introduction to the Translation" for an overview of the evidence for the work's impact as well as, more recently, Austin Harrington and Thomas M. Kemple's "Introduction: Georg Simmel's 'Sociological Metaphysics': Money, Sociality, and Precarious Life" in the December 2012 special issue of *TCS* devoted to Simmel.

and the scope and ambition of its philosophical claims continue to go largely unrecognized.

The *Philosophy of Money* set out to redefine the tasks of philosophical reflection for a world where all that was solid had already melted into air—where, Simmel had come to believe, it was no longer possible to secure a reliable philosophical foundation in the face of the dissolution of the most basic categories: God, truth, subjectivity. In writing the *Philosophy of Money*, he was attempting nothing less than to represent and render comprehensible the complexity of contemporary life as a whole—to give a unified account of a fragmented reality. Its incisive interpretations of the phenomenal world shaped by the modern money economy reflect a larger conceptual and methodological strategy for coming to terms with the dissolution of foundations, the undermining of inherited paradigms, in modernity.

Simmel's most characteristic gesture as a thinker is to move directly from concrete—historically, culturally located—particulars to reflection on their global, spiritual significance. The sociological (but also historical and anthropological, economic and psychological, legal and political) matter that makes up much of his *Philosophy of Money* thereby becomes the mode or vehicle for presenting a new, modernist vision of philosophy. Simmel's approach is phenomenological: an attempt to overcome the dichotomy between materialist and idealist explanation by connecting surface and depth, appearance and essence, the "most external and the most interior" aspects of existence (*GSG* 6: 719). Like Hegel, he sets out to overcome the superficial view that identifies truth and representation and to provide his readers with an experience of philosophizing as a process of living, animated exchange with the world.

Simmel shows that philosophy can, as it were, learn from money how to think historically and sociologically. Money can do such heavy theoretical lifting because it is so deeply imbricated with the ways we think, live in society, and reflect upon and communicate with one another. His *Philosophy of Money* traces those connections in order to reveal their philosophical significance and to provide new strategies for philosophizing in a world where value is relative to human existence—a world, that is, without ultimate foundations.

Simmel begins the book by demonstrating in chapter 1 that money is inseparable from the category of value as such. Chapter 2 goes on to explain how money's ambiguous status as at once substance and function helps account both for the increasing complexity of "techniques of life" and for the felt loss of meaning in modern societies, since, as he shows in chapter 3, it fosters the hypertrophy of means over ends and of quantitative over qualitative modes of valuation. These three chapters taken together constitute the "analytic" part of his *Philosophy of Money*, and they form a compelling analysis of what would come to be known as the reified world. The second, "synthetic," part of the book explores the "intertwining of the monetary principle with the developments and valuations of inner life." Its three chapters parallel the arguments of the first three, focusing respectively on money and individual freedom; on the transmutation of personal value into monetary equivalents; and on the overall cultural impact of money as it makes itself felt in the modern "style of life." If the analytic illuminates the philosophical significance of money as such, explaining the essence and meaning of its existence "out of the conditions and relations of life in general [or, perhaps, collective life: *des allgemeinen Lebens*]," the synthetic part reverses perspectives, interpreting "the essence and formation [*Gestaltung*] of the latter through the effectiveness of money" (*GSG* 6: 11).

In the very letter in which Simmel insisted that the "*sciences sociales* are not my discipline," he goes on to declare that his *Philosophy of Money* "aspires to be a philosophy of historical and social life as a whole."[3] Looking back in 1916, he identified its "attempt to unfold the whole external and internal evolution of culture through the development of a single element, to comprehend the individual line as a symbol of the entire image," as an expression of the same "metaphysical longing" to link "part and whole, surface and depth, reality and idea" that shaped his later writing on cultural phenomena and artists. In retrospect, the *Philosophy of Money* may certainly be regarded as the founding text of the sociology of modernity, but that accomplishment is ancillary to its philosophical objectives. To categorize it as a work of sociology obscures one of Simmel's most decisive contributions to modern cultural theory: "the concept of truth developed out of life" that animates the work, which he saw as one of the "original fundamental motifs" he had "contributed to spiritual-cultural evolution."[4]

It is well worth taking Simmel's title to heart and plunging into his daunting opus with its author's characterization of his full ambition in mind—and not just for the sake of doing justice to the historical significance of author and work. More than a century on, his *Philosophy of Money* unquestionably contains much worthy of sustained attention and extension by contemporary social science. Simmel's account of the impact of the domination of money on social practices and institutions in industrialized and urbanized society remains both provocative and illuminating—and relevant for any effort to theorize the "modern" as opposed to the "traditional" world. It brims with prescient and insightful—and often, even today, unsurpassed—analyses of modern life and trenchant accounts of the relations between forms of individual experience and the economic and symbolic order. But those analyses are not ends in themselves: Simmel's interpretations of historical and cultural phenomena are embedded in a larger philosophical framework. His meditation on money's significance for understanding the development of culture, society, and subjectivity is not in fact about modernity or the modern per se.

Reading Simmel's *Philosophy of Money*

In his introduction to the first English edition of the *Philosophy of Money*, seventy-eight years after its original German publication, David Frisby objected eloquently to the ahistorical approaches of his colleagues in sociology who eschewed the hermeneutic value of "immanent understanding of a work and its own context"

---

3. Simmel to Bouglé, December 13, 1899 (*GSG* 22: 343).
4. Simmel quoted from the other newly published self-assessment, "1916. Wenn ich Bilanz ziehe . . ." (1916. When I give an account . . .) (*GSG* 24: 71).

and approached texts "like a vast rubbish heap of latent hypotheses which may be instrumentally extracted from their context and incorporated into the service of contemporary interests." In particular, Frisby condemned the "constant quarrying into Simmel's works for illuminating insights that can be operationalized in an empirical setting," which, he observed, "hardly aids our understanding of Simmel's work as a whole."[5]

Simmel's undeserved reputation as an unsystematic thinker arises from this mode of reception, which actively sets aside the theoretical and methodological questions and motivations he himself declared to be central. The reception of his *Philosophy of Money* is a crucial case in point. The theoretical and historical significance of Simmel's argumentative strategy is not just obscured when his insights into social and cultural life in the money economy are gleaned and presented as ends in themselves. Stripping his distinctive style of thought and innovative methods for interpreting the interactive complexities of human collective life of their epistemological and metaphysical dimensions simply renders them illegible.

Philosophy's loss is quite literally sociology's gain: Simmel's *Philosophy of Money* has been canonized by reframing it so as to assimilate it into twentieth-century social science. Thus Coser elevated its contributions to "cultural sociology" by suggesting that the book's title was a misleading distraction, an approach that exemplifies—that is, both illustrates and represents—how the selective reading and global rewriting of Simmel's oeuvre helped consolidate the dominant disciplinary self-understanding of sociology. This book's reception as a work of sociology has, moreover, taken the form of a self-reinforcing disciplinary procedure that embodies the very dynamic of specialization and objectification Simmel was theorizing—and criticizing.

Even highly sympathetic sociological readers regularly underestimate how innovative both theoretically and methodologically his strategies of interpretation actually were, and the still-pervasive "constant quarrying" described by Frisby enables Simmel's appropriation by fragments. Selecting passages out of longer arguments and failing to take the philosophical horizon and analytic objectives of his interpretations into account, his sociological readers treat as empirical facts the very phenomena his texts put forward as objects for theoretical reflection. By isolating and reframing particular examples in abstraction from his own arguments, they reify partial aspects of what Simmel represents as a complex and internally diverse phenomenal world and examines from multiple, often incommensurable, angles. This mode of reception obscures his overarching effort to develop a philosophical—and for Simmel, this also meant historical, psychological, and cultural as well as sociological—interpretation of money.

The distorting effects of anachronistic disciplinary perspectives become visible methodologically. Enacting constitutive, largely tacit assumptions about what makes sociology scientific, such appropriative readings perform—both produce and maintain—the very understanding of disciplinarity that has distorted the view

---

5. *The Philosophy of Money*, trans. Tom Bottomore, David P. Frisby, and Kaethe Mengelberg, ed. Frisby (1978; 3rd enlarged ed., London: Routledge, 2004), "Introduction to the Translation," 4.

of his work. "Quarrying" for his purported contributions to problems and debates that came to shape social science discourse in the course of the twentieth century obscures the ways Simmel's *Philosophy of Money* both extends and breaks with the philosophical tradition. In fact, Frisby's own elevation of the work to the canonical "sociology of modernity" simultaneously assimilates it into an historical narrative that Simmel rejected and effaces the centrality for his project of philosophical concerns that are neither about "society" nor specific to "modernity." Simmel was posing questions—concerning the interpretation of phenomenal reality and the creation of value; the impact of technological and sociological developments on human experience; the direction and significance of cultural and historical change—that have lost none of their philosophical and theoretical significance since 1900.

The reception of Simmel's *Philosophy of Money* played out in dramatic historical circumstances. His magnum opus enjoyed considerable initial success: portions of the book appeared in the *American Journal of Sociology* even before its original German publication in 1900, and a second, slightly amended German edition was issued in 1907. It remained in print (it was reissued in 1920, 1922, and 1930) and hence available, yet throughout most of the twentieth century it remained something of a secret tip.[6] There was a long gap between the fifth edition in 1930 and the next printing of *Philosophie des Geldes* in 1958 as the first volume of the original, never-completed, effort to publish an edition of Simmel's collected works after the war.[7]

Toward the end of his life in 1918, Simmel had grown acutely aware of the untimeliness of his thinking. Although his memory remained alive in German cultural and intellectual life after World War I, Simmel's impact on Weimar culture still awaits its historian. After his death, his contributions to philosophy began to be marginalized. Students and former acolytes (Lukács, Mannheim) denied, downplayed, or ignored his influence, obscuring the role of his ideas and methods in subsequent theoretical developments. Explicitly or implicitly encouraged by Simmel's lack of institutional legacy, readers and interlocutors (Husserl, Heidegger, Weber) appropriated his ideas and intellectual strategies without acknowledging or perhaps

6. Consider, by contrast, the reception of its 1900 "siblings," Freud's *Interpretation of Dreams* (actually published in 1899), and Husserl's *Logische Untersuchungen*. See Helmuth Vetter, Brigitta Keintzel, and Ulrike Kadi, *Traum, Logik, Geld: Freud, Husserl und Simmel zum Denken der Moderne* (Tübingen: Diskord, 2001).

7. The volume in question was a reprint of the 1930 edition. Until the 1980s, editorial efforts remained oriented by Gertrud Simmel's original vision of keeping in print those works of Simmel's that had maintained their relevance (*GSG* 24: 1042). Her initial plans for posthumous collections (later misconstrued by Edith Landmann as "complete works") were rendered unrealizable through Gertrud Kantorowicz's loss of papers in 1921, then repeatedly reduced in scope due to postwar economic realities. Regarding the history of the *Nachlaß* and the editions, see *GSG* 20, Editorial Report, and General Editor Otthein Rammstedt's "Zur Geschichte der Georg Simmel Gesamtausgabe" (On the History of the Georg Simmel *Gesamtausgabe*), in *GSG* 24: 1039–90, which describes the monumental struggle to produce a critical edition without designated sponsorship or funding, illustrating Simmel's persistently marginal status in late twentieth-century Germany. Twelve volumes were produced principally through individual grants for related projects "secretly, on the side," seven funded more or less directly, and five "were realized without any specific financial support" (*GSG* 24: 1063). See also Rammstedt, "On the Genesis of a Collected Edition of Simmel's Works, 1918–2012," *TCS* 29, nos. 7–8 (2012): 302–16.

even recognizing his impact on their own work. And in the 1930s, of course, key figures (Benjamin, Kracauer) who situated themselves more explicitly in relation to his work, and whose own achievements are only today attaining belated recognition, were forced into exile.

Simmel had often been regarded as the personification of the "Jewish threat" to universities even during his lifetime, and the Nazis viewed sociology with suspicion. It is thus unsurprising that Simmel's books were banned under the Third Reich. After World War II, from his position at the Freie Universität in Berlin, the Jewish Swiss philosopher Michael Landmann, the son of Simmel's student Edith Landmann, attempted to revive Simmel's heritage in his discipline. But given the unsavory postwar reputation of the philosophy of life and Simmel's association with German nationalism, it was an uphill battle—all the more so as some of the most significant beneficiaries of his unmarked legacy had clear and definite interests in casting Simmel in a minor role in the intellectual history of the prewar period.

The gap between the 1930 and 1958 editions of the *Philosophy of Money* was not simply political. The cultural and intellectual world of the postwar period was leagues away from the fluid environment of Simmel's fin de siècle, the final years of the long nineteenth century. Well before 1958, it had become evident that the lectures that were public cultural events, the salon, vast readership, and wide, international range of interlocutors, indeed, the very cosmopolitan discourse about values and the orientation of modern culture in which Simmel played a key role, all belonged to a world that had disappeared in the Great War.

We have already observed the decisive impact of the increasing professionalization of the discipline of philosophy on Simmel's career. The changes under way in the scholarly world during his lifetime intensified in the postwar period, and the global organization of universities and the structures and specialized practices of academic disciplines evolved even more rapidly between 1930 and 1950. Disciplinary and institutional divisions between philosophy and sociology became further established and enhanced in the United States during this period, so that by the time sociology was reimported into Germany in the 1950s, crucial aspects of Simmel's work were already virtually illegible to the mainstream of the very discipline that claimed him as a founding father.

The increasing marginalization of Simmel's oeuvre was not just a function of the ascendance of new philosophical paradigms and the quantitative, empirical orientation of postwar social science. In the second half of the twentieth century, the sort of wide-ranging philosophical and historical culture, but also linguistic training, shared not only by Small and James but also Merton and Parsons had become the rare exception among social scientists. In the new, highly differentiated scholarly landscape that was emerging in tandem with the ascendance of the American research university to international preeminence, participation in the dialogue with the wider European intellectual traditions that formed the foundation of modern social and cultural theory was itself becoming a distinct specialization. Within the dominant paradigm of postwar social science—and the same holds for the modernized and professionalized discipline of philosophy—it was becoming increasingly challenging for Simmel's own descendants to discern what he had been trying to accomplish in writing a *Philosophy of Money*.

To be sure, Simmel's philosophical conception of sociology had always been marginal in the United States, where a very different vision of social science already held sway during his lifetime. But in the decades after his death, Simmel's vision of social theory did not simply fall out of favor; it grew increasingly foreign to social scientists. Beginning with World War I, the international prestige that German philosophy still enjoyed during Simmel's lifetime was radically undermined. The discipline had evolved, and efforts at the New School in New York to keep a philosophical vision of sociology itself alive were anomalous. Where Simmel's work continued to have a wider impact on the discipline in the United States (insofar as it was not, that is, circulating in the form of unrecognizable "cold cash" through the unacknowledged impact of Simmelian ideas and methods on other thinkers), it tended to take the form of selectively focused readings (Merton's middle-range theories; Coser's sociology of conflict). Decisively, as Günther Roth and others have demonstrated, when sociology was reintroduced in Germany after World War II, what was reimported was a Weberian version of the discipline filtered through the Parsonian structural functionalism that had since come to dominate in the United States. And since Parsons's vision of social theory was influential well beyond the immediate boundaries of the social sciences, his marginalization of Simmel's work helped keep his alternative vision of social and cultural theorizing out of the mainstream not only of social science but also of philosophy.

While an artificially narrowed view of Simmel as sociologist and of the stakes and importance of his work still prevails, since 1989, when the German critical edition of the *Philosophie des Geldes* appeared (co-edited by Frisby and Köhnke, now in its tenth, 2011 printing), its significance has come to be more widely recognized in the scholarly world. The book had long been available in other languages; it was translated into Polish in 1904 and into Italian, French, and Spanish before 1989;[8] since then, it has appeared in a revised and expanded Japanese version (1999), as well as in Hungarian and Serbian (2004), Slovenian (2005), and Chinese (2007). And significantly, in no small part as a consequence of work on the *Georg Simmel Gesamtausgabe*, a considerable specialized secondary literature has grown up around the work in recent years, albeit largely in German, French, and Italian and still primarily within sociology.

This body of work has made increasingly clear that, while surely not in what has become the conventional sense a work of social science, Simmel's *Philosophy of Money* made contributions to economics, political science, social psychology, and anthropology as well as sociology and modern artistic and aesthetic culture.

---

8. Many of these are available but do not necessarily reflect the revisions incorporated into the German critical edition. Thus the 2012 Polish edition is a reprint of the translation of the first edition of the work; the Italian volume is a reprint of the 1984 translation; the Quadrige/PUF French edition (1999; repr. 2007) a reissue of the 1987 translation; and the 2013 Spanish volume contains a translation from 1977. A second, partial translation by Serge Katz also exists in French, with introduction by Olivier Aïm: *Philosophie de l'argent: Partie analytique, 3e chapitre, sections 1 et 2* (Paris: Flammarion, 2009).

Its history of effects is palpable, if not always explicitly recognized, in the qualitative social sciences and in cultural studies today.[9] It remains perhaps the most important mostly unread theoretical work of the twentieth century—and not only within Simmel's own discipline of philosophy.[10] The *Philosophy of Money*'s contributions to economics and especially the resources it offers for thinking through the world financial crisis catalyzed in 2008 by virtualizing market practices remain largely unappreciated. It is noteworthy how little impact the book has had on the burgeoning field of money studies, where ambitious overviews and attempts at new theoretical syntheses continue to be published in which Simmel's name barely appears.[11]

The marginalization of Simmel's philosophical contributions is overdetermined. Institutional, political, cultural, ideological, and sociological factors have converged to create structural blind spots. Recognition and misrecognition intertwine in the disciplining of his memory. Thus while Simmel's work began to be rediscovered in the context of the wider return to culture in the last quarter of the twentieth century, its scope and ambition have continued to go largely unrecognized, often even by his proponents, within the Anglophone world.

Within the dominant paradigm or hermeneutic horizon of contemporary sociology (but by no means only in that discipline) today, "scientific" investigations are generally understood to involve "applying" theories to "empirical" problems or issues. There is little room for questioning fundamental assumptions or investigating the historical origins of the governing conception of "science"—let alone for examining the more or less tacit patterns of thought that define proper disciplinary practice. If questions about the boundaries of the sociological arise, it is as a pragmatic rather than a philosophical matter.

Even within the subfields of sociological history or social theory, when the question of the status of theoretical and methodological frameworks that define social science are discussed, the very limited and highly fragmentary corpus of Simmel's work available in English helps reinforce the received narrative about it. Selective translations and the anthologies in which excerpts have been disseminated (generally recategorized under topics alien to or at least distant from Simmel's own analytic frameworks) foster truncated readings and facilitate the appropriation and assimilation of his work to mainstream social science models in the form of decontextualized

---

9. There is an excellent overview of English sources in Frisby's preface to the 3d ed. of his translation; see esp. xxxv. See also *Georg Simmels Philosophie des Geldes: Aufsätze und Materialien*, ed. Otthein Rammstedt with Christian Papilloud, Natàlia Cantó i Milà, and Cécile Rol (Frankfurt am Main: Suhrkamp, 2003).

10. In a sure sign of Simmel's ascension into the French canon, selections from *Philosophie de l'argent* were, however, included in the "general culture" category in the preparatory exams for entry into the French Grandes Écoles in science and engineering in 2009–10, when one theme was money.

11. To take just a few noteworthy examples, Niall Ferguson's *The Cash Nexus: Money and Power in the Modern World, 1700–2000* (New York: Basic Books, 2002) does not mention Simmel. Adam Kuzminski's *The Ecology of Money: Debt, Growth, and Sustainability* (Lanham, MD: Lexington Books, 2013); Frederick Taylor's *The Downfall of Money: Germany's Hyperinflation and the Destruction of the Middle Class* (New York: Bloomsbury, 2013), and Thomas Piketty's *Capital in the Twenty-First Century* (trans. Arthur Goldhammer; Cambridge, MA: Harvard University Press, 2014) do not even include him in their bibliographies.

passages and ideas—textual practices that further reinforce the dominant categories and obscure the ways in which Simmel's approach calls them into question. Even those who should know better tend thus to read him selectively, to focus on evocative "cases" and to downplay or ignore their complex hermeneutic contexts.

To understand the distinctive way in which Simmel's ideas and methods have come to circulate in modern social thought as well as the significant caesurae in his (official) reception, we need to take seriously the formal challenges his writing poses. Approaching his *Philosophy of Money* as a work of modernist philosophy helps reveal the ways Simmel's thinking transcends the strictures of the contemporary disciplinary imaginary.

Simmel's Philosophical Modernism

Simmel's *Philosophy of Money* is a text of remarkable density and complexity: a book of intricate byways as well as grand highways, and one not amenable to easy summary. There can be no question of addressing its full scope and significance here. Nonetheless, given its author's declared aspiration to produce a "philosophy of social and historical life as a whole," it is necessary to attempt to read this work, the last of his grand philosophical monographs, as a whole.[12]

The conceptual range and theoretical scope of Simmel's *Philosophy of Money* are daunting, and his argumentative strategies can border on the hermetic. But the dialectical tension between his philosophical ambition to comprehend all of "social and historical life" and the perspectivism that leads him so insistently to call such totalizing into question is the hallmark of a distinctive and largely unrecognized contribution to twentieth-century philosophy: the inauguration of a modernist mode of philosophizing.

Incorporating a self-reflexive awareness that the means of understanding and interpreting human life are also part of cultural (historical, psychological, social) reality, Simmel approaches value as at once historically and culturally created and transcendent. The text does jump from topic to topic frequently and often without explicit mediation. Yet it is erroneous to equate this apparent unpredictability with a lack of system. In reading it as a work of modernist philosophy that aspires to a cogent vision of a world in dissolution, I show that Simmel's text does cohere, albeit in an unconventional fashion, for there is systematicity in what many readers have perceived as the apparent arbitrariness of his strategies of composition.[13]

---

12. Simmel to Bouglé, December 13, 1899 (*GSG* 22: 343). Simmel does not make comparable claims to comprehensiveness elsewhere. His later long books are either essay collections or extended essays, rather than treatises; even the "large" *Soziologie* of 1908 is structured as a series of "investigations" rather than as a treatise in the grand mode.

13. Simmel has been repeatedly and eloquently defended against the charge of being unsystematic, and there is a body of literature, especially in German, that situates him broadly in the dialectical tradition. Yet even his theoretical advocates tend not to take him seriously enough as a philosopher and as a writer, often because they begin from anachronistic perspectives—regarding him as a seer of social structure or of a post-productivist New Left—that occlude crucial theoretical and historical questions posed by his style of presentation and thereby unduly simplify the task of reading. Consider Uta Gerhardt's claim that Simmel's *Philosophy of Money* follows "a principle of construction corresponding to Hegel's

This modernist approach to philosophizing is in some ways more easily accessible in the shorter texts and occasional pieces he categorized under the rubric of "philosophical culture." But Simmel's *Philosophy of Money* vividly reveals the theoretical significance of his style of thought and prismatic compositional strategies. It is not simply open to manifold readings; it is distinctly resistant to the closure of definitive interpretation, for it is not just anti-foundationalist but overtly relativist in its ontology. Simmel's text performatively exposes the philosophical limits of the longing for hermeneutic closure by demonstrating the viability of multiple, conflicting interpretations of the phenomena that make up human (sociocultural, historical, psychological) life.

In the memories of his students cited at the outset, Simmel's philosophical and aesthetic sensitivity operated as a sort of barometer for the zeitgeist. Bearing his own complex culturalist conception of the "psychological" in mind, we should beware of reducing this theoretical brilliance to an expression of "subjective" states or "seismographic" capacities à la Hans-Georg Gadamer.[14] Simmel's theoretical style is anything but naïvely representational; its immediacy, what in a novel might be called breathlessness, is a deliberate effect: an artifact of writing.

This point is beautifully attested to by Paul Fechter, recalling a lecture by Simmel he attended:

> It was a genuinely Simmelian *Kolleg*: you did not just hear him, you also saw him thinking. He enabled his hearers to share in his experience, making visible the coming into being, rising up, self-expression of thoughts, their origination out of and in the word-complexes, presented the same old fascinating spectacle of a human being philosophizing with his entire body, who needed not only the head but all limbs as formative means of expression for his inner spiritual processes. (*BdD* 161)

Then Fechter learned from a colleague that this seemingly spontaneous performance had actually been a rerun from years earlier. Simmel had apparently

> without a manuscript repeated the same lecture as before; he knew the text and had used it once again to conjure up the spectacle of thinking before his listeners, perhaps with the same gestures that had accompanied the first lecture.... [His] impressiveness gained a supplement of self-knowledge that made its effect on the listeners even more uncanny.

Although eyewitnesses often emphasize that Simmel's lectures were much more accessible than his published work—as Emil Ludwig put it, "what he spoke in an hour, he wrote on two pages" (*BdD* 154)—Fechter's anecdote suggests that his uncanny

---

dialectical logic" as exemplified by *The Philosophy of Right* (Gerhardt, *Idealtypus: Zur methodologischen Begründung der modernen Soziologie* [Frankfurt am Main: Suhrkamp, 2001], 120). While also emphasizing his relations to Marxian thought and insisting that "far from being a *bricoleur*, Simmel was a systematic thinker" (121), Gerhardt corrects distortions propagated by, among others, the late Lukács and the Weinsteins, at the cost of underestimating Nietzsche's importance for him. As, more recently, for Henry Schermer and David Jary, attention to "form and dialectic" serves to expand understanding of Simmel's contributions to the discipline of sociology (see Henry Schermer and David Jary, *Form and Dialectic in Georg Simmel's Sociology: A New Interpretation* [New York: Palgrave Macmillan, 2013]).

14. Gadamer refers to Simmel's "seismographic refinement" in the context of his 1960 discussion of "lived experience" (*Erlebnis*) (Gadamer, *Wahrheit und Methode* [Truth and Method], *Gesammelte Werke*, vol. 1, *Hermeneutic I* [Tübingen: Mohr/Siebeck, 2010], 6).

capacity "to conjure up the spectacle of thinking" was the effect, in the broadest sense, of writing.

One might of course view philosophy itself as (involving) such a performative (re)enactment of the activity of thinking—as constituting the experience to which it refers. Certainly, Hegel's *Phenomenology of Spirit* and Platonic dialogues operate by evoking the same sort of readerly excitement. My point is not that Simmel is unique but that he is exemplary and that his activities as both writer and teacher need to be seen in the context of the longer tradition of philosophizing as public event, as pedagogic spectacle. Whether in books or lectures, Simmel enacted for his audience the process of thinking, performatively engaging them in the process.[15]

Fechter's story is well worth recalling when considering the paradoxical impression of modernity or contemporaneity Simmel's writings make today. It suggests that the historical-hermeneutic task of reconstructing his thinking must be balanced with a healthy dose of critical awareness regarding the structure of the historical "referent" itself. Not only, to put this point from another angle, does the highly contemporary feel of both the topics and the approach of a man famous for vividly capturing the lived experience of industrializing and urbanizing Europe illustrate once again that in Simmel's work, style is substance. It also underlines the continuing theoretical salience of the thought of the nineteenth-century fin de siècle—even as it points to many unresolved questions concerning its reception.

As a philosophical modernist, Simmel was attempting to describe the fragmentation and dissolution of experience in (still-emergent) mass society in synthetic ways—and thereby to revitalize the conceptual inheritance of the philosophical tradition. Descriptive and conceptual aspects intertwine in his phenomenological approach to the analysis of modern money culture. His somewhat old-fashioned philosophical vocabulary notwithstanding, this mode of theorizing is often less totalizing than his successors'.

Simmel's intellectual agenda was shaped by his conviction that the Western philosophical and more broadly cultural tradition was in the process of dissolution. And yet, like Nietzsche, he maintained faith in the power of (at least some) individuals to achieve new forms of reflective equanimity and to create ethically and aesthetically meaningful lives that carried forward the ideals of that inheritance. Unlike Durkheim or his friend (and fellow Nietzschean) Max Weber, Simmel did not ultimately place his faith in the power of science and the advance of objective knowledge of the social. He insisted on the constitutive importance of ineluctable conflicts between individual existence and the superindividual—social, historical, cultural—worlds in relation to which it takes on contours.

---

15. Simmel's best-selling 1910 *Hauptprobleme der Philosophie* (Main Problems of Philosophy) offers a vivid example of his performative rhetorical strategy. There Simmel deploys a "certain fiction" (*gewisse Fiktion*) to aid him in "representing and examining" a series of central philosophical problems by depicting a philosopher thinking through different, historically changing solutions (*GSG* 14: 12). An index of that book's impact: in the semester Hitler came to power, Adorno offered (with Paul Tillich) a *Proseminar* (introductory course) focusing on *Hauptprobleme*. See *Adorno Handbuch*, ed. Richard Klein, Johann Kreuzer, and Stefan Müller-Doohm (Stuttgart: Metzler, 2011), 481.

Simmel's post-substantialist and perspectivist philosophical vision of human self-understanding and self-reflection is set out most overtly in his late *View of Life*, a work that has had a significant and largely unrecognized history of effects in philosophy. Its influence is especially notable in the case of the resonance between Simmel's reflections on mortality (a preliminary version of which appeared in *Logos* in 1910) and the early Heidegger's existential phenomenology,[16] but his thinking about human historicity also had a significant impact on others who, like Adorno, did not construe the differences and conflicts endemic to social and cultural life in terms of subjective authenticity. Simmel saw metaphysical, ethical, and aesthetic questions as intertwined, and his philosophy of life was in many ways a throwback to the antique sense of practical philosophy Adorno himself later attempted to revitalize: "the teaching of the good life."[17] If his *Philosophy of Money* is less despairing than, say, Adorno's *Minima Moralia*, about the ultimate significance of the changes to subjective experience (and the historical possibilities of individual existence) being brought about through modern "techniques of life," surely this is understandable, given the events that transpired between 1900 and 1945.

In reading Simmel's *Philosophy of Money* as inaugurating an influential modernist style of philosophizing that integrates attention to the phenomena of everyday social and cultural life with nuanced reflection on their philosophical and historical significance, I am thus attempting to draw attention, not only to the work's considerable theoretical ambition and complexity and its continuing interest for cultural theory, but also to a form of influence that has been insufficiently appreciated by philosophers and social scientists alike. The story of Simmel's impact as a writer and thinker cannot be properly told so long as the philosophical and theoretical importance of his modernist style of thought goes unrecognized.

Because Simmel's strategies of writing are integral to his mode of argument, some of the most influential and theoretically significant aspects of his oeuvre have been rendered illegible through what Frisby called "quarrying . . . for illuminating insights." We have already seen the paradoxical consequences of these reading practices: Simmel is indicted as formalist but labeled an unsystematic thinker and praised for the very genial inspirations to the sociological imagination that are represented, theoretically speaking, as accidental. Stylistic features whose philosophical significance would be evident were they placed in historical context are explained

---

16. "Already in 1923 Heidegger spoke to me of Simmel's late writings with admiration. That this was not just a general recognition of Simmel's philosophical personality but indicated substantive philosophical impulses Heidegger had received will be clear to anyone who reads . . . what the doomed Simmel had in mind as his philosophical task," Hans-Georg Gadamer writes. He then goes on to cite a decisive passage from the end of the first chapter of Simmel's *Lebensanschauung* (*GSG* 16: 235) that culminates in the sentence: "I know well what logical difficulties stand in the way of the conceptual expression of this way of viewing life. I have attempted to formulate them in the full presence of the logical danger since in any case here the level is *perhaps* reached where logical difficulties do not necessarily demand silence—since it is the level out of which the metaphysical root of logic itself is first nourished" (Gadamer, *Wahrheit und Methode*, 247n138). See also Gadamer, "Erinnerungen an Heidegger's Anfänge," *Dilthey Jahrbuch* 4 (1986–87): 13–26.

17. Theodor Adorno, "Die Lehre vom richtigen Leben," *Minima Moralia* (1951; Frankfurt am Main: Suhrkamp, 1991), 7.

away as inadvertent expressions of psychological idiosyncracies or simply dismissed as aesthetic or argumentative deficiencies. Yet appropriating Simmel's work by decontextualized fragments serves a constructive, canonizing function that is quite directly self-validating for the discipline of sociology, and these hermeneutically problematic practices have proved highly resilient.

In the first instance this function is methodological. But since the question of Simmel's philosophical and historical significance cannot really be posed from within the dominant, ahistorical mode of reception defined by these reading practices, they have substantial historiographical implications as well. When Simmel is appropriated by fragments, the most tangible evidence of his influence on students and readers appears to be the result of a convergence of topics or gestures—historical or cultural coincidence rather than a marker of intellectual lineage or theoretical relations.

In the dialectical tradition, style and substance are inseparable; larger questions about Simmel's oeuvre cannot properly be posed without critical attention to his strategies of writing. Moreover, such formal issues are simultaneously historiographical: the theoretical significance of his style of thought cannot be understood in abstraction from its philosophical antecedents. Attending to the integral role of style in his strategies of argumentation exposes highly influential and theoretically significant dimensions.

Reading Simmel as a modernist thus helps confront a challenge that is at once philological and philosophical: how to recognize and theorize the interdisciplinary—or, better, transdisciplinary—legacy of a style of thought in order to make Simmel's distinctive influence on twentieth-century thought—his wider philosophical or theoretical "history of effects"—legible. As the case of his reception in sociology illustrates, when his modernist style of thought goes untheorized, Simmel's influence is effectively converted into cold cash: separated from their metatheoretical framing, his innovative philosophical strategies are made appropriable for quite different projects whose "provenance is not apparent" (*GSG* 20: 261).

As much as Simmel's thinking builds and depends on the dialectical philosophical tradition, it also self-consciously inhabits the moment of crisis in which faith in the power of thought was yielding to universalized skepticism in a culture where rationality no longer appeared a safe refuge. His writing must be situated in the wider field of rhetorical, representational, and reflective innovations that make up literary and more generally aesthetic modernism. Far from being unsystematic or aleatory, his innovative strategies of philosophizing evoke the associative logic of living thought itself. Simmel's texts operate in ways that are formally analogous to the modernist remaking of the visual arts, in which inherited representational strategies have come into crisis and the viewer is forced to reflect upon painting (and upon representation and aesthetic practices in general) in new ways. Analyzing his writing calls for the same sort of self-reflexive turn on the part of his reader. His texts aim to open up new perspectives, not just on their ostensible topics, but also on the historical and cultural transformation of modes of experience, perception, and understanding under way in the period.

In thinking about Simmel, as in approaching cultural modernism more generally, it is important to distinguish this broad aesthetic sense of modernism (which of course encompasses a multiplicity of artistic practices, responses, and movements) from the descriptive, historical and sociological usage of the term. The discursive slippage between "modernity" and "modernism" can easily lead via a sort of grammatical reduction to the (often implicit) assumption that "modernist" can be understood as meaning "of modernity" and explained in (ultimately tautological) contextualist terms.

Cultural modernism is tied up with the historical and sociological changes associated with "modernity" and the sociohistorical and political process of "modernization." But modernist works and activities cannot be adequately understood as the reflex or reflection of modern material and cultural conditions, and such reductive forms of explanation obscure not only the theoretical stakes of the stylistic and formal aspects of modernism but also the complex relation between modernist aesthetic practices and their cultural and historical context. It is necessary both to distinguish and to relate the two senses of "modernism" in order to grasp the complex interplay between historically and culturally located practices and transhistorical and -cultural philosophical concerns that define aesthetic modernism—and to do justice aesthetically as well as philosophically to Simmel's style of thought.

Sociologically speaking, Simmel as a philosopher occupied the liminal space between a modernizing and professionalizing discipline and its multiple others—not just the emergent social science disciplines but also the feuilleton and the market in popular philosophical writings more broadly. He was also a modernist philosopher in the sense that he straddled these worlds, and in this respect too, taking Simmel's liminality seriously can help us think more clearly about the cultural phenomenon known as modernism. As a consequence of the *Gesamtausgabe*, Simmel's importance as interlocutor for artists and writers involved with a wide range of aesthetic movements—for naturalists and symbolists, for members of the Stefan George Circle, but also for activists in the new social movements—has become evident even as new translations have made the breadth of his aesthetic and cultural interests increasingly visible to Anglophone readers.

For Simmel, philosophy and engagement with the arts and culture went hand in hand. Nor were his devotion to aesthetics, pursuit of "essayism," and promotion of "philosophical culture" apolitical. On the contrary, Simmel's work is a key site for reflection on the ways philosophical or theoretical and literary or stylistic issues are intertwined in the modernist search for new strategies of representing and interpreting contemporary experience. They can help us recognize the importance of the sociohistorical setting of these practices in a cultural moment when inclusion and democratization were increasingly regarded as virtues.

The breadth and diversity of Simmel's oeuvre is the mark of a paradigmatically modernist thinker: the philosophical style not of a marginal academic but of an internationally famous philosopher and best-selling writer—one whose understanding of his mission as a teacher, whether in the university lecture hall or outside it, was by no means narrowly professional. What is in some ways a premodern conception of himself as a thinker turned out to enable the most progressive aspects of his thought. Like other influential modernists, Simmel was attempting to foster new modes of human self-understanding adequate to a world in radical—aesthetic, cultural, political—flux.

What makes Simmel a *philosophical* modernist, then, is not that his questions are of a different kind or quality from those of other modernist thinkers, writers, artists. I am neither implying that what we conventionally identify as modernism and modernist artistic practices are not philosophical nor suggesting that his rhetorical strategies differ categorically from those employed in modernist literary texts. My point is that Simmel's formal strategies serve explicitly philosophical purposes—and that the vehicle of his reframing of subjective experience is not the mode of narration or representation per se but the very matter of the philosophical tradition. Simmel's texts are modernist *philosophy* in that they performatively engage readers in reflection upon the central dilemma of post-Nietzschean thought, inviting—forcing—us to consider what constitutes philosophizing in a world without secure foundations, where subjectivity itself has entered into flux.

In assessing Simmel's importance, it is crucial to keep in mind that he wrote for the predecessors of what Siegfried Kracauer would in 1926 call Berlin's "homogeneous cosmopolitan audience."[18] By focusing attention on the phenomenological and dialectical strategies of Simmel's modernism, I situate his reflective efforts to come to terms with the challenges of life in a cultural world defined by money—to philosophize in and about what he sometimes called *Geldkultur*, money culture—in relation to modernist culture and cultural modernization more broadly.[19] This helps illuminate why and how his influence extended from figures in the arts and politics to those in social science and philosophy proper.

A great debt is owed the late David Frisby in making the current flowering of Simmel Studies possible. His efforts as translator, editor, and tireless advocate of Simmelian ideas brought wider, cross-disciplinary recognition of Simmel's importance. The hallmark of Frisby's approach was a reading of Simmel as a thinker of modernity that directed attention to his significance as a predecessor of critical theory and the sociology of culture and renewed sociology's image of Simmel for a new, more culturally oriented discipline.

My reading of Simmel as a philosophical modernist parts ways with Frisby's influential account of the pioneering "sociological impressionist" and "sociologist

18. Siegfried Kracauer, "Der Kult der Zerstreuung," in id., *Das Ornament der Masse. Essays* (Frankfurt am Main: Suhrkamp, 1977), 313. Kracauer's argument concerning the "legitimacy" of aesthetic pleasure in new cultural phenomena is clearly Simmelian. Kracauer sought out Simmel soon after his 1907 arrival in Berlin to study architecture and for a time hoped to change careers through work with him. The first chapter of his 1919 monograph, modeled on Simmel's own intellectual biographies, "Georg Simmel: Ein Beitrag zur Deutung des geistigen Lebens unserer Zeit" (Georg Simmel: A Contribution to the Interpretation of the Spiritual Life of Our Time) first appeared in *Logos* in 1920 (now in *Ornament der Masse*). The text, dedicated to Margarete von Bendemann (Susman), is in *Frühe Schriften aus dem Nachlaß*, vol. 9.2 of *Siegfried Kracauer Werke*, ed. Inka Mülder-Bach and Ingrid Belke (Frankfurt am Main: Suhrkamp, 2004), 139–291. On Simmel's intellectual and personal significance for Kracauer, see Mülder-Bach and Belke's editors' report.

19. *Geldkultur* is linked to life lived in pursuit of "the exciting as such" (see *GSG* 6: 336–37).

of modernity" whose writings deployed "fragments of modernity" to represent the subjective experience of modern life and thereby expanded the sociological compass beyond the "objective" effects of industrialization and urbanization. From the perspective I have been developing, Frisby's is but the latest and in many ways most successful effort in a distinguished tradition of attempts to improve Simmel's status in the sociological canon by emphasizing his contributions to questions and problems central to the contemporary discipline. Like those who interpreted him as a formal sociologist or as a sociologist of conflict, Frisby focused attention on important aspects of his work. But reading him as a "sociologist of modernity" anachronistically imports into Simmel's thinking categories that were at best inchoate during his lifetime. The consequence, as in the earlier cases, is that a much more ambitious and ambiguous philosophical program is simplified as his work is assimilated as canonical (and foundational) part of social science.

Frisby's interpretive strategy both fosters and, via the performative logic of the concept, confirms sociology's position as a discipline defined by the project of understanding modernity and modern society. Ironically, even as he drew attention to Simmel's importance as the predecessor of students and readers such as Kracauer and Benjamin, Frisby thereby helped encourage the very tendency he criticized of returning to Simmel's work to mine his texts for unrecognized contributions to the contemporary sociological enterprise—and reinforced sociology's self-representation as a discipline that had parted ways with philosophy in the rigor and precision of its modes of theorizing the world. By definition, a mode of reception centered on Simmel's contributions to the "sociology of modernity" obscures the ways in which his work continues to resonate with other, earlier modes of reflection on human identity and community—and thereby implicitly calls core assumptions of the contemporary discipline of sociology into question. On my reading, Simmel's work decenters the question of what it means to think modernity and radicalizes reflection on sociology's constitutive categories of "society" and "individuality" alike, as well as on the discipline's place in the contemporary theoretical imaginary.

One of Simmel's earliest advocates, the historical economist Gustav Schmoller (1838–1917), suggested in his review of the *Philosophie des Geldes* in 1901 that the "actual purpose" of the book was "to determine what the money economy, especially the modern one of the nineteenth century, has made out of human beings and society, their relations and institutions."[20] To think human being historically and culturally is at once a social scientific and a philosophical undertaking, and Simmel's complex effort to grasp what was becoming of human existence in the rapidly changing world around him was at the vanguard of decisive breakthroughs in twentieth-century thought in what we now understand to be very different fields. His innovative approach to thinking the *geistige*—spiritual, cultural, historical—significance of the socioeconomic formations fostered by industrialization and urbanization still holds important lessons for us.

---

20. Gustav Schmoller, "Simmels Philosophie des Geldes" (1901), in *Georg Simmels Philosophie des Geldes*, ed. Rammstedt et al., 282.

Subsequent developments have made it difficult to perceive the integral connections among Simmel's theoretical legacies, which extend, not just to philosophy and sociology, but also to psychology, anthropology, and even the practices of cultural criticism initially associated with the feuilleton. With its wide-ranging reception history, the *Philosophy of Money* is an exemplary case, one of all the more interest given the book's importance within Simmel's oeuvre. I hope my effort to get at the methodological, historical, and philosophical significance of the work as a whole will persuade readers in many fields to take on this difficult, even daunting, text—to give Simmel's attempt "to delineate the spiritual foundations and spiritual significance of economic life"[21] the reading it deserves.

Focusing attention on Simmel's rhetorical sophistication, in both the argumentative and aesthetic senses, helps reveal the theoretical significance of his writerly modernism. He advances his conception of form as inhering in "living interactivity"—and hence inextricably, dialectically, linked with conflict and change—in a performative demonstration of its value for thinking the complexity of historical and cultural reality. By enacting a modernist approach to philosophizing, Simmel's monumental work carries forward the critique of instrumental reason (and ipso facto of a thinking of the human world in its image) already articulated by Hegel. Drawing on Marx, but also on Goethe and Nietzsche, to develop a vision of cultural evolution as a process of progressive reification and alienation, it provides the lineaments of the argument that would, after Simmel's death, become famous in the work of his erstwhile protégé György Lukács.

Simmel lacks the faith in progress or in collective consciousness that imbued history with salvific resonance for Lukács. In its relativist emphasis on the multiplicity and indeterminacy, the excess and exuberance, of life itself, his *Philosophy of Money* instead sets out a philosophical perspective that identifies possibilities for transcending the stultification of "objective culture" in the very alienating forms and modes of subjective existence and experience that were emerging in the highly developed money economy of the nineteenth-century fin de siècle. Simmel thereby reframed very old philosophical questions—about life and knowledge, about the relation between value and history, and about human freedom—in ways that are, even today, palpably relevant. This is not to say that his work provides the answers to those questions. Indeed, he would surely have balked at any suggestion that the central, decisive problems of human life and thought could in principle be definitively resolved.

And yet, for Simmel, the dilemmas that we have come to identify with modernity—the loss of foundations and of faith in substantial values and stable meaning, the acute awareness of the contingency and historicity of our own, historically situated perspectives and judgments of value—were historical only in an accidental sense. As he often pointed out (and here his thinking is quite consonant with that of many other modernists), the problems themselves were not new. Rather, they

---

21. In the words of the opening sentence of Simmel's own book announcement, published in 1901 and reproduced in *GSG* 6: 719–23.

inhered in human (that is to say, historical, contingent, mortal) existence itself. What was called for was a renewal of the philosophical tradition under circumstances where awareness of problems of meaning had become acute, and skepticism about the possibility of ultimate answers democratized.

Simmel's *Philosophy of Money* regrounds reflection in the (historical, cultural) world of experience. Like the literary modernism of Musil or Proust, Eliot or Woolf, his writing aspires to find the eternal in the transient, transcending (or undermining) the apparent dichotomy between materialism and idealism by deploying and intertwining seemingly opposed rhetorics of reflection on human existence. Thus Simmel summons the language of evolution, of social and psychological determination. But he also revitalizes the dialectic, reinscribing the language of subject and object in a materially and culturally articulated and disenchanted, post-Marxist conception of *Geist*.

Simmel's *Philosophy of Money* is ambiguously situated with respect to the very scholarly divisions it helped to constitute. At once inside and outside of social science, it bears the marks of its historical moment, when the emergent disciplines had not yet established their institutional independence of philosophy. Viewed retrospectively, it is a crucial point of origin for that modern mode of reflection that has come to be called theory.

Such a categorization would perhaps have appealed to Simmel, who occasionally even employs the term "theory" in ways that anticipate its current usage. In quite rigorous and classical senses, it is certainly correct to call his undertakings philosophical. But Simmel's epistemological and metaphysical concerns are inextricable from methodological issues that lend his work the appearance of belonging to rather different intellectual contexts, and in both a theoretical and a practical sense, since his death, his texts have become even more anomalous from the point of view of mainstream philosophy.

To put the point more positively, in its concern with signification as such, Simmel's *Philosophy of Money* is not simply inter- or transdisciplinary. It is a metadisciplinary, a self-consciously and conceptually liminal undertaking: speculative in the concrete sense that we associate today with the category of theory as an enterprise at once epistemological and strategic.

In revising Simmel's place in intellectual history, what is at issue is less the past than the present. In returning to his texts, the challenge is not how best to categorize and assimilate his achievements as a thinker by appropriating new elements and aspects into the sociological analysis or philosophical interpretation of contemporary culture. We need, rather, to recognize and reflect upon the ways in which Simmel's liminal style of thought helps us to understand our own conceptual and disciplinary frameworks and in particular the dilemmas that purportedly less rigorous "humanistic" or "qualitative" modes of inquiry face in an intellectual landscape dominated by the quantitative perspectives of today's mainstream social and natural sciences. His work can help us think the modernity (and modernism) of the enterprise of contemporary theory as an undertaking that cannot be situated in a determinate relation to the global ordering of inquiry into quasi-naturalized disciplinary divisions.

Indeed, Simmel's *Philosophy of Money* provides a model for interrogating the limits of inherited modes knowing that can foster critical reflection on the contemporary disciplinary imaginary as such.

Rethinking Thinking: Culture, Relativism, and *das Geistesleben*

Simmel's disciplinary self-understanding underwent a considerable evolution during the second half of the 1890s, while he was writing what he initially conceived of as a "psychology of money," and there is an internal connection between that evolution and his efforts to develop strategies for thinking about money in its full, complex significance for human cultural life. The *Philosophie des Geldes* owes its existence to Simmel's overcoming of his earlier, proto-positivist faith in (social) science. Both conceptually and biographically, what began as a sociological—and, in the broad, sociocultural sense of that term in *Völkerpsychologie*, "psychological"—study of money led him back to philosophy. And it was in confronting the challenges of conceptualizing money itself and of understanding the sociohistorical and psychic phenomena associated with the rise of the money economy that he elaborated the relativist philosophy and methodology that characterize his mature work.

In Part III we shall look more closely at Simmel's intellectual development from his early conviction (as expressed in 1894's "Das Problem der Sociologie") that in modernity "the science of human being has become the science of human society" to his mature views regarding the scientific status of reflection on the social in his 1908 *Soziologie: Untersuchungen über die Formen der Vergesellschaftung*. His conception of sociology as "Investigations into the Forms of Association" (the book's subtitle) directly reflected the changed understanding of philosophy and its tasks consolidated during Simmel's long labors on his *Philosophy of Money*.

For the moment, though, it suffices to note that by the time he published *Philosophie des Geldes*, Simmel's conception of the "superindividual" and of the nature and purpose of *Wissenschaft* had evolved considerably. To be sure, he was still exploring what Friedrich Tenbruck would describe a half-century later as the "novel perspective and the world of new phenomena" disclosed by recognizing a specifically superindividual, social dimension of reality. But only so long as the epistemological issues surrounding the ways the flux and multiplicity of historical and cultural life took on knowable form seemed to be resolvable methodologically, could Simmel regard social scientific inquiry as supplanting philosophical reflection.

In the brief autobiographical text probably dating from the same period as the second (largely unrevised) edition of *Philosophie des Geldes*, Simmel related how his understanding of what was involved in reflection on the social expanded as his thinking about money opened onto more profound metaphysical and epistemological problems. That work had inaugurated a new theoretical approach, a historically and philosophically self-reflective response to the destabilizing effects of what he memorably described as the "contemporary dissolution of everything substantial, absolute, eternal into the flux of things, into historical mutability, into merely psychological reality": to wit, redefining the "central concepts of truth, of value, of objectivity" relativistically, by replacing the old ideal of "substantial fixed values" with a "living reciprocity of elements" (65620: 304–5).

In his *Philosophy of Money*, then, the paradigm shift embodied in the emergence of modern social science (or to put it in less whiggish terms, the increasing hegemony of psychological, historicist, naturalizing and other anti-foundationalist perspectives on the foundations of culture and experience) was itself rethought— or rather dialectically extended. With his new, self-reflexively relativist concept of foundations, Simmel expanded the "concept of reciprocal interaction" beyond its original "sociological significance" into an "entirely comprehensive metaphysical principle" through a new concept of concepts based on "the living reciprocity of elements."

Simmel's new way of thinking about thinking found direct expression in his distinctive way with what is perhaps the key element of German classical philosophical vocabulary, the category of *Geist*. His *Philosophy of Money* develops a methodological strategy for reflecting on human *Geistesleben*—cultural, intellectual, spiritual life—both with and beyond historical materialism by interweaving ideal and material explanations and interpretations of human experience and (individual and collective) existence. Like his philosophical predecessors, Simmel saw difference and conflict as constitutive for historical existence, but he interpreted the dialectic in contemporary, that is to say, post-Darwinian terms, as cultural evolution.

As noted, in 1903, Simmel helpfully resumed key arguments from the longer work in "Die Großstädte und das Geistesleben," an essay that has become canonical well beyond sociology under the misleadingly psychologizing title of "The Metropolis and Mental Life." In light of Simmel's innovative reframing of the category of *Geist* in the spirit of the *Völkerpsychologie* of his teachers Moritz Lazarus and Hermann Steinthal, the text might better be called "Metropolises and Cultural Life." It enacts what we would call Simmel's interdisciplinary methodological strategy for interpreting the revolutionary impact of the metropolis on individual and collective existence in modernity, integrating sociological, psychological, anthropological, and philosophical perspectives on the new forms of life that were evolving under the sociocultural and material conditions brought about by industrial and political revolutions. Focusing on constellations of phenomena associated with urbanization, Simmel interprets the fin de siècle metropolis as the mise-en-scène of historic transformations in human *Geistesleben*, both describing and theorizing the changes in individual and collective forms of spiritual, mental, cultural life enabled and catalyzed by the conditions in the rapidly expanding cities of the nineteenth century.

The title's provocative juxtaposition of "metropolises" and "spiritual life" foregrounds what Simmel had come to see as a necessary intertwining of conceptual and descriptive, philosophical and empirical, dimensions in any effort to reflect on human identity and community. But it also points to what he would later identify as the "conflict in modern culture," whose source was not modernity but culture itself. He opens the essay by declaring: "The most profound problems of modern life have their source in the claim of the individual to preserve the autonomy and singularity of his or her existence in the face of the overwhelming powers of society, of the historical inheritance, of the outward culture and technology of life—the current reconfiguration of the struggle with nature that the primitive human being had to conduct for his or her *corporeal* existence" (GSG 7: 116).

As this formulation, resonant with Nietzschean pathos, shows, Simmel's mature position significantly reframes the evolutionary principles of his 1890 *Einleitung in die Moralwissenschaft* (Introduction to Moral Science). Simmel returns to the topic of this internal—later, though not always, "tragic"—cultural dynamic at the conclusion of "Die Großstädte." It leads, he says there, to a "crushing superabundance of crystallized, now impersonal forms of *Geist*," which overwhelms the subject, and hence "through the hypertrophy of objective culture to an atrophy of individual culture." Simmel poses the philosophical question of the place of the metropolis "in the world-history of spirit" with this dynamic in mind (GSG 7: 130).

He reads the urban environment of the fin de siècle as the site of a conflict between two modes of understanding subjective existence: the Enlightenment ideal of equality and the romantic vision of individual uniqueness: "The external as well as internal history of our time proceeds through the struggle and changing convolutions of these two ways of determining the subject's role in the totality. It is the function of big cities to provide the site for the strife and attempts at unification between the two" since the "distinctive conditions" of metropolitan life serve as "occasions and stimulations" for the elaboration of both poles of the dialectic of individuation. The metropolis is "one of those great historic configurations in which the opposing currents that comprise life flow together and unfold as if mutually" (GSG 7: 131).

The mature Simmel never lost sight of the conflict internal to modern subjectivity. Even if his philosophical allegiance lay on the side of uniqueness rather than equality, he regarded the two forms or aspects of modern subjectivity as dialectically interdependent. Insofar as the question of the meaning and direction of culture itself is always also necessarily at stake in thinking individuality, the two sides of the equation are intertwined in his contributions to sociology as well. This philosophical context thus helps illuminate Simmel's insistence that sociology was merely a "sideline" for him.

In the absence of the reductivist assurance that there could be a science of morality, sociological problematics centered on the cultural-historical and psychological impact of metropolitan life gave rise to philosophical questions about the vicissitudes (cultural and also individual) of rationality and subjectivity. Reflection on the formation of the modern subject had led Simmel back to a historical and phenomenological rethinking of the tasks of philosophy. The insights and interpretive strategies he had developed in reflecting on social form(ation) were then integrated into a new practice of cultural self-reflection that built on and transformed the resources of the German philosophical tradition. As the mature Simmel understood and represented it, *Geist* was at once individual and super- or transindividual or cultural—its "life" simultaneously ideal and material: a transhistorical reality comprehensible only through reflection on the collective and intersubjective forms of human cultural existence as they evolved in and through time. Subjectivity could not be understood in isolation, nor was individuality reducible to a sociohistorical epiphenomenon.

In reading his *Philosophy of Money*, it is essential to keep this non-psychological, culturalist understanding of *Geist* in mind. The mature Simmel aspired to free human beings from historicism just as Kant had liberated them from naturalism, in order to reassert "the freedom of the spirit, which is forming productivity."[22] This notion of human spiritual freedom resonates with Marxian and Hegelian understandings of historical dialectic, as well as with the Herderian tradition of philosophical anthropology bequeathed to Simmel by Lazarus and Steinthal. The accent had shifted from identifying the "forms of association" as such to interpreting the condensed or consolidated [*verdichtete*] phenomenal "forms" of (objective and subjective) culture. So understood, "superindividual" spiritual life comprises psychology and sociology, the individual and the collective, bodily as well as historical and cultural phenomena.

Simmel's phenomenology of culture was constituted from a point of view that self-reflexively encompassed and related these multiple dimensions of spiritual-cultural life in reflection on philosophical problems as they are lived. In "Die Großstädte," urban life serves as a synecdochic site for posing the question of the world-historical significance of the transformation under way in human social and individual existence. This was the culturalist reframing—with all its philosophical implications for thinking subjects and history alike—that turned Simmel's work on money into an effort to construct "a philosophy of historical and social life as a whole" in which philosophical questions about human freedom and individuality were simultaneously sociological, historical, and philosophical objects. As he put it at the conclusion of his 1900 book announcement, his *Philosophie des Geldes* attempted to give an account of why and how "our time, viewed as whole, despite all that could still be improved, surely has more freedom than any earlier age, yet is so little made happy by it" (*GSG* 6: 723).

Simmel's modernist commitment to overcoming reductivism by rendering human self-determination visible gave rise to a performative philosophical strategy that represented and enacted the movements of spirit it thematized. His *Philosophy of Money* aspires to convey a new way of philosophizing. Like Hegel's *Phenomenology of Spirit*, it seeks to be something more and different than a systematic philosophical treatise: to enact new strategies for approaching epistemological, metaphysical, and ethical questions that resituate philosophy as a scientific discipline (*Wissenschaft*) in relation to historical and social life as a whole. Harking back to Platonic efforts to conjoin the pursuit of certain knowledge (that is, science in the sense of *epistēmē*) and the contingent practices of thought, both Hegel and Simmel target readers who will do more than simply follow the discursive or logical structure of their texts, readers who self-consciously submit to an experience of reflection that aims to change their self-understanding as thinkers and as human beings.

---

22. As Simmel put it in the preface to the second, 1905, edition of *Die Probleme der Geschichtsphilosophie* (*The Problems of the Philosophy of History*), this insight had led to a thorough revision, indeed a "fully new" book (*GSG* 9: 231, 468).

As he developed his *Philosophy of Money*, a profound shift took place in Simmel's understanding of the world and of his task as a thinker. Having lost his optimism about the potential of social science to resolve problems inherited from the philosophical tradition, in his mature work, he set aside foundationalist strategies in favor of a metaphysical relativism and a new concept of concepts that embraced the lived dilemma of contemporary *Geistesleben* in the broadest sense: the dissolution of foundations and apparently of meaning itself in modern culture.

Money, as "relativity itself that has become substance" (*GSG* 6: 134), provided the basis for a rethinking of truth, value, and foundations as such under the sign of his new, relativistic "concept of solidity." Simmel had come to believe that the only way to avoid nihilism, to prevent the slide into bottomless "subjectivism and skepticism," was to affirm the relentless process of relativization—the "contemporary dissolution of everything substantial, absolute, eternal into the flux of things"—as the expression of a more fundamental life process. Simmel thereby converted the problem into a solution, affirming metaphysical relativism "as a cosmic and epistemic principle that replaces the substantial and abstract unity of the world-image with the organic unity of reciprocal interaction" (*GSG* 20: 305).

This, of course, is hardly admissible as "social science" today. And since we tend to equate relativism and nihilism and to oppose both to metaphysics, Simmel's claims for his theoretical and methodological views have sat uneasily even with his partisans. In tandem with his seemingly old-fashioned philosophical vocabulary, the misleading enframing of Georg Simmel's career as moving "from" science "to" metaphysics, from early, foundational contributions to sociology toward the alleged irrationalist abandon of his late "philosophy of life," has helped foster disregard for the relevance of his mature philosophical views for contemporary cultural theory. As the failure of multiple, learned, and eloquent efforts to correct the historical record to generate a real rethinking of Simmel's importance indicates, the story being told about him has a symptomatic quality; its persuasiveness is relatively independent of its (in)accuracy.

The history of sociology as a discipline is not even recognized as theoretically relevant by most practitioners. While the same can be said for most modern disciplines, this fact is of particular salience for those that emerged from what were still often known as the "historical" sciences in Simmel's lifetime. The narrative that leaves so much of his oeuvre out of account has thus been pragmatically far less significant than the pervasive practices of selective reading in establishing Simmel's peculiar status as a (mostly forgotten) founding father of sociology. But those interpretive practices cannot be entirely extricated from the hermeneutically flawed narrative frame that authorizes them.

Simmel's affirmation of relativism began from a clear-eyed recognition of the epistemic situation in which there is in principle no appeal to absolute, transcendent truth or values. From this modernist perspective, he made theoretical contributions that are largely illegible in the terms of the discipline of sociology they helped constitute—which is not to say that they are irrelevant for understanding it. In constructing his *Philosophy of Money* on the basis of a relativism itself overtly relativized as grounded in the "world-imag[e] that I hold to be the most adequate expression of contemporary contents of knowledge and emotional directions" (*GSG* 6: 13), Simmel was not beginning from empirical reality, let alone claiming that his epistemic views followed of necessity from historical and cultural circumstances. Wary of the venerable logical abyss that welcomes those who assert the truth of relativism, he put forward a provisional solution based in historiographical reflection on quite intransigent epistemological and metaphysical dilemmas—dilemmas arising in modernity, but, again, not for that reason comprehensible as modern.

We must thus beware mistaking the phenomenological and logical analyses generated by this relativistic way of seeing as empirical descriptions. Simmel's relativized relativism anchored a new, a modernist, style of philosophizing, and his texts must be read with sensitivity for the theoretical, historical, and methodological sophistication of a self-reflexive approach that frames its own perspectives and conclusions as inherently provisional. As Simmel declared provocatively in the Preface to his *Philosophy of Money*, if his efforts to connect "the particularities and superficialities of life to its most profound and essential movements" and provide an "interpretation of their total meaning" on a relativist basis proved "factually inaccurate," it would only make it easier to recognize "the methodological significance" of its investigations as "the form of future validities" (*GSG* 6: 13).

In light of the fundamental continuity of many of our philosophical dilemmas with those of the nineteenth-century fin de siècle, it is well worth considering whether and to what extent Simmel's self-reflexive strategies of thought and writing remain viable. Certainly his work remains an inspiring model for culturally and historically situated theorizing today, even in cases when his analyses are of primarily historical or exemplary significance, yet as in encounters with other pioneering cultural theorists, we need to beware a presentist collapsing of perspectives and attend to the internally complex, genealogical relationship between his conceptual framework and the assumptions and approaches governing contemporary modes of inquiry.

Simmel's mature style of thought represented an effort to come to terms with methodological difficulties that continue to plague us today—a circumstance both obscured and institutionalized by the existing disciplinary division of labor and often reinforced by appeals to "theory" as a (quasi-) post-disciplinary formation or genre. By characterizing his *Philosophy of Money* as a work of modernist philosophy, I am situating it in the (pre-) history of contemporary cultural theory both inside and outside the social sciences. But in placing his contributions in relation to the advent of theory as a genre, I am neither attempting to claim Simmel as a "post-modernist" avant la lettre nor to canonize him as the founding father of a new sort of disciplinary (or post-disciplinary) enterprise.

The fragmented disciplinary organization of contemporary scholarship is itself a symptom of the epistemic problems Simmel was trying to address with his *Philosophy of Money*. If we are to escape the impasse that results from a falsely naturalized division of intellectual labor that severs the study of society and culture and fragments reflection on art and science, philosophy and history into different disciplines, what is called for—what Simmel was already calling for—was a different kind of understanding of our knowledge practices. The way the disciplinary division of labor prevents an adequate historical perspective on the history of those practices as a whole is illustrated by the very language we use to describe its global forms of organization: the slippery terms that mark the (imaginary, yet very real) distinctions between "the humanities," the social "sciences," and the "natural" sciences belie the contingency and porousness of the categories in which knowledge is classified.

By naturalizing the (historical, social, cultural, human) distinctions among different kinds of objects and ways of knowing, that contemporary disciplinary ordering of inquiry serves both institutionally and conceptually to absolve those situated inside it from self-reflection on the larger cultural, historical, human context of their knowledge practices. The global organization and everyday practices of academic life conspire to prevent those immersed in particular disciplines from recognizing the difficulties involved in generating a science of the social or of human being (but also of the biological or the physical) for the complex philosophical issues they are.

Rather than focusing on identifying what is appropriable in Simmel's texts in the abstract, I am suggesting that we read his modernist philosophy as (to adapt his own terms) both symptom and mirror of an era that was culturally and historically decisive for our own ways of seeing and understanding social and cultural life. To disclose the conceptual resources his texts can offer, we thus need to confront both continuities and discontinuities in that genealogical relationship. Read with a sense of the distance but also the proximity between Simmel's modernity and our own, his work illuminates the disciplinary imaginary: it provides opportunities to interrogate our basic assumptions about what makes for rigor in these matters and to reflect on the largely tacit conceptions that authorize the disciplinary and methodological divisions that constitute the practical conditions of and constraints upon thinking human life in modernity.

The challenges involved in reading historically become evident at every level, but Simmel's sometimes old-fashioned philosophical vocabulary presents a particular hurdle for the twenty-first-century reader. The Anglophone reception tends to translate such difficulties out of the way, in this case through an equation of *Geist* with "mind" or "intellect" that assimilates his ideas to a philosophical framework that, to put it mildly, Simmel did not in fact espouse. As we have seen, his understanding of thinking was decisively shaped by culturalist and materialist philosophical traditions in which the "psychological" is thought as transcending the individual, and he was neither an idealist nor the proponent of a vicious "psychologism." His anti-idealist conception of *Geist* as the human potentiality or capacity that makes culture possible cannot be assimilated to a rhetoric of the human organized around categorical oppositions between body and mind, individual and collective, subject and history.

Simmel's use of the concept of *Geist* is by no means without its problems. But the contemporary universalization of the concept of culture, which is represented and imagined as forming or even producing subjects, as institutionalizing and perpetuating inherited perspectives and practices and stabilizing historically specific and contingent understandings of human being, is beset by many of the very same logical and substantive difficulties.

This is not a coincidence but a complex convergence. Like the current notion of "culture," Simmel's conception of "objective" (or "objectified") spirit has its origins in (philosophical) anthropology. In fact, he uses the term *Kultur* virtually synonymously with *Geist* in developing his account of the relations between "subjective" and "objective" sociocultural and historical developments. The theoretical and political implications of Simmel's redeployment of the vocabulary of idealism certainly bear critical analysis and exploration. But such difficulties should not be confounded with the problems of thinking the relation between individual and society that beset philosophical traditions, whether rationalist or empiricist, that posit unsocialized "natural" individuals who must somehow be turned into social and cultural beings.[23] For Simmel, as for Hegel, or for that matter for Heidegger, there is no problem of nature and nurture, no mystery about how society and culture become possible, no explanatory gap between the embodied beings who act and the products of human reason, broadly understood.

Understood as objective *Geist*, culture, as manifested in science and art, in collective practices and political and social institutions, exists on account of its being produced by beings defined by their capacity for generating such enduring traces of their own thinking, feeling, forming ways of being—by beings who are fundamentally, essentially, cultural beings. The mature Simmel was engaged in an effort to get his readers to recognize that they themselves—we ourselves—embody the "forming productivity" that characterizes human (cultural, social, historical) being as *geistig*, spiritual in a sense that transcends the individual/society dichotomy.

My point is not that *Geist* is superior to "culture" conceptually or terminologically. Nature and nurture, objective and subjective, material and historical reality cannot entirely be disentangled in human existence. Explaining the forms and manifestations of collective life requires concepts that express the distinctive qualities of human (interactive, intersubjective, historical, cultural, in a word, *geistige*) life. The contemporary discourse on culture is still beset by these very issues, which then as now make it so challenging to oppose reductivist psychological accounts of human being effectively.

Here, as so often, lived experience exceeds the conceptual vocabulary at our disposal. Simmel's Goethean emphasis on *Wechselwirkung*, reciprocal interaction, epitomizes the nonreductive, interactive thinking of causality that he believed could enable more philosophically adequate forms of reflection on human (cultural, social, but also psychological) life. In and through the project of developing a philosophy of money, this notion led him to a powerful rethinking of the relations between "parts" and "wholes" and hence to a complex set of strategies for grasping the complexity of

---

23. These remain paradigmatic assumptions for much of the research on the human taking place under the aegis of the natural sciences. The conceptual aporiai that ensue, including the allied mind–body problem, are frequently reimported into humanistic inquiry in the course of attempts to integrate natural scientific perspectives, the often lamentable results of the current vogue for incorporating brain imaging into literary and cultural study being a case in point.

a reality in flux. In redefining *Geist*, Simmel laid the foundations for a new thinking of culture as super- and transindividual, lived phenomenon.

Despite Simmel's undeniable allegiances to *Kultur* in the old, idealist and elitist sense, his work points to the future, using both *Geist* and *Kultur* in a more historical and anthropological way. The resulting tensions are palpable in his ideas about "objective" and "subjective" culture and his account of the "tragedy of culture" that manifests itself in the psychic life, but more generally in the form of existence, of modern subjects. The distance between Simmel's conception of human *Geistesleben* and the contemporary rhetoric of human cultural being should not be overstated. Rather than obscuring the problem through a psychologizing rendering of *Geist*, we need to consider the relationship between these conceptual frameworks genealogically.

In the second section of the final chapter of his *Philosophy of Money*, "The Style of Life," Simmel begins a discussion of "the concept of culture" that provides an important point of orientation. We identify "culture," he writes, with "the refinements, the spiritualized forms of life" that result from the process of exchange with the world in which human beings create "values." From the point of view of the "concept of culture," he adds, "the values of life are but cultivated *nature*" (*GSG* 6: 617). A few pages later, Simmel takes up the relations between such "objectified spirit and culture" and "the individual subject" to explore the relations between this creation of "the sphere of objective spirit" and what he had earlier referred to as "the negative meaning of freedom and the deracination of the personality."[24]

Most of what makes up the "content of our lives," he writes, consists in "the preserved spiritual-cultural work of the species [*Geistesarbeit der Gattung*]," in "preformed contents" that can be realized or actualized by individual subjects [*in individuellen Geistern*] but that have an objective existence, a "determination that persists" beyond that realization. This existence cannot be thought simply as material, for even when such objectified spirit is "bound to matter, as in equipment, works of art, books, it is never identical with what is sensorially perceivable about these things. It inhabits them in a potential form that cannot be further defined, out of which it can be realized in individual consciousness."

Thinking, then, is in the first instance the thinking of the culturally constituted world, the activation or recapitulation of historically accreted human activity. "Objective culture is the historical representation or the—more or less complete—concretion [literally, "condensation," *Verdichtung*] of that objectively valid truth of which our knowledge is a tracing."

Simmel's description of cultural realities up to and including truth itself as the objectification of human formative capacities resonates with the Marxian notion of species work, *Gattungsarbeit*, developed in the then unknown Paris Manuscripts—

---

24. The phrase quoted translates a category, "Der negative Sinn der Freiheit und die Entwurzelung der Persönlichkeit," that appears in Simmel's descriptive table of contents for chapter 5. In the English version of *Philosophie des Geldes*, these categories have been inserted into the text as subsection headings although no subsections are indicated in the German text. With the exception of this phrase, all citations here and in the following paragraph are from *GSG* 6: 626.

but also with Platonic imagery, and not least with the Hegelian conception of historical truth. The text also makes palpable how Simmel's thinking about culture anticipates Lukács's work. Not only the conception of form put forward in Lukács's more overtly Simmelian *Die Seele und die Formen* (1910; *Soul and Form*) and *Die Theorie des Romans* (1916; *The Theory of the Novel*) but the nominally Marxist conception of reification that Lukács advanced in *Geschichte und Klassenbewußtsein* (1923; *History and Class Consciousness*) also owes a great debt to this approach to thinking about human cultural existence and in particular to Simmel's account of the consequences of the increasing "preponderance of objective over subjective culture" (*GSG* 6: 651) in modern life.

This line of thought led Simmel to Schopenhauerian and Nietzschean themes that decentered the idealist legacy in his thinking of history, including the history of philosophy. Yet just a few years later, Lukács's *Geschichte und Klassenbewußtsein* (*History and Class Consciousness*) became one of the founding documents of the Western Marxist tradition that shaped the post-1917 leftist theoretical imaginary by reactivating the same Hegelian historical tropes in a fashion that contributed both directly and indirectly to Simmel's being unjustly relegated to the detritus of an outdated "idealism."[25] What is at stake—and this was of course formulated with exemplary clarity in Jean-François Lyotard's 1979 account of Western culture as having entered into a "postmodern condition"[26]—is less the viability of Marxist theory than of the historical metanarrative that animated it. Lukács stands here *pars pro toto* for the way that, however truncated and subjunctivized, a faith that history would or at least could continue to advance human freedom ran as an undercurrent through the most diverse theoretical traditions in the humanities and social sciences throughout most of the twentieth century. Neither history nor what is still called "progressive" thought has come to an end since 1989, yet this metanarrative framework has largely lost its historiographical plausibility, and new understandings of the relations between politics and subjectivities, history and memory, have reshaped social and cultural theorizing.

In this larger intellectual-cultural context, Simmel's much more skeptical view about the course of history and about the potential of human reflective self-awareness to yield knowledge of historical truth should be reexamined. As his *Philosophy of Money* illustrates, such skepticism is quite compatible with belief in the "forming productivity" of human (collective and individual) "spirit" in the *Kulturprozeß*—in a more contemporary idiom, the ongoing historical and cultural construction of individual and social life. Focusing on the role of money rather than capital enables reflection on this collectively lived, evolutionary "cultural process" as a historical manifestation of the same productive self-reflexivity that constitutes human *Geistesleben*.

Simmel did not, and we need not, conflate such reflection, whether understood as social science or philosophical meta-science, with the imposition on history as a

---

25. To be sure, Lukács subsequently repudiated *Geschichte und Klassenbewusstsein* as infused with the same subjectivism and idealizing Hegelian tendencies he had criticized in his erstwhile mentor's work.
26. Jean-François Lyotard, *La condition postmoderne: Rapport sur le savoir*. (Paris: Minuit, 1979).

whole of ethical or epistemological judgments about its direction or value. For him, as for Nietzsche, what orients the global process in which human being evolves is not reason but life—that is to say, the grounding dimension of existence that is itself not subject to determination by concepts. This life process includes the life of the spirit as the technically unknowable ground of the historical-cultural process as a whole. For Simmel, as for Nietzsche, the distinctive feature of modernity is the way life itself has become a question for human beings—a fact, it should be born in mind, that is just as much a natural scientific as a sociological, cultural, or individual one. This account of subjective experience intersects with another significant source of much of the Simmelian cold cash that ended up in the pockets of those who dismissed him as a bourgeois aesthete: the analysis of the role played by what he called techniques of life in the historical "cultural process."

Epistemic ambiguity and historical indeterminacy have philosophical significance. In the concluding chapter of his *Philosophy of Money*, Simmel emphasized that the growing discrepancy between the objective achievements of historical civilization and the ability of the individual subject to internalize or even encounter its breadth was a two-edged sword. The very same cultural developments that were giving rise to subjective alienation also fostered "the reserve, independent intensification and internal development" of subjectivity. Even as the "culture of things" becomes "a superior power" over individuals and "production, with its technology and its outputs, appears as a cosmos with hardened, so to speak logical determinations and developments," people were being freed of "immediate concerns with and immediate relations to things," making it possible for some to achieve a deep interiority, "a reserve of the subjective, a secretness and completeness of the most personal being" that inherits "something of the religious style of life of earlier times" (*GSG* 6: 651–52).

The fact that money enables such opposed subjective and objective cultural developments indicates an even deeper cultural significance. Like language, Simmel writes, money lends itself to "the most divergent directions of thinking and feeling ... it belongs to those powers whose singularity lies in a lack of singularity" (*GSG* 6: 654). Thanks to its absolute indifference, it facilitates and supports opposed developments on both sides of this and every other equation: "In the extension of its power, incomparable with any other cultural factor, to bear life's most antithetical tendencies equally, [money] reveals itself as the condensation of purely formal cultural energy, which can be appended to any content whatsoever in order to enhance in it its own direction and bring it to ever purer expression" (*GSG* 6: 608).

Money is, in a word, the dialectical phenomenon par excellence. Yet however Hegelian Simmel's conceptual apparatus may appear, the "Nietzschean" moment of indeterminacy and openness, his emphasis on emergent and material forces, is decisive for his historical and philosophical analyses and led, in methodological terms, to a new and theoretically highly significant emphasis on the particular.

Simmel's "tragedy of culture" is the tragedy of subjectivity only in the sense of the objective genitive. He invokes the rhetoric of *Geist* to describe what is more accurately the tragedy of philosophy oriented toward the eventual identity of subjective and objective spirit—the tragedy of the idea of history that strove to impose a clear progressive, unidirectional narrative of sublation on the multiplicity and indeterminacy of historical and cultural life. For Simmel, as for Nietzsche, the question of the direction and outcome of the evolution of culture—of human individual and collective spiritual-historical life—was uncertain, and the meaning of history was open in ways that are of decisive theoretical but also practical importance both in and beyond the human and social sciences.

CHAPTER 5

Performing Relativity: Money and Modernist Philosophy

By the late 1890s, culture, art, and aesthetic practices in general had become crucial reference points for Simmel in defining his philosophical endeavor, in tandem with his deepening engagement with the question of how to understand the spiritual-cultural/historical significance of "science" (*Wissenschaft*) and its truth claims. Indeed, an analogy with the fine arts (*bildende Künste*) helped him to articulate his aspirations for his *Philosophy of Money* as a whole through an innovative "location [*Ortsbestimmung*; literally, definition of the place] of philosophy in general" among the disciplines (*GSG* 6: 9) that is one of the most sustained methodological statements in his oeuvre.

Simmel opens the book by situating the project of philosophy as itself importantly indeterminate or relative to other intellectual undertakings, writing: "Every province of inquiry has two boundaries at which the movement of thought passes from the exact into the philosophical form."[1] The "individual sciences," he emphasizes, "cannot take a step without proof, that is, without presuppositions of a substantive and methodological nature." Philosophy, "in representing and investigating these presuppositions" and those of "cognition as such" pursues the infinitely receding goal of thinking without any presuppositions whatsoever. In any given case, however, it can reach only a provisional finality: the point "where forceful assertion and the appeal to the unprovable" come into play, a point that is itself never definitive since what is provable changes over time.

The rudimentary principles of individual sciences or disciplines and the epistemological "preconditions of cognition" in general, then, constitute the "lower boundary of the exact" that demarcates one end of the "philosophical domain." The other side of that domain begins at the diametrically opposed point, "where the ever-fragmentary contents of positive knowledge demand to be supplemented by definitive concepts into an image of the world and related to the totality of life." Even if the "history of the sciences" actually exposes the "philosophical mode of cognition as primitive, as a mere approximation of the phenomena in general concepts—this preliminary procedure is still indispensable with respect to some questions, namely

---

1. *GSG* 6: 9. All citations in this and the following paragraph are from the same page. Unless otherwise noted, all subsequent citations in this chapter refer to *GSG* 6, *Philosophie des Geldes*.

those which belong particularly to the valuations and most universal connections of spiritual life, questions that we have thus far neither been able to answer exactly nor to renounce."

However insufficient philosophical concepts might be by comparison with the precision of specialized scientific knowledge, there is little to imply that Simmel thought the fundamental questions of human existence could ever be either objectively resolved or definitively renounced. On the contrary, he was suggesting that such aporiai were structurally inscribed in human knowledge practices as such.[2]

Simmel's topology implies that only by failing to reflect upon the conditions of possibility, ethical consequences, and ultimate ends of their own knowledge practices can even the most elementary inquiries define themselves as "natural" sciences. The logico-epistemological, as it were, "lower," infra-disciplinary field that provides the axiomatic basis for a particular mode of inquiry cannot be clearly demarcated, nor can definitive answers to the metaphysical-ethical problems of meaning and purpose encountered at the super- or metadisciplinary "upper" boundary of every disciplinary enterprise be attained. Indeed, at the limit, as philosophizing about money demonstrates, materiality itself must be explained in relation to the ideal—and vice versa.

Here, at the outset of his magnum opus, Simmel makes quite clear that he has set aside all traces of naturalistic determinism. In the very next sentence, invoking a prescient analogy, he declares that philosophy's indispensable attempts to unify knowledge in a coherent vision of life and the world remain in an important sense subjective—or, more precisely, perspectival. Like Nietzsche, he now understood philosophy, like art, as an expression of individual, creative spirit. Indeed, Simmel continues, "perhaps the most perfect empiricism would just as little replace philosophy as an interpretation, coloration, and individually selective accentuation of the real as the perfecting of mechanical reproduction would make the phenomena of the fine arts superfluous" (9).

With its inexact yet totalizing attempt to understand the significance, nature, and value of human "spiritual life," philosophical interpretation, like the original work of art, is anchored in individuality and oriented toward particularity. The properly philosophical relationship between concepts and phenomena is as unlike the precision of objective, empirical knowledge as such a work is unlike its technologically perfect copy. The need to synthesize the "fragmentary contents" of everyday reality into an "image of the world" that relates them to "the totality of life" cannot in principle be eliminated through empirical research, because the phenomena that evoke the need—questions of value and of ultimate meaning—are constitutive of human

2. The Enlightenment imaginary, the Baconian vision of a well-ordered hierarchy of knowledge practices was growing increasingly implausible as the complex intellectual-cultural field of the modern disciplinary order emerged. Scientific practices generate not a clearly differentiated and hierarchically structured arrangement of more and less elementary fields but an array of incommensurable disciplinary knowledge practices that themselves rapidly and constantly proliferate and differentiate into further disciplines and sub- trans-, cross-, and interdisciplines. Simmel expands on the "complete historical unity" formed by the "relations of specialization" in "reciprocal interaction with the money economy" in chapter 6, "Der Stil des Lebens" (The Style of Life) (*GSG* 6: 651).

experience, including the experience of the empirical. The indeterminacy of philosophy is grounded in the indeterminacy and ambiguity of experience—in life itself, which is always lived through particularity.

The *Philosophy of Money* asks, not what money is, but rather what the (historical, cultural) phenomenon of money reveals about human existence and the conditions of reflection on that existence. In the remainder of the Preface, Simmel sets out his vision of a philosophy of money as at once "prior to and beyond the economic science of money" and distinct both from economics and from history in its concern with money's "substantial meaning and significance" in and for human existence (10). As he goes on to explain, the first, "analytic," part of the book explores the "idea and structure" of "the historical phenomenon of money" (10). It allows "the essence of money to be understood from the conditions and relations of life in general," while the second, "synthetic," part reverses the equation, using the "efficaciousness" of money to illuminate "the essence and formation" of life as such (11). There Simmel interprets the spiritual significance of money for human existence: "its effects upon the inner world, upon individuals' feeling for life, upon the linkage of their fates, upon culture in general" (10). Incorporating evidence from history, psychology, anthropology, sociology, law, and political economy, he approaches money as the paradigmatic cultural medium—as at once element and emblem of the symbolic exchange that constitutes the foundation of human collective life.

Simmel rejects the intellectual division of labor that assigns all reflection on economic matters to the economists. The logic of the disciplines is misleading both methodologically and metaphysically. "Just as a poem is not only a literary-historical fact but also an aesthetic, a philosophical, a biographical one . . . the standpoint *of one* science, which is always a specialized one, can never exhaust the totality of a reality" (11). The philosophical perspective on economic facts reveals dimensions of life that economics cannot dream of and leads to an epistemic model of far-reaching philosophical significance. In Simmel's phenomenological approach, money thereby becomes the "means, material, or example for representing the relations that exist between the most external, most realistic, most contingent phenomena and the most ideal powers of existence, the most profound currents of individual life and of history. The meaning and purpose of the whole [book] is only this: to cast a guideline from the surface of economic events into the ultimate values and significances of everything human" (12). Grasped philosophically, money points the way to an overcoming of the instrumental logic it embodies and exemplifies, for such reflection exposes the limits of the narrowed, quantitative understanding of value of which it is, in Simmel's terms, both bearer and symbol.

What money most fundamentally is—to translate the point into more modern terminology, its signifying power—cannot be explained in the reductive and instrumental quantitative terms money itself imposes upon all it touches. As the purest product of the human activity of meaning-making, money is a (lived, instantiated) metaphor for the power of signification, for the specifically human (that is to say, cultural and historical) power of creating a world of value distinct from the world of nature. It is thus the perfect "means, material, or example for representing the relations" between the material and the ideal, the synecdochic link "from the surface of economic events into the ultimate values and significances of everything human." Approaching the monetary form of value as the product of human historical, cultural, social activity made it possible for Simmel to pose new sorts of philosophical questions altogether and to ask old questions in new ways. By exploring the meaning, value, function, and limits of money as a cultural institution, the *Philosophy of Money* develops a new perspective for reflection on the social-cultural world and forms of life money both epitomizes and perpetuates.

At this point, Simmel clearly articulates the methodological ambitions of his modernist approach to philosophizing, at once describing his method as a mode of speculation and distinguishing his undertaking from its idealist predecessors. "The abstract philosophical system maintains such a distance from the individual phenomena, especially those of practical existence," that it can only "*postulate* their redemption from isolation and unspirituality." By contrast, his *Philosophy of Money* sets out to "*realize* [that redemption] through an example" (12). But not just any example.

Not only does money "indicate the indifference of pure economic technique," Simmel continues, "it is so to speak indifference itself, insofar as its entire purpose lies . . . only in its conversion into other values." The phenomenon of money thus embodies the greatest possible tension "between what is apparently the most external and inessential and the inner substance of life." For this reason, if "this particular reveals itself as not only, bearing and being borne, woven into the entirety of the spiritual world, but also as the symbol of its most essential forms of movement" (12), it would amount to a paradigmatic reconciliation of the opposition between phenomenon and essence.

Money, then, is not simply an example; it is the example of examples—or more precisely, the synecdoche of synecdoches. Its workings turn out (to translate once again into more current terminology) to reveal the operations of valuation, of signification, as such. Those operations are exposed via the analysis of money's concrete (historical, social, psychological, cultural, material) functions, by drawing attention to the actual practices through which (objective) meaning and value are created and perpetuated in human historical, cultural, and social—*geistige*—life. "The philosophical significance of money," as Simmel puts it later on in a passage to which we shall return, lies in its making practically visible [literally, in its being "within the practical world the most decisive visibility of"] the "formula of being in general according to which things find their meaning *in one another* and in the mutuality of relations" that makes them what they are (136).

The *Philosophy of Money* is not, then, concerned with sociohistorically conditioned, culturally evolved practices or functions or institutional arrangements per se. The book coheres formally or methodologically rather than substantively: what money reveals about meaning-making as a lived process of negotiating surface and depth, ideal and material, particular and universal, is of ultimate philosophical significance. There is thus a radical difference between philosophical inquiry into money and the approach taken by other disciplines. "The unity of these investigations," Simmel continues, comes not from developing and proving "a proposition about a singular content of knowledge." It lies, rather, "in the possibility (which is to be demonstrated) of finding in every particular of life the totality of its meaning" (12). As the synecdoche of synecdoches, money both instantiates and symbolizes the human power of signification. Its historical vicissitudes illuminate human being and knowing in general.

As Simmel recognizes, his approach to epistemology is more artistic than conventionally philosophical. Without a pause (the passage is introduced by a dash rather than a paragraph break), he continues by noting that the work of art has the "tremendous advantage over philosophy" that it always focuses on "a particular, narrowly delineated problem"—and therefore allows us to experience "every extension of that problem toward the universal, every addition of larger features of world-feeling" to the concrete representation as a "gift," indeed, as "an unearned happiness" (12). To avoid the converse, usual tendency of philosophy—"whose problem is immediately the whole of existence"—to reach disappointingly narrow answers, Simmel proposes to adopt (or rather adapt) the artistic model. Beginning from "a limited and small problem," he will attempt to "do it justice by expanding and elaborating it into totality and the greatest universality" (12–13).

As the *Philosophy of Money*'s Preface attests, a sea change had taken place in Simmel's thinking and in his methods in the second half of the 1890s. His turn from (naturalistic) ethics to (relativist) metaphysics had brought a new concern with aesthetic questions in the broadest sense, that is to say, as rooted in the Greek sense of *aesthēsis* as perception, that would continue to shape his work in the years to come. Epistemological and methodological concerns always remained paramount, but the mature Simmel would approach them from different directions, via new sorts of problems and topics—and by employing innovative, modernist, strategies of writing.

The relativist methodology he developed in thinking about money formed the groundwork for Simmel's later efforts to foster modernist "philosophical culture." In order to clarify why and how this particular topic led him to rethink his methodological and disciplinary orientation, it will be helpful to consider how his understanding of what was at stake in reflection on money changed over the decade he was working on this book. We shall therefore temporarily interrupt our reading of the Preface at this point. Before taking up the passage that follows, in which Simmel goes on to elaborate his relativistic method, it will be helpful to examine the evolution of the project that eventually resulted in his *Philosophy of Money*, for it was during this process that his early naturalism gave way to an anti-idealist ontology and a principled metaphysical relativism.

From a Psychology to a Philosophy of Money

Simmel's interest in the phenomena of the money economy began even before his Kantian turn, when he was still working very much in the idiom of *Völkerpsychologie*. In March 1889, he spoke in Gustav Schmoller's political science colloquium "On the Psychology of Money"—a talk that turned out to be the "seed" for the subsequent book.[3] Simmel mentions "preliminary labors on a larger social-psychological work" to Xavier Léon in a letter on October 5, 1894,[4] but the first clear allusion to the work in progress itself is in a letter to Bouglé in June 1895, where Simmel refers to a "psychology of money" that he hopes to complete in the coming year.[5] However, his conviction that the phenomena he was exploring could be explained in such, broadly speaking, materialist terms quickly faded, as a lecture he gave in Vienna the following year attests.

Simmel begins "Das Geld in der modernen Kultur" ("Money in Modern Culture") by proposing a contribution to "sociology," suggesting that "the contrast between more modern times" and the past, "especially the Middle Ages," lay in the absence of all those "binding affiliations" that once integrated individual human beings into larger (social, cultural, religious) wholes. Such "cohesiveness" or "uniformity" [Einheitlichkeit] had been destroyed: "Modernity [die Neuzeit] has rendered subject and object independent and opposed."[6] But as Simmel goes on to sketch out a number of ideas that would be developed more fully in his *Philosophy of Money*, this apparently clear explanatory paradigm and disciplinary location were quickly abandoned.

Much of what follows could just as well be classified as philosophical even if it is also psychological or sociological. The ever-greater hegemony of money leads to dissatisfaction, despondency, and those "so very modern feelings . . . that the core and meaning of life is always slipping from our fingers," Simmel contends. Yet money's "increasing indifference" also fosters "increasing differentiation" among human subjects. His reflections on the psychological and sociological phenomena associated with the modern money were reaching deeper veins. Simmel conclusion sounds a strikingly metaphysical note: money is one of the "great historical powers" and, as such, is "like the mythical spear that is able to heal the wounds it causes" (*GSG* 5: 186, 188, 196).

Simmel interprets the increasing hegemony of money as an index of "the same transition from stability to lability that characterizes the entire modern image of the world." The "vicissitudes" (*Schicksale*; literally, fates) of the "economic cosmos" describe a partial movement that is "at once symbol and mirror of the whole." This synecdochic perspective—grasping money as symbol and microcosm of the historical-cultural process—enables a new mode of philosophizing. As Simmel continues,

> a phenomenon like the money economy, however much it seems exclusively to obey its own interior laws, nonetheless follows the same rhythm that regulates the totality of the

---

3. Quotations are from Schmoller's review of the finished work, where he also noted that Simmel's talk, "Zur Psychologie des Geldes," had been published the same year in his *Jahrbuch für Gesetzgebung, Verwaltung, und Volkswirtschaft im Deutschen Reich* 13 (1889), 1251–64 (*GSG* 2: 49–65). On the prehistory of the *Philosophy of Money*, see the editors' reports in *GSG* 6: 725–28 and 5: 585–91.

4. Simmel also expresses his enthusiasm about contributing to Léon's *Revue de métaphysique et de morale* and thereby taking part in an undertaking "necessary for maintaining our culture": making "the scientific reciprocal interaction between France and Germany ever more lively and intensive" (*GSG* 22: 129–30).

5. Simmel to Célestin Bouglé, June 22, 1895 (*GSG* 22: 149–50).

6. *GSG* 5: 178–96; here p. 178. Originally a talk delivered to Austrian economists, the text first appeared in Vienna's *Neuen Freien Presse* in August 1896.

contemporaneous cultural movements, even the most remote. In contrast to historical materialism, which makes the entire cultural process dependent on economic relations, the contemplation of money can teach us that although the forms of economic life indeed have far-reaching consequences for the psychic and cultural state of the period, on the other hand, this formation itself receives its own character from the great unified streams of historical life, whose ultimate forces and motives are obviously a divine secret. (GSG 5: 195)

Money's sociohistorical significance is its philosophical significance; the economy is a cultural phenomenon in which the material and the ideal are intertwined in mutual determination. Reflection on this "symbol and mirror" of deeper, metaphysical sources of existence had evaporated Simmel's confidence that social science could replace philosophy.

In an 1897 essay entitled "Die Bedeutung des Geldes für das Tempo des Lebens" ("The Significance of Money for the Tempo of Modern Life"), which the editors of the critical *Gesamtausgabe* text of the *Philosophie des Geldes* call "the first unequivocal preformulation for the planned monograph" (GSG 6, 726), Simmel went even further. His historically and sociologically wide-ranging investigation of the increasing hegemony of the money economy on the perceived tempo of human life concludes with a philosophically more elaborated account of what makes money a synecdochic reflection of the whole:

> There is surely no clearer symbol than money for the character of the world as absolute movement. The meaning of money lies in its being given away; as soon as it rests, it is no longer money in its specific value and meaning . . . it is so to speak *actus purus* [pure actuality]; it lives in continuous self-externalization from every given point and thus forms the antipode and the direct negation of every being for itself.

No "empirical case" could "incorporate with such complete purity" the "character of nature" as unceasingly change. On the other hand, he concludes,

> the possibility of using the representation of money for the absolute presentation of this category casts a bright light back on money itself as on the purest realization of the principle of movement. In this way we attain the abstract and absolute expression for all of the concrete and relative effects that money's position in practical life exercises on the determination of life's tempo. (GSG 5: 234)

Simmel's investigations had disclosed unexpected depths. By the time he published this essay, he had ceased to refer to his work-in-progress as a "psychology of money." His new conception of money as "the purest realization of the principle of movement" (GSG 5: 234) had made a *philosophy* of money both possible and necessary. The new title reflects a global evolution in Simmel's professional self-understanding during the late 1890s. Even though selections from a number of earlier texts found their way into the final version, thinking about money had led him to problems for which psychological or sociological interpretations were clearly inadequate.

Since neither the historical phenomenon of money nor its impact on human individual and collective existence could be exhaustively described, let alone understood, in exclusively materialist or historicist terms, Simmel's deepening philosophical vision of what was at stake in interpreting social life also led him to abandon his earlier understanding of science as a functional and in principle potentially comprehensive division of labor. But (re)identifying with the discipline of philosophy did not mean casting aside sociological (historical, psychological, materialist) explanation per se. Rather, as Simmel attempted to come to terms with the problem of value in human life, he adopted what he later characterized as "relativism as cosmic and epistemic principle"—an approach in which diverse forms of knowledge discovered from various disciplinary perspectives were taken into account and related.

Identifying money's philosophical significance as "symbol and mirror" of a world in absolute flux had inaugurated a decisively modernist philosophical strategy: in Simmel's synecdochic style of thought, the "surface phenomena" of psychological experience and of sociohistorical and cultural life serve to illuminate dimensions of existence that are beyond linear analysis. As the "purest realization of the principle of movement," money was the dialectical vehicle par excellence, connecting different, often incommensurable, perspectives and opposed, even contradictory, aspects of reality without reconciling them via conceptual hierarchies or reductionism. Thus, to recall the passage in the Preface, studying the historical and cultural phenomenon of money's "efficaciousness" as universal symbolic mediator could illuminate "the essence and formation" of human spiritual-cultural, collective life as such (11).

Beginning philosophizing with money thereby simultaneously enabled Simmel's theoretical and conceptual innovations and anchored the relativistic methodology that characterizes a style of thought and writing whose rigor and systematicity have proved so challenging for social scientists and philosophers alike to recognize and acknowledge: Simmel's homeopathic conceptual strategy for coming to terms with the loss of foundations by replacing the old ideal of "substantial fixed values" with a "living reciprocity of elements" themselves subject to the same dissolution in an infinite dialectic of creation and destruction, substance and flux.

In considering this "relativist," anti-foundationalist approach, it is important to keep in mind that Simmel did not see the philosophical dilemmas his *Philosophy of Money* addressed as modern per se. Quite generally, as he put it in the Preface, "the substantial meaning and significance" of phenomena that arise in history are not for that reason to be explained historically: "the importance, the dignity, the substance, of law or religion or knowledge stands in an entirely different sphere than the question of the ways it was historically realized" (10). Through an approach shaped by Kant and Hegel as well as by Schopenhauer and Nietzsche,[7] Simmel was attempting

---

7. Simmel taught the history of modern philosophy throughout his career. The topics of his lecture courses (listed in GSG 24: 607–24) document his ongoing engagement with the nineteenth-century tradition and its critics. His first lectures as *Privatdozent* in Berlin (Summer Semester 1885), already very well attended, were on Kant's ethics, and he continued to hold forth virtually every year on some topic related to Kant until his famous lectures were published as a book in 1904. In his second semester in Berlin, Winter Semester [WS] 1885–86, a course "On Pessimism" drew a remarkable 269 registered listeners (*BdD*, 21). Schopenhauer's significance for Simmel is attested by the explicit mention of his name in later variants: WS 1887–88's "On Pessimism, with Extensive Consideration of Schopenhauer's Teaching" and "On Pessimism, Especially Schopenhauerian" (WS 1890–91 and WS 1894–95).

Simmel's sociological thinking also developed within a broader thematization of the place of philosophy in relation to the sciences. In the Winter Semester of 1886–87, his second year as *Privatdozent*, he offered a lecture course entitled "Philosophical Results of Darwinism." This was succeeded the following

to meet the challenge of thinking cultural phenomena, up to and including the crises besetting attempts to engage in philosophical reflection, both historically and transhistorically.

In lines that resonate with a key passage in the Preface over which we shall have occasion to linger, the author declared in his announcement of the first edition of *Philosophie des Geldes* that he had set out to show that "on the other side of every grounding of intellectual or ethical, religious or artistic existence in the forces and vicissitudes of the material stands the possibility of excavating for the latter a further foundation and grasping the course of history as an interplay between the material and the ideal factors, in which none is the first and none the last" (GSG 6, 719).

Simmel's *Philosophy of Money* can be read as a work of social or cultural theory, but its object is (properly, if not conventionally speaking) metaphysical. Reflection on money involves thinking about foundations and limits of all sorts. And because it demonstrates the ineluctable multiplicity of historical, social, cultural reality, philosophizing about money illustrates the constructedness and ultimate instability of disciplinary boundaries.

In the passage in the Preface where Simmel distinguishes the task of a philosophy of money from economics, he rejects the proprietary logic that would divide up the world into categories of objects, since "the standpoint *of one* science, which is always a specialized one, can never exhaust the totality of a reality." We only have the impression there is such a thing as "'economic facts'" (scare quotes in original) because economics addresses itself to the "most practically interesting . . . most exactly representable" aspect of "the phenomena of valuation and selling, exchange and means of exchange" (11). Phenomenal reality is more complex: "there is no such thing" as an act of exchange whose "content would be exhausted by its economic image."

What is at stake is always also representative: as an interaction, exchange is not simply an "economic fact" but can also be interpreted as a "psychological, as a moral-historical, and even as an aesthetic" phenomenon. Moreover, even viewed qua economic fact, exchange can become "the object of a philosophical contemplation that examines its preconditions in non-economic concepts and facts and its consequences for non-economic values and connections" (11). When situated in this way (literally, in this *Problemkreis* or "circle of problems"), money becomes a site for rethinking the relations between facts and values in a way that surpasses the limits of disciplinary perspectives altogether. It serves as "the means, material,

---

year by "The Most Recent Philosophical Theories, Especially in their Relations to the Natural Sciences," which he offered yearly until 1892, when the title was amended to ". . . the Natural and Social Sciences." At the time of the publication of "The Problem of Sociology," he was offering a course entitled "Philosophical Theories of the Past Thirty Years." Two years later, in 1896, Simmel published his first essay on Nietzsche, and the same year, he gave the crucial lecture on "Money and Modern Culture." "What Does Kant Mean to Us?" appeared in the *Vossische Zeitung* in August 1896.

Nietzsche's name did not appear in course titles until WS 1901–2, but beginning that year, Simmel repeated his lectures on "The Philosophy of the Nineteenth Century, from Fichte to Nietzsche" virtually every academic year (once, in WS 1907–8, with the addendum ". . . to Nietzsche and Maeterlinck") until WS 1909–10. Starting the following year, the subtitle became "from Fichte to Nietzsche and Bergson."

or example for representing the relations that exist between the most external, most realistic, most contingent phenomena and the most ideal powers of existence, the most profound currents of individual life and of history" (12).

The *Philosophy of Money* is a self-reflexive enterprise that sets out to show that thinking money in its indeterminacy and multiplicity (as substance and function, evolving historical institution and universal symbolic phenomenon, etc.) can provide insight into the most fundamental features of human cultural existence. For Simmel, money is the philosophical object par excellence, enabling reflection not only on the foundations and implications of particular disciplinary perspectives but also on the perspectival qualities of knowledge itself. Thinking about money performatively reveals philosophy's own radical relativity as an enterprise poised between the indeterminacy of lived experience and pursuit of the clarity to which scientific thought aspires. For Simmel as for Kant, the pursuit of such scientific—*wissenschaftlich* meaning not empirical or numerical but self-reflexively assured, reliable—knowledge of reality was an unachievable, an infinite task.

The operations of money thus make visible and reflectively accessible the limits of knowledge in general as a function of human existence. Simmel elaborates his point about disciplinary perspectives and economics in his first chapter, "Value and Money." "Human activity" of all sorts, he writes, relies extensively on abstraction: "not just reflection on the economy but the economy itself consists so to speak in a real abstraction out of the surrounding reality of valuation processes" (57). What we encounter sensorially is not yet strictly speaking a world at all; human endeavor as such depends on the a priori constitution of a field of phenomena. "The forces, relations, qualities of things" including our own selves constitute what Kant might have called the manifold of intuition, *ein einheitliches Ineinander*,

> a unified intertwining that is first divided up into a multiplicity of independent series or motives [*Reihen oder Motive*] by the interests we bring to bear in order to act upon it. Thus every discipline investigates phenomena that only have a self-enclosed unity and tidy differentiation from the problems of other disciplines under the point of view it has imposed, while reality itself does not bother with these boundaries, rather every segment of the world presents a conglomerate of tasks for the most manifold disciplines. (57)

These limitations are by no means exclusive to intellectual understandings. On the contrary, as Simmel continues, human praxis in general defines such "one-sided series" and creates larger cultural formations based on pragmatic motives, what he calls "culture's grand systems of interest."[8]

Simmel's perspectivism brings together Nietzschean and Hegelian ways of thinking about the relativity of human existence to embed a phenomenological account of the origins of science in the basic human need to synthesize coherency from experiential flux.[9] One of the "formulas" that capture

---

8. See also the *View of Life*, where Simmel refers to the "worlds" corresponding to the "diverse kinds of spiritual-cultural functions," through which "possible contents" are unified provisionally—"the world in the form of art, in the form of knowledge, in the form of religion, in the form of gradations of value and meaning altogether" (*GSG* 16: 238).
9. There is considerable overlap in these strategies of thought with the late William James.

> the relation of the human being to the world is that out of the absolute unity and entanglement of things . . . our praxis no less than our theory constantly abstracts individual elements in order to consolidate them into relative unities and totalities. Except in quite general feelings, we have no relation to the totality of being: we first achieve a relation to the world determinate in its particulars by beginning from the needs of our thinking and acting, by drawing continual abstractions from the phenomena and furnishing them with the relative independence of a merely internal connection that the continuity of the world's movements denies to the objective being of each. (58)

Our own (pragmatically grounded, relative) concepts circumscribe what is knowable. Science (*Wissenschaft*) of all sorts depends on such a priori lived syntheses. The pursuit of knowledge in general and the formalizations of that pursuit in disciplinary form in particular must be understood in relation to the larger purposive, evolutionary, context of human life interests. This is not because knowledge or scientific endeavor can be reduced to its practical or instrumental function. Rather, without the philosophical perspective that situates human cognitive activity through a broader phenomenological (and at the same time historical, cultural, and psychological) account of embodied, social existence, we cannot come to an adequate understanding of either truth or value. It is only through this relativity to human life—or to translate it into a more familiar idiom, only when we understand truth and value in pragmatic terms—that we genuinely understand what anything means. The cultural-historical, "spiritual," process is the ongoing interactive and transsubjective life process by which value and meaning are created (and destroyed).

Grasped philosophically, the phenomenon of money thus illuminates the generative, history-making power of human existence itself. The "economic system is based on an abstraction," on distinguishing "the reciprocal relation of exchange" from "the actual process" of its realization, which is "inextricably merged into foundation and result: into desires and enjoyments" (58). As in the other "areas into which we dissect the totality of appearances for the purposes of our interests," on an experiential level, the actual "form of existence" of exchange melds the subjective and objective. What makes for "that objectivity of economic value that demarcates the economic realm as independent" is a second-order abstraction: the transindividual, supersubjective validity that value acquires in and through exchange (58–59). From a philosophical perspective, exchange is thus culturally significant independent of its pragmatic, material and socioeconomic functions. The "economic form of value provides one of the clearest justifications for the equation: objectivity = validity for subjects as such" (59). In Hegelian terms, objective value is the (recognized) desire of the other.

Exchange is, then, a highly significant, a paradigmatic, cultural or life-form. According to Simmel, "most relations among human beings can be counted as exchange; it is at once the purest and most heightened reciprocal interaction." Moreover, conversely, "every reciprocal interaction should be regarded as an exchange" (59). Exchange epitomizes human life: in it, the same "spiritual-synthetic process that creates a with- and for-one another [*ein Mit- und Füreinander*] out of the juxtaposition [*Nebeneinander*] of things"—that is to say, the same living subject that confers "the form of its own unity" on what is given to the senses—apprehends "the naturally given rhythms of our existence" and organizes its elements into a meaningful connection (60). Ultimately, "the economy is a special case of the universal form of life of exchange" (67) through which the realm of value—that is to say, culture—comes into being in the first place.[10] Economics points beyond itself, equally to that larger context of meaning and value and to the material a priority of an intersubjective realm in which the "spiritual synthetic process" that is subjectivity is situated.

The *Philosophy of Money* offers a subtle account of how need, desire, and exchange are related and elaborated into the supersubjective, supernatural structures and institutions that make up the human world. What we call culture comes to be in a process with ideal and material, collective and individual dimensions, and as Simmel performatively demonstrates, the phenomena thereby generated—subjectivity, objectivity, value, law—require multidimensional analyses. Situated at the beginning of the twentieth-century discourse on culture, the *Philosophy of Money* asks not what culture is but rather how to think about its becoming—how to understand the change, development, evolution of human values, institutions, practices, and ways of life over time. In and through what Simmel calls the "cultural process," human beings generate, refine, and propagate a social, historical, and psychological world, an interactively created and sustained environment in which life is oriented toward the (transcendent) dimension of value. Money facilitates this process both by enabling the requisite abstraction from concrete particularity and by embodying and representing the forms of value thereby created.

Money in Action: Value, Life, Form

If money is only a means or example, it is one of particular philosophical significance. As Simmel puts it in the Preface to his *Philosophy of Money*, money does not simply exemplify "the indifference of pure economic technique but is, so to speak, indifference itself insofar as its entire purpose lies not in itself but only in its conversion into other values" (12). As the synecdoche of synecdoches or (as Simmel puts it in the first chapter of the "synthetic" second half of the book, "Individual Freedom") because money is "itself nothing other than the representation of the value of *other* objects" in quantitative terms that enable "virtually unlimited" division and addition, money "provides the technical possibility for exact equation among exchange values" (388).

Money thereby enables what Simmel calls the "first step" in the evolution that leads beyond the particularity of individual exchange, with its attendant problem of unequal and indeed incommensurable desires, into the more complex forms of social organization that both overcome and stabilize that difference and complexity by mediating (among) them.[11] In its very purity as means, as the *technē* of quantifica-

---

10. For a sociological interpretation of *The Philosophy of Money* that foregrounds the importance of the problem of value, see Natàlia Cantó Milà, *A Sociological Theory of Value: Georg Simmel's Sociological Relationism* (Bielefeld, Germany: Transcript, 2005).

11. As he puts it later, "the objectivity of money" does not stand outside the dialectical process as "something beyond the antitheses . . . this objectivity signifies from the outset the service of both sides of the opposition" (694).

tion par excellence, money facilitates the intersubjective representation, translation, and manipulation of qualitative differences. Monetary exchange thus provides a formal solution for what Simmel calls "the great cultural problem" that ensues once (things of) value have been created in the first place: how to generate new values by turning "objectively given quanta of value into a higher quantum of subjectively felt value via a mere change in bearer" (388). That is, to phrase it in more current terms, the problem of how to make values (objects) signify. "Next to the original creation of values," Simmel elaborates, "this is clearly the task par excellence for social purposiveness." The "cases" that illustrate money's function in the larger human enterprise of "giving form to the contents of life" and thereby bringing forth "the value latent in them" reveal the significance of its "technical role." They show "that exchange is the essential social way of solving this problem and that in money, exchange itself has become a body" (389).

Money literally enriches the lived world. For Simmel, what is philosophically decisive is not the economic fact but rather the form of exchange—and the generative quality of the inter- and transsubjective relations it embodies and fosters. Money makes visible the creation of value, enabling human beings to weave complex webs of symbolic interrelations and mediations in which subjective and objective effects are intricately intertwined and reflexively accessible. In this realm of culture, of intersubjective, historical life—in what Simmel sometimes calls the world of *Geist* or objective spirit, but often refers to as the *Kulturprozeß*, the cultural process—money's philosophical importance as the means of means is revealed. As a pure representation of value, it is a spiritual/intellectual *technē* in the widest sense, one inextricably tied up with the historical evolution of human (social, cultural) life. The interpenetration of ideal and material factors in its operations helps illuminate why, in Simmel's mature view, social science could not become independent of philosophy.

At this point, it will be helpful to step back to an earlier phase in his argument to examine the account of value that underpins this understanding of money. Simmel begins chapter 1, "Value and Money," by establishing the categorial independence of value from nature. "That objects, thoughts, events are valuable can never be read off of their merely natural existence and content." His position is quite radical: the natural order of things and an "ordering according to value" not only diverge; they lack any connection, positive or negative (23). "The relation between them is absolute contingency" (24). And yet value and being nevertheless have philosophical parity—each is a "comprehensive form and category of the world-image" (25). As a psychological process, to be sure, valuation belongs to the natural world, "but what we *mean* by it, its conceptual *sense*" is so independent as to constitute "the whole world seen from a specific point of view"—one that, furthermore, gives "our whole life . . . meaning and significance" (24–25). Value is, so to speak, the subject's objectivity and, as such, the medium of intersubjectivity.

This distinction between the natural and the social existence of objects is culture's condition of possibility. The initial creation of value may lie in some sense outside the cultural process. Within human society, however, "the value of an object depends on its being desired, but on a desiring that has lost its absolute instinctuality [*Triebhaftigkeit*; literally, 'drive character']" (43).[12] For human sociocultural existence to achieve higher degrees of complexity and refinement, it is necessary both that objects achieve a certain independence and that desiring itself be regulated and socially structured. Money turns out to be crucial for both sides of this dialectic.

Historically speaking, the emergence of money is situated within the (evolutionary) "cultural process" by which institutionalized and intersubjectively mediated forms of exchange supplant what Simmel calls "the subjective forms of appropriation of the property of others, pillage and the gift" (89). (Or again, "the pure subjectivity of the change in ownership represented by pillage and the gift" [86].) The form of exchange itself uncovers the "first supersubjective possibility of social regulation, which in turn first prepares the way for objectivity in the material sense; it is initially via this social standardization that the objectivity which is the essence of exchange first becomes incorporated into that free exchange of property between individuals" (89).

Simmel contends that exchange proper (*Tausch*), like "language, mores, law, religion, in short, all foundational forms of life . . . came into being as inter-individual configurations, as reciprocal interaction" in the group as such (88–89). Dismissing as a "prejudice" the assumption of social contract theory that the institutions of the social represent a systematization of formerly unregulated individual acts that served the same purpose, Simmel insists (with Nietzsche) that the historical precursors of a given cultural institution or practice may have been "a form of relationship of *an entirely different kind*" (89). The evolution of culture is discontinuous. Exchange is "a sociological configuration sui generis, an originary form and function of inter-individual life" (89). As such, it is the condition of possibility for the "value-forming significance" of what then come to be misconstrued as the (causal as well as logical) pre-conditions of exchange: "the qualitative and quantitative constitution [*Beschaffenheit*] of things referred to as usefulness and rarity" (89–90).

Value, again, dwells in intersubjectivity, is a function of the superindividual dimension of existence that is the condition of possibility for subjectivity and objectivity as such. Exchange, the paradigmatic form of human interaction, thereby reveals the metaphysical significance of *Vergesellschaftung*, association, as

> the most immediate illustration of relativity in the material of humanity: society is the super-singular configuration that is yet not abstract . . . the universal that also has concrete vitality. Hence the unique significance for society of exchange, as the economic-historical realization of the relativity of things: it elevates the individual thing and its significance for the individual person out of its singularity, yet not into the realm of the abstract but rather into the vitality of reciprocal interaction that is at the same time the body of economic value. (91)

Exchange is quite literally embodied sociality: the expression of the concrete reality of the super-singular yet nonabstract existence of human historical association, the

---

12. I pursued the implications of this intriguing convergence between Simmel's philosophical analysis and a Freudian perspective in relation to the problem of fetishism in "'Eine specifisch moderne Begehrlichkeit': Fetischismus und Georg Simmels Phänomenologie der Moderne," *Die Philosophin* 13 (May 1996): 10–30.

symbolic cultural mode in which value properly speaking dwells. Viewed in another way, exchange is the medium for the mediation of desire—and hence for the creation and elaboration of objectivity and subjectivity alike.

No wonder that Simmel "sighed and despaired over [his] theory of value."[13] He was attempting to square the circle by demarcating a transcendent realm of value while simultaneously affirming its absolute relativity. If value cannot be located in the (natural) object as such, neither is it purely a function of subjective desire. Only as "the foundation or matter of a—real or imagined—exchange" does an object's desirability (or better, desiredness, *Begehrtheit*) turn it into a value (77). To be precise, "it is always the relation of desires [*Begehrungen*] to one another first realized in exchange that makes its objects into economic values" (83).

There can be no (coherent) economics without philosophical reflection, for it is the human (social) relation that constitutes its objects as objects. Conversely, money's philosophical significance is not outside or different from its sociocultural existence but rather emerges with and through it. The need for a philosophy of money arises from (reflection on) the conditions of possibility and consequences of money's historical reality and effectiveness; money's subjective and cultural significance are bound to its most basic operations. This relation is illustrated in an exemplary fashion by the intrication of "sociological" and "philosophical" aims in Simmel's account of the relations between the (speculative) historical/cultural origins of symbolic exchange and the processes of social differentiation and individuation.

Like Marx, Simmel follows the ethnography of the day in regarding the first step in the evolution of culture as dependent on the formalization of social relations represented by the barter economy. He too emphasizes that what in German is called *Naturalientausch*, literally, the exchange of naturalia, or natural objects, corresponds to a highly static social order. To step beyond it requires a form of symbolic mediation that differentiates value itself through an implicit reference to the role played by the dialectic of desire. Value is—and here Simmel is quite Hegelian—the desire of the other. Money thereby provides the solution for what he calls the "great cultural problem" of awakening reflective awareness of the value that comes into being through that dialectic: concretely, through exchange, which socializes and objectifies (the experience of) desire so that it loses its "absolute drive-character."

As "exchange itself become a body," money is the name for the representation of that universality—a manifestation of that super-singular yet concrete actuality of human interdependence. As such, it is at once substance and function, element and symbol of human sociality. "The significance of money," as Simmel puts it in the conclusion to the chapter, "is to represent in itself the relativity of the things desired, [that] through which they become economic values" (138). Money thereby takes on its already noted exemplary function in the cultural process of giving form to the contents of life: Even as it transforms objects of desire and consumption into things of independent meaning and value, money renders visible how human symbolic practice as such operates. In the very purity of its relativity, as exchange incarnate,

---

13. Simmel to Rickert, August 15, 1898 (*GSG* 22: 304–5).

money enables human beings to recognize and reflect upon the "forming productivity" that makes their existence cultural. Simmel's argument that money makes visible the qualities of being in general accordingly takes a self-reflective and performative, modernist form.[14]

Native to the boundary zones of interaction where concretion gives way to reflection, money (to recall the Preface) is the "symbol of the essential forms of movement" proper to "the spiritual world" as such (12). Simmel's doubled inquiry into the philosophical and historical significance of money therefore leads to metareflection on the historical and cultural process by which meaning as such is produced and perpetuated. Not only, in clarifying the origins and growth of objectivity, does this inquiry illuminate the vicissitudes of subjectivity. As a cultural phenomenon, money sheds light on the relation of thought to positive knowledge more generally. In the topological terms Simmel used to describe the emergence of philosophical reflection at the very outset of the book, "the movement of thought" is led beyond disciplinary boundaries in two directions. On one hand, exploration of money's cultural and historical origins and effects leads "below" the social, toward the logical and ontological realm of reflection on the constitution and operations of value in and for human cultural life as such. On the other, consideration of the meaning and operations of money in human society and culture points beyond "the upper boundary" of scientific exactitude, toward a synthetic vision of reality in which the "always fragmentary contents of positive knowledge" are related to "the totality of life."

The philosophical investigation of money thus generates reflection on the foundations and limits of knowledge as such—and on how foundations and valuations come into being and evolve historically. As Simmel puts it in "Value and Money," "The significance of money as representing the economic relativity of objects in itself" that is the source of its "practical functions" does not enter the world as a "finished reality." Rather, Simmel continues, drawing on Hegelian tropes: "like all historical configurations the phenomenon of money only gradually becomes refined into the purity of the concept" proper to it as an object of thought (133). That refinement is a constitutive dimension of the ongoing historical mediation between human beings and world through which culture develops, "the cultural process." Money's philosophical significance is intricated with that historically unfolding process of continuous change—indeed, its meaning only emerges in and through what can then retrospectively be characterized as the evolution of culture.

At the end of "Value and Money," Simmel returns to his account of money as the synecdochic instantiation of the interactive spiritual-historical, sociocultural process by which value emerges and persists—by which things gain objective meaning—from a slightly different perspective. Here money again appears as a body, but one of a peculiarly ghostly sort. "The gap that drove the subjective and

---

14. In this dialectical sense, money's metaphysical significance is rendered apparent: "It is the symbol, in the narrow and empirical, of the unspeakable unity of being, from whence its energy and reality streams forth into the world in its entire breadth and with all its differences" (695).

the objective out of their original unity with one another has so to speak become embodied in money"; its meaning lies in its ability to bridge and thereby enable us to overcome the resulting distance in exchange (136). Money itself tends to abstractness—tends to lose its meaning as substance and become simply the signifier of its social function. So while many objects do (and in principle every object can [133]) serve as money, naturalia "cease to be money or to be able to be money in proportion as money ceases to be a use-value" (134). "Money becomes ever more an expression of economic value because this is itself nothing other than the relativity of the things as exchangeable with one another." But that very relativity comes in turn to dominate and suppress "all other qualities": money eventually becomes "nothing other than relativity itself that has become substance" (134). This social, historical, cultural development of money from substance to function, object to sign, is philosophically significant.

As the purest and clearest expression of the intersubjective relations through which meaning and value come into being, persist, and circulate, money is the paradigm of reification, but also of sublation. In the abstract form of exchange proper to modernity, we experience the coin or bill not as metal or paper but as the instantiation of value, exchangeability, as such.[15] As already noted, Simmel identifies the "philosophical significance of money" as inhering in this synecdochic being without qualities. Money is that site "within the practical world that is the most decisive visibility, the clearest realization of the formula of being in general" according to which things find their meaning *in one another* and in the mutuality of relations" that makes them what they are (136). Both representing and embodying the fact that meaning is a function of the (social) relativity of beings to and among one another, money is, in my terms, the synecdoche of synecdoches.

In the next paragraph, Simmel translates this point into more concrete terms: "one of the fundamental facts of the psychic world" is the way (social, cultural, social, material) relations between "elements of existence [*des Daseins*]" become "embodied in special configurations" that subsist independently yet "have their *significance* for us only as the visibility of a relation" that is bound up with them. "Thus the wedding ring, but also every letter, every piece of collateral, as well as every official uniform is the symbol or bearer of a moral or intellectual, a juridical or political relation between human beings" (136). Whether they express connections or divisions, he continues, "such substances" have their real meaning not for the individual as such but "in the relations between human beings and human groups that are crystallized in them (136).

These configurations are of great philosophical, metaphysical significance. "The idea of a relation or connection" may appear to be an "abstraction" from the reality of the elements that constitute it—at least so long as cognition does not proceed in Hegelian fashion "beyond its empirical boundaries" in order to "sublate this duality" by "dissolving each [substantial element] into reciprocal interactions and processes"

---

15. The same phenomenon is tangible today in credit cards or, in even purer form, "bitcoins," which are (meant to be) a virtually pure function of quantitative operations.

that will in turn suffer the same dissolution (137). But lived experience transcends the fragmentation and bifurcation of the conceptual. In such crystallized symbolic constellations, "practical consciousness" has given stability to flux and concept alike, capturing both in a type of concrete abstraction that lends form and "substantial existence" to "the processes of relation or interaction in which reality proceeds." And, he continues:

> That projecting of mere relations into special configurations [*Sondergebilde*] is one of the great achievements of spirit, in that spirit is indeed embodied in them, but only in order to make the corporeal into the container of the spiritual and thereby to assure the latter a fuller and more animated effectiveness. With money the capacity for such formations [*Bildungen*] has celebrated its highest triumph. For the purest reciprocal interaction has found in it the purest representation, it is the tangibility of the most abstract, the individual configuration [*Einzelgebilde*] that has the most of its meaning in the superindividualized [*Übereinzelheit*]; and thus the adequate expression of the relation between the world and the human being, who can only ever grasp that relation in something concrete and singular but only really *grasps* it when that [concrete and singular thing] becomes the body of a living, spiritual process which weaves everything individual [*alles Einzelne*] together and thus creates reality. (137)

As the symbolic form of exchange, that is to say, of interaction as such, money reveals—represents and expresses—human spiritual-cultural existence in its complexity as transindividual source and ground of value and meaning. We live not in a world of things in themselves but in a dense, historically, socially, and culturally constituted, inter- and transsubjective network of symbols, meanings, and value. Only by understanding the phenomena of social and cultural life—ultimately, the coherency of the world—as the product of human endeavor can we understand ourselves qua human beings. But this is a lesson that must be learned through practice, by participating in the very (cultural, spiritual) process by which meaning and value are produced, exchanged, and perpetuated in interaction—that is, by reflectively engaging with the social and cultural practices in which meaning and value are communicated and (symbolically) exchanged.

The animating idea of Simmel's *Philosophy of Money*—what makes it possible for him to think of the book as a philosophy of social and historical life as a whole—is at once philosophical and sociological. Reflection upon money as the symbol and bearer of very material processes of abstraction is uniquely suited to fostering insight into the relation between human praxis and signification in general—into the genesis but also the limits of meaning and value as such as functions of human (social, cultural) being.

We shall return to the question just touched upon—what it means to understand ourselves as spiritual-cultural beings living in a world that is in important senses of our own making—and to this passage, for Simmel here goes on to introduce a concept of great methodological significance for his *Philosophy of Money*: the "phenomenal series," or "sequence of appearances" (*Erscheinungsreihe*). Before continuing, however, it will be helpful to consider the historiographical implications of Simmel's relativist account of money as a cultural phenomenon.

Money, Representation, and "the Cultural Process"

In (re)turning to philosophy, Simmel had neither left the empirical-sociological dimension behind nor sundered theory from (knowledge) praxis. On the contrary, he was attempting to integrate a renewed engagement with everyday experience into philosophy. In the historical life of society, relativity becomes concrete. What Simmel later called his "special concept of metaphysics," in which "relativism as a cosmic and epistemic principle that replaces the substantial and abstract unity of the world-image with the organic unity of reciprocal interaction" (*GSG* 20: 305), finds its model in money.

For Simmel, "relativism" functions both as a phenomenological description and as a theoretical account of the relations between social-historical and cultural phenomena and epistemological and metaphysical issues. It is neither the embrace of a generalized contextualism nor an admission of defeat in the face of the apparent "dissolution of everything substantial, absolute, eternal" in modernity. As he described it in the Preface to the *Philosophy of Money*, Simmel's "fundamental intention from a methodological point of view" was to "build a story beneath historical materialism" that captured the indeterminacy of reality by upholding idealist and materialist perspectives in unending dialectical exchange. On his view, "In such alternation and absorption of completely opposed cognitive principles, the unity of things, which appears ungraspable to our cognition and nevertheless grounds its complexity, is rendered practical and animated for us" (13).

Money is the incorporation of relativity as such and as such a dialectical phenomenon that fosters both sides of every opposition it enters. Thus it brings what is far near, near, far; intensifies subjectivity and renders objects more independent, and so on. Money is, as it were, both synthetic and analytic: as a historical phenomenon, even as it facilitates the emergence of larger and more complex forms of social and cultural organization, money also brings about all sorts of fragmentation, notably the breakdown of the long-standing, inherited "forms of life" that had circumscribed human existence in traditional society and thereby stabilized its meaning. Such desubstantializing developments are culturally and historically but also psychologically and metaphysically significant: focusing on money's dialectical effects makes visible the complex interplay between the material and ideal transformations under way in what would come to be called the modernization process.

For example, Simmel reads the increasing importance of money in economic life beginning in what we would now call the early modern period as both a symptom and a catalyst of the decline of landed property and the socially fixed forms of human self-understanding that marked premodern identities. The gradual emergence of industrial capital, that is to say, of a form of wealth radically separable from its origins, went hand in hand with the destabilization of the dominant politico-religious framework of the medieval world, itself fostered and intensified by the rise of "natural" philosophy. Urbanization and industrialization (and, we would add, colonialism) furthered and internationalized the ongoing reorganization of social and cultural life that the ascent of the globalized money economy and its increasing penetration into all life spheres both symbolizes and fosters. As the *Philosophy of Money* demonstrated, the changes thereby brought about are explicable neither in sociocultural and economic nor in psychological or spiritual terms alone.

What I have called the democratization of skepticism in modernity comprises a tendency or disposition to devalue and disqualify all nonmaterialist, nonquantitative forms of explanation—a transformation that calls for a different order of reflection on the cultural evolution that has brought it into being. Reducing questions about the meaning and purpose of human existence to epiphenomenal symptoms of material or social causes was nothing new from a philosophical point of view. Yet the increasing cultural purchase and pervasiveness of such skeptical tendencies in the face of the lived loss of cultural self-evidence that accompanied urbanization, industrialization, and the ascendance of modern science and technology involved more than a demythologization of the old religious worldview a là Feuerbach. As the natural sciences grew more independent of philosophy and cast off their theological underpinnings, an increasingly disenchanted and instrumental but highly effective vision of rationality gained social and cultural force and cogency—bringing with it a new kind of understanding of human being as such and fostering the rise of the modern social sciences.

Simmel's historical and cultural analyses demonstrate that the increasing penetration of the money economy into all spheres of human life was the bearer of an intellectualization and rationalization of aspects and dimensions of existence that had formerly been the province of habit, instinct, and feeling. This is not simply a sociological analysis; his interpretation of the cultural transformations we now associate with modernity is part of a discourse that may be traced back at least to Schiller, and that resonates with both idealist and post-idealist German philosophy. But Simmel's approach cannot be written off as the last gasp of a dying idealism. His *Philosophy of Money* reflects upon the conditions as well as the meaning of the transformations it describes and poses both sociohistorical and philosophical questions about the significance of the historic shift in human thought and self-understanding associated with the double revolution.

In demonstrating how the rise of the money economy was linked both to new forms of identity and self-understanding and to the increasing virulence of problems of meaning in everyday life, Simmel pointed to new, properly philosophical challenges within modern culture whose effects have if anything intensified in the intervening century. His *Philosophy of Money* thereby revitalized the strategies of the dialectical tradition from a perspective that recognizes the seriousness and indeed intransigence of problems of meaning and value in a post-Enlightenment world. By intertwining historical (sociological, psychological) and philosophical perspectives on the lived loss of cultural self-evidence in modernity, it traces a genealogy of the relativism it espouses.

Simmel, again, saw himself as avoiding the danger that "the contemporary dissolution of everything substantial, absolute, eternal" would lead to a bottomless "subjectivism and skepticism"—by rethinking concepts as such, starting with "relativism as a cosmic and epistemic principle," and replacing the "substantial and abstract unity of the world-image" with an "organic" vision of "living reciprocity." By embracing the new, decentered type of coherence proper to modern—that is to say, self-reflexively contextualized—modes of experience, he was attempting to convert the problem into a solution. Whatever our verdict on his metaphysical views, Simmel's way of thinking about the relations between consciousness and its sociohistorical and cultural contexts and of theorizing the nature and limits of self-relativizing modern modes of thought bears careful consideration. Let us therefore look more closely at the historical account of the evolution of subjectivity that led Simmel to regard his relativist philosophical position (as he put it in the Preface to his *Philosophy of Money*) "as the most adequate expression of contemporary contents of knowledge and directions of feeling" (13).

The final chapter of the book's first, "analytic," part, "Money in the Series of Purposes," elaborates the argument touched on in discussing his essay on metropolitan life. Human "life in earlier times," Simmel writes, appears to have been "much more bound to stable given unities" and temporal rhythms, whereas

> the modern age dissolves both into an arbitrarily divisible continuum. The contents of life—ever more capable of being expressed by absolutely continuous, unrhythmic money, in itself foreign to every stably circumscribed form—become fragmented into such small pieces, their rounded totalities so shattered, that every arbitrary synthesis and formation out of them becomes possible. The material for modern individualism and its abundant products is thereby first created. (366)

"Clearly," Simmel adds, "the personality ... creating new life-unities out of such unformed stuff" can do so with "greater independence and variability" than a human being living "in closer solidarity" with the unified and stably persisting institutions and forms of collective life, as in earlier times.

The philosophical radicality of Simmel's account is noteworthy: subjective freedom, indeed subjectivity itself in the modern sense, is quite literally born of historical and cultural destruction. Money is at once bearer and symbol of the sociocultural fragmentation that makes the revaluation of values possible.

All of this is quite resonant with historical materialism, broadly speaking. But here Simmel heads in a different direction, turning his sights from praxis to theory to reflect on the significance of these sociocultural changes. The form and experience of subjective freedom—"modern individualism"—emerged against the background of a radical transformation of the culturally dominant modes of reflection and self-understanding. He situates his own project by creating a self-reflexive account of the tectonic shift through which the pursuit of knowledge itself was being redefined as scientific inquiry took on the properly modern contours in which method, as it were, replaces self-reflection.

Simmel writes that the same essential characteristic that makes money the agent of fragmentation also makes it "the most perfect representative within the historical-psychological realm of an epistemic tendency of modern science altogether: the reduction of qualitative to quantitative determinations (366). He then steps back to reflect on what contemporary intellectual developments were revealing about the cultural process as such—that is to say, regarding the historical evolution of both collective and individual human existence.

The "ambition" of "mathematical natural science" to explain everything in terms of formulae was finding expression in everything from psychological studies of sensory experience to chemical analyses. A "fundamental tendency" to reduction was omnipresent in contemporary intellectual life, and the same "disposition was making itself felt within the historical sciences," as well. Explanations centered on the miraculous origins of "language, art, institutions, cultural assets of every sort" and "the quality of heroic individual personalities" in action were rapidly being displaced by attention to "the quantity of the converged and condensed activities of entire historic groups": the proper "object of historical research" now appeared to be the small everyday processes of spiritual, cultural, political life" (367). From this point of view, historical materialism was more a symptom of than a critical perspective on the historical "cultural process."

The developments Simmel was describing in a sometimes disconcertingly antiquated philosophical vocabulary are intimately familiar today. A global shift in the culturally dominant rhetoric of reflection was palpably under way in the Western world during his lifetime, and Simmel's strategies for thinking the changes that were giving rise to a self-consciously "modern" intellectual and cultural world are genealogically connected to our own modes of understanding those still ongoing processes of cultural transformation.

The dilemma of philosophy in the modern world was already quite apparent to Simmel: To be sure, "the empiricist propensity" that "characterizes the modern era as a whole" was internally connected with "modern democracy" (368). Yet the rise of the Enlightenment ideal of equality was philosophically ambiguous: Western subjects who were coming to understand themselves as free and equal individuals were also approaching the world around them in increasingly reductive, materialist ways. What was at stake was not simply a change in emphasis from individual to group, quality to quantity. A fundamental shift in culturally salient explanatory paradigms was under way: Simmel saw not just the "increasing preponderance of the category of quantity over that of quality" but in fact the

> tendency to dissolve the latter into the former, to shift the elements ever more into a being without qualities [*ins Eigenschaftslose*] . . . to explain everything specific, individual, qualitatively determined as the more or less, the bigger or smaller, the broader or narrower, the more frequent or rarer of those in themselves colorless elements and objects of consciousness [*Elementen und Bewußtheiten*] now actually only accessible through numerical determination. (368)

The wholesale quantification of the qualitative that would so transform human existence in the twentieth century was already well under way by 1900. From the point of view of the author of the *Philosophy of Money*, other perspectives on the nature of reality were being effaced.

Logically or metaphysically speaking, the tendency to displace qualitative with quantitative, ideal with material explanation might never be completely realized, but the psychological and historical importance of the culturally ascendant tendency to reductivism was enormous. In my terms, skepticism was being democratized. Thanks especially to the power of quantitative methods in the thriving new field of scientific psychology, materialist forms of self-understanding were even gaining purchase on what had been thought of as the inner sanctum of subjective experience. "The modern quantitative tendency" was reshaping both individual and collective self-understanding.

Simmel's position was neither anti-modern nor anti-intellectual. He was very sensitive to the growth in subjective freedom that accompanied these changes. But he also saw the increasing dominance of reductive modes of interpretation and explanation as undermining the qualitative perspectives from which larger questions about the purpose and meaning of human life could be posed, and in subjective and objective spheres alike, money was the synecdochic "example, expression, and symbol of the modern emphasis on the quantitative moment" (369). As "the most perfect representative within the historical-psychological realm" of the dominant "epistemic tendency of modern science" as such, money was at once the bearer and facilitator of the quantitative revaluation of value itself.

Grasped as a cultural phenomenon, however, money also exposed the ambiguity of the associated changes—such as the ways in which the flowering of individuality was intertwined with the deepening of problems of meaning in modernity. Through its dialectical capacity to foster diametrically opposed phenomena, money makes visible and thinkable the lived foundation of the ongoing transvaluation of values. That is, even as it fostered the fragmentation that was threatening to lead to a nihilistically boundless subjectivism and skepticism, the phenomenon of money suggested a radical relativism as a sort of homeopathic cure. The genitive in Simmel's *Philosophy of Money* is no less ambiguous than Hegel's in the *Phenomenology of Spirit*.

The *Philosophy of Money* does not conflate cultural development or evolution with historical progress. Simmel was attempting to interpret why and how "the cultural process" gave rise to rationalization and quantification, fostered the dynamics of differentiation, specialization, and democratization—but also to uphold the values of individuality and freedom. Yet, like Weber, Simmel regarded it as unscientific to moralize about the large-scale sociohistorical and cultural shifts he was attempting to understand. Thus he declared at the end of "Die Großstädte und das Geistesleben" that whether or not we care for the internally conflicted form of modern subjectivity fostered by urban existence is beside the point. The metropolis itself is an indisputably significant "place in the development of psychic existence" as such and, in its protean capacity to foster fundamentally opposed tendencies and forces of life, "one of the great historical configurations" that stand "outside of the sphere in which the attitude of a judge is appropriate" (*GSG* 7: 131).

Keeping this distinction between cultural process or development and historical progress in mind, let us turn to the next step in Simmel's self-reflexive historical-cultural argument for the philosophical significance of money. Chapter 3, "Money in the Series of Purposes," demonstrates that as the means par excellence, the tool of tools, money tends to become an end in itself. Once again, Simmel stresses money's function as synecdoche of synecdoches. As the "concrete means" most perfectly "congruent with the abstract concept" of a means, money illuminates the "fundamental motives of life": it "embodies, culminates, sublimates, the practical bearing of the human being . . . [as] the indirect being [*das indirekte Wesen*]" toward objects of interest and desire—toward "the contents of will" as such (265).

Money never rests; "thanks to its absolute lack of content it not only has but is the mere *possibility* of unbounded use." Its excellence as the means of abstraction, the "inner emptiness of meaning" that lends money its "practical significance" in a "conceptual infinity of realms of meaning" (267), drives it into ever new spheres and configurations. As the means of means, it thus intensifies and reinforces the tendency to fragmentation in a self-perpetuating dynamic that psychologically and practically strengthens the disposition to quantification in modern culture quite generally.

As the synecdochic expression of that global transformation, money also expresses in itself the changes of which it is the representative bearer. Thanks to the development from substance to function, traced in Simmel's second chapter, "The Substance-Value of Money," money gains an increasingly universal signifying power. As "things give themselves over to the power of money with ever less resistance, [money] itself becomes ever more devoid of qualities, but precisely for that reason simultaneously gains power with respect to every quality of things" (298). Its dialectical nature, the "inner polarity in the essence of money: to be the absolute *means* and precisely thereby to become for most people the psychologically absolute *end* makes it into a uniquely meaningful image [or allegory: *Sinnbild*]" of what regulates "practical life" (298–99).[16] Thus the subject's "apparently contradictory doubled demand of every moment of life that it be absolutely definitive and absolutely non-definitive . . . finds its ironic fulfillment in money, the most extreme (since beyond all qualities and intensities) configuration of *Geist*" itself (299). The resulting psychological tendency to elevate and revere money had already found expression in the sixteenth-century poet Hans Sachs, who, as Simmel points out, had put the words "money is the earthly God on earth" into the mouth of a "representative of common opinion" in early modernity (307).

The quantitative tendency or disposition reflected not just in science but in modern culture more generally rests on the same psychological foundation. Not only does "the fundamental motive" for money's prominence lie in its being "the absolute means that thereby ascends to the psychological significance of an absolute

---

16. The tendency to increasingly abstract economic forms continues to intensify. The process has been radically enhanced by automated modes of quantification and the impact of phenomena such as high-speed trading on both value and social life. Consider the cultural authority to represent subjective experience as such granted to MRI images that in fact reflect the amalgamated and statistically re-presented "experience" of many individuals.

end" (307). Money's philosophical significance is also a function or expression of this doubling. It is "the strongest and most immediate symbol" of the (apparently) absolute relativity of things: "For it is the relativity of economic value in substance, it is the meaning of every particular that it has as a means for acquiring another, but really only this mere *meaning* as means" (307). As he puts it later, money's "essence" lies in the "unconditioned fungibility, the inner homogeneity" (588) that makes each piece equivalent to every other—that, in theoretical terms, makes its substance tend to collapse into its function.

Money's cultural and sociohistorical importance for human existence lies in this infinitely extensible, because abstract, power of representation and in what money's unlimited capacity for signifying difference makes possible both practically and theoretically. But money's philosophical meaning is embodied in a distinctively concrete form of abstraction. Elaborating on an argument already touched on in our discussion of exchange, Simmel writes: "The significance of money is that it is a unity of value that cloaks itself in the multiplicity of values," thereby enabling people to perceive (the verb is *empfinden,* to feel or sense in general) "qualitative differences among things" in the form of the "quantitative differences of homogeneous currency" (589–90). Money converts the multiplicity of desire into a manageable continuum of measurable and hence manageable specifics. It thus becomes both end and bearer of the *Zweckreihen,* the series or sequences of (partial) ends of which modern life consists, interlacing them "as the means of means, as the most universal technology of external life, without which the individual techniques of our culture would never have come into being" (676). This last, decisive point, made in the final chapter of the *Philosophy of Money,* bears a brief elaboration.

It is not (pace Nietzsche) the masses who have inherited the "spiritual potency" from the individual in modernity; it is, rather, Simmel writes, "the things" that are engaged in a "'slave-revolt' against the autocracy and norm-giving character of the strong individual" (673–74). In an argument whose resonance with both Marx and Heidegger should be noted, he continues: "just as we have on one hand become the slaves of the production process, on the other we are the slaves of the products." Thanks to the mediation of technology, life itself has been decentered by "habits," "distractions," "external needs" of all sorts. "The domination of means" has thereby "gripped the seat of purpose as such" in the individual. "Thus the human being is as it were distanced from himself," with an insurmountable proliferation of means and partial ends "interposed between him and his ownmost, most essential [being]" (674).

Here, strikingly, Simmel continues with a rare invocation of the first person, declaring: "I don't know of any era" free of "such emphasis on the mediating instances of life over its central and definitive significance." Since "human being is oriented to the category of ends and means," being between ends and means is probably the human "destiny" (674). However, the symptoms of this disparity had become acute: "For the present, the dominance of technology which—as cause and effect—clearly means a predominance of clear and intelligent consciousness . . . the spirituality and gathering of the soul, drowned out by the loud pomp of the natural-scientific-technical age, avenges itself as a muffled feeling of tension and disoriented longing" (674–75).

In a passage that exemplifies his emphasis on the intertwining and mutual determination of ideal and material dimensions, Simmel goes on to describe the cultural effects of these psychic phenomena.

> I believe that this secret restlessness, helpless searching below the level of consciousness, that drives the contemporary human being from socialism to Nietzsche, from Böcklin to Impressionism, from Hegel to Schopenhauer and back again—not only stems from the external haste and excitement of modern life, but that conversely the latter is often the expression, the appearance, the discharge of that innermost state. (675)

This argument, recycled virtually verbatim in the metropolis essay, foregrounds the methodological and theoretical payoff of focusing on money for grasping the complex interplay of ideal and material, subjective and objective, individual and cultural-historical dimensions of modern cultural-spiritual life.

Money's importance for that "state [*Verfassung*] of life" stems from the same dialectical doubling that led Simmel to identify it as "the most extreme . . . configuration of *Geist*." On one hand, "money stands in a series with all the means and tools of culture" as the "incrementally highest of all those phenomena" of technical means. But thanks to "the passion with which it is desired" and "its own emptiness," money also exposes "the meaninglessness and the consequences of the teleological displacement" (675–76) of ends into means that shapes human life under the highly mediated social and cultural circumstances of the industrialized world.

Yet money is not only "inside" but also "above" what Simmel calls "the series of existence." Reflection on money as "the means of means . . . the most universal technique of external life, without which the individual techniques of our culture would never have come into being" (676) reveals that in its doubled function of being inside and outside phenomenal reality, money "repeats the form of the greatest and most profound powers of life altogether"; Simmel compares it to religion, which is both a partial "power in life" and "the unity and bearer of existence itself as a whole" (676).

The *Philosophy of Money* thereby establishes a valuable reflective perspective on the psychic and sociocultural phenomena of modern life. Simmel (and here he is emphatically part of the tradition that stretches from Kant and Hegel via Marx and Nietzsche to Lukács and Adorno) is suggesting that it matters a great deal whether we recognize and understand ourselves as producing the world of symbolic forms in which we dwell. Only when the meaning of which money is the bearer is thought as the product of the social relations that it equally embodies can the tendency to nihilism that arises from the preponderance of economic valuation in modern culture be combatted. Money's ultimate philosophical significance lies in its potential to reveal the operations of mediation as meaningful in a larger sense—a capacity rooted in its being the "technique of life" par excellence.

On Simmel's interpretation, money both embodies and exemplifies what Hegel called the "monstrous power of the negative": the capacity of signifying practices to turn everything human beings encounter into conceptual shadows. Comparable to language, "which likewise lends itself to the most divergent directions of thought and feeling, supporting, clarifying, working them out," money "belongs to those powers whose singularity consists precisely in their lack of singularity" (654). As a means of expressing, intensifying, transforming, multiplying, converting and generally increasing the forms of value generated in, by, and through human interaction, money is historically, culturally, sociologically, and psychologically intertwined with human existence as such. Thus, as the social "techniques of life" money enables and enhances grow ever more complex, so too does the hegemony of the modes of valuation of which it is (in a favorite phrase of Simmel's) "both bearer and symbol." "In money, pure economic value has acquired a body" (371). Its ubiquity in complex societies reflects the unique adaptability of this desubstantializing form of signification: as social life becomes more highly mediated by money, its phenomenal correlates—impersonality, abstraction, reification—grow more dominant. The (dialectical) consequence of money's ubiquity as a mode of signification is that it becomes ever more difficult to defend or even discern the importance of types and modes of value that are not quantifiable.

Money's dynamic tendency to become an ever more universal means of representation reconfigures both subject and world. The increasing pervasiveness of the money economy leads both to the intensification of subjectivity and the rationalization and disenchantment of the nonhuman. In language that exemplifies the subtlety of his transformation and resignification of the legacy of idealism, Simmel reframes this Hegelian point in post-Nietzschean terms: "By being both symbol and cause of the leveling [*Vergleichgültigung*; more literally, the neutralization or rendering indifferent] and externalization [*Veräußerlichung*] of everything that can possibly be leveled and externalized, money also becomes the protector of the most interior being, which can then develop within its ownmost boundaries" (653).[17]

Through terminology deeply rooted in the German philosophical tradition, Simmel exposes the "story beneath historical materialism"—and the mutual determination between materiality and ideality in the process known today as subjectivation. When he brings idealist categories into the proximity of money, the phenomenon known as *Veräußerlichung*, externalization or alienation, reveals its internal links to

---

17. The resonance of Simmel's language and the concretizing resignification of idealist tropes with (then still unrecovered) early Marxian texts is apparent. But the notion of *Vergleichgültigung* appears to have its origins in the medieval German mystic Meister Eckhart's *aequaliter stare* (equal station). Eckhart's importance for Simmel would bear a good deal more investigation and elaboration—an undertaking that would help cast light on the convergences and divergences of his thought from Heidegger's on a number of points.

Frisby et al. translate this passage in a fashion that elides the subtlety and philosophical precision of Simmel's analysis, hypostasizing subject and object alike: "In so far as money is the symbol as well as the cause of making everything indifferent and of the externalization of everything that lends itself to such a process, it also becomes the gatekeeper of the most intimate sphere, which can then develop within its own limits" (*The Philosophy of Money*, trans. Tom Bottomore, David P. Frisby, and Kaethe Mengelberg, ed. Frisby [1978; 3rd enlarged ed., London: Routledge, 2004], 475).

very material processes of signification: *veräußern* also means to sell in the sense of "liquidate": to convert material assets into fungible cash.[18]

The ultimate significance for human existence of the mutually reinforcing intensification of subjectivity and objectivity, interiority and exteriority, that is a consequence of the increasing penetration of the money economy into all dimensions of society and culture remained, Simmel thought, uncertain. The passage continues: "To what extent this really leads to that refinement, particularity, and interiorization of the subject, or whether on the contrary it will permit the subjugated objects to become rulers over the human precisely through the ease by which they are obtained—that will depend not on money, but rather on human beings" (653).

As ambiguous as thought itself, money embodies the dialectical capacity of intensifying opposites: its historical and cultural as well as philosophical importance are tied up with a seemingly unlimited power to divide and unite, to render unlike things indifferently equivalent, to convert quality into quantity, but also to dematerialize the most material aspects of life.

For Simmel, neither the sociopolitical and cultural consequences of industrialization and urbanization nor the subjective effects of modern forms of life, including the problems of meaning concomitant with the very material achievements and practices that make up the historical fabric of modern social life, could be understood in purely materialist terms. To recognize the peculiarly modern intensity of the subjective crisis manifested (as Simmel often noted) in the rebellion against reason and the turn to the category of life—a turn itself both reflected in and intensified by the ascent of evolutionary paradigms in the course of the second half of the nineteenth century—was not to explain away the experience of crisis Nietzsche would call the death of God but rather to plumb its depths as a cultural and historical process with tangible phenomenal manifestations. The *Philosophy of Money* develops a self-reflexive account of the philosophical dilemmas that provided the theoretical and historical impetus to move beyond system philosophy by rendering visible the ongoing historical and "cultural process" of interactivity and mediation between ideal and material dimensions that animates both collective life and individual experience.

Simmel's strategy for reframing the (Hegelian) project of intellectual-cultural history is nicely illustrated by the way he incorporates insights from Nietzsche and Schopenhauer into his philosophical interpretation of the cultural evolution of problems of meaning. "Higher cultures" with complex social arrangements, he writes,[19] depend on extensive interpersonal and material networks to guarantee that

---

18. Kant uses the same word in a 1785 essay polemicizing against unauthorized reproductions of books and other writings, and in invoking the correlative Latin terms, he sheds new light on what is at issue, writing that authors' inalienable right to their intellectual property is based in "a mere use of his forces [*opera*] which he can delegate [*concedere*] but never sell [*alienare*]" (Kant, "Von der Unrechtmäßigkeit des Büchernachdrucks," originally in the *Berlinische Monatsschrift* 5 [1785]: 403–41).

19. Clearly, Simmel's notion of "higher" levels of culture has troubling connotations. That being said, his notion of the *Kulturprozeß* does not identify history or evolution with progress, and thus provides a valuable counterpoint both to social scientific theories of "modernization" and to natural scientific discourses that (implicitly) identify evolution with progress.

basic needs are met; they are distinguished by the "diversity and length of the teleological series" operative in everyday life (489). Under these circumstances, human "wishes and desires" and the means to these ends grow ever more intricate, with even provisional means increasingly requiring lengthy series of indirect goals in the form of a "manifold mechanism of interlocking preconditions" for their realization (490). Enmeshed in the web of activities and interests that are treated as ends but known to be mere means, human beings come to struggle with problems of meaning and value as such. A paradoxical psycho-cultural product of the growth of complexity and mediation in the forms of "objective culture," such generalized struggles are from the outset dialectically linked to the elevation of individual existence.

Sociocultural complexity brings an increasingly palpable diremption between subject and objects: highly individuated subjects confront an ever more alienating world—what Simmel later calls the "tragedy of culture." But the "tragic" dynamic describes the process by which (both objective and subjective) culture develop, and it brings not just problems of meaning but also philosophical resources into being. The "abstract representation of purpose and means" stands in a dialectical relation to cultural conditions defined by complexity and deferral. Indeed, according to Simmel, the very "thought of a final purpose" of the whole in which all the conflicting means and ends could find "reconcilation" arises historically as a utopian image of "peace and redemption" out of the very experience of subjective and cultural fragmentation (490).[20]

These passages perfectly illustrate the liminal situation of Simmel's thinking—how, in his usage, the category of culture stands poised between an old-fashioned humanistic and an emergent social scientific understanding.[21] To be sure, *Kultur* signifies for him the historically accreted achievements of the human spirit, yet its existence in this ideal, traditional sense depends upon and inheres in the means that are interjected between desire and its object—the techniques (and results) of human "forming productivity" that cultivate human needs, intensifying, elaborating, and transforming desire, satisfying and etherealizing it. Material—in the broadest sense, psychological—conditions give rise to ideal forms and effects, and those cultural ideals and practices are not disembodied. They shape individual subjectivity, but also the interactive sociohistorical processes and conditions—the superindividual *Geistesleben*—in and through which they are perpetuated, reinscribed, and transformed.

---

20. The German text reads: "in der Zersplitterung und dem fragmentarischen Charakter der Kultur." Simmel reprises these arguments at the opening of his lectures on Schopenhauer and Nietzsche. Thanks to the length and complexity, the sheer extension of "the series of purposes that make life into a technical problem," he writes, "consciousness gets caught on the means, and the final goals that give meaning and significance to the whole development" disappear from sight (*GSG* 10: 176). "Technology, i.e. the sum of means for a cultivated existence, grows into the actual content of the efforts and valuations until one is surrounded on all sides by criss-crossing series of undertakings and institutions that everywhere lack conclusive, definitively valuable ends. It is in this state of culture that the need for a final purpose to life altogether first arises" (*GSG* 10: 177).

21. Simmel's importance for Walter Benjamin is evident here, as in his emphasis on technologies of life. See Marian Mičko, *Walter Benjamin und Georg Simmel* (Wiesbaden: Harassowitz, 2010).

In Simmel's relativist approach to what we now call cultural theory, then, the "ideal" and "anthropological" senses of culture intermingle. Thus it is that despite his frank allegiance to what would come to be called "high" culture, he pioneered new forms of reflection on the everyday world that laid the foundations for a de-centering of the meaning of culture itself in the twentieth century. The historical significance and theoretical influence of Simmel's philosophical attention to institutions, intersubjective arrangements, and material practices is obscured when he is misconstrued as an idealist or (what often amounts to the same thing) read through a critical lens that focuses on his ideological allegiance to the German nation and underplays the ambiguity and multiplicity of his conception of culture as well as the complexity of his account of subjectivity.

The rethinking of the concept of *Geist* entailed by Simmel's relativism involved a post-Darwinian resignification of the philosophical legacy. What has too often been misconstrued as a reinscription of idealism is better understood as a proto-cultural turn aimed at a transformative redemption of fundamental categories of human life such as truth, value, and meaning, which he saw as threatened with dissolution in a world dominated by reductive quantitative modes of valuation. In his approach, Simmel was both a precursor of modern social science and an adherent of the dialectical tradition that understands thought itself as historical and thus regards historical self-reflexivity as a sine qua non for philosophizing adequate to the phenomena—that is to say, in the first instance, to the world as known to and experienced by human beings.

Everyday life in complex socio-cultural organizations generates contradictory effects: alienating experiences of disconnection and lack of larger purpose foster awareness of subjective individuality, thereby nurturing longings for meaning that in turn feed impulses for collective (religious and political) transcendence. Crucially, the desire for unity and cultural purpose makes itself felt not only philosophically, in "conscious formulation," but also as a "mute drive, longing, dissatisfaction of the masses" (490). In line with his anthropological conception of the psychological, Simmel understood "spiritual" symptoms as transsubjective phenomena. All human knowing, feeling, understanding, experiencing is framed by conditioning and enabling inter- and transsubjective, cultural contexts, by the perspectives they bear with them—and by the drive to move beyond those constraints.

Not only is the world of experience constituted by the subjective forms and conditions of its coherence and comprehensibility, as Kant had shown. Sensibility itself has to be understood, Simmel believed, as relative to the historical, cultural, trans-individual psychological process in and through which (experience of) the phenomenal world comes into being and is sustained. A philosophically adequate approach must situate phenomena that are experienced and understood in largely ahistorical and intensely personal ways—including the lived sense of individual freedom and uniqueness that is paradigmatic for modern subjectivity—in a broader historical and cultural framework. This does not mean, however, that Simmel thought philosophical questions could be resolved or eliminated through sociological and historical contextualization. His meditation on the genealogy of modern problems of meaning underlines the complex, dialectical relation between "sociological" and "philosophical" dimensions.

The "mute longing" for ultimate meaning was neither modern nor timeless: "at the beginning of our era, Greco-Roman culture was clearly at this point," Simmel notes (490).[22] Human existence had become an elaborate "network of purposes"; a longing for "the *definitive* purpose of the whole" that would not, like everything else, have merely relative value and purpose was distilled as "focus imaginarius" (virtual focus) out of this experienced complexity and fragmentation.[23] On Simmel's reading, ancient pessimism and hedonism, but also mysticism and aestheticism, were the "expression of that dark searching for a conclusive meaning for life, that anxiety about the ultimate purpose" of the entire complex "apparatus of means." Christianity had, however, provided an answer. With it, "for the first time in western history the masses were offered a genuine final purpose for life, an absolute value for being, beyond everything individual, fragmentary, contradictory, in the empirical world (490–91).

Decisively—and at this point in the argument, Nietzsche's influence is again most evident—"the need outlived its fulfillment" (491). The peculiarly intense experience of the lack of meaning in modernity is the legacy of Christianity, which had over many generations provided human beings with the sense of an absolute purpose beyond earthly life itself. Even as that vision lost its cultural hold, and the tensions endemic to culture as such were becoming palpable as such, the "legacy" of that vast desire persisted, taking the form of "an empty longing after a definitive goal for existence as a whole." Schopenhauer's metaphysics of the will was the perfect "expression of this state of culture, which has inherited the most urgent need for an absolute purpose but lost its convincing content" (491).

Like Nietzsche, Simmel emphasized that as an historically instilled longing, a constitutive element of subjective and cultural life, this intense need for meaning could not be reduced to a philosophical problem—nor could it be hypostasized, a là Schopenhauer, into metaphysical transcendence. Crucially, "The fact that the final purpose has slipped away from the modern human being" was making itself felt not only in the "weakening of religious feeling" but also in "the so vividly revived desire for it" (492)—that is to say, in phenomena rooted in the intensified interiority of the

---

22. Simmel's genealogical understanding of the problem of meaning in history matured in tandem with his *Philosophy of Money*. He also disseminated this account in public lectures on Schopenhauer and Nietzsche in the Viktoria-Lyceum in Berlin in 1902, and as Harry Graf Kessler's notes on Simmel's lectures on nineteenth-century philosophy in WS 1902–3 attest, the larger argument, which plays a key role in his philosophy of life, was already fully developed by that time (*GSG* 21: 352–53). The passage cited here appears once again as the beginning of the first chapter of Simmel's *Schopenhauer and Nietzsche: A Lecture-Series*, "Schopenhauer and Nietzsche's Place in Cultural-Intellectual History" (1906), and may be found, again unchanged, in the critical edition of those lectures (*GSG* 10: 176–78). Simmel's reading is also discussed in my book *Experience without Qualities: Boredom and Modernity* (Stanford: Stanford University Press, 2005).

23. Simmel is alluding to Kant's conception that unrealizable "Ideen der reinen Vernunft (ideas of pure reason)" serve an ineluctable orienting ("regulative") function in thought. The optical term *focus imaginarius* appears in Kant's discussion of the nature and role of such ideas in human understanding in the "Anhang zur tranzendentalen Dialektik (Appendix to Transcendental Dialectic)." Kant, *Kritik der reinen Vernunft* [*Critique of Pure Reason*], ed. Raymund Schmidt (Hamburg: Felix Meiner, 1956), A 644/B 672.

subject brought into being through the history of Christianity's effects. What had not gone the way of the theological ideal of an ultimate purpose to life but remained "active in its legacy" in the modern West was the "valuation of the human soul," an emphasis on the incomparable significance of the individual human being, with all its ethical implications and cultural effects (492). For Simmel, that legacy included Nietzsche's own radical synthesis of evolutionary thought with a negation of all quantitatively grounded understandings of human existence: his view that only "the *quality* of humanity" mattered and "in each case the *sole* highest exemplar decided the value of an epoch" (369).

Simmel's mature philosophy turns on his modernist effort to embrace Nietzsche's perspectivism, to take seriously his predecessor's insight that life itself might be understood as the purpose of life and the basis of thought, without reducing historical life to an epiphenomenon of the will. Placed in the larger context of the history of philosophy, Nietzsche's genealogical account of modern subjectivity itself appears as a symptom of the epochal turn in human self-understanding known as the death of God. The ethical and philosophical challenge posed by the revaluation of values palpably under way in Simmel's lifetime was thus not simply avoiding the sort of facile identifications between power and excellence, egotistical self-regard and historical importance that make Nietzsche's work so seductive intellectually and so dangerous politically. The question was how to proceed beyond the rationalism of the philosophy of the subject without abandoning hope of an ethical orientation and an understanding of the ends of human existence that could escape Nietzsche's seemingly nihilistic elimination of all historical and philosophical horizons beyond that of life itself.

Money and Metaphysics: Relativism as Modernist Method

At the heart of Simmel's magnum opus was an exploration of the modernist problem par excellence: the question of the meaning and value—historical, cultural, philosophical—of individuality. His struggle to find real traction for thought, for a relativist mode of reflection that could overcome the impasse Nietzsche's ethical views seemed to entail, reaches its fulfillment in the ideas about life and form and the vision of an internally relativized subjectivity set out in his 1918 *Lebensanschauung* (*View of Life*), with its conception of the "individual law," aimed at squaring the circle of individualist ethics. But the strategies of thought developed in the *Philosophy of Money* for understanding subjectivity and subjective experience already delineate Simmel's approach to reenvisioning the tasks of philosophy by embracing the seemingly absolute loss of foundations in a relativistic affirmation of the historic transvaluation of values.

Money's significance as a philosophical point of departure becomes visible in the way his *Philosophy of Money* addresses the impasses of efforts at abstract philosophical system-building. In the final paragraph of the "analytic" part of the book, Simmel elaborates on the approach described in the Preface as, like the work of art, wagering everything on expanding and extending a "limited and small problem . . .

into a totality and into the most universal" (12). In a passage that follows upon the discussion of money as "the most perfect representative" of the reductive "epistemic tendency" of "modern *Wissenschaft*," that is to say, of disciplinary knowledge practices (366), Simmel once again distances his approach from idealizing modes of philosophizing: "Metaphysics may succeed in constructing essences absolutely devoid of quality that, ordered into purely arithmetical relations . . . generate the play of the world. But in the phenomenal realm, money alone achieves this freedom" to represent being as determined only quantitatively" (370).

Simmel is by no means claiming that metaphysical problems can themselves be eliminated à la Wittgenstein. Rather, however heretical it might sound, money is the philosophical object par excellence, the ultimate being without qualities. In its purity as means, it actually achieves the freedom to which metaphysical—and for Simmel, as a philosophical descendant of Hegel, this emphatically does not mean ahistorical—reflection aspires.

> While we can never grasp pure being or pure energy in order to derive the particularities of phenomena from their quantitative modifications . . . [in money] pure economic value has acquired a body, out of whose quantitative relations all possible singular configurations now go forth, without it having had to invest anything other than just its quantity. Here too one of the great tendencies of life—the reduction of quality to quantity—thus reaches in money its most extreme and sole complete representation; here too [money] appears as the culmination of a spiritual-historical developmental series [*geistesgeschichtliche Entwicklungsreihe*] and thereby first unambiguously establishes its direction. (370–71)

Money's status as symbolic representative of symbolization, as synecdoche of synecdoches, makes possible Simmel's breakthrough to a new form of philosophizing grounded in particularity. This passage, which attests to the importance of the category of life and its intertwining with the concepts of culture and spirit in his mature thought, renders visible the methodological continuities of Simmel's work with the dialectical philosophical tradition even as it foregrounds the innovations that make his text exemplary for subsequent cultural theory.

In representing money as a paradigmatic phenomenon that "appears" at the apex of a "spiritual- [or cultural/intellectual-]historical evolutionary series," Simmel links the category of spirit to the evolutionary cultural process by deploying a phenomenological concept, the *Erscheinungsreihe*, that is methodologically crucial for his account of how meaning becomes embodied in symbolic formations. At the level of the text, one of the key rhetorical strategies by which the *Philosophy of Money* mediates between sociohistorical realities and philosophical questions is by abstracting such "series of appearances [or phenomena]" from complex lived realities, distributing diverse phenomena in multiple, sometimes overlapping, sometimes opposed, contiguous sequences that reveal particulars as expressing larger cultural developments. His concrete analyses move metonymically through multiple such arrays of appearances, using these conceptual constructs to illuminate larger features of human (historical, spiritual, cultural) life.

Simmel introduces the category of the "phenomenal series" in an argument that links the *Erscheinungsreihe* to the constructive role of figuration in human (cultural, historical) existence via a phenomenological description of human rhetorical-cognitive practice as such. Like other crystallized symbolic constellations, he underlines, a "concept with which we define the essence of a phenomenon" (137) is a form of practical abstraction that facilitates thinking. Such concepts (his examples include "language" and "animal" as opposed to "plant" life) are speculative constructs through which global features of the world and experience can be understood and explored: "The pure concept of a phenomenal series is often an ideal that is nowhere entirely realized in it," but that gives it meaning as a hypothesized point of orientation (138). That is, these concepts and the series of phenomena to which they (implicitly) refer are constituted from particular points of view, with particular interests in mind. No less than the (speculative) a priori foundations that define the analytic "lower boundary" at which disciplinary inquiry gives way to philosophizing, such discipline-defining generic groupings are conceptual objects. They are generated via (synthetic) strategies borne of knowledge interests through which diverse moments and aspects ("parts") of the phenomenal world are interpretively linked into provisional "wholes."

Simmel's modernist, overtly relativist strategy for reading appearances and relating them to one another in multiple, sometimes overlapping, sometimes opposed "series" of conceptually and pragmatically delimited groupings enables him to situate the historical and cultural significance of money and the money economy within the larger speculative phenomenological framework in which all these "historical-spiritual developmental series" are thought as converging: what he calls the *Kulturprozeß*. The *Philosophy of Money* thereby reframes metaphysical questions for an era without foundations.

No less than the "series of appearances," the cultural-intellectual trajectories into which the phenomena of human historical and cultural life may be synthesized from the point of view of historical-philosophical reflection register the practical constraints on thinking experience. Our concepts are not, cannot be, direct expressions of reality, but always begin from the world as it appears to us. As in the case of Weberian ideal types, the direction or ultimate tendency of a phenomenal series is never entirely realized or actualized in historical and cultural life, and we do not, cannot, absolutely know the final meaning or value of the unfolding arrays of appearances, for we ourselves and our processes of reflection belong to the very process in which our concepts are developing historically. Our strategies of thought are inherently perspectival and will need supplementation, redescription, resignification, and so forth, over time.

Simmel does not, as a matter of principle, provide definitive answers or even interpretations. To be sure, the series of historical and social, psychological and anthropological examples and analyses he puts forward advance a larger argument about the *geistige*—spiritual, cultural, and intellectual—significance of money for the historical, inter- and transsubjective process of human cultural development. But the ultimate meaning and value of that development is unclear; its effects are highly ambiguous both from the point of view of the individual and the collective.

What is clear on Simmel's reading is that the evolution of culture and indeed thought as such has been decisively shaped by the historical vicissitudes of the money economy, and that modern subjectivity in all its complexity reflects the impact of the increasing penetration of money's effects into all facets of life. But the purpose of the *Philosophy of Money* is not to analyze these intertwined cultural and subjective effects of money as sociological phenomena, much less to reduce them to their historical-psychological foundations. It is to move readers from the socio-culturally articulated, phenomenal surface to metaphysical heights (or depths), to foster a clearer understanding of the philosophical significance of human cultural existence by exploring and elucidating the metaphysical, epistemological, ethical, meanings and implications of the larger historical and cultural evolution borne along by the money economy: the cultural process in which the phenomena under consideration play an illuminating part.

The *Philosophy of Money* enacts the metaphysical and epistemological relativism that was Simmel's principled response to what he had come to see as the undecidability of questions about the nature and limits of interpretation. Far from advocating for skeptical withdrawal, he aimed to develop hermeneutic strategies appropriately open to lived experience, which always exceeds conceptualization. Simmel's modernist approach to philosophizing in and through multiple, diverse phenomenal series was an attempt to think (and performatively to reflect for his hearers and readers) the ways meaning and value find expression in a world where the absence of stable foundations has become manifest in everyday life. If Hegel found the solution to the problem of life in his turn to system philosophy, Simmel was returning philosophy from system to life.

Following Nietzsche, Simmel understood the value and ultimate significance of any given phenomenon to vary depending on the perspective from which it is viewed, and he rejected the possibility of attaining complete certainty about one's own perspectives, let alone the total self-reflexivity of "absolute knowledge." He understood the evolutionary significance of knowledge and science as (part of) the self-reflexive dimension of what he thought of as a larger culture-defining and -creating sociohistorical "process." At the same time, and this is a critical distinction, because he did not believe it was possible to completely transcend the phenomenal world, Simmel also rejected all reductivist forms of materialism (including the crude sensationalism Nietzsche himself sometimes espoused, as well as Marx's more sophisticated version).

Simmel's relativism is as much ontological as epistemic, for it centers on the reciprocal relations that define the phenomenal locations from which his readings repeatedly move to (partial, perspectival) totalities. Although his published writings are all but silent on Hegel, the modernist dialectical strategy for cultural analysis Simmel thereby developed is the recognizable inheritor of Hegelian phenomenology. As such it is the antecedent of the strategies of thought developed by Lukács in his account of reification and elaborated by Adorno under the aegis of negative dialectics—and set the stage for Walter Benjamin's imagistic reworking of dialectics.

The philosophical (or, perhaps better, "theoretical") achievement of Simmel's *Philosophy of Money* turns not on the facts themselves but on the mode by which he represents them. By examining the highly ambiguous phenomena that make up the money economy from the standpoint of metaphysical relativism, he renders them sociologically (culturally, historically) significant. That is, the social scientific significance of his work is a *consequence* of its (Nietzschean) philosophical achievement. It is not, as some would have it, that Simmel disclosed the relativism of reality (viz., modernity) and overcame metaphysics through his proto-postmodernist strategies of interpretation.[24] Rather, adopting a relativist epistemology entailed a philosophical shift that enabled him to develop the methodological strategies and more broadly the modernist style of thought that characterize his mature writings.

The *Philosophy of Money* thereby self-reflexively and performatively responds to the dilemmas that arise from perspectivism and relativism, understood as doctrines. Simmel's modernist approach needs to be seen against the philosophical horizon of his relativist refiguration of metaphysics as such around the "organic" unity of *Wechselwirkung*, reciprocal interaction. His conceptual and experimental praxis allowed him to confront cultural phenomena in interesting and innovative, yet never definitive ways, keeping open the normative horizon even as he explored the sociocultural (material, historical, psychological) processes by which concrete forms of meaning and value are generated and disclosed. The *Philosophy of Money* thereby developed methods and strategies of thought that proved valuable resources for social sciences and humanities alike.

These reflections on Simmel's self-reflexive grounding of his philosophical approach in a speculative interpretation of the historical-cultural process bring us back once again to the question of method. To put the point in somewhat paradoxical terms, the *Philosophy of Money*, as its author himself stressed, is in very important ways not actually about money. The philosophical problem Simmel poses is what money—at once the most ethereal of human cultural products, a metaphysical approximation of pure number, and the basest reduction of value to substance—reveals about human symbolic existence. To recall his remark in the book's Preface, money is but "the means, material, or example for representing the relations" between the most prosaic and the "most ideal" dimensions of human individual and collective existence (12).

Beginning from reflection on this exemplary phenomenon of human collective life, the *Philosophy of Money* develops a method or strategy for making visible how value and meaning are created, sustained, and transformed in the lived context and sociohistorical framework of human (inter- and transsubjective) interaction. As Simmel frequently observes, money is both the bearer or vehicle, the *Träger*, and the means or mediator, the *Mittel*, of the concrete processes of exchange that constitute society as living interaction and thus functions as both the symbol and mirror for the cultural process as a whole in which the specifically human capacity for world creation is manifest.

24. As Nigel Dodd points out, the soi-disant "postmodernists" (he mentions Weinstein and Weinstein, Baumann, Stauth, and B. Turner) have been prone to a tendency, "naïve in historical terms," to regard Simmel as "a seminal social theorist of their own ilk" (Dodd, *The Sociology of Money: Economics, Reason & Contemporary Society* [New York: Continuum, 1994], 108).

From the very first lines of the book, Simmel makes clear that no less than the conditions of possibility of knowledge as such are at stake, but also that his *Philosophy of Money* is not a purely epistemological but also a strategic undertaking, one concerned with the boundaries or limits of "domains of disciplinary inquiry," with the regions "at which the movement of thought goes over from the exact into the philosophical form" (9).[25] In such transitional zones, thought turns upon itself to reflect on the foundations and ultimate significance of scientific inquiry. At once "prior to [*diesseits*] and beyond [*jenseits*] the economic science of money (10), his *Philosophy of Money* interrogates the status of the assumptions (both logical and cultural) that constitute the scientific domain of the quantitative in order to direct attention to what is beyond the material world of economic reality by asking about the ultimate meaning, value, and purpose of money in and for human existence.

Simmel, then, quite explicitly and systematically locates his project at the interstices between philosophy and social science. While putting forward an innovative method for interpreting social and cultural phenomena, he develops a nuanced account of the sociogenesis of value and meaning that links fundamental metaphysical questions to the phenomenon of money—and thereby demonstrates the inseparability of philosophical issues from social scientific inquiry. It was, I think, in this spirit that Simmel declared to Célestin Bouglé that his forthcoming book "aspire[d] to be a philosophy of historical and social life as a whole."

As a relativist, Simmel eschewed the sort of totalizing epistemic ends that that remark would seem to imply, yet his text is among other things a meditation on what constitutes rigorous reflection on the domain of the human. In this respect, it is part of a conversation that includes other contemporary theoretical undertakings such as Husserl's phenomenology, Rickert's *Kulturwissenschaft*, Weber's *verstehende Soziologie*, Dilthey's hermeneutics, and Cassirer's philosophy of symbolic forms. At the same time, Simmel's work anticipates the directions of the next generation: the philosophically ambitious cultural criticism of Lukács, Kracauer, and Benjamin, as well as the no less ambitious investigations of the social and historical foundations and operations of knowledge by Mannheim and Elias and the very different approaches to thinking about questions of identity and meaning historically developed by Blumenberg and Luhmann.

The intertwining of cultural, historical, psychological, epistemological, and metaphysical questions that is the hallmark of Simmel's work proved challenging to his readers from the very beginning. This work, like its author, simply did not fit in, least of all to a discipline, still centered on the philosophy of the subject, that saw itself besieged by the emergent modern social sciences and especially by psychology and empiricist approaches to the psyche. Simmel was not a proponent of the new (represented, as today, by efforts to supplant philosophical self-reflection with purportedly empirical studies of "consciousness"); nor, with his unconventional

---

25. The theoretical and methodological importance for Simmel of the category of boundaries (*Grenzen*), can hardly be overstated. As he puts on the first page of his final work, *Lebensanschauung*: "Through always and everywhere having boundaries, we also are boundaries" (*GSG* 16: 212).

thinking of *Geist* and *Kultur*, was he a secure ally for the old. He was and remains a liminal figure, poised between nineteenth-century philosophy and the emergent cultural and empirical sciences.

The *Philosophy of Money* definitively established Simmel as one of the most important thinkers of his generation. Yet it by no means ended his difficulties with the philosophical establishment. Not only did many powerful colleagues find his work too close for comfort to their social scientific rivals. Simmel espoused a philosophical position whose very name was tantamount to a direct attack on the establishment. It is hardly surprising that even his defenders often shied away; most professional philosophers would look askance at the invocation of "relativism" even today.[26]

When we interrupted our reading of Simmel's methodological reflections in the Preface, he had just criticized "abstract philosophical system-building" for failing to integrate the concrete phenomena of "practical existence" and described his aspiration to revitalize philosophical reflection by remaking it in the image of artistic practice. Rather than approaching the "entirety of existence" through traditional philosophical strategies of analysis and abstraction from particulars, he proposed to adopt the aesthetic model of generalization grounded in particularity. His *Philosophy of Money* was an attempt to begin philosophizing from "a limited and small problem in order to do it justice by expanding and elaborating it into totality and the greatest universality" (12–13).

As we have seen, money is no ordinary example. In its abstractness, it is less a particular than a signifier of particularity: as "indifference itself," the cultural means by which particularity of all sorts is represented and thereby interrelated—in practical terms, the technology for socializing difference by making all objects of desire exchangeable. As social and cultural life grows more complex, money thus comes to permeate human existence—as Simmel puts it in the book's final section, "as the means of means, as the most universal technique of external life" (676).

Approached philosophically, money can therefore become the "means, material, or example for representing the relations that exist between the most external, most realistic, most contingent phenomena and the most ideal powers of existence, the most profound currents of individual life and of history." Understood as the synecdoche of synecdoches, as a figure for the process by which indifference becomes significant difference—by which meaning emerges—money enables a new form of philosophizing focused on the concrete phenomena of historical and cultural-social life. "The meaning and purpose of the whole [book] is only this: to cast a guideline from the surface of economic events into the ultimate values and significances of everything human" (12). Simmel's *Philosophy of Money* aims neither to establish a universalizing theoretical point of view nor to delineate the foundations of a discipline, but to develop and articulate this interpretive practice, his modernist mode

---

26. A letter to Rickert of May 10, 1898, attests to the centrality and the difficulty of this issue—in particular, of the problem that values had to be both relative and absolute or objective. Simmel was convinced: "I can only stick with my relativism if it is able to solve all the problems that the absolutistic theories pose just as well" as they do (*GSG* 22: 292).

of philosophizing. To start with money is to begin thinking, quite literally, in a new way so as to capture the prismatically shifting complexity of lived experience and explore the processes of (semiotic) exchange through which human beings render their lives meaningful and valuable.

This bring us back to the passage where we interrupted our reading of the Preface. Immediately after setting out his aspirations for this synecdochic strategy of philosophizing—his intention to start from "a limited and small problem in order to do it justice by expanding and elaborating it into totality and the greatest universality"—Simmel goes on to make some of the most explicit and significant methodological remarks in his entire oeuvre, remarks that have proved subject to serious misunderstandings.

"From a methodological perspective," the next paragraph begins, the "fundamental purpose" of the *Philosophy of Money* is to "build a story beneath historical materialism such that the explanatory value of incorporating economic life into the causes of spiritual culture is preserved, but those economic forms themselves are recognized as the result of more profound valuations and tendencies, of psychological and indeed metaphysical presuppositions" (13). The process of analysis cannot stop there, however, and Simmel continues:

> For the praxis of cognition [*Praxis des Erkennens*], this must then develop in infinite reciprocity: every interpretation of an ideal configuration through an economic one must be succeeded by the demand to understand the latter out of more ideal depths, while for these the general economic basis is sought once again, and so on into the unbounded. In such alternation and intertwining of conceptually opposed epistemic principles, the unity of things, which appears ungraspable for our cognition and nevertheless grounds its cohesion, becomes practical and animated for us. (13)

Simmel's proposal to build a "story beneath historical materialism" has often been taken (out of context!) to imply that he was setting out to restore the very idealist, transcendental foundations Marx had attacked. But his conception of what constituted an adequate philosophical grounding for the dialectical strategies of historical materialism was considerably more complex. In building that story, Simmel aimed to "preserve the explanatory value of incorporating economic life into the causes of spiritual culture." At the same time, by situating the "economic forms" themselves in a broader cultural, psychological, and philosophical context, he aspired to deeper insight into their meaning as expressions of human being. In a word, he was attempting to establish a way of thinking those forms themselves as, in his expanded sense of the term, objectified *Geist*: "as the products of more profound valuations and tendencies, of psychological, even metaphysical, presuppositions."

Simmel not only rejected Marx's progressivist philosophy of history; he regarded the reductivist self-assurance of materialist theoretical discourse as such as misguided. While he shared with historical materialism a vision of increasing objectification and alienation as a consequence of sociohistorical and political developments linked to capital, he was both more skeptical about the utopian possibilities of new forms of collectivity and more concerned about the implications of dynamics internal to cultural and individual existence than Marx had been. His account of reification illustrates how much is at stake in this theoretical divergence.

In *Capital*, Marx famously found the commodity to be "full of metaphysical subtleties and theological niceties." Since these could be explained as functions of the capitalist mode of production, nonalienating forms of objectification could be imagined. On Simmel's view, by contrast, no definitive reinversion of the reified world was possible. His underappreciated concept of *Technik* and particularly of "techniques of life" foregrounds the continuity between mediation and means of all sorts in human existence. Simmel understood technology (as the term may also be translated) as constitutive of culture. Instrumental strategies cannot be mastered and placed at the service of human beings, who live in a world both constituted and constantly being transformed by institutionally mediated means that we ourselves produce and performatively sustain. The very constitution of human existence is in permanent flux. There is no separating *technē* from *Kultur*—the realm of the instrumentally rational from its higher human purposes: *Geist*, intellect, means, and value are all ambiguous in their historical significance.

For Simmel, it was thus not capital but money itself, "as the means of means, as the most universal technology of external life," that led into metaphysical and historical depths. As the symbol and bearer of the alienation and abstraction proper to capitalist production and the engine of individuation, money is an apparently universal signifier that reveals the limits of signification. Consolidating the theoretical advances of historical materialism required a mode of analysis that could integrate the lived significance of objectification and abstraction as such.

Simmel's metaphor for his undertaking—inserting a new story beneath historical materialism—is rather misleading. He was not, as the image seems to suggest, setting out to provide a more fundamental foundation. Neither "economic forms" nor their ideal "depths" can provide ultimate explanations. As Simmel describes his method for extending the dialectic by adopting a mimetic relationship to the complexity of lived reality, with materialist and idealist interpretations proceeding via "alternation and intertwining" and "in infinite reciprocity" on "into the unbounded" (13), his anti-foundationalism becomes explicit. Insofar as his *Philosophy of Money* aims to make visible the (culturally, historically) generative movement of thought as it proceeds through the (in principle infinite) reciprocity of opposed interpretations, it arguably has more in common with Hegel than Marx. But this is not to say that Simmel was an idealist. The resonance so evident in this passage between his approach to the cultural logic of reification and Adorno's negative dialectics bears careful consideration.

For Simmel, there is no ultimate, unrelativizable foundation. From a point of view at once Kantian and Nietzschean, Simmel presents the distinctions between the material and ideal, historical and transhistorical, life and form, as dialectically constituted ways of describing a reality we experience as exceeding our conceptual grasp, yet open to being approached and understood in multiple ways, from intersecting, indeterminately bounded disciplinary and philosophical perspectives. The *Philosophy of Money* sets out to overcome the distance from particulars that had prevented philosophy from doing justice to the complexity of cultural-historical life through a relativist method or knowledge practice, a *Praxis des Erkennens*, that precisely in refusing to seek secure foundations aspires to generate a "philosophy of social and historical life as a whole." Simmel aims, then, to attend to and represent lived experience in its full—social, historical, cultural, psychological, philosophical—complexity by extending into infinity the tracing of the dialectical relations between material and ideal, life and form.

The stakes of this relativist practice, which mimetically adopts multiple and conflicting perspectives and ways of knowing without insisting that they be reconciled or synthesized, are metaphysical. By rendering "practical and animated" what cannot be directly known or apprehended—the dialectical process of unending "alternation and intertwining of conceptually opposed cognitive principles" that constitutes the human effort to understand the world—Simmel's text generates an experience of the unity-in-multiplicity of the reality human beings are continually attempting and repeatedly failing to understand from partial perspectives.

What Simmel characterizes as an in principle "infinite reciprocity" between (apparently opposed) materialist and idealist accounts of any given phenomenon finds expression in a strategy of writing centered on the interpretation and reinterpretation of particulars. Following upon one another in series, often anchored in contrasting, even contradictory aspects of the larger topic or aspect of reality under consideration, these particulars become the starting points for (partial) totalizations and thereby repeatedly reveal themselves as synecdochic openings onto the prismatically shifting appearance of the significance of existence as a whole.

In proceeding through "phenomenal series"—or, as Simmel characterized it in his book announcement, through "tracings" of the "connections between the most external and most intimate [literally, most interior, *Innerlichste*]" matters—his *Philosophy of Money* aspired to "demonstrate that it is possible to cast a plummet from every point on the most indifferent, most un-ideal surface of life into its ultimate depths, that every single one of its particulars bears and is borne by the totality of its meaning" (*GSG* 6: 719). This aspiration should not be confused with a belief or desire that all these perspectives resolve into a single, total vision of life. Simmel's method accentuated the multiple and perspectival nature of reality and the incompleteness of every particular vision of the whole. Far from being the mark of a failure of sociological or philosophical systematicity, Simmel's synecdochic, modernist style of thought expresses a metaphilosophical conviction that the world, that is to say the intersubjective, sociocultural world, is already in fragments.

As he put it, "The life of earlier times appears much more bound to stably given unities" and their steady rhythms. "Modernity dissolves these into an arbitrarily divisible continuum." Money bears and intensifies the rationalizing and intellectualizing tendency, paradigmatically evident in the modern natural sciences, to experience and understand life not as a whole but in isolated, quantifiable parts. Simmel's perspectival approach to philosophizing is an attempt to come to terms self-reflexively with the seemingly ineluctable advance of this cognitive tendency.

The *Philosophy of Money* aspired to no less than "the redemption" of individual phenomena, "especially those of practical existence, from their isolation and unspirituality" and apparent "contrariety"—but not by reintegrating them into a (postulated, abstract) totality à la system philosophy. Written from a modernist point of view that takes the fragmentation of the world as a given, the book reveals particulars as synecdoches, as a significant parts of a perspectival whole. Simmel's apparently associative mode of writing captures the fragmentary multiplicity of experiential reality through sequences of such partial and contingent totalities, in and through a relativist "knowledge practice" that traces successions of diverse phenomenal "series" to make visible how value and meaning are created, sustained, and transformed in the lived context of human interaction.

By embracing epistemic uncertainty, Simmel develops a model for philosophizing without foundations that takes the ineffable unity of life as its model. He emphasizes that the process of relativization, of relating and transforming interpretive perspectives, must continue in principle into infinity. In this performative, modernist mode of philosophizing, a self-reflexively relativist and relativizing knowledge practice is unified by a style of thinking that enacts the contingency of lived experience—and in that very enactment achieves a modernist philosophical perspective that self-reflexively transforms circumstances that might otherwise appear to be grounds for despair into the lineaments of a new, lived understanding of human existence itself, in which, again, "In such alternation and intertwining of conceptually opposed epistemic principles, the unity of things, which appears ungraspable for our cognition and nevertheless grounds its cohesion, becomes practical and animated for us" (13).

The vertiginous rhetorical movement characteristic of Simmel's work, in which diametrically opposed interpretations follow on one another without mediation or explanation, reflects an effort to grasp the supplementary relation between the opposed epistemic principles that underlie divergent explanatory paradigms. Simmel never lets any definitive interpretation stand as the ultimate word. If he is in principle committed to a synecdochic model of reality, according to which it is possible to find "in every particular of life the totality of its meaning," his texts proceed metonymically, via the proliferation of possible meanings along a line of association. In this way, the Simmelian text demonstrates—or better, performs—a fundamentally Kantian agnosticism about the ultimate nature of "the unity of things" that is the counterpart of our modes of knowing.

Keeping in mind the performative process by which "phenomenal series" function in Simmel's texts as relativist knowledge practice, let us bring our reflections on what is at stake in his modernist mode of philosophizing to conclusion by completing our reading of the Preface. In its final lines, the argument takes an unexpected turn as Simmel relativizes his claims for the *Philosophy of Money* as a whole by extending his agnosticism to his own text. The philosophical value of his work, its "intentions and methods" can only lay claim to "correctness in principle," he writes, if they can serve thinking that begins from "a substantive diversity of fundamental philosophical convictions." The synecdochic strategy of interpretation that provides the text's methodological unity is ontologically neutral. He continues: "The linkage between life's particularities and superficialities and its most profound and essential movements and their interpretation according to its total meaning can take place on the foundation of idealism or realism, of rationalist or voluntarist, of an absolutist as well as a relativist interpretation of being." At this point, Simmel invokes the first person to relativize even his own relativism, proceeding to the following remarkable conclusion:

> That the following investigations are based on one of these world-images, which I hold to be the most appropriate expression of the contemporary states of knowledge and emotional tendencies, while decisively excluding the opposite, would in the worst case give them the role merely of an exemplary case whose methodological significance as the form of future correctness stands out all the more if it is substantively inaccurate. (13)

Simmel's claim for his modernist approach could hardly be stronger. It is the style rather than the substance of thought that is at stake. Even if his relativistic epistemology does not get at the deepest structures of being, even if it is simply a reflection of the limits to knowledge and human self-awareness inscribed in the social, cultural, historical circumstances in which he is writing, his synecdochic method, as "the form of future correctness," will retain its value for human self-reflection—we would say, for cultural theory—whatever its metaphysical basis.

Simmel's claim is, in a Kantian sense, a logical one: that his relativist method reflects the necessary phenomenological foundation of human thought. Human beings *must* think about life in a way that links "particularities and superficialities and its most profound and essential movements," must attempt to interpret phenomenal reality "according to its total meaning." His modernist knowledge practice attempts to do justice to the fragmentation, multiplicity, and uncertainty of the world of experience, to the (post-Kantian and, even more, post-Nietzschean) reflective certainty that nothing is really certain, without belying the lived imperative to make sense of it. Simmel's avowal of the necessity of orienting thinking to experience in the face of the uncertain meaning of being reveals further affinities between his modernist mode of philosophizing and Heideggerean anti-foundationalism, on the one hand, and the perspectival experiments of Adorno's explicitly essayistic modernism, on the other.

CHAPTER 6

Disciplining the *Philosophy of Money*

Simmel rightly emphasized the methodological contribution of his *Philosophy of Money*, which unsettles the distinctions between the ideas and methods proper to epistemological and metaphysical reflection and to historical and empirical inquiry. In Gustav Schmoller's formulation, Simmel turns the results of historical and economic, ethnological and political research into "raw material" for higher-level analysis.[1] This modernist mode of theorizing, which intervenes in multiple discourses without becoming part of the disciplines that generate them, destabilizes what have since become very real boundaries between philosophy and social science.

Simmel's exploration of money as an historical, cultural, and social phenomenon leads into philosophical depths, revealing the generative movement of thought in the boundary zones where precision gives way to reflection and enabling metareflection on the process by which scientific knowledge itself is produced and perpetuated. The *Philosophy of Money*'s disciplinary location was thus uncertain from the beginning. Embracing the unstable boundaries between different modes of inquiry into the phenomena of human collective existence but also the indeterminacy of the disciplines themselves, it blurred the lines separating philosophy from its others to become a foundational text for what has come to be called cultural or critical theory. Returning to this liminal work, situated at the cusp between (nineteenth-century) philosophy and (twentieth-century) theory can therefore reopen questions that have been not so much resolved as forgotten.

Simmel's chef d'oeuvre was published during a period of great intellectual and cultural ferment, when the limits of the dominant modes of philosophizing were becoming evident, yet before the social sciences had acquired confidence that they had put metaphysics behind them. The borderlines between those new disciplines and their intellectual and cultural predecessors were still unsettled, and boundaries we take for granted—between practical and theoretical, professional and non-professional approaches to reflection on the social; between humanistic and empirical study of culture; between science and history—were still inchoate. Inquiry had not yet been imaginatively and institutionally ordered in and through the metadisciplinary and

---

1. Gustav Schmoller, "Simmels *Philosophie des Geldes*," in *Georg Simmels Philosophie des Geldes: Aufsätze und Materialien*, ed. Otthein Rammstedt, with Christian Papilloud et al. (Frankfurt am Main: Suhrkamp, 2003), 282–89; here p. 282.

bureaucratic divisions that systematize, sanction, legitimate, and perpetuate research, scholarly paradigms, and professionalized knowledge practices today.

A Disciplinary Rorschach: Early Responses to the *Philosophy of Money*

The *Philosophy of Money* appeared in December 1900. Unlike some of Simmel's later books, it was not an instantaneous success. In May, Gustav Schmoller, who had just published a very positive review of it, assured Simmel's publisher, who had complained of poor sales, that "It is a very brilliant, significant book. But certainly no more than a hundred people in Germany will read it, even if more buy it. . . . However, you will nonetheless perhaps be able to issue a second printing in fifteen years."[2]

In fact, Simmel was already enjoying sensational public success and was well-established as a figure of interest in modernist cultural circles in Germany and beyond by 1900. The *Philosophy of Money* was one of the first works Max Weber read after his nervous breakdown, and Hugo von Hofmansthal is even said to have envisioned making it into a libretto.[3] Sales turned out to be such that a second, slightly expanded edition would be issued at the beginning of 1907.

Simmel's accomplishment was recognized in major international journals representing a range of academic disciplines.[4] Even more skeptical reviewers singled out its author's creativity and intellectual fecundity, though as Émile Durkheim's abrasive assessment of Simmel's approach as *spéculation bâtard* attests, the protean text was not to everyone's taste. But let us begin by considering the very positive reception of the *Philosophy of Money* by two founding figures of modern social science.

Schmoller, Simmel's former teacher, welcomed the work as a major breakthrough, a brilliant reimagining of the boundaries of scholarship. Its author, he declared, had "blazed new paths through a previously unexplored primeval forest." Simmel's study was a "substantial scientific advance; anyone who wants to elucidate the general significance of the money economy in the future will have to build upon it."[5]

Simmel's purpose was nothing less than "to determine what the money economy, especially the modern one of the nineteenth century, has made out of human beings and society, their relations and institutions," Schmoller wrote (282). With his "productive imagination," this "philosophically and dialectically trained thinker who at the same time has an exceptional command of political economy as well as legal and economic history" had disclosed entirely new questions, connections, and perspec-

---

2. Schmoller to Carl Giebel, May 8, 1901, cited in *GSG* 22: 380–81.
3. On January 27, 1900, Simmel wrote to Heinrich Rickert that he had "ca. 315" students in his seminars (*Privatkollegien*), adding, "It is wonderful to see what interest these people take in the very most difficult and profound questions" (*GSG* 22: 345). See Marianne Weber's account of Weber's recuperation in id., *Max Weber: A Biography* (New York: Wiley, 1975), 254. Regarding Hoffmansthal, see Frisby, "Preface to the Third Edition of *The Philosophy of Money*," xxxi.
4. Selections had appeared in English and Russian as well as German even before 1900, and a Polish translation of the work as a whole was published in 1904. Regarding the English reception, see Frisby's invaluable "Introduction to the Translation."
5. In Otthein Rammstedt et al., eds. *Georg Simmels Philosophie des Geldes* (Frankfurt am Main: Suhrkamp, 2003), 297. Subsequent citations are given parenthetically in the text.

tives (297). The *Philosophy of Money* thus had implications for many disciplines (besides economics and legal and economic history, Schmoller also mentions sociology, philosophy, cultural history, political science, and psychology). And in addition to "enriching the political and social sciences," Simmel had succeeded in "illuminating the great ethical life-questions of our time and our culture" (298).

Like the American philosopher George Herbert Mead (1863–1931), who declared that the book "demonstrates . . . not only the legitimacy, but the value of approaching economic science from the philosophic standpoint," Schmoller emphasized the methodological implications of Simmel's syncretic and transdisciplinary approach for the social sciences, broadly understood. As Schmoller put it, the *Philosophy of Money* "takes what we know about money, historically and in terms of political economy, as raw material, so to speak, in order to turn it to account sociologically and philosophically, in order to derive psychological, social scientific, cultural conclusions from it" (282).[6]

Mead was in nominal agreement, declaring Simmel's work of interest to economists for its sociological and philosophical perspective on money. The *Philosophy of Money* "analyzes the form of the economic object rather than its content" and thereby casts light on the philosophical problem of value, he explained (616). However, Schmoller's decided emphasis on the historical character of both object and inquiry is absent from his review. For Mead, a pragmatic theorist of the social self, "the chief aim of the treatise is to follow out in money and its use the relation of the individual to the community" (619).[7]

The contrast is noteworthy. As I have shown, Simmel's reception is marked by dichotomous readings, corresponding to the basic tension within his work between the formal and historical, theoretical and empirical dimensions. What makes his *Philosophy of Money* so significant methodologically speaking is, so to speak, anterior to the difficulty of categorizing its accomplishment in well-defined disciplinary terms and, as these differing responses attest, relates to the formal and stylistic qualities of the text itself.

Both Mead and Schmoller drew attention to what the former called the "dismayingly massive" dimensions of the book, on top of which, as the latter noted, "in presenting the economic-psychical and economic-institutional changes, it repeat-

---

6. George Herbert Mead, "*Philosophie des Geldes* by Georg Simmel," *Journal of Political Economy* 9, no. 4 (1901): 616– 19; here p. 619. Subsequent citations are given parenthetically in text. Schmoller's language attests to the still inchoate boundaries among various modes of inquiry that would become established social scientific disciplines. Here as throughout, virtually without exception, he refers to disciplinary *perspectives* rather than disciplines, using adjectives rather substantives. The difficulty of laying the emphasis properly in translation underlines a problem that is by no means merely semantic. Schmoller's account in the preceding paragraph refers to what he actually calls "disciplinary practices," but there is no English term for this that does not implicitly reinscribe the assumption that such perspectives and practices have institutional homes in (specialized, professionalized) disciplines.

7. Although Mead taught a popular course in social psychology and is best remembered today as the founding father of symbolic interactionism, he was a professional philosopher who chaired the department at the University of Chicago. Mead had studied with pioneering experimentalists Wilhelm Wundt and G. Stanley Hall at Leipzig, then taken his PhD in Berlin, where he heard Simmel but worked with Dilthey.

edly becomes necessary to compress the quintessence of centuries and millennia into three or four pages. There allusions must suffice which only the connoisseur understands" (298). Thanks to its scope and compass, to the strikingly diverse range of topics and theoretical interventions that populate its densely argued pages, the *Philosophy of Money* came to function as a sort of disciplinary Rorschach test.

Simmel's contemporary readers encountered challenges symptomatic of the ways in which disciplinary styles of thought and hence ways of reading were diverging. Schmoller conceded that it could be difficult to grasp what Simmel was after, but he saw this as a consequence of the author's effort to do justice to all sides. As a writer who "sees the light and shadow sides of every phenomenon," Simmel presented the reader with a mimetic image of human life itself: "the eternal play of peak and valley, of rise and fall of historical processes" (298). Although written in a "lively, attractive, sparkling style," the book was aimed at readers with a certain intellectual independence and critical perspective. Those who lacked philosophical training or historical knowledge would have difficulty following Simmel's argument and "clearly surveying the connections" among its diverse materials (298). Indeed, Schmoller predicted, the "philistines among the political economists" would cast it aside, contemptuous of its excessive refinement. However, "the genuine scientific world of the nobly educated will be all the more grateful to [Simmel]; those who are capable of reading each difficult chapter two or three times will do so with enjoyment and increasing benefit" (299).

This is the *Philosophy of Money* as high modernism: a kaleidoscopic succession of perspectives resolving into a cohesive whole that is nothing less than a "sociological-philosophical treatment" of life in the modern economy. Simmel asked "what money and the money economy has made out of the thinking, feeling, and desiring of individuals, out of the societal connections, out of the social, legal, and economic institutions. The repercussions of the most important institution of the modern economy, of money, for all aspects of cultural life, that is his theme" (297). Not only did his contribution range over "all realms of knowledge," Schmoller continued. Because answering such questions involved "ultimate decisions concerning not only the intellect but also the heart and character of the individuality in question," his topic could not be exhausted or even addressed in a fashion that everyone could accept (297).

In short, the text's prismatic, modernist mode of cohesion made Simmel's relativism palpable. As he put it in the Preface, "the unity of these investigations lies not in a claim about a singular content of knowledge" but rather in an effort to shape a new way of seeing by demonstrating "the possibility of finding the totality of life's meaning in every particular" (*GSG* 6: 12). His kaleidoscopically changing representations of modern life invited readers to think further. With its constantly shifting topics and foci, Simmel's *Philosophy of Money* stands in a complex relation to social scientific strivings for objectivity and empirical knowledge, challenging its audience to become more self-reflective about matters of interpretation and to ask how ultimate philosophical questions are related to and indeed embedded in everyday experience.

Sympathetic as he was to this project, Schmoller did not entirely do justice to the reasons for the measured response to the *Philosophy of Money* within many academic circles. Simmel was not simply ranging over multiple disciplinary territories. The boundaries between political economy and sociology, psychology and history, legal history and political science, and all the other fields he touched on were hardly solid in any case. He was also posing the sort of questions that many who identified themselves as social scientists had hoped to consign to the dustbin of history.

In a period of rapid professionalization in higher education, even as his colleagues were attempting to establish sociology as a distinct and officially recognized scientific discipline, Simmel was drawing attention to the questionable epistemological and ontological presuppositions and philosophical consequences involved. His meditations on money suggested, for instance, that the sort of objectivity understood to characterize the natural sciences could not be achieved in the domain of the social, raising the issue of whether the category of "laws" could be legitimately applied to investigations into historically and culturally varying matters at all.[8]

Unsurprising, then, if the *Philosophy of Money* provoked palpable anxiety among those with strong disciplinary allegiances—or more precisely, those with significant investments in the institutional framework of the modern research university that was taking shape during this period. As the painful ups and downs of his career attest, Simmel's work did not really fit in. Indeed, the book's scope and range appear to disqualify it as a "proper" work either of philosophy or of social science even today.

The reception of the *Philosophy of Money* illustrates once again that the problem was not simply the relation between Simmel's sociological work and the discipline of philosophy. Neither his topics nor his strategies of thought had a proper place in the professionalized order of knowledge being consolidated during this period in and through the organizational form of the modern research university. They are also incompatible with, even hostile to, the narrowed vision of philosophy centered on *Wissenschaftstheorie* that arose on the ashes of the old, more encompassing understanding of the discipline that had included what we now think of as social scientific (sociological, but also psychological, political, and legal and historical) questions and problems. In this respect, Simmel was becoming historical in his own lifetime.

Durkheim's rather vicious response to the *Philosophy of Money* is a case in point. As we have seen, the two had been early allies of a sort, but by the late 1890s their paths were diverging. Simmel had by no means abandoned his activities on behalf of the discipline of sociology, but he had moved away from the Spencerian and naturalist premises of his early works and grown more focused on epistemological and metaphysical questions. Durkheim, who retained his faith in scientific objectivity throughout his life, had never been friendly to philosophical and humanistic approaches to the study of the social. While Simmel was writing the *Philosophy*

---

8. The virtually complete absence of discussions of Simmel's work from economics is telling, for his analyses of money and exchange relations show how problematic it is to build models based on a conception of human beings as rational actors.

of Money, he was building the conceptual and practical foundations for what would be a colossally successful academic career, negotiating ongoing theoretical skirmishes with the philosophical establishment, and engaging in social scientific institution-building on a redoubtable scale. He had published his *Les règles de la méthode sociologique* (*The Rules of Sociological Method*) in 1895, and in 1896, the first issue of his *L'année sociologique* appeared. Directed, as he put it in the preface, "to all those who long to see sociology finally leave the philosophical phase and take its place among the sciences,"[9] Durkheim's journal would become the vehicle through which he advanced his work and that of his students and publicized and consolidated his vision of the discipline.

Most of the inaugural issue of *L'année sociologique* was devoted to presenting research from allied fields as material for sociological analysis. Notably, just two essays appeared in the original contributions section: Durkheim's own "The Incest Prohibition and its Origins [La prohibition de l'inceste et ses origines]" and, from Simmel, "How Social Forms are Preserved [Comment les formes sociales se maintiennent]," which again advanced his view that sociology should "become an independent science" by "abstracting the form of association from the concrete states, interests, sentiments, that are its content" (*GSG* 19: 106). Simmel's essay had been shortened in translation from the original German version (over 150 pages and entitled "The Self-Preservation of Society") in a process that contributed to the estrangement between the two men.[10] Durkheim was "far from being an enthusiast where Simmel is concerned," as he reminded his nephew and collaborator Marcel Mauss in June 1897. But he found it expedient to include Simmel's work in the inaugural issue, and the conflict over the cuts notwithstanding, Simmel initially remained unaware of his colleague's reserve; he published another essay, "On the Sociology of Religion," in *L'année sociologique* the following year.[11]

The gap between their visions of sociology soon grew all too apparent. As Durkheim's review of the *Philosophy of Money* makes clear, Simmel's turn back toward philosophy was tantamount to a personal affront for him. Writing in *L'année sociologique*, Durkheim dismissed the *Philosophy of Money* as an unsuccessful "treatise in social philosophy."[12]

With the vituperousness of a man whose hopes in his colleague had been betrayed, Durkheim declared that the book's many "ingenious ideas, lively observations" and "wealth of historical and ethnographic facts" were assembled "without accuracy or proof." Twisting Simmel's introductory remarks concerning disciplinary

---

9. Émile Durkheim, "Préface," *L'année sociologique* 1 (1896–97): vii.

10. Durkheim objected to including passages that he read as resonating with (his own) Jewish identity out of fear they would be professionally deleterious. Simmel, resistant for his own political reasons to the changes, was first unhappy with the way editorial processes were handled and eventually bewildered at being accused of anti-Semitism. See Otthein Rammstedt, "Das Durkheim-Simmelsche Projekt einer 'rein wissenschaftlichen Soziologie' im Schatten der Dreyfus-Affäre," *Zeitschrift für Soziologie* 26, no. 6 (1997): 444–57.

11. My discussion follows the editorial notes to the essay in *GSG* 19: 392–401; the letter to Mauss is cited on p. 401.

12. Émile Durkheim, "Review of the *Philosophy of Money*," *L'année sociologique* 5 (1900–1901): 140–45.

boundaries and method in the Preface into the inference that he "believes, in point of fact, that unlike the sciences proper, philosophy is not subject to the common obligations of proof; the unprovable is philosophy's domain," Durkheim objected to the very innovative qualities he initially seemed to praise. "Imagination, personal feelings are thus given free reign here, and rigorous demonstrations have no relevance," he declares. Simmel's approach thus amounted to an "illegitimate speculation [*spéculation bâtard*], where reality is expressed in necessarily subjective terms, as in art, but also abstractly, as in science. For this very reason, it can offer us neither the fresh and living sensation of things that the artist arouses nor the precision which is the scientist's goal."

In an effort to make visible the interconnectedness of a world whose complexity he believed could not be reduced to a single point of view, Simmel was intentionally bringing aesthetic perspectives to bear in theorizing the social. But Durkheim was unable to recognize, or simply refused to acknowledge, that Simmel's mode of argument was a means of engaging very real issues of epistemic foundations and disciplinary boundaries. For a man with Durkheim's commitments, the *Philosophy of Money* was neither fish nor fowl.

Similar anxieties about the transgression of disciplinary categories were produced on the other side of the increasingly palpable divide between the social and human sciences. Thus Erich Adickes, who included the *Philosophy of Money* in his survey of "The Philosophical Literature of Germany in the Years 1899 and 1900" for the *Philosophical Review*, began his remarks by consigning the book to "the boundary domain of philosophy."[13] His review was largely laudatory, but Adickes objected to the purportedly "philosophical procedure" followed in its second part. He took exception to the very passage that had evoked Durkheim's ire: the book's opening, where Simmel declares that since the boundaries of the disciplines are not and cannot be fixed, one of philosophy's responsibilities is to provide conceptual resources for approaching phenomena that are not yet susceptible of precise empirical investigation, even if so in principle. For Adickes, such undertakings could not be regarded as philosophical at all. He proceeded to erect a boundary with Simmel on the other side, thereby protecting not just philosophy but the emergent disciplinary order itself: "Philosophy could only bring deserved discredit upon itself were it, from the fact of there being a domain whose exact and detailed investigation had not yet been made, to seek justification therein for interfering in this discipline."

Fortunately, the *Philosophy of Money* did not really endanger the order of things in this way, since "in the second part, Simmel does not speak as a philosopher but as a sociologist." Adickes went on to call the book "suggestive and full of novel points of view" and to "heartily commend this work to the reading public." In fact, he concluded, it was not only instructive but possessed "a quality still higher than instructiveness, the highest quality a book can possess—stimulation to think for

13. "The Philosophical Literature of Germany in the Years 1899 and 1900," *Philosophical Review* 10, no. 4 (1901): 386–416. All the following citations are from the pages on *Philosophy of Money*, 414–16. This text is reproduced in *Georg Simmel: Critical Assessments*, ed. David Frisby (New York: Routledge, 1994), 161–62.

one's self." In light of his dismissal of Simmel's philosophical objectives, Adickes's recommendation of him as brilliant outsider sounds a good deal like damning with faint praise.

While Durkheim dismissed Simmel's contribution to the social sciences on the grounds that his method was too philosophical, too subjective, and insufficiently scientific, Adickes embraced its philosophical suggestiveness but consigned what its author regarded as the constructive theoretical achievements of the *Philosophy of Money* to sociology. Durkheim and Adickes were policing opposite sides of an emerging disciplinary division that Simmel's work clearly transgressed—one, moreover, whose theoretical coherence he denied, and whose practical and institutional consequences he arguably disdained. As is the case with Simmel's reception history more generally, those who identify primarily as historians rather than practitioners of the social sciences seem better equipped to address the complexities of a mode of argumentation that is philosophical without ceasing to be sociological. For it is from within a cosmopolitan historicism that Simmel advances his theoretically nuanced and culturally and sociologically situated interpretation of modern subjectivity and culture.

The economist S. P. Altmann took up the question of the *Philosophy of Money*'s problematic disciplinary location with disarming forthrightness in a review essay published in 1903 in the *American Journal of Sociology*. In praising the book's interdisciplinary breadth and innovative approach, he addressed the very methodological issues that had vexed Durkheim and Adickes. However, Altmann wrote, "Simmel's *Philosophy of Money* does not belong to any special branch of science, and therefore to all; this the competent representatives of the sciences in question will never pardon him, and yet they all of them can learn a great deal from him, the lawyer as well as the economist, the aestheticist as well as the historian." Although the work of an "absolute master," he continues, it bears "a tragic stain," for "every thought" is burdened "with the fate of the eternal Jew . . . eternal restlessness, the longing after ever deeper knowledge and insight . . . a tragic fate for him who is seeking after truth."[14]

Altmann's long review, headed by an epigraph from Emerson, "The difference between persons is not in wisdom, but in art,"[15] then concludes on a note at once poetic and sober. Invoking a phrase he attributes to Simmel, Altmann declares: "Only the narrow pride of a scientific bureaucracy can refuse to accept" his accomplishment in presenting new knowledge "in the form of artistic intuition." And yet "the circle of those for whom he has written will unfortunately be small, and the *Philosophy of Money* ought to be introduced" by Stendhal's dedication "To the happy few."

Altmann's assessment proved prescient. Simmel's innovative approach to philosophizing inspired modernist artists, writers, and activists, but the reception of his

---

14. S. P. Altmann "Simmel's Philosophy of Money," *American Journal of Sociology* 9, no. 1 (1903): 46–68; here p. 67.

15. Ibid., 46. Howard Becker, "On Simmel's *Philosophy of Money*," in *Georg Simmel, 1858–1918*, ed. K. H. Wolff (Columbus: Ohio University Press, 1959), 216–32, also drew attention to the importance of Altmann's essay.

masterpiece within the academy was very different. In a nutshell, the very idea of a philosophy of money appeared problematic—and not only to philosophers.

As the modern, professionalized, university emerged, and the "scientific bureaucracy" I am calling the modern disciplinary order took form, scholars increasingly understood themselves as specialized professionals whose identity was defined by their interest and expertise in narrowly demarcated areas and fields. Simmel's Nietzschean perspectivism was an uneasy fit. His explicit concern with the unstable boundaries between different modes of inquiry into social and cultural phenomena, as well as with the philosophical problems of theorizing human historical existence, drew unwanted attention to the indeterminacy of disciplines still in the process of differentiation, professionalization, and institutionalization. And while the *Philosophy of Money* has, after a fashion, entered the canon, even today, many potential readers (and by no means only within the social sciences) might well still endorse Durkheim's description of Simmel's method as "bastard speculation."

Simmel's methodological relativism represents a serious practical and theoretical challenge that it has proved more convenient to avoid than to confront. As the reviews of the *Philosophy of Money* underscore, the incompatible charges against him—that he was unsystematic and overly formalist, too critical and too metaphysical—were not just misunderstandings but defenses. Simmel was transgressing boundaries around which careers were being made. His philosophical views, notably his epistemological position that generalizations in the historical sciences have an ineluctably speculative dimension, were an affront to the self-understanding of the emergent modern social sciences. Writing him off as a metaphysical relic of the philosophical prehistory of those disciplines enabled Simmel's successors to avoid confronting what remain, even today, unresolved theoretical and methodological issues—not least the lack of a clear referent for the ostensible object of the new disciplines, "the social."[16]

As the modern disciplinary ordering of inquiry took shape, Schmoller's (doubtless idealized) "genuine scientific world of the nobly educated" was indeed being displaced by very different institutions and ideals and new sorts of scholarly practices. The same tendencies to differentiation and specialization that shape modern life as a whole are operative in the university, and the institutional and more generally practical benefits of such rationalization have continued to catalyze the emergence of new disciplines focusing on ever more narrowly defined areas. Altmann's description may seem somewhat of an exaggeration for 1903, but today's intellectual landscape, with its balkanized disciplines and subdisciplines, its thousands of journals and series and professional organizations and conferences, its suspicion of "generalists" and bias toward empirical and verifiable "results," is surely not inaccurately described as a "scientific bureaucracy."

If the sort of reflection on the conditions of possibility of knowledge of human social reality that animates Simmel's work appears old-fashioned today, then it is in no small part because the overarching philosophical questions concerning

---

16. See Olli Pyyhtinen, *Simmel and 'the social'* (New York: Palgrave Macmillan, 2010).

knowledge and science he was asking have themselves been turned into the province of specialists. In his own time, questions of certainty and verification were on the ascendant, and the pursuit of truth was already beginning to acquire a ring of quaintness. The transformation of philosophical reflection on natural science in the context of the emergence of the elaborate modern organization of disciplines is the index of highly significant historical developments.[17] The Rorschach-like responses of some of Simmel's most prominent reviewers to the account offered at the beginning of the *Philosophy of Money* illuminate key features of (emerging) disciplinary consciousness—and unconsciousness.

The culturally dominant understanding of knowledge was changing. Tensions within the enlightenment view of progress were coming to the fore. The integrative, ultimately theological ideal of human fulfillment through the pursuit of truth was gradually being supplanted by a seemingly disenchanted, utilitarian view of science. This instrumental orientation and the focus on observation and quantifiability constitutive for the empirical social sciences increasingly excluded philosophical questions of the sort Simmel was asking—about judgment, about the meaning and purpose of the knowledge enterprise of modern science as a whole.

Simmel saw disciplines as bounded both from above and below: by logical presuppositions and ontological foundations, but also by questions about the purpose and meaning of systematic inquiry. He took it for granted—and here he was by no means alone, though it does perhaps mark him as a man of the nineteenth century—that metaphysical, theological, ethical issues were and should still be of concern in and for the social sciences. Logical and substantive questions intertwined in the boundary zones between disciplines.

In the century since his death, intellectual, sociohistorical, cultural, political and economic (and at the same time very material, concrete, practical, and technical) developments have created a very different intellectual environment. At least within the institutional context in which knowledge is professionally pursued, validated, verified, and disseminated and "knowledge workers" are recruited, certified, regulated, and supported, the boundaries between disciplines are palpable realities. In this milieu, questions about the ultimate purpose of disciplinary practices and boundaries are posed mostly in pragmatic, instrumental and bureaucratic terms. A quasi-naturalized division into distinct professionalized domains underpins and sustains a regime of knowledge practices that fragments inquiry into "hard" and "soft," "natural" and "social" sciences, and isolates questions about the meaning and significance of the relations among disciplinary practices in a ghettoized "humanities."

Today "science" has come to be virtually synonymous with technoscience, and "ethicists" scramble to generate procedures to prevent or at least complicate the unbridled pursuit of the technologically possible. In an intellectual culture in which expertise too often supplants critical reflection, Simmel's work reminds us why in-

---

17. Here it is worth noting that well into the twentieth century, the most important work on the history and philosophy of science was still being done by (former) practitioners.

tellectual boundaries are not, and cannot be, fixed. His perspectival account of the relations between disciplinary formations and philosophical questions not only directs attention to the limitations of modern, highly specialized and professionalized, knowledge practices themselves. It illuminates the problematic status of the disciplinary imaginary—of the embodied and encultured acceptance of the intellectual division of labor into "areas" and "fields" that underpins scientific—and not only scientific—bureaucracy.

The *Philosophy of Money* as "Social Theory"

Ironically, yet perhaps not surprisingly, given Durkheim's rejection of it as unscientific in form and conception, the *Philosophy of Money* entered the modern social scientific canon under cover, its philosophical ambitions going largely unrecognized. Today, thanks in no small part to the late David Frisby's tireless editorial and scholarly efforts on Simmel's behalf, the book has come to be widely celebrated in the Anglophone world as the first *sociology* of modernity—a designation that, however capacious, cannot possibly do justice to its author's ambition to write "a philosophy of historical and social life as a whole." Even with a full translation of the text available, its size and sheer difficulty and the institutional triumph of a very un-Simmelian vision of what makes social science scientific have continued to encourage selective appropriation.

Decisively, the practice of reading the final chapter, "The Style of Life," in isolation from Simmel's larger argument about money remains comfortably institutionalized within sociology today. A key case of the appropriation by fragments that has helped render his ideas accessible to the disciplinary mainstream, this highly selective approach both reflects and reinforces the pragmatic methodological attitude of a discipline oriented toward investigating "empirical" questions about the social using quantitative methods and resolving problems that arise within the practice of normal science without reflecting either historically or theoretically on the limitations of that quantitative orientation itself. The specifically hermeneutic issues surrounding reading and understanding texts, foundational or otherwise, are not generally recognized as *sociological* problems. As in political science or psychology, such issues tend to be the purview of (subdisciplinary) specialists in history and/or theory.

Reframing the *Philosophy of Money* as a work of sociology epitomizes the global rewriting of his philosophical achievements that performatively legitimates the very practices of selective reading through which Simmel's theoretical contributions are obscured. For a methodological worldview that treats the language in which sociological problems are represented as a neutral conveyer of concepts, questions about the way theoretical claims are formulated are logical or semantic matters. The sorts of inquiries that stand at the center of so much theoretical work on society and culture in the continental philosophical tradition—interrogations of the language (the rhetoric, metaphorics, the conceptual imaginary) that is historically and culturally embedded in social scientific discourse—simply do not arise for those who understand sociology as "science." Issues that humanistically oriented thinkers regard as central are marginal at best to them.[18]

From this perspective, Simmel's thinking continues to be criticized as unsystematic despite a series of distinguished and compelling demonstrations to the contrary. To render visible the constructive role of this misunderstanding, it will be helpful to examine a specific example that illustrates the difficulty of reading him from within the disciplinary horizons of sociology. Gianfranco Poggi's *Money and the Modern Mind: Georg Simmel's Philosophy of Money*, a thoughtful and engagingly written effort to make Simmel's opus magnum "more accessible to readers,"[19] remains the only English-language monograph devoted to the work more than twenty years after its publication. Declaring his allegiance to a "'presentist' approach" (2) focused on the "enduring significance" of Simmel's "persistently valid or at any rate highly thought-provoking insights into a wide range of social phenomena," Poggi simultaneously construes the *Philosophy of Money* as a classic of (sociological) social theory and occludes the work's philosophical agenda.[20] Systematizing and summarizing Simmel's central ideas without regard for the form of their presentation, he reframes the task of reading the book in a way that eliminates the need to encounter the text on its own (modernist) terms.

As Poggi explains in his Preface, he "deals with [the book's] content in a relatively selective manner" to "assist" Simmel's readers, by "focus[ing] their attention on four main themes": "the nature of modern society," "the nature of money (which is of course the book's eponymous theme)," and two topics that, as Poggi concedes, Simmel himself does not thematize: "the nature of action in general and economic action in particular, and the notion of objective spirit" (x). He aspires "to be more systematic in the treatment of these topics than Simmel himself is" by "assembling from the text numerous, fragmented, and dispersed arguments about a particular topic, and rendering them as components of a unified treatment" (x).[21] Finally, Poggi aims to aid those who are "daunted by the size" of the *Philosophy of Money*

---

18. I am no means claiming that these hermeneutic practices are exceptional to Simmel or even to the social sciences: selective translations and pedagogically oriented anthologizations that resituate arguments with very different valences in new conceptual frameworks are constitutive elements of many disciplines today.

19. Gianfranco Poggi, *Money and the Modern Mind: Georg Simmel's Philosophy of Money* (Berkeley: University of California Press, 1993), 1. Subsequent citations in text.

20. Approximately the first third of Poggi's book consists a lively albeit historiographically outdated account of "The Context" (chap. 1) and "The Author and the Book" (chap. 2), a breezy overview of Simmel's life that helpfully situates his *Philosophy of Money* in relation to his career and the development of his thought.

21. Poggi remarks at the outset of his chapter on "Action and Economic Action," that its topic was derived from Talcott Parsons's foundational act of social theorizing, from which Parsons, "for reasons which are of no concern to us here," had excluded Simmel despite his "quite elaborate if not systematic theory of social action" (Poggi, *Money and the Modern Mind*, 71). On the surface, Poggi's blunt refusal to consider the relation of Parsons's own exclusion of Simmel's approach to the conceptual foundations of "social theory" while importing the Parsonian conception of "action in general" into Simmel's text is a far more problematic operation than drawing attention to the role of the idea of "objective spirit," a concept indigenous to Simmel's own theoretical idiom. But in both cases the familiar systematizing assumptions and dehistoricizing procedures are deployed.

by adopting a "more accessible manner" of expression, and in offering a "shorter" and "clearer" book, "a less demanding way of familiarizing [readers] with that text's contents" (xi).

Poggi thus runs Simmel's text through a Parsonian filter, reframing its theoretical "insights into a wide range of social phenomena" in terms Simmel would hardly have endorsed. He thereby imposes a "scientific" theoretical rhetoric on an argument structured to resist the intellectual strategies, including such dehistoricizing hypostasization, through which the Parsonian understanding of "social theory" as a self-sufficient intellectual formation came into being in the first place.

In assimilating the *Philosophy of Money* to the intellectual world of late twentieth-century sociology, Poggi recycles and updates the hoary and contradictory tropes of the secondary literature. For all his "thought-provoking insights," Simmel is "notoriously unsystematic," and his arguments are fragmented and in need of "assembling"; yet he is simultaneously a species of Platonist whose philosophy is ultimately concerned with the "nature" of money, action, and "modern society." Fortunately, however, Poggi believes, it is possible to sever form from "content" and reassemble Simmel's work into a significant contribution to (ahistorical, systematic) "social theory."

In advancing his account of Simmel as a diagnostician of "the modern mind" and redescribing his larger theoretical enterprise in terms of a purported focus on modern society, Poggi reinscribes the assumptions of "systematic" Parsonian theorizing for a new generation of Simmel's readers. He fails to do justice to the complex relation between the historical and philosophical, the cultural and psychological, aspects of the *Philosophy of Money* and misleadingly abstracts ideas and concepts very much in flux from Simmel's self-reflexively critical, cultural-intellectual frame.

For example, rather than engaging with the distinctive uses of the term *Geist* in the *Philosophy of Money*, Poggi posits a unified German intellectual tradition with a monolithic notion of objective spirit or mind. Simmel, he writes, "derived it (by way of . . . Lazarus and Steinthal) from the Hegelian heritage in German philosophy," albeit perhaps "almost unawares" since he "belonged to the neo-Kantian generation in German philosophy, of which some have said that it no longer had any idea of what Hegel was all about" (108).[22] According to Poggi, "Simmel's use of the concept of objective spirit . . . constitutes a significant episode in a prolonged exploration of that concept within German social theory . . . that begins with Hegel and culminates in the work of Arnold Gehlen" (117). Since Simmel fails to provide "anything resembling a typology of its manifestations [*sic*]" (113), Poggi fills out that narrative with an extended discussion of Hans Freyer's conception of "objective spirit,"[23] supplemented by what he contends is Karl Popper's evocation of the "same" conceptual structure as an autonomous "third world" (117–31). On the basis of this reconstruc-

---

22. A strategically placed footnote referring to an essay by Michael Landmann suggests that this claim was his; this is not the case (Poggi, *Money and the Modern Mind*, 217).

23. Freyer was a student of Simmel's and went on to enjoy an all-too-successful career under National Socialism. See Jerry Z. Muller, *The Other God That Failed: Hans Freyer and the Deradicalization of German Conservatism* (Princeton, NJ: Princeton University Press, 1987).

tion, Poggi arrives at Parsonian articles of faith, moving from Simmel's contention that the "law" of gravity is valid independently of human awareness to the conclusion that he holds there to be an "intrinsic *normativity* of human action" even if that notion "is not conspicuously present" in the *Philosophy of Money* (129).

In advancing a reading of the role of objective *Geist* that situates Simmel in a line from Hegel to Hans Freyer and Arnold Gehlen, Poggi whiggishly inscribes his thinking of human cultural and historical life into the ambit of conservative cultural criticism, even as he tries to identify its positive contributions to a theory of modernity. He thereby perpetuates the ambivalence about Simmel and the ambiguous legacy of his thought within leftist cultural criticism and continental philosophical and social theory more generally. While insisting the *Philosophy of Money* is "about" modernity, Poggi fails to recognize the modernism of Simmel's text. Confident that he can abstract content from "unsystematic" form and transport the book's "persistently valid or at any rate highly thought-provoking insights into a wide range of social phenomena" out of their time without distortion, he misreads the structure of the book and occludes Simmel's profound systematic insight into the role of historical and cultural self-reflexivity after the sociohistorical, cultural turn in modernity.

Following in the footsteps of Lewis Coser's anti-philosophical reading of the *Philosophy of Money*, Poggi goes so far as to call the "neatly symmetrical layout of the work" as a whole, its organization into analytic and synthetic parts, each further divided into three chapters with three subdivisions, "rather deceptive." Having just described what would seem to be a classically and overtly dialectical structure, Poggi continues: "Simmel was not a systematic thinker," and "the transitions between one topic and another, or between one aspect and another of a given topic, are often as unpredictable in this book as they are in most of his other writings" (61).

Predictability, though, is hardly the most desirable quality in a thinker. Simmel's *Philosophy of Money* is clearly not a deductively ordered treatise, but it is highly misleading to call its author unsystematic. To be sure, its arguments are not linear. But the overtly dialectical structure of the book, like its "unpredictable" shifts of perspective and multiple, often seemingly contradictory, lines of argument, reflect Simmel's striving to do justice to the lived complexity and multiplicity of the phenomenal world. His style of argument embodies a formal effort to capture the dialectical experience of thought itself: to move readers repeatedly from the particular to the general, from local detail to historico-cultural totality, without presenting any particular totalization or synthesis as absolute, and thereby to foster self-reflexive awareness of the intrinsic relativity of every perspective. Its formal complexity serves to foster recognition of the lived need for multiple points of view, engaging readers by confronting them with the impossibility of achieving a completely reflexive total understanding of reality.

Moreover, the *Philosophy of Money* makes quite explicit this aspiration to represent the experience of encountering a world in flux and attempting to capture it in thought—a project that, for all its Nietzschean aspects, carries forward the Hegelian legacy that intertwines historical self-consciousness and subjective freedom. The reader who learns to think the social as a process, to abstract "forms" from diverse "contents," and to recognize the constructive role of thought in synthesizing perspectives that make sense, however partially and provisionally, of the complex totality of the world of experience, becomes aware of the "super-individual"—the mode of immanent transcendence traditionally known in German as *Geist*—that makes human existence human.

Money and the Modern Mind repeats a pattern already familiar from the history of Simmel's reception: even his most sympathetic sociological readers approach his texts in ways that demonstrate how illegible his thinking has become from the point of view of the discipline he helped found. As the significant rewriting embedded in the very title of his book betrays, Poggi has missed the import of Simmel's dialectical rhetorical strategies. What appear to a sociological audience as leaps in argumentation are invitations to the reader to participate in synthesizing a vision of modern life that can revitalize the philosophical tradition in a changing culture.

Poggi's approach underlines the methodological and theoretical significance of the misrecognition involved in approaching Simmel as an "unsystematic" thinker. The self-reinforcing effects of dominant sociological knowledge practices, especially those concerning reading theoretical texts, are further obscured by the endemic failure to situate his work properly in the philosophical tradition. But depicting Simmel as an unsystematic thinker does not merely serve to justify the hermeneutic laxness that fails to meet the challenge his modernist texts pose of grasping the underlying logic behind such apparent unpredictability. Even more significantly, it reflexively authorizes selective modes of appropriation that further obscure the strategies—as much stylistic and representational as conceptual—through which Simmel in fact quite methodically develops his philosophical perspective on money and the money economy.

Representing Simmel as unsystematic occludes what remain crucial theoretical contributions to modern social science—not least concerning what constitutes the object of study itself. It legitimates a mode of reception that continues to convert Simmel's thinking into appropriable "cold cash" by focusing on particular, selected instances or examples and isolated elements of larger lines of argument and by setting aside his often very explicit theoretical and methodological claims regarding the meaning of the instances, examples, and elements he analyzes. Paradoxically and tellingly, it is by misreading Simmel and in particular by failing even to attempt to give an account of his *Philosophy of Money* as a "philosophy of historical and social life as a whole" that such selective readings render the text appropriable as a canonical work of sociology.

Money and the Modern Mind sets out to provide a sympathetic reading, to mediate and facilitate the reception of the *Philosophy of Money* by stressing its contributions to contemporary sociology. In doing so, however, Poggi betrays how illegible Simmel's philosophically nuanced vision of the place of social and cultural self-reflection in and for everyday modern life has become from the perspective of mainstream social science. His approach to the *Philosophy of Money*, which sets aside Simmel's own argumentative strategies unexamined and relates selected instances and examples to one another in frameworks foreign to the author's own project, illustrates with particular clarity how much is at stake in the hermeneutically questionable practices that have shaped Simmel's reception within mainstream social science more generally.

As I demonstrated in Part I, strikingly selective reading strategies and sharply truncated interpretative frameworks reflect much larger problematics concerning the relation of the social sciences to philosophy. The mode of canonization I am calling the appropriation by fragments is a self-reinforcing operation through which the discipline of sociology (or in this case, the subfield of social theory) reproduces its own blind spots as it differentiates itself from philosophy. Poggi's selective modes of reading literally convert Simmel's theoretical contributions into cold cash.

When the dialectical structure of the *Philosophy of Money* is discounted, the question of what Simmel meant in claiming that his investigations were unified by an effort to demonstrate "the possibility of finding in each of life's particularities the totality of its meaning" cannot even be posed. Poggi's approach misses the critical value of this self-reflexive, modernist reframing of disciplinary knowledge practices and obscures Simmel's strategic use of *Erscheinungsreihen*, "phenomenal series," in organizing the global arguments of the *Philosophy of Money*. As these series (or "arrays of appearances," as the term might also be translated) illustrate, the "unpredictability" Poggi predicates of the text is for Simmel a feature of the world he is describing and analyzing. Formally speaking, the *Philosophy of Money* is constructed to draw the reader who submits to its demands into a performative demonstration of the very relativity that underlies that unpredictability. This mimetic strategy provides one of the methodological cornerstones of Simmel's mature theoretical approach. As we shall see in Part III, such arrays or series also serve to illustrate the viability of the sorts of formal generalizations about human interaction that are at the heart of the distinctive theoretical and methodological strategies in his 1908 *Soziologie*.

Interdisciplinarity before Disciplines: Simmel's Phenomenology of Culture

In his early years, Simmel regarded a turn to social science as a critical affirmation of the loss of transcendence in modernity and advocated a sociological approach to inherited philosophical questions, most notably in his multivolume effort to develop a "science of morality" as an epiphenomenon of the social. But his thinking shifted considerably in the mid-1890s, and as he pursued the project of theorizing money, the question of the epistemological and ontological foundations of method loomed ever larger. Affirming the turn to the social—in the terms of 1894's "Das Problem der Sociologie," the shift from the science of man to the science of human society—no longer seemed a sufficient response to the dissolution of foundations in modernity. Indeed, Simmel had come to regard reductivism and materialism in modern scientific knowledge practices as symptomatic of the same historic transformations.

By the late 1890s, while he continued to espouse the nominalist view of the social put forward in "Problem," Simmel had set aside his naturalism. He had grown more skeptical about progress and developed a more differentiated notion of *Wissenschaft* and its limits. With the *Philosophy of Money*, he returned to epistemological and metaphysical questions bearing the fruits of his sociological, psychological, and historical labors and reframed the tasks of philosophical reflection for a world where all that was solid had already melted into air.

By now an acute reader of Nietzsche as well as Marx, Simmel recognized that the ongoing dissolution of philosophical foundations might well lead to a pernicious nihilism. With History and Nature rapidly going the way of God, Truth, and the Subject, new theoretical practices were called for. Simmel was, of course, by no means alone in seeking to reframe the relations between knowledge and value, ethics and epistemology via new approaches to interpreting human collective life. It was at this juncture—in the historico-conceptual space defined by the cultural circumstances we have come to call modernity—that the modern social sciences were taking shape. But now better-known contemporaries rarely shared Simmel's philosophical views.

Distancing themselves from the philosophical tradition, practitioners of the rapidly differentiating modern social science disciplines—psychologists and economists, sociologists and anthropologists—defined themselves and established the institutional autonomy of their disciplines by modeling their work on the natural sciences. Comte, Spencer, and Mill, academic outsiders all, had leavened their scientific visions with ethical, political, and even theological aspirations. But their heirs were embracing a more narrowly materialist rhetoric of reflection, and with it a pronounced tendency to reduce questions of meaning to quantifiable factors. The new knowledge-formations were taking shape both institutionally and methodologically under the sign of scientific progress.

Simmel was largely unsuccessful in his effort to persuade his more literal-minded colleagues that an overtly nominalist approach to the social would provide the firmest conceptual and methodological grounding for sociology. By 1900, other leading figures in the emerging institutional and disciplinary formations saw the turn to the social less as a philosophical solution than as the beginning of the end of philosophy, convinced that social science was at last in the process of overcoming the problems that plagued human collective life. Even as Simmel's effort to embrace the vertiginous epistemic circumstances of modern life led him back to philosophy, his colleagues were busy institution-building. Many hoped—and here the ambitions of Simmel's onetime supporter Émile Durkheim may be taken as paradigmatic—to develop a scientific practice that could compensate for the loss of inherited foundations and traditional modes of social cohesion and thereby reestablish moral traction in modern society.

The break between Simmel and Durkheim that took place during this period attests to the high stakes of this parting of theoretical ways. Durkheim's classic 1897 study *Le Suicide: Étude de sociologie* epitomized the increasingly dominant tendency to redefine problems of meaning as epiphenomena of the social that could—and should—be studied in terms of quantifiable factors. Simmel's mature approach was not simply opposed but antithetical. The *Philosophy of Money* is the work of a methodological and epistemological relativist, and it advances an internal critique of the ideal of quantifiability. No wonder its argument was so unacceptable from Durkheim's point of view that he dismissed it as *spéculation bâtard*, charging that Simmel's neglect of empirical methods could only lead sociology back toward metaphysics.

Durkheim's indictment of Simmel's methods helped establish a pattern of reception that is only now being overcome.[24] He and his students dominated French social science both institutionally and intellectually for generations to come, and his hostile misreading foreshadowed Simmel's reception in mainstream twentieth-century sociology.

Even as the emerging social sciences strove to distance themselves from their philosophical origins, Simmel's attitude toward that legacy, including the problem of foundations, had become more nuanced. Taking the phenomena of everyday cultural life as his point of departure, Simmel integrated the insights he had gained from sociology and *Völkerpsychologie*, from art history and economics, into a properly philosophical account of the genesis of meaning and value in human interactive exchange (*Wechselwirkung*).

Simmel's sociological and psychological analyses serve a philosophical end: persuading his readers to adopt a new way of thinking based on his relativist concept of concepts, to leave substantialism and foundationalism behind in favor of a phenomenologically grounded and intersubjectively articulated understanding of truth and of value. He was systematically fostering a rethinking of the meaning of the "superindividual." Again, on Simmel's account, the socio-genesis of value, the process or activity of association, *Vergesellschaftung*, "is the most immediate illustration [literally, making-visible: *Veranschaulichung*] of relativity in the material of humanity: society is the super-singular configuration [*Gebilde*] that is yet not abstract . . . the universal that also has concrete vitality [*Lebendigkeit*]."

Exchange, "the economic-historical realization of the relativity of things," thus has "singular importance" for human beings. It "elevates the individual thing and its significance . . . into the vitality of reciprocal interaction that is at the same time the body of economic value (*GSG* 6: 91). Value—the meaning of objects for people—is not a quality of the things themselves but a function of the interactive totality of human association.

For Simmel, whose thinking here resonates with that of contemporaries such as William James and Henri Bergson, relativism signified not nihilistic (in)decisionism but a reflective affirmation of our epistemic limits in the face of the lived complexity of the world. It was a considered response to the experience of human existence as at once embedded in social, cultural, historical context and radically

---

24. See also my discussion in chapter 2 of Durkheim's misprision of Simmel's conception of form in Émile Durkheim, "The Realm of Sociology as a Science" (1900), trans. Everett K. Wilson, in *Georg Simmel: Critical Assessments*, ed. Frisby, 1: 82–97. Although his *Philosophy of Money* has in recent years found a warmer reception in French sociology, the image of Simmel as less scientific than Durkheim or Weber remains deeply entrenched. To be sure, contemporary readers tend to cast what formerly seemed a deficit in a more positive light.

individualized and embodied. Focusing on money, which represents by instantiating that very relativity of human life, enabled him to theorize its objective and subjective, shared and individual, complexity and indeterminacy while attending to the concrete interactive phenomena through which meaning and value exist in and through human social, cultural, historical—"spiritual"—life.

In demonstrating that it was possible to philosophize about money, Georg Simmel made a decisive contribution to the much larger debate about the status of values in modernity. In positive terms, money expresses and fosters the all-encompassing interdependency of human association or becoming-social, *Vergesellschaftung*, as the spiritual-cultural medium and process in which values attain independence of their material conditions and instantiations. As a universal means, "the relativity of economic value in a substance," money is, in Simmel's terms, at once bearer and symbol of the entire sociohistorical "cultural process" by which human activity generates a realm distinct from nature: a world of values. And as the dialectical sign and embodiment of the (inter- and trans-subjective, spiritual-cultural) process of representation, money epitomizes the ambiguous role of abstraction in that creative process, which leads to a reified world neither experienced nor comprehended as a human product.

Simmel's account emphasizes the dimension of signification in what Marx called exchange value. Money expresses the "meaning of every individual thing" qua object of exchange—that is, its "mere *significance* as means, disconnected from its concrete carrier" (*GSG* 6, 307).[25] With it, the principle of abstraction penetrates all life spheres, simultaneously creating higher orders of value and meaning and evacuating particularity by rendering what cannot be signified in quantitative terms valueless, meaningless. Money, that is, both bears along and represents the rise of a new regime of signification. As localized and historically and culturally thick forms of social organization and interaction are displaced (or colonized) by complex, highly differentiated, but also relatively abstract modes of association, money tends to become the dominant, even the sole end and measure of value. It is "the absolute means, that precisely in this way attains the psychological significance of an absolute end" (*GSG* 6, 307).

Thanks to the fundamentally reciprocal nature of human (interactive, cultural, embodied) existence, this power of universal signification in turn fuels the increasing hegemony of the money economy over other life spheres in the modern world. As Simmel shows again and again, non-quantitative ways of thinking about ends are undermined when they are forced into relation to money. Inherited "substantial values" prove "unable to sustain their claim to absoluteness" in a world of multiple orders of signification and pervasive value conflict, even as money, "the most powerful and immediate symbol" for the circumstance that "the only absolute" seems to be universal relativity, cannot itself be relativized.

---

25. See *Philosophy of Money*, chap. 5, pt. 3, on the inadequacy of the labor theory of value to account for the phenomena generated through social interaction and exchange, which for Simmel are the primary economic factors.

There is no turning back from the new regime in which change, movement, and transformation have come to dominate meaning itself. All that is solid melts into air; at the extreme, the very notion of ultimate values and purposes that escape or even transcend the instrumental and quantitative logic that dominates modern life comes to seem antiquated and romantic. As illustrated by Max Weber's reading of the *Philosophy of Money* at a crucial moment in the evolution of his thinking, Simmel's account of the process of rationalization and intellectualization has had a powerful, yet largely unrecognized, influence.

The *Philosophy of Money* offers a compelling account of the role of human "forming productivity" in value-creation, demonstrating repeatedly how the eclipse of traditional, unchanging foundationalist understandings of value as substance has fostered individual freedom and ethical self-determination. Just as Simmel did not see the "cultural process" as a unified rational development, he did not regard it as simply increasing individual autonomy. The very historical and social developments that were refining subjectivity and demonstrating the power of human rationality were also increasing individual and collective awareness of human unfreedom, recognition of the limits of the subject but also of the determinative power of external forces.

Reflection on the cultural-historical process—and here again, Simmel is not simply a post-Hegelian but also a post-Nietzschean thinker—thus opens the possibility for human beings to attain an entirely new relation to questions of truth, meaning, and value. In linking philosophical questions about money to the historical evolution of the money economy, Simmel was attempting to provide his readers with resources for coming to terms with the sociocultural transformations wrought by capitalism in nineteenth-century European life. Like Marx (and in good Hegelian tradition), he sought to identify the fundamental features of human existence that were being expressed and revealed by a revolutionary process that was very palpably under way in the fin de siècle. On his view, what was being brought to light was not just the world-historical function of capital but the essence of money as a social and historical institution—one with psychological, cultural and (in the widest sense) anthropological significance. As a culturally and historically situated, variable phenomenon, money in turn raised philosophical questions about the fundamental meaning, the metaphysical significance, of what Simmel, introducing the term, identifies as the *Kulturprozeß*, the cultural process that "transmutes the subjective states of drive and enjoyment into the valuation of objects" (*GSG* 6: 50).

Near the end of the second chapter, "The Substantial Value of Money," Simmel elaborates on the cultural-historical relationship between subjectivity and urban life that he describes in quasi-Darwinian terms at the start of his essay on the metropolis, "Die Großstädte und das Geistesleben," as the synecdochic site of the contemporary "reconfiguration of the struggle with nature that the primitive human being had to conduct for his or her *corporeal* existence (*GSG* 7: 116). The *Philosophy of Money* presents the development of social organization that "frees individuality" from immersion in group life and the emergence of the metropolis as a new form of collective life as two "sides of the cultural process": both depend on the "cultural tendency to condensation of powers" tied up directly and in mediated ways with the "monetary form of value" (*GSG* 6: 245).

What had been "traditionally accounted among money's main duties," being a "means of preserving and transporting value," are in fact "merely secondary appearances of that founding function" of condensation, which is "clearly without any internal relation whatsoever to money's being bound to a [particular] substance," making "palpable that what is essential about money are the representations that, far beyond the inherent significance of its bearer, are invested in it." History shows—and here, via a slight, Latinizing shift in terminology, Simmel is introducing a technical, electrical, metaphor into vocabulary inherited from the philosophical tradition—that as the "role of money as the condenser of value [*Wertcondensator*]" grows, its substance becomes "ever more inadequate to the plenitude, flux, multiplicity of values that are projected onto its representation and condensed [*kondensiert*] into it." Indeed, Simmel continues, "One could characterize this as an increasing spiritualization of money [*Vergeistigung des Geldes*]. For the essence of spirit is to impart to multiplicity the form of unity.... Reciprocal interaction in exchange procures this spiritual unity for values. Thus money, the abstraction of reciprocal interaction, can only find a symbol in everything spatial-substantial" (*GSG* 6: 245–46).

But money does not ever entirely become a function. The substantialized form in which its activity is realized cannot be completely set aside; money is not really the ideal it incarnates. In this constitutive ambiguity, too, it exemplifies and enables the human form of embodied, immanent spirit ever in the process of formation. At the end of the chapter, Simmel returns to this problem in relation to concept-formation:

> The whole development of the modern, naturalistic spirit tends to dethrone universal concepts and emphasize the particular as the sole legitimate representational content. In the theory as in the praxis of life, the universal is treated as the merely abstract.... However, the feeling for the significance of the universal that once reached its zenith in Plato has not disappeared, and we will only attain an entirely satisfying orientation to the world when every point of our image of it reconciles the material reality of the singular with the profundity and depth of the formal-universal. (*GSG* 6: 252)

Simmel ties this point directly to the enterprise of (scientific) self-reflection in which he is engaged at that particular point in the first, "analytic" half of the *Philosophy of Money*: "Historicism," he continues, "and the social *Weltanschauung* is an attempt to affirm the universal and still deny its abstractness ... for society is the universal that is not abstract." In the course of the historical-cultural process in and through which human self-reflexivity emerges, form or function gains independence of content, as when "religious feeling" is distinguished from "the contents of belief" or "cognition" from the "particular objects" of knowledge. Money's tendency to become a function is thus of quite general significance: the "feeling of value makes itself independent" of the substance that represents it in a function that is "universal and yet not abstract." Its substance becomes form, and this "form or function" develops into "an independent value" in which "the bearer is entirely secondary" and extrinsic to our "perception of value"—but not for that reason unnecessary or eliminable (*GSG* 6: 253).

Money is both substance and function: the "condenser of value" in which the limits of each of these perspectives on the sociohistorical, cultural process and activity of signification are embodied. It thus provides the performative demonstration that human life is of such complexity and multiplicity that the interlocking limitations of (material and ideal) perspectives cannot be definitively overcome. As both bearer and symbol of the essential human activities of forming productivity and interactive association, money, qua object of reflection, facilitates insight into symbolization itself. It is the principle (or, perhaps better, embodies the practice) of abstraction as such. As the substantialization of value in which desubstantialization is realized, money is the universal means and the means by which all substantive ends can be transformed into means.

Briefly reviewing one of the book's central themes, the dialectical relation between what Simmel would later come to call objective and subjective culture, will help to make this connection between money and meaning somewhat more concrete. Simmel shows that money fosters both economic and social specialization and subjective particularity and individual freedom through its role in intensifying and diversifying the division of labor. The dominance of the money economy, which is predicated on abstracting from the significant differences among things and subjecting them all to a universal point of view, simultaneously reifies the human surround by reducing objects to commodities and generates highly individualized, nominally autonomous and self-determining subjects.

But Simmel's analysis does not stop here. The *Philosophy of Money* shows how these subjects are confronted with a range of problems stemming from the eclipse of qualitative by quantitative reasoning, problems that ultimately call that very autonomy and self-determination into question. As the hegemony of the economic point of view undermines and destroys other modes of valuation, meaning itself as traditionally understood is threatened. The *Philosophy of Money* attempts to account for the way the money economy points beyond itself to dimensions and realms of experience that it cannot capture even as it forecloses access to them by rendering it difficult for people even to recognize and experience forms of value that cannot be quantified.

These processes are quite concrete. They encompass not only the material effects of specialization and the division of labor but also, more broadly, the spiritual consequences of the mode of life associated with *Geldkultur*, monetary culture—with the dominion of intellect over feeling, objectivity over subjectivity, with the ways speed, distance, and technology come to dominate the social world and to determine the lived quality of human existence in modernity.

Sociohistorical analysis of money's ambiguous—dialectical—effects becomes the proof of the philosophical point that there is no universally valid point of view. For Simmel, the relativity of truth, experience, knowledge, to the position of the observer is demonstrated by the evolution of money as a historical phenomenon. In his hands, what is often taken to be the negative consequence of the increasing penetration of the money economy—the way the universal functionality of money leads to the dissolution of all other orders of valuation and the transmutation of all other forms of value into its own currency—becomes a proof of money's transcendent significance. Philosophizing about money generates reflective knowledge of the circumstance that money is also the universal means in a philosophical sense: that through it, the essential constitutedness of value can be represented and lived. In this his work resembles that of the early Marx, who (in texts Simmel could not have known) set out to show that capitalism confronts human beings with the truth of their existence as producers of their own world.

For Marx, of course, what was at stake was the course of history. His thinking attempts to intervene from a philosophically validated point of view in the historical process. Simmel was far from seeing his theoretical intervention in this sense. Indeed, he consistently denied that there could be laws of history at all, let alone that consciousness of those laws would proceed with a quasi-inevitability and foster necessary historical progress, as Marx seemed inclined to believe. He had a fundamentally different vision of dialectics. For Simmel, negation does not entail annihilation: seemingly incompatible alternatives coexist all the time in the real world. Diverse points of view need not be synthesized, conflicts need not be resolved into higher or larger unities. His *Philosophy of Money* registers, reflects, and thematizes the circumstance that no universally valid point of view can be achieved, mediating between divergent perspectives through a synecdochic strategy of thought that exemplifies and demonstrates a new way of doing philosophy: what I call his phenomenology of culture.

Simmel's reflections on money and the cultural transformations associated with the money economy are paradigmatic for the multivalent significance of phenomenal reality in his mature work. The empirical and historical evidence concerning the development and operation of the money economy is open to multiple interpretations and conflicting valuations. This circumstance—itself an historical, cultural, material reality with philosophical implications—forms Simmel's point of departure. Almost none of the material he draws on appears to be unambiguous, but the *Philosophy of Money* transmutes this indeterminacy into a theoretical strength. Breaking decisively with the progressivist version of history inherited from the Enlightenment and embracing the need for multiple perspectives to account for the phenomenal complexity associated with money and the money economy, Simmel develops a relativistic view of reality that integrates historical, philosophical, and natural and social scientific dimensions.

Eschewing linear development, Simmel's argument glides repeatedly from "the surface of economic events" to the "ultimate values and significances of everything human." These synecdochic movements are in turn linked metonymically into *Erscheinungsreihen*, phenomenal series, consisting of prismatically shifting successions of partial totalities. In this way, his analyses performatively display the formal multiplicity and ambiguity of the "cultural process" itself—the process in and through which subjectivity and objectivity are at once differentiated and connected, and desire and drive are transmuted into valuation. Simmel represents social life as a process of endless becoming, in which complexity and abstraction, freedom and alienation, being and value, quantity and quality, develop in tandem, and dialectical opposites are both mutually constitutive and reciprocally destructive.

Money—substance, function, means of means, synecdoche of synecdoches—embodies and fosters this relativity. Precisely in its endless (because self-reflexive) relativity as cultural phenomenon, money thus exposes the complex relations between surface and depth, substance and function, individual and totality, being and becoming, that constitute human life. It is "the expression and means for the relationship, for the interdependency and relativity of human beings that makes the satisfaction of the wishes of the one ever mutually dependent on the other." In fact, he continues, "there is no place to be found where there is no relativity at all": so long as human beings have need of one another, require the other to satisfy their desires, they are in relation (*GSG* 6: 179).

The *Philosophy of Money* is a self-reflexive attempt to illuminate the phenomenon of signification as a dimension of human cultural life. Thus it is that in terms of the "type and range of its historical power," money can "at best be compared with language, which likewise lends itself to the most divergent directions of thought and feeling, supporting, clarifying, working them out" (*GSG* 6: 653–54). Money, as embodied relativity, as the "expression and means" both through which human beings relate to one another and by which everything in their world as a whole is related, becomes the signifier of signifiers and "the symbol, in the narrow and empirical, of the unspeakable unity of being" (*GSG* 6: 695). Becoming aware of the relativity of reality, of the interdependency and reciprocity of sociohistorical life and of the processual character of culture as a whole fostered by the modern money economy enables a new form of human self-understanding that can invigorate theoretical reflection on collective life.

Metaphysical Relativism and Modernist Praxis

This brings us back to the difficulty that it is by no means immediately clear how Simmel's perspectivism and methodological relativism can be reconciled with his aspiration to write "a philosophy of historical and social life as a whole." One might argue that on his own terms, any such totalizing effort was doomed in advance, but it was in fact in and through this self-reflexively relativist ontological perspective that his strategy for thinking cultural reality in its multiplicity and manifold complexity—and in that sense, as a whole—took shape.

It was the challenge of grasping money itself and the phenomena associated with it in both sociohistorical and philosophical terms that prompted Simmel to elaborate the relativist dialectic of form and life that characterizes his mature work. The *Philosophy of Money* performs, exemplifies, a kind of theorizing that negotiates the challenges of human existence as situated in culturally mediated forms of life, in multiple contexts and worlds that are both the products of human endeavor and forces in their own right with their own independent logics and structures.[26]

---

26. In this connection, Simmel is an important predecessor of Niklas Luhmann. On the latter's role in the beginnings of the *Gesamtausgabe*, see Otthein Rammstedt, "Zur Geschichte der Georg Simmel Gesamtausgabe" (*GSG* 24: 1038–90), published in an abbreviated English version as "On the Genesis of a Collected Edition of Simmel's Works, 1918–2012," *Theory, Culture and Society* 29, nos. 7–8 (2012): 302–16.

Simmel's book addresses its reader as a modern subject struggling to make sense of a chaotic world, a subject whose experiences of alienation, abstraction, fragmentation, provide a point of entry into the interpretive nexus.

In and through his attempt to philosophize about money, Simmel's distinctive conception of form attained the philosophical weight and significance that would bear fruit in the more overtly modernist essayism of the ensuing years. Reading the *Philosophy of Money* as a self-consciously modernist text places the distinctive coherency of his mature oeuvre into relief, revealing the argumentative and analytic strategies that make Simmel's writing so distinctive stylistically as direct expressions of his mature philosophical position. Since, as his often puzzling reception history attests, efforts to extract substance from form obscure the theoretical significance of his work, my approach also helps explain why so many would-be Simmel renaissances have withered on the vine.

Foregrounding the performative dimension of his writing helps account for one of the most paradoxical features of Simmel's afterlife as mostly forgotten founding father: the way his distinctive style of thought was effectively converted into "cold cash" and passed on, even as its philosophical and methodological significance went unrecognized or at least unacknowledged. By the same token, recognizing the complexity and sophistication of his modernist mode of philosophizing underlines the ongoing challenge of maintaining an appropriately holistic view of Simmel's work—of coming to terms with him as a writer and doing justice to him as a thinker—without losing critical perspective and historical distance.

Simmel was a man of the previous fin-de-siecle, and there is much that calls for critique or outright rejection—notably, his views on gender and his attitude toward racial others. What is ultimately at stake in returning to him is the relationship between our thinking and that particular past: a historical and theoretical—genealogical—relationship that calls for reflection. In disentangling our own modernity from Simmel's, we establish perspective on our present theoretical (and institutional/disciplinary) situation.

In the Preface to the *Philosophy of Money*, Simmel explicitly distinguishes his undertaking from "abstract philosophical system-building" with its "distance from individual phenomena, especially those of practical existence" (*GSG* 6: 12). Here, he is no longer the author of his 1894 manifesto "Das Problem der Sociologie" attempting to establish a new discipline. He is, rather, trying to disseminate a new sort of theoretical practice, methodology, or strategy of thought that takes his self-reflexive conception of form as a point of departure. As a performative demonstration of the power of Simmel's self-reflexive, modernist knowledge praxis for understanding human life and culture—of the value of the strategy of reading or style of interpretation that enacts his concept of truth grounded in life—the *Philosophy of Money* seeks to be a "philosophy of historical and social life as a whole."

The Preface alerted readers considering embarking on this adventure that the work's coherence did not rest on an effort to prove "a claim about a singular content of knowledge" at all. It was methodological, or more properly, speculative: "The meaning and purpose of the whole" of Simmel's modernist reimagining of philosophical inquiry in emulation of art's life-enhancing movement from the particular to the universal was to connect "the surface of economic events to the ultimate values and significances of everything human." Undertaken from the point of view of what Klaus-Christian Köhnke calls the "universal self-reflexivity" (*Der junge Simmel*, 28) of his epistemic agnosticism and correlative methodological relativism, the great achievement of Simmel's *Philosophy of Money* is his demonstration that it is possible to rethink conceptual consistency by developing "a new concept of cohesion" (*Festigkeitsbegriff*).

To be sure, Simmel's invocation of the language of metaphysics can be off-putting. His metadisciplinary claims that it is possible "to find in each of life's particularities the totality of its meaning" or to move from "the surface of economic events to the ultimate values and significances of everything human" are framed in language that is admittedly unsettling to twenty-first century sensibilities. But his approach in the *Philosophy of Money* actually differs significantly from the romantic holism with which such remarks resonate. These are, as it were, post-Nietzschean synecdoches.

Simmel's modernist mode of thought, which treats all totalities as transient, contingent, human constructions, straddles the boundaries between what we have come to think of as "sociological" (or more broadly social scientific) and "philosophical" perspectives. As many readers have noted, his mode of writing anticipates many intellectual moves of postmodernism.[27] In situating these ideas and strategies instead within the ambit of modernism, I am not simply underlining the problematic status of the distinction between the modern and the postmodern, at least where Simmel is concerned. The metatheoretical debates concerning this distinction have by and large lost their purchase in the decades since 1989. As in the case of other, analogous categories that operate as signifiers both of genre and of conceptual and aesthetic substance ("enlightenment," "romanticism"), whether and how we should distinguish between the modern and the postmodern, or indeed the post-postmodern, depends largely on the context. But what we might anachronistically call Simmel's trans- or interdisciplinary mode of theorizing can help revitalize important critical perspectives on the existing disciplinary order that were central to the discourse on the "post"modern.

Focusing on his (modernist) phenomenology of culture will make the methodological point clearer. Simmel's approach, it must be emphasized, is less Husserlian than Hegelian or even Aristotelian. The relativistic argument of the *Philosophy of Money* proceeds through sequences of interlocking reflections organized around very large topoi (value and meaning, substance and function, means and ends, freedom and equality). Simmel arrays series of examples metonymically to display the symbolic structures he is using them to reflect upon to explore money first as a "historical phenomenon [or appearance: *Erscheinung*]" and then "in its effects on the inner world" and on "general culture" (*GSG* 6: 10).

---

27. See esp. Deena Weinstein and Michael Alan Weinstein, *Postmodern(ized) Simmel* (New York: Routledge, 1993).

As noted, Simmel introduces the category of the "phenomenal series" (*Erscheinungsreihe*) in an account of human rhetorical-cognitive practices that foregrounds the cultural significance of figuration. Concepts, too, are crystallized symbolic constellations or configurations, practical abstractions that facilitate thinking. Such "series of phenomena" thus reflect the practical conditions of thinking about lived experience: the concept itself is emphatically perspectival, and Simmel deploys such series in ways that underline their relativity to particular interpretive points of view. Arrays of examples succeed one another in turn, circumscribing different, often very explicitly opposed series of phenomena or appearances that illustrate or embody dialectically related aspects of the topos under consideration.

On the final page of chapter 1 ("Value and Money"), having already invoked the concept of phenomenal appearances, *Erscheinungen,* in multiple contexts, Simmel introduces the concept of the "series" or "array" of phenomena using developmental and evolutionary analogies. We do not define "the essence of language," he avers, based on "the first stammerings of a child," nor are we troubled in defining animal life by a certain indefiniteness in the transitional forms between plant and animal. In the first instance, the notion of an *Erscheinungsreihe* describes how human thinking operates in practice by grouping phenomena and creating concepts or definitions to account for them. Simmel continues on an Aristotelian note: "We often first apprehend in the highest phenomena of psychic life the meaning of the lower, even if we cannot possibly prove it there. Indeed, the pure concept of a phenomenal series is often an ideal that is not completely realized anywhere in it, but that nonetheless, since it is striving toward it, provides a valid interpretation of its meaning and content."[28]

But cultural phenomenology is not (merely) description. By multiplying and juxtaposing such series of cases, the *Philosophy of Money* develops a synthetic perspective on a wide range of interrelated and (dialectically) opposed phenomena that characterize the money economy. Thus, for example, in chapter 6, Simmel employs divergent phenomenal series to illustrate how money's capacity to facilitate action at a distance both extends the individual human being's range of action and possibilities for interaction and isolates and alienates people from one another. Through the intercession of money, "the most distant comes closer at the price of expanding the distance to what is closer" (*GSG* 6: 663).

The *Philosophy of Money* demands a reader attentive to the dialectical possibilities in the contradictions that appear as Simmel repeatedly traces such related and opposed phenomenal series, successively generating relative truths and relative totalities that are in turn reframed and recontextualized in other contexts later on

---

28. In the original, the final lines read "der reine Begriff einer Erscheinungsreihe ist oft ein Ideal, das in ihr selbst nirgends restlos verwirklicht ist, aber dennoch dadurch, daß sie ihm zustrebt, ihren Sinn und Gehalt gültig deutet" (*GSG* 6: 138). Frisby et al translate: "The pure concept of a series of phenomena is often an ideal that is never completely realized, the approach towards which, however, makes possible a valid interpretation of the concept" (*The Philosophy of Money*, trans. Tom Bottomore, David P. Frisby, and Kaethe Mengelberg, ed. Frisby [1978; 3rd enlarged ed., London: Routledge, 2004], 128). In unfortunately typical fashion, this rendering introduces significant idealizing confusion into Simmel's text that has helped solidify the pattern of hypostasizing misprision I have been tracing.

in the book. By exploring divergent lines of interpretation and juxtaposing these to illustrate the need for multiple, non-congruent perspectives on the same social and cultural phenomena, Simmel simultaneously represents the multiplicity and indeterminacy of sociocultural reality and develops his own self-reflexively relativist philosophy. His modernist approach, which is too easily dismissed, if not inaccurately described, as "essayism," underscores that (our) reality is flux and multiplicity. As he performs these repeated encounters with the limits of particular interpretive frameworks, Simmel develops his "special concept of metaphysics" out of the "organic," relativistic unity of reciprocal interaction and begins to unfold a vision of individuality that would disclose new and generative philosophical perspectives in the years to come.

If (as he himself recognized) the ultimate metaphysical status of the relativistic worldview reflected in his phenomenological approach to culture must remain uncertain, Simmel's basic theoretical claims were surely correct: that the seemingly contradictory (psychic, social, cultural) effects associated with money signal its importance for understanding human collective life—and that the ambiguity and multiplicity of the phenomena with which it is associated embody that philosophical significance. As Simmel puts it on the final page of the book: "The more the life of society becomes an economic life, the more effectively and clearly does the relativistic character of being imprint itself in conscious life, since money is nothing other than the relativity of economic objects embodied in a special configuration that signifies their value" (*GSG* 6: 716).

This crucial concept of a "special configuration" first appears just before Simmel introduces the notion of phenomenal series, in the already cited passage at the end of "Value and Money" where he describes such forms as the bearers and mediators of culture as such, declaring "That projecting [*Projizierung*] of mere relations into special configurations [*Sondergebilde*] is one of the great achievements of spirit" (*GSG* 6: 137).

For Simmel, such objectifications are both ideal and material, super- and trans-subjective historical cultural formations, themselves interwoven in multiple forms of relations and connection. He explores them through the complex rhetorical-representational strategy, itself a kind of mimesis of human creative cultural life, of describing "phenomenal series" in and through which the flux of the underlying generative process can be grasped. Such series of appearances are themselves then (thought as) arrayed in larger, speculative spiritual-cultural-historical "developmental series."

These historical configurations and configurations of configurations, imaginatively constituted from particular interpretive perspectives, make the cultural process thinkable. By deploying such figurations or embodied representations, the *Philosophy of Money* can account for the coherency of experience while insisting on the contingency of the metaphysical perspectivism it performs. Simmel's claim is at one level a historical assertion quite compatible with historical materialism: as the "life of society" becomes dominated by money, that is to say, as the object-world increasingly comes to be experienced as a world of commodities, experience itself becomes an experience of "the relativistic character of being." Human beings, as Marx would have put it, can recognize themselves as the (collective) makers of their world. But, Simmel insists, neither this process nor the configurations that result can really be explained in materialist terms, however historical. Precisely because it is grounded in a concrete praxis of self-reflection, the understanding of being as relative rather than absolute (metaphysically univocal) must recognize itself as historically, culturally contingent; the perspective on perspectives disclosed in and through Simmel's modernist approach to philosophizing fosters his reader's awareness that no worldview can legitimate, give an account of itself, in materialist or idealist terms alone. The most that can be said—and these are the concluding lines of his *Philosophy of Money* as a whole—is that

> just as the absolutistic vision of the world [*Weltansicht*] represented a specific intellectual developmental phase, in correlation with the corresponding practical, economic, emotional formation of human things [*der menschlichen Dingen*]—so too the relativistic appears to express, or perhaps better, to be, the momentary adaptive relation of our intellect, confirmed through the counterimage of social and subjective life, that has found in money at once the real and effective bearer and the mirroring symbol of its forms and movements.

Money, in remaking the world in its image, not only creates but also reveals "the general relativity of the world" (*GSG* 6: 715). That is to say, in and through their remaking of the world under the absolute sign of quantification, modern human beings are collectively revealing the metaphysical and epistemological limits of materialism. Through the universal hegemony of money, we come to experience reality as flux, movement, change—and, if we follow Simmel, to reflect that being itself, at least for embodied beings such as ourselves, can only be grasped perspectivally, that is to say, under the sign of value, and hence in an historically, culturally situated fashion.

The philosophical significance of Simmel's concept of "phenomenal series" can be made clearer by considering his approach to the topos of distance, an area in which his pioneering importance as a social theorist is widely recognized. Even as his conceptual framework underlines Simmel's debt to Kant and Hegel, his handling of this topos attests to how much he learned from Nietzsche. On his account, both social distantiation and the correlative objectification of social life that accompany the infiltration of money into virtually every sphere of human existence simultaneously foster the interiorization of subjects. For modern, individualized subjects, the objective world created by the money economy has become a condition of survival, and the lived meaning of existence itself is suffused by money and monetary effects.

As Simmel elaborates in the book's concluding section, with the domination of money even in familial relationships, in the "forms of modern existence," a thirdness and "new strangeness" enters into human relations as such: the very "significance of the human being for the human being is increasingly dependent (if often in a dissimulated form) on interests of a financial sort." Such (mediated) social distance makes "the modern form of life possible." As he puts it, "The monetariness [*Geldhaftigkeit*] of relationships—either apparent or concealed in a thousand forms—inserts an invisible, functional distance between human beings that is an inner protection and compensation against the all-too-crowded closeness and friction of our cultural life" (*GSG* 6: 664–65).

The *Philosophy of Money* demonstrates repeatedly how objectification and (as we would say) subjectivation are intertwined materially, ideally, and "stylistically" in the forms of life fostered by the domination of money. But if money, as "both symbol and cause of the leveling" or neutralization of the external world "also becomes the protector of the most interior," the ultimate historical and cultural outcome—whether the cultural process will lead to a "refinement, distinctiveness, interiorization of the subject" or to the domination of commodified things—"depends not on money but on the human being" (*GSG* 6: 653). Money is simply the bearer of what is ultimately the fundamental human power: the capacity for symbolization, for the creation of worlds of meaning and value distinct from the natural. This is not to say that the diremptions of modernity are soluble by thought alone. As for his predecessors and successors in the German dialectical philosophical tradition, the decisive question for Simmel was whether human beings will gain genuine reflective autonomy and integrate the powers of rationality into forms of life that encompass the fullness of human being.

Before his alleged late turn to metaphysics and the "philosophy of life," before the Great War, which was for him the beginning of the end of the cultural world he cherished, Simmel saw the logic of the economic world—the quantitative calculation of ends and means—as increasingly overshadowing human existence and even dominating the powers of life itself. That is, the objectified and reified reality of the modern money economy was obscuring its own nature as a product and expression of the creative power of human "superindividual" existence—the fact that money and the money economy are ultimately rooted in the human power to create value through *lebendige Wechselwirkungen*—the generative, "living," processes of material, social, cultural interaction, interchange, reciprocity that constitute the fabric of collective life.

Simmel's years of effort writing the *Philosophy of Money* were animated by the hope of fostering reflective understanding of modern life—of creating a form of self-conscious social being adequate to the intellectual-spiritual-cultural task of living in the post-Kantian, post-Nietzschean world. Such philosophical and theoretical reflection—emphatically, for him, inseparable from *Wissenschaft*, systematic historical-social-cultural knowledge practices—was the necessary first step toward ways of living that would enhance and cultivate, rather than isolate and alienate, modern human beings.

All of this provides, of course, considerable challenges for the reader, who is confronted with a text not simply without footnotes (hardly extraordinary for 1900) but with barely an overt acknowledgement of its author's (intertextually often quite evident) predecessors and interlocutors. Philosophically demanding as well as rhetorically challenging, the *Philosophy of Money* is indeed directed at "the happy few": an audience whose wide-ranging and sophisticated culture and familiarity with the Western intellectual and especially philosophical tradition, as well as with the most fundamental contemporary issues of the human and emergent social sciences, is taken for granted.

It is standard practice for social scientists—though by no means only social scientists—to approach canonical texts by extracting passages from longer works, taking up and testing the claims made in them in (relative) isolation from the larger arguments in which they appear. Simmel's sociological readers have tended to pick and choose particular examples and to jump, as it were, to his conclusions without much attention to text and context. In the case of the *Philosophy of Money*, the widespread assumption that Simmel was an unsystematic thinker has helped authorize ignoring larger and even mid-range structures such as the phenomenal series. Partial lines of his larger arguments have typically been redeployed sociologically without attending to other (competing, often contradictory) series of cases he also discusses—let alone to the question of the overall logic of an argumentative strategy that repeatedly decenters its own apparent claims through relativizing juxtapositions of metonymically linked and logically opposed, inverse or obverse phenomenal series.

The consequence has been a mode of reception that canonizes Simmel's descriptions of particular elements, moments and features of social and cultural life while failing to take account of the ways in which his mode of writing is a dimension of his philosophical project.[29] Recognizing Simmel's modernism, his explicit effort to get at the multiplicity and interconnectedness of the social and historical reality that arises through the mediation of money, can help counteract the misleadingly one-sided, undialectical characterizations of his thinking that result when particular analyses are isolated from their contextual frameworks.

The reception strategies and practices by which Simmel is simultaneously canonized and forgotten are theoretically and methodologically self-reinforcing. Through them, his ideas and methods have been converted into "cold cash" and all too often invested in precisely the sort of projects he was explicitly criticizing. As the case of the *Philosophy of Money* illustrates, when examples are extracted from the *Erscheinungsreihen* in order to put his claims about particular phenomena or categories of phenomena to theoretical use within sociological, anthropological, psychological, or other disciplinary frameworks, the multiplicity and nuance of Simmel's world-view and understanding of scientific inquiry tend to disappear from view along with the larger argument in which his discussions of the cases themselves are embedded. And as such selected instances take on disciplinary lives of their own, questions about what the phenomenal examples represent in Simmel's own texts no longer arise. The reception of the *Philosophy of Money* thus exemplifies how the appropriation by fragments turns him into a mostly forgotten founding father of sociology: in a single movement his work is canonized and what animated Simmel's thinking consigned to oblivion.

Readings that turn on abstracting individual cases from Simmel's larger philosophical account of the historical and trans-historical meanings of money have cre-

---

29. As Becker put it candidly in 1959, "many of Simmel's abstract analyses are illustrated in such a way that, for some readers, the illustration is a greater interest in the analysis" (Becker, "On Simmel's Philosophy of Money," in *Georg Simmel*, ed. Wolff, 229).

ated an impoverished vision of his theoretical objectives and achievements, which then encourages the tendency to treat Simmel as an unsystematic thinker—and validates and justifies the practices of selective reading themselves. The resulting one-sided accounts of his positions actively occlude the very point of the sort of reflection on socio-cultural reality the *Philosophy of Money* aimed to cultivate. What is at stake in these hermeneutically and methodologically dubious self-reinforcing reception practices turns out to be nothing less than the relationship between the social sciences and their philosophical origins.

Taken on its own terms, the *Philosophy of Money* is far from unsystematic. Simmel's declared purpose can properly be described as metaphysical: to "demonstrate the possibility of finding in every particular of life the totality of its meaning" (GSG 6: 12). In a phenomenological effort to establish, as it were, an antifoundational foundation for the relativist epistemology he espouses, he deploys strategies of argument firmly situated in a dialectical tradition of reflection that cohere, both globally and locally, in that idiom. To be sure, his texts may appear unsystematic from the point of view of an instrumental understanding of theory that decontextualizes readings of particular social, cultural, and psychological phenomena both textually and methodologically, yet the same practices of selective reading have also authorized a complementary, equally misleading image of Simmel as "formalist." Both takes miss his metatheoretical project: establishing the viability of a relativist hermeneutic strategy—and modernizing philosophy.

The interpretive moves that have shaped Simmel's reception in modern social science cannot be adequately understood as errors in an empirical sense, however problematic their hermeneutic and scholarly bases may be. What is at stake, ultimately, is itself metaphysical—in Simmelian terms, a conflict of worldviews. His is a philosophy of becoming, not of being, a mode of thought in which every substance dissolves into function, and every moment of stability, every form of conceptual stasis, is set into motion. Sometimes ambiguities and contradictions disappear (are sublated) when the connection between particular interpretations and the higher-scale or -order logics he is describing are taken into account. But often such tensions are not eliminated at a "higher" level. The fundamental principle that neither ideal nor material explanations are sufficient holds throughout. The resulting conception of the social is not easily assimilated into either (implicitly or overtly) positivist or (tacitly or residually, if no longer affirmatively) structuralist predilections of mainstream social science.

The modus operandi of modern disciplinary knowledge practices has led to a fragmentation of Simmel's oeuvre, where his sociological contributions are isolated from their philosophical "other," with the latter being consigned to (antiquated) metaphysics.[30] What I, very much with Simmel, am disputing, is whether his socio-

---

30. This trope echoes even in its general editor's account of the *Gesamtausgabe*'s origins, which credits the success of the second effort to create a critical edition, begun in 1980, principally "to the impetus coming from sociology. After the Second World War, Simmel as philosopher . . . seemed to merit only a footnote in the history of philosophy, whereas Simmel's sociological ideas had initiated a plethora of new approaches in American sociology [and here Rammstedt provides a footnote identifying social

logical contributions can really be separated from their philosophical horizon in this fashion.

That the reading practices through which this separation has been achieved are methodologically unsound has long since been established by historically inclined readers, but to little institutional effect, since that hermeneutic perspective is explicitly rejected by sociological theorists of a "systematic" stripe. Separating these disciplinary "parts" from their philosophical "whole"—or rather, from the speculative or perhaps ironical perspectival "unity" of this highly fragmented text—thus continues to perpetuate seemingly willful blindness to the enduring importance for social and cultural theory of the metaphysical and epistemological questions Simmel was raising. The value of his *Philosophy of Money* for contemporary social and cultural theory includes its performative disclosure of this larger horizon of historical-critical reflection on the boundaries of the modern disciplinary imaginary.

The same holds for Simmel's 1908 *Soziologie*. As he insists there, "the philosophy of society has no justification for evading the advantages or disadvantages of its belonging to philosophy as such by constituting itself as a special science of sociology" (*GSG* 11: 41). From a contemporary perspective, the obstacles to overcoming the inadequacies of reductively sociological (or historicist) modes of interpretation are, like the readings of particular cases themselves, symptomatic of a larger problem that is by no means exclusive to Simmel. How can modern social and cultural theory return to and learn from thinkers whose very conception of the enterprise in which they were engaged poses a challenge to the institutions and practices, the intuitions and assumptions, that shape the intellectual and rhetorical horizons of the contemporary disciplinary imaginary?

If we are to identify and access the theoretical and methodological resources the *Philosophy of Money* makes available, it is necessary to bear in mind that Simmel was attempting to think the social as such as an emergent phenomenon of and in modern life. In his intellectual world, such theorizing was not a practice within an existing field of discursive and disciplinary possibilities. Questions about the nature, methods, and limits of social science as a distinct form of inquiry were still being formulated. What would come to be understood as distinct branches of inquiry—historical, psychological, economic, psychological, anthropological—were still relatively undifferentiated from one another. Simmel's work could neither appeal to nor depend on a theoretical assumption that has come to seem so obvious that it is no longer easily recognized as the highly mediated postulate it is: that there is such a thing as the social or society.

Modern social science is not properly conceived of as the result of attempts to understand an existing object of study. Simmel and his interlocutors—Marx, Spencer, and Nietzsche no less than Lazarus, Rickert, Weber, and Durkheim—were

---

scientists and historians of social science] that in turn demonstrated Simmel's relevance to German sociology. This intersected with a burgeoning discussion about the classics of sociology in the wake of the 'self-historicization of the social sciences' . . . motivated by a search for validation of the social sciences in times of crisis" (Otthein Rammstedt, "On the Genesis of a Collected Edition of Simmel's Works, 1918–2012," *TCS* 29, nos. 7–8 [2012]: 302–16; here p. 307). These assertions reappear in *GSG* 24: 1049–50.

in the process of creating new ways of categorizing and comprehending the phenomena of human collective life. Their thinking took place in medias res, as part of a (social, historical, cultural, political as well as conceptual) process of invention and discovery that reflected and reflected upon changes under way and by its very nature helped generate the very object ("the social," "society," "nature," "culture") that it studied.

Viewed from this rhetorical perspective, the emergent modernist enterprise of (social, cultural) theory is situated rather differently than from the point of view of the disciplines. The conceptual, historical, and institutional developments associated with all these thinkers can, of course, be interpreted as innovations within the older disciplines of history or political philosophy, just as they can be understood as the inaugural, canonical, moment of modern disciplines, whether sociology, history, or political science. But to take a disciplinary perspective is to situate what is in play in narratives of development within intellectual traditions that appear more clearly defined from our own perspective by far than they were at the time. In any case, only some of what was new about the idea of the social or society (*Gesellschaft*) can be captured in such narratives. As Nietzsche taught, many compelling philosophical tendencies—notably faith in logic and conceptual consistency and the corollary assumptions that what does exist has always existed or that we may take for granted the survival of what is just coming into being—render us ill-suited to the urgent challenge of understanding the momentous cultural and historical change under way in the modern world.

In our own intellectual context, when the problems with disciplinary divisions of all sorts are becoming all too evident conceptually, methodologically, and institutionally, it is valuable to attend to how very much was in flux at the time when modern social and cultural theory were coming into being—that is to say, when the human and social sciences began to take drastically separate paths. In reading Simmel as a modernist philosopher, I am also attempting to foreground the conceptual novelty at the origin of the modern social sciences—the process of the invention of the "social" and "society." For (to invoke Nietzsche once again) emphasizing the potentiality and indeterminacy of the past can help free us to rethink what is apparently stable and self-evident in the institutions and practices of the world we ourselves inhabit. I cannot make the more general case for such a reframing of disciplinary history here. But I do hope to have shown that Simmel's reception as (mostly forgotten) founding father of sociology casts light on the problems that arise when the crucial role played by the modernist turn to self-reflection is left out of our thinking about the origins of the modern social sciences—and when philosophy is implicitly exempted from the problematics of modernism altogether.

The categorization of the *Philosophy of Money* as a work of sociology depends on a practice of selective (mis)reading that is institutionally significant as well as theoretically self-reinforcing. Recontextualizing and dehistoricizing his overtly philosophical project to assimilate it to sociology, a discipline that inherited some but by no means all of Simmel's theoretical concerns, legitimates and facilitates a mode of reception that simultaneously obscures the theoretical significance of

Simmel's (re)turn to philosophy and hypostasizes the assumptions and preoccupations proper to a very different horizon of inquiry.

Precisely in its silences, however, this mode of reception points to what makes Simmel's work most important for understanding the philosophical—theoretical—significance of the contemporary disciplinary imaginary—and identifying its lacunae. When it is read with an awareness of Simmel's self-reflexive intellectual-historical location at the juncture where the modern distinction between "society" and "culture" was coming into being, the *Philosophy of Money* illuminates the historical and conceptual foundations—and fault lines—of what came to be disciplinary paradigms that continue to dominate our thinking about society and human sociality. Not only does Simmel's intellectual biography underline the importance for him of the question of the future of philosophy in the face of developments in the social sciences. The very project of the *Philosophy of Money* involves a phenomenologically articulated approach to theorizing the relations between disciplinary knowledge practices, an approach whose considerable virtues have gone largely ignored by discipline-centric historiographies.

Reading the *Philosophy of Money* through the prism of subsequent developments and interpretive practices occludes the ways Simmel's text both directly and indirectly calls into question the presuppositions and methods of the social sciences as they have taken shape in the intervening century. By the same token, though, the profound challenge his book poses for the discipline of philosophy has also gone unrecognized. Indeed, on my reading, what leads to the virtual illegibility of the *Philosophy of Money* as a whole from the point of view of mainstream sociological ways of seeing likewise accounts for its virtual absence from contemporary philosophical discourse. Neither of these forms of silence is amenable to easy remedies, for Simmel's absence is a symptom of lacunae constitutive for the modern disciplinary imaginary. This pervasive difficulty in seeing the work whole has helped keep the *Philosophy of Money* the most important mostly unread theoretical work of the twentieth century.

PART III

The Case of Simmel

Georg Simmel was doubtless the most significant and interesting transitional phenomenon in all of modern philosophy.

György Lukács (1918)

CHAPTER 7

Thinking Liminality, Rethinking Disciplinarity

Method and Change: Thinking Liminality

Part I used the vagaries of Georg Simmel's reception to illustrate how, as the cultural and social sciences evolved, the very philosophical questions that motivated their inaugural thinkers were occluded. Part II explored the methodological consequences for the reception of the *Philosophy of Money*, identifying the traces of a process of forgetting in the objectifying, ostensibly ahistorical perspective of contemporary cultural and social theory on this work. In showing how Simmel became a mostly forgotten founding father of sociology, I also demonstrated why what is at issue methodologically cannot be addressed simply by recalling the facts about the origins of the social sciences. Rather, it entails self-reflexive attention to the theoretical and practical consequences of those constitutive enframings of disciplinary knowledge practices.

The case of Simmel's reception within sociology illustrates a more general feature of the cultural and intellectual history of the disciplines: the operative historical narratives of contemporary practitioners tend to be a rather poor reflection of what actually gave rise to the governing practices—methods, standards of evidence, framing assumptions—of a field. Myths and pseudohistories, a misremembering of origins that flatters the present with a veneer of necessity, help consolidate and maintain disciplinary boundaries. Like other social institutions and cultural formations, scholarly disciplines depend for their stability on silencing and even foreclosing (parts of) their histories and maintain cohesion by regulating which questions and problems are to count as interesting or relevant—or even coherent. If we are to move beyond the conceptual and practical impasses that attend on the proliferation of specialized and increasingly autonomous disciplinary perspectives in our own time, we need to understand the rhetorical transformation that brought into being the disciplinary unconscious, as it were, of the modern social and cultural sciences.[1]

The case of Simmel, whose fame and knack for making deep and difficult issues accessible to broad audiences contributed from early on to his devaluation as

---

Part III epigraph: Lukács obituary of Georg Simmel, reproduced in *BdD*, 171.

1. *Social Knowledge in the Making*, ed. Charles Camic, Neil Gross, and Michèle Lamont (Chicago: University of Chicago Press, 2011), addresses these issues from the perspective of concrete knowledge practices.

a "popular" philosopher, underlines that this mode of forgetting is proper, not to the social sciences per se, but to the modern professionalized academic disciplinary ordering of inquiry itself. In institutional terms, philosophy, like theology, has long since become a discipline among other disciplines. Attempts to address philosophical questions and issues for a general audience mostly fall outside the domain of professional work. Much of the philosophical legacy has resettled in the grey zones of the self-help genre or been marooned in what has come to be called "metaphysical literature," but since the arts and especially literature have never ceased to be concerned with these matters, a great deal that once fell under the rubric of philosophy has also been appropriated by other disciplines.

From the perspective of a narrowly analytic understanding of what is properly philosophical, the migration of certain kinds of philosophical issues and approaches into other (inter)disciplinary locations might be applauded as a continuation of the process of institutional-intellectual differentiation in and through which philosophy modernized and professionalized—the same process in and through which the social sciences emerged out of the larger "philosophical faculties" in Germany as the modern research university came into being. But the same dynamics of specialization and professionalization continue to effect increasing disciplinary and subdisciplinary fragmentation—and to encourage the cultivation (and colonization) of "interdisciplinary" methods and approaches. Sociologically speaking, the constantly increasing level of technical specialization and differentiation within the discipline of philosophy has helped foster the very explosion of cultural and critical theory that now appears to encroach on "philosophical" territory.

Simmel's fate, including the dispersed history of effects of a small number of his writings in far-flung humanistic as well as social scientific disciplinary contexts is, then, in part a function of the vicissitudes of academic philosophy in the twentieth century. That evolution places in particular relief the tendency of professionalized "humanities" disciplines to disqualify the "naïve" approaches of nonexperts to the objects, nature, and foundations of their knowledge (practices). Within the ambit of humanistic inquiry, the unfortunate result has been a debasement of public discourse even as the technical sophistication of professional literatures increases—precisely the sort of development Simmel described as a cultural effect of the elaboration of a complex money economy.

Directing critical attention to the genealogy of the contemporary disciplinary ordering of inquiry and especially to the historicity of contemporary theoretical practices can help increase the methodological sophistication of interdisciplinary discourse and thereby contribute to the larger rethinking our contemporary theoretical and disciplinary impasse demands. Simmel's oeuvre, both philosophical and sociological, deserves greater attention in itself; his significant history of effects needs to be written into the history of modern cultural and social thought; and the distinctive trans- or interdisciplinary mode of theorizing exemplified by the *Philosophy of Money* has gained in currency in light of developments since 1989. Returning to his work thus provides an opportunity to reexamine core practices and assumptions of contemporary cultural inquiry. If we can find ways to integrate the theoretical reach and methodological force of his style of thought, Simmel's theorization of money both in its sociohistorical and cultural effects and "as symbol of the most essential forms of movement" of the *geistige Welt*—the super- and transindividual cultural, spiritual, intellectual world—may even help contemporary cultural theory to overcome some of the aporias that are the legacy of the disciplinary fragmentation that has ensued since Simmel's death.

Part I approached the question of Simmel's philosophical significance in the first instance from the point of view of his dominant reception as a sociologist. But as Part II demonstrated, that disciplinary perspective systematically and symptomatically underestimates and marginalizes him as a thinker through a historically inaccurate and theoretically misleading mode of canonization that also helps occlude the (philosophical) origins of modern social science itself. At this point, it becomes possible to pose the question of Simmel's philosophical significance in a way that does better justice to his actual contributions as a thinker—and to the fact that of all the disciplines, philosophy is probably least suited to being reduced to a scholarly specialization.

To reprise, whether Simmel was "really" a philosopher was not at all at issue during his lifetime. His somewhat rocky educational path notwithstanding, his intellectual distinction was acknowledged early on by his senior colleagues. After qualifying in 1885, Simmel quickly gained a following as a lecturer with a range of introductory classes. He was still a *Privatdozent* in 1897 when he was asked to step in to replace Dilthey's lectures on logic during the latter's illness.[2] Throughout his career, Simmel continued to teach logic and the history of philosophy, but also to cover all of the other major areas of the discipline, with regular courses on ethics and aesthetics as well as metaphysics and epistemology. From early on, his offerings integrated reflection on natural as well as social scientific and psychological topics. Yet with the exception of the brief period in the mid-1890s when he hoped that what he would come to see as his idiosyncratic vision of sociology might carry the day, Simmel always identified as a philosopher.

To be sure, he never ceased to reflect on social life or to attempt to promulgate his vision of what the discipline of sociology ought to be—one of his very last books was entitled *Grundfragen der Soziologie (Individuum und Gesellschaft)* (translated as "Fundamental Problems of Sociology (Individual and Society)" and known as the "small" *Soziologie*). Simmel's sociological activities—as a teacher, writer, and institution-builder—were considerable, yet they remained, as he put it, a "sideline." He was famous in his lifetime as a philosopher, and all of the positions he held were in philosophy, as were all of those for which he was considered.

The difficulties that beset Simmel's academic career cannot be entirely disassociated from his identification with sociology, then a new and slightly suspect discipline. In practical terms, though, what was at stake professionally was whether and

---

2. Köhnke suggests in his notes to a letter of January 7, 1896, from Simmel to Hugo Münsterberg (who had returned to Freiburg after three years in William James's department at Harvard, where he would take up permanent residence as professor of experimental psychology in 1897) that Simmel may also have done so in WS 1895–96 (*GSG* 22: 169). See also the notes to *GSG* 21: 1034.

how a man with his unconventional and in many ways unacademic approach could find a place in the institutional context of the modernizing discipline of philosophy. Like so many of his best-remembered predecessors, Simmel did not entirely fit in, and while the social sciences were gaining traction institutionally, there were still no positions in sociology per se. Under these circumstances, Simmel's sometime identification as a sociologist was, like his purported Jewishness, more fodder for those who questioned his eligibility in the sense of his suitability for the status of *Ordinarius*.

Over many years, the efforts of figures such as Rickert, Husserl, and Weber notwithstanding, lesser men consistently received prestigious professorships that had seemed within Simmel's grasp. It speaks volumes that, when it finally came, his chair in philosophy was not in Berlin or Heidelberg or Freiburg, but in Strasbourg, literally at the margins of Germany. By the time the ultimately successful appointment process was under way, Simmel was nearly fifty-six.[3] The repeated failure of such efforts in the face of cynical opposition at the highest levels illustrates how anti-Semitism and hostility to sociology intertwined in Simmel's very real problem of perception: what he described to Rickert, after learning that his name was under discussion in Strasbourg, as the persistent "myth" that he was not interested in a regular professorship, as well as his "reputation for political and other 'radicalism.'"[4]

Still, to put it bluntly, the practice of attributing Simmel's professional tribulations to his being, in reality, a sociologist flies in the face of historical evidence. Far from being a heroic voice in the wilderness fighting for a fledgling discipline against its traditionalist enemies, he enjoyed very considerable public and professional success as an internationally regarded philosopher and best-selling author, whose lectures drew crowds; he was called to Strasbourg in Alsace in 1914 with the understanding that his prominence would help build up the university by raising the profile of German philosophy there.[5] Simmel's aspiration to foster a genuine "philosophical culture" in the newly expanded landscape of southern Germany would be thwarted by the Great War. But during the next four years in Strasbourg, a city at one point virtually on the front lines, Simmel had ample opportunity to test his views on society, culture, and community—as well as his understanding of

---

3. At that time, the average age for such appointments was forty. See Christian R. Ferber, *Entwicklung des Lehrerkörpers der deutschen Universitäten* (Göttingen: Vandenhoeck & Ruprecht, 1956), 32, cited in Lewis Coser, *Masters of Sociological Thought: Ideas in Historical and Social Context* (1971; 2nd ed., New York: Harcourt Brace Jovanovich, 1977), 197.

4. Simmel went on to assure Rickert in letter dated May 12, 1913, that he took these machinations coolly, and that "in this semester once again many hundreds of students comfort me in the face of my academic misfortune" (*GSG* 23: 225).

5. What is today the Université de Strasbourg is a venerable institution located in the former imperial free city of Strasbourg that traces its royal charter to 1631. After Alsace, largely Francophone since the French Revolution, was annexed to the German Second Empire following the Franco-Prussian War, it became the Kaiser-Wilhelm-Universität, which it remained until 1918. In Simmel's day, it was expanding rapidly. See Maurice Blanc and Freddy Raphaël, "Strasbourg, carrefour des sociologies (1872–1972)," *Revue des sciences sociales*, no. 40 (2008): 8–11. In the same issue, see also Heribert Becher, "Georg Simmel à Strasbourg (1914–1918): Trois entretiens avec un témoin: Charles Hauter (1888–1981)," 42–49.

the German national and imperial project. It was as a philosopher that Simmel set out the resulting insights in his essays on war, and it was as a philosopher that he composed his great last essay on social themes, "Der Konflikt der modernen Kultur" ("The Conflict in Modern Culture"), published in 1918, shortly before his death.

Simmel never ceased to see philosophical questions of all sorts as intricated with sociological, psychological, and anthropological issues, because he regarded knowledge as constituted in and through categories and modes of perception and valuation generated and sustained in sociocultural, historical processes. His philosophical writings often expand on ideas—about subjectivity, history, culture, individuality, freedom, identity—that he had initially explored from a sociological perspective; they develop rather than abandon the concerns of his earlier work. But most of this later work has barely registered within mainstream social science, and as a series of distinguished historians of sociology have learned to their chagrin, drawing attention to the continuities in Simmel's thought—or to the historical and biographical facts regarding his career—by no means suffices to overcome established views.

It is necessary to take a step back in order to explain the resilience of a mode of reception that involves ignoring so much evidence. As I have demonstrated, forgetting (or dismissing) the fact that Simmel understood himself and was understood by his contemporaries first and foremost as a philosopher helps anchor a narrative about the emergence of the sociological discipline that remains important for its continued cohesion. Severing his sociological from his philosophical contributions makes it possible to claim him as founding father while simultaneously distancing the discipline from the very questions he regarded as central.

An inaccurate or at best misleadingly narrow account of Simmel's life and work is part and parcel of an account of sociology's origins whose effectiveness at establishing and reinforcing disciplinary boundaries comes at the expense of historical accuracy. And since the same anachronistic assumptions about intellectual boundaries also inflect the self-understanding and disciplinary memory (as it were) of philosophy, Simmel has been largely disregarded and forgotten in the discipline he called his own as well. His philosophical contributions have been written out of the story, quite literally in the case of the *Philosophy of Money*.

Simmel's view that the "constitution of a special science of sociology" neither resolved nor eliminated the questions proper to social philosophy (*GSG* 11: 41) provides a crucial missing link between the preoccupations of "theory" (in the broader sense in which that term is used in the contemporary, increasingly "interdisciplinary" humanities and qualitative social sciences) and the regnant questions and problems of a hundred years ago—that is, of the philosophical and historical moment in which the modern disciplinary order was coming into being. What has been framed in anachronistic terms as Simmel's disciplinary marginality is better understood as theoretical and methodological liminality.

This liminal position must be grasped in historical and cultural as well as biographical and institutional terms. As a famous philosopher with considerable status in the intellectual culture of his era who spent most of his career as a marginalized semi-outsider in the professionalizing academy, Simmel was a different kind of thinker than the institution-builders and historians who would in various ways go on to claim his legacy for sociology. Given the manifest practical and personal challenges of his professional position, the tendency to frame his story as a tragic case of nonrecognition is understandable. Yet Simmel's own well-attested sense of his importance and his demonstrable influence over colleagues and students, as well as readers further afield, do not square easily with this view, and he was in fact very far from regarding himself or his life as tragic or unfulfilled.

As both philosopher and sociologist, Simmel developed practices of thought that even today do not comfortably fit into existing institutional frameworks. His advocates within the contemporary social sciences tend to argue that those frameworks should be modified to accommodate his work, for example, by expanding the field of cultural sociology or, more recently, interpellating a subfield devoted to "sociological metaphysics."[6] But the strategy of intradisciplinary differentiation—which could equally be described as the internalization of interdisciplinarity—does not address the problems attendant on categorizing his oeuvre in (anachronistic) disciplinary terms. Creating a third place, however designated, does not overcome or even effectively call into question the tendency, shared by mainstream social scientists and professional philosophers, to neglect or demean Simmel's theoretical accomplishments by excluding him from their respective disciplines.

Indeed, insofar as it exacerbates the fragmentation of intellectual life, incorporating Simmel into the contemporary intellectual landscape via this sort of pigeon-holing, for example, as a canonical philosopher of culture, arguably makes matters worse. The concerns of social and cultural theory are at once empirical and theoretical, social scientific and philosophical. To proliferate yet more inter- and intradisciplinary subdivisions with distinct assumptions and interpretive practices obscures rather than addresses this circumstance. Moreover, turning Simmel into the lineal ancestor of present developments effaces the significance of his (historically, culturally, theoretically) persistently liminal position between philosophy and sociology and, by reinforcing the limits of received intellectual and cultural models, distorts the intellectual and cultural history of the disciplinary order as a whole.

---

6. The 2012 special issue of *TCS* includes a series of investigations into what the editors, Thomas Kemple and Austin Harrington, call "Simmel's metaphysics of the social, or what he himself called his 'sociological metaphysics'": an "idiom of thinking in Simmel's work encompassing core ideas and basic problems central to the modernist project of critical reflexive knowledge about the social conditions of human existence." It designates "an insistence that the traditional philosophical field of metaphysics has a sociology" but also "the idea that compelling grounds exist for probing the liminal area at the intersection of experiences that are open to definite empirical scientific observation and to other dimensions of reality that can only be disclosed by other means" (*TCS* 29, nos. 7–8 [2012]: 10–11). Kemple and Harrington suggest valuable new lines of inquiry for social theory at the boundaries of the empirical. Yet sociological metaphysics so conceived aims to enrich the existing disciplinary formation by incorporating this metaphysical (for Simmel, philosophical) dimension of self-reflexivity into sociology, thereby obscuring something of great theoretical and practical importance that is of at least equal concern to Simmel: that the extradisciplinary dimension at the boundaries of science and experience is not just supplementary but constitutive for sociology and philosophy alike—that just as philosophy has a sociology, sociology has a metaphysics.

Liminality generates irregular reception and unofficial modes of transmission. Rather than attempting to counteract or overcome the resulting history of effects by retroactively and anachronistically assimilating Simmel to (invented) disciplinary traditions, I propose attending to his overdetermined liminal position as a site that enabled theoretical innovation. Doing so can help us to read for the resources his writings may still hold for efforts to think beyond disciplinary boundaries in confronting the complex and interpenetrating theoretical and practical challenges of a globalized cultural world. Since Simmel is hardly the only significant thinker with a vexed relationship to the professionalized and specialized knowledge practices taking hold in the late nineteenth and early twentieth centuries, this approach should be of more general applicability for enriching the resources of a historically self-reflective cultural theory.

Neither 1900's *Philosophie des Geldes* nor 1908's "large" *Soziologie* can be understood without taking into account Simmel's style of thought, which transgresses the conventions, not only of contemporary empirical social science, but also of the principal social theory traditions. To extract sociological "content" from the formally complex larger argumentative structures of these works distorts the meaning of his analyses: Simmel's phenomenological strategies are themselves philosophically significant, and his specific mode of methodological rigor is rendered illegible when style, form, and content are disconnected and his modernist philosophical approach is represented as unsystematic or misconstrued as an expression of his purported "aestheticism." This holds true whether being unsystematic or aestheticizing are being celebrated or condemned.

Simmel's cultural phenomenology embodies the legacy of the dialectical tradition: discrete analyses of particular "appearances" and forms of life are taken as synecdoches, approached as "parts" of larger "wholes," in an interpretive strategy that, as he put it in the Preface to the *Philosophy of Money*, strives to link "the particularities and superficialities of life to its most profound and essential movements" to provide an "interpretation of their total meaning" (GSG 6: 13). I would hesitate to suggest that we are in a better position than Simmel to determine whether his "relativist interpretation of being" is ontologically warranted. But perhaps we have arrived at the point where it becomes possible to recognize "the methodological significance" of his investigations as "the form of future validities" (ibid.): as valuable independently of the question of the verifiability of his framing metaphysical assumptions.

A history of tendentious misreadings and surprising exclusions attests to the challenges texts organized in a relativist fashion have posed for professional readers, notwithstanding the intuitive purchase of Simmel's style, attested to by his popularity during his lifetime and the fascination his writing holds for nonacademics even today. But his accessibility, ingenuity, and imagination as a cultural exegete, so often dismissed as marks of superficiality, anchored a phenomenological approach that helped disclose new questions and fields of philosophical as well as sociological inquiry. As Siegfried Kracauer emphasized, attention to "seemingly insignificant superficial phenomena" can reveal deeper historical truths: "The fundamental content of an epoch and its unnoticed stirrings are mutually illuminating."[7] Simmel persuaded his students and readers of the value of attending to the complex and multiple relations of interactivity and mutual determination between seemingly insignificant or superficial phenomena of everyday social and cultural life and larger historical, sociological, and philosophical dimensions and questions—and thereby helped inaugurate cultural criticism in the modern mode.

That today Simmel is virtually absent from the intellectual history of the twentieth century even in areas where his contributions are well documented calls for reflection. As in other cases where exclusions have distorted the historical record, rectifying the story depends on changing our understanding of its meaning. Reconstructing the history of misreading that has obscured Simmel's achievements as a thinker makes it clear that however inspiring and valuable his writings remain when removed from their context, his theoretical contributions cannot entirely be rendered legible without critical attention to that reception. There is no returning to "the text itself," not least because the meaning of the phenomena he described has itself often changed over time.

In nuce: what appears from a contemporary perspective as marginality is symptomatic of the difficulty of thinking before, beyond, and outside the reigning categorical and disciplinary frameworks. Simmel's reception thus provides a particularly clear illustration of how disciplinary paradigms foreclose the protean complexity proper to the predecessors and antecedents of contemporary practices, methods, and styles of thought. To take a page from Kracauer, his historical and conceptual liminality is an apparently superficial cultural phenomenon that illuminates larger features of our own epoch.

Simmel was often represented as somehow personifying the zeitgeist, and his professional difficulties were not unrelated to his reputation for being too popular, too fashionable, too much of his time. Yet many serious thinkers took Simmel quite seriously indeed. That his fame as a philosopher proved fleeting entails neither that it was undeserved nor that his influence was insignificant. On the contrary, that Simmel has been so thoroughly marginalized today, that he has been virtually excluded from the memory of his own discipline of philosophy, should encourage us to explore how much is at stake in such forgetting—both for individual thinkers such as Heidegger and for the discipline as a whole. When his liminal status is foregrounded, "Simmel" appears both as a figure for the disavowed philosophical origins of the modern social sciences and as a reminder to philosophy of the importance of situating thought itself by reflecting on the historical, cultural, sociological, and psychological location of the most transcendent insights.

For all these reasons, the problematic history of Simmel's reception cannot be redressed by extending the network of disciplinary categories with one tailored to erase his liminal position between philosophy and sociology. Whether his writing

---

7. Siegfried Kracauer, "Das Ornament der Masse" (1927), in *Das Ornament der Masse: Essays* (Frankfurt am Main: Suhrkamp, 1977), 50–63, 50. Once again, the underlying logical structure here is Simmelian: a synecdochic plumbing of the depths that reveals meanings via attention to relativistic *Wechselwirkung*.

is rechristened "social theory," "cultural studies," "sociological metaphysics," or "philosophy of culture," attempts to redefine the liminal space where his thinking unfolded all come down to efforts to claim Simmel for contemporary disciplinary and institutional battles. Such efforts of necessity beg the question of the status of present (disciplinary) assumptions and styles of thought and effectively reinscribe Lukács's view of him as "the most significant and interesting transitional phenomenon in all of modern philosophy" (*BdD*, 171), that is, as a thinker whose time has passed.

Such contemporary rereadings and rediscoveries are not just formally continuous with past efforts to define or contest Simmel's place in the sociological canon (or outside it). As I have shown, his identification as a sort of internal other evolved through a history of would-be renaissances and proposed remappings of his contributions that shadow the intellectual and institutional development of the contemporary discipline of sociology and reflect the process of its (apparent) emancipation from its "metaphysical" roots in philosophy. Simmel's evolving role as (mostly) forgotten founding father, epitomized by his frequent depiction as "The Stranger" he famously theorized, can thus serve us (to invoke a Simmelian formulation) as at once symbol and mirror, illuminating the significance of the divide between sociology and philosophy and, more generally, of the bifurcation between social scientific and humanistic reflection on human life.

Integrating Simmel into the larger narrative of twentieth-century intellectual and cultural history is challenging. It is perfectly legitimate to reframe and thereby assimilate work that has been represented as marginal to extend and refine current thinking. Yet attempts to enrich cultural sociology or social theory today by retroactively introducing Simmel's more overtly philosophical writings into the sociological canon function as means of containing and neutralizing the challenge his liminality continues to pose. Even when they foster valuable theoretical developments, such presentist readings risk circumventing the critical theoretical potential of a return to his work to further consolidate the contemporary disciplinary imaginary.

Whatever the virtues and value of (social, critical, cultural) theory as a distinct academic specialization, it cannot (any more than contemporary philosophy or neurology) be understood as an autonomous formation. Even the most timeless idea of truth comes enrobed in the specificity of its historical and cultural formation. Inventing or expanding (theoretical) areas or subfields in Simmel's name not only fails to address the circumstance that for most mainstream philosophers and social scientists, his thinking remains largely illegible, his texts safely foreign. Retroactively integrating his "interdisciplinary" work effectively reifies his (historically constituted) marginality, subverting the question of what Simmel's persistently liminal position reveals about the limits of the dominant ways of seeing and understanding human life, culture, and society.

The disciplinary organization of scholarship is not simply a matter of ideas and methods, however, but very much an institutional and political reality. As such, it functions as a sort of intellectual bureaucracy that thwarts efforts to think in complex and comprehensive ways about challenges that are not in fact bounded, let alone contained, by the conceptual strategies we bring to bear on them. As Simmel always emphasized, the world exceeds our thinking. Reality does not correspond to the disciplinary subdivisions, which are contingent, historical and cultural formations whose air of authority is often rooted in institutional rather than intellectual power. Just as the task of subjective self-understanding has been transformed in the aftermath of Freud's "discovery" of unconscious motivations, we need to learn to recognize and maintain awareness of the effects of what I am calling the disciplinary imaginary on our ways of perceiving and understanding the world.

A series of Simmel "renaissances" that presumed the inevitability of the very disciplinary organization they set out to explain have already failed to render his historical and theoretical significance more widely legible. To grasp the unrealized potential of his intellectual legacy, we must think in different ways about culture and identity, philosophy and sociology, history and theory—confront the limits of the disciplinary imaginary that enframes our own highly specialized knowledge practices.

The difficulty in thinking outside or beyond disciplinarity except in terms of an additive "interdisciplinarity" is a significant symptom of a historic dilemma. Especially in the increasingly dominant form of intradisciplinary subspecialization, "interdisciplinarity" makes it possible to acknowledge, and, to a certain extent, to address the limitations of the contemporary intellectual division of labor without calling its institutional hegemony in the academy (and beyond) into question. On an individual level, it enables innovation while preserving the considerable professional advantages of membership in a disciplinary community.

Yet however innovative interdisciplinary moves may be within the contemporary scholarly game, they cannot point the way beyond the constitutive problems of the sociocultural ordering of knowledge practices as such. Insofar as the fragmentation, specialization, and lack of historical self-reflection that characterize the norms of the contemporary disciplinary order are epistemological and methodological symptoms of the worldview born of the hegemony of the modern money economy, the proliferation of increasingly differentiated inter-, trans-, and post-disciplinary practices reinforces rather than challenges the philosophical—ethical, but also metaphysical—insufficiencies of the modern disciplinary imaginary.

The case of Simmel provides an occasion for critical reflection on the ever-proliferating varieties of ("inter-," "trans-," "post-) disciplinary divisions and subdivisions in contemporary scholarship. Because his liminality reveals the boundaries and limits of our own ways of seeing (and reading), it has a good deal to teach us about both history and theory—most especially about what has been rendered invisible from within intellectual milieux shaped by the established assumptions and certainties of the specialized, professionalized, and highly differentiated disciplinary ordering of inquiry we have come to take for granted. His work directly challenges the hypostasization of humanistic, social, and natural scientific "areas" and "fields," not because Simmel was both sociologist and philosopher, but because he was, in today's understanding of the terms, neither.

Keeping Simmel's liminality in mind helps illuminate the theoretical and historical significance of his contributions. To achieve an adequate, critical perspective on his reception—on the "history of effects" (to literalize the German term) that has shaped his memory—it is necessary to address how and why those aspects of his work that transgress (and thereby implicitly call into question) the naturalized disciplinary divisions of contemporary intellectual life have been consistently occluded and excluded. To recover what has become, what has been rendered, illegible in disciplinary memory thus entails returning to Simmel's texts in a new way and moving back beyond interdisciplinarity, so to speak, in an effort to encounter the very different possibilities of the conceptual space that preceded the hollow certainties and dubious clarities of the contemporary division of intellectual labor.

To step imaginatively into this space of uncertain possibility requires setting aside our assumptions about what knowledge is (good for) and calling into question our explicit and implicit faith in the power of the specialized vocabularies and routinized methods that have come to structure, not just academic life, but what Simmel would have called our *Geisteskultur*, our intellectual culture, as a whole. His work invites us to rethink the larger narratives that enframe our (disciplinary and interdisciplinary) knowledge practices and to question not just the forms and techniques of thought and life proper to that culture but also the dubious certainties of the contemporary disciplinary imaginary itself.

Beyond the (Philosophy of the) Subject: Thinking Relatively and the "Problem of Sociology"

In an essay titled "Das Abenteuer" ("The Adventure"), which appeared in an illustrated paper in 1910, Simmel wrote that the adventurer "treats what is incalculable in life in the way we ordinarily only behave toward what is calculable with certainty." Revising the collection *Philosophische Kultur* (Philosophical Culture), in which the essay was reprinted, in the final months of his life, he added: "Therefore the philosopher is the adventurer of the spirit. He makes the hopeless, but not for that reason senseless, attempt to form the soul's comportment toward life [*Lebensverhalten der Seele*], its disposition [*Stimmung*] toward itself, the world, God, into conceptual knowing. He treats this irresolvable as though it could be resolved."[8]

Simmel embraced change as a philosophical object, and at its best, his writing conveys this exhilaration of thought. Following his suggestion, we may read his evolving praxis as a writer and thinker as a series of philosophical adventures, efforts to forge strategies of thought that integrated new ways of interpreting the world into experiences, however provisional, of life as an object of knowledge. Simmel's intellectual evolution maps onto his shifting disciplinary allegiances during the final

---

8. Originally published in *Der Tag* (in a version now in *GSG* 12: 97–110), "Das Abenteuer" was included in *Philosophische Kultur: Gesammelte Essais* in 1911. I cite from the critical edition of *Philosophical Culture*, which follows the revised edition (Leipzig: Kröner, 1919) that had been corrected by Simmel shortly before his death (*GSG* 14: 159–459; here p. 175). The interpolation is noted in that volume's varia, *GSG* 14: 493. The essay was translated by David Kettler in *Georg Simmel, 1858–1918*, ed. K. H. Wolff (Columbus: Ohio University Press, 1959), 243–58; repr., under the subheading "Social Types," as "The Adventurer" in *Georg Simmel on Individuality and Social Forms*, ed. Donald N. Levine (Chicago: University of Chicago Press, 1971), 187–98.

years of the nineteenth century. His modernist style of philosophizing emerged out of his engagement with the problem of thinking the social when the still-inchoate boundaries between the humanities and social sciences were beginning to take on their modern contours.

Simmel's understanding of the possibilities and limits of historical and cultural inquiry changed considerably in the early years of his career. Leaving behind the "extreme sociologism" of the 1890s' *Einleitung in die Moralwissenschaft* (Introduction to Moral Science), which represented the human subject as a "point of intersection of social circles,"[9] and the associated faith that empirical laws of history could be discovered, Simmel developed his distinctive notion of sociology as the study of social forms. Then, for a period in the mid-1890s, he believed that focusing on the modalities of *Wechselwirkung*, reciprocal interaction, by which society is realized in becoming-social—in forms of association, *Vergesellschaftung*—would provide ample tasks for a lifetime of work. However, he soon grew disillusioned with the philosophical limitations of this approach.

Simmel's autobiographical account of the next major shift in his thinking captures his sense of intellectual adventure: the internal dynamics of his distinctive concept of the social extended the idea of "living reciprocal interaction" into "an entirely comprehensive metaphysical principle," which in turn became the basis for the relativist re-visioning of the "central concepts" of philosophy—"truth, value, objectivity, etc."—that culminated in the *Philosophy of Money*. In the ensuing years, Simmel's self-reflexive embrace of intellectual transformation, his attempt to "treat the irresolvable as though it could be resolved," found formal reflection in a modernist style of thought and writing that gives expression to his philosophical and theoretical engagement with the diverse modes of social and cultural inquiry evolving around him. Comparing the 1894 and 1908 versions of his seminal essay "Das Problem der Sociologie" exposes the theoretical and methodological stakes of his shifting disciplinary self-understanding.

Like so many of the most interesting minds of his generation, the young Simmel believed that philosophy in the traditional sense had reached its end. In 1894, he regarded it as an established fact that (in the words of the first version) "the science of the human [*Wissenschaft vom Menschen*] ha[d] become the science of human society [*Wissenschaft von der menschlichen Gesellschaft*]" (*GSG* 5: 52). The question was how to organize the modern, social scientific study of human (cultural, psychological, historical) life and thereby face the challenge of theorizing human existence in the absence of transcendental foundations. But the revised version of "Problem" that introduced his 1908 *Soziologie* no longer represents sociology as the inheritor of philosophy's mantle; instead, Simmel reasserts the role of (suitably reinvigorated and modernized) philosophical inquiry in the newly differentiated disciplinary landscape.

To understand the theoretical and historical significance of Simmel's mature work, it is necessary to attend to the ways in which his later thinking was both

---

9. As Köhnke pointed out (*Der junge Simmel*, 28–29), Simmel criticized his own earlier view of subjectivity in these terms in his 1913 essay, "Goethe's Individualism" (*GSG* 12: 388–416; here p. 391).

continuous and discontinuous with his earlier, breakthrough conception of sociology. Quite radical in his initial turn to the social, Simmel also quickly arrived at a clear-headed recognition of the philosophical limits of the resulting theoretical paradigms—which is not to say that he entirely abandoned the ideas and strategies of thought that defined his approach to sociology in (re)turning to philosophy. Both continuity and discontinuity play a decisive role in Simmel's intellectual development, and both aspects must be taken into account in assessing the historical and theoretical significance of his oeuvre and situating it in the larger story of the evolution of the disciplines in the early twentieth century.

Even if "human studies" have not (yet, entirely) been replaced by disciplines of the social, the historical transformation Simmel described in 1894 as an "overcoming of the individualistic way of seeing" has been institutionalized and naturalized in the intervening generations. As the history of his failed renaissances in sociology illustrates, the perspectival and contingent status of that discipline's own way of seeing has thereby been rendered invisible to its practitioners. As the history of reading and misreading traced in Part I shows, there are significant methodological stakes in this narrative enframing of social "science," and reflecting on the evolution of the modern disciplinary order through the prism of Simmel's reception can help call the assumptions of a whiggish progressivism into question.

Simmel's star has risen in light of the recent "rediscovery" of "the cultural." Yet his work is still mostly being appropriated by bits and pieces to bridge explanatory gaps, rather than as a theoretical resource that might help the social sciences reframe constitutive assumptions in more philosophically adequate terms.[10] Simmel's mature understanding of *Wissenschaft* and especially his views about the powers of argument and interpretation in relation to human social and cultural life could not be more profoundly opposed to a paradigm oriented to causal models and quantitative explanations.[11] For him, contingency extends, not just to particular interpre-

10. For example, the only (brief) discussion of Simmel's contributions to sociology in the fifth edition of Stephen Seidman's celebrated introductory textbook *Contested Knowledge: Social Theory Today* (Malden, MA: Wiley-Blackwell, 2013), occurs in a section on "The Rise of Post-Disciplinary Theory" in the chapter on "Theories of the 'Other'"; it conforms to the pattern of treating Simmel himself as "stranger" (309).

11. Simmel's approach may be fruitfully contrasted with what John T. Hall has characterized as Andrew Abbott's effort to reorient quantitative sociology on a "third path": like Weber and Simmel, acknowledging the "socially constructed character of concepts" without falling prey to a vicious relativism and "leaving the discipline stranded in a wasteland of texts, unable to engage in empirical analysis" (Hall, "Measurement and the Two Cultures of Sociology," in *Social Theory and Sociology: The Classics and Beyond*, ed. Stephen P. Turner [Cambridge: Blackwell, 1996], 184–85).

Abbott has tried to foster methodological reexamination of regnant sociological models, in particular via an internal critique of the practices and assumptions surrounding statistical practices. His 2001 essay collection *Time Matters* reviews his ambitious and nuanced efforts at what he calls "transcending general linear reality"—that is to say, the "set of deep assumptions about how and why social events occur" that shape sociology's standard (quantitative) methods—by persuading his colleagues that those assumptions "prevent the analysis of many problems interesting to theorists and empiricists alike" in the discipline. Andrew Abbott, *Time Matters: On Theory and Method* (Chicago: University of Chicago Press, 2001), 37–38. But in a long footnote to this very sentence, Abbott reveals the limits to how far such a reflexive rethinking of models and methods may go if it is still to count as social science: "I assume throughout that *theory exists to provide comprehensible and logically rigorous accounts of facts.* Definitations, but to the very existence of sociology, and indeed of social science as such. A founding figure who avowed a relativism that extended even to his own results and methods should provide a powerful provocation to deeper rethinking, of sociological objects and knowledge practices—and of the vexed relationships between "culture" and "society" and social and natural scientific forms of knowing, all the more as the category of life and the analogy with the life sciences shapes his thinking of the social.

Simmel poses questions—about facts, values, objectivity, laws, the definition of society and culture—that have lost none of their importance for the social sciences today in a fashion that connects them with the pressing matter of how to grasp the historical, cultural, human meaning of modern science as a function of human cultural life. Thus the *Philosophy of Money* explores the social, historical, and cultural meaning of quantification, linking it to the role of rationality in human life as such in ways that cannot be assimilated to approaches that take the actual operations of the social as a given or treat the reigning social logics as their primary object of analysis. Crucial questions about the structure and logic of social and cultural life today cannot be posed unless we problematize what quantifying approaches represent—configure—as accounts of "empirical" facts.

In the first, 1894, version of "Das Problem der Sociologie," Simmel presents the social sciences in general and sociology in particular as having inherited philosophy's task of understanding human being. He begins with a bold assertion: "The overcoming of the individualistic way of seeing [*die Überwindung der individualistischen Anschauungsart*] is generally regarded as the most significant and consequential advance historical science, and the understanding of human being altogether, has made in our time" (*GSG* 5: 52).

Although he initially identifies the historic "overcoming of the individualistic way of seeing" in science and subjective experience alike as a sign of intellectual-cultural progress, his own text in fact supports interpretation of the change as a shift in the dominant Western rhetoric of reflection. By the end of the nineteenth century (as the introductory paragraph just quoted continues), the question of "individual fates" no longer "stood in the foreground of the historical image [*des historischen Bildes*]." Instead, explanations in terms of "social forces and collective movements" predominated in which it was "rarely possible to distinguish the contribution of the individ-

---

tions of comprehensibility, logicality, and facticity are of course debatable. Some theorists believe that empiricists' 'facts' are uninteresting or artifactual while some empiricists believe that theorists' theories are incomprehensible or esthetic. But despite their *disagreements about content, the two sides agree that theory aims to explain why facts are what they are*" (38n; my emphases). Notable ontological and epistemological assumptions are in play here, which remain unquestioned. To concede that sociologists may disagree regarding "comprehensibility, logicality, and facticity" while insisting that "theory aims to explain why facts are what they are" is to illustrate how effectively intellectual culture shaped by a narrow understanding of scientific ideas and methods helps place the domination of logics of quantification beyond critique. As Simmel's genealogy of quantitative logics and knowledge practices in the *Philosophy of Money* demonstrates, what is at issue is formal in a philosophical sense: what counts as "explanation" or even as "logic"—and therewith the ontological status of social facts and the constitutive opposition between "empirical" and "theoretical" inquiry itself: the very liminal space identified in Simmel's *View of Life* as nourishing the "metaphysical root of logic itself."

ual with complete certainty: the science of human being has become the science of human society. No object of humanistic inquiry can escape this turn..." (*GSG* 5: 52).

In thus setting out "the problem of sociology," Simmel was pointing to a phenomenologically verifiable internal shift in the rhetorical means and ends, not just of science, but of reflection itself, a change in the objects of knowledge that was already a fait accompli at the end of the nineteenth century. This "overcoming of the individualistic way of seeing" was a broadly cultural, as opposed to intellectual or academic, phenomenon and reflected transformation in the "understanding of the human" as such: "the tendency to trace every individual occurrence back to the historical situation, to the needs and accomplishments of the totality" was making itself felt everywhere: in the arts, in religious and economic life, in "morality as in technical culture," in politics and in medicine (*GSG* 5: 52). As the *Philosophy of Money* would demonstrate, the hermeneutic implications of the new style of thought extended into every sphere of collective and individual life, even reaching into the intimacy of subjective experience itself.

On Simmel's view, then, the historical (but also empirical, psychological, cultural) turn embodied in the universal tendency to reframe explanation in terms of social or historical totalities was itself a matter of historical, phenomenological experience by the end of the nineteenth century. The ubiquitous tendency to historicize, to contextualize and de-individualize, gave rise to "the problem of sociology," that is to say, of distinguishing the discipline from the general tendency it epitomized.

In 1894, Simmel's essay "Das Problem der Sociologie" proposed his solution. The socially oriented way of knowing (*Richtung des Erkennens*; literally, "tendency or direction of cognition") was so generally admissible as to constitute a "regulative principle for all humanistic inquiry and for that very reason could not ground *any particular independent discipline*" (*GSG* 5: 52). Any attempt to universalize the social as a ground of explanation risked reproducing the same sort of logical errors that had befallen its idealizing predecessor, philosophy. Without naming names, Simmel was arguing that it was time for the discipline to move beyond the all-encompassing "sociological" visions of philosophers such as Spencer and Comte. The new, post-individual rhetoric of reflection that had become the general condition for all thought and inquiry was a new paradigm rather than a principle in the sense of an *archē* that could ground a new discipline or science per se.

A vast array of aligned and competing knowledge practices taking a "historical," that is to say, contextualizing, approach to the study of cultural and social life were percolating in the fin de siècle German intellectual universe. As we now know, the cornerstones of what would become modern psychology, political science, economics, geography, history, Jewish studies, and other disciplines were also being laid. In this context, Simmel was warning against understanding "sociology" so broadly that it would become "nothing more than a collective *name* for the totality of the *Geisteswissenschaften* approached in a modern way" and thus fall prey to the "very empty generalities and abstractions that had spelled the fate of philosophy." The idea of a universal science of the social was vacuous at best. Understood "as the history of society and all its contents, that is, in the sense of an explanation of everything that happens by means of social forces and configurations," sociology would not be a discipline at all, but rather, like induction, "a method of cognition, a heuristic principle" applicable to "an infinity of diverse areas of knowledge" (GSG 5: 52–53).

To resolve the problem he had identified, Simmel proposed focusing on the "forms of association [*Vergesellschaftung*]." Establishing a distinct object of inquiry would enable the discipline to become a scientific study of the social as such and thus neither "a mere methodology [*Methodik*] for other sciences nor just a new word for the complex of all historical sciences" (GSG 5: 60–61)—to avoid the "empty generalities and abstractions" of an obsolete idealism and champion "the overcoming of the individualistic way of seeing" that characterized "modern" approaches in the cultural and humanistic disciplines (GSG 5: 52–53). In 1894, then, Simmel aimed squarely at replacing philosophy with sociology as the master discipline and paradigm for inquiry in the *Geisteswissenschaften* as a whole. This was the Simmel who wrote Bouglé that he would henceforth be "devoting [him]self entirely to sociological studies."

Simmel's faith that sociology could be established on a firmer footing via his methodological strategy was such that he enthusiastically disseminated "Das Problem der Sociologie," which was translated into multiple languages and published in the most important new social science journals over the next few years. But his conviction that sociology would be able to displace philosophy with a general science of the social was relatively short-lived. As Simmel delved into what he initially conceived of as a "psychology of money," he confronted methodological difficulties that provoked serious rethinking: the fundamental problem of how to theorize value could not be resolved in sociological—in self-referentially contextualist—terms. In and through money, the social formation of value acquired historical and cultural force and re-acted upon its conditions of genesis in material and ideal ways that called for more complex theorization.

In working on *Philosophie des Geldes*, Simmel encountered phenomena such as emergent properties and downward causation that would eventually be construed as counterevidence against the reductively quantitative, positive views of social reality then just beginning their ascendance in (social) science. But as his thinking matured and evolved, significant, countervailing institutional developments were also under way. Simmel's attempt to negotiate his conflicts with Durkheim over sociological methods had proved (to put it mildly) unsuccessful, and by 1899, he was distancing himself from the social sciences as a whole, representing himself as the isolated proponent of a "distinctive" version of sociology even in Germany. To be sure, Simmel would continue to advocate defining sociology as the study of social forms. But as the radically revised version of "Problem" that served as the first chapter of 1908's "large" *Soziologie* attests, his claims for and about that discipline and the social sciences in general had changed profoundly by then.

As the author of *Philosophie des Geldes* (1900), Simmel no longer held that the developments that had given rise to the modern social sciences had consigned the discipline of philosophy to the dustbin of history. Indeed, his confidence that historical-cultural "overcoming of the individualistic way of seeing" represented a progressive development that was leading to the universal dominion of the "science of human society" had evaporated (*GSG* 5: 52–53). He had developed a very robust sense of the contingency and transiency of every analytic perspective, and while the second version of "Problem" carries forward a number of ideas from the first, it is a radically different essay.[12]

As he put the finishing touches on his "large" *Soziologie: Untersuchungen über die Formen der Vergesellschaftung* (Sociology: Investigations into the Forms of Association) in 1908 in response to the exciting possibility of a professorship at Heidelberg, Simmel was all too clearly aware of the negative effects of his continuing identification as the author of the *Einleitung in die Moralwissenschaft*—that is to say, with precisely the reductive and debunking, evolutionist mode of philosophizing that characterizes the opening of 1894's "Das Problem der Soziologie." In his revised account of "the problem of sociology," Simmel defended his concept of the discipline but at the same time attempted to redraw philosophical lines of demarcation.

Simmel prefaces his 1908 *Soziologie* with a two-paragraph statement that foregrounds the inaugural and exploratory—and thus, in his mature sense, philosophical—nature of these "investigations into the forms of association." Unlike a study that follows the previously "legitimated epistemic ends and methods of an established science," he emphasizes, a novel undertaking such as his cannot even assume that its "problematic [*Fragestellung*]" will be recognizable. Since "the line that it traces through the phenomena" lacks precedent, "the determination of its place in the system of the sciences, the explication of its methods and their possible fruitfulness" is a "new and independent task" that must precede the investigation proper. He warns the reader of his attempt to "give the vacillating concept of sociology a univocal content governed by *a single* methodologically reliable thinking of the problem [*Problemgedanken*]" to keep the "problematic developed in the first chapter" continuously in mind, lest the rest of the work appear to be "an accumulation of disconnected facts and reflections" (*GSG* 11: 9).

The revised version of "Problem" opens with a hypothetical invocation of a naturalistic account of the origins of knowledge, thereby situating the project of the *Soziologie* in dialectical relation to the very sort of excessively "critical" or analytical approach with which Simmel was unjustly identified. In this new passage, the sea change in his thinking finds expression in a modified account of the meaning of the

---

12. Simmel had reworked and expanded the essay for publication in Italian in 1899 ("Il problema della sociolgia," *GSG* 17: 107–17) and sent the revised version of "Problem" to Bouglé with the very letter of December 13, 1899, in which he declared that he was not a sociologist at all. In his account of the genesis of the 1908 *Soziologie*, Rammstedt notes that this rewritten version, which included some passages from Simmel's earlier work on group cohesion, was incorporated "with only slight changes" into the new version of "Problem" that served as the introductory chapter of the 1908 volume (*GSG* 11: 893) Although that new, 49-page version includes crucial opening and concluding passages not present in the (10-page) Italian version, in striking contrast to the usual practice in other volumes of the *Gesamtausgabe*, no attempt was made to collate the differing versions of "Problem" and identify varia; in editorial terms, the 1908 version has been treated as a new text with the same title.

rhetorical shift that he had identified as defining "modern" approaches in the social and human sciences in 1894:

> If it is correct that human cognition developed out of practical necessities, since knowledge of the truth is a weapon in the struggle for existence both with respect to extra-human being and in the competition of human beings among one another—even so it has long since become unbound from this origin, and changed from a mere means for the ends of action into a definitive end in itself. (*GSG* 11: 13)

Here Simmel reprises one of the key insights of the *Philosophy of Money*: the products of human culture—objects, but also forms of association—gain independent value and existence and create a "superindividual" realm of their own. This realm, the world of objective culture, can be understood neither in individualistic nor in instrumental terms.

In gaining independence and self-sufficiency as an end in itself, Simmel continues, knowledge, even scientific knowledge, has by no means "severed all relations to the interests of praxis." But these now appear as "reciprocal interactions between two realms with their own independent laws." Thus cognition leads "in technology to the realization of external willed ends," even as a "need for theoretical insight" arises in the realm of praxis. The practices and techniques of life that make up objective culture give rise to new, higher-order forms of reflection. Accounting for this *Wechselwirkung*, this reciprocity, between knowledge, reflection, and the social world was at the heart of Simmel's philosophy of life. As the next lines make clear, Simmel has taken both Nietzsche and Marx to heart. Not only do

> inner and outer practical circumstances alike acquire the need for theoretical insight; sometimes new directions of thought arise whose purely abstract character nonetheless only extends the interests of a new feeling and desiring into the problematics and forms of intellectuality. Thus the sorts of claims made by the science of sociology are the theoretical extension and reflection of the practical power that the masses have gained over the interests of the individual during the nineteenth century. (*GSG* 11: 13)

The rhetorical gesture with which Simmel began the first version of "Problem"—appealing to general consensus about progress in "the understanding of the human" altogether—has disappeared; he no longer situates the "problem of sociology" in relation to a positively connoted, objectively perceivable progressive "overcoming" of the "individualistic way of seeing" in modern knowledge practices. The "problem" is, rather, the direct reflection within the social formation that is science of the historic rise of mass society. Sociology as "theoretical extension and reflection" of the masses' "practical power": Simmel's importance for Karl Mannheim, and not only Mannheim, is evident.

The "concept of 'society'" itself, Simmel continues, both embodies the new "feeling of significance" acquired by "the lower classes" in the nineteenth century and reflects the "social distance" that caused them to appear, not as individuals, but as a "unified mass" to the upper classes who were generating those concepts.[13] As Sim-

---

13. The same erasure is also evident in English usage, but the apparent unity of this "mass" finds vivid expression in the German collective singular *die Masse*. The common linguistic roots of both words are

mel put it, "precisely that distance" between the classes—that is to say, the absence of the sorts of substantive connections that had integrated human communities in the past—found expression in this new theoretical abstraction: the only "aspect" through which the upper and lower classes were "connected in principle" was that they "formed 'a society' together" (*GSG* 11: 13).

The emergence of the modern sciences of the social was thus symptomatic, to employ more contemporary jargon, of a new constellation of power-knowledge: "as a consequence of the practical relations of power," Simmel wrote, "theoretical consciousness" was directed at the "classes whose impact lay not in the perceptible significance of individuals but in their being-'society' ['*Gesellschaft*'-*Sein*]." A new perspective on the relation between subjectivity and knowledge entirely was emerging, one that represented a historic shift in human self-understanding in the context of mass society: "All at once," Simmel continues, "thinking [*das Denken*] perceived that absolutely every individual phenomenon is determined by an infinity of influences" in its human surroundings—a new, relativistic perspective that was soon extended historically. Society, both present and past, now "appeared as the substance that formed individual existence, as the sea the waves," so that the social now seemed to be "the foundation whose forces would alone make it possible to explain the particular forms into which it had shaped individuals" (*GSG* 11: 14).

The "overcoming" of the subject-centered perspective construed in 1894 as a straightforward sign of epistemic progress now appears as a historically contingent and metaphysically significant shift in perspective. Sociology is no longer represented as the modern, scientific successor to philosophy but as a historically located knowledge formation whose ideas and methods must likewise be contextualized. Simmel's new historical and methodological self-reflexivity finds expression in a reframing of his understanding of sociology in terms of the philosophical (cultural, historical) significance of the emergence of modern social science. A historic cultural shift based in very real material changes had transformed the way subjectivity and subjective experience could be understood. If sociology is the intellectual expression of "the interests of a new feeling and desiring," and its scientific claims, "the theoretical extension and reflection of the practical power that the masses have gained over the individual during the nineteenth century," then developing a methodologically adequate form of theoretical self-reflexivity entails more than recognizing the historic change in perspective as such.

As a lived metaphor for the new, decentered understanding of human super- and transsubjective being, "society" was displacing religion. Simmel's modernist emphasis on the figurative transformation involved, on the generative, metaphoric force of the new experience of human being, is significant—as is the way he links the experiential-conceptual innovation at the heart of the new paradigm of human

---

ancient (Latin *massa*; Greek *massein*), but according to the *OED*, "the masses" was first used in the sense of "a large number of human beings, collected closely together or viewed as forming an aggregate in which their individuality is lost" (II 9a) by Sir Walter Scott. Christian Borch rightly begins his penetrating *The Politics of Crowds: An Alternative History of Sociology* (Cambridge: Cambridge University Press, 2012) by invoking Simmel.

self-understanding to the conditions and context of its emergence in the modern metropolis.

The introductory methodological chapter of Simmel's purportedly "formalist" *Soziologie* continues with a reflection on the historical and philosophical significance of the theoretical and methodological transformation—the paradigm shift—in and through which what I call the modern disciplinary imaginary was coming into being. In a passage that exposes the theoretical significance of his modernist self-reflexivity, Simmel comments on the implications of the new way of representing, of figuring, human life that had emerged:

> This tendency of thought [*Denkrichtung*] supported modern relativism, the inclination to dissolve the singular and substantial in reciprocal interactions; the individual was only the place where social threads were intertwined, the personality only the particular form in which this happened. Having brought to consciousness that all human action takes place in society and nothing can escape its influence, it seemed to follow that everything that was not the science of external nature must be the science of society. (*GSG* 11: 14)

That universalized and reductive contextualism gave rise to the "idea [*Vorstellung*] of sociology as a science of the human as a whole" that comprised all the cultural and social disciplines, "ethics as well as cultural history, political economy as well as religious studies, aesthetics as well as demography, politics as well as ethnology" (*GSG* 11: 14). The implicit metaphor of society as the universal container of all things social led to theoretical as well as methodological confusion: an idea of sociology as the overarching science of the social rendered reflection on the new way of seeing brought about by the historic shift in perspective not just impossible but superfluous and unnecessary. Here Simmel doubles back in a self-reflexive commentary on the original version of "Problem." "Since the objects of these sciences were actualized within the framework of the social: the science of the human was supposed to be the science of society" (*GSG* 11: 14).

A very significant distance has been traversed. To be sure, Simmel still objects to the representation of sociology as the generic master science of the social. He goes on at this point to reprise and extend his 1894 argument addressing what we would call the genetic fallacy: just as the fact that "their objects are actualized only in human consciousness" does not turn sciences such as "chemistry, botany, and astronomy" into part of psychology, the fact that "human thinking and acting takes place in society and is determined by it" does not "make sociology into a comprehensive science" of thought and action (*GSG* 11: 14). Yet Simmel distances himself very explicitly from the notion that the social sciences have displaced philosophy. He identifies the apotheosis of the discipline that he is criticizing—the "idea of sociology as a science of the human as a whole"—not just as an unwarranted overextension of the discipline but as a misapprehension of the nature and meaning of the epochal change in human self-understanding that had brought into being a whole new way of understanding human knowing, including scientific activity as such.

For the mature Simmel, then, the "problem of sociology" lay in the tension between the comprehensive and universalizing impulse—the "new direction of thought" striving to find expression in "theoretical insights" and take scientific, that is to say intersubjectively valid, form—and the conceptual weakness of a reductive paradigm that can only explain by subsuming. The methodological crux was the pervasive misapprehension of the nature of the social epitomized by the representation of society as container, whose conceptual correlative is the understanding of sociology as the universal and most general science of the social.

Simmel still emphasized the historic shift in human self-understanding that had taken place, the "realization" that human being and doing in all its expressions is shaped and "defined by living in reciprocal interaction with other human beings" (*GSG* 11: 15)—beings, that is, who could not be understood in the reductive terms of the dominant natural scientific model of causal explanation, but only through the mutually determining interactions with others and with the "superindividual" sphere of culture that such *Wechselwirkung* generates and sustains.

But the implications of that shift itself had been drastically misunderstood. The new perspective neither eliminated the need for philosophy nor provided the foundation for a general or comprehensive science of human collective life. Rather, as a historic "insight," a revolution in human self-understanding, it entailed a transformation in knowledge practices tout court. The consciousness of the social as such catalyzed by industrialization, urbanization, and political change in the course of the nineteenth century had given rise to a new mode of historical self-reflexivity, "to a new mode of observation [*Betrachtungsweise*] in all the so-called human sciences [*Geisteswissenschaften*]"—and thereby inaugurated a new scientific era.

The eclipse of subject-centered philosophy—of "the science of the human"—was, then, still a fait accompli. But in 1908, in an implicit critique of his own earlier, less methodologically and philosophically reflexive views regarding the implications of that eclipse, Simmel now describes the change that had taken place as a consequence of the rise of mass society even more explicitly as a shift in the culturally dominant rhetoric of reflection. The passage continues:

> It is now no longer possible to explain historical facts in the most broadest sense of the term, the contents of culture, the types of economy, the norms of ethics, from the individual human being, his understanding and interests and, where this fails, to turn immediately to metaphysical or magical causes.... Rather we now believe that historical phenomena can be understood through the reciprocal interactions and cooperation of individuals, the summation and sublimation of countless individual contributions, through the incorporation of social energy in configurations that stand and develop beyond the individual. (*GSG* 11: 15)

The notion of form and formation in play here is hardly formalist. Simmel goes on to give language and religious institutions as paradigmatic examples of the sort of objectively existing, historically persisting transindividual sociocultural configurations he calls *Gebilde*.

Along with the rest of the *Geisteswissenschaften*, philosophy had to change. Human being and doing simply could not any longer be understood in terms of the inherited rhetoric of (transcendental, ahistorical) subjectivity. For all his cultivation of aesthetics and individuality, his efforts to revitalize metaphysics and ethics in a new key, Simmel never abandoned this conviction that any adequate form of human self-understanding had to encompass reflexive awareness of its own historical, cultural, and social situatedness. As in the case of his revitalization of the figure of "objective culture," Simmel's insistence on the constitutive importance of the sociocultural situation of thought for philosophy marks him as both the inheritor of the Herderian and Hegelian traditions and a key precursor of critical theory. This is the same point from which he would go on in his late work to reformulate the insights embodied in that tradition in ways that were influential on thinkers, including Heidegger, who rejected the social turn on principle.

Like every historically situated form of consciousness, the revolutionary new perspective that had emerged in modernity had both limits and perils. Not only, as Simmel would continue to argue throughout his life, are there aspects of human existence that cannot be explained in social (superindividual) terms. The concept of society may also, in itself, be a cause of significant confusion. Earlier on, Simmel had seemed to suggest that a kind of transcendence or absoluteness could be predicated of the forms of association as such.[14] In the course of writing *Philosophie des Geldes*, he had become more cautious in his epistemic views and developed a more sophisticated account of the reflective conceptual foundations of disciplinarity.

Simmel's larger claim for sociology as the study of the unity of interactive form is accordingly more cautiously posed. "If there is to be a science whose object is society and nothing else," he writes, its sole possible object must be

> these reciprocal interactions, these types and forms of association. For everything else that is within "society," realized through it and in its frame, is not society itself but only a content that has taken on this form of coexistence or that this form of coexistence has taken on [*anbildet*] and that only together with it brings into being the real configuration [*reale Gebilde*] that is called "society" in the broader and usual sense. (*GSG* 11: 19–20)

Founding a "special science of the social as such" requires a constitutive act of "scientific abstraction" because only through such abstraction is the complex reality of social process, "the facts we designate as social-historical reality, really projected onto the level of the purely social." In an act of thought, a discipline-defining process of abstraction, "the forms of reciprocal interaction [*Wechselwirkung*] or association [*Vergesellschaftung*; literally, becoming-social] are brought together and placed methodically under a unified scientific point of view" (*GSG* 11: 20).

This "real configuration" that is the referent of the notion of "society" has a distinctive sort of existence: it can be seen as an objectively existing reality with actual effects, yet its existence is virtual or conceptual. The "social" is a phenomenon of objective culture, which is by no means to say that it is merely "ideal." That the actual historical phenomena which constitute social reality, the "highly complicated facts of historical society" cannot be brought together "under a *single* scientific point of view," gives rise to the multiplicity of social sciences: "The concepts of politics, the economy, culture, etc., generate conceptual series [*Erkenntnisreihen*]" along their

---

14. Simmel speaks of "a field that can justifiably be abstracted: that of association itself and its forms" (*GSG* 5: 55).

own lines, each of which gets at different aspects of the historical-cultural phenomena of the social as a whole by constructing "unique historical processes" out of "certain parts of the facts" (*GSG* 11: 17). The "problem of sociology," then, is what it would mean for sociology to generate a similar, "methodological-scientific unity" from which to approach that phenomena in a way distinct from other, particular social sciences:

> If there is to be a special science of sociology, the concept of *society* [or the social: *die Gesellschaft*] as such . . . must be able to subject the social-historical givens [*gesellschaftgeschichtliche Gegebenheiten*] to a new abstraction and collation in such a way that certain determinations that have until now only been observed in other diverse combinations are recognized as belonging together and therefore as objects of a *single* science. (*GSG* 11: 17)

The perspectival construction of reality (and, as we shall see shortly, the metaphorical quality of the form/content distinction) comes into play here. "Society as such," Simmel writes, does not exist, for there is no such thing as "interaction as such," but only interactions of "definite types" that, in taking place, as he emphasizes, are "neither the cause nor the effect" of society but rather, "already, immediately, society itself" (*GSG* 11: 24). At times, Simmel sounds very close to a contemporary such as Ernst Mach or Fritz Mauthner. Philosophically, though, he is closer to Spinoza, to Aristotle—and at times to the ancient Skeptics.

At this point, Simmel takes a very interesting turn, in which his mature nominalism provides a new perspective on sociology and simultaneously on the emergent disciplinary order as a whole. It is "only the limitless breadth and diversity" of these constantly operative macro- and microscopic interactions, he adds, that

> has given the general concept of society [*Allgemeinbegriff Gesellschaft*] an apparently independent historical reality. It is perhaps in this hypostasization of a mere abstraction that the cause of the distinctive exaggeration and uncertainty that has attached itself to this concept and to the discussions regarding general sociology up to now lies—just as one did not really make progress with the concept of life as long as science treated it as a unified phenomenon of immediate reality. (*GSG* 11: 24–25)

Simmel is here criticizing the very sort of hypostasization of form for which he has so often been unjustly condemned. The very concrete, encultured process of abstraction that he has just argued constitutes the necessary basis of the science of society produces, as it were, its own transcendental illusion. And Simmel's analogy (not mentioned in 1894) between the methodological and conceptual shifts that inaugurated the life and social sciences respectively bears deeper consideration—particularly since it is followed by the oft-cited passage in which he develops the image of sociology as a kind of geometry of the social.

Abandoning the tendency to hypostasize abstractions and learning to think of the universal in a decentered way, via a focus on localized "individual processes," enabled scientific progress in the study of life as such, and a similar attention to the particulars, to the study of social processes in their diversity, must precede genuine understanding of the social. Thus far, as Simmel puts it later in the chapter, the objects of the social sciences had been those large-scale "social phenomena" that make up, as it were, the "large organs and systems" of social life in which the "reciprocally interacting forces have already crystallized out of their immediate bearers" and become "at least ideally unities"—that is to say, institutions, structures, regularized practices, and objectified organizational forms (GSG 11: 32).

But beyond "objective configurations" that have condensed the "singular and primary processes" of "immediate, inter-individual living and acting" into an "abstract existence," there are also countless "forms of relation and modes of reciprocal interaction between human beings" that, as Simmel puts it, "insert themselves between the comprehensive, so to speak, official social formations and thereby first bring society as we know it into being." Just as the "living body" cannot be explained in terms of major organs such as heart and lungs alone, so too "the actual life of society given in experience cannot be explained through configurations of the sort that formed the traditional objects of social science." Understanding social life requires attention to the plenitude of "apparently insignificant social forms" that are "generally not yet solidified into stable, superindividual configurations but show society as it were in *status nascens,*" as the "eternal flowing and pulsing" of lived interaction that is its permanent state of becoming (GSG 11: 32–33).

Simmel's conception of "living interactivity" (in the terms of the autobiographical text that, following Köhnke's dating, is roughly coeval with the completion of the *Soziologie*) was his methodological response to the loss of epistemic orientation, the "contemporary dissolution" of subject and object, truth and value. On his view, every modern discipline must establish sufficient methodological and epistemological self-reflexivity to ground its knowledge practices and, at least in a provisional sense, assure the validity of investigations undertaken in its sphere. The search for new strategies of thought that could do justice to a world gripped in eternal transformation—where inherited understandings of conceptual foundations and indeed of thinking itself were being rendered obsolete—thus led Simmel to a mature vision of sociology shaped by the same emphasis on becoming and the dialectic of life and form as his overtly metaphysical late work.

Laws, Norms, and the Relativity of Being

When he first formulated his vision of sociology as a science with social forms as its object, Simmel appears to have regarded the epistemological and ontological assumptions associated with his claims as relatively unproblematic. To be sure, in 1894, he already held that "there is probably no longer any doubt that 'laws of history' cannot be discovered; for history is on the one hand such a tremendously complex configuration [*Gebilde*] in itself, on the other, such an uncertain and subjectively bounded selection from the cosmic process, that there can be no unified formula for its development as a whole."[15] And yet, he continued, there was no need to entirely "abandon the hope of understanding history as a lawful development." However indivisible it might be in reality, the study of history as a whole could be divided

---

15. Simmel contends in one of his rare footnotes that he had proved this in *Die Probleme der Geschichtsphilosophie*.

up among diverse specialized disciplines, *Sonderwissenschaften*, whose objects were relatively "simple and internally homogenous partial processes." If the untenable aspiration to discover universal laws was set aside, this disciplinary division of intellectual labor would make possible "an approach to 'laws'" for the well-defined regions of sociohistorical reality (*GSG* 5: 60).

In particular, Simmel concluded "Das Problem der Sociologie" in 1894, the "qualitative simplicity" of the specifically sociological domain he proposed to distinguish from the rest of the "total historical process by distilling out the function of association and its countless forms and developments as a special area" would render "the discovery of specific laws less chimerical" than it seemed when facing the undifferentiated complexity of actual historical formations. Abandoning its inherited "high-flying pretensions" would enable the discipline (and here the metaphor of borders, so important to Simmel, takes a very distinctive form) to "found a securely bordered home based on clearly defined property rights" (*GSG* 5: 61).

By 1899, Simmel had set aside the residual traces of his early Spencerianism and with it the allied hope that causal laws governing particular aspects of historical and cultural life could be discovered. His new perspective on the nature of the social in general and on the status of social forms in particular had profound implications for his understanding, not just of sociology, but of social science altogether. While the second version of "Problem" still speaks of identifying systematic laws within particular areas of investigation, Simmel's views on the status of those laws had changed along with his understanding of scientific inquiry itself. Crucially, he no longer thought about the study of social life as capable of being divided in its totality into discrete *Arbeitsgebiete*, disciplinary domains. In a passage that echoes his remarks in the introduction to the *Philosophy of Money*, he writes: "It is always *one* reality, which we cannot encompass scientifically in its immediacy and totality, and which we must take up from a series of distinct standpoints and thereby shape into a multiplicity of mutually independent scientific objects" (*GSG* 11: 36).

For the mature Simmel, the complexity of lived cultural and historical reality was neither reducible to material causes nor entirely analyzable into ideal forms such that it could be capable of being understood as a sum of its parts. Although the proliferation of disciplines is a consequence of human efforts to come to terms with the world's complexity, such differentiation and specialization does not in fact resolve the epistemic difficulty that brings it about. On the contrary, as Simmel had demonstrated at a quite general level in the *Philosophy of Money*, the profusion of knowledge practices increases the density and complexity of human experience by disseminating ever-new, non-congruent modes of knowing the world. These partial views do not add up to a single coherent whole but rather to multiple possible wholes; the synecdochic "parts" result in a multiplicity of relative visions of reality in its entirety. Relativism and fragmentation go hand in hand with specialization and the advance of science.

Simmel's vision of sociology and of the status of its tasks had been transformed accordingly. In particular, his understanding of the distinction between form and content had undergone a sea change. In 1894, he had attempted to define a distinctive role for the discipline: apprehending and studying "the actual forces and elements as such, the forms of association" themselves (*GSG* 5: 54)—that is, the dimension or existence of modes of interactivity invisible to or unrecognized by the social and cultural sciences engaged in investigating particular contents of historical life. In reframing "Das Problem der Sociologie" in 1908, Simmel emphasized not the particularity of distinct disciplinary objects but the distinctive perspective and point of view from which scientific inquiry is constituted in each case. "Every science rests on an abstraction insofar as it observes the totality of some thing, which we cannot grasp as unified through a single science, from one of its aspects, from the point of view of a single concept" (*GSG* 11: 16).

Simmel still regarded the forms of association as the proper focus of sociology. But he now understood form in a relativist idiom, as a "methodological-scientific unity" abstracted from a more complex total reality. He conceived of social scientific inquiry in terms, not of knowledge of contents, *Inhalte*, as such, but of concept-governed interpretive relations to states of affairs. Perhaps it is not a coincidence that the key Wittgensteinian term *Lebensform* has such strong Simmelian echoes.[16]

Simmel goes on to invoke the account of knowledge practices familiar from the *Philosophy of Money*: "Faced with the highly complicated facts of historical society, which cannot be brought together at all under *a single* scientific point of view, the concepts of politics, economics, culture, etc.," generate *Erkenntnisreihen*, "knowable series," of empirical elements. That is to say, each groups experiential "content" along a formally distinct line of reflection, what he had described in the *Philosophy of Money* as *Erscheinungsreihen*, phenomenal series or arrays of appearances. Depending on the case, the evidence generated by such a disciplinary perspective may either account for "unique historical processes" or make it possible to identify a more general "timelessly necessary connection" (*GSG* 11: 17). The particular sciences are grounded in the phenomenology of historical culture itself, the dialectical counterpart of knowledge practices in the "historical sciences"—that is, in our terms, in the humanities and the social sciences.

But what is the status of these governing concepts or perspectives—what we would call disciplinary paradigms—themselves? On what basis, to extend our earlier discussion of the speculative (or, in the Kantian sense, problematic) status of the series themselves, could such concatenations of diverse phenomena be understood as unified objects of knowledge? On one hand, Simmel held that every such partial point of view could in principle illuminate reality as a whole. Thus adopting the sociological *Gesichtspunkt* illuminated sociohistorical life by drawing a distinction between the "contents" of social life—the drives and goals that bring about the interactions that constitute social reality—and the "forms" of association (and disassociation)—that is, the patterns and structures in and through which those interactions occur. On the other hand, he recognized that each discipline or "scientific point of

---

16. In his discussion of the similarities between Wittgenstein's thinking and life-philosophy, Nicholas F. Gier notes the convergence with Simmelian terminology but avoids the question of intellectual influence (Gier, *Wittgenstein and Phenomenology: A Comparative Study of the Later Wittgenstein, Husserl, Heidegger, and Merleau-Ponty* [Albany: State University of New York Press, 1981]).

view" generated a hypothetical and partial (political, economic, literary-historical, etc.) vision of the world.

Simmel was defending the methodological value of his concept of society or the social even as he conceded that the "distinction between form and content of society" was actually just an "analogy," an image dependent for its power on its resemblance to other knowledge-practices. To invoke an image from Simmel's later work, the emphasis on the figurative or constitutive force of the distinction on which the sociology of forms was founded had brought about an axial turn in his account of what makes sociology a discipline at all.

The distinction, however figurative, between social form and particular contents founds a consistent and cogent theoretical point of view, a paradigm for inquiry that enables diverse (series of) phenomena to be grasped as "belonging together and thus understood as the objects of a *single* science." Differentiating between "forms" and "contents" does not, then, simply identify but actually constitutes an object for sociology, one that would, and, Simmel argued, should, give it a well-defined place among the other human sciences—that is to say, an epistemic perspective and the authority to recognize and investigate an *Erkenntnisreihe* of its own.

Social form cannot be understood as the ideal "container" for or "structure" of social "contents." Simmel's conception of form—a mode of scientific abstraction that enabled him to focus on reciprocal interaction across a wide range of phenomena—describes a synecdochic disclosure of new dimensions and aspects of human existence from the point of view of a hypothetically or speculatively articulated concept. Grouping phenomena associated with space and spatiality, superordination and subordination, conflict or secrecy, to name a few of the 1908 *Soziologie*'s central categories, thus illuminated the lived reality of human social existence in new ways.

At the most elementary level, to identify a social form is to identify and relate the elements of experience via a particular type of *Erkenntnisreihe*, an epistemic series, into a conceptual or figurative whole. The same process reflected in this praxis of bringing together seemingly disparate "contents" (related to spatiality, hierarchy, quantity, etc.) under comprehensive "forms," helps human beings achieve self-reflective insight into their own social existence. But Simmel's insight into the (speculative) unity of social forms is conveyed performatively, through a self-reflexive experience of the limits of the social—so that sociological reflection leads back to the philosophical problems of individual existence.

From a relativist philosophical perspective, sociohistorical reality cannot actually, but only ideally or virtually, be subdivided into different disciplinary realms. Each discipline has its own legitimate vision of holism, and the hypothetical or even metaphorical stakes of the unifying concept that constitutes a knowable scientific object for sociology represents a theoretical, a philosophical advance—the imaginative constitution of a sociological way of seeing. This perspective subjected a wide range of phenomena to a process of abstraction and interrelation and thereby rendered them knowable in a new way, as socially and historically constituted features of human collective existence.

Simmel's mature work reflects his distinctive combination of Kantian and Nietzschean philosophical impulses. He regarded laws as a synthetic product of human intelligence attempting to come to terms with the multiplicity of the world; like money, they both express and make fungible the relativity of being, in a Kantian sense, to human subjectivity. But Simmel goes further. To clarify this point, it will be helpful to return briefly to the *Philosophy of Money*, which neither posits value and meaning as transcendent qualities of things themselves nor presents them as products of a subjective a priori synthesis of the objects of human experience. Rather, Simmel argues, they arise perspectivally, in and through human sociality: value and meaning are what we would call emergent qualities of the relations among things that come about in and through the living interaction of human beings and the world they constitute.

Significance is socially produced. Money's philosophical importance reflects its intrication in the (intersubjective, social) processes by which meaning and value arise. As a switching point between social reality and its symbolic superindividual organization—"valuation petrified into substance"—money illuminates the nature, powers, and complexity of human historical and cultural existence: it "expresses the relativity of things, which itself constitutes value" (*GSG* 6: 124). And just as money is "the sublimate of the relativity of things," so, too, "the norms of reality are not subject to the same relativity that dominates reality, and this not despite but precisely because their contents are the relationships among things which have achieved independent animation, meaning, and stability. All being is lawful, but precisely for this reason, the laws that underlie it are not themselves lawful" (*GSG* 6: 124).

For Simmel, being is never static; although the concepts, values, and interpretations through which it is captured may pretend to stability, in fact, by their very (historically and culturally variant) nature, they reflect the flux of being-in-process. And at a higher level, as it were, the same goes for the generalizing philosophical operations that attempt to capture the nature of the relationships that govern "the fundamental movements of thought."

> So the norms—whether these are called with Plato and Schopenhauer the ideas, with the Stoics the logoi, with Kant the apriori, with Hegel the stages of the development of reason—are nothing but the types and forms of relativities themselves that develop between the particulars of reality in forming it. They [the norms—EG] are not themselves relative in the same sense as the particulars subject to them, for they are their relativity as such. On this basis, it becomes comprehensible that money, as the abstract value of wealth, expresses nothing other than the relativity of things, which constitutes value and yet at the same time stands over and against it, as the still pole of its continual movements, oscillations, adjustments. (*GSG* 6: 124–25)

The human effort to grasp reality generates the forms and norms in and through which knowledge becomes possible and through which a kind of grounded transcendence emerges. Laws and norms embody and name the relativities of the particulars that they subsume. Like money, the "norms" of metaphilosophical accounts externalize and express (however accurately or completely) the ongoing human effort to understand, to give structure and regularity to, a world in perpetual transformation. As a metaphysical relativist, Simmel is not committed to a concept of truth that transcends the expressive function of reflection on the human contribution to the foundation of reality. To be sure, the laws are not themselves lawful—but because they instantiate or subtend the ontological relativity of what they subsume.

Simmel saw that the historically evolving effort to systematize and express the multiplicity of "reality, which we cannot encompass scientifically in its immediacy and totality" from any single disciplinary point of view, had in effect fractured reality into a number of "independent scientific objects" (*GSG* 11: 36). Epistemological reflection might seem to move us even further from the complexity and multiplicity of the real. However, this is not how Simmel understands the symbolic function.

The third-order reflective concepts that he here calls "norms" are themselves generated out of the phenomenality of thought, as attempts to describe and name "the types and forms of the very relativities that develop between the particulars of reality in forming it." As the paradigmatic case of money demonstrated, the value of such spiritual-cultural products is not entirely separable from this in-between-ness and hence from the contingent and historically situated activity of interpretation. Like money, philosophical "norms" express the relativity of things as a function of human self-reflection. However abstract these forms of forms may seem, as efforts to grasp "the fundamental movements of thought" as such, they are (metaphorical) expressions of and about the human relation to phenomenal reality. But Simmel does not stop at this ("neo-") Kantian point. Philosophical metaconceptions are conventions for intellectual self-reflection. They expose the relativity of being the only way it can be exposed, by converting it into value. They give the ineffable multiplicity of reality an intersubjectively accessible form and render it (relatively) meaningful. Whether we speak of Ideas or of the a priori, it is this attempt to grasp the bases of thought and of knowledge that is at stake. This brings us back to the question of the social.

While knowledge is not simply "a weapon in the struggle for existence," it cannot be entirely abstracted from that struggle, that is, from its sociocultural significance. Diverse, historically changing philosophical idioms—in my terms, metaphorics or rhetorics of reflection on the nature and status of knowledge—are constitutive elements of the ongoing sociohistorical "cultural process." And since neither subjectivity nor objectivity can be understood as independent of that process, the philosopher's habit of taking the discipline's own inherited modes and categories of metareflection as the final (literal) word on knowledge had to be overcome. The same historic self-reflexive turn that had brought the social-historical-cultural sciences into being—the realization that life is lived in perpetual reciprocity with other human beings and with the natural world—had given rise to new ways of seeing, new modes of understanding altogether. After Nietzsche, but just as much after the rise of modern technoscience, there could be no turning back to a world of stable unities and substances. Being had been revealed as becoming, the very possibility of thinking (metaphysical, religious, epistemic) foundations had yielded to the reality of flux.

A few pages before the end of the *Philosophy of Money*, Simmel interpreted the dichotomy between an ideal realm of laws completely capturing the causal structure of reality and the "concrete, historical, experienceable phenomenon of the world in that absolute flux" described by Heraclitus, as follows:

> If the world-image is brought into this opposition, everything enduring, pointing beyond the moment altogether is taken out of reality and gathered in that ideal realm of mere laws; in reality itself, things do not endure for any time at all, through the restlessness with which they offer themselves in every moment to the application of a law, every form is already being dissolved in the very moment of its coming to be, it lives only so to speak in its being destroyed, every solidification of form to enduring—however briefly enduring—things is an incomplete view that is unable to follow the movements of reality in its own tempo. (GSG 6: 714)

The opposition between an ideal realm of laws and an utterly transient material existence appears absolute, yet in this complementarity, a greater unity appears: "Thus," he continues, "it is the enduring as such and the non-enduring as such into whose unity being as a whole is absorbed without remainder." But human—symbolizing, interpretive, disclosive—being is itself this dialectic. The two realms are interdependent functions of human perspectives on the ineffable multiplicity of existence: "There is surely no clearer symbol than money for the absolute movement-character of the world" (GSG 6: 714).

The perspective represented here is no longer that of the man who had confidently declared that the individualistic point of view had been overcome and the science of the human replaced with the science of society. The author of the *Philosophy of Money* was a modernist in a different key, with a deepened sense of cultural and historical variability as well as of the implications of epistemic uncertainty. His understanding of both subject and object of knowledge were deeply inflected by awareness of the limitations, by no means exclusively epistemological, inhering in embodied human existence. Simmel had become more sensitive to the ramifications of the experience of individuality (or to translate into more contemporary language: the implications of singularity) and thereby to the significance of the point of view of the knower who understands knowledge, identity, and experience as historically and socially constituted and culturally situated. His conception of form had deepened, and he no longer assumed that historical and cultural life could be divided up neatly into simple and homogeneous partial areas of study according to a quasi-naturalistic disciplinary division of labor. Indeed, Simmel's erstwhile hope of attaining definitive scientific truths had been tempered by an increasingly profound awareness of the inevitable multiplicity of perspectives on a world gripped in change—as well as of the wider implications of the contingency and partiality of human knowledge in general.

Form, Figuration, and the Disciplinary Imaginary

The mature Simmel continued to struggle with the consequences of the ways the world, including the academic world, was changing. His writings bear the traces of his effort to retain his deepest commitments as a thinker and human being in the face of what he understood as utterly fundamental, historic transformations of human

Geistesleben—of cultural-intellectual-spiritual life—in modernity. Despite the continuity of many of our dilemmas with his, Simmel's way of understanding what was happening differs profoundly from the perspectives and vocabulary we bring to bear on understanding these changes from within the contemporary disciplinary order.

We encounter his thinking across an abyss and out of forms of seeing whose contingency and metaphoricity is all but entirely forgotten, through modes of reading psychologically as well as institutionally embedded in the highly developed objective forms of late modern cultural-intellectual life, including knowledge practices of seductively great disclosive power generated in and through disciplinarity. It is necessary to attend carefully to the constitutive role of metaphor in and for our own ways of thinking and seeing if we are to grasp the difference between the ways Simmel is actually using terms like *Geist* and what we happen (for reasons more or less entirely unrelated to what he actually says) to believe he must mean. We have already encountered the effects of hypostasized metaphors like "social structure" and "modernity" for knowledge practices in and outside the social sciences. The conceptual and terminological flux in Simmel's texts can be instructive, reminding us, for example, that even if the historical changes taking place in Simmel's lifetime have come to be regarded retrospectively as the dawning of a new era in the West—the emergence of a genuinely modern world—"modernity" is a theoretical, interpretive, and cultural, rather than an empirical, descriptive sociological category.

As those who have lived through the epochal technological and geopolitical revolutions of the past thirty years will recognize, it is no simple matter to discern when a new world is dawning, to separate essential from incidental, material from imaginary changes, let alone to know how to evaluate the process as a whole. For Simmel, as for Hegel, what was decisive about the modern was the shift within theoretical praxis to self-reflexive awareness of thinking about society and culture as historically evolving phenomena. At this juncture, when the assumption that we are or have ever been "modern" has been so radically called into question (see, e.g., Bruno Latour's *Nous n'avons jamais été modernes* [1991]), without our being able to set it aside, Simmel's strategies of thought are of considerable interest. But it must be kept in mind that in 1908, or even 1918, the "modern" world—in which human religious, socioeconomic, political, and gendered identity is no longer grounded in inherited institutions and practices, and the very experience of subjective individuality has become unmoored—was just coming into being.

The self-reflexive shift in Simmel's thinking about the emergent modern social science disciplines is significant. Embracing the "contemporary dissolution of everything substantial, absolute, eternal" in the flux of experience and replacing the lost ideal of a "substantial and abstract unity of the world-image" with the "organic unity of reciprocal interaction" in the *Philosophy of Money* had indeed opened up new philosophical—theoretical—possibilities. The strategies of thought Simmel developed there renewed the resources of dialectical thought by setting aside both the material determinism of positivist social scientific approaches and the idealism of the philosophical tradition in ways that are paradigmatic for modern cultural theory more generally.

The new concept of concepts that formed his point of departure in the *Philosophy of Money* enabled Simmel to capture the interpenetration of form and process in human historical life in powerful new ways; it also anchored the philosophy of life that was his crowning achievement as a thinker. His innovative methods of cultural interpretation and his speculative efforts to reframe philosophy itself beyond both materialism and idealism have had a largely unacknowledged, significant history of effects in twentieth-century thought. The lineaments of both were laid down in his philosophical approach to sociology as the study of the way intersubjectivity becomes something more than the sum of its "parts" in "superindividual" forms of association.

Simmel's new concept of concepts is at work in all his mature work. In his reformulation of "the problem of sociology," form or formation [*Formung*] is self-consciously approached as an "object abstracted out of reality" (*GSG* 11: 26), and the search for laws (or rather lawfulness) is complemented by attention to the historical process in which such epistemological self-reflexivity emerged. To be sure, Simmel is still fighting many of the same battles as in 1894, albeit with a radicalized sense of their institutional and theoretical stakes. A few pages later, invoking a category, *Gesellschaftswissenschaft*, that does not appear in the first, 1894 version of "Das Problem der Sociologie" at all, he asserts that sociology, understood as "the theory [*Lehre*] of association as such," is "the only science justified in taking the name of social science as such" (*GSG* 11: 39). Unlike other such disciplines, which are "defined by a particular content of social life," sociology is demarcated by a "new complex of individual problems" pertaining to the forms of association as such. In sharp contrast to his earlier optimism, Simmel sounds a note of general skepticism regarding the ability of sociology (and ipso facto any other such social (historical, cultural) sciences to address, let alone to resolve, basic philosophical questions about the nature, meaning, and significance of the social.

He concludes the revised text with an incisive meditation on the limits of the discipline, arguing that sociology can neither absorb nor replace "the philosophy of society," that is, the domain of questions and "claims about society as such and as a whole" (*GSG* 11: 39) that we might also call social or cultural theory. Simmel's new emphasis on the importance of historical and cultural self-reflexivity in all kinds of theorizing registers a self-understanding at once "sociological" and "philosophical" that had transformed his understanding of the "problem of sociology" since 1894.

Sociology, like other social and cultural sciences, had its limits. From his new relativistic point of view, Simmel no longer regarded it as sufficient to focus on the forms of association or becoming-social [*Vergesellschaftung*] to grasp "what is genuinely 'society' in society." Defining those forms as the discipline's unique "object" no longer appeared theoretically adequate; to address the significance of the new ways of seeing that constituted the social, it was also necessary to reflect philosophically on the nature, historical-cultural constitution, and ultimate value of those forms of social life as such—and to incorporate self-reflexive awareness of the epistemic position and mode of observation of the cultural exegete.

Defending the claim that sociology was the science of the social par excellence thus entailed clarifying the discipline's relationship to philosophy, which likewise aspires "to establish claims about society as such and as a whole." Reprising the argument regarding disciplinarity that opens the *Philosophy of Money*, Simmel goes on to emphasize that like every "exact" and empirically oriented discipline, sociology is "bounded by two philosophical regions." Below, as it were, lies the epistemological, the "conditions, fundamental concepts, presuppositions" that make any particular inquiry possible. On his expansive conception of the a priori, these comprised not merely logical, but also psychological and historico-cultural preconditions of a given mode of thought. At the other, so to speak, upper, boundary are the "metaphysics of the particular domain in question," where the disciplinary sphere touches on "questions and concepts that have no place in experience as immediately given knowledge," in this case, those that situate society and social forms in larger speculative wholes and address their value and ultimate purpose (*GSG* 11: 39–40).

For Simmel, questions about the meaning and ends of the social, no less than those concerning its foundation and constitution, lack the "categorial independence, that unique relation between object and method" that would enable them to "ground sociology as a distinct new science." Simply put, the deepest problems of sociology are not sociological problems but, properly speaking, "*philosophical questions* . . . that take society as their object." They "extend a way of thinking that is structurally speaking already given into a new area. Whether or not one recognizes philosophy as a science at all: The philosophy of society has no justification for evading the advantages or disadvantages of its belonging to philosophy as such by constituting itself as a special science of sociology" (*GSG* 11: 40–41).

Even if philosophy should be thought of as a science—in our terms, as a discipline—it must be recognized as different in kind from other such knowledge formations since its questions and problems precede and transcend specialized object domains. What he calls the "philosophy of society [or the social]," which is neither entirely different from nor entirely congruent with the enterprises that go by the names of social or cultural theory or the philosophy of the social sciences today, is not simply distinct from sociology proper. It belongs to a different sphere: If sociology involves a particular way of seeing, the philosophy of society entails reflection on the problems and limits of that perspective. Yet it is not clearly and distinctly separable from sociology, for the boundary conditions of ways of seeing are not themselves entirely articulable.

Insofar as any discipline is defined by a particular perspective, a way of seeing and constituting its objects and questions, it is constitutively unable to address philosophical problems concerning the nature and constitution of its objects. Because the category of society or the social itself is problematic, this circumstance is more acute in sociology than in disciplines with more readily recognizable objects. Simmel still holds that to focus on the forms of association or becoming-social, *Vergesellschaftung*, is to grasp "what is genuinely society in society."[17] But his understanding of the stakes in thinking about the social had expanded considerably in the

---

17. This phrase appears in both the 1894 version of "The Problem of Sociology" and in the revised and expanded 1908 version: *GSG* 5: 54 and 11: 25.

course of writing his monumental meditation on money as the paradigmatic cultural medium or form, the bearer and emblem of the practices of symbolic exchange that constitute the foundation and reality of human collective life as such. For Simmel, "most relations among human beings can be counted as exchange; it is at once the purest and most heightened reciprocal interaction" (GSG 6: 59). Money is the synecdochic instantiation of the interactive, value-creating processes of human association as such, which generate configurations and constellations that transcend particularity to bring a meaningful world into being. As the symbolic representation of value and the medium of human interaction par excellence, money epitomizes the cultural-historical process in and through which inter- and transsubjective interactions create and perpetuate that realm of value and meaning—the sphere of forms that are, in the terms of his late philosophy, "more than life."

Simmel's new rhetorical self-reflexivity is strikingly evident in the way he relativizes his own 1894 definition of the social. In 1908, the notion that "society in the broadest sense clearly exists whenever several individuals enter into interaction" is reframed as a hypothetical consequence of the "analogy" that grounded Simmel's concept of sociology in the first place, the (figurative) distinction between form and content. In place of his ambitious earlier claims for his conception of social forms, which had culminated in the assertion that "their sum constitutes concretely what one designates by the abstraction society" (GSG 5: 54–55), he now accentuates the process of "scientific abstraction" and emphasizes the nominalist and relativist character of the discipline-grounding distinction between "form" and "content," which are "in reality inseparable elements of every social being and event" (GSG 11: 19).

Simmel's mature approach to sociological forms self-reflexively emphasizes the boundaries to the philosophical and thereby the perspectival quality of every particular analysis. He consistently raises the question of the meaning, value, and limits of this way of seeing—for the sociological point of view cannot, by definition, give an adequate account of its own meaning or interpret the significance of the historic shift in human self-understanding that constitutes its own condition of possibility. The point is quite general: seeing from within a disciplinary paradigm always means failing to see what it constitutively excludes. Only at sociology's limit can questions be posed concerning the meaning of the historical-cultural process in which "society" has emerged, for these are also questions about the significance and value of the new, scientific mode of reflection on the forms—the lived and instantiated structures and practices—that constitute social life. But the emergence of the science of the social par excellence makes confrontation with the constructedness of knowledge in general unavoidable.

Having distanced himself from the uncritical affirmation of the "overcoming of the individualistic way of seeing" in the first version of "Problem" and deepened his understanding of the meaning of attention to the modes of reciprocal interaction that make up social life, Simmel's theoretical focus opens toward the subjects who provide the "content" for the forms of association that constitute and differentiate the social. After all, it is the particular drives, interests, and ends of individual human beings that "achieve social reality through a form or type of reciprocal interaction among the individuals"; and it is these "forms of reciprocal interaction" that "make the 'social'... into society [*die 'Gesellschaft'... zur Gesellschaft*]" (*GSG* 11: 19).

Thus, in the 1908 version of "Problem," in place of straightforward assertions that social forms exist and that the abstract term "society" can be used to refer to the social totality, we find Simmel's nominalist insistence on the value of a hermeneutic perspective that approaches the complex reality of human collective existence as though it were structured in forms and contents. Not only had Simmel's concept of concepts grown considerably more sophisticated since 1894, along with his understanding of the social and indeed of science itself. Not only had he reframed his old definition of sociology (now situated four pages into the essay) as a hypothetical; his former claim that the science of man was giving way to the science of human society is foregrounded at the outset as a corollary to the sociologism that Simmel was indicting. He now argued that a new awareness "that all human action takes place within society and nothing can evade its influence" had come into being as a consequence of the rise of the masses and that that epochal shift in human historical consciousness suggested the seductive but ultimately nonsensical notion that "everything that was not a science of external nature must be a science of society" (*GSG* 11: 14).

But that totalizing vision of social science in general and of sociology in particular depended on a false hypostasization of the social as a sort of universal container. Society "appeared as the all-encompassing field, in which ethics and cultural history, political economy and religious studies, aesthetics and demography, politics and ethnology came together because the objects of these sciences were realized within the framework of society: the science of the human being was [supposed to be] the science of society" (*GSG* 11: 14).

Simmel's self-critique is quite explicit. His earlier faith that social science was displacing philosophy now appears as part of the same illusion he had been criticizing all along: the grandiose "idea of sociology as the science of everything human altogether." The expansive tendency exacerbated by the fact that "sociology" was "a *new* science" is evocatively described. All sorts of unresolved and uncategorizable problems had rushed into the new discipline for the same reason that "a newly discovered region always becomes the El Dorado of homeless and rootless existences at first: the initially unavoidably indeterminate and undefended borders permit everyone the right to take refuge there."[18]

However (and here Simmel reprises an argument from the 1894 version) throwing "all historical, psychological, normative sciences into a big pot" and labeling it 'sociology' was no way to define a science. "That human thought and action occur in and are defined by society" does not turn sociology into "a comprehensive science" of the social any more than the circumstance that the objects of "chemistry, botany, and astronomy" depend on being realized in human consciousness turns those sciences themselves into contents of psychology (*GSG* 11: 15).

---

18. This passage cited here and in the next paragraphs is from *GSG* 11: 15 and was introduced in the 1899 Italian version, *GSG* 19: 107–8.

To hypostasize the social was not just to make a logical error—we would call it a category mistake—it was to misconstrue the meaning of the historical and cultural shift in perspective that had given rise to the modern social sciences tout court: "The insight that the human being is determined in its entire being and all expressions by the fact that this being lives in reciprocal interactions with others must certainly lead to a new *mode of observation* in all the so called human sciences" (*GSG* 11: 15). Simmel was not only realigning his relation to sociology. He was reinterpreting the meaning of the very existence of the modern social sciences, placing his methodological claims in a new light to gain philosophical purchase on the emergence of the sociological point of view. The perspectival shift he had earlier represented as a quasi-organic development, a historical overcoming (Nietzschean *Überwindung*) of the individualistic way of seeing, itself called for further interpretation. The "problem of sociology" now opened onto "humanistic," philosophical questions about the historical and cultural meaning of the paradigm shift in and through which the modern social science disciplines and knowledge practices had been constituted.

Canonization Reprised

By 1908, both Simmel's understanding of his method and his conception of the intellectual mission and historical significance of the discipline he had helped found had undergone a sea change. While this transformation was tied to his interpretation of the historical-cultural processes and social changes we have come to identify with "modernity," he was not putting forward a "theory of modernity," much less of modernization.

As we have seen, the distance between Simmel's earlier views and the philosophical vision of sociology he articulated after 1900 has been underplayed or elided entirely in the dominant reception of his work within sociology.[19] This neglect is in part simply a quite ordinary and predictable effect of the growth and success of the sciences of society in the century since Simmel's death. As in other disciplinary formations, an early preoccupation with foundations and methodological self-justification faded in importance as sociology became better established institutionally and attention turned to the pragmatic demands of constituting and perpetuating research programs. But other factors were also involved in the creation and dissemination of accounts that elided or ignored key moments of sociology's prehistory.

---

19. As so often in the history of Anglophone social science, the history of translation has played a key role in obscuring substantive concerns in Simmel's work. Both the 1894 and 1908 versions of "The Problem of Sociology" had quickly appeared in English, in 1895 and 1909 respectively. Kurt Wolff published a new translation in 1959 in *Georg Simmel, 1858–1918*—that is, *not* in the 1950 volume entitled *The Sociology of Georg Simmel*, which would not be supplanted as the primary source for translations from the 1908 *Soziologie* for more than fifty years, but rather in a collection of essays and translations that enjoyed considerably less circulation (according to WorldCat, Wolff's 1950 volume is held by 1,221 libraries worldwide, nearly twice as many as the 1959 collection, held by 620). Wolff's rendering of the 1908 version appears in Donald Levine's 1971 collection, *Georg Simmel on Individuality and Social Forms*, which is still in print. However, the crucial passages from the beginning and end of the essay in which Simmel reflects on sociology's situation among the sciences and its relation to philosophy have been omitted (without comment) from the translation.

By the time Simmel was rethinking his position on the powers and limits of sociology in the second half of the 1890's, the study of the social had already begun to lose its specifically philosophical tenor. The meaning of science itself was shifting, with Marx's star on the ascendant, and the speculative systems of Comte and Spencer giving way to investigations rooted in practices of empirical research along the lines being pioneered by contemporaries such as Gustav von Schmoller, Ferdinand Tönnies, Émile Durkheim, and Max Weber. Even as Simmel continued to treat empirical evidence as "raw material" for ongoing inquiry into history and human life in general, sociological practice was coming to be defined by confidence in identifying "social facts" and making claims to objectivity and scientificity.

As seeing "the social" took hold and became second nature, a significant rhetorical shift took place. Questions about the monumental transformations of human collective life in process were increasingly cast in terms of purportedly straightforward empirical—historical, cultural, psychological—facts and treated as though they were amenable to practical (and hence, aspirationally at least, to political) solutions. The pragmatic legacy of the social survey movement gained force as new technologies of measurement and statistical calculation began to reveal even more impressive scientific powers in practices of quantification. Soon enough, history was being displaced by systematics as sociology's formative orientation toward interpreting the lived human environment came into tension with the power of quantitative technologies to disclose unseen and unthought "structures" of social life.

This tension continues to animate disciplinary developments. It is often construed historically as a conflict between the hermeneutic ("philosophical," "humanistic") orientation of German sociology and the "positivistic" orientation of the Durkheimian and American traditions. On my reading, however, the tension between the empirical and the conceptual is a constitutive feature of sociology better understood as a performative internalization of sociology's formative opposition to philosophy. Thus the bifurcation between a (humanistic, interpretive) focus on experience and the drive to quantification also finds expression in the division between the Weberian-Parsonian action-orientation of mainstream social theory and the data-driven practices of the quantitatively oriented majority.

The changes in the emphasis, focus, practices, and self-understanding of practitioners that marginalized Simmel did not happen overnight. Sociology emerged out of the wider field of the modernizing and professionalizing social sciences to become a discipline in the contemporary sense over the course of several generations. The process of establishing the discipline was not truly completed until after World War II, with the reimportation of a version of Weberian sociology into the vanquished Germany. It should be kept in mind that many of the first sociologists to hold academic positions in the United States came, not just from other disciplinary backgrounds, but from reform traditions outside academia altogether.[20]

---

20. See Stephen P. Turner and Jonathan H. Turner, *The Impossible Science: An Institutional Analysis of American Sociology* (Newbury Park, CA: Sage, 1990).

As Andrew Abbott has written in relation to Simmel's most distinguished advocate in the United States: "[Albion] Small was not, in the modern sense, a member of a discipline. Rather, he and his peers were trying to found a discipline." Like their European counterparts, they created institutions (professional organizations, journals, and in the United States, departments) that "aimed at anchoring a type of inquiry (as yet unclear in any detail) in a particular institutional setting." A pragmatic orientation—sociology as a science aimed at discerning rational means for the improvement of society—was widespread even among the more theoretically inclined. As Abbott emphasizes, "What they desired to found was not necessarily what resulted, of course. Small did not by any means want reformism to disappear from sociology."[21]

The tension between these poles was constitutive for sociology's disciplinary becoming. By the 1920s, as we have seen, Albion Small—the first professor of sociology and the first chair of a department devoted to social science in the United States and a redoubtable institution-builder—was lamenting that the growing institutional and practical success of the discipline had led to a general neglect of theoretical questions concerning sociological method. As the discipline professionalized and became institutionally established, the battle between empiricists and theorists was internalized and configured as competing subfields. History-writing being in the first instance the province of the victors, both sociology's philosophical lineage and the myriad connections between the emergent discipline and the "new social movements" of the time, with their strivings to place social studies in the service of welfare and social reform, were thereby obscured.

One of the great challenges of historical sociology, both as a practice within the larger discipline and as a scholarly endeavor in its own right, is how to maintain an appropriate level of self-reflection about sociology's own contingency and historical constitution. That is to say, reflection on the historical becoming and evolution of the discipline leads to theoretical questions of its own. As Abbott emphasizes, "the continuous name 'sociology' should not beguile us into thinking that 'sociology' in 1910 denoted either an institution like the discipline of today but smaller or a 'linear ancestor' whose only descendant is the modern discipline. Both of these statements embody assumptions about the social process that are radically ahistorical."[22] It is no simple task to attempt to think the becoming of the discipline in an appropriately multidimensional way. What retrospectively appear to be border disputes with philosophy, as Simmel's shifting meditations on the "problem of sociology" illustrate, go to the heart of what it means to speak of social "science."

Albion Small, George Mead, Thorstein Veblen, and other leading figures in the generation that founded the first departments of social science saw not just Comte and Spencer, but also Adam Smith and Montesquieu, as their precursors. The leg-

---

21. Andrew Abbott, *Department & Discipline: Chicago Sociology at One Hundred* (Chicago: University of Chicago Press, 1999), 180. See also Ellen Fitzpatrick, *Endless Crusade: Women Social Scientists and Progressive Reform* (New York: Oxford University Press, 1990) for accounts of the lives and careers of important female scholars and activists with roots in the Chicago "school."

22. Abbott, *Department & Discipline*, 87n.

acy of the Enlightenment, the faith in the progress of reason in history, was largely intact. And what made sociology a science was still framed in terms of the broader conception of inquiry captured by the German term *Wissenschaft*. As for their peers in other social science disciplines (say, Boas in anthropology or G. Stanley Hall in psychology) speculative, interpretive, and empirical questions had not yet been clearly distinguished. Theory and practice were deeply intertwined in their lives as scholars and in their different understandings of the academic's responsibilities to a broader public audience.

However, a narrower conception of science was rapidly taking hold in sociology, as Small's complaints about the dearth of methodological self-reflection attest. On the empirical side, the struggle between exponents of the "social survey" movement and those who advocated a statistically driven and causally oriented discipline goes back to the very beginning of American sociology.[23] By the time Talcott Parsons launched the inaugural version of the system that would come to dominate the theoretical idiom of the discipline in its postwar heyday, the problem- and reform-oriented survey movement had lost the empirical ground to the decontextualizing power of quantification. A new, more (natural) scientific method, statistically driven inquiry into populations, was on the ascendant.

To be sure, canonical thinkers continue to play a role in training and in the theoretical self-understanding of practitioners and schools of thought. But as the discipline of sociology evolved during the twentieth century, the terms of debate shifted decisively away from the sort of questions that had animated Simmel's work, even as their suppression issued in further subdivision of the field. What had been unproblematic in his lifetime became anomalous—for example, that someone whose primary teaching responsibility lay in the history of philosophy was also Berlin's resident expert in sociology. In the mainstream discursive construction of the disciplinary past that emerged, it was by no means Simmel alone who was diminished.

In the course of the twentieth century, social scientific training increasingly diverged from that of students of culture in the traditional sense. As new canons expanded and specifically social scientific methods took shape, familiarity with the traditions of philosophical, literary, and historical reflection that had still formed the common ground of intellectual life during Simmel's lifetime no longer defined disciplinary identity. The ascendance of the positivist philosophy of science further devalued inherited modes of historical and philosophical reflection. The intellectually robust and, soon enough, institutionally powerful Parsonian appropriation of the tradition provided sociological theory with an alternative, methodologically oriented model that, with its formulae and protocols, could stand its ground in the battle for a scientific rhetoric of reflection on society. In the Anglophone academy, "social theory" as a distinct field with a pragmatic social and political orientation

---

23. In 1901, Columbia's Franklin Giddings published *Inductive Sociology*, a work that in Abbott's words "makes causal understanding the goal of sociology and conceives of causality as a sufficient combination of necessary causes . . . deep down, his idea of theory was simple empirical generalization" (206). For a defense of Chicagoans' alternative "contextualist" approach to the study of the social, see Abbott, *Department & Discipline*, chap. 7 passim.

helped consolidate the social sciences while dialectical and critical traditions became identified with continental philosophy. Particularly as many important works were either only partially translated or entirely unavailable in English, questions concerning the complex history and origins of sociology, including its relation to critical forms of social and cultural theory, tended to be taken up, if at all, either by intellectual historians or within what increasingly became the specialized subfield of "historical sociology."

As the case of Simmel's reception illustrates, the field of sociology as we know it in the United States took shape around a very different set of problems than those its German founders had regarded as central. Within that discipline, established institutionally and operating in the mode of Kuhnian normal science, the theoretical efforts of most sociologists were focused on methodological as opposed to philosophical questions, especially before the cultural turn in the late twentieth century.[24]

Neither the social theorists who followed in the wake of Talcott Parsons and Robert K. Merton nor the empirical sociologists who swam in the discipline's parallel current were much troubled by the sort of fundamental philosophical questions that still occupied Simmel and his peers. Lewis Coser's concerted elimination of "metaphysics" from his presentation of Simmel as a "master of sociology" is a case in point: From the point of view of mainstream practitioners, the matter of the viability of the discipline's founding assumptions was settled—as, indeed, it largely continues to appear to be. For most sociologists, the role of "theory" is to provide framing for facts understood as in need of causal explanation. Today, when the sociological way of seeing has long since been naturalized and the power of social science in general and big data in particular to disclose truth is taken for granted, asking "What is sociology?" or how the discipline is related to philosophy looks suspiciously like tilting at windmills.

Despite the much-vaunted "crisis of sociology"[25] catalyzed in the early 1970s by internal criticisms from the left, the dominance of this particular scientific rhetoric has never seriously been called into question since its establishment in U.S. sociology. To place Marx alongside Durkheim and Weber in the classic triumvirate was to call for a more self-critical and historical understanding of science. Yet that development also led to further displacement and forgetfulness of Simmel's achievements. It has not helped that his legacy includes strategies of thought that have become identified with phenomenology and existentialism and modes of historical and cultural self-reflexivity usually associated with the Frankfurt School's perspective on social and cultural theory, both of which remain decidedly minority concerns in the quantitatively oriented disciplinary formation of U.S. sociology.

A broader canon of thinkers helped shape postwar European social and cultural theory and practice, but opposition to empiricist sociology, whether in the name of a phenomenological understanding of the social or a "critical" understanding of

---

24. Abbott's discussion of struggles at Chicago to define the department in 1950s illustrates the narrowing of the concept of method after Small's time. See also Turner and Turner, *The Impossible Science*.

25. Alvin Gouldner's *The Coming Crisis of Western Sociology* (New York: Basic Books, 1970) is the locus classicus.

theory, enjoys a very marginal presence in American sociology. First-generation critical theorists like Adorno and their postwar successors, including Jürgen Habermas, have been far more influential in U.S. philosophy and literature departments than in the social sciences. This continues to hold for other European sociological traditions as well, including British cultural studies. For most practicing sociologists, questions about the ontology of the social and problems of principle such as how to think about the systematicity of a mode of inquiry that cannot aim to discern laws in a natural scientific sense are nonissues, at best outsourced to philosophers of social science.

My point is not that such questions have disappeared. Theory continues to exist, of course, as a sociological subspecialization, as in political science, where the development toward quantification and away from historical-critical reflection on origins and philosophical reflection on foundations followed a similar path. But the social scientific usage of the category of "theory" is equivocal. Not only do the problems and philosophical concerns that animate such theorizing precede the establishment of the modern social sciences and transcend their purview institutionally. The relationship of these forms of reflection to their philosophical origins remains at issue in the very practices of thought themselves.

To recall Simmel's point, if philosophy can be regarded as a discipline, theoretical issues readily become configured as border disputes with(in) the (social) sciences. To be sure, the exclusion of a wide range of historical and philosophical questions from the disciplinary mainstream of these fields contributed to the migration of social, cultural, and political theorizing to other institutional locations in the contemporary academy. Both inside and outside the social sciences, "theory" also took on independent and quasi-disciplinary forms during the twentieth century. These configurations had their own vicissitudes, and (the discourse on) theory and the interdisciplinary practices associated with it proceeded along paths not necessarily taken by the mainstream disciplines to encroach on the territory of the social and even natural sciences.

The predictable result was even more subspecialization. In perpetuating themselves institutionally, theoretical schools fragmented the very fields from which they had emerged, further weakening already marginalized interpretive approaches to human existence, often in the name of (soi-disant) scientific methods or philosophical programs. The broader development of "theory" into a quasi-disciplinary formation by the late twentieth century accompanied and, in a paradigmatic illustration of Simmel's point about reciprocal interaction across boundaries, reinforced and was reinforced by the dynamic of specialization and professionalization in and through which the disciplinary order of contemporary scholarship was growing more elaborate.

Symptomatic of this history is that by no means all of the works and practices we refer to as "social" or "cultural" or "political" theory are part of social science, even as social theory understood as the basis for social science "methodology" in the more narrowly empiricist Anglophone tradition is hardly recognizable as theory to the critical social or cultural theorists operating in the continental philosophical tradition. Not only is (much of) what non-sociologists think of as social or cultural or political theory illegible to social scientists as such; within those "humanistic" traditions, to understand oneself as a social or cultural theorist is generally to see oneself in principled opposition to mainstream social science.[26]

Within the (discourse on) theory, attempts to overcome these gaps by expanding the compass of the signifier "theory" are in effect strategies for one party in an institutional, pragmatic dispute over the methods and aims of reflection on the social to get a leg up. Sociology's version of "social theory" continues to provide answers to these questions that help maintain the boundaries between social science and the discipline and traditions of philosophy—a boundary, often configured as an opposition, that traces the wider bifurcation between "humanistic" and "social scientific" practices of thought in twentieth-century intellectual life.

In 1894, Simmel presented his conception of social form as providing sociology with a definite object of study. Otherwise, he warned, it was in danger of becoming simply "a collective name for the totality of the human sciences approached in a modern way." Understood as "an explanation of all events in terms of social forces or configurations," sociology would be not a discipline at all but just "a method of cognition, a heuristic principle" of general application, like induction (GSG 5: 52–53). The discipline that Simmel later deemed "the only science justified in taking the name of social science as such" in fact sounds very much like just such a transdisciplinary method—but with a critical difference in the Kantian sense.

In 1908 Simmel wrote that the "special field" of sociology should be defined by drawing a line that transversed the other social sciences to distinguish "the pure fact of association according to its manifold forms." Sociology was a "specialized discipline" like epistemology, which abstracted the "categories and functions of cognition" out of the diverse modes and forms of knowledge. Unlike disciplines defined by a focus on specialized objects of study that could be subsumed with others under a larger umbrella concept,[27] these were, rather, "the type of disciplines that examine an entire field of objects from a particular point of view." Such forms of inquiry are distinguished by a perspectival, self-reflexive quality: "Not their object but their mode of observation, the special abstraction realized by them, differentiates them from the other historical-social sciences."

> The concept of society has two meanings that need to be strictly distinguished . . . first the complex of socialized individuals, the socially formed human material, which constitutes the entirety of historical reality. But then "society" is also the sum of those forms of relation thanks to which society in the first sense comes to be out of the individuals. (GSG 11: 23)

These two meanings or aspects indicate the need for a quasi-transcendental investigation. A sociology that focuses on forms of reciprocal interaction among human beings allows the social to become an object of knowledge without systematically

---

26. That these are territorial disputes is nicely illustrated by Abbott, who even as he espouses a Whiteheadean perspective on temporality dismisses "the confused reasoning humanists call theory" in an offhand comment (Abbott, *Time Matters*, 26).

27. Simmel does not actually name such a concept but, in a parenthetical aside, simply provides examples: "classical philology and German studies, or optics and acoustics."

(methodologically) eliminating its constitutive ambiguity. The enterprise of sociology as a whole is anchored epistemologically and metaphysically in the larger philosophical undertaking of thinking about human life historically and culturally—that is to say, it is a mode of self-reflection on the absence of secure epistemic foundations.

Simmel's mature approach is inflected throughout with a self-reflexive awareness of the constitutive distance from the empirical as such embedded in the sociological way of seeing. No longer does he confidently assert: "Society in the widest sense is clearly present where multiple individuals enter into reciprocal interaction [*Wechselwirkung*]" (*GSG* 5: 54).[28] Rather, after emphasizing the figurative nature of his pivotal distinction between form and content, Simmel once again stresses the contingency of his own interpretive perspective with an unusual invocation of the first person: "I thereby begin from the most general concept of society and the one that as much as possible avoids the conflict over definitions: that it exists wherever multiple individuals enter into reciprocal interaction" (*GSG* 11: 17).

In Simmel's thoroughgoing nominalism and relativism, his Kantianism cannot be distinguished from his Nietzscheanism. Just as he understood the apprehension of form as the product of a synthetic act of interpretation, he objected to hypostasizing society or the social into something distinct in reality from the interactions that constitute it. His mature concept or vision of the social has a hypothetical, self-reflexive quality: the distinction—itself metaphorical—between form and content enables a perspectival focus on interaction as such that synthesizes the flux of sociohistorical experience into a whole that can be studied. "These reciprocal interactions mean that out of the individual bearers of the drives and ends that instigated them a unity, that is, a 'society' comes to be" (*GSG* 11: 18). As in the case of epistemology, the claims that can be made regarding the theoretical object, "society," are inseparably tied to claims regarding the subject of that knowledge.

The category of the social thus gains its singular importance for the epistemological underpinnings of thought and scientific inquiry. With this self-reflexive turn, Simmel's sociology takes on the dimensions of a philosophy of culture. Indeed, the second sense of *die Gesellschaft* as the sum of forms of intersubjective and collective relations arguably refers to what we might call "the cultural." If in Simmel's reception, form has come to be thought as structure, then because "society" has become abstracted from "culture" by dehistoricizing and dephilosophizing his vision of the enterprise, not just of sociology, but of the social sciences altogether. For Simmel, reflection on society had a metaphysical dimension, just as his conception of the a priori was cultural.

In the 1908 *Soziologie*, as in the *Philosophie des Geldes*, Simmel's epistemology links the most general philosophical questions to the concrete challenges of reflection on human cultural existence. Metaphysics is inseparable from social theory: "Unity in the empirical sense is nothing other than the reciprocal interaction of

---

28. In a vivid illustration of the truth of Simmel's claim that his sociological concept of *Wechselwirkung* had been the point of departure for his mature thinking, the term's sole appearance in the 1894 version is this epistemologically blunt assertion.

elements" (*GSG* 11: 18). But that unity must be grasped with the help of a concept of form that implicates self-reflexivity in describing the multiplicity that constitutes the interactive unity of (cultural, social) life. The "problem of sociology" thus leads Simmel to the book's first excursus, on the question of the conditions of possibility of society itself—that is to say, to reflection on the "elements" or "parts" whose unity is being conceived of in the theoretical terminology of the sociologist. These are, of course, human "subjects" and the interactions of beings whose "drives" and aspirations are self-reflexively involved with sociohistorical and cultural structures and processes—beings whose a priori cultural existence is also the condition of possibility for social and cultural life itself.

In the years to come, Simmel's interest in and engagement with the emergent discipline of sociology persisted in the context of his ongoing philosophical concern with how new knowledge practices come into being and legitimate themselves. He was too historically sophisticated to conflate change, intellectual or otherwise, with progress, and as a philosopher of history, he denied that scientific progress per se could be predicated either of history in general or of the history of thought in particular. Methodologically speaking, Simmel was thus not in search of a single right answer. As the years went on and his theoretical interests diversified, he developed a range of strategies for thinking the multiplicity and complexity of reality, including that of human social and cultural life. Yet as Simmel himself rightly emphasized, his discovery that society could be thought of as consisting of forms of interactive process was the point of departure for an intellectual journey that culminated in his mature philosophical conception of *lebendige Wechselwirkung*, living reciprocal interaction, as a phenomenological description of the metaphysical reality of constant change. Hypostasizing his conception of form risks obscuring the theoretical significance of his relativism.

In arguing that the discipline of sociology should focus on the social as form and on forms of association, Simmel had set out to square the methodological circle: to unify sociological inquiry through a mode of self-conscious abstraction that did not reify its own categories and thereby eliminate or oversimplify the complexity of reality. His approach embraced the constitutive multiplicity of historically changing social and cultural life, with all its tensions—between individual and collective, permanence and change, temporality and spatiality; between centrifugal and centripedal, qualitative and quantitative, differentiating and unifying tendencies.

Simmel was no idealist. From the beginning, he used "form" to refer to highly diverse sorts of practices, structures, and dimensions of human interaction. And since his discussions always link particular examples of social and cultural forms to their opposites, others, and differential effects, in drawing attention to the significance of social and cultural forms, his work simultaneously pointed to the ineluctability of the historically, culturally, politically various "particular interests and contents that are realized in and through association" (*GSG* 5: 54), in the interactive reality of human cultural-social life. The recurring charge that Simmel was unsystematic or inconsistent—or, in its more recent, positive iteration, an impressionist or flâneur of modern life—misses the performative quality of his textual strategies for capturing the phenomenal and conceptual complexity of a modern, self-conscious experience of that reality—and thereby his contemporary significance.

If the *Philosophy of Money* has a large-scale architecture, the 1908 *Soziologie* has a fragmented form. This fragmentation has often been wrongly construed as reflecting its author's inability to integrate diverse lines of thought, many of which had been developed in pieces previously published in a variety of contexts, into a unified whole. But the tensions among the disparate elements that constitute the *Soziologie*'s parts are theoretically and methodologically significant; they reflect his effort, as he put it in the Preface, to "give the vacillating concept of sociology a univocal content."

Simmel anticipated the misunderstandings that were to come, emphasizing that it was necessary to "bear continuously in mind the central problematic set out in the first chapter" lest the book's remaining pages appear to be "an accumulation of disconnected facts and reflections" (*GSG* 11: 9). His text demands an active reader, one thinking along with the unfolding series of examples, actively engaged in a synthetic enterprise of consciously experiencing the modernist mode of formal coherence through which he was attempting to do justice to a multifaceted and fragmented reality. The viability of his approach can only be assessed by a reader sensitized to form, one attending to and testing the book's performative methodological strategy through reflection on the phenomenal series or sequences of appearances, the *Erscheinungsreihen,* in which his arguments unfold. Like the *Philosophy of Money*, Simmel's *Sociology* makes dialectical demands on its reader, phenomenologically enacting a way of thinking in order to demonstrate its value.

In a long footnote near the end of the revised version of "Problem" that serves as that first crucial chapter, Simmel invokes the "infinite complications of social life" itself to justify his experimentalist approach: "from the point of view of method, this book's chapters are thought as examples, from the point of view of content, only fragments of what I must hold to be the science of the social" (*GSG* 11: 30). The very breadth and diversity of material, the mixing of generalization and particularity, attest to the potential compass of the discipline he envisions. In "foregrounding the fully fragmentary and incomplete character of this book itself," he is attempting to make his methodological purpose clear. With the same, self-reflexive, skeptical gesture he had made toward the achievements of the *Philosophy of Money*, Simmel explains that since he is simply sketching out a conception for a new discipline, any claim to "systematically definitive completeness would be at best a self-deception"; if the "indubitable contingency in the selection of individual problems and exemplifications should appear to be an error from the point of view of the ideal of objective completion, this would only prove that I have not known how to make its fundamental idea sufficiently clear" (*GSG* 11: 31n).

From the point of view of Simmel's highly self-reflexive conception of disciplinarity, it was not just that systematic inquiry grounded in an understanding of human being as relative to and constituted by its social, historical, cultural context was still in its infancy. In contrast to the disciplines concerned with particular aspects of human social life, sociology's object was the indeterminacy and multiplicity of "society" or the social itself as a living and changing configuration of human cultural-historical existence. The discipline must therefore comprise, multiple, sometimes contradictory, sometimes overlapping perspectives. The forms of the social exist at different scales and intensities from the micro to the macro and thus entail attending to different, perhaps incommensurable metaphysical and epistemological points of view, and the ultimate nature and origin and final meaning and purpose of the forms of interaction that constitute social life must remain unknown to us.

The text as a whole is a performative demonstration of the modernist principle that (dialectical) thought does not, cannot, end in a totalizing integration. As Simmel puts it in the conclusion to the revised account of "Problem" in his chapter 1, "Like every other exact science directed toward the immediate understanding of the given," sociology opens toward questions it cannot contain: on one hand, toward "the epistemology," and, on the other, toward "the metaphysics" of the social field. Then, in a passage that indicates how the aesthetic-cognitive function of forms or figures in his writing reflects his modernist self-understanding as a thinker, he continues: "The dissatisfaction with the fragmentary character of individual cognitions, with the premature end of what can be objectively ascertained and of the series of proofs, leads to the completion [*Ergänzung*] of what is incomplete by the means of speculation; and these also serve the parallel need to complete [*ergänzen*] the disconnectedness and mutual alienation of these pieces into the unity of a total image" (*GSG* 11: 39–40).

Here as elsewhere, the formal multiplicity of Simmel's writing is thus radically unlike an accumulation of "disconnected facts and reflections." In its very diversity, the 1908 *Soziologie* is oriented toward representing social formations as distinctively human, historically extended and objectified cultural configurations of meaningful trans-, super-, and intersubjective "living reciprocal interaction." Reflections on the relations between theoretical method and style in Simmel's thinking lead the reader back once again to the problematic unity of (social) life—and to what the Introduction to the *Philosophy of Money* called "the possibility . . . of finding in every particular of life the totality of its meaning" (*GSG* 6: 12).

Beginning from money as "indifference itself," as a pure means whose "whole meaning and objective purpose lies . . . in its conversion into other values"—that is to say, in representing and relating difference—had enabled Simmel to establish a perspective for reflection on practices of symbolization in which the tensions between and within that indifference were exposed. As the symbol of symbols, the switching point between substance and function, money was "revealed as the symbol of the essential forms of movement of the spiritual world," but at the same time the product and bearer of the "cultural process" by which the natural world is encountered, appropriated, and transformed. The reader who followed Simmel's investigations of money's protean operations learned that life and the world need to be approached in multiple ways since ultimate epistemic certainty regarding the nature of truth is probably not attainable.

The reader of the *Soziologie* is urged to bear in mind the problematic status of the social itself, the perhaps unresolvable question of how to think about a unity that is not unified. Simmel's Kantian but also Nietzschean insistence on the undecidability of ultimate questions provided philosophical motivation for defining the discipline methodologically and shaped his performative, self-reflexive account of form. Even as Simmel identified and analyzed the forms of association as such, his text thus drew attention to the role of difference and conflict, tension and ambiguity, not just among diverse forms, but also in the multiplicity of modes in which such forms become identifiable in social reality. His distinctively self-reflexive approach to analysis and complex conception of form as interactive flux paved the way for a philosophy of life that takes important steps beyond both Schopenhauer and Nietzsche.

Simmel's exploration of the constitutive non-identity of the social as such is one of his vastly underrecognized contributions to modern thought. Grounded historically and methodologically through his *Philosophy of Money*, that exploration was developed conceptually and deepened theoretically in the "essayistic" and overtly modernist mode of philosophizing on cultural life for which, by 1908, he was already famous.

CHAPTER 8

The Stranger and the Sociological Imagination

For Georg Simmel, philosophy was less a scholarly discipline than a form of life. Unlike so many of the prominent philosophers of his generation, he embraced the new and the modern, attempting both to theorize the world transforming around him and to imagine a way of being that carried forward the best of the European cultural traditions through his principled relativism.

Simmel's efforts on behalf of "philosophical culture" in the years after the publication of *Philosophie des Geldes* in 1900 reflect this ambivalent affirmation of the ever-accelerating transformation of European life. Like other modernist writers and artists, he strove to do justice aesthetically and conceptually to circumstances where the relative certitudes of the nineteenth century had palpably disintegrated. Yet he remained a philosopher in a sense that the Great War and its aftermath would bring to an end forever. Like Bergson or James, who can also helpfully be categorized as modernist philosophers, Simmel was influential far beyond the university. His books were read and his lectures attended by a wide, educated, and (in the Kantian sense) cosmopolitan public: by an audience that would effectively cease to exist in Germany in the 1930s.

Simmel's distinctive style of philosophizing is immediately recognizable in the prismatic shifts of topic and perspective and the extreme self-reflexivity that render his writings at once mesmerizing and fatiguing. His singular combination of popular success and philosophical impact attests to the theoretical value of these influential modernist strategies of thought, in which the highly personal converges with the eminently imitable. In this sense, it is necessary to embrace the criticism that what he did was to *simmeln*—"Simmelize"—the world.

Foregrounding his style of thought opens up a new perspective on the intellectual legacy of the man György Lukács ambiguously eulogized as "the most significant and interesting transitional phenomenon in all of modern philosophy."[1] Rather than attempting to trace the diverse lines of Simmel's influence, I am striving to illuminate the topography, as it were, of his absence from twentieth-century intellectual history and render visible his shadowy presence and considerable impact

---

1. Lukács's 1918 obituary is reproduced in *BdD*; here p. 171. Simmel would be the object of a visceral attack by Lukács in the latter's 1954 polemic, translated as *The Destruction of Reason*.

as a modernist "transitional phenomenon" between nineteenth-century philosophy and twentieth-century theory.

My discussion of Simmel's reception in the social sciences has made clear that it is both anachronistic and theoretically misleading to categorize his work in terms of his contributions to disciplines or fields as we understand or define them today. It is necessary but not sufficient to recognize the value of his interventions in sociology and economics or to discuss the new paths he forged in cultural, literary, and art historical studies. For doing so cannot clarify what is so difficult to grasp from the point of view of our own, highly fragmented and professionalized intellectual culture: how and why Simmel retained his core philosophical interests and commitments on his forays into seemingly foreign territory.

In a period of ever-accelerating scientific and technological change and rapidly proliferating new knowledge practices, Simmel experimented with new topics and strategies of thought with an inspirational openness to the flux of the modern world he inhabited. Through his writings on the arts and on significant artists and writers no less than his essays on diverse, often seemingly insignificant social and cultural phenomena, he strove to extend philosophical reflection into new spaces.

Both directly and through those who adopted and adapted his ideas and interpretive strategies, Simmel's philosophical modernism helped shape what today is known as cultural or critical theory across disciplinary boundaries. More Nietzschean than Marxist in orientation, Simmel may surely be regarded as a critical theorist in the expansive sense in which the term is used today. He was, moreover, a significant predecessor of those who advocated critical theory in the primary sense given the term by Max Horkheimer. Simmel's conception of form as well as his attention to the "seemingly insignificant details on the surface of life" helped shape the thinking of Walter Benjamin, Ernst Bloch, Siegfried Kracauer, Lukács, Karl Mannheim, and others; like his impact on a series of lesser figures, this influence is well-documented.[2] It is worth briefly considering the case of the avowedly modernist philosopher Theodor Adorno (1903–69), whose metaphysical views and cultural allegiances resonate with Simmel's.

We know that Adorno taught Simmel and emphasized the philosopher's importance to his students.[3] In his struggles with Walter Benjamin over the methodology of the Arcades Project, however, Adorno squabbled with Benjamin, who had experienced Simmel as teacher, about the latter's legacy, and especially about the *Philosophy of Money*. At a decisive point in their correspondence in 1939, Benjamin remarked that he found Simmel's "critique of Marx's theory of value" to be "striking" and gently questioned Adorno's "skewed view" of their predecessor, going so

---

2. Concerning Simmel's impact on the Frankfurt School, see David P. Frisby, *Fragments of Modernity: Theories of Modernity in the Work of Simmel, Kracauer, and Benjamin* (Cambridge, MA: MIT Press, 1986). Frisby's introduction to the *Philosophy of Money* and his prefaces to its successive editions also remain invaluable resources.

3. Peter Gorsen, *Zur Phänomenologie des Bewußtseinsstroms: Bergson, Dilthey, Husserl, Simmel und die lebensphilosophischen Antinomien* (Bonn: Bouvier, 1966), 12. See also above, p. 148n15.

far as to venture "isn't it about time for us to respect the progenitor of cultural Bolshevism in him?"[4]

The following year, Adorno spoke on Simmel at a crucial professional juncture, an introductory lecture in Robert MacIver's Columbia University sociology seminar. Approaching him as a "philosopher of culture" whose "epistemological analyses" provided a distinctive perspective on "the problem of causality in the social sciences," Adorno developed a subtle account of Simmel's views on individual freedom. Disciplining gestures—"Simmel's life-philosophy belongs despite all contradictions to German neo-Kantianism"—frame the talk, attesting that the commonplaces of the reception had already been firmly established by 1940. Nonetheless, Adorno's reading clearly indicates his own debt to a predecessor whose thinking, he argues, leads to a call to reconceive both universals and individuals. Adorno's ambivalent gesture of canonization is epitomized by a concluding remark, apparently intended to open discussion: "in all its difficulties and contradictions, [Simmel's hypothesis about individual freedom] expresses how things stand today with respect to causality and freedom, arbitrariness and necessity."[5]

Long afterward, in the very different world of 1965, Adorno launched a frontal attack on Simmel in a polemical essay, "Henkel, Krug, und frühe Erfahrung" ("Handle, Pot, and Early Experience"). While acknowledging him as the "first" and still "canonical" thinker who had initiated the "return of philosophy to concrete things," Adorno accused Simmel of "psychological idealism." He contrasted his interpretation of the "handle" unfavorably with Ernst Bloch's more materialist "pot," charging Simmel with superficiality and banality and representing his approach as bourgeois affirmation of the existing world. Rather than "deciphering objects," he proffered "*Bildung*"; the very notion of "philosophical culture" was "annoyingly complicit," his "thesis undialectical" and of "static generality."[6] Adorno's charges reframe in leftist terms the plaint of Simmel's own conservative philosophical elders that he had uncritically embraced everything modern. With his perspectival view of truth and agnosticism about the direction of history, Simmel was perhaps too much of a Nietzschean for Adorno's taste. Yet his principled opposition to reductionism of all stripes and emphasis on the dialectical openness of concepts to the unthought, Simmel's philosophical views, and even more his style of thought and vision of the public responsibilities of a philosopher have an unmistakable resemblance to Adorno's own.[7]

Simmel's undeserved reputation as a philosophical idealist cannot be understood simply as a product of his reception in American sociology, for it was also shaped

---

4. Walter Benjamin to Adorno, February 23, 1939, in Benjamin, *Briefe*, vol. 2 (Frankfurt am Main: Suhrkamp, 1966), 808. Benjamin's *scheeler Blick* can also be translated as "envious view."

5. Theodor Adorno, "Über das Problem der individuellen Kausalität bei Simmel," *Frankfurter Adorno Blätter* (Frankfurt am Main: edition text + kritik) 8, ed. Rolf Tiedemann (2003): 42, 59.

6. Theodor Adorno, "Henkel, Krug, und frühe Erfahrung," in *Noten zur Literatur IV*, vol. 11 of *Adorno, Gesammelte Schriften* (Frankfurt am Main: Suhrkamp, 1974), 558, 559.

7. In "Georg Simmel als Prügelknabe [as Whipping Boy]," *Philosophische Rundschau* 14, no. 4 (1967): 258–74, Michael Landmann invoked the Freudian "narcissism of small differences" to account for the vituperative quality of Adorno's attack on his predecessor.

quite directly by the inheritors of Simmel's legacy within the German tradition—thinkers like Adorno and Lukács whose representations of his impact smack of self-interest. The ongoing challenge of discerning Benjamin's theoretical legacy and differentiating his perspective from the reception history framed by those who were, if not victors, at any rate survivors, and as such the authors and editors of the earliest accounts of Benjamin's work, should serve as a cautionary tale in approaching the sources in question. In critical theory, Simmel too is included in the mode of one who does not quite belong.

As a rule, Simmel goes entirely unmentioned in Anglophone histories of philosophy. Nor is it clear where he could fit into the dominant narrative—as illustrated, for example, by Anthony Kenny's 2010 *A New History of Western Philosophy,* according to which the course of "Philosophy in the Modern World" is captured (so its chapter titles) in three movements: from "Bentham to Nietzsche" and "Peirce to Strawson" to "Freud to Derrida."[8] Although Simmel's name appears a number of times (nineteen at last count) in the online *Stanford Encyclopedia of Philosophy* (http://plato.stanford.edu), there is no entry (even projected) in it that addresses his own contributions as a philosopher.[9] This lacuna may be regarded as exemplary. As currently conceived, the Stanford Encyclopedia will also lack entries on Emil Lask and Wilhelm Windelband, for instance. As a member of the last generation of German philosophers whose fealty to the national philosophical tradition was unembarrassed, yet unalloyed with anti-European chauvinism, Simmel—even more than contemporaries such as Dilthey and Cassirer, Rickert and Cohen—became forgettable for historical reasons both positive and negative.

As in the case of the genealogy of modern social science, the topography of Simmel's exclusion from the intellectual and cultural history of modern philosophy has a symptomatic quality. Methodological influence is often interpreted in relation to political lineage. But a wide range of modern political (and indeed more generally cultural) phenomena attest to the fact that the underlying historiographical assumptions are flawed—consider, to take two of the most obvious cases, right- and left-wing Hegelians and National Socialists. Simmel's complex philosophical legacy, which reaches into Western Marxism and new social movements, into the Stefan George Circle and that highly ambiguous formation, life philosophy, demonstrates, not that strategies of thought or modes of treating evidence are politically neutral, but that they are inherently open to diverse modes of deployment. Efforts to control (or to police) such openness are probably doomed. They are, at any rate, politically dangerous, as the fate of leftist utopianism in Eastern Europe illustrates. Precisely because Simmel's account of the constitutive non-identity of the social antedated the developments that sharpened and hardened such divisions, his work can be a valuable resource for contemporary efforts to rethink the category of the political in the aftermath of the debacles of the twentieth century.

---

8. Anthony Kenny, *A New History of Western Philosophy* (New York: Oxford University Press, 2010).
9. http://plato.stanford.edu/projected-contents.html#s (accessed August 15, 2016).

Reading Simmel: Appropriation by Fragments

Simmel is a more challenging thinker than initially meets the eye. The fascination of his writing is easily perceived, but it is far more difficult to situate his ideas adequately or to translate his way of thinking into our conceptual world. Read in isolation from the dialectical philosophical tradition in which they are at home, many of Simmel's argumentative moves can seem arbitrary. His shorter texts in particular often strike readers as intuitively accessible and illuminating even as his approach remains somehow inchoate. This has fed the tendency to read him selectively, to extract interpretations from rhetorical context—and to canonize "parts" while disregarding their relation to his textual and argumentative "wholes."

The images of Simmel that correspond to and authorize these ways of reading—the unsystematic thinker enthralled by novelty, the bricoleur and seismograph, the *Modephilosoph* (a "fashionable" as opposed to serious philosopher)—are misleading. He was deeply engaged with the Western philosophical tradition and strove to bring its historical legacy, including rigorous, dialectical reflection on everyday life, into the modern world. Genuinely open to the transformations under way in urbanizing Berlin, fearless in the face of the naïve and the recondite alike, Simmel forged a mode of philosophizing suffused with awareness of the larger social, cultural, ethical, and historical context of thought. As a thinker so perfectly of his times, he became both a phenomenal success and an anomaly in a rapidly professionalizing discipline whose leading questions and practices were growing ever more technical, specialized, and sober. Marginalized at least in part due to his popularity, lecturing and writing for a broad, cosmopolitan, international audience, Simmel introduced a whole new range of topics into philosophical discourse.

Paradoxically, the very aspects of Simmel's writing that have done so much "to stimulate the sociological imagination," in Lewis Coser's words, have fed his undeserved reputation as an unsystematic thinker. In the decisive postwar phase of disciplinary consolidation, Simmel's admirers in the social sciences occluded the philosophical stakes of his sociological oeuvre by attributing the difficulties in the reception of his work to the insufficiently developed state of those disciplines in his day. Thus for Friedrich Tenbruck "explanation of the formalistic misunderstanding" should be sought neither "in any shortcomings on Simmel's part, nor in any failures on the part of his interpreters" but rather in the fact that "when Simmel was writing, the social sciences did not have available the conceptual tools which he needed to express his thought articulately. He had to work mainly with such non-specific concepts, illustrations, and images as the 'cultural' sciences of his day could offer him." Fortunately, "progress in conceptualization and methodology" had made it possible (and here Tenbruck cites Kant) to understand Simmel "'better than he understood himself.'" However, to find it necessary, as Tenbruck put it, to "wrest meaning from [Simmel's] text" by recasting his ideas in more modern, "sociological" terms is to set aside not just the author's own self-understanding but an entire tradition of reflection on concept-formation and scientific inquiry.[10]

---

10. Lewis A. Coser, *Masters of Sociological Thought: Ideas in Historical and Social Context* (New York:

Tenbruck's interpretive point of departure, the assumption that social science had emancipated itself from philosophy and more generally from the imprecision of humanistic approaches to "culture," is nourished by a whiggish and very un-Simmelian view of history that tropes disciplinary evolution as conceptual progress. All of this calls for reexamination, especially after the "cultural turn" in the social sciences themselves. In fact, the underlying disciplinary narrative performs the very operation it purports to describe.

Coser's account of Simmel as a "master of sociology" makes the methodological and institutional implications of this rhetoric even more explicit. He, too, represents Simmel's thinking as mired in unscientific prehistory, venturing that since the category of form is "freighted with a great deal of philosophical ballast," it perhaps "frightened away certain modern sociologists intent on exorcising any metaphysical ghosts that might interfere with the building of a scientific sociology." Canonization slides blithely into anachronism: "Had Simmel used the term *social structure*—which, in a sense, is quite close to his use of *form*—he would probably have encountered less resistance" since, Coser claims, it would have been easier to discern the proximity of his "formal conceptualizations" to the intellectual world of modern sociology (181).

Coser's markedly circular logic circumscribes a blind spot surrounding sociology's problematic relations to its philosophical origins. Considerable methodological and historiographical, not to mention epistemic, assumptions are involved in construing the difference between Simmel's ideas and contemporary sociological categories such as "*status, roles, norms*, and *expectations* [understood] as elements of social structure" (181) as primarily a terminological matter. In downplaying the many ways in which his concern with form and the processes in and through which it is produced and sustained play out across Simmel's diverse writings, Coser was setting aside questions about the ways his mode of analysis and vocabulary relate to and engage with the philosophical tradition—questions decisive both historically and conceptually for the constitution of sociology itself. But to ask how "form" and "structure" relate or differ would disclose the disturbing possibility that the conceptual apparatus of social science might itself be haunted by metaphysics.

As Coser candidly reveals, his approach called for a rather labored hermeneutic strategy: "Despite the unsystematic and often willfully paradoxical character of Simmel's work, it is possible to sift and order it in such a way that a consistent approach to the field of sociology emerges (215)."[11] What I call appropriation by frag-

---

Harcourt Brace Jovanovich, 1971; 2nd ed., 1977), 215. (The following citations to Coser in the text also refer to this work.) Tenbruck is quoted from *Georg Simmel, 1858–1918*, ed. K. H. Wolff (Columbus: Ohio University Press, 1959), 63.

11. Coser belonged to a generation of sociologists trained in Europe and fluent not only in multiple languages but also in a wide range of cultural and scholarly traditions. He is remarkably frank about the tensions between his effort to construct a canon for sociology and his striving to write an intellectual history of its origins, making explicit that he is leaving Simmel's contributions to cultural criticism and expressly philosophical works out of his account (while elsewhere singling out Simmel's specifically philosophical impact on other "masters" such as Mannheim). Both method and the relationship between ideas and context have become utterly confused a generation later in Martin Slattery's *Key Ideas in*

ments misconstrues the role of paradox and (apparent) contradiction in Simmel's dialectical mode of systematicity. It literally renders illegible what is most interesting about his oeuvre. We have seen repeatedly how the hermeneutic practices associated with extricating social scientific "content" from philosophical form quite directly and overtly serve to "discipline" Simmel into (contemporary) sociology. With striking frequency, such "sifting and ordering" has been framed by a very specific sociobiographical rhetorical framework, which gains plausibility by foregrounding his liminal position while failing to theorize its methodological implications. Coser's interpretation is its locus classicus: "Simmel, the marginal man, the stranger, presented his academic peers not with a methodical, painstakingly elaborate system but with a series of often disorderly insights, testifying to amazing powers of perception" (214).

To recognize in a mode of writing that did not aspire to the status of a "system" something more than the trace of unrelated flashes of insight requires theoretical attention to Simmel's conception of form. Instead, Coser appeals to one of Simmel's most famous texts, an excursus from the 1908 *Soziologie* on *der Fremde*, the "foreigner" or "stranger," in a fashion that transmutes (theoretical) writing into a mode of testimony. Synthesizing the basic lines of what became the dominant sociological interpretation of Simmel as a sort of free-floating intellectual *avant la lettre*, Coser goes so far as to assert that Simmel developed his remarkably "acute analytic skills" (215) as a consequence of this status as internal outsider in the academy.

In a single stroke, text and author become classics of a peculiarly alien type. Troping historical and conceptual difference as "strangeness" cloaked significant theoretical and methodological assumptions in biographical finery. Moreover, Coser's turning of the tables of sociological analysis on a subject he was ushering into the sociological canon as a "master" quickly became paradigmatic. Simmel's brief text on the stranger would be invoked again and again, construed as an act of self-revelation, to represent and define its author as the prototypical stranger, very often in the context of an underexamined link to Simmel's "Jewishness."[12]

Like many of Simmel's most famous and influential writings, the pages in question are almost always read out of context. His 1908 "large" *Soziologie. Untersuchungen*

Sociology (Cheltenham, England: Nelson Thornes, 2003), a study analogous to Coser's *Masters of Sociological Thought*. "Simmel's focus on micro-sociology and his enthusiasm for 'sociological imaginations' rather than sociological experiments informed and inspired the development of phenomenology and its various offshoots such as symbolic interactionism and ethnomethodology, the Chicago School of Sociology [*sic!*] and studies of urban life in America in the 1920s and 30s," Slattery writes (38).

12. Coser's enframing remains resonant and continues to be frequently redeployed. Jeffrey Alexander extends Coser's rhetorical and narrative framework in a chapter in *The Dark Side of Modernity* (Cambridge: Polity Press, 2013) entitled "Despising Others: Simmel's Stranger" that, in its disconnection from the history of scholarship that calls the reading it perpetuates into question, epitomizes the problematic scholarly practices regularly criticized from the historical side of the aisle. Ignoring Levine's repeated attempts to address the difficulties and complexities of the text's reception history and passing in silence over the entire European secondary literature—not just the efforts by Frisby, Köhnke, Rammstedt, Dahme, and others to establish Simmel's importance as a cultural theorist but also the very existence of the formidable enterprise in which that work unfolded, the *Georg Simmel Gesamtausgabe*—Alexander advances his critique of Simmel's conception of the stranger on an artificially created tabula rasa, referring neither in the body of his essay nor in the bibliography to the extensive secondary literature after Coser.

über die Formen der Vergesellschaftung (Sociology: Investigations into the Forms of Association) would not be translated into English in its entirety for over a century, but the "Exkurs über den Fremden" (Excursus on the Stranger) from its penultimate chapter entered the Anglophone sociological canon in 1921 via Park and Burgess's *Introduction to the Science of Sociology*. Reframed as an essay entitled "The Stranger," it quickly came to be regarded as a sociological classic. As such, it has been regularly anthologized, taught, and cited for nearly a century and remains prominent among the small selection of Simmel's writings that have an indisputable place in the sociological canon.[13]

The fate of this excursus epitomizes the canonization of the "large" *Soziologie* via the intensive reception of a small number of fragments that have long circulated widely independently of the work as a whole.[14] Many portions of the book had been originally published as freestanding essays, so this mode of reception is not without some hermeneutic justification.[15] But this text, barely seven pages long, first appeared as the last of three excurses to chapter 9, "Space and the Spatial Orderings of Society," and it is not, strictly speaking, an essay at all. The "Excursus on the Stranger" has, however, led a life of its own, so to speak, disassociated from its original textual and argumentative context by a reception principally oriented by questions about the role and social functions of strangers and outsiders.

Such an appropriation by fragments is not, per se, illegitimate; ideas and methods found in canonical works are ever being reappropriated and resignified for new contexts. Thus I have not demonstrated that the reception of the *Philosophy of Money* has been constrained by narratives oriented by "social scientific" topoi like "modernization" and "rationalization" in order to argue that these interpretive frameworks or the selective readings they generate are false or even irrelevant, since Simmel's work is clearly significant for sociological theorizing in this key.

But selectively appropriating his ideas in this way prevents critical examination of the categories and theoretical assumptions, narratives and hermeneutic frameworks it reinforces. As discursive aspects of the objectively existing, humanly

---

13. *Introduction to the Science of Sociology*, ed. Robert E. Park and Ernest W. Burgess (Chicago: University of Chicago Press, 1921). In *The Flight from Ambiguity: Essays in Social and Cultural Theory* (Chicago: University of Chicago Press, 1985), 73–88, Donald Levine presented the history of appropriations of "Stranger" as a paradigmatic case of the "useful confusions" fostered by the "undisciplined way in which classic authors have been incorporated into American sociology." On his generous interpretation, the lush variety of misreadings of Simmel's essay provided multiple "points of departure for fruitful theoretical developments" (73). Distinguishing a typology of strangers ("Guest, Intruder, Sojourner, Inner Enemy, Newcomer, Marginal Man" [84]), Levine turned the ways "the stimulating ideas from his essay had been applied and misapplied" in the secondary literature (88) into suggestions for future lines of research. For more recent efforts to extend the category, see the *Journal of Intercultural Studies*, 33, no. 6 (December 2012), an issue devoted to "Strangers," esp. Mervyn Horgan, "Strangers and Strangership" and Vince Marotta, "Georg Simmel, the Stranger and the Sociology of Knowledge." See also Zeena Feldman, "Simmel in Cyberspace," *Information, Communication & Society* 15, no. 2 (2012): 297–319.

14. As noted, while Simmel's 1908 *Soziologie* itself was unavailable in English until 2009, a collection including translations of excerpts from that work and others circulated for many years under the title *The Sociology of Georg Simmel*, trans. and ed. Kurt Wolff (New York: Free Press, 1950).

15. The editors of the *Gesamtausgabe* list no fewer than eighteen distinct essays published between 1905 and 1908 that were eventually integrated into the 1908 volume (*GSG* 11: 896–97).

created cultural reality of social scientific inquiry, these should be subjected to philosophical critique and to socio-historical and cultural contextualization. Both forms of reflection are part of the ongoing, super-and transindividual, cultural and historical process of world-creation in and through which our knowledge practices evolve—itself an important aspect of the "cultural process" Simmel was rightly urging us to reflect upon in complex, multifaceted ways and from multiple, sometimes incompatible perspectives.

Subordinating Simmel's philosophical intentions to his social scientific contributions seems, prima facie, less problematic in the case of his 1908 "large" *Soziologie*. In the final analysis, however, when these "investigations into forms of association" are filtered through the lens of the contemporary disciplinary mainstream, serious misunderstanding obscures the work's theoretical and methodological contributions.

The "large" *Soziologie* encompasses reflection on the meaning and nature of human social and cultural existence as such, and on the metaphysical, ethical, and epistemological implications of self-reflexive awareness of human being-social both for modern knowledge practices and for social and cultural life more generally. But in assimilating Simmel's work into the sociological canon, his reflections on such matters have too often been left out of account—or quite literally omitted, as in the case of the most accessible English edition of the revised version of "The Problem of Sociology." Precisely because "sociological" and "philosophical" dimensions are so profoundly intertwined in Simmel's account of this particular social form, the case of "der Fremde" renders visible how much is at stake theoretically and methodologically for the discipline of sociology in isolating selected ideas from larger arguments and inserting decontextualized passages into conceptual frameworks he was, implicitly or explicitly, criticizing.

As we have seen repeatedly, through this reception by fragments, readers perform, enact, the very thing they set out to establish: that, and in what sense, Simmel is to be understood as a sociologist. The reception of the "Excursus on the Stranger" is paradigmatic, for the performative creation of "Simmel" as at once a "stranger" and founding father simultaneously constitutes the theoretical and methodological blind spots of sociology as a discipline—which is to say, makes "Simmel" into a name for the constitutive blind spot around which a specifically sociological way of seeing coheres.

As we know from optics, the existence of blind spots is a material condition of the possibility of vision, a direct result of the placement of the optical nerve. Under ordinary circumstances, their existence (or rather the absence they demarcate) is obscured in and through a second-order (unconscious) process in the brain that (re)constitutes a continuous visual field. We become aware of such points of occlusion only indirectly, as a consequence of distortions that arise in perception under certain conditions.

The fate of the "Excursus on the Stranger" epitomizes the transformation of Simmel's philosophical vision of sociology in its mainstream reception, exposing how his methodological strategies were brought to serve the constitution of a disciplinary way of seeing by construing them in a fashion that obscures their declared theoretical significance. Representing Simmel as a stranger—as an outsider to, rather than a famous and cosmopolitan participant in, a vibrant and in many ways very modern cultural and intellectual world—is less a way of remembering than of forgetting him as a thinker. Yet that image helps authorize the practices of selective reading through which the philosophical legacy embedded in his conception of form is retooled to undergird inquiry into hypostasized social "roles" and "structures."

The theoretical and methodological blind spots this way of reading creates are further occluded by the sociological way of seeing it enables. The figure of Simmel as sociological stranger reveals and conceals at once, effacing the historical and philosophical complexity of his liminal position while reframing and appropriating his strategies of thought. It thereby enables his assimilation to a discipline that assumes precisely what he did not: that there is such a thing as the social or society outside of its performance by human beings.

That performance *is* the phenomenon of form as Simmel understood it. But the practices of inclusion and exclusion, decontextualization and recontextualization that continue to structure the performative disciplinary strategies through which Simmel is repeatedly reinscribed as a canonical "sociologist" have obscured or occluded entirely the philosophical questions he was raising about (knowledge of) the social.

Placing what Simmel had to say about strangers and strangeness back into its textual context reveals how much is at stake not just for sociology but for contemporary cultural theory more generally in reading him differently. It helps clarify the specificity of his philosophical modernism and to disclose the conceptual and textual space of a way of seeing that both precedes and exceeds the contemporary disciplinary imaginary. By focusing attention on the significance of Simmel's theoretical situation as a thinker between what we have come to think of as "the social sciences" and "the humanities," such a return to the "Excursus on the Stranger" may help enable the renewed and genuinely interdisciplinary interest in his work to foster new forms of reflection on the institutional and intellectual fragmentation that constrains our modes of thinking about our (social, cultural, historical) world as a whole.[16]

What is at issue is not simply that but also how and why Simmel's achievements have been and continue to be forgotten and misconstrued through his canonization as a sociologist. Recall Harold Bloom's strong interpretation of poetic legacies, according to which productive misappropriations are the rule rather than the exception in the case of canonical thinkers and founding fathers. So too in the case of Simmel: his reception is of genealogical interest, for what is being forgotten and obscured enabled the discipline of sociology to become what it is and thus has a good deal to teach us about the theoretical and historical stakes of the genesis of the modern disciplinary order as a whole.[17]

---

16. I elaborate on these arguments in "Sociology as a Sideline: Does It Matter that Georg Simmel (Thought He) was a Philosopher?" in *Anthem Companion to Simmel*, ed. Thomas Kemple and Olli Pyyhtinen (London and New York: Anthem Press, 2016), 29–57.

17. I am by no means alone in drawing attention to Simmel's theoretical significance or to the problems in his mainstream reception. But very few of these efforts have been made by American scholars. Important recent additions to this tradition in historical sociology include two books by Horst Helle,

I am not advocating (another) return to Simmel's work as a point of origin for an alternative mode of canonization. An antiquarian orientation cannot disclose what we most need: ways of thinking differently, strategies that do not just expand the self-perpetuating resources of established disciplinary traditions, but reorient them. We cannot reconstitute the scholarly imaginary of a bygone era or find refuge in the moment before the cultural and social sciences took their leave of philosophy. The challenge confronting critical historical and theoretical reflection (and by no means only in the case of Simmel) is, rather, to find ways imaginatively to enter the conceptual space before the splitting of cultural inquiry into "scientific" and "humanistic" branches.

Revisiting modernism's radical questioning of inherited modes of reflection may help us to recognize unrealized possibilities and potentialities in what turned out to be the beginnings of both "cultural" and "social" theory. Such a critical genealogy of our own ways of thinking about science, knowledge, and human life can open up new theoretical horizons and provide deeper understanding of the continuities and discontinuities of contemporary dilemmas with those of the previous fin de siècle, when the reductivist paradigms and specialized knowledge practices we take for granted today were just beginning their ascendance.

Reading Simmel as a modernist philosopher entails a self-reflexive consideration of what is involved in the imaginative return to this particular *temps perdu*. If we can recognize his importance while also embracing the complexity of our relation to a modernism that can no longer be ours, the example of Simmel's innovative and open-minded, experimental encounter with a world in flux may inspire new thought practices at our own moment of great cultural and social transformation.

Reflecting on what is representative and constitutive—synecdochic—in Simmel's persistent liminality for both sociology and philosophy makes visible the limitations of the narratives and methodological assumptions that constitute and stabilize the modern disciplinary ordering of inquiry as a whole. Simmel's thinking does not simply transgress our analytic categories; his modernist concept of concepts, which relativizes the very mode and ideal of coherence that still animates disciplinary knowledge practices, points the way toward what is (still) unthought in our (theoretical, disciplinary) past itself.

Rereading Rereading: Estranging the Stranger

The "Excursus on the Stranger" is the third and final excursus in the penultimate chapter of Simmel's 1908 "large" *Soziologie*, "Space and the Spatial Orderings of Society." It directly follows a discussion of the evolution of the labor market since

---

Georg Simmel: Einführung in seine Theorie und Methode = Georg Simmel: Introduction to His Theory and Method (Munich: R. Oldenberg, 2001) and *The Social Thought of Georg Simmel* (London: Sage, 2015); Alan Scott and Helmut Staubmann's translation of Simmel's 1916 *Rembrandt: An Essay in the Philosophy of Art* (New York: Routledge, 2005); and the 2012 *TCS* special issue edited by Thomas Kemple (Vancouver) and Austin Harrington (Frankfurt, now Leeds), which also includes a trove of newly translated material from Simmel's cultural and aesthetic writings. Harold Bloom's thesis was set out in *The Anxiety of Influence: A Theory of Poetry* (New York: Oxford University Press, 1973).

the Middle Ages that emphasizes the interplay between modalities of wandering and social organization.[18] The excursus begins by situating "the sociological form of the 'stranger'" in relation to the two extremes of the human relation to space: the "detachment" [Gelöstheit] of those who wander as opposed to the "fixity" [Fixiertheit] of those who remain in the same social space all their lives (GSG 11: 764). Simmel is sensitive to the social function of very concrete relations to space that condition and enable class-differentiated forms of mobility. However, his analysis of strangeness emphasizes dimensions of existence that cannot be understood in these terms and that indicate the constitutive impact of (transindividual) sociality on the spatial organization of human life.

Unlike the wanderer who "comes today and goes tomorrow," he writes, the stranger "comes today and stays tomorrow"; he is "the so to speak potential wanderer who . . . has not entirely overcome the dissolution of coming and going." Simmel anchors this interpretation in his phenomenology of cultural life by invoking explicitly philosophical language to introduce his analytic construct, "the sociological form of the 'stranger.'" Because that form "represents in a certain sense the unity of the two determinations"—that is, the poles of detachment and fixity that constitute human spatiality as a social phenomenon—it "reveal(s)" one of the basic theoretical lessons of the *Soziologie*: "that the relation to space is on one hand the condition, on the other hand the symbol of relations to human beings" (GSG 11: 764).

As a sociological form, "strangeness" is at once symbolic and concrete, ideal and material. The stranger, qua stranger, is a figure of symbolic significance: not simply other or different, but a being in and for whom a particular "constellation" of transpersonal interaction, the "unity of intimacy and distance" (GSG 11: 768–69) that is a feature of every human relation, takes on the symbolic form of otherness. The sociocultural position of the stranger, the potential wanderer, cannot be understood in privative terms, as a lack of identity, nor is strangeness the otherness of one who fails to belong to the community. On the contrary,

> Being-strange [das Fremdsein] is of course an entirely positive relation, a specific form of reciprocal interaction; the inhabitants of Sirius are not actually strange to us . . . rather they entirely do not exist for us, they stand beyond near and far. The stranger is an element of the group itself, not unlike the poor and the manifold "inner enemies"—an element whose immanent position as member simultaneously encloses something external and juxtaposed. (GSG 11: 765)

This subject position has a very distinctive topology. In the next sentence, Simmel describes the entire configuration as a (dialectical) whole in which "the repelling and distancing moments . . . constitute a form of being-together and of reciprocally interacting unity" (GSG 11: 765). Stranger and other, that is, are co-constitutive. Social formations resemble Aristotelian or indeed Hegelian dialectical wholes. But this is merely a resemblance. "Being-strange" is a relationship of reciprocal interaction, a

---

18. First elaborated in an excerpt from his work-in-progress published in Schmoller's *Jahrbuch für Gesetzgebung, Verwaltung und Volkswirtschaft im Deutschen Reich* in 1903 as "Soziologie des Raumes" (GSG 7: 132–83), this discussion remains of considerable interest in an era of mass migrations.

form of social life that implicates both subject and other even as it exposes spatiality as a socially organized phenomenon, one at once social and material, simultaneously product and condition of human existence. In Simmel's account, spatiality is not, pace Kant, a "form of intuition," but the material and ideal effect of movement in and out of, around, within, and between human collectivities, a reflection of the complex interplay of historical, social, psychological, and cultural context that defines all human interaction as such. It is, in a word, a culturally constituted category, at once a material and ideal condition of possibility for social life as such.

The conception of social form in play here accords with Simmel's mature understanding of the significance of Kantian insights, in which the a priori has received a Hegelian twist and is understood as constituted and shaped historically—that is to say, culturally, socially, psychologically. His sociological reflections are shot through with a philosophical effort to understand how subjects and objects come into being, interact, change, and evolve: social forms are culturally and historically situated negotiations and enactments of inter- and transsubjective constellations of relations, and spatiality is both *Bedingung*—condition of possibility—and *Symbol*—symbolic framework for understanding those relations (*GSG* 11: 764).

Simmel's Fremde resonates with Plato's Eleatic Stranger, with the alienated subject depicted by fellow modernists such as Nietzsche and Strindberg, and with politically significant discourses on foreigners and foreignness in Wilhelmine Germany. For him, the figure of the stranger exemplifies how sameness and difference in general constitute both group and individual identities. In its mixture of philosophical universality and sociological and historical particularity as well as its preoccupation with the ways in which being-strange [*Fremdsein*] constitutes both self and other, Simmel's discussion anticipates the discourse on alienation [*Entfremdung*] in the next generation, with its central trope of "spiritual homelessness," but the figure is also the harbinger of what would later be dubbed the deterritorialization of the subject.[19]

Conflict is not eliminated within the social totality; difference is not subordinated to identity, which remains external to itself. Thus the sociological form of the stranger, whose "immanent position as member simultaneously encloses something external and juxtaposed" (*GSG* 11: 765), makes visible—is a figure for—something quite fundamental about human existence. Strangeness turns out, as it were, not to be strange but to be internal to subjectivity itself. In describing the distinctive topology of "being-strange" as a "specific form of reciprocal interaction," Simmel extends and as it were inverts a basic dialectical point that the relation to the other reflects and is partly constituted by a relation to self.

As he puts it earlier in the book in a passage to which we shall return, it is only apparently paradoxical that human beings must "understand themselves and view one another" under such categories in order to become subjects who "so formed, can produce empirical society," since the individual's "mode of being-social [or being-in-society: *Vergesellschaftet-Seins*] is determined or co-determined by his mode

---

19. On the genealogy of the "homeless" modern subject, see Philip Webb, *Homeless Lives in American Cities: Interrogating Myth and Locating Community* (New York: Palgrave Macmillan, 2014).

of not-being-social [*Nicht-Vergesellschaftet-Seins*]" (*GSG* 11: 51–52). "The stranger" is both a constitutive element of the group and a figure in whom this interpenetration of symbolic and spatial dimensions in human sociality becomes uniquely visible.

Reflection on the social form of "strangeness" sheds light on an important "constellation," a key mode of differentiation not only within social groups but also within intimate relations: what we might call the thirdness of human (social) being.[20] The analysis of strangeness can thus help us parse a variety of social and cultural phenomena, some of which we have come to think of as features of subjective identity, others as aspects of group dynamics. For Simmel, these are consequences or effects of the a priori feature of human existence just noted: human identity is external to itself; being-social is internally fractured, wrought with difference and constituted in and by relations that reveal the subject's own otherness to itself. In one of Simmel's recurrent metaphors, being-fragmentary is the human way of being: "we are all fragments" (as he puts it a few pages earlier) "not only of human being in general, but also of ourselves" (*GSG* 11: 49).

In describing what we would call the (sociocultural) process of subjectivation, that is to say, the co-constitution of subjects and the social—which though not spatial, takes place in space—Simmel calls "the objectivity of the stranger" an "expression" of the spatio-symbolic "constellation" of proximity and distance, movement and fixity, that describes strangeness as a social formation. The "special attitude of the 'objective one,'" he writes, "does not signify a mere distance and impartiality, but rather a specific configuration out of distance and intimacy, indifference and engagement" (*GSG* 11: 766–67).[21]

Simmel's view of objectivity as a relative rather than an absolute phenomenon, so central to the methodological conception of the *Philosophy of Money*, is of both formal and substantive significance in the 1908 "large" *Soziologie* as well. His "stranger" is not a role or an identity but a social form that arises in and through a trans- and interpersonal, sociocultural, configuration—the name for a position in an interactive field of human practice. Thus "being-strange" is "an entirely positive relation, a specific form of reciprocal interaction . . . the stranger is an element of the group

20. My "Simmel's Stranger and the Third as Imaginative Form," *Colloquia Germanica* 45, nos. 3–4 (Fall 2015): 239–63, expands on the troping of Simmel's strangeness and its philosophical significance.

21. My "specific configuration out of distance and intimacy" is a more literal rendering of the phrase "*ein besonderes Gebilde aus Distanz und Nähe*," translated by Kurt Wolff, in the version that has had such significant effects in U.S. sociology, as "a particular structure composed of distance and nearness" (*The Sociology of Georg Simmel*, 404). Wolff's choice of "structure" for *Gebilde* is a strong intervention along the lines suggested by Coser's roughly contemporaneous suggestion for reforming Simmelian terminology; either "form" or "formation" would have been more consonant with the conceptual universe of the original.

Because I regard Simmel's relatively systematic use of *Gebilde* as both rhetorically and philosophically significant, I have consistently translated the term as "configuration" in order to emphasize that continuity and draw attention to the connection with the semantics of *Bild*—"image" or "figure"—and *bilden*—"to shape or form." In this context, it is worth noting that *Form* and *formal* appear four times in the excursus; *Konstellation*, three times. Given the subsequent vicissitudes of the latter concept, which goes to the (metaphoric) heart of critical theory, it is worth underlining that *Konstellation* (frequently used in *Philosophie des Geldes*, and here translated consistently as "constellation") plays a role in Simmel's thinking that to my knowledge has not been acknowledged by his successors.

itself." The stranger's objectivity is a function of that particular constellation, an attitude that expresses a reciprocal relationship, neither a being-inside nor a form of exclusion or difference, but rather a way of being the boundaries, a mélange of distance and intimacy, indifference and engagement. No absolute outside or utter exclusion is involved; strangeness is a particular mode of being-related to the dominant perspective, and it is embedded in a social relation or configuration that includes *both* perspectives.[22]

We should beware the philosophical misprision that distorts Simmel's conception of subject and object alike, translating his "form of association" into "social structure"—and hypostasizing his "attitude" that "expresses" a form or "constellation" of intersubjective relations into a "subject position." A far more nuanced account of culture and society, language and form, meaning and embodiment animates his understanding of the difference that is strangeness. Particularly as his own "strangeness" from a contemporary perspective continues to figure Simmel's place in the sociological imaginary, it is worth considering carefully that, in the larger context of the *Sociology*, the figure of the stranger serves to catalyze the reader's recognition that internal difference constitutes both human identity and sociality—that, as he puts it earlier, "the a priori of empirical social life is that life is not entirely social" (*GSG* 11: 53). For Simmel, we are all strangers in the strange land of social life.

Becoming Social, Figuring Strangeness

What Simmel has to say about "the sociological form of the stranger" (literally, of the "foreigner") should be placed in dialogue with Freud's 1919 meditations on that particular species of the anxiety-provoking (*des Ängstlichen*) known as "the uncanny" (*das Unheimliche*; literally, the "unhomelike"). In a remarkable essay on the subject that he frames as aesthetic, in the sense that it concerns "the theory of the quality of our feeling," Freud grounds the strange familiarity of the uncanny in the paradoxical combination of meanings of its nominal opposite, *Heimlich* ("secret"; literally, "homelike"), which, he writes, "is a word that develops its meaning according to an ambivalence until finally it collapses with its opposite, the uncanny [*das Unheimliche*]. Uncanny is somehow a species of secret." What is secret, unknown, yet intimately familiar, is of course the unconscious. A sense of uncanniness arises when what has been repressed returns, when infantile desires and fears rooted in the experience of indifferentiation between self and world are reactivated: the uncanny is the "formerly homelike, the long-familiar," returning as other.[23]

What Freudian psychoanalysis calls "the uncanny" relates to the social position that in Simmelian sociology is occupied by the stranger. *Das Fremdsein*, being strange, is "an entirely positive relation," a specific form of reciprocal interaction that is one

---

22. Simmel notes that the objectivity arising in and through the social form or constellation of strangeness led to a "dominant position of those foreign to the group" under certain circumstances, as in the Italian city-states where such outsiders served as judges for intragroup conflicts.

23. Sigmund Freud, "Das Unheimliche," *Imago: Zeitschrift für Anwendung der Psychoanalyse auf die Geisteswissenschaften* 5 (1919): 302–3, 318.

pole of the "unity of intimacy and distantiation contained in every relation between human beings." Simmel sums up the paradox in one of his characteristic bons mots: "The distance internal to the relationship signifies that the one who is close is distant; strangeness [or being a stranger, *das Fremdsein*], that the one who is distant is close" (*GSG* 11: 765).

Dwelling on the rhetoric of strangeness helps explain the robustness of patently flawed readings in the reception history through which Simmel has become a (mostly) forgotten founding father. Both identifying him as a stranger and categorizing his texts as strange or anomalous have helped authorize the sifting and ordering of what is (pace Coser) "unsystematic" or even "willfully paradoxical" into what appears from the hegemonic disciplinary point of view as "a consistent approach to the field of sociology." At once stranger and founding father, Simmel belongs to the discipline in the manner of one who does not quite fit in. This mode of reception betrays a half-submerged awareness that his allegiances may lie elsewhere—an uneasy suspicion that the "potential wanderer" and his ideas might take flight at any time into the philosophical land from whence he came.

The rhetoric of strangeness, the discursive and narrative framework generated by identifying Simmel as sociology's internal other, is entangled with reading practices and theoretical commitments that in turn anchor the normative self-understanding of sociologists. In this discourse, as quite generally when the rhetoric of strangers and foreignness is invoked, boundaries are being policed. To recall Coser's metaphors, the disciplinary institution comes into being by differentiating sociology proper from the "philosophical ballast" of the past, with its "metaphysical ghosts" and unsystematic and unscientific dependence on imagination, on individual perception and insight. This tendentious narrative and the reading practices that support and reinforce it help naturalize the founding assumptions of the modern social scientific paradigm and thereby lend those assumptions the air of necessity for those whose work depends on the understandings of truth, reality, evidence, science, and so forth they embody.

Modes of reading that disregard the sophistication of Simmel's conception of form and formation and excise fragmentary examples from their textual fabric and philosophical context have facilitated the selective appropriation of his ideas and methods into a disciplinary tradition Simmel would hardly have recognized. Such strategic incorporation remains constitutive for a way of thinking about sociology and its history that continues to disseminate the misapprehension that dialectical thinking is unmethodical.

The absence of English translations of acknowledged major works has also powerfully reinforced Simmel's virtual absence from the historiography of philosophy and even cultural theory. He remains, as it were, a stranger in both social scientific and humanistic domains. The resulting negative configuration is both symptom and figure for the genuine difficulty in giving a systematic account of his mode of thought from within the contemporary disciplinary order. Reading Simmel instead as a modernist philosophical adventurer engaged in a "hopeless but not for that reason senseless" effort to forge concepts adequate to the complex multiplicity and incommensurability of life itself can help free the possibilities enfolded in this doubled liminality.

Simmel's mature thinking is situated at the juncture where modern cultural theory came into being as the social sciences differentiated from philosophy. He was not, like Durkheim or Weber, trying to establish a science of the social; nor was he, like Heinrich Wölfflin or Dilthey, attempting to define alternative methodologies for the study of culture. His investment was not, like Rickert or Husserl's, in establishing firm boundaries around philosophy proper. The distinctiveness of Simmel's disposition as a philosopher (and as a Kantian) found reflection in a capacious conception of philosophical vocation that included writing for feuilletons as well as scholarly journals; public lectures as well as private salons; that tied metaphysics to pedagogy and both to politics and culture. In his oeuvre, questions about the nature and possibility of the distinctions between and relations among the intersubjective and the social, culture and the psyche, subjectivity and history remain in flux.

In Simmel's thinking, as in psychoanalysis, the boundary between the unconscious and the (linguistic, cultural, historical) context cannot really be clearly demarcated—nor, for that matter, can the distinction between description and interpretation. In reading him, this lack of differentiation can be just as aggravating, albeit for different reasons, for his inheritors in the contemporary social sciences as in the humanities, tempting both to celebrate isolated insights while consigning his larger ambitions to the dustbin of history. But Simmel's work also provides an opportunity to revisit the uncanny, liminal moment before the false certainties of our bifurcated theoretical paradigms and to reflect on the enduring modernist insight that our most basic categories—the human, the social, culture, identity—remain radically indeterminate.

Rethinking the unrealized possibilities in Simmel's work will not enable us to bridge the abyss between the humanities and the social sciences. But it may provide a perspective on what is at stake in maintaining the conceptual and methodological bifurcations that constitute, not just division but, to a remarkable degree, mutual alienation between different disciplinary spheres and knowledge practices. Simmel's thoroughgoing nominalism can thereby become an important resource for reflection upon the status both of the social and of the subject in our own time.

Situating the "Excursus on the Stranger" both thematically and formally within Simmel's sociology as a whole exposes the theoretical significance and methodological subtlety of the understanding of form that ties his thinking on culture and society to his views about human being as such—and thereby makes clear how consequential his appropriation by fragments has been.

The sociological reception has passed over this fact as though unawares, but the figure of *der Fremde* makes its first appearance, not in the famous text near the end of the 1908 *Soziologie*, but rather in a supplement to chapter 1—that is, to the radically revised version of "Das Problem der Sociologie" that serves as the book's introduction.[24] In that chapter, in an "Excursus on the Problem: How Is Society Possible?",

---

24. Both that excursus and "Stranger" were first published in the 1908 *Soziologie*.

the stranger enters the text in the company of "the enemy," "the criminal," and "the pauper"—all "types," Simmel writes, whose "sociological significance is fixed in its very core and essence by their being somehow excluded from the society for which their existence is significant" (GSG 11: 51). The "stranger," that is, figures a way of meaning that exists in and through a generic sort of interactive social configuration, exemplifies a form of existence that is of quite general significance in and for the understanding of the social as such. Like the people who bear such labels, these culturally and institutionally mediated "forms of association" cannot be understood in isolation but are cases of a particular modus of interactive mutual relation, of *Wechselwirkung*, between individuals and society.

The "stranger" functions, then, as a figure in the technical, rhetorical sense—one whose philosophical significance should not be underestimated. The form of exclusion it figures helps Simmel to demarcate the parameters of the "sociological a priori," the categories "under which subjects understand themselves and view one another such that they, so formed, can give rise to empirical society" (GSG 11: 50–51). Unlike Weber's "ideal types," these "types" are idealized but not abstract: metaphors grounded in historical and cultural reality. Simmel's emphasis on the ordinariness of the process of abstraction involved is significant: such figures or forms cannot be understood as formalized theoretical constructs; they exemplify and embody the internal difference that is at once a constitutive feature of human subjectivity and one of society's a prioris.

Simmel's way of thinking about the role of otherness in human sociality conjoins phenomena that are now theorized in quite different ways. Strangeness is configured in relation both to otherness understood as in itself un- or a- or pre-social—and thus to the sort of phenomena generally explained today by invoking an unconscious. But it also comprises a relation to otherness in the sense of the non- or extra-social, phenomena thought as structurally excluded from, yet coeval with the social or society as such, that are generated as its constitutive outside. In Simmel's conception, then, the figure of strangeness encompasses both psychological and cultural dimensions, both the pre- and the non- or extra-social.

Simmel can doubtless be criticized from an anachronistic point of view that lays claim to certainty concerning theoretical priority—whether with regard to unconscious or sociohistorical processes, the internal or the externalized other. A great deal of contemporary cultural theory is absorbed with just such attempts to demonstrate the theoretical prerogatives of particular conceptions of otherness. But in reading him, it is worth suspending, at least hypothetically, the certainty that it is possible to distinguish between the pre-and the post social, the infra- and super-individual, not least because Simmel's work suggests that, given their underlying reductive agenda, such efforts are probably doomed to fail.

Simmel does not simply happen not to draw the lines as we would. His theoretical and methodological framework precedes the bifurcations that have become our commonplaces—between reflection on subjectivity and intersubjectivity and theories of the social, between philosophy and sociology, between humanistic and social scientific thought practices. What he figures, paradigmatically, as being-strange cannot be understood as doubled or ambiguous and in need of differentiation; it is a third, liminal sort of category.

I am not arguing that we can or should simply abandon our distinctions and return to the imaginative space before our disciplinary divisions or elide the differences between diverse forms of otherness—least of all between the unconscious and the social. We cannot and should not attempt to read Simmel in a way that sets aside the intervening history, including the history of interpretation. Rather, to put a twist on Lukács' notion, my hope is that embracing his strangeness as the most significant transitional phenomenon in all of modern philosophy can open a new perspective on the cultural-intellectual situation of contemporary theory.

In a period when the methodological differences that would develop into an abyss between the humanities and social sciences were still fluid and contested, Simmel embraced and attempted to theorize that very fluidity and conflict in a modernist approach to philosophizing that directly addressed fundamental questions about the relationship between disciplines and modes of interpretation. He should not be faulted for failing to draw distinctions that seem obvious to us. Instead, tracing the distinctive path of Simmel's ways of thinking can serve to help us both understand the origins of some of our most unquestioned assumptions and habits of thought and to recognize and appreciate the untapped resources of the moment—historical, cultural, social, political, theoretical—when the modern disciplinary imaginary was just beginning to take on its twentieth-century contours.

For Simmel, what brings the social into being also subtends the process of subjectivation. Human beings are constituted as social in a way that involves a presocial (-cultural, -linguistic) outside—what used to be called nature, but is today more usually conceived of in the language of the unconscious (a vocabulary Simmel sometimes uses, albeit not in a Freudian sense)—and the supersubjective, transindividual realm of the "superindividual." Otherness, difference, encompasses both sorts of "outside," and the extrasocial existence of the individual involves both, not necessarily in a clearly distinguishable way. The doubling and ambiguity of strangeness as an exemplary constellation of being-social thus illuminates the complexity of subjectivation—in his terms, illustrates one of the a prioris of empirical social existence, of the existential-ontological modes of interrelation between subjects and the social. Again: "being-strange" is "an entirely positive relation, a specific form of interaction." Simmel's "stranger" or "foreigner" inhabits an "immanent position as member [that] simultaneously encloses something external and juxtaposed" to the group (*GSG* 11: 765).

The constellation exemplified by (figures like) the stranger manifests a positive characteristic of the *social* as such: its being constituted by beings who are in but not entirely of it. But this constellation is a sociological form also in the sense that it makes visible a fundamental feature of *subjectivity* as such. It is a synecdoche of becoming-social, for the socialization process as a whole in both object and subjective senses.

It is now possible to place the passage cited earlier in a larger context.

In his "Excursus on the Problem: How Is Society Possible?" in the 1908 *Soziologie*, Simmel writes: "every element of a group is not only part of society but also in addition something else." But this something else, the non- or incompletely social aspect of individuality, is "not merely a [being] outside of society." In the dialectical tradition to which Simmel belongs, subjectivity depends on the inter- and transsubjective; the notion of a simply nonsocial form of identity is incoherent. He articulates this principle, which has crucial consequences for his understanding of social life, in an admirably straightforward fashion: "the fact that with certain sides of his being the individual is not an element of society forms the positive condition for his being so with other sides: his mode of being-social is determined or co-determined by his mode of not-being-social [*die Art seines Vergesellschaftet-Seins ist bestimmt oder mitbestimmt durch die Art seines Nicht-Vergesellschaftet-Seins*]" (*GSG* 11: 51).

These modes or ways (or, to translate *Art* somewhat differently, kinds or species) of "being social" are practices or forms of life or experience. Among other things, Simmel is warning against hypostasizing "parts" of the self. Just as, after Kant, we must recognize that we cannot understand nature independently of critical reflection on our own practices of thought, we can only assure our knowledge of the human world if we remain reflective about the difficulties of thinking about our own role in its symbolic constitution.

It is in the lines that immediately follow that Simmel introduces the figure of the foreigner or stranger for the first time, in the series of "types" whose sociological significance is also constituted by this exemplary form of "exclusion." The "enemy," the "criminal," the "pauper," and the "stranger" are all social forms—figures who embody and thereby come to represent what is a quite general and only apparently paradoxical condition of possibility for society as such: that the social is constituted by beings whose being is defined by their not entirely belonging to the whole of which they are the constitutive elements or parts. Society is defined, to put the point from another perspective, by figurative boundaries, in and through symbolic forms that are also enacted, identity-defining practices, objectifications.

The philosophical significance of the figure of thought Simmel is introducing here has been obscured by the translation by Kurt Wolff in which this passage has entered the Anglo-American social scientific canon: "the fact that in certain respects the individual is not an element of society constitutes the positive condition *for the possibility that* [my emphasis—EG] in other respects he is: the way in which he is sociated is determined or codetermined by the way he is not."[25]

Wolff's wanly objectivizing "in certain respects" eliminates Simmel's robustly philosophical "sides of his being [or essence: *Wesen*]" from view, preparing the way for an even more significant intervention from the point of view of this text's theoretical (and, more broadly, Simmel's philosophical) history of effects: the recasting

---

25. "How Is Society Possible?" in *Georg Simmel*, ed. Wolff, 345 (this version is partially reproduced in *Georg Simmel on Individuality and Social Forms*, ed. Donald N. Levine [Chicago: University of Chicago Press, 1971], 12). Kurt Wolff's postwar efforts brought Simmel's work to a wider audience, but typically, Albion Small first translated the essay (*AJS* 16, no. 3 [November 1910], 372–91).

of his phenomenological-metaphysical interpretation of a fundamental configuration of human social being into a more "scientific" vocabulary.[26]

For Simmel, *Vergesellschaftung* comprises both the becoming-social of the individual and coming-into-being of society. Wolff's "way he is sociated" obscures Simmel's descriptively accessible, phenomenologically sensitive account of the tenuous and conflicted way in which individual human beings both belong and fail to belong to the societies in which they live behind the screen of a technical vocabulary that hypostasizes lived complexity in a fashion inimical to Simmel's entire approach.[27] Wolff's rendering also distorts his culturalist conception of the a priori, interpellating a "possibility" not in the original text at all and effacing Simmel's point that the a prioris of *Vergesellschaftung* are conditions of individual and society alike—that neither intersubjectivity nor the "superindividual" sphere can be understood as something added to individuality, since both are constitutive of it.

In reframing Simmel's philosophically resonant formulation—a quite contemporary-sounding insight that being-social depends on and is conditioned and shaped by the ways the individual beings who are society's "elements" are also in fact *not* social beings—with a more "scientific" terminology, Wolff's rendering facilitated the assimilation of Simmel's thinking into the contemporary discipline of sociology in a fashion that rendered both the historical and theoretical—the dialectical—stakes of the original invisible.

Wolff's translation occludes the ontological dimension of human sociality that makes Simmel's conception of subjectivation proximate to its nominal antipode in the Freudian unconscious: his insistence that the individual's partial non-belonging to society is constitutive for subject and culture alike. What Simmel actually wrote—that "his mode of being-social is determined or codetermined by his mode of not-being-social"—is a claim about the ontology and genealogy of the human mode of being that resonates quite obviously with Heidegger but also with more contemporary thinkers of difference.

The text in which the figure of the stranger first appears is framed explicitly by an analogy with "the fundamental question of [Kant's] philosophy: how is nature possible" (*GSG* 11: 42). The "Excursus on the Problem: How Is Society Possible?" follows immediately upon Simmel's reflections on the need to distinguish social philosophy from sociology in the conclusion to the revised version of "The Problem of Sociology" that opens the book. It devotes a densely argued twenty pages to a quasi-transcendental inquiry into the conditions of possibility for the existence

---

26. The 2009 English translation obscures Simmel's account even further behind a hypostasized vision of social existence: "the fact that the individual is in certain respects not a member of society creates the positive condition for it being just such a member in other respects. What kind a person's socialized being is, is determined or co-determined by the kind of one's unsocialized being" (*Sociology: Inquiries into the Construction of Social Forms*, trans. and ed. Anthony J. Blasi et al. [Boston: Brill, 2009], 45).

27. In his notes to "The Problem of Sociology" in *Georg Simmel*, ed. Wolff, 335, Wolff refers the reader to his remarks on translation in his 1950 edition of *The Sociology of Georg Simmel*, lxiii–iv. There he notes that Small and Spykman translated *Vergesellschaftung* as "socialization," while Abel used "societalization," and credits his own choice, "sociation," to J. H. W. Stuckenberg.

of society as such. As Simmel demonstrates, "society," like "nature," must be understood as the product of a synthesis: it is a logical as well as ontological error to hypostasize "society" or "the social" as such as though it were independent of the human subjects that constitute it. Indeed, the epistemic challenges posed by scientific reflection on human social existence are even greater than in the case of the science of the natural world.

The unity of the social is not imposed by the "observing subject" on "sensory elements that are in themselves unconnected." Rather, "since they are conscious and synthetically active, the social unity is realized directly by its elements and requires no observer.... Here the consciousness of forming a unity with the others *is* in fact the whole unity in question." However, what constitutes the unity of the social is not, Simmel continues, "abstract awareness of the concept of unity," but rather "countless singular relations, the feeling and knowledge with respect to the other of this determining and being determined." Such lived awareness of being-social is categorically distinct from scientific or synthetic knowledge that arises from the perspective of "an observing third party," and that difference is constitutive for the subject as such (*GSG* 11: 43–44).

This is not idealism. Both society and subjectivity are external to their own concepts; their being is constituted in part by their nonbeing. The differentiation of these differences is probably not entirely graspable in concepts: the distinction between society and the subjects that constitute it is not an ideal or psychological distinction, even though it is a function of the fact that the elements of society are thinking beings. As spiritual, historical, and cultural existences, their identity is constituted by the social and cultural world that comes into being through their "forming productivity"—yet it is this very surround that human beings then experience as an opposed and even alien force over and against their subjective individuality and will to freedom and autonomy.

The intersubjectively configured, performative and experiential knowledge of being-social is enacted in "social forms," that is to say, lived in configurations and constellations of superindividual existence. There is no human subjectivity without a relation to the dimension or function of sociohistorical objectification that constitutes human culture. Simmel's apparently Kantian conception of the subject has taken an idiosyncratic "Hegelian" turn, as his invocation of the objective genitive indicates: "Die Gesellschaft aber ist die objektive, des in ihr nicht mitbegriffenen Beschauers unbedürftige Einheit [Society, however, is the objective, independent unity of the observer who is not included in [literally thought along with] it" (*GSG* 11: 44).

Human subjectivity is constituted through intersubjectivity, but intersubjectivity is not the same thing as the social. One of Simmel's great and largely unrecognized theoretical contributions is to have articulated so clearly the tensions between the two. That is, to have identified the theoretical importance of the "third" as figure for or dimension of understanding, conceptualizing human existence both in its individual and in its sociocultural dimensions.

A passage elaborating what is at stake in this nonidentity of intersubjectivity and the social that demonstrates Simmel's significance for what would come to be known as existentialism is worth citing in full:

> The feeling of being I has an unconditionality and imperturbability that cannot be attained by any particular representation of a material externality. But this very certainty also includes for us [*für uns*], whether justifiably [*begründbar*] or not, the fact of a you [*des Dus*]; and as cause or as effect of this certainty, we feel the you as something independent of our representation of it, something that is just as much for itself as our own existence. That this for-itself of the other does not stop us from making it into our representation, that something which is in no way resolvable into our representing nonetheless becomes the content, thus the product, of this representing—that is the most profound psychological-epistemological schema and problem of becoming-social. (*GSG* 11: 44–45)

To ask "How is society possible?" is, then, to ask about the often alienating implications of representation and of our existence as beings who represent ourselves to ourselves, who are others for ourselves. Simmel's philosophical concerns extend to the objectifications of that process: the various modes in which human (historical, cultural) existence endures in the diverse realms and spheres, defined ultimately by value (legal, cultural, religious, etc.), that form the "third" dimension of sociality, the superindividual dimension that exists in and through but also beyond, before, and above the interactions of individual human beings.

To ask what makes society possible has "an entirely different methodological meaning" than its Kantian counterpart concerning "nature" (*GSG* 11: 45). Nothing corresponds to the "forms of cognition" that make it possible to synthesize the manifold into a causally comprehensible phenomenal world. What is in question in this case are, rather, "the conditions that lie a priori in the elements themselves, through which they really connect themselves into the synthesis 'society.'" Thus (reminding the reader of his prefatory remarks concerning his aspiration to establish "a new and independent task" for sociology and thereby determine its place in the "system of the sciences"), Simmel goes on to say that "in a certain sense the entire content of this book" is "an attempt to answer this question. For it seeks out the processes, ultimately realized in individuals, that condition their being-society—not as the temporally prior causes for this result, but as the partial processes of the synthesis, that we, subsuming, call society [or the social, *die Gesellschaft*]" (*GSG* 11: 45–46).

Sociology is, then, the study of the forms (configurations, constellations) of association and interaction through which these syntheses come into being and persist. Its objects are very far from being formalistic, abstract structures. Although expressible in general terms, social forms always exist in and through particular, historically, socially, and culturally realized, locations, beings, and events. There is no society independent of human actions and passions, no transcendent formal structure manifesting itself in diverse realities, and the institutions, structures, and objective historical realities of all sorts that impinge on individual existence must be understood as cultural products, as configurations ultimately created and sustained in and by human interaction.

"Society" is a process of historical flux: "technologies of life" and "cultural process" are historically and culturally configured instantiations of the very generative transindividual cultural life that such concepts attempt to grasp; there is no stepping outside to achieve an absolute perspective. The appeal to types, figures, and forms is a strategy for capturing the role of metaphor, of valuation, of semiosis, in the process of reciprocal interaction that is the becoming of the social, *Vergesellschaftung*, the essential feature of which is symbolic exchange. Reflections on "types" whose (social) identity is positively defined by exclusion is a means of exploring the materialized, situated, symbolic and social processes in and through which identities come into being in the first place. Sociological (psychological, historical) reflection on these matters points beyond its own limits. What is at stake are the conditions of possibility and the meaning and purpose of the web of reciprocal interaction that constitutes not the abstraction "society" but actual social and cultural life.

Identifying types or social forms such as "the stranger" both exemplifies and enables reflection on the quasi-transcendental features of human sociality that Simmel calls "sociological a prioris"—in this case, the principle that "the a priori of empirical social life is that life is not entirely social." As this formulation, with its significant invocation of the category of life, shows, the theoretical stakes are, in Simmel's sense of the term, metaphysical. Human beings are not simply (socially formed) subjects, and lived self-awareness of the limits to individual belonging to society, if not necessarily conscious, is constitutive of both the experience and the reality of society: "Societies are configurations out of beings that stand simultaneously inside and outside of them" (*GSG* 11: 53).

In Simmel's hands, reflection on the social opens up new dimensions for philosophical reflection in and on those aspects of existence that Heidegger, who rejected the category of social science, would later place under the category of "being-with" (*Mitsein*). In contrast, too, to Hannah Arendt, who regarded the emergence of the category of the social as obscuring the problems of reflection on human existence, for Simmel, society, social being, generates "perhaps the most conscious, at least the most universal elaboration [*Ausgestaltung*] of a fundamental form of life as such: that the individual soul can never stand inside a relation that it does not simultaneously stand outside of, that it is not placed in any order without finding itself juxtaposed to it. This holds from the most transcendent and very most universal contexts all the way to the most singular and accidental" (*GSG* 11: 53).

Here the *Sociology* anticipates the philosophical interpretation of human being as "*Grenzwesen*," as being constituted equally by boundaries and transgressions of boundaries, developed in the book Simmel thought of as his philosophical testament, the *Lebensanschauung* [*View of Life*] of 1918. More generally, the account of subjectivation presented in his introductory exploration of the "sociological a priori" explores questions about the relations between life and form and the epistemological and ethical implications of his relativist ontology that would continue to concern Simmel qua philosopher in the years to come.

In the case of natural determination, he writes, the individual enjoys a "feeling of being for itself" as entirely independent of all contingent causes, even though "this

I with all its freedom and being-for-itself, its opposition to mere nature, is nonetheless a part of it." The same complexity characterizes the "relation of individuals" to the "concept or feeling of being-social altogether": "We know ourselves on one hand as the *products* of society: the physiological series of ancestors, their adaptations and fixities, the traditions of their work, their knowledge and belief, the whole spirit of the past crystallized in objective form." But if our subjectivity depends on, is a product of, the objective achievements of human historical culture, we are also the makers of that culture and that history: "On the other hand we know ourselves as a *member* of society, just as heteronomously interwoven in the simultaneity of its life process and its meaning and purpose as in the succession [of natural causation]" (*GSG* 11: 54–55).

Creativity and subjective alienation, constraint and freedom, are inextricably entangled. No ultimate resolution (pace Hegel and Marx) can be envisioned. Subjective individuality and social being are interdependent but distinct categories: "The standpoint out of which the existence of the individual can be ordered and conceived of can just as well be taken from inside as from outside itself" since "the totality of life" encompasses both perspectives. "The fact of association brings the individual into a doubled position . . . it is comprised by it and at the same time juxtaposed to it, is a member of its organism and at the same time itself a closed organic whole, a being for [society] and for him or herself" (*GSG* 11: 55–56). The apparent opposition between our individual and social being, however great it may seem, is thus an illusion:

> between individual and society the inside and the outside are not two determinations that persist alongside one another . . . they refer to the entire unified position of the human being living socially. His existence is not only, in a dividing up of its contents, partially social and partially individual; it stands under the fundamental, formative, category of a unity that we cannot express in any other way than through the synthesis or simultaneity of the two logically opposed determinations of membership and being-for-oneself. (*GSG* 11: 56)

Here, in the midst of an argument seems to wear its Hegelian heart on its sleeve, Simmel takes a rather surprising turn, one that again anticipates developments in twentieth-century thought well beyond sociology—developments that, although in many cases galvanized by his students and readers, have generally been seen as entirely unrelated to Simmel's thinking. The passage continues:

> society consists not only of beings that are partially not socialized but out of those that feel themselves to be on the one hand fully social existences, on the other, while preserving the same contents, fully personal. And these are not two standpoints that lie without any relation alongside one another, as when one regards the same body now with respect to its mass and again with respect to its color, but rather the two form a unity that we call the social being. (*GSG* 11: 56)

This inherently conflicted and ambiguous "social being" is, he adds the "synthetic category" that unifies the elements of individual and society into an "a priori unity," just as the category of causality unifies cause and effect. An argument that began in Kant and Hegel ends with Nietzsche: strangeness (or foreignness) figures the way individual subjectivity tout court is inseparably intertwined with social being. Human beings live a life that is at once fully social, "produced and encompassed by society," and entirely individual, a life "for itself" lived "out of one's own center and for the sake of that center" (GSG 11: 54).

Simmel's stranger is a figure of philosophical as well as sociological significance, at once a synecdoche for the decentered subject and a microcosm of the form or configuration that defines the (modern, internally differentiated and fragmented) social totality. Like the other "types" whose "sociological significance" is defined "by their being somehow excluded from the society for which their existence is significant," the figure of the stranger exposes what Heidegger would call the *Existentiale* of human "being-in-the-world": being- and existing-with others.[28] Just as sociology cannot evade the philosophical questions that frame all reflection on human being, philosophy cannot begin from the individual alone. Subjects and subjectivation are simultaneously sociocultural, historical, political, psychological, and material processes, and "sociological" questions about them are simultaneously philosophical, since the fact that the individual human being is at once "a being for [society] and a being for him or her self" (GSG 11: 56) is an empirically and theoretically significant feature of both individual and collective life.

Disciplinarity and the Cultural Process

Simmel's 1908 *Soziologie* expands his analysis of many of the central concerns of the *Philosophie des Geldes*, tracing the ambiguous, and often mutually contradictory, historically unfolding effects of "the cultural process" in the modern life forms that foster individual autonomy and subjective differentiation, but also objectification and depersonalization. Here, too, Simmel focuses on the consequences for both "subjective" and "objective" culture of the ways individuals become integrated into ever larger, increasingly alienating, systems and (partial) totalities in industrialized, urbanized society.

Writing before the ascendance of Marxism in the historically decisive sense, Simmel attempted in his *Philosophy of Money* to do justice to both sides of the dialectic, setting out to "construct a story beneath historical materialism" by analyzing "economic forms themselves as the result of more profound valuations and tendencies, of psychological and even metaphysical preconditions," even as he accorded "economic life" its due "explanatory value" in clarifying "the causes of spiritual culture" (GSG 6: 13). For Simmel, values and facts are intertwined; epistemological and ontological reflection cannot be cleanly distinguished from social scientific investigations. In availing himself of a figurative language of "social forms" and "configurations" and in approaching cultural phenomena from multiple perspectives, he was neither conceptually confused nor unsystematic. His *Soziologie*, too, is the work

---

28. Heidegger writes of "structures of existence that are coeval with being-in-the-world, being with and existing with," the latter (*Mitdasein*) being that mode of being (*Seinsart*) in which the everyday mode of subjectivity he calls *das Man* ("the they") is "grounded" in Heidegger's (decidedly un-Simmelian) opinion (Martin Heidegger, *Sein und Zeit* [Tübingen: Max Niemeier, 1979], 114).

of a metaphysical relativist who understands disciplines as contingent formations of knowledge practices, a philosophical adventurer attempting to think together matters that the contingencies of institutional development and intellectual convenience have since accustomed us to thinking apart.

Shortly after the figure of the stranger appeared in the "Excursus on the Problem: How Is Society Possible?" Simmel reprised an important observation from the *Philosophy of Money* about the way "Modern culture, culture defined by the money economy [*modernen, geldwirtschaftlich bestimmten Kultur*]" shapes the intimate sphere of personality, inflects subjectivity itself. As people become identified with their social functions,

> the human being approaches the ideal of absolute objectivity [*Objekivität*]—as producer, as buyer or seller, generally as one accomplishing something; except in very high, leading positions, individual life, the tone of the total personality, has disappeared from the accomplishment, human beings are but the bearers of a reconciliation of doing and reciprocating according to objective norms, and all that does not belong in this pure objectivity [*Sachlichkeit*] has in fact been eliminated from [such exchange]. The personality with its special coloration, irrationality, inner life, has fully absorbed this "besides" into itself. (*GSG* 11: 52)

"Social activities or attunements" are experienced as entirely external as such subjects, vacillating between the extremes of personalization and abstraction, come to recognize that even "the consciousness" of what is excluded from their social being, the "energies and determinations directed toward their inner center, prove to have some sort of meaning for the activities and attitudes [*Gesinnungen*] directed toward the other" (*GSG* 11: 52–53). These are the conditions that foster estrangement—but also the recognition that, like oneself, the other is not entirely a social being, and even, as Simmel puts it, that "the apriori of empirical social life is that life is not entirely social" (*GSG* 11, 53).

Creating a canonical sociological "essay" by decontextualizing his "Excursus on the Stranger" from its (literal and conceptual) place in his "large" *Soziologie* has not only effaced what Simmel explicitly depicted as the theoretically significant exemplarity of the figure of "the stranger." It has obscured the way his meditation on the figure of the stranger and strangeness intervened philosophically at a crucial historical and cultural moment in the politically as well as intellectually decisive process of constituting the modern disciplinary imaginary. Disconnecting the topos from Simmel's discussion of the social a priori and turning "being-strange" into a "social role" occludes the philosophical significance of the figure as a mode of representing and reflecting on human existence as such. This doubly decontextualizing appropriation by fragments epitomizes the way the sociological reception of Simmel's work actively forecloses consideration of the philosophical questions he understood to be intricated with all thinking about human historical, cultural, and social life. In "forgetting" that Simmel, in a highly self-reflexive account of the ways philosophical questions arise "above" and "below" disciplinary boundaries, introduces this figure of internalized otherness as exemplifying the challenges confronting the new knowledge practices coeval with the emergence of the modern concept of society itself, the sociological reception that relegates such challenges to a constitutive outside becomes unable to give a theoretically adequate account of its own ends and practices.

The *Philosophy of Money* had attempted to counter just such an evacuation of ends through a performative demonstration of the necessity of historical-critical self-reflection on knowledge practices in the face of the instrumental understanding of reason gaining sway over human existence. The tradition of appropriating Simmel by fragments not only fails to do justice to his achievements and influence as philosopher and social and cultural theorist. It misses the opportunity his work provides to achieve a more adequate, historically self-reflexive purchase on the conceptual foundations of the contemporary disciplinary imaginary—and thereby on the deep theoretical and practical connections between the concerns of the social sciences and those of humanistic inquiry.

Our established disciplinary conventions and boundaries, which oppose the concerns of cultural and social, qualitative and quantitative inquiry, performatively obscure the urgent question of what knowledge itself means in modern society. As Simmel demonstrated, the instrumental, natural scientific understanding of rigorous inquiry and the correlative knowledge practices that have attained hegemonic status in modern life well beyond the ivory tower go hand in hand with a failure to reflect (philosophically but also historically, socially, and culturally) on the limitations of those perspectives and practices—and on the consequences of those limitations for the human and the natural world.

Because that very institutional-disciplinary ordering of knowledge practices renders historical self-reflection on the cultural-epistemological configuration of inquiry as a whole a matter for specialists, we fail to pose questions that, in ethical terms, we are obligated to ask. Indeed, those who are operating most effectively (both in psychic and pragmatic senses) within highly developed institutional environments circumscribed by webs of disciplinary and subdisciplinary specialization often have the greatest difficulty recognizing and reflecting upon the theoretical limitations and political consequences of their own knowledge practices—let alone on what the modern disciplinary imaginary, with its many regimes and practices of knowledge, itself includes and excludes.

The institutionalized amnesia involved is by no means exclusive to the social sciences, any more than the ahistorical conception of theory it anchors. It is probably the rule rather than the exception that disciplines, like so much else, come of age by disavowing their origins. Philosophy itself took form via such a repudiation of its predecessor and "antistrophe" (Aristotle), rhetoric, defaming thought that paid too much attention to its audience as sophistry. At stake in the genealogical recovery of the complex origins of sociology is our ability to recognize the paradigmatic contours of a forgetfulness that remains consequential for the contemporary disciplinary imaginary.

The actual historical origins of sociology were multivarious, but as it became institutionalized in universities, the discipline evolved toward a mode of self-legitimation rooted in Comtean positivism and elaborated in Durkheim's vision of a science of social facts. As what I have been calling the modern disciplinary order took shape in the early twentieth century, the men (and they were almost without exception men) who established the institutional and methodological foundations of the modern social sciences modeled their research paradigm on the natural sciences, focusing on questions of causation and empirical as opposed to hermeneutic methods, elaborating systems and testable models and neglecting historical and cultural context.[29] The "systematic" mode of reflection on disciplinary foundations, which deliberately sets aside whatever residual philosophical elements cannot be assimilated to the scientific paradigm, led to a virtual erasure of history by theory. Ironically, the ascendance of the (increasingly quantitative) social sciences in the second half of the twentieth century thereby fostered idealized and idealizing, unhistorical ways of thinking about theory and methods that continue to play a largely unexamined role in the self-understanding of contemporary mainstream social scientists, particularly in the Anglophone world.[30]

Professional training in most social science disciplines involves minimal attention to institutional and disciplinary history and prehistory. For many if not most practicing social scientists today, it simply does not matter where ideas or theories came from if they are capable of being operationalized to achieve interesting or important results. The study of "theory" and "methods" is treated as a largely technical matter that can proceed without any serious attention to the historical and cultural context in which ideas emerged—let alone intensive study of the philosophical precursors of modern social science. In this respect, the professional training of most U.S. sociologists today resembles that in the contemporary natural sciences, where scant attention is paid to disciplinary prehistory. As in physics or biology, the focus is on conveying the state of the field, so that students can begin building upon established questions and problems.

There is, then, a pronounced tendency to understand the origins of social science disciplines in ways that resonate with the heroizing narrative of Enlightenment. The historical and philosophical dubiousness of the story that has scientific rationality emerging out of the obscurity of metaphysics and proceeding to ever greater historical triumphs over superstition and prejudice need hardly be rehearsed here. Yet the cultural power of the narrative persists, and thanks to robust, largely tacit assumptions about knowledge and science, a highly idealized way of understanding the cultural and intellectual history of the disciplines—one that obscures the material processes by which science, including social science, took on its contemporary

---

29. This disciplinary ordering of knowledge emerged in tandem with the increasingly complex sociopolitical machinery of the bureaucratized nation-state and extends beyond the internal organization of scholarship and universities into the network of institutionalized strategies for managing and professionally administering populations. In our increasingly globalized and transnationally organized world, the prestige of the social sciences and the influence of expertise based in those disciplines has continued to grow—consider the deployment of anthropologists to Iraq by the U.S. Army, the role of psychologists in facilitating "enhanced interrogation" in the war on terror, or the integral place of social scientific knowledge practices in institutions from the IMF to the NGOs that help manage the highly globalized economy.

30. As I have argued elsewhere, these are tied up with highly problematic views about human existence—consider the role of assumptions about "rational actors" in social scientific modeling.

institutional form—enjoys forms of resilience that are not grounded in the quality or plausibility of the underlying ideas.

Academic disciplines are sociohistorical and cultural formations, historically shifting aggregations of knowledge and knowledge practices that are only to a rather limited extent matters of ideas at all. That the modern social sciences came into being and took root institutionally in a historical and cultural process that very directly involved differentiating out of and struggling for territory with philosophical predecessors continues to have significant direct and indirect effects that make themselves felt, symptomatically as it were, in the idealizing enframing of disciplinary evolution as progress.

To be clear: I am not attempting to reopen the pseudo-debate about the virtues and vices of "positivism." The disciplinary ordering of contemporary inquiry came about as a consequence of convergent intellectual, cultural, and institutional changes that register a truly epochal paradigm shift in the cultural role of knowledge of the human, and there is no turning back the clock. The social sciences could not possibly be "reabsorbed" into philosophy, itself changed irrevocably since psychology, sociology, anthropology, etc. became established as independent, empirically oriented modes of inquiry.

Disciplines are social and cultural formations whose boundaries evolve over time. While these adaptive changes may not constitute progress, they embody the irreversibility that, for good and bad, history brings. Since scholarly knowledge (like specialized knowledge of other sorts) is organized, maintained, and perpetuated in and through socially and culturally embodied structures, even when the conceptual blinders of disciplinary boundaries fail to serve a constructive intellectual purpose, transversing them in any given case is not simply an intellectual or conceptual challenge.

The question of what constitutes (the boundaries of) "society" or "the social" has never been settled with any scientific certainty. Yet what might seem to a philosopher to be an insurmountable problem does not appear to be even a serious difficulty for practicing social scientists. The operative assumption that there is an empirical object of study suffices to generate the possibility of investigation. Methodological and theoretical attention falls, by and large, on the considerable technical and pragmatic challenges involved in successfully engaging in the intricate and challenging knowledge practices of statistically organized social science.

What Simmel called intellectual culture has been disciplined, and the sort of unanswered fundamental questions that disturb humanist colleagues barely register in scholarly communities focused on answering questions about large-scale institutional and social phenomena by modeling and measuring behavior and opinions. From within today's methodologically oriented knowledge practices, (much of) what philosophers regard as matters of epistemological or even ontological import appears accessible to contextualist explanation. The resulting disregard is quite compatible with skepticism concerning a conception of progress based in an Enlightenment ideal of natural science for the Comtean question of whether the social sciences have inherited the mantle of philosophy need no longer arise.

In the fragmented disciplinary and interdisciplinary culture of the contemporary university, the fundamental problems Simmel and his contemporaries identified as constitutive for the social and cultural sciences are still unresolved. Yet the demands and rewards of participation in the normatively organized activities of modern social science constrain the ability and motivation of practitioners to step back to reflect, for example, on the question of what constitutes the social or whether questions of value are sufficiently understood when approached empirically. Under these circumstances, the recent "cultural turn" can comfortably coexist with hope that an even more radicalized materialism—in its most fashionable form currently framed as a turn to the neurological—can enable inquiry into human social and cultural existence to become positively scientific.

That disciplinary differences are cultural rather than (simply) intellectual is the source of some of the most serious challenges in the contemporary university. The problems of the twenty-first century are multifaceted and multiform; phenomena such as global warming or nuclear proliferation cannot be addressed adequately from within any particular disciplinary perspective.[31]

It can be invaluable to explore the liminal strategies of thought developed before the social and natural sciences were clearly differentiated from the humanities. But the guiding questions and problems, the evidentiary and methodological orientations that define disciplinary cultures have evolved. We cannot return to the conceptions of culture, society, science, or human being that were current at the turn of the twentieth century to resolve our own very different dilemmas. For better and for worse, we live in a world in which the most everyday realities of social life are shaped more by economic and international than cultural and national interests—and where the measurable forms of knowledge produced by chemists and sociologists rather than the questions generated by philosophers or in the study of literature and the arts are valorized.

It can hardly be regarded as surprising that under these circumstances the university's once largely unquestioned role in the perpetuation of cultural traditions of all sorts has become the object of both internal and external critique, even as a very different, technical and instrumental, vision of knowledge and of the aims of education gains hegemony in modern societies. In what Simmel called "money culture"—or even more pointedly, in relation to the fates of individual subjects striving to live meaningful lives in such a world, "modern culture defined by the money economy"—the dominance of quantitative values and practices of quantification has long since placed other standards and measures of value on the defensive.

---

31. The "problem-oriented" mode of interdisciplinarity that predominates in the contemporary natural sciences is clearly an improvement over the "silo" model. But bringing a variety of different disciplinary knowledge practices to bear on an issue, in itself, promises only a marginal improvement. Collaborations between disciplines that share large bodies of common assumptions do not necessarily foster genuine innovation. And collaborations across disciplinary lines where more profound differences are at stake tend to break down when conflicting fundamental assumptions (regarding evidence, for example) come into play and, at least insofar as institutional realities permit, thanks to the underlying dynamic of specialization tend themselves to generate new sub- and interdisciplines, as opposed to dialogic mutual reconsideration of perspectives and commitments.

There is much to be learned about the strengths and limits of our accustomed ways of thinking culture, subjectivity, and the social from a return to Simmel. His texts, at once resonant and foreign, can help us gain critical perspective on our own modernity and identify what is at stake both theoretically and historically today, when not just the disciplinary order of the university but also the socially dominant paradigms of human self-understanding are once again, still, in extreme flux.

To integrate Simmel's effort to develop a relativist "philosophy of social and historical life as a whole" into the intellectual and cultural history of the twentieth century, we need to grasp what the story of his reception reveals about the constraints on thought in a world of disciplinary knowledge practices. In telling this story, I hope to have at least disclosed the possibility that we may come to see our own ways of thinking and seeing, and hence the dilemmas of our time, differently. The encounter with Simmel's modernism can provide new perspective on our own contingent modes of understanding, not least by reminding us that today's highly specialized, technologically driven knowledge practices are situated at the end of a development whose beginning was already marked by the (disavowed) failure of the "science of human society" to fulfill its initial promise to render philosophy obsolete.

Simmel's relativist conviction was that human beings could not ever reach final explanations, since neither form nor that which exceeds and dissolves form—what he called life—can be adequately understood in terms of the concepts and language we bring to bear. His skeptical attitude toward the possibility of reaching definitive answers to questions that had troubled human beings for eons was shaped by his reflections on the shifting organization of knowledge and inquiry in the modern university. It is in this context that the question of Simmel's relation to philosophy gains its real importance.

Simmel, like his modernist contemporaries, understood himself to be observing the dissolution of traditional understandings of meaning—of subjective identity, ethical obligation, artistic value. Even as the technological capacities born of modern scientific progress revolutionized human life, the limits of rationality and of the possibilities of scientific knowledge were becoming apparent culturally. The questioning of foundations that gave rise to such important developments in all cultural spheres was well under way by the 1890s. In science and philosophy, in religion and the arts, inside and outside the university, the institutional and cultural transformations of the dawning twentieth century were implicitly and explicitly shaped by this larger modernist crisis of meaning.

Today, as the spell of the short twentieth century fades, it is easier to see that these crises and these developments neither began in 1914 nor ended in 1989. By the end of Simmel's life, the inherited consensus about (or, to put it less politely, the hegemonic vision of) what counted in and as humanistic and more generally culturally and historically oriented knowledge no longer really existed. Yet as the bloody history of the twentieth century and the reinvigoration of religion as a self-conscious defense against the depredations of the modern in the early twenty-first century attest, the efforts of intellectuals to turn the experience of dissolution into a new, modernist (non)foundation have not exactly been met with popular success.

The disciplining of the study of literature and the arts, religion, history, and culture has created a class of experts with their own professionalized, often highly technical knowledge practices. However valuable the results may be, the ensuing disconnection and even alienation from the everyday has come at a high cost. With technoscience on the ascendant, the social and cultural marginalization of the disciplines primarily concerned with the meaning, value, and purpose of human life has proceeded apace. The widespread assumption that it is naïve to be concerned with such questions—that meaning, purpose, and value are matters for one's private rather than professional attention—has become widespread within the academy, by no means exclusively outside the "humanities." The organization of the contemporary university makes manifest how the study of nature and of society and culture have been split off from philosophical reflection. Sociologically, and culturally too, the specialized ordering of inquiry is symptomatic of the dilemma of knowledge in the contemporary Western world more generally.

What can today be recognized as a tectonic cultural shift began as a fault line in Simmel's own discipline. The modern disciplinary order arose in and through the institutional fragmentation of philosophy. In the fluid intellectual context of the nineteenth-century fin de siècle, as scholarship modernized and professionalized, as technoscience and modern medicine emerged and the social sciences gained autonomy and institutional self-determination, philosophy itself entered into a paradigm crisis concerning not just the scope but also the nature of its concerns and knowledge practices.[32]

As philosophy professionalized, it was deeply transformed by the loss to other disciplines (psychology, political science) of huge areas of traditional concern, by developments in the natural sciences, both physical and biological, and by the ascendance within the discipline itself of efforts to achieve a scientific method in the modern sense. Particularly in the Anglo-American context, the aspiration to provide a theory of knowledge adequate to the burgeoning natural and social scientific disciplines increasingly overshadowed concern with the questions that had traditionally dominated the Western philosophical tradition.

These changes, too, were packaged in the idiom of scientific progress. The logic of inquiry was being revolutionized, and foundational categories—metaphysics, spirit, consciousness—were jettisoned in favor of a new mode of symbolic representation that facilitated the abstraction of philosophical "questions" and "problems" from their context in what became the hegemonic "analytic" approach to philosophy. As in other fields, in the course of the twentieth century, interest in the history of the discipline itself became a relatively marginal subspeciality.

Both directly, through the influence of philosophers and indirectly, via the considerable impact of these new ways of thinking about evidence, proof, and argument beyond philosophy proper, the dialectical tradition Simmel represented was

---

32. Simmel, it should be recalled, was the contemporary not just of Husserl, Weber, and Rickert but also of Frege and Mach (one and two decades older, respectively) and Russell (somewhat more than a decade younger).

marginalized. In the course of the twentieth century, the philosophical concerns that animated his work came to seem like relics of the past. The growth of modern technoscience and statistically driven social science undermined the prestige of the forms of knowledge associated with humanistic inquiry and grounded in culturally and historically oriented reflection. Particularly outside the ambit of Western Marxism, the critical resources for calling into question the models of science, scholarship, and indeed of thought itself grew ever weaker.

That Simmel fails to be remembered as a philosopher is arguably as much due to these tectonic shifts in cultural valuation and philosophical practices as to his actual contributions to sociology. The global devaluation of humanistic inquiry in general and of modes of philosophizing that maintain an allegiance to dialectical complexity and critical self-reflexivity in particular contribute quite directly to the difficulty in rendering his importance as a thinker legible. But there are also specific challenges in recognizing the power of Simmel's idiosyncratic style of thought and writing from within poststructuralist theoretical frameworks. The same decontextualizing and dehistoricizing strategies of thought and skepticism about categories such as intention and purpose, meaning and value proper to the analytic philosophical tradition have been disseminated in and through theoretical practices with very different epistemic outlooks. That Simmel's frank concern with problems of ultimate meaning and value appears naive or idealistic obscures the power of his culturalist vision of epistemological self-reflexivity and the sophistication of his account of how modern technologies of life have undermined our access to fundamental (ethical, but also metaphysical) questions.

To respond to the social, political, and environmental challenges of the twenty-first century, we need, not just fresh approaches to already recognized problems or recombinations of previously existing knowledge practices, but new ways of thinking the human relation to the world altogether. Such a deep rethinking entails calling into question our most basic assumptions about modes of categorizing knowledge: it requires a critique of the disciplinary imaginary itself. Rather than succumbing to the pessimism of Adorno's "no life in the untrue" or the terrifying despair of Heidegger's "only a God can save us now," we may at least attempt to ask ourselves how it is possible to think differently about our collective circumstances.

The challenges we confront, the perils that threaten the future of our collective life, are so momentous; our inherited science and technology, our culture and ways of life so implicated in the creation of those threats, that anything less than a radical paradigm shift seems doomed to inadequacy. Our habitual, disciplinary, habits of thought are so deeply imbricated with the powerful, market-driven paradigms of techno- and social science that they can hardly be expected to help us address the dangers posed by the interpenetrating and accelerating ecological, economic, and sociopolitical crises to the future of human society and much of the rest of life on the earth.

Simmel, who never abandoned his conviction that human beings could learn to experience a world in becoming, may perhaps provide a touchstone for strivings to think differently. Within his self-reflexively relativist "image of the world"

[*Weltbild*], it is necessary to embrace the transgression of boundaries and to interrogate the ethical and metaphysical implications of every assumption and apparent certainty, to question the foundations of every knowledge practice. Simmel's example might just thereby, as he put it, have proved "its methodological significance as the form of future correctness" (*GSG* 6: 12).

Epilogue: Georg Simmel as Modernist Philosopher

In February 1911, Georg Simmel sent Edmund Husserl his latest work, a "little booklet" entitled *Hauptprobleme der Philosophie* (Main Problems of Philosophy). He modestly warned that it would probably not contain anything new to his "revered friend," adding: "As a measure of our philosophical culture, though, it is not entirely uninteresting."[1]

Simmel's *kleines Büchelchen* was the "Jubilee" volume Crayen had commissioned in 1908, and it had sold 13,000 copies in ten weeks. "Such a thing would have been utterly impossible twenty years ago," Simmel declared, adding that he was proud to have contributed as teacher and writer to bringing about the change. He hoped that this, his latest work, "which makes no concessions to popularity," would also do its part "to awaken the need for philosophy as a world concept [*Weltbegriff*]." That is, to spell out Simmel's allusion to Kant, for a worldly conception of philosophy, one "that concerns that which necessarily interests everyone."[2]

As for *Hauptprobleme*, itself, it was merely supplementary, a *parergon*. In an early allusion to the project that would eventually come to fruition in his last book, *Lebensanschauung* (The View of Life), Simmel confided to Husserl that he was "occupied with very difficult investigations" with no end in sight.[3] But he had temporarily interrupted those labors to assemble what would become the influential collection of essays that recast Kant's cosmopolitan conception of philosophy as *Philosophische Kultur* (Philosophical Culture).[4]

In 1983, after *Philosophische Kultur* had been out of print in German for sixty years, Jürgen Habermas wrote, in introducing a new edition, that Simmel's approach had "changed the mode of perception, the themes, and writing style of an entire intellectual generation." Today, more than thirty years on, Habermas's judgment still

---

1. Rather less modestly, he added in parenthesis: "except perhaps in the interpretation of the fundamental motifs of the Platonic theory of ideas and Spinoza's substance, and maybe in the presentation of Hegel." Simmel to Husserl, February 19, 1911 (*GSG* 22: 940–41). Subsequent citations in the text are to the same letter. Before the decade was out, 37,000 copies of *Hauptprobleme* were in print (*GSG* 14: 476).
2. Kant opposes a worldly to a scholastic conception of philosophy (*Kritik der reinen Vernunft*, B867).
3. He wondered, he wrote, whether he would "experience their conclusion."
4. That volume, first published in November of 1911, includes thirteen essays, ten of which had first been published between 1909 and 1911. The second edition (with a few emendations by the author) appeared shortly after Simmel's death in 1918; the book was reprinted again in 1923. Now *GSG* 14: 159–459.

rings true: "For us, Simmel as a critic of culture is in a distinctive way at once distant and close."[5]

Philosophische Kultur includes, inter alia, essays on fashion, religion, adventure, the Alps, and Rodin as well as a series of extended meditations on gender and culture, including the very important and often misconstrued "Der Begriff und die Tragödie der Kultur" ("The Concept and the Tragedy of Culture").[6] Simmel's Introduction sets out the modernist concept of philosophy that justifies unifying such heterogeneous topics under a single cover: a focus on the process of thinking as opposed to its content or results. "What is essential" to philosophy, he writes, "is a certain spiritual attitude toward world and life, a functional form and way of taking things up and dealing with them within oneself." He calls for "an entirely principled turn from metaphysics as dogma . . . to metaphysics as life or as function"—to a new mode of philosophizing defined by "the unity of the movement of thought" itself (*GSG* 14: 165).[7]

Simmel's understanding of "philosophical culture" includes, but is not reducible to, a historical perspective on "the philosophical process" as a whole in and through which different positions are developed, advanced, and laid aside over time. "What is essential and significant in philosophy" turns just as much on the "formal being-in-motion of the philosophizing mind [*Geist*]" as on the substantive positions attained and defended. Pursuing philosophy in a modern way means recognizing the independence of this "spiritual-intellectual attitude [*geistige Attitüde*] to life and world" from all particular claims: "such a division between the function and content, the living process and its conceptual result, signifies an entirely universal orientation of the modern spirit [*des modernen Geistes*; perhaps, 'modern culture']" (*GSG* 14: 162).

But the project of philosophical culture is not just oriented, methodologically defined, by a mode of formal self-reflexivity historically identifiable as modern. Foregrounding the modern "spiritual-cultural attitude" makes possible a new mode of philosophizing with deep affinities to other literary and cultural modernisms. In it, form, as it were, returns as being, and "the metaphysical drive, the process or

---

5. Jürgen Habermas, "Georg Simmel über Philosophie und Kultur," repr. in Habermas, *Texte und Kontexte* (Frankfurt am Main: Suhrkamp, 1991), 161, 157.

6. The book itself is not available in English, but many of the essays have been translated. See Thomas M. Kemple, "Simmel in English: A Bibliography," in *Anthem Companion to Georg Simmel*, ed. Thomas Kemple and Olli Pyyhtinen (London and New York: Anthem Press, 2016), 191–98. *Simmel on Culture: Selected Writings*, ed. David P. Frisby and Mike Featherstone (Thousand Oaks, CA: Sage, 1997), renders the Introduction.

7. Simmel's conception of philosophical culture was neither abstract or idealistic; it stood for the anti-systematic vision of philosophizing he had already been performatively disseminating for over a decade. Long passages of the text discussed here reappear in the preface to the collection of French translations Simmel published in 1912 under the rubric of "Relativist Philosophy," subtitled *Contribution à la culture philosophique*. And the very day after his appointment in Strasbourg was finalized, Simmel wrote Rickert to propose that they work to create a regional philosophical culture by convincing "as many students as possible to move between the three universities [Strasbourg, Freiburg, and Heidelberg]" in a philosophical *Bildungsgang*—an educational journey. Eventually, Simmel hoped, they could "seek to expand the concept of 'philosophical culture' and introduce a certain, philosophically oriented cooperation among the universities in neighboring fields as well" (Simmel to Rickert, January 28, 1914 [*GSG* 23: 284]).

the spiritual attitude that flows out of it, can be grasped as a character or a value" in itself (*GSG* 14: 163). This liberation from a traditional orientation toward "objective problems" and results brings a new, historically and culturally self-reflexive, performative—modernist—mode of philosophizing into being.

Distinguishing form from content in this way inaugurates the development that would culminate in what we have come to call "theory," enriching and deepening philosophy itself by disclosing new kinds of objects and sites for reflection. As Simmel puts it, recognizing "the functional, the attitude, the profound orientation and rhythm of the thought process as that which makes it philosophical" renders the range and extension of possible objects "a priori unlimited." And identifying "the mode or form of thought [*Denkart oder Denkform*]" as the unifying element makes possible a new kind of philosophical writing, which gathers "the most substantively heterogeneous investigations" into a prismatic, modernist unity. The individual essays that make up *Philosophische Kultur* are as much illustrations of that principle as is the book's subdivision into sections "On the Philosophy of the Sexes," "On Aesthetics," "On Artistic Personalities," and so on. "Philosophical culture" is both enacted and produced through a mode of thought and writing that aims not to reach unchanging truths but to display the delicate fluctuations of thinking itself—and thereby to evoke in its readers a self-reflexive, experiential "need for philosophy as world-concept" (*GSG* 14: 163)

Beginning with money and all its synecdochic, metaphorical (and metaphysical) movements and metonymic social and cultural effects, Simmel had developed a performative style of thought that revealed the philosophical significance of the most diverse aspects of culture and experience—everything from fashion and flirtation to Michelangelo and Goethe, from the modern metropolis to Venice and Rome. But this distinctively modernist, formally oriented conception of reflective unity generated a philosophical oeuvre that can easily appear fragmented, incoherent, even internally contradictory—and a mode of writing that precisely in the richness and diversity of its topics and complex performative strategies has all too often been misconstrued as unmediated description.

Here as elsewhere, Simmel articulates the metaphilosophical position that ought to have prevented his being misread as an unsystematic thinker but that has arguably had quite the opposite effect: "Historical experience" has revealed that whenever human "metaphysical orientedness" is tied to a determinate content, "tremendous cosmic and psychic regions" are excluded from "philosophical interpretation and exploration [*Vertiefung*]" (*GSG* 14: 163). The difficulty lies not just with "the ever-relative capability of each absolute principle" but in the ways in which adherence to any particular foundational point of view tends to foreclose exploration of the ambiguity and complexity of everyday life.

To be true to its calling, Simmel insists, philosophy must embrace the world, must begin from the richness and multiplicity of lived experience and encompass even "life's most transient and isolated superficial phenomena" (*GSG* 14: 163). No "single metaphysical foundational concept [*Grundbegriff*]" can possibly suffice: "If the philosophical process is really to take the universal breadth of existence as its point of departure," it must proceed in an "unlimited number of directions" and issue in a genuine multiplicity of ultimately incommensurable metaphysical perspectives (*GSG* 14: 163–64). In sharp contrast to the analytic aspiration to remake philosophy on the model of natural scientific explanation, Simmel advocates embracing, not reducing, complexity. He sees a "most inner relationship between the full plenitude of existence as it is given … and the entire plenitude of possible metaphysical absolutisms" (*GSG* 14: 164).

Simmel's distinctive style of thought anchors a self-reflexively modernist, self-consciously performative mode of philosophizing that also finds expression in the architecture of his books. His self-relativizing practice as a writer, his constant shifting of perspective within individual essays, his penchant for bringing together disparate topics and forms of evidence, his habit of enfolding incompatibly dissonant, even contradictory positions within a single line of argument—all of this is his method for imparting "philosophical culture." His texts enact "the being-in-motion [*Bewegtheit*] of spirit," which is "in itself metaphysical" (*GSG* 14: 164). Thinking is most adequate to the complexity and multiplicity of the real "precisely in such giving itself up to the metaphysical function"; "dogmatic crystallization" is inimical to this being-in-motion "of philosophical life itself" (*GSG* 14: 164)—to the pursuit of the love of wisdom in which the way and the goal are inseparable.

Simmel emphasizes that his "point of view is most profoundly distinct from eclecticism and readiness to compromise [*Kompromißweisheit*]" (*GSG* 14: 164). Thinking that does not grasp its own genealogy reinscribes the transcendental illusions of the naïve image of truth as certainty. In advocating a focus on thought as process, on the activity of "philosophical life" as such, Simmel is calling for a far more radical embrace of the incommensurability of interpretive perspectives. His principled relativism accents the multiplicity of human cognitive, embodied experience of the world and draws attention both thematically and formally to the role of tacit, mediated, and enacted configurations of knowing and valuing. What is at stake is no less than "an entirely principled turn from metaphysics as dogma to metaphysics as life or function" (*GSG* 14: 164). A turn, that is, from philosophy understood as a contemplative search for ultimate substances or foundations to an emphasis on the form and process of theorizing itself as a cultivated practice of relating thoughtfully to the world—in Simmel's terms, on the "unity of the movement of thought" in which all philosophical paths begin (*GSG* 14: 165).

Such a mode of self-understanding, in which the thinking subject is acutely self-aware of, yet profoundly distanced from, his or her own metaphysical predilections and commitments, constitutes a distinctively modernist form of philosophical self-reflexivity. Simmel regards this "shift of accent in metaphysics [*Akzentverlegung der Metaphysik*]" as "the condition of a 'philosophical culture' in a broader and modern sense. For this culture does not consist in the knowledge of metaphysical systems or the avowal of individual theories but in a continuous spiritual relation to all existence [*Dasein*]" (*GSG* 14: 165).

To be philosophically cultured in the modern sense is, then, self-reflexively to embrace intellectual-spiritual "being-in-motion": to take up the task of grasping life itself in all its multiplicity and apparent incommensurability from the self-relativizing, historically and culturally self-aware perspective of the modern human being. The tectonic shift in and through which metaphysics itself had become relativized to the lived experience of the philosophical adventurer thus discloses a constructive conceptual strategy for coming to terms with the loss of ultimate foundations and the dearth of absolute truths in modernity.

Simmel emphasizes that his conception of metaphysics departs radically from those of the "genial creators in the history of philosophy," whose "spiritual individuality" was such that form and content were radically inseparable and a "philosophical attitude toward life" had to be projected onto "a fully and univocally determined world-image" (GSG 14: 165). Such an absolute and integral unity of thought and being was a thing of the past. But a relativistic, post- and anti-dogmatic "shift of accent in metaphysics" from the search for totalizing systems to a "comprehensive spiritual relation to all of existence" could provide the basis for a modern philosophical culture, just as religiosity could still provide the guiding value to shape an existence no longer organically unified by orthodoxy.

Thinking itself thereby comes to be understood in a new, modern way: moving beyond the search for timeless, context-independent truths in and through such a self-reflexive shift in perspective reveals the institutional and historical significance of the philosophical effort to capture the complexity and multiplicity of the world in thought as a "bearer, an element, or a form of culture altogether." For Simmel, the practice of thought that constitutes such a modernist philosophical culture must remain "unsettled [labil]," able "to see and to move back from every singular theory to the functional commonalities of all of them. The results of these efforts may be fragmentary, but the effort itself is not" (GSG 14: 166).

Here as elsewhere, Simmel emphasizes the performativity of his strategy for re-envisioning philosophy, his pragmatic solution to the Hegelian "problem of beginning." The reader would have to judge whether he had succeeded and in particular whether his "fundamental concept of philosophical culture bears or is borne by" the diverse material treated in *Philosophische Kultur*. "Depending on the point of view taken, the work depends on the presumption or sets out the proof: it is a prejudice that ... what one could call *giving meaning* [*Sinngebung*] must necessarily lead to *a single* final point and float unmoored in the air if it does not receive its orientation from such a point."

Simmel both insists on the philosophical or theoretical value of his own anti-foundationalism and emphasizes the aesthetic quality of his conception by closing the introduction to *Philosophische Kultur* with a "fable" that illustrates his vision of modernist metaphysics. The children of a farmer, by searching long and in vain for treasure their father claimed to have buried, render the land they have inherited three times more fertile. So too in Simmel's unending dialectic: "We shall not find the treasure, but the world that we have dug up looking for it will bring threefold fruit to the spirit—even if in reality it was never a question of the treasure at all but of the fact that this digging is the necessity and inner determination of our spirit" (GSG 14: 166–67).

Simmel's constant shifts of perspective and topic, his aleatory, seemingly stream-of-consciousness lines of argument, and the complex, by no means transparent, articulations of his writing perform a self-reflexively modernist affirmation of the self-relativizing process of thought itself that remains of considerable theoretical and methodological interest more than a century later. Focusing on his modernist conception of philosophical form reveals a truly distinctive and significant philosophical achievement and helps account for the wide-ranging influence of his innovative style of thought. Not only did his efforts to preserve and foster what he called "philosophical culture" disclose, often for the very first time, the theoretical significance of everyday phenomena such as gender, urban life, fashion, and the role of technology in society that subsequently became established arenas of inquiry in modern cultural theory. By teaching his readers to distinguish the philosophical value and distinctiveness of the "metaphysical drive" and the "spiritual attitude" associated with it from the pursuit of absolute truth claims, Simmel's writings demonstrated that the multiplicity and inner heterogeneity of modern experience could be addressed through a self-reflexive shift in philosophical perspective.

Although he insisted on the historicity and cultural relativity of thought, including his own, Georg Simmel by no means saw his philosophical convictions and strategies as limited in their significance to his own time. His mature texts participated, however, in the broader "modernist" transformation in ways of thinking about and representing human experience and stand, thematically as well as formally, in an explicitly self-reflexive relation to the epochal sociocultural and spiritual-intellectual paradigm change then under way.

Simmel understood all too intimately that philosophy in a traditional sense was at an end, even if the partisan of "philosophical culture" had long since ceased to celebrate its eclipse by the "science of human society." A visionary account of the evolution of modern *Wissenschaft* is at the heart of his monumental analysis of the genesis and operations of the modern money economy as both product and vehicle of the displacement and de-valorization of non-monetary modes of valuation. As the *Philosophy of Money* showed, the ever more specialized, technically oriented disciplinary organization of knowledge practices both expresses and fosters the general modern tendency to intellectualization and rationalization, and hence to the privileging of mechanistic, reductive, instrumental approaches and modes of valuation over those less easily quantified, even to the foreclosure of larger questions of meaning and value. His writings, both "sociological" and "philosophical," performatively address the limits of the "scientific" approaches to human sociocultural and historical life that stand in reciprocal relation to—are enabled by and reinforce—the disenchanted understanding and experience of human being that corresponds to "culture defined by the money economy" (*GSG* 11: 52) and disclose new perspectives for reflection on philosophical questions concerning the conditions of possibility of thought itself.

In his self-described philosophical "testament," the *View of Life*, Simmel develops this modernist understanding of philosophical culture into a conception of relativism as a "positive metaphysical world-image." It will be impossible to do more here than gesture toward that late, great work, which merits and rewards the closest reading. The stature of its ambition is vividly illustrated by the next piece of the fragmentary evidence that has been preserved of his friendship with Husserl.

A few weeks after the letter cited above, Simmel wrote again to thank him for sending "Philosophy as Rigorous Science." After warmly reassuring Husserl that he had by no means been angered by it, Simmel emphasizes their shared opposition to philosophy professorships being taken over by "*Experimentators*," and, alluding once again to Kant, declares that all who "have philosophy at heart" should rejoice at Husserl's critique of experimental psychology.

> With respect to your determinations on philosophy, science, worldview—admittedly, I draw the lines differently. But I find the multiplicity through which our poor souls attempt to say the unsayable and solve the insoluble a wonderful thing; we have after all been given the capacity (which more and more appears to me as an ultimate foundation of all spirit), to stand *opposite* even our own opinion and regard it on the same plane as that of the other.[8]

The philosophical equanimity that accompanied Simmel's mature relativism was no merely theoretical attitude. He goes on to add a few words about the latest failed attempt to secure a regular professorship that illuminate his liminal situation on the fault lines of the modern life of the mind:

> naturally there can be for me *objectively*, no more favorable and more influential position than the one I have here, and the thought of a chair (*Ordinariat*) fills me with horror. But after I have spent an entire lifetime in Berlin, I'd like, purely for reasons of internal development to exist for a series of years elsewhere, which for the sake of the economic basis I cannot really do other than on the foundation of an appointment.... If I were a rich man, I would probably go as a *Privatdozent* to some south German university or other.

As we know, things turned out very differently. Soon enough, even as his long-denied wish for a chair in philosophy was fulfilled, the world in which it was possible to retreat into the provinces and devote oneself to philosophy would, at least for Simmel, be shattered forever.

Simmel in Strasbourg

During the final years of Georg Simmel's life, the Great War raged on seemingly without end. Exiled, as it were, from Berlin beginning in March 1914, he had landed, ironically, right back in the midst of things—in what almost immediately became the "citadel" (*Festung*) Strasbourg. Like so many others, Simmel was swept up in the patriotic fervor of August 1914. By early the next year, though, he was already—very publicly—expressing deep concern about the disastrous cultural consequences of the war for Europe as a whole. In April 1915, in Simmel's judgment, "Europe as spiritual configuration [*geistige Gebilde*]" was already "so torn to pieces that its growing together again seems to me to lie at a very great distance"; in July, he wrote in the *Berliner Tageblatt* of "the suicide of Europe."[9] This sort of thing did not sit well with

---

8. Simmel to Husserl, March 13, 1911 (*GSG* 22: 950–51).

9. Simmel to Helmer Key, April 12, 1915 (*GSG* 23: 514), published in the *Svenska Dagbladet* on May 16, 1915 in both German and Swedish (as "Kulturarbetet efter krigets slut"); Simmel, "Europa und Amerika," *Berliner Tageblatt*, July 4, 1915 (*GSG* 13: 139).

the authorities, and in early August, proceedings were initiated against Simmel for his purportedly "unpatriotic way of thinking."[10] He defended himself passionately and successfully against this quite unjust charge, avoiding the danger that he would be removed from the professorship that he had, at long last, attained, but he was warned against further political engagement.

It cannot be said that Simmel entirely heeded this warning, for he continued publicly to express his views about the cultural and spiritual significance of the war, and in 1917, he published a best-selling collection of essays and speeches titled *Der Krieg und die geistigen Entscheidungen* (The War and the Spiritual Decisions) that aspired, as he put it in the Preface, to provide "interpretations of the inner side of the world's destiny."[11]

> Today, when every present and future victory must be paid for with the loss of the most precious human beings and with the suicidal destruction of enduring European values, who will dare to decide whether our great-grandchildren will curse or bless this catastrophe? . . . The cohesive spiritual-intellectual configuration [*geistige Einheitsgebilde*] that we called "Europe" is destroyed and its reconstruction is not to be foreseen.[12]

I do not want to defend Simmel's war writings, but I think it is fair to say that accusations that he chauvinistically placed his philosophy at the service of the war hardly do justice to a thinker who with foresight and temerity defended "the idea of Europe" from within Alsace. Simmel viscerally experienced what we now know as World War I as an epochal turning point in European life, including through his very public estrangement from his French colleagues. In March 1915, he confided to Margarete Susman: "Since the war [began] my imagination has been lamed, every thought is so burdened with the weight of the German and European fate that it cannot move forward."[13]

The war seemed quite literally to punctuate the ending already implicit in Simmel's departure from Berlin. That July, he wrote other friends:

> As I stepped down from the rostrum in Berlin for the last time, I knew: It is over! I knew that life's highlands, on which I had walked so long, would now slowly incline down—knew it without complaint. . . . But the war placed a period where I had at first only expected a semicolon. I am convinced that a new world period is beginning . . . & that I shall belong to the old. Certainly I thought I was in various ways acting into the future; but the world has taken a turn in which in all likelihood the future I had helped to prepare does not lie.

---

10. The accusation was based on public statements in which fidelity to the "idea of Europe" appeared to trump national loyalty. Regarding the procedures undertaken, see Simmel's letter to Hans von Dallwitz, imperial governor in Alsace-Lorraine of August 16, 1915, in which he responds to the charges (*GSG* 22: 548–52). Other documents related to the proceedings are in *GSG* 24: 417–29.

11. Simmel's *Der Krieg und die geistigen Entscheidungen* (The War and the Spiritual Decisions) (*GSG* 16: 7–58; here p. 9) included an essay and a lecture from 1916 as well as (somewhat revised) earlier material; it was published in June 1917 and sold so well that a second printing was immediately necessary (*GSG* 16: 431).

12. Simmel, "The Idea of Europe" (*GSG* 16: 55). Revised from a version published in March 1915 in the *Berliner Tageblatt* (*GSG* 13: 112–16).

13. Simmel to Susman, March 5, 1915 (*GSG* 23: 489–90). Simmel also affirms his intention to begin working again, presumably on the book on metaphysics he had set aside in 1913 (*GSG* 23, *Editorischer Bericht*: 491) and reports that he and Gertrud are resuming their *jours*, the Monday salon, in their new city.

That is what is *personally* hard in this time. . . . That my acting and thinking stretched into a future that will not become present, that I have strewn the seeds where there is not fertile ground.[14]

Simmel's late work lies, then, under the sign of impossibility. Extending the analyses he had developed in the prewar years, he struggled to express a perspective he himself experienced as at once timely and untimely.

Simmel's mature philosophy of life must be read in this context—in a very real sense, a tragic one. Its fullest expression may be found in the late work with a title at once grand and modest: *Lebensanschauung: Vier metaphysische Kapitel* (Life-View: Four Metaphysical Chapters).

Simmel finished the book when he knew he was dying of liver cancer and was in considerable pain, refusing morphine until he had finished writing.[15] What is genuinely remarkable is not simply that he managed to complete this impressive and widely (albeit often stealthily) appreciated work under such difficult personal conditions. In the face of a war he correctly regarded as the end of the world that had been his, a war that, furthermore, he saw as the fulfillment of the darkest potentials of the modern, Simmel, good Nietzschean that he was, managed to write a book that wrings hope from that very ending. His meditations on life's self-transcendence disclose the possibility of meaning in mortality; his conception of the "individual law" locates ethical action within the very fragmentation and disenchantment of post-theological existence; his vision of cultural life as self-overcoming creation of form affirms human being in a world devoid of enduring standards of truth or value, where the nihilism of instrumental reason and the vacuity of the forms of objectivity fostered by the money economy were becoming apparent.

What was at stake in and for philosophy in the modern, that is to say, godless and ontologically ungrounded, world, was not at all abstract or scholastic for Simmel. By focusing on embodied existence and on the concrete social and cultural phenomena through which epistemological and ethical dilemmas are lived, he disclosed a new, existentially oriented practice of thought. Here as elsewhere in his "essayistic" work, Simmel makes questions about the meaning and ends of science and knowledge and the vicissitudes of human self-reflection in modern life accessible—thereby anticipating, prefiguring, and preparing the way for the emergence of cultural and critical "theory" as the disenchanted inheritor of philosophy. By opening thought to a new sort of practice, a style of interpretation that comes to terms with the lack of ultimate foundations by disclosing the profundity of the everyday, Simmel's vision of philosophy as oriented toward the "transcendence of life" at once extended and destabilized the dialectical tradition. His modernist mode of philosophizing wagered everything on a performative self-overcoming of the skeptical dissolution of foundations guided by this vision of life as itself "more than life"—according to

---

14. Simmel to Anna and Ignaz Jastrow, July 13, 1915 (*GSG* 23: 534–35).

15. Versions of three of the four essays had already been published in *Logos*. But two, including the remarkable and influential "On the Metaphysics of Death" were so changed, on the author's view, "that they had to be viewed as new works" (*GSG* 16: 236).

which, as he put it in 1916, "every moment of its continuous becoming-other is not a part but the whole of life in the form of this specific moment."[16]

Simmel was hardly unaware of the intellectual and practical perils of his metaphysical views, but he understood his responsibility as teacher and philosophical author to include this Nietzschean affirmation of the aporetic epistemic circumstances of modern existence. In a world where there is in principle no longer any appeal to absolute, transcendent truths or values, human individuals must be both (ethically) autonomous and (self-consciously) social beings. In continuing to work on behalf of "philosophical culture"—of a future that was not to be—Simmel was struggling for the meaning of his life.

After 1914, Simmel's philosophical position deepened as he watched the worldly conditions for his aspirational "philosophical culture" worsen. His clear-eyed awareness from early on of the gravity of the crisis of meaning in European life and hence of the world-historical cultural significance of the Great War seems to have fostered a kind of tranquility, a stoic acceptance of the historic necessity of what he vividly experienced as the destruction of the cultural world that had given meaning to his life. In his final four years, working, not just under the globally terrible conditions of wartime, but in the acute circumstances of the garrison town, Simmel produced a series of essays and talks in which he strove publicly to convey that vision—a striving that culminates in the beautiful and profound work that he would call his "last word in wisdom."[17]

Simmel had long recognized that human beings were collectively producing a world that they individually found increasingly unlivable—a paradoxical consequence internal to the "cultural process." In his late work, this analysis becomes ever more nuanced as it is linked in richer ways to a metaphysical account of historical development as part of a larger life process, an account that stands in a complex relationship to historical materialism.

Deploying key concepts from the *Philosophy of Money*, Simmel describes in 1916's "The Crisis of Culture" how "the configurations of the historical-spiritual work of the species [*Gebilde der geistig-geschichtliche Gattungsarbeit*]"[18] lose their mediating function and come to be experienced as independent forces, as ends in themselves. The nuance and elaboration of his analysis of the consequences of cultural objectification suggests that Simmel, rather than Lukács, should be credited with the conceptual breakthrough that anticipated the rediscovery of Marx's Paris Manuscripts. "Crisis" presents what would come to be known as reification as both a material consequence of the "historical cultural process" and, at the same time,

---

16. This is Simmel's characterization of two of the "original fundamental motifs" he had developed (in the newly available "accounting" of 1916; *GSG* 24: 71).

17. "Its completion was so important to him and occupied him until the end of his power. Therefore, I send it to friends really as a testament. Near the end Georg often used to say: this book, it is my last word in wisdom, slight as it may be," Gertrud Simmel wrote Hermann Graf Keyserling on January 22, 1919 (*GSG* 23: 1026).

18. Originally a lecture in Vienna, "Crisis" was published in the *Frankfurter Zeitung* on February 13, 1916; it appeared in revised form in 1917's *Der Krieg und die geistigen Entscheidungen*; this passage is unchanged (*GSG* 16: 37).

as unfolding the internally conflicted concept of culture itself, understood as the "cultural path of subjective spirit."

Simmel emphasized that "the tremendous, internal and external growth of our technology—which is by no means exclusively the technology of material realms" had given rise to the "tremendous internal danger of all highly developed cultures": that objective culture would overwhelm subjective—ultimately, that the realm of ends itself might be eclipsed as a consequence of living in circumstances complicated by such highly developed forms and technologies of life (*GSG* 16: 37–38). And yet this very dynamic historical-cultural-spiritual process had also brought forth the highly individualized modern form of subjectivity. No ultimate end could be envisioned to the problematic situation of the nominally autonomous and free modern subjects, whose lives become so entangled in and with means that they lose sight of higher ends, for crisis, conflict, and change are inherent in the cultural process itself. Nor did Simmel hold out utopian hope for the return of the certainties of traditional community: the highly differentiated modern form of subjectivity elaborated in the same process could never be reintegrated into a sublated totality.

Simmel's commitment to forging a modernist philosophical culture in which people could face this complexity squarely—could come to terms with the indeterminacy and moorlessness, the intense awareness of subjective particularity and experience fostered by the loss of secure metaphysical referents and epistemological foundations—is beautifully illustrated by an essay published in July 1918, "The Conflict of Modern Culture," that had its origins in lectures first held for military audiences the previous December.[19] Simmel explores the implications of "the tragic conflict of life as spirit" (*GSG* 16: 200)—of the opposition between life and form he saw as a basic fact of human cultural existence and the source of the dynamism that represented life's "self-transcendence" in and through historically and culturally developed forms. "Conflict" places this constitutive and generative dynamic in relation to the epochal self-reflexive shift in human self-understanding through which life itself had come to be understood as "the central concept of the worldview" and turned in an existential sense into the "metaphysical primal fact and essence of being altogether" in modernity (*GSG* 16: 198).

In every sphere of human existence, Simmel writes, "thinkers filled with the modern feeling for life turn against the closed system, in which the earlier epochs still dominated by the classical idea of form had sought their philosophical salvation" (*GSG* 16: 199). Under these conditions, the "primal fact" of life, that its mode of being is self-division and self-overcoming, makes recognizing conflict as internal to life practically inescapable. "The tragic conflict of life as spirit ... becomes "more palpable" (*GSG* 16: 200) through life's (culturally mediated) self-reflexive turn—whence the oft-noted rebellion against form as such that Simmel had long regarded as a distinctive feature of modern cultural existence. Again, what distinguishes modernity

---

19. Initially entitled "Problems of Contemporary Culture," these were reframed as "Philosophy of Modern Culture" in Berlin and Amsterdam in early 1918. Simmel reworked the text again before publishing it at the end of July.

are not the diremptions of cultural life—these are "revelations of the most profound internal self-contradictions of spirit" insofar as it is cultural, that is, formed—but rather the "clarity with which our epoch has revealed this [chronic conflict] as its fundamental motif" (*GSG* 16: 206).[20] The self-reflexive elevation of the category of life to the metaphysical center of human existence had brought the stakes of historical change, of cultural evolution as such, into relief.

We have arrived at a point that has tempted many readers to project their own, clarifying retrospective visions of Simmel as an alleged warmonger into his philosophical statements and to equate his assessment of the historical and philosophical appropriateness of the way of seeing embedded in his philosophy of life with a coded advocacy of "blood and earth" (*Blut und Boden*). This reading underestimates the philosophical seriousness of Simmel's approach to the historical, political, and cultural phenomena of his modernity and in particular the complexity of his attitude to the Great War as historical experience. It also fails to sound the philosophical depths of his indictment of the war as early as 1915 in the name of a European culture that was even then in the process of becoming a museum piece.

In keeping with the dialectical tradition that so deeply shaped his thinking, Simmel emphasized the role of difference and struggle in generating historical and cultural transformation, dismissing the notion "that all conflicts and problems are there to be solved" as an "entirely philistine prejudice" (*GSG* 16: 206). Yet—and here it is important to bear in mind that this essay had its origins in Simmel's effort to bring the philosophical perspective that had gripped his life to a military audience—the present was so contradictory, "the bridge between the before and after of cultural forms so entirely severed" that it suggested the need for "a more fundamental transformation" than the usual supersession of historical forms. Clearly, Simmel's high modernism still had a foot in the nineteenth century and in the romantic pursuit of timeless universals. His lucid assessment of the world-historical significance of the Great War notwithstanding, "The Conflict of Modern Culture" closes with a reassuring invocation of faith that Europe's fragmented culture could still somehow be shaped into an associative unity, a new, if not organic, then at least quasi-organic, cultural configuration.

But Simmel is misunderstood when he is grouped with the conventional German "mandarins" whose inability to come to terms with the challenges of modernity would have such devastating political effects (in Fritz Ringer's famous analysis).[21] Although his writings on art and culture sometimes resonate with the commonplaces of cultural conservatism, his alliances with the forces of modernization were also very real. Simmel's thinking, whether on epistemological, metaphysical, or eth-

---

20. For Simmel, rebellion against form as such was evident in phenomena as diverse as modernity's turn away from the classical ideal of education, the questioning of sexual mores and gender roles (*GSG* 16: 200–201), and the ascendance of mysticism over organized religion (*GSG* 16: 202).

21. Fritz K. Ringer, *The Decline of the German Mandarins: The German Academic Community, 1890–1933* (Cambridge, MA: Harvard University Press, 1969). While Simmel still belonged to a world where Bildung and Kultur were identified, especially in his later writings, the foundations of a hegemonic world-view had palpably begun to tremble—as in the speculations on gender that, however problematic their ontological commitments, unmask the masculinity of the category of culture itself.

ical questions or on political and social matters, reflected a constructive conversation with the changes under way around him.

That self-reflexive engagement with modern life, in which attention to form is inseparable from an exploration of difference and conflict, multiplicity and ambiguity, remains an important model. We cannot, however, adopt Simmel's approach, much less his views, without reserve. With the advantage of political and historical hindsight, we can discern both "regressive" and "progressive" elements and tendencies in his thinking. He took up ideas and problems the mandarins disdained and treated more traditional topics in ways that, as his career attests, hardly met with their approval. With his self-conscious attempt to affirm the relativity of perspectives, he was a thinker at once exemplary and unusual, for whom his own liminality became a positive condition for theorizing the phenomenal complexity of the world he encountered.

Identifying Simmel as a modernist philosopher is less a positive claim about his disciplinary identity than a way of suggesting that the question of whether he was "really" a philosopher or a sociologist is itself ill-posed. What today appear clear distinctions—between philosophy and sociology, between humanistic and social scientific inquiry—were by no means well-defined in his lifetime. Simmel became the rarest of thinkers, a public scholar and teacher whose influence extended over an entire generation, because his thinking about society, culture, and human existence cannot be placed on either side of these divides. Today, with the disciplinary and institutional ordering of knowledge practices once again in radical flux, taking an integrated view of his oeuvre reveals how much was at stake in his striving to foster a self-reflexively modernist "philosophical culture"—and hence the significance for us of the failure of that project.

As a philosophical adventurer, Simmel rethought the oldest questions and inspired new ones, maintaining a cosmopolitan, self-reflexive skepticism about the possibility of finding ultimate answers. His modernist style of philosophizing remains a model of innovation, and his concerns and topics could not be more contemporary. But precisely because the world has indeed long since "taken a turn in which...the future [he] had helped to prepare does not lie," the question of his theoretical significance cannot be posed in terms of the correctness or applicability of his ideas today. Indeed, the untimeliness of his work merits special attention.

In the twenty-first century, in the face of daunting challenges both inside and outside the university, for which professionalized expertise as we know it is proving both indispensable and insufficient, it is necessary to critique the inherited conceptual and methodological blinders that shape, enable, and constrain our modes of thinking and acting. As I have shown, the history of Simmel's reception illuminates the genealogy of the contemporary disciplinary imaginary. Read against the grain, that history can help us understand the complex origins of our theoretical models and disciplinary paradigms and recognize the operations and effects of crucial, largely tacit assumptions and intuitions about knowledge and scientific inquiry—and thus to apprehend the contours of the very real, yet in many ways artificial limits built into what Simmel called our *Geisteskultur*. It can thereby help us gain reflective purchase on the contingency of the disciplinary frameworks that sustain and perpetuate the knowledge practices and techniques of life of our highly bureaucratized sociocultural world and, perhaps, to imagine strategies for moving beyond the networks of values and beliefs, practices and technologies, that have shaped the destructive path of Western culture in the century since Simmel's death.

. . .

During the final weeks of his life, Georg Simmel wrote a series of moving letters to his closest friends, in which he proved himself, as Marianne Weber recalled in her memoirs, the "true philosopher who affirms his fate."[22] On September 5, 1918, he wrote Agathe and Hugo Liepmann:

> My life, objectively insufficient and in so many ways run awry as it was, now appears to me surprisingly rounded, it has attained a wonderfully clear conclusion through this consciously experienced death (of the sort I have always wished for, if not quite the present one, through which I gradually starve to death over months). The world has given me so much and more than I deserved and expected, I have given back, at least by the measure of my modest forces—the reckoning is finished, what could still have come would not have been an *essential* "increase of the realm" for myself or for others. (*GSG* 23: 1006–7)

He had enjoyed "the extraordinary happiness" of finishing his last book, which was being rushed through the press, and no fewer than four other books of his were in the process of being reprinted. "For all my present suffering, I do not for a moment lose the feeling of being the favorite of the gods.... I depart with the deepest thanks for all the love that has been given me."

These themes—acceptance of fate, gratitude for a life fulfilled by meaningful work, love, and friendship—run through the last letters. Again and again Simmel affirms the sense of completeness his impending death has brought to his life.

In taking leave of Max and Marianne Weber, he wrote: "I go at the right moment without any sort of melancholy or resignation.... Despite everything incomplete, painful, fragmentary, I am deeply thankful that I was permitted to live this life and that it is ending thus."[23] And to the painter Sabine Lepsius (to whom, with her husband Reinhold, he had dedicated *Philosophie des Geldes* in 1900): "The world has given me and I have given it what my powers permitted.... Now I actually have nothing more to say. Everything particular has fallen away from me, and I hope to bear this difficult ending without complaint and with dignity."[24]

Even during these final weeks, Simmel was not entirely freed from his concern about the "spiritual future" of Europe and the long-term cultural consequences of the Great War, so often voiced in his wartime letters. To be sure, the final book that he liked to call his "last word in wisdom" carries not a single overt reference to the tumult around him.[25] It moves in dimensions where such references could only be jarring. But this is to say that, like the letters, it is written from a perspective that

---

22. Marianne Weber, *Lebenserinnerungen* (Bremen: Johs. Storm, 1948), 390.
23. Simmel to Max and Marianne Weber, September 15, 1918 (*GSG* 23: 1024).
24. Simmel to Sabine Lepsius, September 11, 1918 (*GSG* 23: 1015).
25. Aside from a rather labored discussion of conscientious objection.

Simmel himself arguably experienced not simply in the relativist hypothetical but in the actively counterfactual mode. For he saw quite clearly that the world from which he was departing no longer had a place for philosophical adventurers who set out against the tides of the experience of fragmentary hyper-self-awareness to imagine, to write into being, a syncretic sense of self and life: no place for philosophizing, as it were, in a major key.

In "Die Transzendenz des Lebens" (The Transcendence of Life), the first chapter of that last book, the 1918 *Lebensanschauung* (*View of Life*), Simmel describes the human "position in the world" (*Weltstellung*) as a being-between boundaries (*Grenzen*) that are ever being overcome. The resulting self-reflexive relation to limits constitutes self-consciousness: "Spirit first shows itself as the living as such through this movement into the transcendence of itself" (*GSG* 16: 217). Channeling the early Hegel, Simmel declares that the movement of self-consciousness must be grasped as "life's original phenomenon [*Urphänomen*]." That "we are the absolute over our relativities" epitomizes the way life relativizes every opposition; it reveals "the transcendence of life as the true absoluteness, in which the opposition between relative and absolute is sublated," and thereby the "fundamental fact, that transcendence is immanent to life" (*GSG* 16: 223–24) Even the fact that "death inhabits life from the outset, that too is a way life reaches beyond itself" (*GSG* 16: 229).

Simmel conjures wholeness out of fragmentation by evoking a relativist "vision of life" that imaginatively reconfigures the old ideal of a philosophical subjectivity, of a self grounded in reflective unity, into a decentered, experiential totality. As he had described it to Rickert in 1916, his conception of "relativism as a positive metaphysical world-image [*Weltbild*]" was "as little skepticism as the physical relativism of Einstein or Laue." Rather, building on his understanding that "truth is a relation"—that is, that truth, like gravity, consists in the mutual relations and interactions among elements—Simmel aimed to secure a metaphysical conception of truth as "infinite relativity" that could ground logic itself.[26]

As a modernist, Simmel self-reflexively underlined the contingency of his relativist, explicitly "modern worldview" of life as immanent transcendence in a continuous process of self-overcoming (*GSG* 16: 234). He foregrounds the uncertainty and fragmentation of his own synthetic efforts, encouraging readers to take up and extend philosophical culture by deepening their own singular self-understandings in and as relation to the superindividual configurations of social and cultural life. In the book's final pages, Simmel speaks of the need to abandon what he calls "objectivity of the old style," to recognize the insuperable "discrepancy between the *nature* of reality and that of our concepts" and hence the impossibility of realizing the longing for totality in a universe in flux (*GSG* 16: 418).

Life as spiritual-cultural life—that is to say, the life of human beings existing together in worlds they have not made and whose meaning they cannot entirely comprehend—is, for both better and worse, always transcending its boundaries, always "more-life" and "more-than-life." As Simmel puts it in "Life's Transcen-

---

26. Simmel to Heinrich Rickert, April 15, 1916 (*GSG* 23: 638–39).

dence," the "relativistic process" that produces objectivity out of subjectivity, and in which the incompleteness of each particular vision of ultimate truth is eventually overcome in the continuous "unforseeability of the cultural process," is the embodied "life of spirit," at once tragic and creative, fulfillment and despair, life's self-wounding (*GSG* 16: 296). It is, to invoke Hegel, life in death. We must, I think, be very cautious about turning all of this into a "philosophy of culture" or attempting to revitalize Simmel's effort to reconceptualize ethics in a modernist key as "individual law." To embrace life's perennial self-transcendence is to accept that the theoretical and practical challenges involved in shaping our collective existence can never be definitively resolved because the future remains fundamentally—necessarily—open.

Select Bibliography

Writings by Georg Simmel

"Anfang einer unvollendeten Selbstdarstellung" (Beginning of an Unfinished Self-Representation). In *Buch des Dankes an Georg Simmel: Briefe, Erinnerungen, Bibliographie. Zu seinem 100. Geburtstag am 1. März 1958*, ed. Kurt Gassen and Michael Landmann. Berlin: Duncker & Humboldt, 1958. Reproduced as "Fragment einer Einleitung" (Fragment of an Introduction) in *GSG* 20: 304–5.

"Die Bedeutung des Geldes für das Tempo des Lebens" (The Significance of Money for the Tempo of Life). *Neue Deutsche Rundschau (Freie Bühne)* 1, no. 8 (1897): 111–22.

The Conflict in Modern Culture and Other Essays. Edited by K. Peter Etzkorn. New York: Teachers College Press, 1968.

Einleitung in die Moralwissenschaft. Eine Kritik der ethischen Grundbegriffe (Introduction to Moral Science: A Critique of the Foundational Concepts of Ethics). Berlin: W. Hertz, 1892–93.

"Exkurs über den Fremden" (Excursus on the Stranger). In *Soziologie. Untersuchungen über die Formen der Vergesellschaftung*, 509–12. Berlin: Duncker & Humblot, 1908. *GSG* 11: 764–71.

Fragmente und Aufsätze: Aus dem Nachlaß und Veröffentlichungen der letzen Jahre. Edited by Gertrud Kantorowicz. Munich: Drei-Masken, 1923.

"Das Geld in der modernen Cultur." *Zeitschrift des Oberschlesischen Berg- und Hüttenmännischen Vereins* 35 (1896): 319–24. Translated by Mark Ritter and Sam Whimster as "Money in Modern Culture" in *Simmel on Culture* (Thousand Oaks, CA: Sage, 1997).

Gesamtausgabe, vol. 2: *Aufsätze 1887 bis 1890. Über sociale Differenzierung (1890). Die Probleme der Geschichtsphilosophie (1892)*. Edited by Heinz-Jürgen Dahme. Frankfurt am Main: Suhrkamp, 1989.

Gesamtausgabe, vol. 3: *Einleitung in die Moralwissenschaft. Eine Kritik der ethischen Grundbegriffe*, vol. 1. Edited by Klaus Christian Köhnke. Frankfurt am Main: Suhrkamp, 1989.

Gesamtausgabe, vol. 4: *Einleitung in die Moralwissenschaft. Eine Kritik der ethischen Grundbegriffe*, vol. 2. Edited by Klaus Christian Köhnke. Frankfurt am Main: Suhrkamp, 1991.

Gesamtausgabe, vol. 5: *Aufsätze und Abhandlungen, 1894–1900*. Edited by Heinz-Jürgen Dahme and David P. Frisby. Frankfurt am Main: Suhrkamp, 1992.

Gesamtausgabe, vol. 6: *Philosophie des Geldes*. Edited by David P. Frisby and Klaus Christian Köhnke. Frankfurt am Main: Suhrkamp, 1989.

Gesamtausgabe, vol. 7: *Aufsätze und Abhandlungen, 1901–1908*, vol. 1. Edited by Rüdiger Kramme, Angela Rammstedt, and Otthein Rammstedt. Frankfurt am Main: Suhrkamp, 1995.

Gesamtausgabe, vol. 8: *Georg Simmel: Aufsätze und Abhandlungen, 1901–1908*, vol. 2. Edited by Alessandro Cavalli and Volkhard Krech. Frankfurt am Main: Suhrkamp, 1993.

Gesamtausgabe, vol. 9: *Kant; Die Probleme der Geschichtsphilosophie (zweite Fassung, 1905/1907)*. Edited by Guy Oakes and Kurt Röttgers. Frankfurt am Main: Suhrkamp, 1997.

Gesamtausgabe, vol. 10: *Philosophie der Mode (1905). Die Religion (1906/1912). Kant und Goethe (1906³/1916). Schopenhauer und Nietzsche (1907)*. Edited by Michael Behr, Volkhard Krech, and Gert Schmidt. Frankfurt am Main: Suhrkamp, 1995.

Gesamtausgabe, vol. 11: *Soziologie. Untersuchungen über die Formen der Vergesellschaftung*. Edited by Otthein Rammstedt. Frankfurt am Main: Suhrkamp, 1992.

Gesamtausgabe, vol. 12: *Aufsätze und Abhandlungen, 1909–1918*, vol. 1. Edited by Rüdiger Kramme and Angela Rammstedt. Frankfurt am Main: Suhrkamp, 2001.

Gesamtausgabe, vol. 13: *Aufsätze und Abhandlungen, 1909–1918*, vol. 2. Edited by Klaus Latzel. Frankfurt am Main: Suhrkamp, 2000.

Gesamtausgabe, vol. 14: *Hauptprobleme der Philosophie. Philosophische Kultur*. 1911; rev. ed. 1919. Edited by Rüdiger Kramme and Otthein Rammstedt. Frankfurt am Main: Suhrkamp, 1996.

Gesamtausgabe, vol. 15: *Goethe. Deutschlands innere Wandlung. Das Problem der historischen Zeit. Rembrandt*. Edited by Uta Kösser, Hans-Martin Kruckis, and Otthein Rammstedt. Frankfurt am Main: Suhrkamp, 2003.

Gesamtausgabe, vol. 16: *Der Krieg und die geistigen Entscheidungen. Grundfragen der Soziologie. Vom Wesen des historischen Verstehens. Der Konflikt der modernen Kultur. Lebensanschauung*. Edited by Gregor Fitzi and Otthein Rammstedt. Frankfurt am Main: Suhrkamp, 1999.

Gesamtausgabe, vol. 19: *Französisch- und italienischsprachige Veröffentlichungen. Mélanges de philosophie relativiste*. Edited by Christian Papilloud, Angela Rammstedt, and Patrick Watier. Frankfurt am Main: Suhrkamp, 2002.

Gesamtausgabe, vol. 20: *Postume Veröffentlichungen. Ungedrucktes. Schulpädagogik*. Edited by Torge Karlsruhen and Otthein Rammstedt. Frankfurt am Main: Suhrkamp, 2004.

Gesamtausgabe, vol. 21: *Kolleghefte, Mit-und Nachschriften*. Edited by Angela Rammstedt and Cécile Rol. Frankfurt am Main: Suhrkamp, 2010.

Gesamtausgabe, vol. 22: *Briefe 1880–1911*. Edited by Klaus Christian Köhnke. Frankfurt am Main: Suhrkamp, 2008.

Gesamtausgabe, vol. 23: *Briefe 1912–1919. Jugendbriefe*. Edited by Otthein Rammstedt and Angela Rammstedt. Frankfurt am Main: Suhrkamp, 2008.

Gesamtausgabe, vol. 24. *Nachträge • Dokumente • Gesamtbibliographie • Übersichten • Indices*. Edited by Otthein Rammstedt with contributions by Angela Rammstedt and Erwin Schullerus. Frankfurt am Main: Suhrkamp, 2015.

Goethe. Leipzig: Klinkhardt & Biermann, 1913. Rev. 3rd ed. 1918.

"Die Großstädte und das Geistesleben." In *Die Großstadt. Vorträge und Aufsätze zur Städteausstellung. Jahrbuch der Gehe-Stiftung Dresden*, ed. Th. Petermann, 9 (1903): 185–206. In *GSG*, vol. 7. Trans. Edward Shils as "The Metropolis and Mental Life" in *Second-Year Course in the Study of Contemporary Society (Social Science II), Syllabus and Selected Readings*, 5th ed. (and subsequent editions) (Chicago: University of Chicago Bookstore, 1936), 221–38; repr. in *Georg Simmel on Individuality and Social Forms*, ed. Donald N. Levine (Chicago: University of Chicago Press, 1971). Also translated by Hans Gerth in *The Sociology of Georg Simmel*, ed. Kurt H. Wolff (New York: Free Press, 1950).

Grundfragen der Soziologie (Individuum und Gesellschaft). Berlin: de Gruyter, 1917. The "small" *Soziologie*. Translated by Kurt H. Wolff as "Fundamental Problems of Sociology (Individual and Society)," in *The Sociology of Georg Simmel* (New York: Free Press, 1950), 3–84.

Hauptprobleme der Philosophie (Main Problems of Philosophy). Leipzig: G. J. Göschen, 1910.

Kant und Goethe. Zur Geschichte der modernen Weltanschauung. Berlin: Bard Marquardt, 1906 (*GSG* 10: 119–66). Translated by Josef Bleicher as "Kant and Goethe: On the History of the Modern Weltanschauung," *Theory, Culture & Society* 24, no. 6 (2007): 159–91.

Der Konflikt der modernen Kultur. Ein Vortrag. Munich: Duncker & Humblot, 1926. Trans-

lated in *The Conflict in Modern Culture and Other Essays* (New York: Teachers College Press, 1968).
Der Krieg und die geistigen Entscheidungen: Reden und Aufsätze (The War and the Spiritual Decisions). Leipzig: Duncker & Humblot, 1917.
Lebensanschauung. Vier metaphysische Kapitel. Leipzig: Duncker & Humblot, 1918. Translated by John A. Y. Andrews and Donald Levine as *The View of Life: Four Metaphysical Essays with Journal Aphorisms*, with an introduction by Donald N. Levine and Daniel Silver (Chicago: University of Chicago Press, 2010).
Philosophie des Geldes. Leipzig: Duncker & Humbolt, 1900. Translated by Tom Bottomore, David P. Frisby, and Kaethe Mengelberg, ed. Frisby, as *The Philosophy of Money* (1978; 3rd enlarged ed., London: Routledge, 2004).
Philosophische Kultur: Gesammelte Essais (Philosophical Culture: Collected Essays). Leipzig: W. Klinkhardt, 1911. Rev. 2nd ed. Leipzig: Kröner, 1919.
"Das Problem der Soziologie." *Jahrbuch für Gesetzgebung, Verwaltung, und Volkswirtschaft im Deutschen Reich* 18 (1894): 257–65. Translated as "The Problem of Sociology," in *The Annals of the American Academy of Political and Social Science* 6 (1895): 52–63.
"Zur Psychologie des Geldes." *Jahrbuch für Gesetzgebung, Verwaltung, und Volkswirtschaft im Deutschen Reich* 13 (1889): 1251–64. Translated by Mark Ritter and David Frisby in *Simmel on Culture* (Thousand Oaks, CA: Sage, 1997).
Rembrandt: An Essay in the Philosophy of Art. Translated and edited by Allan Scott and Helmut Staubmann. New York: Routledge, 2005.
Schopenhauer und Nietzsche: Ein Vortragszyklus. Leipzig: Duncker & Humblot, 1907. GSG 10: 167–408. Translated by Helmut Loiskandl, Deena Weinstein, and Michael Weinstein as *Schopenhauer and Nietzsche* (Amherst: University of Massachusetts Press, 1986).
Simmel on Culture: Selected Writings. Edited by David P. Frisby and Mike Featherstone. Thousand Oaks, CA: Sage, 1997.
The Sociology of Georg Simmel. Translated, edited, and with an introduction by Kurt H. Wolff. New York: Free Press, 1950.
Soziologie. Untersuchungen über die Formen der Vergesellschaftung. The "large" *Soziologie.* Leipzig: Duncker & Humblot, 1908. Translated and edited by Anthony J. Blasi, Anton K. Jacobs, and Mathew Kanjirathinkal as *Sociology: Inquiries into the Construction of Social Forms* (Boston: Brill, 2009).
View of Life. See *Lebensanschauung* above.

Secondary Sources

Abbott, Andrew. *The System of Professions: An Essay on the Division of Expert Labor.* Chicago: University of Chicago Press, 1988.
———. *Department & Discipline: Chicago Sociology at One Hundred.* Chicago: University of Chicago Press, 1999.
———. *Time Matters: On Theory and Method.* Chicago: University of Chicago Press, 2001.
Abel, Theodore. *Systematic Sociology in Germany: A Critical Analysis of Some Attempts to Establish Sociology as an Independent Science.* New York: Columbia University Press, 1929.
———. "The Contribution of Georg Simmel: A Reappraisal." *American Sociological Review* 24, no. 4 (1959): 473–79.
Adickes, Erich. "The Philosophical Literature of Germany in the Years 1899 and 1900." *Philosophical Review* 10, no. 4 (1901): 386–416.
Adorno, Theodor. *Minima Moralia.* 1951. Frankfurt am Main: Suhrkamp, 1991.
———. "Der Essay als Form." In Adorno, *Gesammelte Schriften*, vol. 11, *Noten zur Literatur IV*, 9–33. Frankfurt am Main: Suhrkamp, 1974.
———. "Henkel, Krug, und frühe Erfahrung." In Adorno, *Gesammelte Schriften*, vol. 11, *Noten zur Literatur IV*, 556–66. Frankfurt am Main: Suhrkamp, 1974.

———. "Über das Problem der individuellen Kausalität bei Simmel." *Frankfurter Adorno Blätter* (Frankfurt am Main: edition text + kritik) 8, ed. Rolf Tiedemann (2003): 42–59.

Alexander, Jeffrey C. "Parsons' 'Structure' in American Sociology." *Sociological Theory* 6, no. 1 (1988): 96–102.

———. "Against Historicism/For Theory: A Reply to Levine." *Sociological Theory* 7, no. 1 (1989): 118–20.

———. "Formal Sociology Is Not Multi-Dimensional: Breaking the Code in Parsons' Fragment on Simmel." *Teoria sociologica* 1, no. 1 (1993): 104–14.

———. "Despising Others: Simmel's Strangers." In id., *The Dark Side of Modernity*, 78–98. Malden, MA: Polity Press, 2013.

Altmann, S. P. "Simmel's Philosophy of Money." *American Journal of Sociology* 9, no. 1 (1903): 46–68.

Aronowitz, Stanley. "The Simmel Revival: A Challenge to American Social Science." *Sociological Quarterly* 35, no. 3 (1994): 397–414.

Backhaus, Gary. "Georg Simmel as an Eidetic Social Scientist." *Sociological Theory* 16, no. 3 (1998): 260–81.

———. "Husserlian Affinities in Simmel's Later Philosophy of History: The 1918 Essay." *Human Studies* 26 (2003): 223–58.

Backhaus, Gary, and Richard Owsley. "Simmel's Four Components of Historical Science." *Human Studies* 26 (2003): 209–22.

Becher, Heribert. "Georg Simmel à Strasbourg (1914–1918): Trois entretiens avec un témoin: Charles Hauter (1888–1981)." *Revue des sciences sociales* 40 (2008): 42–49.

Becker, Howard. "On Simmel's *Philosophy of Money*." In *Georg Simmel, 1858–1918*, ed. Kurt H. Wolff, 216–32. Columbus: Ohio University Press, 1959.

Bedorf, Thomas, Joachim Fischer, and Gesa Lindemann, eds. *Theorien des Dritten. Innovation in Soziologie und Sozialphilosophie*. Munich: Fink, 2010.

Belke, Ingrid, ed. *Moritz Lazarus und Heymann Steinthal. Die Begründer der Völkerpsychologie in ihren Briefen*. Tübingen: Mohr (Siebeck), 1971.

Blanc, Maurice, and Freddy Raphaël. "Strasbourg, carrefour des sociologies (1872–1972)." *Revue des sciences sociales* 40 (2008): 8–11.

Blegvad, Morgens. "A Simmel Rennaissance?" *Acta Sociologica* 32, no. 2 (1989): 203–9.

Bloom, Harold. *The Anxiety of Influence: A Theory of Poetry*. New York: Oxford University Press, 1973.

Blumenberg, Hans. "Geld oder Leben. Eine metaphorologische Studie zur Konsistenz der Philosophie Georg Simmels." In *Äesthetic und Soziologie um die Jahrhundertwende: Georg Simmel*, ed. Hannës Böhringer and Karlfried Gründer, 121–34. Frankfurt am Main: Klostermann, 1976.

Böhringer, Hannes, and Karlfried Gründer, eds. *Äesthetik und Soziologie um die Jahrhundertwende: Georg Simmel*. Frankfurt am Main: Klostermann, 1976.

Borch, Christian. *The Politics of Crowds: An Alternative History of Sociology*. Cambridge: Cambridge University Press, 2012.

Bouglé, Célestin [Jean Breton, pseud.]. "Notes d'un étudiant français: Heidelberg–Berlin." *Revue de Paris*, June 1, 1894. http://gallica.bnf.fr/ark:/12148/bpt6k207971w.image.r=Revue+de+Paris.f500.pagination.langEN (accessed July 19, 2016).

———. *Notes d'un étudiant français en Allemagne: Heidelberg–Berlin–Leipzig–Munich*. Paris: Calmann Lévy, 1895.

Buxton, William J. "From the 'missing fragment' to the 'lost manuscript': Reflections on Parsons's Engagement with Simmel." *American Sociologist* 29, no. 2 (Summer 1998): 57–76.

Caillé, Alain. "Introduction to Symposium: Does the Prospect of a General Sociological Theory Still Mean Anything (in Times of Globalization)?" *European Journal of Social Theory* 10, no. 2 (2007): 179–83.

Calhoun, Craig J., ed. *Sociology in America: A History*. Chicago: University of Chicago Press, 2007. American Sociological Association centennial volume.

Cantó i Milà, Natàlia. *A Sociological Theory of Value: Georg Simmel's Sociological Relationism*. Bielefeld, Germany: Transcript, 2005.

Camic, Charles, ed. *Reclaiming the Sociological Classics: The State of the Scholarship*. Malden, MA: Blackwell, 1997.

———. "The Formation of Intellectual Fields: American Social Science, c. 1880–1910." In *Bourdieu and Historical Analysis*, ed. Philip S. Gorski, 183–214. Durham, NC: Duke University Press, 2013.

Camic, Charles, Neil Gross, and Michèle Lamont, eds. *Social Knowledge in the Making*. Chicago: University of Chicago Press, 2012.

Cauvin, Jean-Paul. "A New Machine for Thinking: Historical Epistemology in Twentieth Century France." PhD. diss., Emory University, 2014.

Chris, James J. "Albion Small." In *Fifty Key Sociologists: The Formative Theorists*, ed. John Scott, 156–59. New York: Routledge, 2007.

Coser, Lewis A., ed. *Makers of Modern Social Science: Georg Simmel*. Englewood Cliffs, NJ: Prentice-Hall, 1965.

———. "The Stranger in the Academy." In id., *Georg Simmel*, 29–39. Englewood Cliffs, NJ: Prentice-Hall, 1965.

———. *Masters of Sociological Thought: Ideas in Historical and Social Context*. New York: Harcourt Brace Jovanovich, 1971; 2nd ed., 1977.

———. "The Many Faces of Georg Simmel." *Contemporary Sociology* 22, no. 3 (1993): 452–53.

Dahme, Heinz-Jürgen. "On the Current Rediscovery of Simmel's Sociology—A European Point of View." In *Georg Simmel and Contemporary Sociology*, ed. Michael Kaern, Bernard S. Phillips, and Robert Sonné Cohen, 13–37. Dordrecht: Kluwer Academic, 1990.

Dodd, Nigel. *The Sociology of Money: Economics, Reason & Contemporary Society*. New York: Continuum, 1994.

Durkheim, Émile. "Préface." *L'année sociologique* 1 (1896–97): vii.

———. "The Realm of Sociology as a Science." Translated by Everett K. Wilson. In *Georg Simmel: Critical Assessments*, ed. David P. Frisby, 1: 82–97. New York: Routledge, 1994. Originally published as "La sociologia ed il suo dominio scientifico," *Rivista italiana di sociologia* 4 (1900): 127–48.

———. "Review of the *Philosophy of Money*." *L'année sociologique* 5 (1900–1901): 140–45. http://hdl.handle.net/2027/mdp.39015033525125 (accessed April 28, 2016).

———. *Suicide: A Study in Sociology*. Translated by John A. Spaulding and George Simpson. Edited by George Simpson. New York: Free Press, 1997. Originally published as *Le Suicide: Étude de sociologie* (Paris: Félix Alcan, 1897).

Feldman, Zeena. "Simmel in Cyberspace." *Information, Communication & Society* 15, no. 2 (2012): 297–319.

Ferber, Christian R. *Entwicklung des Lehrerkörpers der deutschen Universitäten*. Göttingen: Vandenhoeck & Ruprecht, 1956.

Fitzi, Gregor. *Soziale Erfahrung und Lebensphilosophie: Georg Simmels Beziehung zu Henri Bergson*. Konstanz: UVK Verlagsgesellschaft, 2002.

Fitzpatrick, Ellen. *Endless Crusade: Women Social Scientists and Progressive Reform*. New York: Oxford University Press, 1990.

Fleck, Ludwik, Lothar Schäfer, and Thomas Schnelle, eds. *Entstehung und Entwicklung einer wissenschaftlichen Tatsache. Einführung in die Lehre vom Denkstil und Denkkollektiv*. Frankfurt am Main: Suhrkamp, 1980.

Freud, Sigmund. "Das Unheimliche." *Imago: Zeitschrift für Anwendung der Psychoanalyse auf die Geisteswissenschaften* 5 (1919): 297–324.

Frisby, David P. *Fragments of Modernity: Theories of Modernity in the Work of Simmel, Kracauer, and Benjamin*. Cambridge, MA: MIT Press, 1986.

———, ed. *Georg Simmel: Critical Assessments*. 3 vols. New York: Routledge, 1994.

Frischeisen-Köhler, Max. *Georg Simmel*. Berlin: Reuther & Reichard, 1919.

Furniss, Edgar S. "The Contribution of Nicholas John Spykman to the Study of International Politics." *World Politics* 4, no. 3 (1952): 382–401.

Gadamer, Hans-Georg. "Erinnerungen an Heidegger's Anfänge." *Dilthey Jahrbuch* 4 (1986–87): 13–26.

———. *Gesammelte Werke*. Vol. 1: *Hermeneutic*. Tübingen: Mohr/Siebeck, [1960] 2010.

Gassen, Kurt, and Michael Landmann, eds. *Buch des Dankes an Georg Simmel: Briefe, Erinnerungen, Bibliographie. Zu seinem 100. Geburtstag am 1. März 1958*. Berlin: Duncker & Humboldt, 1958.

Gerhardt, Uta. *Idealtypus: Zur methodologischen Begründung der moderne Soziologie*. Frankfurt am Main: Suhrkamp, 2001.

———. "Dialektik." In *Georg Simmels Philosophie des Geldes: Aufsätze und Materialien*, ed. Otthein Rammstedt, with Christian Papilloud, Natàlia Cantó i Milà, and Cécile Rol, 117–57. Suhrkamp: Frankfurt am Main, 2003.

———. "Much More than a Mere Translation—Talcott Parsons's Translation into English of Max Weber's *Die protestantische Ethik und der Geist des Kapitalismus*: An Essay in Intellectual History." *Canadian Journal of Sociology* 32, no. 1 (2007): 41–62.

Gier, Nicholas F. *Wittgenstein and Phenomenology: A Comparative Study of the Later Wittgenstein, Husserl, Heidegger, and Merleau-Ponty*. Albany: State University of New York Press, 1981.

Godspeed, Thomas W. "Albion Woodbury Small." *American Journal of Sociology* 31, no. 6 (1926): 1–14.

Goodstein, Elizabeth S. "'Eine specifisch moderne Begehrlichkeit': Fetischismus und Georg Simmels Phänomenologie der Moderne." *Die Philosophin* 7, no. 13 (1996): 10–30.

———. "Georg Simmels Phänomenologie der Kultur und der Paradigmenwechsel in den Geisteswissenschaften." In *Aspekte der Geldkultur. Neue Studien zu Georg Simmels Philosophie des Geldes*, ed. Willfried Geßner and Rüdiger Kramme, 29–62. Berlin: Edition Humboldt, 2002.

———. *Experience without Qualities: Boredom and Modernity*. Stanford: Stanford University Press, 2005.

———. "Simmel's Stranger and the Third as Imaginative Form." *Colloquia Germanica* 45, nos. 3–4 (Fall 2015): 239–63.

———. "Sociology as a Sideline: Does it Matter That Georg Simmel (Thought He) Was a Philosopher?" In *Anthem Companion to Georg Simmel*, ed. Thomas Kemple and Olli Pyyhtinen, 29–57. London and New York: Anthem Press, 2016.

Gorsen, Peter. *Zur Phänomenologie des Bewußtseinsstroms: Bergson, Dilthey, Husserl, Simmel und die lebensphilosophischen Antinomien*. Bonn: Bouvier, 1966.

Gouldner, Alvin. *The Coming Crisis of Western Sociology*. New York: Basic Books, 1970.

Grafton, Anthony. *The Footnote: A Curious History*. Cambridge, MA: Harvard University Press, 1997.

Grossheim, Michael. *Von Georg Simmel zu Martin Heidegger: Philosophie zwischen Leben und Existenz*. Bonn: Bouvier, 1991.

Gumbrecht, Hans Ulrich. "Modern, Modernität, Moderne." Vol. 4 of *Geschichtliche Grundbegriffe. Historisches Lexikon zur politisch-sozialen Sprache in Deutschland*, ed. Otto Brunner, Werner Conze, and Reinhart Koselleck, 93–13. Stuttgart: Klett-Cotta, 1972–97.

Habermas, Jürgen. "Georg Simmel über Philosophie und Kultur." 1983. Reprinted in Habermas, *Texte und Kontexte*, 157–69. Frankfurt am Main: Suhrkamp, 1991.

Hall, John T. "Measurement and the Two Cultures of Sociology." In *Social Theory and So-

ciology: The Classics and Beyond, ed. Stephen P. Turner, 181–208. Cambridge: Blackwell, 1996.

Harrington, Austin, and Thomas M. Kemple. "Introduction: Georg Simmel's 'Sociological Metaphysics': Money, Sociality, and Precarious Life." *Theory, Culture & Society* 29, nos. 7–8 (2012): 7–25.

Heidegger, Martin. *Sein und Zeit*. 1927. Tübingen: Max Niemeier, 1979.

Helle, Horst J. *Dilthey, Simmel und Verstehen: Vorlesungen zur Geschichte der Soziologie*. Frankfurt am Main: Lang, 1986.

———. *Georg Simmel: Einführung in seine Theorie und Methode = Georg Simmel: Introduction to His Theory and Method*. Munich: R. Oldenberg, 2001.

———. *The Social Thought of Georg Simmel*. London: Sage, 2015.

Horgan, Mervyn. "Strangers and Strangership." *Journal of Intercultural Studies* 33, no. 6 (2012): 607–22.

Jalbert, John E. "Time, Death, and History in Simmel and Heidegger." *Human Studies* 26, no. 2 (2003): 259–83.

Jaworski, Gary D. *Georg Simmel and the American Prospect*. Albany: State University of New York Press, 1997.

———. "Contested Canon: Simmel Scholarship at Columbia and the New School." *American Sociologist* 29, no. 2 (1998): 4–16.

Johnston, Barry V. "Sorokin Lives! Centennial Observations." *Footnotes* 17, no. 1 (January 1989): 1, 5. www.asanet.org/about/presidents/Pitirim_Sorokin.cfm (accessed July 19, 2016).

Jones, Robert Alun. "The New History of Sociology." *Annual Review of Sociology* 9 (1983): 447–69.

———. "On Merton's 'History' and 'Systematics' of Sociological Theory." In *Functions and Uses of Disciplinary Histories*, ed. Loren Graham, Wolf Lepenies, and Peter Weingart, 121–42. Dordrecht: D. Reidel, 1983.

———. *Emile Durkheim: An Introduction to Four Major Works*. Beverly Hills, CA: Sage, 1986.

Kaern, Michael, Bernard S. Philips, and Robert Sonné Cohen, eds. *Georg Simmel and Contemporary Sociology*. Boston: Kluwer Academic, 1990.

Kaesler, Dirk. "Oppenheimer, Franz." *Neue Deutsche Biographie*, vol. 19, s.v. Berlin: Duncker & Humbolt, 1999. http://daten.digitale-sammlungen.de/0001/bsb00016337/images/index.html?seite=586 (accessed July 19, 2016).

Kalberg, Stephen. "A Cross-National Consensus on a Unified Sociological Theory? Some Inter-Cultural Obstacles." *European Journal of Social Theory* 10, no. 2 (2007): 206–19.

Kant, Immanuel. "Von der Unrechtmäßigkeit des Büchernachdrucks." *Berlinische Monatschrift* 5 (1785): 403–41. http://flechsig.biz/V04Kant.pdf (accessed May 8, 2016).

———. *Kritik der reinen Vernunft*. Ed. Raymund Schmidt. Hamburg: Felix Meiner Verlag, 1956.

Kemple, Thomas M. "Simmel in English: A Bibliography." In *Anthem Companion to Georg Simmel*, ed. Thomas Kemple and Olli Pyyhtinen, 191–98. London and New York: Anthem Press, 2016.

Kemple, Thomas M., and Austin Harrington. "Georg Simmel's 'Sociological Metaphyiscs': Money, Sociality, and Precarious Life." *Theory, Culture & Society* 29, nos. 7–8 (December 2012): 7–25.

Kemple, Thomas M., and Olli Pyyhtinen, eds. *Anthem Companion to Georg Simmel*. London and New York: Anthem Press, 2016.

Kenny, Anthony. *A New History of Western Philosophy*. New York: Oxford University Press, 2010.

Klein, Richard, Johann Kreuzer, and Stefan Müller-Doohm, eds. *Adorno Handbuch*. Stuttgart: Metzler, 2011.

Köhnke, Klaus Christian. *Enstehung und Aufstieg des Neukantianismus: Die deutsche Univer-*

sitätsphilosophie zwischen Idealismus und Positivismus. Frankfurt am Main: Suhrkamp, 1986.

———. *Der junge Simmel in Theoriebeziehungen und sozialen Bewegungen*. Frankfurt am Main: Suhrkamp, 1996.

Kracauer, Siegfried. "Der Kult der Zerstreuung." In *Das Ornament der Masse: Essays*, 311–17. 1963. 2nd ed. Frankfurt am Main: Suhrkamp, 1977.

———. "Das Ornament der Masse." In *Das Ornament der Masse: Essays*, 50–63. 1963. 2nd ed. Frankfurt am Main: Suhrkamp, 1977.

———. "Georg Simmel: Ein Beitrag zur Deutung des geistigen Lebens unserer Zeit [1919]." In *Frühe Schriften aus dem Nachlaß*. Vol. 9.2 of *Siegfried Kracauer Werke*, ed. Inka Mülder-Bach and Ingrid Belke, 139–291. Frankfurt am Main: Suhrkamp, 2004.

Kramme, Rüdiger, "Wo ist der Nachlaß von Georg Simmel? Spurensuche zwischen Klein- und Großkriminalität." *Simmel Newsletter [Simmel Studies]* 2, no. 1 (1992): 71–76.

———. "Brücke und Trost? Zur Georg Simmels Engagement in *Logos*." *Simmel Newsletter [Simmel Studies]* 3, no. 1 (1993): 64–73.

Kruse, Volker. *Geschichte der Soziologie in Deutschland*. Konstanz: UVK Verlagsgesellschaft, 2012.

Landmann, Michael. "Konflikt und Tragödie. Zur Philosophie Georg Simmels." *Zeitschrift für philosophische Forschung* 6, no. 1 (1951): 115–33.

———. "Georg Simmel als Prügelknabe." *Philosophische Rundschau* 14, no. 4 (1967): 258–74.

———. "Ernst Bloch über Simmel." In *Äesthetic und Soziologie um die Jahrhundertwende: Georg Simmel*, ed Hannes Böhringer and Karlfried Gründer, 269–71. Frankfurt am Main: V. Klostermann, 1976.

Laz, Cheryl. "Albion Small." *American National Biography Online*. www.anb.org.proxy.library.emory.edu/articles/14/14-00569.html?a=1&n=albion%20small&d=10&ss=0&q=1 (accessed July 19, 2016).

Lazarus, Moritz. *Grundzüge der Völkerpsychologie und Kulturwissenschaft*, ed. Klaus Christian Köhnke. Hamburg: Meiner, 2003.

Lazarus, Moritz, and Heymann Steinthal. *Moritz Lazarus und Heymann Steinthal: Die Begründer der Völkerpsychologie in ihren Briefen*, ed. Ingrid Belke. Tübingen: Mohr, 1971.

Leck, Ralph. *Georg Simmel and Avant-Garde Sociology: The Birth of Modernity, 1880–1920*. Amherst, NY: Humanity Books, 2000.

Levine, Donald N. *The Flight from Ambiguity: Essays in Social and Cultural Theory*. Chicago: University of Chicago Press, 1985, 1988.

———, ed. *Georg Simmel on Individuality and Social Forms*. Chicago: University of Chicago Press, 1971.

———. "Parsons' *Structure* (and Simmel) Revisited." *Sociological Theory* 7, no. 1 (1989): 110–17.

———. "Simmel and Parsons Reconsidered." *American Journal of Sociology* 96 (1991): 1097–116.

———. "Simmel Reappraised: Old Images, New Scholarship." In *Reclaiming the Sociological Classics: The State of the Scholarship*, ed. Charles Camic, 173–207. Malden, MA: Wiley-Blackwell, 1997.

———. "*Soziologie* and *Lebensanschauung*: Two Approaches to Synthesizing 'Kant' and 'Goethe' in Simmel's Work." *Theory, Culture & Society* 29 (2012): 26–52.

Levine, Donald N., Ellwood B. Carter, and Eleanor Miller Gorman. "Simmel's Influence on American Sociology. I." *American Journal of Sociology* 81, no. 4 (1976): 813–45.

———. "Simmel's Influence on American Sociology. II." *American Journal of Sociology* 81, no. 5 (1976): 1112–32.

Lichtblau, Klaus. *Kulturkrise und Soziologie um die Jahrhundertwende. Zur Genealogie der Kultursoziologie in Deutschland*. Frankfurt am Main: Suhrkamp, 1996.

Lukács, Georg [György]. *The Destruction of Reason*. 1954. Translated by Peter Palmer. Atlantic Highlands, NJ: Humanities Press, 1981.

———. *History and Class Consciousness: Studies in Marxist Dialectics.* Translated by Rodney Livingstone. Cambridge, MA: MIT Press, 1971. Originally published as *Geschichte und Klassenbewußtsein* (1923).
———. *Die Seele und die Formen.* Berlin: Egon Fleischel, 1911. Translated as *Soul and Form.* London: Merlin, 1974.
———. *The Theory of the Novel: A Historico-Philosophical Essay on the Forms of Great Epic Literature.* Cambridge, MA: MIT Press, 1971. Originally published as *Die Theorie des Romans: Ein geschichtsphilosophischer Versuch über die Formen der großen Epik* (1916).
Lyotard, Jean-François. *La condition postmoderne: Rapport sur le savoir.* Paris: Minuit, 1979.
Macdonald, Lynn. *The Early Origins of the Social Sciences.* Quebec: McGill/Queens University Press, 1993.
Mamelet, Albert. *Le relativisme philosophique chez Georg Simmel.* Paris: Alcan, 1914.
Marotta, Vince. "Georg Simmel, the Stranger and the Sociology of Knowledge." *Journal of Intercultural Studies* 33, no. 6 (2012): 675–89.
Mead, George Herbert. "*Philosophie des Geldes* by Georg Simmel." *Journal of Political Economy* 9, no. 4 (1901): 616–19.
Merton, Robert King. *On Theoretical Sociology: Five Essays, Old and New.* New York: Free Press, 1967.
———. *Social Theory and Social Structure.* New York: Free Press, 1968.
Mičko, Marian. *Walter Benjamin und Georg Simmel.* Wiesbaden: Harrassowitz, 2010.
Mülder-Bach, Inka. "'Weibliche Kultur' und 'stahlhartes Gehäuse': Zur Thematisierung des Geschlechterverhältnisses in den Soziologien Georg Simmels und Max Webers." In *Triumph und Scheitern in der Metropole: Zur Rolle der Weiblichkeit in der Geschichte Berlins*, ed. Sigrun Anselm and Barbara Beck, 115–40. Berlin: Dietrich Riemer, 1987.
Muller, Jerry Z. *The Other God That Failed: Hans Freyer and the Deracialization of German Conservatism.* Princeton, NJ: Princeton University Press, 1987.
Nietzsche, Friedrich. *Sämtliche Werke: Kritische Studienausgabe.* Vol. 1. Edited by Giorgio Colli and Mazzino Montinari. Munich: Deutscher Taschenbuch, 1999.
Oakes, Guy, ed. *Georg Simmel on Women, Sexuality, and Love.* New Haven, CT: Yale University Press, 1984.
Park, Robert E., and Ernest W. Burgess, eds. *Introduction to the Science of Sociology.* Chicago: University of Chicago Press, 1921.
Parsons, Talcott. *The Structure of Social Action: A Study in Social Theory with Special Reference to a Group of Recent European Writers.* New York: McGraw Hill, 1937.
Pattullo, E. L. [Harvard University Department of Psychology] "History." http://psychology.fas.harvard.edu/history (accessed July 19, 2016).
Penny, H. Glenn, and Matti Bunzl, eds. *Worldly Provincialism: German Anthropology in the Age of Empire.* Ann Arbor: University of Michigan Press, 2003.
Poggi, Gianfranco. *Money and the Modern Mind: Georg Simmel's Philosophy of Money.* Berkeley: University of California Press, 1993.
Pollini, Gabrielle, and Giuseppe Sciortino, eds. *Parsons' "The Structure of Social Action" and Contemporary Debate.* Milan: Franco Angeli, 2001.
Porter, Theodore M., and Dorothy Ross, eds. *The Modern Social Sciences.* Vol. 7 of *The Cambridge History of Science.* Cambridge: Cambridge University Press, 2003.
Portioli, Claudia. "La fascination des sens par la marchandise entre anesthésie et hyperesthésie: Sur l'une des acceptions de l'esthétique chez Simmel." *Revue des sciences sociales* 40 (2008): 50–59.
Pyyhtinen, Olli. *Simmel and "the social."* New York: Palgrave Macmillan, 2010.
Rammstedt, Otthein, ed. *Simmel und die frühen Soziologen: Nähe und Distanz zu Durkheim, Tönnies und Weber.* Frankfurt am Main: Suhrkamp, 1988.

———. "Das Durkheim-Simmelsche Projekt einer 'rein wissenschaftlichen Soziologie' im Schatten der Dreyfus-Affäre." *Zeitschrift für Soziologie* 26, no. 6 (1997): 444–57.

———. "On the Genesis of a Collected Edition of Simmel's Works, 1918–2012." *Theory, Culture and Society* 29, nos. 7–8 (2012): 302–16.

———. "Zur Geschichte der Georg Simmel Gesamtausgabe." Appendix to *GSG*, vol. 24.

Rammstedt, Othein, with Christian Papilloud, Natàlia Cantó i Milà, and Cécile Rol, eds. *Georg Simmels Philosophie des Geldes: Aufsätze und Materialien*. Frankfurt am Main: Suhrkamp, 2003.

Ringer, Fritz K. *The Decline of the German Mandarins: The German Academic Community, 1890–1933*. Cambridge, MA: Harvard University Press, 1969.

Ross, Dorothy. *The Origins of American Social Science*. Cambridge: Cambridge University Press, 1991.

Scaff, Lawrence. *Max Weber in America*. Princeton, NJ: Princeton University Press, 2011.

———. "Simmel Redux." *Contemporary Sociology: A Journal of Reviews* 40, no. 1 (2011): 1–4.

Schermer, Henry, and David Jary. *Form and Dialectic in Georg Simmel's Sociology: A New Interpretation*. New York: Palgrave Macmillan, 2013.

Schmoller, Gustav. "Simmels *Philosophie des Geldes*." In *Georg Simmels Philosophie des Geldes: Aufsätze und Materialien*, ed. Othein Rammstedt, with Christian Papilloud, Natàlia Cantó i Milà, and Cécile Rol, 282–89. Frankfurt am Main: Suhrkamp, 2003.

Sciortino, Giuseppe. "The *Structure of Social Action*'s 'Missing' Chapter on Simmel: An Introduction. Appendix: Talcott Parsons, Letter to J. C. Alexander, January 19th, 1979." In *Parsons' "The Structure of Social Action" and Contemporary Debates*, ed. Gabrielle Pollini and Giuseppe Sciortino, 45–69. Milan: Franco Angeli, 2001.

Scott, John. *Fifty Key Sociologists: The Formative Theorists*. New York: Routledge, 2007.

Seidman, Steven. *Contested Knowledge: Social Theory Today*. 5th ed. Malden, MA: Wiley-Blackwell, 2013.

Sica, Alan. "Acclaiming the Reclaimers: The Trials of Writing Sociology's History." In *Reclaiming the Sociological Classics: The State of the Scholarship*, ed. Charles Camic, 282–98. Malden, MA: Blackwell, 1997.

Simmel, Hans. "[*Lebenserinnerungen*] 1941/43." *Simmel Studies* 18, no. 1 (2008): 9–135.

Slattery, Martin. *Key Ideas in Sociology*. Cheltenham, England: Nelson Thornes, 2003.

Small, Albion. *An Introduction to the Study of Society*. New York: American Book Co., 1894.

———. *General Sociology: An Exposition of the Main Development in Sociological Theory from Spencer to Ratzenhofer*. Chicago: University of Chicago Press, 1925.

———. Review of *The Social Theory of Georg Simmel* by Nicholas J. Spykman. *American Journal of Sociology* 31, no. 1 (July 1925): 84–87.

Sorokin, Pitirim. *Contemporary Sociological Theories*. New York: Harper & Brothers, 1928.

Sprague, Joey. "Holy Men and Big Guns: The Can[n]on in Social Theory." *Gender and Society* 11, no. 1 (1997): 88–107.

Spykman, Nicholas J. *The Social Theory of Georg Simmel*. 1925. Reprint, New York: Russell & Russell, 1964. Reissued with intr. by David Frisby. New Brunswick NJ: Transaction, 2004.

Steinmetz, George, ed. *The Politics of Method in the Human Sciences: Positivism and Its Epistemological Others*. Durham, NC: Duke University Press, 2005.

Steinthal, Heymann. *Der Ursprung der Sprache im Zusammenhange mit den letzten Fragen alles Wissens*. Berlin: F. Dümmler, 1888.

Stocking, George W. "Franz Boaz and the Culture Concept in Historical Perspective." *American Anthropologist* 68, no. 4 (1966): 867–82.

———. "The History of Anthropology: Where, Whence, Whither?" *Journal of the History of the Behavioral Sciences* 2, no. 4 (1966): 281–90.

———, ed. *Volksgeist as Method and Ethic: Essays on Boasian Ethnography and the German Anthropological Tradition*. Madison: University of Wisconsin Press, 1996.

Susman, Margarete. *Die geistige Gestalt Georg Simmels*. Schriftenreihe Wissenschaftlicher Abhandlungen des Leo Baeck Instituts, 3. Tübingen: Mohr-Siebeck, 1959.
Teggart, Frederick J. "In Memoriam: Nicholas John Spykman, 1893–1943." *American Journal of Sociology* 49, no. 1 (1943): 60.
Tenbruck, Friedrich H. "Formal Sociology." In *Georg Simmel, 1858–1918*, ed. Kurt H. Wolff, 77–96. Columbus: Ohio University Press, 1959.
Tönnies, Ferdinand. *Gemeinschaft und Gesellschaft*. Leipzig: Fues, 1887.
Tribe, Keith. "Talcott Parsons as Translator of Max Weber's Basic Sociological Categories." *History of European Ideas* 33, no. 2 (2007): 212–33.
Turner, Stephen P., ed. *Social Theory and Sociology: The Classics and Beyond*. Cambridge: Blackwell, 1996.
Turner, Stephen P., and Jonathan H. Turner. *The Impossible Science: An Institutional Analysis of American Sociology*. Newbury Park, CA: Sage, 1990.
Vetter, Helmuth, Brigitta Keintzel, and Ulrike Kadi. *Traum, Logik, Geld: Freud, Husserl und Simmel zum Denken der Moderne*. Tübingen: Edition diskord, 2001.
Vogt, W. K. "Un durkheimien ambivalent: Célestin Bouglé, 1870–1940." *Revue française de sociologie* 20 (1979): 123–39.
Ward, Lester. "Sociology at the Paris Exposition of 1900." U.S. Bureau of Education, *Report of the Commissioner of Education, 1899–1900*, chap. 28. Washington, DC: GPO, 1901.
Webb, Philip. *Homeless Lives in American Cities: Interrogating Myth and Locating Community*. New York: Palgrave Macmillan, 2014.
Weber, Marianne. *Max Weber: A Biography*. New York: Wiley, 1975.
———. *Lebenserinnerungen*. Bremen: Johs. Storm, 1948.
Weber, Max. *Die protestantische Ethik und der Geist des Kapitalismus*. 1904–5. 2nd ed., 1920. Translated by Talcott Parsons (London: G. Allen & Unwin, 1930) and by Stephen Kalberg (Oxford: Blackwell, 2002) as *The Protestant Ethic and the Spirit of Capitalism*.
———. "Georg Simmel as Sociologist." Translated by Donald Levine. *Social Research* 39 (1972): 155–63.
———. *Essays in Sociology*. New York: Oxford University Press, 1994.
Weingartner, Rudolph H. *Experience and Culture: The Philosophy of Georg Simmel*. Middletown, CT: Wesleyan University Press, 1962.
Weinstein, Deena, and Michael Alan Weinstein. *Postmodern(ized) Simmel*. New York: Routledge, 1993.
Wiese, Leopold von. "Neuere soziologische Literatur—Kritische Literaturübersichten." *Archiv für Sozialwissenschaft und Sozialpolitik* 31 (1910): 882–907.
Winch, Peter. *The Idea of Social Science and Its Relation to Philosophy*. London: Routledge & Kegan Paul; New York: Humanities Press, 1958.
Wolff, Kurt H., trans. and ed. *The Sociology of Georg Simmel*. New York: Free Press, 1950.
———, ed. *Georg Simmel, 1858–1918. A Collection of Essays with Translations and a Bibliography*. Columbus: Ohio University Press, 1959.
Yui, Kiyomitsu. "Parsons' 'Lost Fragment' on Simmel: Pivoting around an Unpublished Manuscript." *Annual Reports of Humanities and Social Sciences, Kobe University* 17 (March 1998): 1–22.

Index

Abbott, Andrew, 99n13, 261n11, 286, 287n23, 288n24, 290n26
Abel, Theodore, 75, 100, 101, 317n27. *See also* Columbia University
Adickes, Erich, 217–18. *See also* Philosophy of Money
Adorno, Theodor, 46, 48n72, 85, 148n15, 149, 193, 202, 207, 210, 289; as reader of Simmel, 297–99, 330
Aesthetics, 16, 20, 22, 37n48, 47, 51, 152, 251, 268, 269, 283, 333
Alexander, Jeffrey, 101n19, 302n12
Althusser, Louis, 74
Altmann, S. P., 218–19. *See also* Philosophy of Money
Arendt, Hannah, 319
Aristotle, 18n10, 116n38, 271, 323
Aronowitz, Stanley, 103
Association. *See* Forms of association; *Vergesellschaftung*

Bastian, Adolf, 126
Baudelaire, Charles, 30
Becoming Social. *See* Forms of association; *Vergesellschaftung*
Benjamin, Walter, 2, 46, 105, 143, 153, 196n21, 202, 204, 298, 299
Bergson, Henri, 5n7, 39n54, 56n, 61, 86, 116n38, 119, 176n, 228, 296
Berlin Universities: Freie Universität, 143; Friedrich-Wilhelms-Universität, 16, 19, 23–25, 59, 126n45; Humboldt Universität, 37n48
Big data, 288. *See also* Quantification
Bildung (cultural formation/education), 6, 28, 79, 128, 185, 298, 332n11, 342n21. *See also* Cultural process; *Philosophische Kultur*

Blind spots (methodological), 44, 113, 145, 226, 304–5. *See also* Disciplinarity
Bloch, Ernst, 19, 63, 88, 89, 297, 298
Bloom, Harold, 306
Blumenberg, Hans, 12, 127n47, 204
Boas, Franz, 126, 287
Böhm, Franz, 19n15, 94
Borch, Christian, 267n
Bouglé, Célestin, 39–43; and *Philosophy of Money*, 41, 91, 140, 146, 204; and project for a "Psychology of Money," 91, 173; and sociology, 2n2, 19n13, 39–43, 91, 138, 140n3, 146n12, 264–65
Bourdieu, Pierre, 104
Buber, Martin, 2, 16n5, 19, 87n36
Burgess, Ernest, 100, 115, 303

Camic, Charles, 111
Canonization, 2–4, 53–57, 98n6, 111–21, 244, 251, 284–95; appropriation by fragments, 105, 150, 225–26, 241, 254, 300–6, 315; and cultural philosophy, 127–28; and disciplinary formation, 48, 92, 114; and French canon, 145n10; and sociology, 36, 39, 42, 45, 53, 99–100, 110n29, 129, 142, 153, 257, 304; status of Simmel's texts, 112, 157, 219, 221, 321
See also Bouglé, Célestin; Liminality; *Philosophy of Money*; Simmel, Georg (in Berlin): marginality, sociologist; Simmel, Georg (reception history); Stranger
Cassirer, Ernst, 49, 54n7, 67n, 128, 204
Chicago School, 99, 286n21, 287n23, 288n24, 302n100. *See also* Small, Albion; Park, Robert
Cohen, Hermann, 49, 54n7, 299

Columbia University, 100, 101, 115–16, 124n42, 287n23, 298. *See also* Abel, Theodore; MacIver, Robert; Merton, Robert

Commodification, 36, 131, 207, 232, 238, 240. *See also* Reification

Communist Manifesto, 26, 84, 139, 227, 230. *See also* Cultural process; Flux; Marx, Karl

Configuration. See *Gebilde*

Coser, Lewis, 17n8, 19n15, 114n34, 144, 60n12; as canonizer of Simmel, 67n23, 75nn27, 28; 102n21, 103, 141, 288, 300–2, 309n21, 311; as reader of the *Philosophy of Money*, 44, 137, 138, 224;. *See also* Simmel, Georg (reception history)

Comte, Auguste, 42, 64, 97n5, 132, 227, 263, 285, 286, 323, 325

Crayen, Wilhelm, 53, 331

Critical theory, 125–33 passim, 152, 250, 257, 297; and *Philosophy of Money*, 211, 297, 309n21; Simmel marginalized in, 52, 113, 152, 270, 299; Simmel as precursor of, 30–31, 125–27, 152, 211, 270, 297, 309n21, 339

Cultural formation. See *Bildung*

Cultural process (*Kulturprozeß*), 106, 165, 180, 195n19, 201, 230; and disciplinarity, 321–30; and human existence, 164–66, 185, 240, 304, 340–41, 346; money and, 179–83, 186–99, 202, 203; money as symbol and bearer of, 173–74, 282, 294; and *Philosophy of Money*, 106; society and, 319; sociohistorical, 81, 277; as substance and function, 229–33. *See also* Money; *Philosophy of Money*

Cultural studies, 52, 104, 145, 257, 289, 297

Cultural theory, 254; academic specialization, 249–51, 257, 288, 290, 323; history of, 33, 92, 103–4, 113, 123, 132, 311; modernist enterprise of, 2, 3, 143, 149, 210, 244, 305, 306, 313, 336; phenomenology of, 226–34; Simmel's contributions to, 105, 109, 125, 140, 128, 160–61, 211, 297; Simmel's innovations for, 46–49 passim, 53n6, 61, 197, 200, 243, 255, 279–81 passim, 339; Simmel as resource for, 8, 44, 71, 80, 112, 126, 176

Culture: disciplinary order and cultural practices of modern, 25–35; Simmel and performative, 156–67; Simmel and theory of, 78–83; 125–33. See also *Bildung*; Cultural process; *Geist*; Metropolis; Money; *Philosophische Kultur*

Dahme, Hans-Jürgen, 302n12, 43n64

Dallwitz, Hans von, 338n10

Dante, 64

Darwin, Charles, 79, 119, 126, 132, 157, 175n7, 197, 230

Dialectic, 84, 85, 121, 202, 207, 233; dialectical strategies, 109, 112, 119, 121, 124, 152, 186, 225, 339; dialectical tradition, 81, 108, 124, 150, 187, 197, 200, 225, 240, 288, 300, 328 *See also* Essayism; Exchange

Dilthey, Wilhelm, 23, 49, 59, 82n31, 128, 132, 213n7, 251; canonization and, 54n7, 204, 299, 312; *Einleitung in die Geisteswissenschaften*, 28n39, 45n69

Disciplinarity, 32–35, 45–53, 81–83, 121–25, 249–72 passim, 279, 321–30 passim; and history, 12, 50, 58; sociology and, 67, 71, 80, 121–42 passim, 280–81, 93–94. *See also* Sociology; Cultural process; Simmel, Georg (university career); Social sciences; Technoscience; Interdisciplinarity; Ways of seeing

Disciplinary imaginary, 9–12, 31–35, 45–53, 121–33, 146, 156, 162, 220–21, 242–45, 256–59, 268, 278–84, 305, 314, 321–330, 343. *See also* Disciplinarity; Style of thought

Durkheim, Émile, 1, 8, 96, 97, 111n30, 131–32, 243, 285, 288; ASA centenary session, 100n18; break with Simmel, 227–28; as canonizer of sociology, 39–41, 103; difficulties with Simmel's work, 43n64, 71–75, 91n45, 212, 264, 312; response to *Philosophy of Money*, 215–19; and science, 148, 323; trained as philosopher, 99n14

Education. See *Bildung*

Elias, Norbert, 104, 204

Ellbogen, Ismar, 88n

Ellwood, Charles A., 98

Emerson, Ralph Waldo, 218

Engels, Friedrich, 26, 132. See also *Communist Manifesto*

Enlightenment, 25, 132, 169n2, 187, 236, 287; idea of equality, 106n28, 158, 189; view of progress, 220, 324, 325. *See also* History as progress

Epigones, 63, 88, 89. *See also* Menzer, Paul
Epistemology, 5, 16, 32n42, 84n32, 91, 133, 172, 227, 242, 251, 290, 291, 294
Erkenntnisreihen (conceptual series), 270–71, 274–75.
Erscheinungsreihen (phenomenal series, sequence or array of appearances [of phenomena]), 108, 185, 199–210 passim, 226, 233–42, 274–78, 292–95. *See also* Simmel, Georg (theoretical categories); Flux; Formation; Phenomenology; Phenomenology of culture; Relativism; Style of thought
Essayism, 47, 81, 119, 151, 235, 238. *See also* Style of thought
Exchange, 36; as abstraction, 322; as interactive (*Wechselwirkung*), 186, 228–31; money as technology, 205–06; *Philosophy of Money*, 176, 178–182, 184–85, 192, 203; as process, 97, 139, 164, symbolic, 170, 282, 319. *See also* Marx, Karl; Money

Featherstone, Mike, 332n6
Fechner, Gustav, 82
Fechter, Paul, 16, 147, 148
Figure/figuration, 72, 200–1, 203, 237, 262, 270, 278–84, 294, 309; as embodied representation, 237–238; money and, 205–6; Simmel as, 205, 256, 305, 310–11; of the stranger, 305, 307–21, 322, 323. *See also* Formation; *Gebilde*; *Konstellation*; Stranger
Fitzi, Gregor, 5n7, 39n54,
Flux: disciplinary order, 94, 125, 343; and experience, 177, 312; and Heracleitan, 84, 86, 277–79; knowable form, 74, 76; method, 71; and money, 239; and nervous stimulation, 105–6; and phenomenal series, 238; and self-reflexivity, 156, 223, 291, 295; world in flux, 5, 83–85 passim, 87, 130, 152, 160, 164, 175, 185, 207, 224, 231, 238, 244, 276, 297, 306, 319, 327, 345. *See also* Form; Formation
Form, 77, 89, 231, 276; Simmel's conception of, 66–78 passim, 126, 129, 154, 165, 168, 174, 177n8, 203–5, 216, 234–35, 255, 272–78, 297–99, 280–84, 308–10, 327, 332–33, 339. *See also* Forms of association; Formation; Stranger
Formal sociology, 43n 64; Simmel as "formal sociologist," 50, 61, 66–78, 83–92, 120, 153, 216, 242, 268–72, 272–94 passim; Tenbruck on 66–78, 156, 300–301
Formation (*Formung*), 26–32 passim, 64–78 passim, 78–87, 105–8, 140, 158, 157–59, 173–75, 188, 200, 230, 238–39, 272–73, 280, 311, 342; in fragmentary "Self-Representation," 65–66, 68–9, 76–78, 80–87. *See also* Cultural process; Disciplinarity; Form; Forms of association; *Gebilde*; Simmel, Georg (theoretical categories)
Forms of association (*Formen der Vergesellschaftung*), 66–78 passim, 156–59, 177–79, 290–95, 304–21 passim; sociology of 38, 42, 66, 73–74, 81, 90–93, 216, 260–84 passim, 294–95. *See also* Stranger
Foucault, Michel, 104n25, 131
Foundational motif or motive. See *Grundmotiv*
Foundations: disciplinary, 78, 90, 126, 197, 201–2, 217, 220, 245, 250, 284, 289, 324–25; money and 175–178, 183–188, 190–92, 245, 282; in *Philosophy of Money*, 139, 147, 154–72, 181–3, 199–210 passim, 239, 249; relativist rethinking of: 27, 84–90, 152, 228–234, 242, 260, 277, 291, 330, 333–44 passim. *See also Gebilde*; Metaphysics; Phenomenology of culture
Frankfurt School, 288, 297n2. *See also* Adorno, Theodore; Benjamin, Walter; Habermas, Jürgen
Frege, Gottlob, 328n32
Freud, Sigmund, 1, 8, 96, 105, 142n6, 181n12, 258, 298n7, 299, 310, 314, 316; and uncanny, 310–311
Freyer, Hans, 38n49, 223, 224
Frisby, David, 149, 221, 302n12; as co-editor of *Philosophie des Geldes*, 144, 237n28, 145n9; and renewed interest in Simmel, 103, 115, 138n2, 140–42, 149, 152–53; Simmel's impact on Frankfurt School, 297n2; translator of *Philosophy of Money*, 194n17; 212nn3, 4

Gadamer, Hans-Georg, 147, 149n16
Gassen, Kurt, 25
Gebilde (configuration), 47, 69, 106, 158, 181–94 passim, 200, 206, 228–30, 237–40, 264, 269–72, 282, 289–95, 307, 309–10, 311, 313–25 passim, 334, 337–38, 340, 342, 345. *See also* Cultural process; *Erkenntnisreihen*; *Erscheinugsreihen*;

Formation; Forms of association; *Geist*;
Sondergebilde
Gehlen, Arnold, 223, 224
Geiger, Abraham, 88n
Geist (spirit/culture): changing understanding of, 79, 133, 155, 162, 223–25; and concept of culture, 163–64; as formative force, 65, 68, 332; *Geisteskultur*, 259, 343; money as configuration of, 191–94; as objective culture, 82, 180, 206; Simmel's conception of, 105–7, 126, 157–67 passim, 197, 205, 207, 279. *See also* Cultural process; Formation; Money; *Völkerpsychologie*
Geistesleben (cultural life), 105–7; 109, 156, 157, 160, 164–65, 196, 279. *See also* Simmel, Georg, works (mentioned): "The Metropolis and Mental Life"
Geisteswissenschaften, 28n39, 45n69, 67, 104, 125n43, 263, 264, 269, 310n23. *See also* Humanities
Geldkultur (money culture), 148, 152, 232, 326. *See also* Cultural process; Money; *Philosophy of Money*
Genealogy, 6, 104, 110, 133, 161–64, 306, 316, 344; of disciplines, 9, 31, 47, 53, 124, 126, 130, 250, 262n, 299, 323, 343; of meaning, 197; of relativism, 186–99 passim, 334. *See also* Disciplinarity
Georg Simmel Gesamtausgabe, 1n1, 3–4, 61, 103, 144, 151, 174, 265n12, 303n12, 303n15; project of, 24n30, 52–4, 142n7, 234n26, 242n30. *See also* Köhnke, Klaus Christian; Rammstedt, Angelika
George, Stefan, 16, 58, 61, 151, 299
Gerhardt, Uta, 99n6, 146n13
German Empire, 24, 34
Giddens, Anthony, 104n25
Giddings, Franklin, 287n23
Goethe, Johann Wolfgang von, 6, 29, 84, 114n36, 137n, 151, 154, 163, 260n9, 333.
Groethuysen, Bernhard, 19
Gründerzeit (era of economic take-off), 26, 34, 78
Grundmotiv (foundational motif or motive), 65, 68, 76, 88n 39, 140, 191, 331, 340, 342

Habermas, Jürgen, 13, 15n, 104n25, 331–32
Hacking, Ian, 127n48
Halévy, Élie, 40n56
Hall, G. Stanley, 213n7, 287

Hall, John T., 261n11
Hampe, Karl, 21n19
Harrington, Austin, 138n2
Harvard University, 45n70, 75, 99n14, 100, 101, 251n2. *See also* History of the disciplines; James, William; Parsons, Talcott; Sorokin, Pitirim
Hayes, Edward, 98
Heidegger, Martin, 18, 46, 128, 142, 274n16; affinities between Simmel and, 85, 149, 163, 192, 194n17, 210, 256, 270, 316, 319, 321; charisma compared to Simmel's, 19n12
Hegel, Georg Friedrich Wilhelm, 10n14, 52, 116n38, 175, 193, 279, 320, 331n1, 345–46; and Berlin University, 24; critique of instrumental reason, 154; *Phenomenology of Spirit*, 148, 159, 190, 346; and reciprocal interaction, 74; Simmel influenced by, 10, 18, 74, 139, 175, 200, 202, 239; Simmel's unwritten book on, 89n39
Hegelian: philosophical tradition(s), 18, 193, 223–24, 230, 270, 299; strategies of thought, 10, 30, 83–85, 148, 162–66, 177, 182–84, 202, 236, 307–8, 317; understanding of dialectic, 18, 84, 146 n13, 159, 165, 178, 194–95, 276, 320, 335
Heinze, Max, 62, 63
Herder, Johann Gottfried von, 106, 126; Herderian, 27, 82, 159, 270
Hiller, Kurt, 15, 126n44
Historical image (*Bild*), 66, 67, 69, 262
History as progress, 26, 84, 117, 132, 154, 165–67, 206, 220, 227, 233, 261–72 passim, 284–92 passim, 301, 325–28. *See also* Enlightenment
History of the disciplines, 36–51, 96–121; *See also* Berlin Universities; Chicago School; Columbia University; Harvard University; New School for Social Research; Simmel, Georg (university career)
Hobhouse, Leonard, 97n5
Hofmannsthal, Hugo von, 212
Horkheimer, Max, 297
Humanities: in academic culture, 32, 34, 37, 46, 67; devaluation of, 131, 326–29; and social sciences, 70, 112, 123, 133, 162, 165. *See also Geisteswissenschaften*, Disciplinarity; Social sciences
Humboldt(ian), 27, 94, 126, 130, 131

Husserl, Edmund, 16, 20n18, 54n7, 93n49, 128, 252, 312, 328n32; friendship with Simmel, 18, 142, 337; *Philosophy of Money* and Simmel's phenomenology, 46, 127n47, 204, 236; sharing assessment of philosophical culture with, 331

Idealism, 122, 130, 133, 164–65, 239; and culture, 28, 105–6; and dualism, 86, 155, 210, 279, 280; "psychological," 105, 126, 162, 298; Simmel part of outdated, 165, 187, 264, 298; Simmel's redeployment of, 77–87 passim, 162–63, 171–72, 186–87, 279–80, 317–29, 332n7; transforming legacy of, 27–28, 58, 90, 139, 155, 194–210 passim, 264, 292, 317
Intellectual history: and the disciplines, 115, 118, 249, 324; margins of: 44, 143; narrative of, 2, 50, 257, 327; Simmel's absence from, 137, 256, 296, 299; Simmel's place in, 4, 6, 31, 36, 46, 119, 122, 129, 155; Simmel's strategy for reframing, 195. *See also* Idealism; Simmel, Georg (reception history); Social sciences; Sociology
Interdisciplinarity, 32, 127, 169, 226–234; and categorizing Simmel's work, 44, 65, 129, 150, 157, 218, 236, 249–59 passim, 305; dilemma of, 258; and institutional divisions, 46, 71, 131, 250, 289; moving beyond, 259; in natural sciences, 326. *See also* Disciplinarity; Simmel, Georg (reception history)
Intersubjectivity, 85, 158, 163, 179–85, 228, 276, 280, 291, 294, 310–21 passim. *See also* Forms of association; *Vergesellschaftung*

James, William, 45n70, 143, 177n9, 228, 251n2, 296. *See also* Harvard University
Jastrow, Anna and Ignaz, 339n14
Jaworski, Gary, 97n4, 99n11, 101n20, 113–16, 118, 119
Jellinek, Georg, 2n2, 20, 21, 22n23, 36n45, 39, 43, 52n3, 87n36, 92, 93. *See also* Simmel, Georg (university career): Heidelberg
Jones, Robert Alun, 40n58, 110, 111, 117, 122n41

Kalberg, Stephen, 88n6, 104
Kant, Immanuel, 18, 74, 79, 116n38, 126, 175, 193, 195, 198, 274, 276, 296, 300, 308, 320, 331, 337; Simmel's prize-winning paper on, 23; Simmel's writings on, 23, 30, 89, 114n36, 159, 172–79 passim, 331, 337
Kantian(ism): neo-, 40n58, 78, 223; Simmel's, 4–6, 58, 64–65, 68, 71, 73, 77–78, 80, 83–89, 119, 159, 162–67 passim, 183, 194–99 passim, 206–10 passim, 223, 230–32, 239–40, 272–78, 290–91, 295, 298, 306–21, 317; and worldly conception of philosophy, 15–25 passim, 89, 126, 129, 143, 152, 218, 296, 300, 305, 331, 337, 340, 343. *See also* Formation
Kantorowicz, Gertrud, 1n1, 55n9, 142n7
Kemple, Thomas, 43n65, 114n36, 115n, 138n2, 254n6, 305n16, 306n, 332n6
Kenny, Anthony, 299
Kessler, Harry Graf, 198n22
Keyserling, Hermann Graf, 5, 35n44, 340n17
Kierkegard, Søren, 117n38
Köhnke, Klaus Christian, 236, 251n2, 260n9, 302n12; dating of "Self-Representation," 62–63, 156, 272; and *Georg Simmel Gesamtausgabe*, 4, 47, 53, 61, 174, 302; and *Philosophy of Money*, 47, 144; on Simmel as classic of cultural philosophy, 4, 53–65, 68, 125–30 passim; on Simmel's professional woes, 23n28, 36n46, 37n48, 39n54, 45n69; on Simmel's "Self-Representation," 55–57, 61–66, 81–90 passim, 94; Simmel's social democratic activities, 15n1
Konstellation (constellation), 47, 157, 185, 201, 267, 282, 307–10, 314, 317–18. *See also* Simmel, Georg (theoretical categories); *Gebilde*
Kracauer, Siegfried, 49, 143, 152, 153, 204, 255, 256, 297
Kuhn, Thomas, 32n41, 117, 121, 288
Kulturprozeß. See Cultural process
Kulturwissenschaft (science of culture), 45n69, 82n31, 128, 204. See also *Geisteswissenschaft*; Humanities, Simmel, Georg (reception history); *Wissenschaft*

Lacan, Jacques, 74
Lacuna, 82, 100, 124, 245, 299
Lazarus, Moritz, 27n38, 58n10, 82n31, 126, 223, 243; and conceptual strategies assimilated by Simmel, 64–65, 68, 82, 91, 159; and philosophical anthropology, 159; and religious studies, 82n31, 87n37;

as Simmel's teacher, 27, 58n10, 64–65, 68, 157, 159, 223
Landmann, Edith, 142n7
Landmann, Michael, 16nn4, 5, 56, 57, 62, 63nn15, 16, 85, 88n38, 143, 223n22, 298n7
Lazarsfeld, Paul, 116
Lebensform (form of life), 7, 47, 274
Leck, Ralph, 126n44
Lepsius, Sabine, 344
León, Xavier, 5n7, 40n58, 91n45, 173
Levi-Strauss, Claude, 74
Levine, Donald, 96–104 passim, 108, 110–15 passim, 119–21; and concept of the stranger, 302n12, 303n13; as editor of Simmel, 284n19, 315n25
Lichtblau, Klaus, 15n1, 94
Lidz, Victor, 101n19
Liminality, 4–12, 26–31, 35, 44–51 passim, 55, 64–65, 196–97, 204–205, 211, 262n, 337, 343; challenges of theorizing, 9, 54–55, 96, 106, 122–23, 151, 155, 249–59, 302–14 passim, 326. *See also* Disciplinarity; Simmel, Georg (in Berlin): as modernist philosopher; *Philosophy of Money*: reception of; Simmel, Georg (reception history)
London School of Economics, 99n14, 100n15
Ludwig, Emil, 16n5, 147
Luhmann, Niklas, 104, 204, 234n26
Lukács, György, 2, 19, 193; Simmel's influence on, 52, 142, 154, 165, 202, 204; on Simmel's legacy, 147n13, 247, 249n, 257, 296, 297, 299, 314, 340
Lyotard, Jean-François, 165

Mach, Ernst, 271, 328n32
MacIver, Robert, 298
Mannheim, Karl, 19, 142, 204, 266, 297, 301n11
Marcuse, Ludwig, 17, 18, 19, 25n34, 37n47
Marx, Karl, 36, 233; exchange value, 229, 297; as founder of sociology, 103, 288; influence on Simmel, 82, 84, 104n25, 131–32, 147n, 154, 182, 192, 230, 239, 243, 266, 340; and philosophical tradition, 26, 159, 164–65, 193, 202, 206–7, 227, 285, 297, 320; strategies of thought, 1, 10, 97, 126, 130–31, 194n17, 233. *See also Communist Manifesto*
Marxist/Marxian: metanarrative, 26, 84, 103, 125–26, 130–31, 321, 329; and Simmel's legacy, 155, 165, 297, 299, 321

Mass Society, 26, 132, 148, 266, 267, 269; Simmel on concept of masses: 192, 197–98, 266–67, 283
Mauthner, Fritz, 271
Mead, George Herbert, 213. *See also* University of Chicago
Menzer, Paul, 90n42
Merton, Robert, 143, 144; and Columbia University, 115–18; exclusion of philosophy, 116n38; and history of sociology, 110, 111n, 114n34; and Talcott Parsons, 101, 102n21, 288
Metaphysics, 16, 73, 169–70, 190, 198, 251, 324, 328, 334, 341–42; metaphysical questions, 5, 51, 80, 149, 161, 173–74, 215, 227, 243, 329; Simmel's books on, 16n3, 44, 61, 338n13, 339; sociology and, 44, 73–75, 104, 108–9, 137–39, 211, 219, 228, 254–59 passim, 288, 291–94, 301–21 passim. *See also* Simmel, Georg (reception history); Social sciences; Sociology
Metropolis/metropolitan life, 3, 17, 24, 333, 336; new mode of philosophizing, 24, 81, 159, 269, 300; and sociological research, 97, 108; subjective experience of, 105–9, 148, 158, 188, 190, 195, 230, 321; urbanization, 25–26, 79, 81, 131–32, 140, 153, 157–58, 186–87; *See also* Simmel, Georg, works (mentioned): "The Metropolis and Mental Life"; Benjamin, Walter
Michelangelo, 333
Mill, John Stuart, 227
Misrecognition, 83, 101, 104–114, 122, 145, 225. *See also* Blind spots; Canonization; Simmel, Georg (reception history)
Money: as dialectical phenomenon, 166, 170–71, 177, 180–88 passim, 190–96, 199–210, 201, 232, 234, 237, 278, 282, as symbol, 135, 140, 170, 173–75, 184–85, 187, 190, 192, 194, 204, 207, 228–40 passim, 240; as synecdoche of synecdoches, 171–72, 179–85, 191, 200, 205, 234, 294; system of exchange, 176–82; as *Wertkondensator* (Condenser of value), 230–32. *See also* Cultural process; Exchange; *Geist*; *Philosophy of Money*; Quantification; Value; *Zweckreihen*
Montesquieu, 286
Musil, Robert, 1, 3, 155

Natorp, Paul, 89n41

Natural sciences: development of, 25, 28–29, 79–80, 187, 289, 328; emulation of, 45n70, 71–74, 227, 300–1, 309n21, 311, 315, 316, 328; institutional divisions, 46, 118, 132, 324–26 passim; knowledge practices, 155, 162, 169, 208, 262, 323–34 passim; objectivity and laws of: 71, 215, 269; philosophy of, 32n42, 133, 163n23,175n1–176n, 220. *See also* Humanities; Quantification; Social sciences;

New School for Social Research, 115, 144

Nietzsche, Friedrich, 1, 12, 18, 21, 26, 28n39, 87–88, 116n38, 117, 154, 192, 193, 243–44, 308, 320; cultural/philosophical impact on, 29–30, 128, 147–48, 154, 165–67 passim, 169, 175, 181, 230, 236, 243–4, 266, 277, 339–40; legacy of, 126n44, 192–6 passim, 198–99; perspectivism, 33, 85, 124, 128, 152, 177, 199–210 passim, 219, 284; relativism, 90, 202, 203, 207, 210, 240, 266, 277; Simmel as reader of, 5–6, 88–90, 107, 124, 126n,44, 175–77, 181, 194–99, 224, 227, 272, 239, 291–99 passim, 339–340 passim; stranger and alienated subject; 308, 320; subjectivity, 10, 87–90, 148, 169

Objectivity, 2, 73, 83, 85, 87, 130, 132; and economic value, 178–83 passim, 339; Kantian a priori, 71, 73; Simmel's relativism and: 37, 68, 83–95 passim, 157, 179–82, 260; and sociology, 111, 117, 124, 214–15, 262, 285, 262; and subjectivity, 30–31, 77, 109, 124, 182–83, 195, 232–33, 277, 309–10, 322, 345–46. *See also* Dialectic: dialectical strategies

Pareto, Vilfredo, 97n5
Park, Robert, 2, 43n64, 98, 99, 303
Parsons, Talcott, 44n64, 71, 98n6, 99n14, 101, 114n34, 143, 144, 222n21, 288. *See also* Harvard University
Patullo, E. L., 45n70
Performativity, 304–05; mode of philosophizing, 122, 147, 152, 177, 170, 209, 221, 232, 243, 273, 331–40; process of thinking, 148, 154, 202; and relativism, 86, 203, 226; and social form, 76–77, 305, 317; sociology, 285, 305; strategy, 75, 87, 117, 153, 159, 233–35, 292–95 passim, 323. *See also* Money; Style of thought

Perspectivism, 71, 85, 89, 219, 234; *Philosophy of Money*, 146, 177, 199, 203, 238. *See also* Nietzsche, Friedrich; Performativity; Relativism

Phenomenology, 18n9, 107, 127, 149, 159, 204, 226, 233, 236, 237, 255, 274, 288, 302n; of culture, 159, 226–234, 237, 255 (*see also* Cultural process; *Erscheinungsreihen*)

Phenomenology *Philosophische Kultur* (philosophical culture), 27, 30, 58, 61–62, 128, 143, 147, 151, 172, 252, 296–98, 331–36 passim, 340–41, 343–52

Philosophy of Money (Philosophie des Geldes), 139–41; and cultural process, 186–199; disciplinary location of, 172–79, 211–21 passim, 250–51; as modernist mode of philosophizing, 146–56, 187–88, 192–96, 199–210, 234–45; reception of, 142–46, 212–22; as work of sociology, 44, 124, 138–42 passim, 221–26, 288, 301–2;. *See also* Coser, Lewis; Cultural process; Dialectics; Disciplinarity; Durkheim, Émile; Frisby, David; *Gebilde*; Money; Poggi, Gianfranco; Schmoller, Gustav; Performativity; Perspectivism; Relativism; Simmel, Georg (reception history); Simmel, Georg, works (mentioned)

Plato, 116n38, 231, 277, 308; Eleatic Stranger, 308; Platonic, 89, 148, 159, 165, 223, 331n1
Poggi, Gianfranco, 221–26. See also *Philosophy of Money*
Political science, 38, 39, 42, 99n14, 144, 172, 213, 215, 221, 244, 263, 289
Poovey, Mary, 127n48
Popper, Karl, 223
Poststructuralism, 74, 76, 104, 329
Pyyhtinen, Olli, 43n65, 115n, 219n16, 332n6

Quantification: 75, 189, 190, 191, 239, 261n11, 262, 285, 287, 289, 325–26, 329. *See also* Reductivism; Social sciences

Rabinbach, Anson, 127n48
Radbruch, Gustav, 19
Rammstedt, Angelika, 62n15
Rammstedt, Otthein, 1n1, 3, 43n66, 78, 81, 92n47, 142n7, 145n9, 153n20, 211n1, 212n5, 216n10, 234n26, 242n30, 243n, 265n12, 302n12

Reductivism, 35, 170, 187–195, 200, 243, 268–269, 306, 313, 336; of early work, 53, 65–69; opposed in mature thinking, 107, 151, 158–159, 163, 197, 202, 206–10, 226, 264–265

Reification, 154, 165, 184, 194, 202, 207; reified reality, 240, reified theory, 108, 123; reified world, 139, 207, 229. *See also* Marx, Karl; Lukács, György

Relativism: and being, 272–84; epistemic, 83–90; metaphysical, 6, 61–63, 83, 85–90, 155–61, 169, 172, 202–210, 234–45 passim, 254–78, 281, 322; as modernist method, 199–210; perspectival, 6–9, 202, 210, 291. *See also* Cultural process; *Geldkultur*; Genealogy; Nietzsche, Friedrich; Objectivity; Performativity; *Philosophy of Money*

Rhetoric of reflection, 96, 120–22, 125, 155; current crisis in, 125, 133; Marxist. 130–31; paradigm shift in, 82, 189, 249, 262–63, 266, 269, 285; philosophical, 75, 155, 162, 164, 269; (social) scientific, 78, 109, 111, 117–23, 221, 223, 227, 263, 277, 287–88

Rickert, Heinrich, 18, 55n8, 182n13, 212n3, 243, 328n32; and academic appointments, 20, 22n24, 93n49, 94, 205n26, 252, 332n7, 345; disciplinary approach, 45n69; 49, 68n; philosophical tradition, 89n, 128, 204, 299, 312; Simmel's friendship with, 5, 16

Ringer, Fritz, 343
Romanticism, 106n28, 236
Ross, Dorothy, 96n1, 113, 114n33, 127n48
Roth, Günther, 144
Russell, Bertrand, 328n32

Sachs, Hans, 191
Salomon, Albert, 115. *See also* New School for Social Research
Schäfer, Dieter, 19, 93
Scheler, Max, 16
Schiller, Friedrich, 79, 187
Schmoller, Gustav, 219, 285; as reader, 153, 173n3, 211–215; as Simmel's mentor, 39n49, 126, 172, 307n18
Schopenhauer, Arthur, 63, 114n36, 116n38; and culture, 196n20, 198; and philosophical tradition, 18, 52, 165, 175, 193, 195, 276, 295; and unity of philosophy, 88–89

Simmel, Georg (in Berlin), 16–25; cosmopolitanism, 16–19 passim, 87n37, 88, 129, 143, 218, 305, 343; and cultural conservatism: 342–43; marginality: 1, 3, 15, 90, 98, 103, 253, 256, 257; as modernist philosopher, 3, 12, 17–18, 22, 29, 31, 36–37, 46, 55, 89, 113, 123, 129, 151–52, 175, 244, 255, 296, 306, 311–12, 331–46; as neo-Kantian, 4–5, 68, 80, 83–84, 89n41, 119, 223, 277, 298; and postmodernism, 52, 119, 165, 203n24, 236; as sociologist, 19n13, 36, 54–55, 65–71, 78, 90

Simmel, Georg (reception history), 4–11, 48–61, 66–67, 125–33, 137–56, 211–20, 240–45, 249–59, 284–95, 305, 342–344; misreading in, 83, 96–125 passim, 137–39, 141, 221–26, 240–45, 249–59 passim, 279, 293–94, 299–317, 322–30 passim; Simmel as Jew, 20, 60, 63–64, 143, 218, 252, 302; Simmel as philosopher, 15–25, 46–48, 85–95 passim, 154–56, 202–210 passim, 296–99, 319, 328–29, 331–32; Simmel as sociologist, 35, 38–45, 71–78, 90–104, 113–25, 137–40, 144–46, 152–54, 160, 215–28 passim, 251–54, 261–62, 284–90. *See also* Canonization

Simmel, Georg (theoretical categories). *See* Cultural process (*Kulturprozeß*); *Erkenntnisreihen*; *Erscheinungsreihen*; Formation (*Formung*); *Gebilde, Geistesleben, Konstellation, Lebensform, Philosophische Kultur, Sondergebilde, Verdichtung, Vergesellschaftung, Wechselwirkung, Weltbild, Zweckreihen*

Simmel, Georg (university career): as academic outsider, 20, 37, 52, 60–61, 98, 218, 254, 302–4 passim (*see also* Stranger); Berlin, 16–25; Greifswald, 23n29; Habilitation, 23, 28n39, 41, 60, 64; Heidelberg, 19–21, 23n29, 36nn45, 46, 39, 43, 52, 90, 93, 99n14, 252, 265, 332n7; Privatdozent, 23, 39, 175n7, 251, 337; Professor Extraordinarius, 23; Strasbourg, 1n1, 20, 22n24, 23–24, 39n53, 252, 332n7, 337–46.

Simmel, Georg, works (complete). *See Georg Simmel Gesamtausgabe*

Simmel, Georg, works (mentioned), "The Adventure" ("Das Abenteuer"), 259–60, 311, 322, 335; "The Conflict in Modern Culture" ("Der Konflikt der modernen Kultur"), 157–58, 253; "The Crisis of Culture, 340–41; "Excursus on the Problem: How is Society Possible," 312–22; "Excursus on the Stranger" ("Exkurs über den Fremden"), 302–304, 322; "Feminine Culture" ("Weibliche Kultur"), 29, 86n35, 332; *Fundamental Questions of Sociology* (*Grundfragen der Soziologie*), 42, 251; *Goethe*, 137n; "How Social Forms are Preserved," ("Comment les formes sociales se maintiennent"), 216; *Introduction to Moral Science* (*Einleitung in die Moralwissenschaft*), 20, 21, 51, 59n11, 64, 90, 158, 260, 265; *Kant und Goethe*, 114n36; *Main Problems of Philosophy* (*Hauptprobleme der Philosophie*), 36, 52, 148n15, 331; "The Metropolis and Mental Life" ("Die Großstädte und das Geistesleben"), 80, 105–6, 108, 157, 158, 159, 190, 230; *Philosophical Culture* (*Philosophische Kultur*), 62n14, 136–37, 259, 331–35; *Philosophy of Money* (*Philosophie des Geldes*), 20, 23, 40, 41, 44, 48n, 51, 55, 62, 91, 92, 106, 125n43, 142, 144, 145n9, 153, 156, 159, 164, 168n1, 174, 176, 212n5, 264, 270, 275–82 passim, 294–95, 296; "The Problem of Sociology" ("Das Problem der Sociologie") (1894), 7n11, 40n58, 42, 59, 65n19, 66–70, 76, 78, 90, 91, 92, 156, 176n, 226, 235, 260–65, 269, 272–74, 280, 281n7, 282, 284n19, 312; "The Problem of Sociology" (1908), 70, 77, 80, 260, 264, 265, 272–76 passim, 280–284 passim, 293–94, 304, 312–14; *The Problems of the Philosophy of History* (*Die Probleme der Geschichtsphilosophie*), 58, 59, 64, 65, 66n22; *Rembrandt*, 114n36, 137n, 306n17; "The Significance of Money for the Tempo of Modern Life" ("Die Bedeutung des Geldes für das Tempo des Lebens"), 174; *On Social Differentiation* (*Über soziologische Differenzierung*), 36, 58, 59n11, 64; *Sociology: Investigations into the Forms of Association* (*Soziologie: Untersuchungen über die Formen der Vergesellschaftung*), 36, 42–43, 54, 70, 78, 89, 93, 114, 146n12, 156, 226, 243, 255, 260, 264–65, 268, 272, 275, 284n19, 291, 293, 294, 302–22 passim; *View of Life* (*Lebensanschauung*), 51, 149, 199,

204n25, 319, 331, 339, 345; *The War and the Spiritual Decisions* (*Der Krieg und die geistigen Entscheidungen*), 338. See also *Philosophy of Money*; Stranger

Simmel, Georg, works (posthumous fragment) "Self-Representation" (disputed title), 59, 61, 61n5

Simmel, Gertrud (wife), 55n9, 127, 137n, 142n7, 338n18, 340n17

Simmel, Hans (son), 16n4, 19n14, 24, 25n35, 55n9, 81n30

Skepticism, 29, 83–84, 87, 94, 150, 160, 165, 280, 321–45 passim; democratization of, 155, 187–90

Skeptics, 68, 271

Slattery, Martin, 301n11, 302n

Small, Albion, 98–100, 112, 286, 315n25

Smith, Adam, 286

Social forms. *See* Forms of association

Social sciences: division of inquiry, 28–29, 34–37, 46, 211, 250, 253–54, 325–26; and historiography, 126–27, 130, 287–89; management of populations: 131–32; method, 67, 69, 75, 271, 274, 284, 300, 314, 324; philosophical origin, 79–80, 204, 226, 242–43, 249, 260, 262; roots in humanities, 131; rise of 2, 21n19, 48, 61, 76–77, 227, 240; and Simmel, 4, 7–9, 41–42, 45, 54, 63, 68, 86, 90, 95, 106, 109, 112, 118, 138, 140, 144, 160–67 passim, 213, 252, 266, 280, 297, 312, 323, 326; Simmel's contribution dismissed, 218–20, 228; Simmel on mode of observation: 290–91. *See also* Bouglé, Célestin; Coser, Lewis; Durkheim, Émile; Forms of association; Merton, Robert; Parsons, Talcott; Simmel, Georg (reception history); Small, Albion; Sociology, Tenbruck, Friedrich

Social survey movement, 285, 287

Socialism, 20n18, 38n49, 58, 80, 93, 94, 193, 223n23

Sociology: foundations of, 36–38, 58–59, 65–66, 92–93, 97, 100nn15, 16, 104, 112, 138, 217, 226–28, 291; and philosophy, 15–6, 18, 21n19, 80; systematic approach to sociology, 67–76, 100–101, 110–11, 115–25 passim, 222–26, 243, 285, 287–89, 301–302, 311, 323–24. *See also* Chicago School; Columbia University; Cultural process; Durkheim, Émile; Formation;

Forms of association; Frankfurt School; Harvard University; Levine, Donald; New School for Social Research; Simmel, Georg (reception history); Simmel, Georg, works (mentioned): "The Problem of Sociology"; Tenbruck, Friedrich; *Vergesellschaftung*

Socrates, 21, 24
Sombart, Werner, 54n7, 132
Sondergebilde (Special configuration), 185, 238
Sorokin, Pitirim, 75, 99n14, 100, 101. *See also* Harvard University
Spencer, Herbert, 40, 42, 58
Spinoza, Baruch, 271, 331n1
Spykman, Nicholas J., 19, 99n11, 100, 101, 316n27
Steinthal, Heymann, 27, 58n10, 64, 88n, 91, 126, 157, 159, 223
Stöcker, Helene, 15n1, 126n44
Stocking, George W., 27n38, 58n10, 121–22
Stranger, 300–321; "essay" as sociological classic, 300–6, 322; and Freud's uncanny, 310–11, 313–14, 321; Simmel as stranger, 257, 261n10, 302, 311–12; synecdoche of becoming social: 314, 321; and *Vergesellschaftung*, 308–9, 315–21; strangeness as configuration, 306–317. *See also Gebilde, Konstellation*
Strindberg, August, 308
Structuralism: assumptions of, 118; challenge to, 71, 76; legacy of: 121, 123; as research program, 116
Stuckenberg, J. H. W., 316n27
Style of thought, 17, 32, 43, 121–25, 130; innovative, 3, 59, 133, 263, 296; legacy of, 46–47, 102, 110, 113, 119–20, 133, 150–51, 235; modernist, 6, 22, 133, 149, 150, 161, 175, 203, 208, 210, 214, 260; theoretical significance of, 50, 78, 85, 102, 110, 112–13, 119–20, 147–51 passim, 150–51, 155, 224, 251–57 passim, 296–98, 329, 331–36;
Subjectivity, 10, 30–31, 44, 47, 55, 68, 106, 139, 140, 152, 166, 179, 181, 182–183, 186, 194, 197, 253, 269, 276, 306, 320–21; ethical, 87; evolution, 105, 188; and flux, 152; intensification, 194–95; knowledge, 267; metaphysics, 89; metropolitan, 107; modern: 69, 158, 190, 199, 202, 218, 230, 232, 341; and objectivity, 31, 77, 179, 182, 195, 232–33, 346; rethinking, 133; as social form/configuration, 312–15, 317, 327; understanding, 77. *See also* Flux; Intersubjectivity; Metropolis/metropolitan life; Stranger
Susman, Margarete, 6–7, 19, 25n35, 26–28, 62, 152n18, 338
Synecdoche, 18, 171–72, 159, 179, 184, 191, 200, 205, 209, 234, 236, 255, 314. *See also* Money; *Philosophy of Money*; Stranger; *Verdichtung*
System philosophy, 64, 86, 88, 159, 202, 341–42; Simmel's opposition to, 6–10 passim, 17–18, 62, 146–47, 171, 195, 199–210 passim, 235–45, 265–72, 290–95, 302, 318, 331–36. *See also* Idealism

Tarde, Gabriel, 97n5, 132
Technologies of life, 34, 158, 196n20, 319, 329
Technology, 25, 79, 106, 166, 192, 205, 207, 232, 266, 336
Technoscience, 28, 220, 277, 328–29
Tenbruck, Friedrich, 67, 75–78, 156, 300, 301
Thiess, Frank, 18
Tönnies, Ferdinand, 49, 54n7, 67n, 101n19, 132, 285
Tribe, Keith, 98n6
Turner, Jonathan, 285n20, 288n24
Turner, Stephen, 96n2, 203n24, 261n11, 285n20, 288n24

Ueberweg, Friedrich, 62, 63, 89
Université de Strasbourg, 252
University of Chicago, 99, 100, 213n7. *See also* Chicago School

Value, 176–82, 230–32. *See also* Cultural process; Exchange; Money; *Philosophy of Money*
Veblen, Thorstein, 132, 286
Verdichtung (condensation), 47, 159, 164, 189, 272
Vergesellschaftung (association, becoming social), 66, 92, 181, 228–29, 260, 280–81, 294, 308–9, 315–21. *See also* Forms of association; *Wechselwirkung*
Völkerpsychologie: and experimental psychology, 82, 156; influence on Simmel, 27, 64, 65, 68, 87n37, 126, 157, 228; and self-reflexivity, 90. *See also* Lazarus, Moritz; Steinthal, Heymann

Wagner, Adolph, 38n49, 40n56
Way(s) of seeing: disciplinary styles, 161–62, 214, 245, 258; individualistic, 67–68, 72, 80, 84; sociological, 42, 257, 261–64, 275, 280–82, 288, 291, 304–5, 342. *See also* Liminality; Perspectivism; Simmel, Georg (theoretical categories)
Weber, Marianne, 15, 22n24, 126n44, 212n3, 344
Weber, Max, 1, 8, 49, 86n35, 99n14, 104n25, 115, 128, 132, 190, 204, 228n24, 252, 285, 312, 328n32; Anglophone reception of, 98n6; dispute about value in sociology, 42n63; and ideal types, 201, 313; and *Philosophy of Money*, 212, 230; Simmel's friendship with, 16, 148, 344; Simmel's professional woes, 21–22, 22n24, 36n46, 38n49, 67n22, 93–94, 142; and social science, 96, 97, 243; as sociological founder, 43n64, 103, 288; and "third path," 261n11
Wechselwirkung (reciprocal [inter]action), 66, 74, 83–84, 86, 163, 203, 228, 240, 257n7, 260, 266, 269, 270, 291, 292, 313. *See also Gebilde*; Simmel, Georg (theoretical categories)
Weisbach, Werner, 17n8
Weltbild (world image), 86, 160,180, 186, 188, 210, 278, 279, 335, 336, 345. *See also* Simmel, Georg (theoretical categories)
Whitehead, Alfred, 290n26
Wissenschaft (science), 6, 34, 69, 90, 121, 156, 159, 168, 177, 178, 200, 261, 287, 336; and disciplinary consolidation, 54, 60, 63–64 passim, 69, 215; inseparable from philosophy, 11, 55, 156, 240; modern, 6, 34, 54; positivist conception of, 55, 59, 287. *See also Geisteswissenschaften*; Humanities; *Kulturwissenschaft*; Simmel, Georg (reception history); Social sciences; Sociology,

Wiese, Leopold von, 17n8, 19, 38n49, 43n64
Wilhelminian Germany (Emperor Wilhelm II), 53, 63
Windelband, Wilhelm, 21n19, 22n24, 59, 99n14, 299
Wittgenstein, Ludwig, 200, 274

Wolff, Kurt, 67n23, 102, 218n15, 241n29, 259n8, 284n19, 301n, 303n14, 309n21, 315–16
Wölfflin, Heinrich, 312
World War I (Great War): 1, 19n12, 26, 34, 128, 296; and disciplines, 38, 78–79; German culture, 142, 144; and new generation, 27, 49; philosophy of life, 240; postwar and disciplinary consolidation, 300; Simmel's death and, 7, 25; Simmel's view of, 35n44, 338–40, 342, 344
World War II, 115, 285, 242n30; and Columbia, 116; and emigration of scholars, 102; and reintroduction of sociology in Germany, 143–44
Worms, René, 39
Worringer, Wilhelm, 20n17
Wundt, Wilhelm, 213n7

Zeller, Eduard, 23
Zweckreihen (series or sequences of purposes), 192. *See also* Simmel, Georg (theoretical categories)

Lightning Source UK Ltd.
Milton Keynes UK
UKOW05f0252231117
313207UK00018B/973/P